DOS® Programmer's Reference

Reference

3rd Edition

Terry Dettmann
Revised for 2nd Edition by Jim Kyle
Revised for 3rd Edition by Marcus Johnson

PROGRAMMING
SERIES

DOS Programmer's Reference
3rd Edition

Library of Congress Catalog No.: 91-66203

ISBN: 0-88022-790-7

95 94 93   8 7 6 5 4 3

Interpretation of the printing code: the rightmost double-digit number is the year of the book's printing; the rightmost single-digit number, the number of the book's printing. For example, a printing code of 91-1 shows that the first printing of the book occurred in 1991.

This book was written for DOS versions through DOS 5.0. The examples in this book should work with the following versions of MASM, TASM, Microsoft C, Turbo C and Turbo C++, Borland C++, QuickBASIC, QBasic, and Turbo Pascal (unless noted otherwise):

Borland C++ through version 2.0
MASM versions through 6.0
Microsoft C versions through 6.0
QBasic version 1.0
QuickBASIC versions through 4.5
TASM versions through 2.0
Turbo C and Turbo C++ versions through 2.0
Turbo Pascal versions through 6.0

This book is dedicated to friends who were hackers before hacker *became a dirty word, for without them much of the information in this book would not be as freely available as it is.*

Terry Dettmann

I second the motion.

Jim Kyle

And to the new breed of hackers, who, while avoiding that title, continue the tradition of seeking and spreading information.

Marcus Johnson

Publisher
Richard K. Swadley

Publishing Manager
Joseph Wikert

Managing Editor
Neweleen Trebnik

Technical Editors
Greg Guntle
Gordon Arbuthnot
Alan Plantz

Editor
Susan Pink, TechRight

Project Managers
Cheri Clark
Rebecca Whitney

Editorial Assistants
Molly Carmody
Rosemarie Graham

Illustrations
Barbara Bennett

Cover Design
Dan Armstrong

Index
Jeanne Clark

Book Design
Scott Cook
Michele Laseau

Production
Claudia Bell
Brad Chinn
Brook Farling
Denny Hager
Bob LaRoche
Laurie Lee
Anne Owen
Howard Peirce
Cindy L. Phipps
Tad Ringo
John Sleeva
Kevin Spear
Bruce Steed
Suzanne Tully
Susan VandeWalle
Johnna VanHoose
Phil Worthington

Composed in ITC Garamond and Macmillan Digital by Que Corporation

Terry Dettmann

Terry Dettmann's love affair with computers began in the 1960s and has continued sporadically ever since. He has written numerous articles about computers, has taught computer courses, and has been a consultant, programmer, and editor. Mr. Dettmann has done doctoral work in electrical engineering and computer science. Currently, he is the Chief scientist for Digital Systems International, Inc., in Redmond, Washington, where he designs computer-based solutions to productivity problems in the telecommunications and banking industries.

Jim Kyle

Like Terry Dettmann, Jim Kyle has been involved with computers since the 1960s, working first with mainframes and then with minis before getting into micros. A prolific writer since 1948, with some 14 books and hundreds of magazine articles bearing his byline, he is currently primary forum administrator for the Computer Language Magazine forum of COMPULSIVE, and MIS Administrator for a major manufacturer of mainframe peripherals for the banking industry. For fun, he disassembles operating systems in search of undocumented features.

Marcus Johnson

Marcus Johnson has been working with computers since the mid-1970s and with micros since the early 1980s. He has written articles about computers and has been a programmer and a consultant. Currently, he is a senior systems engineer with Precision Software in St. Petersburg, Florida, where he designs firmware for digital telephone systems.

CONTENT OVERVIEW

Introduction 1

Part I   An Overview of DOS

1 An Introduction to DOS 9
2 The Structure of a DOS System 21
3 The Dynamics of DOS 55
4 The DOS and BIOS Interface 87

Part II   Character Devices and Serial Devices

5 Output Devices 117
6 Input Devices 161
7 Serial Devices 191

Part III Disks, Directories, and Files

8 Disks 229
9 Directories and Files 261

Part IV Memory Management and Miscellaneous Topics

10 Program and Memory Management 285
11 Interrupt Handlers 359
12 Device Drivers 417
13 Miscellaneous Functions 461

Part V   Reference

BIOS Function Reference 485
DOS Reference 593

Appendix A   The ASCII Character Set 937
Appendix B   Selected Memory Locations 941
Appendix C   A Resource List 945
Appendix D   A Standard TSR-Identification Technique 949
Appendix E   The Reserved DOS Functions 955

Index 1005

TABLE OF CONTENTS

Introduction 1

I An Overview of DOS 7

1 An Introduction to DOS 9

What Is DOS? 9
History of DOS 10
  Version 1.0 12
  Version 1.1 13
  Version 1.25 13
  Version 2.0 13
  Version 2.1 14
  Version 3.0 14
  Version 3.1 15
  Version 3.2 15
  Version 3.3 15
  Version 4.0 15
  Version 5.0 16
  And the Future 16
The Structure of DOS 16
The Programmer's Interface to DOS 18
Summary 19

2 The Structure of a DOS System 21

The "Virtual Machine" Concept 21
The Physical Machine 23
The Processor 24
  8086 Memory Addressing 24
  The 8086 Register Set 27
    General-Purpose Registers 28
    Segment Registers 29
    Offset Registers 31
    The Flags Register 32
  The 80286 and Beyond 32
  Identifying the CPU Chip 33
  Math Coprocessors 36
  Identifying the Math Coprocessor 37
Memory 40
I/O Channels 40
  The Keyboard 41

The Display Screen 42
    Types of Display Adapters 43
    Memory Mapping and Display Adapters 44
The Printer 45
The Serial Port 45
The Mouse 46
Storage Devices 46
Physical Disk Structure 47
Logical Disk Structure 48
    The Boot Record 49
    The File Allocation Table 49
    The Root Directory 49
The Software 50
The BIOS 50
The DOS Kernel 51
The Command Processor 52
Device Drivers 53
Summary 54

3   The Dynamics of DOS 55
The DOS Boot Sequence 55
Command Processing 59
Programs under DOS 61
COM Programs 61
EXE Programs 64
Some High-Level Language Examples 72
A Turbo Pascal Program 73
A Compiled C Program 73
Comparing Different Versions of a Program 74
    COM versus EXE Programs 75
Interrupts 76
Internal Interrupts 78
The Non-Maskable Interrupt 78
Hardware (Maskable) Interrupts 79
Software Interrupts 79
Memory Allocation and Management 82
Summary 85

4   The DOS and BIOS Interface 87

Accessing DOS and BIOS from Your Programs 88
   A Simple Call to DOS 90
   Passing String Addresses to DOS 90
High-Level Language Resources 91
   The C Programming Language 93
      Accessing Registers and Generating Interrupts 93
      Getting and Setting File Attributes 96
   Turbo Pascal 103
      Accessing Registers and Generating Interrupts 104
      Reading a File's Date and Time Stamp 105
   QuickBASIC 108
      Accessing Registers and Generating Interrupts 109
      Finding Files That Match a File Specification 111
Summary 113

II   Character Devices and Serial Devices 115

5   Output Devices 117

Basic Character Devices 117
How the Display System Works 118
   Storing and Displaying Video Data 120
   Video Display Formats 123
      Text-Mode Display 125
      Graphics-Mode Display 127
   Identifying the Video Display Adapter 128
Video Functions 145
   Programming with DOS and BIOS Video Functions 146
   Using Multiple Display Pages 154
Printer Functions 157
Summary 159

6   Input Devices 161

Keyboards 162
   How the Keyboard Works 162
   Reading the Keyboard from BASIC 168
   Accessing the Keyboard Using Int 16h 170

Accessing the Keyboard Using Int 21h 174
Identifying the Level of Keyboard Support 181
The Mouse 183
How the Mouse Works 184
Initializing the Mouse Driver 184
Where Is the Mouse? 184
Summary 189

7   **Serial Devices** 191
Serial Interfaces 192
PC Serial Conversion: The 8250 UART 196
The Transmitter Holding Register (THR) 198
The Receiver Data Register (RDR) 198
The Baud Rate Divisor (BRD) 198
The Interrupt Enable Register (IER) 199
The Interrupt Identification Register (IIR) 200
The Line Control Register (LCR) 200
The Modem Control Register (MCR) 200
The Line Status Register (LSR) 202
The Modem Status Register (MSR) 202
Initializing the Communications Port 203
Modems 207
Writing a Terminal Program 208
Duplex Considerations 208
The Controlling Program: Term.c 209
Supporting Functions 210
Initialization: Setup( ) Function 210
An Initialization Alternative 211
Keyboard Control: Keybd( ) Function 213
Receiving Characters: Serial( ) Function 216
Using Term.c 219
Directly Accessing the 8250 UART 220
Assembly 220
C 221
BASIC 221
Pascal 221
Modifying Term.c 221
Loopback Testing 223
Evaluation of the Serial I/O Services 224
Summary 225

III   Disks, Directories, and Files 227

8   Disks 229

Disk Internals 230
   The Partition Table 231
   The Boot Record 234
   The File Allocation Table (FAT) 239
      The 12-Bit FAT 241
      The 16-Bit FAT 243
      More FAT Information 245
Using Disk Functions 246
   Drive Information 247
   Formatting Disks 254
Summary 260

9   Directories and Files 261

Disk Directories 262
   The Root Directory 262
   Directory Entries 264
      File Name (Offset 00h) 264
      File Extension (Offset 08h) 266
      File Attribute (Offset 0Bh) 266
      Time of Last Update (Offset 16h) 267
      Date of Last Update (Offset 18h) 268
      Beginning Disk Cluster (Offset 1Ah) 268
      File Size (Offset 1Ch) 269
   Subdirectories 269
   Volume Labels 270
What Is a File? 271
How Files Are Handled Through DOS 271
   Standard File Control Blocks 272
   Extended File Control Blocks 272
   Basic FCB File Handling 273
   When To Use FCB Functions 274
   Handle Functions 275
   Basic Handle File Handling 276
   When To Use Handle Functions 276
   Directory Searching: A Practical Example 277
Summary 281

IV   Memory Management and Miscellaneous Topics 283

10   Program and Memory Management 285

How Memory Works 287
Memory Management 291
    Shrinking Program Memory 293
    Getting More Memory 294
Expanded Memory 296
    Determining Expanded Memory's Availability 296
    Using Expanded Memory 299
Extended Memory 304
    Determining Extended Memory's Availability 305
    Using Extended Memory 306
Program Execution 344
    The EXEC Function 344
    Program Exits 348
    Possible EXEC Problems 349
    Entering a Command to DOS 350
    Superseding DOS's Internal Commands 352
    Why Some EXE Files Cannot Be Converted to COM Files 353
    The Program Segment Prefix 353
Memory-Resident Programming 355
Summary 357

11   Interrupt Handlers 359

What Is an Interrupt? 360
How Interrupts Work 362
The Intel 8086 Family Interrupts 363
    Internal Hardware Interrupts 363
    External Hardware Interrupts 365
    Software Interrupts 365
Interrupt Vectors 366
Getting and Setting Interrupt Vectors 366
When Should You Write an Interrupt Handler? 367
Writing a Ctrl-C Handler 369
Writing a Critical Error Handler 375
Revisiting TSRs 406

Interrupts Essential to TSRs 408
   The Keyboard Interrupt 408
   The InDOS Flag, DOSOK Interrupt, and Timer Interrupt 409
Summary 416

12   Device Drivers 417
Driver Types 419
   Character Device Drivers 419
   Block Device Drivers 419
How Device Drivers Work 420
Device Driver Structure 422
   Device Header 423
   Strategy Routine 428
   Interrupt Routine 430
      Driver Initialization 435
      Media Check 438
      Build BIOS Parameter Block 441
      I/O Control Read 443
      Read 445
      Nondestructive Read 445
      Input Status 446
      Flush Input Buffers 447
      Write 447
      Write with Verify 448
      Output Status 448
      Flush Output Buffers 448
      I/O Control Write 448
      Open 449
      Device Close 449
      Removable Media 449
      Output until Busy 450
      Generic IOCTL 450
      Get and Set Logical Device 450
The Whole Driver 451
   Assembling the Driver 456
   Installing the Driver 457
   Debugging the Driver 457
Making a Practical Driver 458
Using the Device Driver 459
Summary 460

13 Miscellaneous Functions 461

DOS Version Information 461
Equipment Information 466
Date and Time Functions 469
Extended Error Processing 474
Undocumented Features 480
Summary 481

V Reference 483

BIOS Function Reference 485

The BIOS Functions 487
BIOS Function Quick Reference 489
The VESA BIOS 586

DOS Reference 593

How DOS Services Are Invoked 593
Reentrancy 594
DOS Function Chart 595
Reserved Functions 609
Undocumented Functions 609
How DOS Services Are Presented 610
    Interrupt Number 610
    Function Number 611
    Subfunction Number 611
    DOS Version Availability 612
    Purpose 612
    Description 612
    Calling Registers 612
    Return Registers 612
    Comments 613
DOS Services 613
Mouse Functions: Int 33h 796
The EGA Register Interface 817
EMS Functions: Int 67h 822
XMS Functions 862
DPMI Functions 872
Task Switching 923

Data Structures 923
    SWAPIINFO 923
    SWCALLBACKINFO 924
    SWINSTANCEITEM 925
    SWSTARTUPINFO 926
    SWVERSION 926
Notification Functions 927
Service Functions 932

A   **The ASCII Character Set** 937

B   **Selected Memory Locations** 941

C   **A Resource List** 945
Hardware 945
MS-DOS and BIOS Programming 946
Programming Languages 946
General Programming 947
General DOS 947

D   **A Standard TSR-Identification Technique** 949
The User Parameters Block 950
Function 00h (Check Install) 951
Function 01h (Return User Parameter Pointer) 953
Other TesSeRact Functions 954

E   **The Reserved DOS Functions** 955
Four Types of Reserved DOS Functions 956
    The Useful Group 956
    Numbers Not Really Used 956
    Hooks for the Future 957
    Who Knows? 957
Using Function 52h: The Configuration Variable Table 957
    Content and Layout of the CVT 957
        The Version 2 CVT 958
        The Version 3 CVT 960
        The Version 4 CVT 963

CVT3: A Program for V3 967

The Data Structures 967

Utility Functions 968

Tracing the DPBs 968

Tracing the BCBs 969

Tracing the DCBs 969

Tracing the MCB Chain 970

LDT Tracing 971

The Main Routine 971

CVT4: Updating the Program to V4 972

Buffer Control Block and EMS Links 972

The Memory Control Block 973

The Drive Parameter Block 973

The Device Control Block 973

The Logical Drive Table 974

The CVT Definition Itself 974

Utility Routines 974

The Main Routine 974

Summary 974

Index 1005

In building on the impressive work of Terry Dettmann and Jim Kyle, I owe them an incalculable debt. In addition, I am grateful to the community of computer professionals for making DOS the vibrant and fascinating system it has become. Finally, my thanks and love to my wife, Joan, and children, Chelsea and Trevor, for putting up with my passion for computers.

Marcus Johnson

TRADEMARK ACKNOWLEDGMENTS

Que Corporation has made every attempt to supply trademark information about company names, products, and services mentioned in this book. Trademarks indicated below were derived from various sources. Que Corporation cannot attest to the accuracy of this information.

1-2-3, Lotus, and VisiCalc are registered trademarks of Lotus Development Corporation.

3Com is a registered trademark of 3Com Corporation.

86-DOS is a registered trademark of Seattle Computer Products, Inc.

ANSI is a registered trademark of American National Standards Institute.

Apple DOS and Macintosh are registered trademarks of Apple Computer, Inc.

Ashton-Tate is a registered trademark of Ashton-Tate Corporation.

COMPAQ Deskpro 286 and COMPAQ Portable Computer are registered trademarks of COMPAQ Computer Corporation.

CompuServe Incorporated is a registered trademark of H&R Block, Inc.

CP/M and CP/M-86 are registered trademarks of Digital Research Inc.

DESQview is a trademark of Quarterdeck Office Systems.

Epson RX-80 is a trademark of Epson America, Inc.

Guide is a registered trademark of Owl International, Inc.

IBM, IBM PCjr, OS/2. and PS/2 are registered trademarks of International Business Machines Corporation.

Intel is a registered trademark of Intel Corporation.

MCI Mail is a registered servicemark of MCI Communications Corporation.

Microsoft, Microsoft C, Microsoft C Compiler, Microsoft Macro Assembler, Microsoft QuickBASIC, Microsoft Windows, Microsoft Word, and MS-DOS are registered trademarks of Microsoft Corporation.

Norton Utilities is a trademark of Peter Norton Computing.

PC Tools is a trademark of Central Point Software.

Quadram is a registered trademark of Quadram Corporation.

SideKick, Turbo BASIC, Turbo C, and Turbo Pascal are registered trademarks of Borland International, Inc.

TesSeRact is a trademark of the TesSeRact Development Team.

TRS-80 and TRSDOS are registered trademarks of Radio Shack.

UNIX is a trademark of AT&T.

1 An Introduction to DOS
10 Program and Memory Management

2 The Structure of a DOS System
11 Interrupt Handlers

3 The Dynamics of DOS
12 Device Drivers

4 The DOS and BIOS Interface
13 Miscellaneous Functions

5 Output Devices
BIOS Function Reference

6 Input Devices
DOS Reference

7 Serial Devices

8 Disks

9 Directories and Files

Introduction

Welcome to *DOS Programmer's Reference*, 3rd Edition. This book was written for two reasons. First, we wanted to demonstrate to people programming at the DOS level how using DOS (and BIOS) functions can help their programming. Second, we wanted to encourage high-level language programmers to use DOS functions to extend their control of the PC system.

Most books about DOS or BIOS programming seem to focus on assembly language. A few discuss using DOS functions from high-level languages, but most are spotty in their coverage and virtually useless as references. *DOS Programmer's Reference*, 3rd Edition, exemplifies a range of techniques that serve as a starting point for greater use of the DOS or BIOS functions in your programs. You will want to keep it next to your computer—not on a dusty bookshelf.

To make this book as useful as possible, we have tried to strike a balance between breadth and depth of coverage to give you a start into any one programming topic. Entire books could be written about many programming topics and techniques. This book does not provide exhaustive coverage of any particular technique. Instead, you are shown a starting point and given enough information to get you "down the path."

DOS Programmer's Reference, 3rd Edition, covers each major area in which BIOS and DOS functions can be applied. The discussion and examples in this book should help beginners learn how to use these functions and give more advanced programmers a way to organize what they have learned. We emphasize the *why* wherever possible.

A book like this is truly useful only if it provides programmers with pertinent reference information. The last part of this book is devoted to a detailed function-by-function listing of all DOS and BIOS functions (including many that are otherwise undocumented). For each function, the available information is summarized and details of register requirements are provided. The function listings alone should make this a useful reference for any DOS programmer, whether you work in assembly language, BASIC, C, or Pascal.

A book like this is useful only if it is up-to-date. This edition covers MS-DOS 5.0, including information on extended memory drivers, expanded memory drivers, and mouse drivers. The sections on hardware describe how to identify what CPU chip is in use, what coprocessor is available, and what video board your system is using.

This edition offers several added features not available in the second edition of *DOS Programmer's Reference*. In addition to more "how-to" code, we have included coverage of XMS, DPMI, and DOS 5.0, including the task-switching API. We are sure that you will benefit from the enhanced information available only in this edition.

In some cases, information on undocumented features may appear incomplete or sketchy. It is presented because programmers need the widest variety of information on DOS and the BIOS and only by distribution of the known data can the full set of undocumented features be uncovered. Use of these features is risky; because they are not documented, there is no guarantee that they will operate the same in all DOS implementations or that they will even be present in any specific implementation.

Purpose of This Book

A principal aim of this book is to show you how to work at appropriate levels to program the DOS system. Available functions are discussed, but you do not *always* have to resort to assembly language to use them. Some programming tasks can be done efficiently only in assembly language. (Some things, in fact, can be done only by going "right down to the bare metal"—even BIOS and DOS services sometimes get in your way.) But working at the highest possible level has definite benefits. This book provides the information you need to decide which level to use in your own programming.

The examples are oriented toward high-level interfaces to the DOS and BIOS routines. Although we minimize the use of assembly language, we do not neglect it. By emphasizing that you can access and effectively use routines from C, BASIC, or Pascal, we hope to make these techniques more widely usable.

Who Should Use This Book?

If you are a programmer interested in working with DOS to make the most effective programs possible, *DOS Programmer's Reference* is for you. It deals with DOS at many levels, from high-level programming-language services down to the BIOS interrupts.

This book is intended for programmers who have some experience in C, BASIC, or Pascal and are comfortable with assembly language. We assume that you are familiar with at least one programming language, curious about others, and familiar also with MS-DOS or its cousin, IBM's version of DOS.

A fundamental assumption is that you want to speed up your programs or access facilities unavailable in your language. We will go after these facilities through DOS and BIOS functions. This book deals with advanced program design and freely uses elements from high-level languages as well as assembly language.

Although a certain technique may be illustrated in a particular programming language, the *technique*—not the *language*—is of primary interest. After you learn how to use a technique, it is equally applicable whether you use it in C, Pascal, BASIC, or assembly language. It will apply, in fact, in any language that provides access to DOS and BIOS interrupts.

What You Should Know To Use This Book

This book is written for C, BASIC, or Pascal programmers. It includes little or no explanatory information about how to program in assembly language. If you want to learn more about this topic, we suggest that you read *Using Assembly Language, 2nd Edition*, also published by Que Corporation, or some of the other books listed in Appendix C.

The examples in *DOS Programmer's Reference* are drawn from assembly language, BASIC, C, and Pascal, with a tendency toward C. We have tried to make the examples clear, no matter what your programming background may be. The listings help demonstrate the actual use of the DOS and BIOS functions.

How To Use This Book

This book is divided into five parts. Readers interested in learning the fundamentals of DOS programming will want to start with Part I. Those who want specific information about various aspects of programming at the system level can find useful information in Parts II, III, and IV. More advanced programmers who simply want a quick reference should concentrate on Part V.

The four chapters in Part I, "An Overview of DOS," lay the groundwork. You first look at some of the history of the system and at how DOS works, both statically and dynamically. Then you are introduced to the general principles of programming at the DOS level and to the language resources available for this type of work. Finally, we explore the "nitty-gritty" of programming at the DOS level.

In Part II, "Character Devices and Serial Devices," Chapters 5 and 6 cover output devices (the video display and printer) and input devices (the keyboard and mouse). Chapter 7 deals with serial input and output devices; the 8250 UART is discussed also.

Part III, "Disks, Directories, and Files," contains two chapters. Chapter 8 describes the partition table, boot record, and file allocation table (the FAT) and discusses disk functions. Chapter 9 covers the root directory, directory entries, subdirectories, and volume labels. You also learn in this chapter about how files are handled through DOS—about file control blocks (FCBs) and handle functions and when to use them.

Part IV, "Memory Management and Miscellaneous Topics," covers program and memory management (Chapter 10), interrupt handlers (Chapter 11), and device drivers (Chapter 12). Chapter 13, "Miscellaneous Functions," provides information on such topics as equipment information and extended error processing.

Each chapter in Parts II, III, and IV introduces you to the subject and illustrates it with practical examples that you can use as the basis for your own library of functions.

All of the sample programs illustrate basic techniques only. If you learn a basic technique from one of these simple programs, you can then extend it to your own programming.

Part V is a reference section. Typography, icons, and other design elements were carefully planned to make this section easy to use. The BIOS and DOS services are presented in numerical order. Each function is listed in a standard reference format, with cautions or restrictions for the various functions included in the comments. In addition to the BIOS and standard DOS functions, Part V includes sections on the functions of the mouse (DOS Int 33h), expanded memory (DOS Int 67h), XMS, DPMI, and task switcher.

Five appendixes are filled with additional information. Appendix A contains the ASCII character set; Appendix B is a table of selected memory locations; Appendix C is a resource list of other titles; Appendix D describes a proposed standard for TSR interfacing; and Appendix E discusses the use of undocumented features of DOS, including two sample programs for exploring them.

Talk to Us

Many people have worked on this book to make it the best possible programmer's reference available. As with any book of this magnitude, there could be errors. Let us know of any errors or omissions you find so that the next edition can be even more complete.

And please take a moment to fill in and mail the registration card at the back of this book. Que Corporation is interested in your reaction to *DOS Programmer's Reference*.

PROGRAMMING

Part I

An Overview of DOS

PROGRAMMING

An Introduction to DOS

It will be helpful for you to have a clear idea about what DOS is before you read further. This chapter provides an overview of DOS, as well as a short history of the operating system; original sources were used for details of how DOS came to be. In addition, this chapter touches on DOS structure and interfacing. Because this is a cursory examination, do not be concerned if some terms are unclear. Each is explained in detail in later chapters.

What Is DOS?

DOS consists of four basic modules:

- *The boot record:* This record begins on track 0, sector 1, side 1 on every disk formatted by the DOS FORMAT command. On fixed disks, the boot record is on the first sector of the DOS partition. This record, which requires one sector of space, identifies the disk and contains the initial boot program for the disk.

1

CHAPTER

- *The BIOS:* The basic input/output system (BIOS) is located in ROM. This low-level interface to the physical machine is responsible for hiding the vagaries of the hardware from all other software. It is augmented, for DOS, by the I/O system loaded from disk.

- *The DOS programs:* Two programs implement DOS. One, the I/O system, is an interface module loaded from disk that augments the ROM BIOS functions and usually contains a set of standard device drivers. The other, the disk operating system itself (DOS), is the high-level interface for all programs that run on the computer, whether or not they make use of the disk.

- *The command processor:* Most people think of this module as DOS. The command processor, the normal interface to DOS services for people working with the system, generates the command prompt (C>), accepts commands, and executes programs requested by users of the system.

Each of these modules is covered in detail in Chapter 2, "The Structure of a DOS System," and Chapter 3, "The Dynamics of DOS." At this point, however, some basic explanations are in order.

The BIOS provides a series of functions that programmers can use to perform operations without having to concern themselves with the details of the underlying hardware. Throughout this book, BIOS functions are used to perform necessary operations in programming examples. Part 5 of this book, "Reference," contains a function-by-function reference to the capabilities of the BIOS.

Even though the BIOS is powerful, it is far from comprehensive. DOS, built on the platform provided by the BIOS, provides many services essential to programming. In the early days of computers, before general-purpose operating systems (such as DOS) became available, programmers wrote programs that included the functional equivalent of DOS. This made the process of debugging applications terribly complex.

With the DOS functions already programmed by Microsoft (and other vendors), the authors of DOS become our partners in program development. Although you should not assume that *everything* in DOS works without error, you can assume that (unless proven otherwise) DOS is solid. Part 5 contains a function-by-function breakdown of the DOS functions.

History of DOS

Over the years, DOS has emerged as the primary operating system for microcomputers. DOS has more users today than any other operating system. It has become a sophisticated environment with tools and applications to meet a wide spectrum of needs.

DOS's foreseeable growth involves expansion to handle more sophisticated microprocessors such as the 80386 and 80486. Future releases of DOS may even handle multitasking and multiuser operations (some may question this statement, in light of the emergence of OS/2).

DOS was first marketed by Seattle Computer Products as 86-DOS for that company's line of computers. The original DOS was written by Tim Paterson starting in April 1980, and first shipments were made in August of that year. At that time, Digital Research's CP/M was the most widely used microcomputer operating system. 86-DOS was specifically designed to make porting applications from CP/M easy: it kept the same structure for file control blocks and functions so that a mechanical translator could convert a program directly to 86-DOS.

Because 86-DOS worked only with 8086/8088 CPU chips, which were just coming into the marketplace in 1980, few people even knew that it existed. Those who did use the 8086 CPU on their S-100 systems as an upgrade from the 8-bit 8080/Z80 standard and CP/M found 86-DOS useful, and Seattle Computer Products established a base of several dozen customers, including at least one other hardware manufacturer. Then Microsoft approached SCP about writing a customized version for an anonymous customer. Though at the time no one knew it, IBM was looking for an operating system. By January 1981, Paterson knew who the customer was, and Microsoft had taken out a license to distribute 86-DOS under its own name. In April of that year, Paterson left Seattle Computer Products and joined Microsoft, where he spent the next several months tailoring the system to IBM's needs.

In July 1981, Microsoft bought from Seattle Computer Products all rights to 86-DOS. When IBM released the PC on August 10, 1981, Microsoft was ready with MS-DOS 1.0 (Personal Computer DOS, *not* PC DOS, for IBM machines; IBM never accepted the popular term *PC DOS* in reference to the system, and the latest IBM versions are identified simply as *DOS*).

Paterson's direct involvement with DOS ended during 1982, but he remains active on the PC scene, most recently as a consultant to Phoenix Technologies Inc., the clone BIOS experts.

After the PC's original release, DOS still was not prominently displayed in some stores. IBM had selected CP/M-86 and Softech's p-system as alternative PC operating systems. But vendors were slow to deliver both products, and few languages were available for development under those operating systems. Microsoft already had earned a reputation for programming languages. IBM released its own software using DOS, and developers rapidly picked up the ball, which has never stopped rolling. CP/M-86 and the p-system never got off the ground as serious contenders in the PC marketplace.

DOS has been changed officially many times (and several versions exist that were not available for general use). Although improvements and bug fixes both have figured in this evolution, each release usually has involved a response to some hardware change—particularly, a change in disk-drive format or capability.

Table 1.1 lists each major official DOS release (to date) and the primary change involved. (Some minor releases have been omitted from this list.)

Table 1.1. DOS Versions

Version	Date	Hardware Change
86-DOS	August 1980	Seattle Computer Products' version (begun in April 1980, by Tim Paterson)
1.0	August 1981	Original PC, single-sided disk
1.1	March 1982	Double-sided disk, date-time stamping
1.25	March 1982	First OEM version (ZDOS), VERIFY added
2.0	March 1983	PC XT, including hard disk
2.1	October 1983	IBM PC*jr* and Portable PC
3.0	August 1984	Personal Computer AT, including high-capacity disk
3.1	March 1985	Networking
3.2	December 1985	Enhanced support for new media
3.3	April 1987	Support for PS/2
4.0	June 1988	Support for disk drives larger than 32M; integration of EMS memory capability
5.0	June 1991	Support for XMS, upper memory blocks, and the HMA

As you look at table 1.1, consider the trade-off between memory and features that each new version of DOS has required. DOS V1.0 could exist in 16K of memory, and the original IBM PC was available with only 64K. Version 2 needed at least 24K of memory (more, if device drivers were installed). Any useful programming required a minimum of 128K of memory. As of V3, DOS needed 36K of memory (and could require much more for file sharing and installed device drivers). Machines with less than 512K were almost impractical. And with V4, 512K became essentially a requirement and more than 640K (expanded and extended memory, see Chapter 2) was definitely desirable. As DOS continues to expand, machines will need megabytes of memory to do practical work.

Let's look at each version of DOS to see what was involved in each change. Throughout this book, *V1*, for example, refers to a generic subversion of V1, and *V1.n* means a specific subversion *n*.

Version 1.0

DOS V1.0 was the original support for the PC system. It supported the basic single-sided, eight-sector disk format and provided all the basic disk services. Changes (from CP/M) included a much improved disk-directory structure that managed file attributes and exact file size. Version 1.0 also added to the original

86-DOS improved disk allocation and management, better operating-system services, and an AUTOEXEC batch file for start-up initialization. IBM was the only vendor to ship this version. Interestingly, this version of DOS did not include the date-time stamping of files that later became known as one of the major distinguishing features of DOS.

Version 1.1

In V1.1 (the last IBM-only edition), the date-time stamp and support for double-sided disk drives were added, as were some bug fixes. It was released in March 1982.

Version 1.25

V1.25 was the first version to be distributed by original equipment manufacturers (*OEMs*) other than IBM. (The jump in version numbers from 1.1 to 1.25 reflects the difference between IBM's version count and Tim Paterson's private revision control system, in which IBM V1.1 was known as V1.24.) The VERIFY capability was added in this version, as was the 00h end-of-directory flag byte (which did not appear in IBM versions until V2.0).

V1 was far from a uniform standard; Microsoft did not distribute it directly to end users, but rather licensed it to OEMs, who were free to modify it or even to rename it (as Heath-Zenith did in March 1982, naming it ZDOS, which was the first non-IBM use of DOS).

Version 2.0

In DOS V2.0, support was added for double- and single-sided nine-sector diskettes, fixed disks, and cartridges that would be used on the PC*jr*. DOS services were enhanced significantly. This version also added hierarchical file systems similar to those in UNIX. Here are some of the significant changes incorporated into DOS V2.0:

- File handles
- I/O redirection
- Pipes
- Filters
- Print spooling
- Volume labels

- Expanded file attributes

- System-configuration file

- Program-environment block maintenance

- ANSI display driver

- Dynamic control of memory by programs

- Support of user-customized command processors

- International support

As with V1, V2 was licensed to OEMs, who made changes. By this time, though, most OEMs were aware that the marketplace was demanding near-total compatibility with the IBM machines; therefore, the changes were much less wide-ranging. Some, such as Tandy with the Model 2000 (their first MS-DOS machine, which used DOS V2), went so far as to provide dual vectors in their BIOS interfaces for IBM BIOS compatibility.

Some variations between editions bearing the same version number but coming from different OEMs can still be found. This is true of all V2 editions.

Version 2.1

In V2.1, only timing changes were made to allow better handling of IBM's PC*jr* and Portable PC. The MS-DOS version, known as 2.11, is still sold in some machines; one Toshiba laptop unit has V2.11 burned into ROM.

Version 3.0

DOS V3.0 was the earliest version offered for the Personal Computer AT. This version added support for high-capacity (1.2M) diskettes and additional hard disk formats, as well as the foundation for support of networked disks. Some major new features include the following:

- Control of the print spooler by applications

- Extended error reporting

- Suggested error-recovery codes

- Support for file and record locking

The release of V3 marked the end of near-total freedom on the part of the OEMs to change the structure of DOS, although some variations between Microsoft and IBM editions continue today. IBM, for example, provides most of the support utilities as COM files, and Microsoft supplies them in EXE format. Other less obvious changes abound in the code itself.

Support for network operations, however, made it necessary to enforce stricter standards on the structure of DOS and especially on its internal data formats, and the OEM contracts were changed to reflect this requirement. Life for independent developers became simpler because the key parts of DOS became essentially stable at this time.

Version 3.1

DOS V3.1 added networked disks, including support for file sharing, as well as some bug fixes. This version has been standard for some time with many vendors.

Version 3.2

V2.3 added support for 3½-inch floppy disks. It also integrated formatting control into the peripheral device drivers. Version 3.2 was the first version to be sold to the end-user market by Microsoft under its own name.

Version 3.3

In DOS V3.3, two new user commands (NLSFUNC and FASTOPEN) and two new functions were added, many other services upgraded, and device support expanded to cover IBM's PS/2 line. Effective with this version, the maintenance and development responsibility for DOS was transferred from Microsoft to IBM, freeing Microsoft to devote its resources to OS/2. (As part of the trade, IBM relinquished its own OS/2 development responsibilities to Microsoft.) Both firms continued to release and support their own unique versions of both products, however.

Version 4.0

In DOS V4.0, many user commands were enhanced, several more functions were added, and a graphic user shell program was introduced. The most significant changes, however, were the addition of support for hard disk drives of more than 32-megabyte capacity and the inclusion of expanded-memory drivers as a standard part of DOS. (Both features had been available for some time as add-on options.)

Two months after Version 4.0 was released by IBM, an update—identified *only* on the disk labels as V4.01—was released to correct several problems. The VER command still identifies the version as 4.00, though; the only way to distinguish the versions is by the file dates on the two hidden files and on SHARE.EXE. V4.01 bears dates of 08/03/88 or later, and V4.00's date is 06/17/88. Microsoft delayed its own release of V4, and its V4.00 is the equivalent of IBM's 4.01. However, Microsoft has also released V4.01, which has additional corrections.

Version 5.0

In DOS V5.0, support for extended memory was added, many user commands were enhanced, and new user commands were added, notably UNDELETE, UNFORMAT, MIRROR, and a mouse-aware, full-screen text editor. A task switcher API (application program interface), which is supported in the shell program, was added. The kernel was restructured, resulting in DOS taking up less space for the first time. In addition, DOS can now be run from ROM. SHARE is no longer necessary to safely support DOS partitions in excess of 32M.

DOS V5.0 is the first real update of DOS from Microsoft since V3.3; Microsoft's support of V4.0 was a result of reverse-engineering IBM's DOS V4.0.

And the Future

As DOS continues to evolve, new services and options become available to programmers. The advent of windowed environments such as Microsoft Windows and DESQview has made sophisticated new services available for DOS-level programmers. Each new service hides more of the machine from our programs and allows us to do more without having to reinvent the proverbial wheel. The cost of any high-level service, however, tends to be a compromise in the maximum amount of speed and responsiveness that can be achieved. But as processors get faster, the need for lower-level tricks will diminish. Applications programs will use the services of DOS and its cousins. Only systems-level programmers working inside DOS, Windows, or DESQview will have to worry about direct access to the machine or its services. Such is progress.

The Structure of DOS

As this book examines DOS and the PC system, you will notice a layering of functions. Figure 1.1 should help you visualize this layering.

Fig. 1.1. *System layering.*

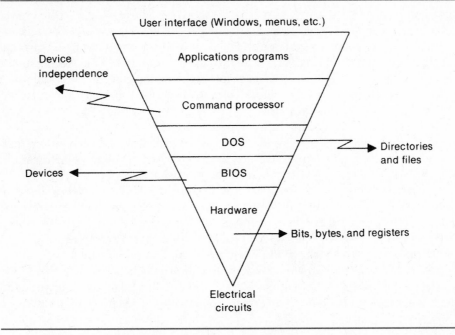

Fundamental to the design of the whole DOS/PC system is a kind of system-within-a-system approach to design. Starting with the electrical circuits at the bottom of the system, for example, you will notice that the circuits implement a device (called a computer) with definite capabilities and features.

The BIOS integrates this circuitry level into a new "computer system" with well-defined features and functions. The BIOS level is characterized by the presence of devices that have standard features. No matter which kind of display you use or whose keyboard you bought, the BIOS makes them all respond similarly. Taken together, all of the BIOS's features make it capable of supporting a programming environment. Within this environment, DOS was developed. To standardize the interface between DOS and the various BIOS conventions used by different manufacturers, the DOS designers introduced a cushioning layer that we can call the I/O system. It is often considered to be part of BIOS. But the I/O system comes on disk as part of the DOS package (and changes when necessary to meet DOS requirements), so technically it should be thought of as an entity unto itself, associated more with DOS than with the BIOS.

The DOS environment defines yet another computer system—but at a much higher level. A computer language that can manage files and file systems is introduced at this level, as are the devices on which the language is based. And at this level DOS integrates the features we need to operate in a standardized environment.

Whether you use a Toshiba or Maxtor disk drive, the operating system treats them the same way. To programs working with DOS, the lower-level details are unimportant.

On the next level (that of the command processor) is yet another computer: an interactive one characterized by device independence. At this level, you can deal with devices and files as though they were the same. Although DOS has to keep things straight, at the command-processor level you can direct output (that was supposed to go to the screen) to a file. You do not have to worry about the implications of speed or differences between the devices.

Up one more level is a computer system defined by your applications programs. The system is even simpler when it interfaces with users rather than programmers. Now the "computer language" consists of menu selections and windows. This layer, like all the others, is built on what precedes it.

As you read this book, working your way down through these levels (or layers), keep in mind what you gain (and lose) by skipping parts of the system hierarchy. Because DOS is built on the BIOS routines, programs that skip around DOS to the BIOS *can* affect the way DOS works. You could use the disk read and write functions, for example, to write your own file handling at the BIOS level. But you probably would need to work for years to make it work as well as DOS does. Conversely, you can stay at the highest level, but all the lower levels will eat away at your program speed. There are trade-offs up and down the hierarchy. The choice is yours.

The Programmer's Interface to DOS

Programmers who work in high-level languages are accustomed to working with predefined functions. In BASIC, all the functions (like PRINT and INPUT) are defined in the language. Pascal also defines the standard functions that you can access. C compilers come with a standard set of library functions. For many people, these functions represent the limits of the language.

In fact, the functions provided with BASIC, C, and Pascal are based on a much lower level of interaction with DOS and the BIOS functions. The language functions are written to handle requests for services in standard ways. In some cases, language functions are defined to be compatible with national or international standards. But to be implemented, the functions must refer directly to DOS, the BIOS, or the hardware.

Ordinarily, you are protected from the world of functionality beneath the level of language functions. Because language functions are written for general use by many people who could not "program their way out of a paper bag," these functions must provide error checking and control for generalized cases. Generalizing slows things, but you do not have to give up on speed. DOS and BIOS services are directly available from any language, if you take the time to learn how to work with that language.

The software interrupt is the mechanism for using DOS and BIOS services. (Chapter 11, "Interrupt Handlers," is devoted to interrupts.) In the present context, think of a software interrupt as a high-level language's subroutine call. You have to set entry parameters and you get a result. But you can run into trouble if you do not have the language functions to smooth the way.

By going beyond the language functions, you give up not only their error-checking, control capabilities, and the reliability of standard libraries, but also a considerable amount of portability. C programs written in standard Microsoft or Turbo C functions often can be taken, with few changes, directly to a UNIX system. DOS and BIOS functions cannot, but you can build in your own error checking and control based on what you need, not what a Microsoft or Borland programmer thought would be suitable for the mass market.

By slipping down to the DOS and BIOS level, you regain a degree of control and speed your programs. The cost (some extra programming effort) is minimal. For the highest speed possible, you need to access the hardware directly. Doing so makes sense for some devices such as screen displays and serial ports, but makes little or no sense for other devices such as disks.

Ordinarily, a slow program that works correctly can be made faster by recoding critical modules at a lower level or by changing the programming algorithm. Throughout this book, the pros and cons of working at the various programming levels are presented. *You* decide what is appropriate for your application. As a general rule, however, you should always work at the highest possible level. When software works for you, errors are easier to find. The lower you go, the more subtle the errors—and the harder they are to locate.

Summary

The IBM-compatible line of computers has been built on a firm foundation of BIOS and DOS. BIOS provides the low-level interface to the outside world; DOS provides the functionality of higher level services that augment the development of computer programs. As the most popular operating system in the world, each successive version of DOS has provided a solid footing upon which to build.

How you develop your programs—which language you use, whether you use BIOS or DOS services, and so on—depends largely on your programming needs. There are trade-offs to any programming decision you make. As you think through options and formulate strategies, you will begin to find ways to make your computer system work for you (not against you). *DOS Programmer's Reference* is designed with that end in mind: to make your programming experience the best it can be by making full use of your computer environment.

In the next chapter, which covers the structure of DOS, you look more closely at the conceptual foundation upon which DOS is built and how it relates to your programs. You also examine the tools, resources, and building blocks available to you as a programmer in a DOS environment.

The Structure of a DOS System

The structure of DOS involves the whole machine—not just the operating system, but the whole computer from the hardware up. You must understand the structure of DOS if you are to make the best decisions about which functions to use and how to use them.

The "Virtual Machine" Concept

A useful way to think about a DOS system is to view it as a hierarchical structure in which functions are distributed among subsystems. Each level in the hierarchy provides a well-defined set of services upon which the next higher level can build. Thus, each level becomes a virtual machine; it is the computer to the next higher level. Figure 2.1 illustrates this concept in relation to a DOS system.

2

CHAPTER

Fig. 2.1. *The virtual machine hierarchy.*

The physical machine, or hardware, is the lowest level of the hierarchy. At this level there are many differences between systems.

The common threads among the various machines include:

- A processor from the Intel 8086 family: the 8086, 8088, 80186, 80286, 80386, or 80486

- A similar mapping of physical equipment within the system (in other words, similarly assigned interrupts and addresses)

- One of a limited number of bus designs

One of the major purposes of DOS is to hide physical differences between machines so that there is a standard method of accessing the computer's capabilities at both the programming and user levels. DOS quite successfully provides a uniformity that has made it the operating system of choice on a wide variety of IBM-compatible computers.

The Physical Machine

The greatest differences between machines occur at the hardware level, the level at which you generally discover whether "compatibles" are truly compatible. Programs that operate at this level will not work on machines with any major hardware differences.

The physical computer system (see fig. 2.2) can be broken down into several major components:

- The central processing unit (CPU), which performs the operations of the computer system

- ROM and RAM, which hold programs and data

- The input channel(s), which feed information to the computer

- The output channel(s), which feed information to the user

- The storage devices (floppy disks and hard disks) used to hold information temporarily or permanently

Fig. 2.2. *Block diagram of the basic computer.*

Disk drive

Keyboard

RAM   ROM

CPU

Video display

An understanding of each of these elements of the computer system is integral to the successful development of quality software—particularly when you use DOS and BIOS functions. Let's look at each of these elements.

The Processor

The *central processing unit* (CPU) used in a PC or compatible is a member of Intel Corporation's 8086 series of processor chips. You are likely to see an 8088, 80186, 80286, 80386, or 80486 chip in the computers you program. Each of these chips not only implements unique qualities that set it apart from its predecessors but also retains compatibility with its earlier versions. Thus, an 80186, for example, can do all that an 8086 or 8088 can, as well as its own unique operations.

This book does not explore specific differences between the chips, but you should be aware that DOS is based on the capabilities of the 8086 or 8088 chip. In the discussions of DOS, the BIOS, and programming, the examples run on the 8086 or 8088 (without taking advantage of the unique capabilities of the newer chips). Throughout this book, all references to the 8086 imply the entire family of processors: the 8086, 8088, 80186, 80286, 80386, 80486, and so on. Some of the newer additions and enhancements to DOS require knowledge of the differences between the CPU chips; examples requiring such knowledge are clearly identified.

CPUs are basic processing engines that perform only the simplest of operations. Because you need to know something about this basic processor engine, this section provides an overview of microprocessors in the 8086 series. If you are already familiar with the subject, you can skip this section. If you want details about programming the 8086 family, see the bibliography at the end of this book.

Later in this section, the CPU registers that are accessible to you as a programmer are discussed. But first, because memory addressing is fundamental to many of the programming operations you perform at a DOS level, it is important that you understand how the 8086 addresses memory. Let's take a look at this area.

8086 Memory Addressing

Some programmers criticize the 8086's segmented memory-addressing scheme. Memory segmentation limits the sizes of data items and complicates pointer arithmetic. For DOS programmers, however, segmented memory is here to stay. It represents a reasonable solution to a problem inherent in the 8086's design: finding the best way to represent 20-bit address values using the 16-bit registers of the 8086. The 8086 has 20 address pins, which allows the addressing of 2^{20} (1,048,576, or 1M) unique memory locations, yet its registers are only 16 bits wide (register usage is discussed shortly).

The solution is to divide an absolute memory address into "pieces" that can be stored individually in the 16-bit registers. Thus, two registers are used to represent a single address; one of these registers stores a base (or segment) address, and the other stores an offset from that base. Theoretically, such a method can generate 2^{32} (more than four billion) unique addresses. Even though such an address range would require 32 address lines for the microprocessor and therefore is beyond the capabilities of the 8086, an example that uses this address range is helpful.

Figure 2.3 shows the four corners of a memory space containing 100000000h (4,294,967,296, or 2^{32}) locations. Each row is a portion, or *segment*, containing 10000h (65,536, or 2^{16}) locations. The address of each location in a segment can be expressed as an offset from where the segment begins, with the first location at offset 0. The convention for writing addresses in this segment-offset form is *segment:offset*, and is always expressed in hexadecimal notation.

Fig. 2.3. *Memory segments with 10000h-byte intervals.*

All numbers are hex except those with the *d* suffix, which denotes decimal.

The last byte of the first segment (at 0000:FFFFh) is followed immediately by the first byte of the next segment (at 0001:0000h). Therefore, the absolute address of each memory location—its ordinal position, counted from the very first memory location—can be calculated from the following formula:

actual_address = (segment_number * segment_interval) + offset

Figure 2.3 shows that when the segment interval is 10000h, the segment number forms, in effect, the four most-significant digits of the 8-digit absolute address. Similarly, the offset address can be regarded as the four least-significant digits of the absolute address.

In practice, the relationship between the base address and the absolute address does not have to be as simple as that shown in figure 2.3. Sophisticated hardware can rapidly perform address translations equivalent to those we humans use to calculate absolute addresses from segments and offsets.

Even though an understanding of this example is helpful, it still leaves us with a quandary: the 8086 uses 20 (not 32) bits for addresses. Thus, this example must be adapted to the reality of the situation. The addressing scheme developed by Intel regards the contents of the segment register (the segment portion of the absolute address) as the 16 most-significant bits of the absolute address; the 4 least-significant bits are assumed to be zero. In other words, the segment register contains the four most-significant hex digits of the address, and the least-significant (rightmost) digit is zero. Adding the contents of the offset register to this calculated address results in the desired absolute address. Figure 2.4 shows how an absolute address is determined from a segment-offset pair under the Intel addressing scheme.

Now that you have a conceptual basis of how the 8086 addresses memory, let's look at the register set of the 8086.

8086 Memory Addressing

The 8086's use of segment-offset pairs for addressing memory results in an interesting anomaly: virtually every absolute memory address can be addressed in a multitude of ways. For instance, all of the following valid segment-offset pairs reference the same absolute memory address:

```
0101:FFF0       1000:1000
03F1:D0F0       1001:0FF0
0900:8000       1002:0FE0
0CB7:4490       1003:0FD0
0FFF:1010       1100:0000
```

All of these segmented addresses refer to the same absolute address: 011000h. Notice that for each increment or decrement of the segment portion of the address there is a corresponding increase or decrease of 10h in the offset portion. As you can see, memory segments can overlap in many different ways.

Fig. 2.4. *Calculating an absolute-memory address.*

The 8086 Register Set

The 8086 family uses 14 separate 16-bit registers that can be grouped, by purpose, into the following four categories:

- General-purpose registers

- Segment registers

- Offset registers

- The flags register

Clearly, when you deal with individual registers, you work directly with the CPU at a hardware level. Note that although this usually is accomplished through assembly language, high-level languages such as BASIC, C, and Pascal have ways to access the registers. (Some techniques used to do this are covered in Chapter 4, "The DOS and BIOS Interface.")

As mentioned, the 8086 register set can be divided, according to purpose, into four categories. Let's examine each category and its registers.

The registers and their categorization are shown in table 2.1.

Table 2.1. *The 8086 Register Set*

Register	Category	Use
AX	General purpose	
BX	General purpose	
CX	General purpose	
DX	General purpose	
CS	Segment	Code segment
DS	Segment	Data segment
ES	Segment	Extra segment
SS	Segment	tack segment
SP	Offset	Stack pointer
BP	Offset	Base pointer
SI	Offset	Source index
DI	Offset	Destination index
IP	Offset	Instruction pointer
Flags	Flags	Status flags

General-Purpose Registers

The general-purpose registers, as their name implies, are used for such general purposes as the storage of immediate results or other temporary needs. When you use a DOS or BIOS function, you load these registers with values needed for the completion of the function. You will always include a value that represents the specific function, as well as other parameters that may be needed. Upon return from a DOS or BIOS function, values that can be used by your program may be returned in the registers.

The general-purpose registers are AX, BX, CX, and DX. To facilitate use of 8- and 16-bit values, each of these 16-bit registers can be addressed also as a pair of 8-bit registers. The register names AL, AH, BL, BH, and so on are used to address the lower or higher 8 bits (*L* and *H* signify low and high, respectively). Figure 2.5 shows this relationship.

Fig. 2.5. *The 16-bit registers can be addressed as a pair of 8-bit registers.*

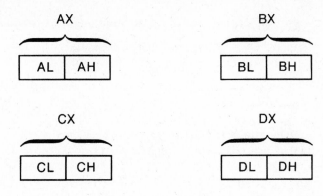

These registers are used extensively in programming, whether you are working in assembly language or using high-level language calls to access the DOS or BIOS routines.

Segment Registers

The segment registers play an important role in the 8086's memory-addressing scheme. They store 16-bit values representing the base addresses of 64K memory segments. As you may recall, these values represent the upper 16 bits of a 20-bit base address; the lower 4 bits are assumed to be zero. The 8086's memory-addressing hardware combines these base addresses with offset values stored in one of the CPU's offset registers, which are discussed in the following section.

The segment registers are

- The CS (code segment) register

- The DS (data segment) register

- The ES (extra segment) register

- The SS (stack segment) register

Each segment register specifies a distinct segment. As a programmer, you are free to use these segment registers in any way you choose, within certain limits (described shortly). In Chapter 3, "The Dynamics of DOS," you will see how programs are developed and how the segment registers are put to use. The segment registers are designed to be used in the following manner:

- CS holds the base address of the segment containing the code currently executing

- DS holds the base address of the segment containing the program's data

- ES supplements the DS register, holding the base address of an "extra" segment often used for data

- SS holds the base address of the program's stack, which is used for temporary storage of data

The previously mentioned limits on the use of segment registers include restrictions on the use of the CS and SS registers. To operate properly, the 8086 expects that the CS register will *always* point to the segment of the program that currently is executing and that the SS register will *always* point to the current stack (which is necessary for 8086 operations).

The Stack

Processors in the 8086 family use a structure called a *stack* to keep track of information during function calls and other operations. The processor puts registers on the stack whenever a subroutine is called (a PUSH operation) and takes them off (a POP operation) on return from the subroutine. Each PUSH causes the stack pointer to point to a lower address than before; each POP reverses this "movement" of the pointer. These effects on SP are built into the '86 chips and cannot be changed. The practical effect is that SP must initially be set to point to the top of the stack memory space rather than to the bottom as you might expect.

Programmers use the stack to store intermediate values in calculations or to pass values to subroutines. Programming languages make extensive use of the stack for the same purpose.

The stack works like a stack of dishes in a cafeteria: as items are added (PUSHed on) to the stack, the stack gets larger. When something is removed (POPped off), the first item to come off is the last item added to the stack. This type of structure is called a *last-in first-out* (LIFO) structure.

Offset Registers

The offset registers, as the name implies, generally are used as the offset portion of memory addresses. The segment portions of the addresses usually are stored in the segment registers.

Because the addresses are split between a segment register and an offset register, each offset register is (by default) paired with a specific segment register that contains the "other" part of the address. These pairings are automatic, unless they are overridden by specific commands.

The five offset registers, and the associated default segment register for each, are

- The SP (stack pointer) register (paired with SS)

- The BP (base pointer) register (paired with SS)

- The SI (source index) register (paired with DS)

- The DI (destination index) register (paired with ES)

- The IP (instruction pointer) register (paired with CS)

Because the registers in this group differ in their common uses, they frequently are subdivided into two separate classes: pointer registers and index registers.

Pointer Registers

The pointer registers provide a convenient way to access values, typically from the current stack segment. SP always points to the current top of the stack and is updated automatically by various assembly language instructions. The other pointer register, BP, typically is used as a base (or reference) pointer for indexed operations. For instance, some programmers use BP to point to a fixed position in the stack. This position then is used as a reference point for retrieving variables that were placed on the stack before the subroutine was called. With high-level language compilers, this use of the BP register is a standard means of accessing parameters.

The instruction pointer (IP) holds the offset address of the next instruction to be executed by the CPU. When the IP and code segment (CS) registers combine, they point to the absolute address of the instruction. (The CS:IP register pair is always used in this manner.) The value of IP is incremented automatically by the CPU after each instruction is fetched from the current code segment.

Index Registers

The index registers, SI and DI, are specialized offset registers. Typically, SI and DI are used with the DS and ES segment registers. In string operations, for example, you would use DS:SI to point to the address of the source string and ES:DI to point to the destination string. In nonstring operations, programmers generally use SI and DI for what their name implies—an index (offset) to the source or destination data.

The Flags Register

The flags register uses 9 of its 16 bits as flags that reflect the processor's status or control its operations. These flags are divided into two categories: status flags and control flags.

The status flags are

- The CF (carry flag)
- The PF (parity flag)
- The AF (auxiliary carry flag)
- The ZF (zero flag)
- The OF (overflow flag)
- The SF (sign flag)

These flags report on the status of the last instruction executed. If the last instruction generated a value of zero, for example, the zero flag is set. The status flags are set and cleared automatically, but programs also can set and clear the flags. Many DOS and BIOS routines use the carry flag to signal errors.

The control flags are

- The DF (direction flag)
- The TF (trap flag)
- The IF (interrupt flag)

The direction flag controls certain aspects of the 8086's instructions for copying ranges of memory. The trap flag puts the CPU in "single-step" mode (which debuggers use to control program execution). The interrupt flag enables or disables hardware interrupt response.

The 80286 and Beyond

Beginning with the 80286, it became possible to break out of the 1M memory limitation imposed by the 8088/8086 segmented architecture. The CPU could be programmed in real mode, which has the same programmer's model and the same limitations as the 8086 and 8088, or in protected mode.

In protected mode, *descriptor tables* are constructed. These tables contain the information previously found in segment registers—the base addresses of the segments—plus information about the segments, such as whether they can be written to. Segment registers are now *segment selectors,* indices to descriptor tables.

In protected mode on the 80286, a descriptor table entry contains a 24-bit base address. Thus, when the 80286 is running in protected mode, it can access up to 16M of memory.

The 80386 continued the expansion of memory addressing capabilities. Like the 80286, it can be programmed in protected mode, but now the descriptor table entries have 32-bit base addresses, which allows access to more than 4 billion bytes (4 gigabytes) of memory. In addition to this addressing leap, the general-purpose, offset, and flags registers now have 32-bit versions: EAX, EBX, ECX, EDX, ESP, EBP, ESI, EDI, EIP, and EFLAGS. The old 16-bit registers (AX, BX, and so on) still exist as the least significant words of their 32-bit counterparts.

Not only can the CPU access 4G of memory, a single segment can span the full 4G of memory. That, and the fact that 32-bit arithmetic can now be performed as easily as 16-bit arithmetic, has created a market for 80386/80486-specific software in the DOS environment, including two competing protected mode environments: the DOS protected mode interface (DPMI) and the virtual control program interface (VCPI).

In addition, there are DOS extenders, which are programs that allow 80386/80486-aware software to operate in protected mode while allowing access to the real mode DOS and BIOS functions. DOS extenders allow programs to be created that use DOS and BIOS facilities while taking advantage of the 32-bit power of the CPU. Such programs tend to run faster than their 16-bit equivalents and are not restricted by DOS memory constraints.

Identifying the CPU Chip

To exploit the advanced capabilities of the 80286, 80386, and 80486 CPUs, the software has to know that it is running on one of the chips, and it has to know which one it is running on. There are three solutions to the problem of finding out which chip is present. The first is based on the fact that the 80386 and 80486 tell you who they are at power-up with an ID byte (3 or 4) in the DH register. The second is to ask the users which chip they are using. The third is to deduce which chip is present from known differences between the chips.

The first method involves reprogramming the BIOS chips, which is beyond the scope of most programmers, and intrusive for the user. It also cannot be used to tell an 80286 from an 8086. The second assumes the user knows what CPU is under the hood; in too many cases, this is not a valid assumption. The third is more work than the second but far less than the first, and is reliable.

The code in listing 2.1 demonstrates how to determine which CPU is present. The first test performed differentiates the 8088, 8086, 80188, and 80186 from the

80286 and above. When a value is pushed onto the stack on the 8088, the stack pointer is decremented before the value is written to the stack. Beginning with the 80286, the value is written first, then the stack pointer is decremented. By pushing the stack pointer itself, you can check the value written to the stack to see whether the stack pointer was decremented before or after the value was written. If it is determined that an 80286, 80386 or 80486 is present, you can attempt to set bits in the flags register that the 80286 does not use. The 80286 will not let you meddle with those bits, but the 80386 and 80486 will. If you can change the bit values, the chip is either an 80386 or an 80486. A similar trick is used to differentiate an 80386 from an 80486. Notice that we use the 66h size override prefix to force the 32-bit flags register to be pushed and popped. This is perfectly safe; at that point, we know it is at least an 80386.

Listing 2.1

```
        page 55,132

comseg     segment

        assume   cs:comseg
        assume   ds:comseg
        assume   es:comseg
        assume   ss:comseg

        org  0100h
;
;       Determine whether the CPU in use is an 8088/8086, an 80286,
;       an 80386 or an 80486. Print the CPU and return an
;       errorlevel of 0, 2, 3, or 4 for or 4, for 8088/8086, 80286,
:       80386, or 80486, respectively.
;
;       Assembled with MASM 5.10a. Linked with LINK 3.05.
;
;       MASM /Ml /n /p /w2 /Zd CPU;
;       LINK CPU;
:       EXE2BIN CPU CPU.COM
;
check      proc near
        ;
        ;       The first step is to determine whether the chip is
        ;       an 8088/8086.
        ;
        ;       The key difference is based on what the CPU does when
        ;       it executes the PUSH instruction.  The 8088/8086
        ;       decrements the stack pointer first, then writes the
        ;       saved value to the stack. The 80286, 80386, and 80486
        ;       write the value to the stack, then decrement the
        ;       stack pointer. Thus, when SP is pushed, and the
```

```
;       pushed value is popped off, the value popped off will
;       equal the current stack pointer, unless the chip is an
;       8088 or 8086.
;
push sp                 ; push SP
pop  ax                 ; get back the value pushed?
cmp  ax,sp              ; if same, it is 80286 or higher
jne  short is_86        ; otherwise, it is 8088/8086
;
;       The second step is to determine whether the chip is
;       an 80286.
;
;       The key difference is the IOPL bits in the flags
;       register; the 80386 and 80486 have them, the
;       80286 does not. The 80286 will not allow them to
;       be set; the 80386 and 80486 will.
;
pushf                   ; push flags
pop  ax                 ; retrieve them
or   ax,03000h          ; set IOPL bits
push ax                 ; stuff back
popf                    ; pop flags back—this is where the
                        ;   80286 will put them back the way
                        ;   they were
pushf                   ; push them back
pop  ax                 ; see if the CPU overrode the IOPL bits
test ax,03000h          ; if the IOPL bits are reset, the CPU did
                        ;   and the chip is an 80286
jz   short is_286       ;
;
;       The third step is to determine whether the chip is
;       an 80386.
;
;       The key difference is the alignment check bit in the
;       flags register; the 80486 has one, the 80386 does not.
;       As with the 80286 and the IOPL bits, the 80386 will not
;       let you set that bit, but the 80486 will.
;
db   66h                ; (32 bit)
pushf                   ; push extended flags register
pop  ax                 ; read low word
and  ax,00FFFh          ; clear IOPL bits—level zero
pop  dx                 ; read high word
or   dx,00004h          ; set alignment check bit
push dx                 ; push flags back
push ax                 ;
db   66h                ; (32 bit)
popf                    ; pop flags register—this is where
                        ;   the 80386 will undo your work
```

continues

Listing 2.1 *continued*

```
        db   66h              ; (32 bits)
        pushf                 ; push flags back
        pop  ax               ; read what we did
        pop  dx               ; find out if the CPU reset the
                              ;   alignment check bit
        test dx,4             ;
        jnz  short is_486     ; if it didn't, the chip is an 80486
        mov  dx,offset say386    ; otherwise, it is an 80386
        mov  al,3             ; get errorlevel
sayso:
        push ax               ; save errorlevel
        mov  ah,9             ; call DOS write string function
        int  21h
        pop  ax               ; retrieve errorlevel
        mov  ah,04Ch          ; terminate process with return code
        int  21h
is_486:
        mov  dx,offset say486
        mov  al,4             ; errorlevel 4
        jmp  sayso
is_86:
        mov  dx,offset say86
        mov  al,0             ; errorlevel 0
        jmp  sayso
is_286:
        mov  dx,offset say286
        mov  al,2             ; errorlevel 1
        jmp  sayso
check   endp

say86   db   "8088 or 8086$"
say286  db   "80286$"
say386  db   "80386$"
say486  db   "80486$"

comseg  ends

        end  check
```

Math Coprocessors

The Intel 80x86 family of processor chips, from the 8088 to the 80386, can perform only integer arithmetic. For many applications, integer arithemtic is all that is needed. For applications that require floating-point arithmetic, the math must be performed by specially written procedures. For most applications, the overhead of performing the calculations in software is not noticeable to the user. For math-intensive applications, however, the overhead becomes a problem, and a math coprocessor becomes essential; some applications will not even run unless the system has a math coprocessor.

The math coprocessor can handle floating-point math with the same ease with which the processor handles integer arithmetic. Further, it performs its math in parallel with the processor. Aside from loading data to and from the coprocessor and directing the coprocessor's activities, the processor is free to go about its business while the math coprocessor is performing its functions.

Identifying the Math Coprocessor

Three math coprocessors designed by Intel work with their processor chips: the 8087, the 80287, and the 80387. There is no 80187; the 8087 works with the 80186 and 80188. And there is no 80487; the 80486 has the equivalent of an 80387 coprocessor built in.

Identifying the math coprocessor is not simple. Seemingly disparate pairings of processor and coprocessor can occur, particularly the combination of an 80386 CPU and an 80287.

As in the method for differentiating one CPU from another, the technique for identifying the math coprocessor is based on exploiting subtle differences between one chip and its successor. Complicating the task of discerning which math chip is in the system is the possibility that there is no chip. (The math chips have never been so inexpensive—and applications requiring them have never been so common—that vendors automatically put them in the system. On the other hand, few vendors want to put their products in a position of losing 100% compatibility by locking out applications that do require a math chip. As a compromise, they put a socket for a math chip on the motherboard, and the user may, as an option, install a math coprocessor.)

To find out if a math chip is present, a bit pattern is written to memory, and an attempt is made to initialize the math chip. The math chip is then instructed to write the coprocessor status word to that memory location. If the chip is present, a new value is written to memory. If the chip is not present, we can tell from the bit pattern written—it will not be valid for the coprocessor status word.

After you know that a math chip is present, you can differentiate an 8087 from the 80287 and 80387 by disabling interrupts on the math chip and reading the control word. This has an effect on the 8087, but not on the 80287 or the 80387. An 80287 can be differentiated from an 80387 by creating a positive infinity value (dividing positive 1 by 0), creating a negative infinity value, and then comparing the two values with the math coprocessor. The 80387 differentiates between the two; the 80287 does not.

Listing 2.2 is a procedure that can be called to determine what math coprocessor, if any, is present.

Listing 2.2

```
            page 55,132
            name math_id
            ;
            ;    Procedure for identifying a math processor.
            ;
m_data          segment para 'M_DATA'

scratch         dw   (?)  ; have the math chip store data here

m_data          ends

m_code          segment   para 'M_CODE'

assume          cs:m_code
assume          ds:m_data
            ;
            ;    Procedure for identifying a math processor.
            ;
            ;    If it returns:
            ;               AX = 0000, no math processor was detected
            ;               AX = 0001, an 8087 was detected
            ;               AX = 0002, an 80287 was detected
            ;               AX = 0003, an 80387 was detected
            ;
_math_ident     proc far

        push    ds              ; save caller's DS
        mov     ax,seg m_data   ;
        mov     ds,ax           ; get new DS
        fninit                  ; initialize the math coprocessor
        mov     scratch,055AAh  ; the math coprocessor will not
                                ;   write this
        fnstsw  scratch         ; have the math coprocessor write
                                ;   its status word
        cmp     byte ptr scratch,0  ; check lsb; it should be 0
        jne     no_math         ; if not, return
        fnstcw  scratch         ; now have the math coprocessor
                                ;   write its control word
        mov     ax,scratch      ; read the value
        and     ax,0103Fh       ; mask expected bits
        cmp     ax,0003Fh       ; this is what we should see
        jne     no_math         ; if different, no math chip
        ;
        ;    Now that we know we have a math coprocessor,
```

```
        ;    which one is it?
        ;
        and        scratch,0FF7Fh ; clear interrupt bit
        fldcw      scratch        ; load the control word
        fdisi                     ; disable interrupts
        fstcw      scratch        ; write the control word back
        test       scratch,00080h ; any effect on the word?
        jnz        found_8087     ; if so, it is an 8087
        ;
        ;     The chip is not an 8087, so it is an 80287 or 80387.
        ;
        finit                     ; reinitialize the chip
        fld1                      ; push +1.0 onto the chip's stack
        fldz                      ; push 0.0 onto the chip's stack
        fdiv                      ; produce positive infinity
        fld        st             ; produce negative infinity
        fcompp                    ; compare
        fstsw      scratch        ; write the status word
        mov        ax,scratch     ;
        sahf                      ; copy AH into the flags register
        je         found_80287    ; if Z bit set (equal), the
                                  ;   coprocessor found positive and
                                  ;   negative infinity equal

        ;
        ;     The chip is an 80387.
        ;
        mov        ax,3; AX = 3
return_result:
        pop        ds             ; restore DS
        ret                       ; return
no_math:
        xor        ax,ax          ; AX = 0
        jmp        return_result  ;
found_8087:
        mov        ax,1           ; AX = 1
        jmp        return_result  ;
found_80287:
        mov        ax,2           ; AX = 2
        jmp        return_result  ;

_math_ident     endp

public     _math_ident

m_code     ends

    end
```

Memory

PCs and compatible computers have four classes of memory:

- *ROM (read-only memory)* is permanent memory installed in the computer. Usually it holds a portion of BIOS specific to the physical machine.

- *RAM (random-access memory)* holds nonpermanent program code and data.

- *Extended memory* (memory above one megabyte) can be accessed by an 80286 processor running in protected mode.

- *Expanded memory* is added to the system and is not part of the memory mapped directly by the processor. This memory is accessed through a special expanded memory driver system.

You may hear also about PROM (programmable read-only memory) and other variations, but all such memory is under the ROM heading. Although purists may object to this move, from the standpoint of those programming the DOS system, PROM and other such variations represent permanent memory.

The memory map in figure 2.6 shows how the basic system memory is allocated.

In Chapter 10, "Program and Memory Management," which discusses in greater detail the allocation and uses of memory, you will learn how to control memory and how to use it for your programs.

I/O Channels

The standard input/output (I/O) devices on the PC and compatibles are the keyboard, the video monitor, and the printer (see Chapter 5, "Output Devices," and Chapter 6, "Input Devices"). In addition to these standard devices, you frequently will see a mouse and one or more serial ports (see Chapter 6 and Chapter 7, "Serial Devices").

You also can add custom devices, such as touch-sensitive screens and sensors of all types, to a PC system. Although a discussion of such specialized devices is beyond the scope of this book, Chapter 12, "Device Drivers," shows you how to write your own drivers for specialized devices.

Fig. 2.6. *Memory map for a machine with one megabyte of memory.*

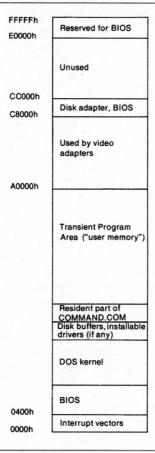

```
FFFFFh      ┌─────────────────────┐
E0000h      │  Reserved for BIOS   │
            ├─────────────────────┤
            │                      │
            │  Unused              │
            │                      │
CC000h      ├─────────────────────┤
C8000h      │  Disk adapter, BIOS  │
            ├─────────────────────┤
            │  Used by video       │
            │  adapters            │
A0000h      ├─────────────────────┤
            │                      │
            │  Transient Program   │
            │  Area ("user memory")│
            │                      │
            ├─────────────────────┤
            │  Resident part of    │
            │  COMMAND.COM         │
            │  Disk buffers, installable
            │  drivers (if any)    │
            ├─────────────────────┤
            │  DOS kernel          │
            ├─────────────────────┤
            │  BIOS                │
0400h       ├─────────────────────┤
            │  Interrupt vectors   │
0000h       └─────────────────────┘
```

The Keyboard

The PC keyboard knows nothing about *what* you type. The keyboard does not interpret your keystrokes—it simply tells the computer that a given key has been pressed or released. The keyboard does not assign meaning to the keys, but does assign a unique number (a *scan code*) to each key. This scan code is passed to the PC for interpretation by the BIOS. Figure 2.7 shows the scan codes of the original 84-key version; later keyboards added more keys and codes, which are fully described in Chapter 6.

DOS
PROGRAMMING

Fig. 2.7. *The keyboard scan codes.*

As you type, the keyboard notifies the computer (through Int 09h) that a key has been pressed or released. When the processor executes Int 09h, the BIOS takes momentary control of the computer and reads the key's scan code, checking first for toggle keys such as Shift and Num Lock. If a toggle key has been pressed or released, the BIOS updates the keyboard status bits kept in memory addresses 0417h–0418h. Next, the BIOS checks for special key combinations (such as Ctrl-Alt-Del) and, if necessary, executes their special handlers.

If the scan code still has not been "weeded out" as a special-purpose character (such as Num-Lock, Ctrl-Alt-Del, Shift, or Ctrl), BIOS translates it into its ASCII equivalent. If no corresponding ASCII character is available for the key, it is given an ASCII value of zero. Then the ASCII character, along with its original scan code, is stored in the keyboard buffer. This buffer is large enough to hold 15 characters and their scan codes. If the buffer is full, BIOS issues a "beep" (signaling that the keyboard buffer is full) and then discards the character.

After the character is in the keyboard buffer, it is available for use by any program (including DOS) currently running. Because the computer usually responds in a fraction of a second, the chances of filling the keyboard buffer are slim, *unless the computer is busy performing another task.*

This overview of the keyboard should suffice for now. Programming the keyboard is discussed in greater detail in Chapter 6, "Input Devices."

The Display Screen

The PC supports several types of video adapters, and most adapters work in more than one text or graphics mode. Writing programs to accommodate the various kinds of adapters is not as difficult as you might think, however, because DOS provides facilities for determining the kind of adapter and the current mode.

Chapter 6 discusses these matters in detail. The following sections are an introduction to typical kinds of adapters.

Types of Display Adapters

For most PC programming, you should be familiar with six types of display adapters. (Others exist but are used for special applications.)

The original "standard" display was the Monochrome Display Adapter (MDA). This system, with its crisp, clear characters and a nice professional appearance, was expected to be the standard for business use of the computer. Other video adapters (the CGA, EGA, HGA, MCGA, and VGA) became available as users began to demand different display enhancements. Table 2.2 lists these display adapters and the year each became available.

Table 2.2. *Display Adapters and Year Each Became Available*

Adapter	Year Introduced
MDA	1981
CGA	1982
HGA	1982
EGA	1984
MCGA	1987
VGA	1987

In addition to the monochrome adapter, the Color Graphics Adapter (CGA) was available for those to whom color was important. The CGA display shows color and graphics, but the characters are not as sharp as those displayed by the MDA. This difference in sharpness is due to the number of dots, or pixels, used to create each character. The MDA uses a 9×14 character box to create characters, whereas the CGA uses an 8×8 box. Because of this difference in resolution, the characters on the CGA tend to look "fuzzy" when compared to the MDA.

The Hercules Graphics Adapter (HGA) display, which combines the monochrome screen's clear characters with the graphics capabilities of the color graphics display, produces high-resolution monochrome displays that rapidly became the standard of comparison for text and graphics. HGAs cannot produce color, but this lack was not a big drawback.

With the introduction of the Enhanced Graphics Adapter (EGA) color graphics system, people (and businesses) began to discover that color added a rich new dimension to their work. Highlighting alone is never adequate for showing a wide range of things on-screen; you can call attention to many more things with color.

The standards for displays have again been revised, albeit only slightly, by the introduction of the Multi-Color Graphics Array (MCGA) for IBM Personal System/2

Models 25 and 30 and the Video Graphics Array (VGA) for IBM PS/2 Models 50, 60, and 80. The MCGA is similar to the CGA but has higher resolution. (The MCGA's resolution is 320×400; the CGA's resolution is 320×200.) The VGA's resolution (640×480) is a modest extension of the EGA (640×350). The big improvement in both displays is that they use analog rather than digital monitors. By working with analog signals, these new video systems can display palettes of 256 colors (of the possible 262,144 colors available).

Memory Mapping and Display Adapters

The video displays of the IBM family all use *memory mapping*. In other words, what you see on the screen is a direct reflection of what resides in the memory area controlled by the display adapter. To put it simply, characters are written to the display memory, then the display adapter reads the characters from the display memory and shows them on the video screen. In graphics modes, the display adapter treats the data in the video memory as an array of individual bits that control the dots on the screen. The memory areas used by the different display adapters vary according to the type of display. Table 2.3 details the starting memory locations and length of video buffers for each display adapter.

Table 2.3. Memory Configurations for Display Adapters

Display Type	Mode	Buffer Segment Address	Buffer Length	Display Pages
MDA	Text	B000h	4K	1
CGA	Text	B800h	16K	4/8
	Graphics	B800h	16K	1
EGA	Mono	B000h	— varies —	
	Text	B800h	— varies —	
	CGA graphics	B800h	— varies —	
	Graphics	A000h	— varies —	
MCGA	Text	B800h	64K	8
	CGA graphics	B800h	64K	1
	Graphics	A000h	64K	1
VGA	Mono	B000h	256K	8
	Text	B800h	256K	8
	CGA graphics	B800h	256K	1
	Graphics	A000h	256K	1/2/4/8

Although this section provides an overview of the way display adapters function, you should refer to Chapter 5, "Output Devices," for more detailed information. That chapter provides specifics on how the display adapters interpret the video memory and how to use the BIOS and DOS functions to display information.

The Printer

In this book, the term *printer* generally refers to a printer attached to the parallel printer port, not to the serial port. (Serial ports are touched upon in the next section; Chapter 7, "Serial Devices," discusses them in greater detail.) With a parallel printer interface, you can send the printer an initialization message and read the printer's status to find out, for example, whether it is out of paper. This is typically what you will do at the DOS level with a printer. Printer gymnastics are beyond the scope of this book.

In Chapter 5, "Output Devices," you learn how to write programs that access the printer directly, using the BIOS and DOS functions. You can access several printers (LPT1, LPT2, and so on) and interpret the return codes to determine the printer's status.

The Serial Port

With a parallel printer connection, you have limited control of the parallel printer port. The hardware has been designed to handle almost every task. You can buy a printer off the shelf and be confident that it will run correctly as soon as you plug it in. But serial ports are different.

Most of today's computers are equipped with at least one serial port. Used predominantly to drive serial printers or modems, serial ports pose special problems. Their parameters must be set identically on both sides of the connection; if the parameters are not set correctly, nothing gets through. These parameters include baud rate, parity, stop and start bits, and data length. Although standards govern the way that wires are physically connected for most (but not all) devices, the parameters have not been completely standardized. Even if you make the correct physical connections, you still have to make the correct *logical* connections.

There is no quick-and-easy way to make these connections. Serial port parameters specify the number of bits per second at which information is transferred; the number of bits that make up a character; whether there is parity checking and, if there is, the type of parity; and the number of stop bits used to indicate the end of a character. You may have to specify flow control over the line with software, such as XON/XOFF or ETX/ACK; or you may have to use a special line protocol, such as Xmodem or Kermit. It is no wonder that beginners rarely succeed in getting their computers connected to the telephone line the first time they try.

In Chapter 7, which is devoted to the intricacies of serial channels and how to program them, you will find the meaning of all the serial port parameters and determine how best to incorporate this information into the programs you write.

The Mouse

When the original PC was designed, the mouse was not considered an important device. Routines inside the BIOS allowed programmers to access the more popular joysticks and light pens. But times (and users) change—today, the mouse has a sizeable following.

Generally, a mouse is connected to a PC either through a custom hardware board that plugs into the PC's internal system bus or through one of the installed serial ports. The mouse driver software determines the location of the mouse and handles the interface to the board.

The Mouse

In its simplest form, a mouse is a device with a small ball fitted on the bottom. When you roll the mouse across a flat surface, sensors measure the device's movement in both X and Y directions. The mouse sends signals indicating changes in position to the computer system. An *optical mouse* does not use a ball; rather, it tracks the movement of the device across a reflective grid. No matter which type of mouse you use, the computer responds to the changes in position by moving a visible pointer on the screen. All this activity is handled at the driver level.

In addition to movement sensors, the mouse usually is fitted with one, two, or three switches (called *buttons*) that can be tested and used to control program actions.

DOS Int 33h accesses the mouse when you use the standard mouse driver software. The interrupt provides information about the mouse and its movement, and permits control of this data. Even though the mouse is an add-on to the DOS system, you can learn more about it in Chapter 6, "Input Devices."

Storage Devices

As DOS has evolved, so have its capabilities for greater disk storage capacity. Table 2.4 shows the increases in floppy disk capacity and in the number of drive formats supported.

Table 2.4. *Floppy Disk Capacities*

DOS Version	Floppy Disk	Capacity
1.0	5¼-inch SSDD	160K
	5¼-inch DSDD	320K
2.0	5¼-inch SSDD	180K
	5¼-inch DSDD	360K
2.1	5¼-inch DSHD	1.2M
3.2	3½-inch DSDD	720K
3.3	3¹/2-inch DSHD	1.44M

Physical Disk Structure

The recording surface of a disk is divided into concentric tracks, and each track is divided into sectors. The number of tracks and sectors varies according to the type of disk (floppy disk or hard disk; single sided or double sided; double density or high density; 3½-inch or 5¼-inch). Figure 2.8 shows the arrangement of tracks and sectors on the disk.

Fig. 2.8. *Disk track formatting.*

Because hard disk drives (also known as "fixed disk" drives, as opposed to drives with removable media) contain more than one platter, hard-disk space is divided into cylinders. Each cylinder includes one track on each side of each platter present in the drive. Figure 2.9 shows how tracks combine to make cylinders.

Fig. 2.9. *A fixed disk.*

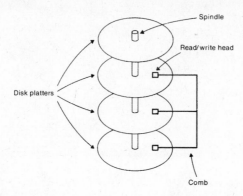

In Chapter 8, which deals with disk structure, you will find a more detailed discussion of the disk's physical format. Chapter 8 also shows how to access the internal formatting routines that control the lowest level of the track-formatting operation.

Logical Disk Structure

The FORMAT program establishes not only the disk's sector structure but also a logical structure, unique to DOS, that controls how data is stored on the disk. Figure 2.10 shows this logical structure.

Fig. 2.10. *The disk's logical structure.*

FORMAT's largest, most time-consuming task is that of formatting the disk—dividing the physical disk into logical tracks and sectors and filling them with an initial value.

After formatting the disk, the FORMAT program creates three areas on the disk: the boot record, the file allocation table (FAT), and the root directory. The rest of the disk (the portion not included in any of these areas) is the file-storage area.

The Boot Record

The *boot record* is the first sector on every logical disk. Beginning with DOS V2, the boot record contains the disk boot program (which is only a few hundred bytes long) and a table of the disk characteristics. When the system is started, the boot program is loaded into memory, then the boot program loads the operating system files from the disk. If those files are not found, the boot program gives you an error message. The booting process is covered in greater detail in Chapter 3, "The Dynamics of DOS."

The File Allocation Table

The *file allocation table* (*FAT*) is a map of the disk. It tracks which portions of the disk are assigned, which are unassigned, and which are not assignable (because of formatting errors, for example). Areas of the disk are assigned to files in clusters, with each cluster represented by an entry in the FAT. Depending on the disk's size, clusters can vary in size from one to eight or more sectors. To accommodate the increased storage capacity of hard disks, FAT entries (originally 12 bits per entry) may now be as large as 16 bits per entry. The FAT-entry size is one of the most significant differences between DOS V2, V3, and V4.

It should be stressed that the FAT is essential to the proper functioning of DOS in relation to a disk. The FAT makes it possible to have files larger than 512 bytes, and any damage to the FAT can chop off files and programs. A detailed description and discussion of the FAT would be premature at this point; for more detailed information on the FAT, see Chapter 8, "Disks."

The Root Directory

The last part of the system information on the disk, the *root directory*, is located immediately after the FAT. It contains the following information about each file accessible through the root directory:

- An eight-byte file name

- A three-byte file extension

- The file size (in bytes)

- A date and time stamp for the file

- The starting cluster number for the file

- The file attribute codes

Each entry is 32 bytes long, with extra space reserved for future expansion. The root directory for a given disk is a fixed size. On 160K, single-sided disks, the root directory can accommodate 64 entries; on a 20M hard disk, it can hold 512 entries. Directory size is limited so that DOS can tell where the disk's data area begins. In DOS V2 and later versions, this limitation is not a problem; you can bypass the limit on the number of files by creating subdirectories, which have no size limit.

For a more detailed discussion of the structure of disks and directories, see Chapter 8, "Disks," and Chapter 9, "Directories and Files."

The Software

Above the physical machine, the software provided with a PC or compatible system builds another layer on the virtual machine. This software starts with the BIOS, which builds a standard view of the machine that attempts to hide the specifics of the installed hardware. Above the BIOS, DOS builds the machine you are familiar with (in terms of files and directories).

The BIOS

The first software level in the virtual machine is the BIOS (basic input/output system). This software forms the lowest-level machine you normally will deal with.

The true BIOS consists of firmware contained in a ROM that implements the most basic machine functions. Many descriptions also include the I/O system software as part of the BIOS. This software, loaded from disk, extends the BIOS functions so that they can handle all system input and output requests. The purpose of the BIOS is to insulate higher levels of software from possible hardware changes in the computer; that of the I/O system is to cushion the interface between the BIOS itself and DOS. Together, the BIOS and the I/O system provide a uniformly defined set of services as a base for higher software levels.

Each computer manufacturer (including IBM) provides the BIOS, and customizes the I/O system, for its machines. Microsoft provides a module called SYSINIT (see Chapter 3), which manages system initialization and the loading of DOS. The BIOS and the I/O system combination must meet certain specifications for the higher-level software to function properly. For example, Microsoft's DOS kernel uses BIOS services to implement many of its own operations.

PC-compatible computers often come with versions of the BIOS ROM provided by the manufacturer. None of them can duplicate the code in an IBM BIOS ROM, but they can provide BIOS services by handling the same interrupt structure and using the same data table areas used by the IBM BIOS. Although the code is different, they provide the BIOS services needed to run DOS.

If third-party BIOS ROMs are accessed through the defined BIOS interrupts, you can expect them to work the way the IBM PC services work. If you write a program that depends on knowledge of the undocumented BIOS ROM functions to get something done, all bets are off. A common example of such code is a program that toggles the speed switch on multispeed compatibles; because the IBM PC never had such a feature, no standard exists for interfacing to it and you must work by trial and error.

The "BIOS Function Reference" section at the back of this book describes the BIOS interrupt functions in detail. All of these functions work with the BIOS ROMs provided by all manufacturers of IBM-compatible computers.

The DOS Kernel

Microsoft provides the DOS kernel as a proprietary program based on the standard BIOS services. The DOS kernel provides hardware-independent services that can be used by application programs on a variety of systems. You will spend a great deal of time working with these DOS services. *Note:* "DOS" refers to IBM's version of DOS *or* to MS-DOS unless specifically mentioned otherwise.

DOS services can be divided arbitrarily into the following categories:

- Character I/O

- Directory operations

- Disk control

- Dynamic memory allocation

- Error handling

- File operations

- Miscellaneous system functions

- Network functions

- Program initiation and termination

You can access the DOS services in two ways. Some services are accessed directly through software interrupts. Most DOS services, however, are accessed through DOS function calls by placing a function number in register AH and then executing Int 21h. The "DOS Reference" section at the back of this book describes the DOS interrupt functions in detail. These interrupts are available on all PCs and compatibles. Known differences between systems are pointed out in this section.

The Command Processor

To most people who work with a PC, the command processor (or shell) *is* the operating system. These people are used to thinking of the C> prompt as coming from the operating system and not from a program. Only a few years ago, interactive operating systems *were* built this way.

Today, however, shell interfaces are the standard. The shell makes the process of changing and adding new features easy, because only one part of the operating system has to be changed. Although the shell interface was not invented by the designers of UNIX, this type of program (COMMAND.COM, for example) was popularized by the UNIX operating system. UNIX systems have several standard shells (csh, ksh, and sh, to name a few).

The structure of COMMAND.COM is important to its operation. The program has three parts: an initialization section, a resident section, and a transient section.

When COMMAND.COM starts, the initialization and resident sections are loaded from disk. The initialization section sets up the system, runs the AUTOEXEC.BAT file, and then loads and turns control over to the transient section. As its name implies, the transient section comes and goes (according to the demands of memory); the resident section, which "is always there," is responsible for reloading the transient section, among other things.

If all the capabilities of COMMAND.COM were coded in a single program, the program would take up a substantial amount of memory (more than 20K). This amount of memory is a drop in the bucket compared to that required by most applications, but if you were trying to get the last few paragraphs into a document or the last few cells into a spreadsheet, it could be considerable. To minimize the program's memory consumption, the COMMAND.COM code for normal operations and the code for the program's built-in commands are kept in the transient section. Because this section is sometimes overwritten by another program, COMMAND.COM's resident section checks to see whether the transient section needs to be reloaded and, if it does, reloads it.

COMMAND.COM executes programs from three categories of commands:

- *Internal commands* (built into COMMAND.COM)

- *External commands* (stored on the disk)

- *Batch files* (stored on the disk)

The transient section of COMMAND.COM includes the code for the internal commands. When the user types a command name, COMMAND.COM first searches to see whether the command is an internal command. If COMMAND.COM does not find the named command among the internal commands, the program searches for it first in the current directory and then along the search path. COMMAND.COM searches for an external command with the .COM extension, and then for one with the .EXE extension. If it finds neither of these in a given directory, COMMAND.COM looks for a batch file (extension .BAT) with the appropriate name.

Batch files are a special type of "program" allowed by a command processor. These files consist of scripts of commands to execute in a given sequence, with a small control language that allows for parameter substitution, decisions, and branching within the batch file. Batch files are executed by COMMAND.COM on a line-by-line basis. Each line consists of a command to be executed: either an executable command or an internal control command allowed only in batch files. Actual operation is simple. The transient portion of COMMAND.COM takes one line of the batch file, performs any parameter replacements, and then uses the DOS EXEC function to execute the command. As each line is finished, COMMAND.COM gets the next line and executes it.

Device Drivers

Most advances in the art of software have involved ways to make the underlying hardware disappear. High-level languages, for example, are an advance because they do not require the programmer to know about registers, bits, and bytes. (Not everyone will agree with that statement.) Similarly, operating systems are a big improvement over the days when we all had to write our own drivers for each device we wanted to use.

CP/M used standard devices for handling the console and printer. DOS has gone a step further by making the devices more interchangeable and making it possible to install your own devices without having to recompile the entire operating system. Think about it! Previously, if you wanted to add new devices to a system, you had to get down to the internals of the operating system to make your devices work. Today, DOS includes a more flexible driver model that allows you to write a driver for a device and to choose whether to add it when the system starts. To understand how this works, you need to understand a little about device drivers.

The operating system software includes a set of device drivers (the resident drivers) that run the hardware. Each driver meets certain specifications for its calling interface so that DOS can operate the hardware *without having to know how the hardware works*.

When you boot the computer, DOS initializes all the drivers through standard initialization entry points, as you will learn in Chapter 3, "The Dynamics of DOS." For now, all you need to know is that you operate a device through a series of functions defined by standard entry points. The type of device you are trying to control determines which entry points are meaningful. In Chapter 12, "Device Drivers," you will learn a great deal about device drivers—in fact, you will create a simple one.

DOS divides devices into character devices and block devices. *Character devices* operate on a character-by-character basis (the keyboard and video display, for example); *block devices* (disks and RAM disks) operate on a block-transfer basis. Each type of driver has entry points appropriate for handling specific functions.

You can write your own device drivers and then add them to your CONFIG.SYS file. These device drivers will be added to the system the next time you boot the system. Your drivers will operate on an equal footing with the resident drivers. You can even replace an existing character driver with completely new code, as ANSI.SYS and other drivers do for the video display.

Installable drivers let you add new equipment, not envisioned in the original design, to the system. (MOUSE.SYS does this for the mouse; EMM.SYS, for expanded memory.) In short, DOS has created an environment that you can expand to meet your needs as new equipment becomes available.

Summary

In this chapter, you learned that DOS systems exist as a hierarchy of "virtual computers." Starting with the hardware at the lowest level and continuing up through the BIOS and DOS systems, each level provides a consistent logical computer with special functions needed to implement the next level of the computer system.

The lowest level, hardware (the combination of components that a system comprises) can vary widely between systems. At the next level, the BIOS provides a "computer" with defined services that we can depend on to work in the same way from one system to another. These basic input/output services allow raw access to the devices on the system. DOS provides a higher level of services (and therefore a higher level of abstraction) than the BIOS. The DOS services create what we commonly think of as "the system"—files, directories, and so on. At the highest level, COMMAND.COM provides a user interface that gives you control of the different services.

Now that you understand something of the statics of DOS, let's move on to DOS in a dynamic environment and learn how it all works.

The Dynamics of DOS

Chapter 2, "The Structure of a DOS System," described the layout of DOS, its hardware support, and its basic software modules. This chapter shows you what happens when these elements operate in a dynamic environment. You see what happens as the system starts up, how it processes commands, and how programs are executed.

Then, having gained an overview of system and program operation, you take a more detailed look at interrupts and memory management under DOS. This chapter and the next lay the groundwork for the practical programming in Chapters 5 through 13.

The DOS Boot Sequence

When you power up or reset a system based on the 8086 family of microprocessors, the microprocessor automatically starts program execution at address FFFF:0000h. This happens because of the processor design and has nothing to do with DOS. The ROM BIOS at FFFF:0000h provides a jump instruction to the beginning of the hardware test routines and the ROM bootstrap code. (In the following discussion, *ROM BIOS* applies to PCs and compatibles.)

When a system is turned on (a cold start), a series of hardware tests called the *power-on self test* (POST) check the amount of installed memory and test which peripheral devices are available and operable. At this point during startup, most machines show rapidly changing memory-size figures and report on serial ports, parallel ports, and so forth.

If the system is being warm-booted (typically through the use of the Ctrl-Alt-Del key combination), the POST is skipped. The computer knows whether a cold or warm boot is in effect by the value stored at memory location 0040:0072h. If the value is 1234h, a warm boot is assumed. Any other value causes a cold boot. This special value is placed there by the interrupt handler for Ctrl-Alt-Del.

Regardless of whether a warm or cold boot is occurring, control is transferred next to the ROM bootstrap initialization procedure.

The bootstrap initialization routine sets up important parts of the interrupt vector table in low memory (especially vectors for hardware located by the POST). The routine also initializes the ROM BIOS tables at memory location 0400:0000h, and may do some hardware setup, such as starting dynamic memory refresh. The routine then searches the memory area from A000:0000h through F000:0000h to locate other ROM extensions; these extensions are marked with a unique byte sequence that identifies them as ROM. (Typical ROM extensions are the EGA graphics ROM and the PC XT fixed disk controller ROM.) The bootstrap routine initializes any ROM extensions it finds. After initialization is complete, the ROM bootstrap code starts the system itself.

The ROM bootstrap routines now read the disk bootstrap code from the first sector (the *boot sector*) of the boot disk. The bootstrap code is a minimal-services routine responsible for getting the system up and running. The ROM bootstrap routines check all bootable disk drives, starting with drive A, for the presence of a boot sector on the disk. The first such disk found is used; this feature makes it possible to regain control by booting from a backup floppy, should the hard disk become damaged. If no boot sector is found, an IBM PC transfers control to ROM BASIC and starts up as a diskless system; PC compatibles prompt you to insert a system disk and then wait for you to press a key. The exact procedure varies from one manufacturer's ROM to another.

When a boot sector is located, the ROM bootstrap loads it into high memory (at address 007C:0000h), away from where DOS itself will be loaded. Control is then transferred to the disk bootstrap routine.

After the disk bootstrap code has been loaded and has control, it looks back to the disk to locate the IO.SYS and MSDOS.SYS files.

Note: On an IBM PC and many compatibles, these files are named IBMBIO.COM and IBMDOS.COM. In this discussion, *MSDOS.SYS* refers to two modules (MSDOS.SYS and IBMDOS.COM) and *IO.SYS* refers to two others (IO.SYS and IBMBIO.COM). Unless a specific difference is pointed out, all operations are performed alike in either set of modules.

The disk bootstrap does not know about file systems or disk structures—indeed, it can't. All details of the disk's file layout are built into the MSDOS.SYS file and, because that file has not yet been loaded and initialized, that data is not available. Therefore, the following requirements are imposed on a boot disk:

1. IO.SYS must be the *first* entry in the root directory.

2. MSDOS.SYS must be the *second* entry in the root directory.

3. The IO.SYS file itself *must* be the first file on the disk and must be stored in contiguous clusters in the correct order. Originally, the second file was required to follow the first and also be in contiguous clusters, but beginning with Version 3, it may be located anywhere on the disk and may be fragmented. This made it possible to upgrade easily from Version 2 to the significantly larger Version 3 (the differences between Version 1 and Version 2 were so great that ease of upgrading was not a consideration).

Now you know why the SYS.COM program "complains" when it tries to make bootable a disk that already has had something stored on it. A bootable disk must be built when the disk is empty (or appears to be empty; that is, the first directory entry begins with a byte containing 00h, indicating that it has never been used). Otherwise, SYS.COM will not work.

If the disk bootstrap does not know about the file system, how does it know about the directory entries and where the files are located? It learns this information from the *BIOS parameter block* (BPB)—the area of the boot sector from byte 0Bh through 17h (see fig. 3.1).

Fig. 3.1. *The boot sector.*

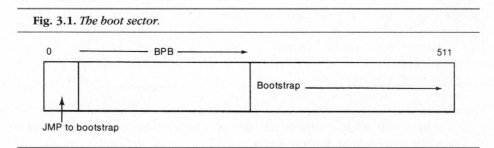

The BPB tells the boot program enough about the disk layout that the boot program can locate the beginning of the directory and the file space. After locating the files, the boot program copies IO.SYS (IBMBIO.COM) into low memory above the BIOS tables. Then, depending on which system you are using, either the boot program or the IO.SYS initialization routine copies MSDOS.SYS to memory in an area above IO.SYS.

Note: Before Version 3, no use was actually made of the BPB even though it was introduced with Version 2. Because of this, many non-IBM manufacturers failed to include the BPB in their boot sectors. Disks formatted under such versions of DOS may not be readable by Version 3 and later, but can be made so by copying the boot sector from a Version 3 disk of the same characteristics over the original one to provide a BPB. This incompatibility has given rise to legends about Version 3 not being fully compatible, but it was the offending Version 2 variant which was incompatible with DOS standards.

There are two parts to IO.SYS. The system manufacturer (IBM or some other firm) supplies the first part—the BIOS. The BIOS contains resident device drivers together with hardware-specific initialization code that is run only when the BIOS is loaded. Microsoft supplies the second part: a module called SYSINIT.

When IO.SYS takes control of the computer, it runs any hardware-specific initialization the system may need. During initialization, IO.SYS checks the BIOS-table area of low memory (set up earlier by the ROM BIOS initialization) to see what hardware is being used. Unneeded drivers may be deleted automatically at this point; most versions of DOS, however, provide only bare-bones drivers in IO.SYS and make no changes. Control is then transferred to the SYSINIT module.

SYSINIT checks the available memory and relocates itself into high memory. No permanent memory space is allocated for SYSINIT, because it is a temporary module whose services will be needed for only a short time. The relocation of SYSINIT to high memory allows the module to serve its purpose, but gets it out of the way so that all low memory is available for DOS.

The high-memory copy of SYSINIT copies MSDOS.SYS over the IO.SYS initialization code (which means that the original copy of SYSINIT is also copied over). This operation makes available to DOS all of the memory used for system initialization. Next, using the DOS Int 21h file services (which became available when MSDOS.SYS was copied into RAM), SYSINIT opens the CONFIG.SYS file (if it exists). The entire file is loaded into memory, all characters are converted to uppercase, and CONFIG.SYS is interpreted (one line at a time) for system configuration information.

Memory is allocated for file tables, disk buffers, and file control blocks. Default values are assigned if CONFIG.SYS does not exist or does not specify explicit values through the FILES, BUFFERS, and FCBS directives. Additionally, any drivers referenced in CONFIG.SYS are loaded, initialized, and linked into the list of drivers maintained by the system, at the front of the list. (If new character drivers and resident drivers have the same name, the new character drivers are always found first when access to a driver is needed, thereby effectively replacing the existing driver.) The initialization function for each device driver checks the driver's status, initializes the hardware, sets up any interrupts serviced by that driver, and then releases any excess memory that was used when the driver loaded.

When configuration is complete, SYSINIT calls the MSDOS.SYS initialization code. This initialization code sets up internal tables and the interrupt vectors, then initializes the original drivers resident in IO.SYS.

MSDOS.SYS also determines how many disk drives are attached to the system, and examines the BIOS parameter block for each to determine the largest disk-sector size for all these disk drives. MSDOS.SYS uses this value to set up a disk-sector buffer for use by the system. Finally, MSDOS.SYS displays the DOS copyright and returns control to SYSINIT.

After completing the initialization process, SYSINIT closes all file handles and opens the console device (CON) as standard input, standard output, and standard error; the printer device (PRN) as standard list; and the auxiliary device (AUX) as standard auxiliary. Finally, SYSINIT calls the DOS EXEC function to load and execute COMMAND.COM or the shell specified by CONFIG.SYS. (The EXEC function is described in this chapter's "Command Processing" section.)

After control transfers to the shell, SYSINIT is no longer necessary. It is therefore overwritten when COMMAND.COM initializes itself.

When COMMAND.COM is loaded, it immediately relocates part of itself into high memory. The low-memory section of COMMAND.COM (the resident section of the code) contains code essential for restarting COMMAND.COM when it regains control, as well as handlers for three interrupts: Int 22h (Terminate Address), Int 23h (Ctrl-C), and Int 24h (Critical Error). The high-memory section of COMMAND.COM (the transient portion) holds the code necessary for the internal commands and for batch-file processing. By splitting itself in two, COMMAND.COM tries to use the smallest possible amount of memory for functions that *must* remain in memory at all times.

When first loaded by SYSINIT, COMMAND.COM sets up the vectors for Interrupts 22h through 24h. COMMAND.COM then executes the AUTOEXEC.BAT file (if one exists). When that step is complete, control is transferred to the transient portion of COMMAND.COM, the DOS prompt is displayed, and the system is ready to go.

Now that all the software necessary for running the computer has been loaded and initialized, let's see how COMMAND.COM processes commands.

Command Processing

COMMAND.COM is a shell program that controls access to system resources and provides a working environment for users. This working environment consists of defined ways in which users can locate and execute functions on the system. When you ask COMMAND.COM to execute a command, the program tries to locate the command in the following manner:

1. By searching for the requested operation in the list of internal commands (such as DIR, COPY, DEL, and so on)

2. By searching for an executable file (with the extension .COM, .EXE, or .BAT) in the current directory, as external commands

3. By searching for a program in the directories listed in the PATH environment variable

When COMMAND.COM searches a directory, it looks first for the command file with the .COM extension, then with the .EXE extension, and then with the .BAT extension, thereby setting up a precedence of program types for execution. If two programs in the same directory have the same root name but different extensions (FORMAT.COM and FORMAT.EXE, for example), DOS will always execute the COM file. The extension is disregarded. Even if you enter FORMAT.EXE, DOS will execute the COM file. (A common misconception, repeated in some other books, is that by entering the extension you can "force" DOS to run the executable file of your choice. You cannot! However, you *can* force the EXE file to be run first by renaming the COM file to have some other extension, and renaming the EXE file to COM; the loader ignores the extension when determining the file type, and relies instead on information contained in the file.)

When a program is identified as either a COM or an EXE file, COMMAND.COM calls the DOS EXEC function to execute that program. The EXEC function:

1. Checks whether enough memory is available to load the program. If sufficient memory is available, the required memory is allocated. If the memory is not available, EXEC issues an error message and does not execute the program.

2. Builds a program segment prefix (PSP) at the bottom of the allocated memory area (see fig. 3.2). (For a more detailed discussion of the PSP, see Chapter 10.)

3. Loads the program into the memory space above the PSP and determines whether the program is COM or EXE by examining the first two bytes of the program. COM programs are simply copied as a memory image; EXE programs are loaded according to the loading information in the header.

4. Transfers control to the program's entry point. COM files *always* have an entry point at 100h (just after the PSP), whereas the entry points for an EXE file are specified in the EXE program header.

5. Returns control, when the program terminates, to the resident portion of COMMAND.COM. The resident portion of COMMAND.COM does a checksum of the area occupied by the transient portion. If the checksum is OK, control of the computer is transferred back to the transient portion, and the system prompt reappears; otherwise, the transient portion is reloaded from disk and regains control. If, for any reason, a reload of the transient portion of COMMAND.COM is required and cannot be performed, the system displays an error message to the effect that COMMAND.COM is "bad or missing" and halts operation. Rebooting is necessary to restart the system in such a case.

A shell program intended to replace COMMAND.COM *must* provide handlers for Interrupts 22h through 24h; the shell can provide other features as needed. On Hewlett-Packard systems, COMMAND.COM has been replaced by a simplified shell that is friendlier to novice users.

Fig. 3.2. *Program segment prefix (PSP).*

Programs under DOS

Applications programs under DOS take two basic and significantly different forms: COM files (COM programs) and EXE files (EXE programs). You must have a thorough understanding of the differences if you are to do useful work on the system.

COM Programs

COM programs are the smallest and simplest of programs. On disk, they exist as memory images; in memory, they are loaded into a single 64K memory segment. Even though COM programs are supposed to exist totally within a single segment, they frequently stray outside. COM programs that access video memory directly, for example, *must* access memory outside their assigned 64K memory area.

Early programs for the PC and compatibles often did much more than simply access video memory. Frequently, because the rest of memory was assumed to be available for its use, a program would set up tables, load program overlays, or control the extra memory in any way needed for its function. Some fairly nice programs acted this way (under Version 1, some programs even did their own assignment of temporary files by going directly to the disk, bypassing the entire DOS file structure).

If DOS assumed that a COM program used only its assigned segment of memory, another program executed by DOS could easily mess up a program that was already there. To eliminate the problem, DOS gives all of free memory to a COM program that is being executed. Later in this chapter (and again in Chapter 10), you will learn in greater detail about the way this memory is assigned.

A COM program easily can exceed the assumed bounds of the data area. It simply modifies the processor's segment registers to point to memory areas that the program needs to access. For example, by modifying the data segment (DS) register, a COM program can manipulate data in any portion of memory. This capability is absolutely necessary if the program is going to modify the screen memory directly instead of using DOS services for video output, because the screen memory cannot be in the program's data segment.

Although you may consider access to all of the system's memory a great capability, it leaves DOS with the possibility that a program can modify anything—thus, nothing is "safe." To obviate this problem, DOS takes the safe way out by assigning all available memory to the program. (Technically, this statement is only partly correct; for a more detailed explanation, check the section on memory allocation, at the end of this chapter.)

If you write a COM program that uses DOS's EXEC function (the program and overlay loader) to execute another program, your COM program should release any memory it is not using. DOS provides memory-management functions that can be used to allocate, deallocate, and change the size of memory blocks used by your programs. These functions are detailed in the last part of this chapter and in the "DOS Reference" section at the end of this book (see DOS Functions 48h through 4Ah). Because high-level languages handle memory-management automatically, you will not need to worry about memory management unless you are programming in assembly language, or are writing memory-critical applications such as TSR programs (discussed more fully in Chapter 11).

Listing 3.1, a sample COM program written in assembly language, is the simplest of programs. It uses a standard DOS function (09h) to write a string to the screen.

Listing 3.1

```
;                         Sample COM Program
       name           dosbook
;
; Democm.asm - .COM file version of simple print
; Prints "DOS Programmer's Reference"
;
;------ Beginning of the CODE Segment ------
cseg  segment        para public 'CODE'
      org            100h               ; Program origin
;
; All of the segment registers are set to point
; to the same segment (required for a
; COM program)
      assume         cs:cseg,ds:cseg,es:cseg,ss:cseg
;
;------ Procedure Book ------
```

```
; PURPOSE:        To illustrate programming for
;                 a .COM file. Displays a defined
;                 string on the screen
; USES:           DX, AX
; RETURNS:        Nothing
;
book   proc       near
       mov        dx,offset msg  ; Get message location
       mov        ah,9           ; Output character string
       int        21h
       mov        al,0           ; Exit code zero
       mov        ah,4ch         ; Terminate
       int        21h
book   endp
;------ End of Procedure Book ------
msg    db         'DOS Programmer',027h,'s Reference',0dh,0ah,'$'
cseg   ends
;------ End of the CODE Segment ------

       end        book
```

Let's go through the program, line-by-line, to see what it does.

After the initial comment section, a segment instruction declares the start of the program's code segment, and the program's origin is established at location 100h. Starting at 100h allows space in the segment for the program's PSP. (See Chapter 10 for a discussion of the PSP's layout and use.)

Another comment section precedes the next step, the assume statement, which tells the assembler that all of the segment registers will point to the code segment. Because all the segment registers point to the same location and a segment can refer to only 64K of memory, the program effectively is limited to 64K of space.

With the program established, the next step is that of creating the program's only procedure (book) and declaring it a NEAR procedure (all references will be within the single segment). The body of the program is simplicity itself. It consists of these steps:

1. Put the offset address of the message into the DX register.

2. Set the AH register to 9 (the code for the DOS function that writes a string to the screen).

3. Execute Int 21h to invoke the DOS interrupt processor.

4. Set the AL register to 0 (the exit code for the program) in preparation for program termination.

5. Set the AH register to 4Ch (the function number for a DOS program-termination call).

6. Make a final call to Int 21h to return control to DOS.

At the end of the procedure, the data string for printing is defined in memory with special ASCII characters 27h (the apostrophe), 0Dh (carriage return), and 0Ah (line feed). The DOS function requires that the string be terminated with a dollar sign.

When you assemble the program, the macro assembler creates an object file from the assembly language source code. This object file is a direct translation of the source file into machine code acceptable to the CPU chip.

Before the program can be executed, though, it must have memory address information added, and be linked to any library routines specified in the source code; the linker creates an EXE file, which is an executable version of the original program.

To turn this EXE file into a COM file, you use the EXE2BIN program. (Beginning with Version 3.3, EXE2BIN is no longer supplied as a part of the basic DOS package; it is now included in the extra-cost "Disk Operating System Technical Reference" manual add-on. A work-alike called EXECOM has been made available as free software by its creator, Chris Dunford, and may be found on CompuServe and many local bulletin boards.)

As you can see from figure 3.3, which shows a COM program dump as it exists on disk, only the program code is kept in the file. The program uses minimal disk space.

EXE Programs

EXE programs are much more complex and versatile than COM programs. Instead of being limited to a single memory segment, EXE programs frequently occupy several segments and may include more than one segment of code and data. EXE program files have a special header area, which is used by the DOS EXEC function to load the program. This header block contains information that DOS uses to relocate the file and determine memory requirements. The program header is essential if the program is to operate because, unlike a COM program, which is stored as an absolute memory image, an EXE program is stored as a relocatable memory image. The system can adjust such an image to conform to overall space and memory-usage needs as determined by DOS.

EXE programs are more flexible than COM programs, and sometimes much larger (reaching the limits of memory). They also coexist better in memory because they can be broken into discrete segments and assigned to available free space. This coexistence is of little use on PC systems in a single-user, single-task environment. Coexistence will become more and more of a problem, however, as we move into multitasking (using systems such as Microsoft Windows or DESQview) or to OS/2. Programs that ignore the possibility of coexistence may not run.

The sample COM program (in listing 3.1) can be rewritten as an EXE program, as shown in listing 3.2. Because this EXE program does not fit into one segment of memory, EXE2BIN will fail if you try to run it on this output program.

Fig. 3.3. *A COM program dump.*

```
0000   BA 0D 01 B4 09 CD 21 B0-00 B4 4C CD 21 44 4F 53   ......!...L.!DOS
0010   20 50 72 6F 67 72 61 6D-6D 65 72 27 73 20 52 65   Programmer's Re
0020   66 65 72 65 6E 63 65 0D-0A 24 00 00 00 00 00 00   ference..$......
0030   00 00 00 00 00 00 00 00-00 00 00 00 00 00 00 00   ................
0040   00 00 00 00 00 00 00 00-00 00 00 00 00 00 00 00   ................
0050   00 00 00 00 00 00 00 00-00 00 00 00 00 00 00 00   ................
0060   00 00 00 00 00 00 00 00-00 00 00 00 00 00 00 00   ................
0070   00 00 00 00 00 00 00 00-00 00 00 00 00 00 00 00   ................
0080   00 00 00 00 00 00 00 00-00 00 00 00 00 00 00 00   ................
0090   00 00 00 00 00 00 00 00-00 00 00 00 00 00 00 00   ................
00A0   00 00 00 00 00 00 00 00-00 00 00 00 00 00 00 00   ................
00B0   00 00 00 00 00 00 00 00-00 00 00 00 00 00 00 00   ................
00C0   00 00 00 00 00 00 00 00-00 00 00 00 00 00 00 00   ................
00D0   00 00 00 00 00 00 00 00-00 00 00 00 00 00 00 00   ................
00E0   00 00 00 00 00 00 00 00-00 00 00 00 00 00 00 00   ................
00F0   00 00 00 00 00 00 00 00-00 00 00 00 00 00 00 00   ................
0100   00 00 00 00 00 00 00 00-00 00 00 00 00 00 00 00   ................
0110   00 00 00 00 00 00 00 00-00 00 00 00 00 00 00 00   ................
0120   00 00 00 00 00 00 00 00-00 00 00 00 00 00 00 00   ................
0130   00 00 00 00 00 00 00 00-00 00 00 00 00 00 00 00   ................
0140   00 00 00 00 00 00 00 00-00 00 00 00 00 00 00 00   ................
0150   00 00 00 00 00 00 00 00-00 00 00 00 00 00 00 00   ................
0160   00 00 00 00 00 00 00 00-00 00 00 00 00 00 00 00   ................
0170   00 00 00 00 00 00 00 00-00 00 00 00 00 00 00 00   ................
0180   00 00 00 00 00 00 00 00-00 00 00 00 00 00 00 00   ................
0190   00 00 00 00 00 00 00 00-00 00 00 00 00 00 00 00   ................
01A0   00 00 00 00 00 00 00 00-00 00 00 00 00 00 00 00   ................
01B0   00 00 00 00 00 00 00 00-00 00 00 00 00 00 00 00   ................
01C0   00 00 00 00 00 00 00 00-00 00 00 00 00 00 00 00   ................
01D0   00 00 00 00 00 00 00 00-00 00 00 00 00 00 00 00   ................
01E0   00 00 00 00 00 00 00 00-00 00 00 00 00 00 00 00   ................
01F0   00 00 00 00 00 00 00 00-00 00 00 00 00 00 00 00   ................
```

Listing 3.2

```
;                       Sample EXE Program
      name        dosbook
;
; Demoex.asm - EXE version of simple print
; Prints 'DOS Programmer's Reference
;
;------ Beginning of the CODE Segment ------
cseg  segment     para public 'CODE'
      assume      cs:cseg,ds:dseg,ss:stack
;
;------ Procedure Book ------
; PURPOSE:        Demonstrates programming for
;                 an .EXE file
; USES:           AX, DX
; RETURNS:        Nothing
;
book  proc        far
      mov         ax,dseg       ; Set data segment register
      mov         ds,ax
```

continues

DOS
PROGRAMMING

Listing 3.2 *continued*

```
            mov         dx,offset msg   ; Get message location
            mov         ah,9            ; Output character string
            int         21h
            mov         al,0            ; Exit code zero
            mov         ah,4ch          ; Terminate
            int         21h
book    endp
;------ End of Procedure Book ------\
;
cseg    ends
;------ End of the Code Segment ------
;
;------ Beginning of the Data Segment ------
dseg    segment     para 'DATA'
msg     db          'DOS Programmer',027h,'s Reference',0dh,0ah,'$'
dseg    ends
;------ End of the Data Segment ------
;
;------ Beginning of the Stack Segment
stack segment       para stack 'STACK'
        db          20 dup ('stack   ')
stack ends
;------ End of the Stack Segment ------
;

            end         book
```

You can see immediately that the EXE version of the program in listing 3.2 is longer and more complex than the COM version in listing 3.1. The program code does the same job in both versions but, in the EXE version, more program lines are needed to do that job. If you compare the COM and EXE versions, you will find that many portions are identical but that significant differences also are apparent.

In both versions, the CODE segment is declared in the same way. But the assume statements are different. In the EXE version, this statement assigns different values to every segment register. Each register points to a different section of the program. (Notice that SS now points to a defined stack segment.)

In listing 3.2, the book procedure starts with a FAR label, which indicates that book can be called from other segments.

Because the EXE program has a data segment, you must explicitly set the data segment register to the beginning of the data segment. The first step in this procedure puts the address into the AX register; the second step moves the address into the DS register.

Then you create the body of the EXE program with the same six steps used for the COM version:

1. Load the offset address of the message into the DX register.

2. Set the AH register to 9 (the code for the DOS function that writes a string).

3. Execute Int 21h to invoke the DOS processor.

4. Set the AL register to 0 (the exit code for the program) in preparation for program termination.

5. Set the AH register to 4Ch (the function number for program termination).

6. Make a final call to Int 21h to return to DOS.

But the EXE program does not end here. Now you must declare the data segment as a separate part of the program. (In this program, the data segment contains one string—the same constant string that is used in the COM version.) And you have to declare and initialize the stack segment. This stack was created with the repeating string 'stack ' in it, to make memory dumps more readable. (Stacks are discussed briefly in a sidebar in Chapter 2.)

Figure 3.4 shows a complete dump of the disk image of the EXE program. Because it includes the EXE header and the relocation table, this program is much larger than the COM version. The EXE version needs considerably more disk space and is slower to load than its COM counterpart.

Fig. 3.4. *An EXE program dump.*

```
0000   4D 5A E0 00 02 00 01 00-20 00 00 00 FF FF 04 00    MZ.....  ......
0010   A0 00 9A CF 00 00 00 00-1E 00 00 00 01 00 01 00    ................
0020   00 00 00 00 00 00 00 00-00 00 00 00 00 00 00 00    ................
0030   00 00 00 00 00 00 00 00-00 00 00 00 00 00 00 00    ................
0040   00 00 00 00 00 00 00 00-00 00 00 00 00 00 00 00    ................
0050   00 00 00 00 00 00 00 00-00 00 00 00 00 00 00 00    ................
0060   00 00 00 00 00 00 00 00-00 00 00 00 00 00 00 00    ................
0070   00 00 00 00 00 00 00 00-00 00 00 00 00 00 00 00    ................
0080   00 00 00 00 00 00 00 00-00 00 00 00 00 00 00 00    ................
0090   00 00 00 00 00 00 00 00-00 00 00 00 00 00 00 00    ................
```

continues

Fig. 3.4. *continued*

```
ØØAØ  ØØ ØØ ØØ ØØ ØØ ØØ ØØ ØØ-ØØ ØØ ØØ ØØ ØØ ØØ ØØ ØØ    ................
ØØBØ  ØØ ØØ ØØ ØØ ØØ ØØ ØØ ØØ-ØØ ØØ ØØ ØØ ØØ ØØ ØØ ØØ    ................
ØØCØ  ØØ ØØ ØØ ØØ ØØ ØØ ØØ ØØ-ØØ ØØ ØØ ØØ ØØ ØØ ØØ ØØ    ................
ØØDØ  ØØ ØØ ØØ ØØ ØØ ØØ ØØ ØØ-ØØ ØØ ØØ ØØ ØØ ØØ ØØ ØØ    ................
ØØEØ  ØØ ØØ ØØ ØØ ØØ ØØ ØØ ØØ-ØØ ØØ ØØ ØØ ØØ ØØ ØØ ØØ    ................
ØØFØ  ØØ ØØ ØØ ØØ ØØ ØØ ØØ ØØ-ØØ ØØ ØØ ØØ ØØ ØØ ØØ ØØ    ................
Ø1ØØ  ØØ ØØ ØØ ØØ ØØ ØØ ØØ ØØ-ØØ ØØ ØØ ØØ ØØ ØØ ØØ ØØ    ................
Ø11Ø  ØØ ØØ ØØ ØØ ØØ ØØ ØØ ØØ-ØØ ØØ ØØ ØØ ØØ ØØ ØØ ØØ    ................
Ø12Ø  ØØ ØØ ØØ ØØ ØØ ØØ ØØ ØØ-ØØ ØØ ØØ ØØ ØØ ØØ ØØ ØØ    ................
Ø13Ø  ØØ ØØ ØØ ØØ ØØ ØØ ØØ ØØ-ØØ ØØ ØØ ØØ ØØ ØØ ØØ ØØ    ................
Ø14Ø  ØØ ØØ ØØ ØØ ØØ ØØ ØØ ØØ-ØØ ØØ ØØ ØØ ØØ ØØ ØØ ØØ    ................
Ø15Ø  ØØ ØØ ØØ ØØ ØØ ØØ ØØ ØØ-ØØ ØØ ØØ ØØ ØØ ØØ ØØ ØØ    ................
Ø16Ø  ØØ ØØ ØØ ØØ ØØ ØØ ØØ ØØ-ØØ ØØ ØØ ØØ ØØ ØØ ØØ ØØ    ................
Ø17Ø  ØØ ØØ ØØ ØØ ØØ ØØ ØØ ØØ-ØØ ØØ ØØ ØØ ØØ ØØ ØØ ØØ    ................
Ø18Ø  ØØ ØØ ØØ ØØ ØØ ØØ ØØ ØØ-ØØ ØØ ØØ ØØ ØØ ØØ ØØ ØØ    ................
Ø19Ø  ØØ ØØ ØØ ØØ ØØ ØØ ØØ ØØ-ØØ ØØ ØØ ØØ ØØ ØØ ØØ ØØ    ................
Ø1AØ  ØØ ØØ ØØ ØØ ØØ ØØ ØØ ØØ-ØØ ØØ ØØ ØØ ØØ ØØ ØØ ØØ    ................
Ø1BØ  ØØ ØØ ØØ ØØ ØØ ØØ ØØ ØØ-ØØ ØØ ØØ ØØ ØØ ØØ ØØ ØØ    ................
Ø1CØ  ØØ ØØ ØØ ØØ ØØ ØØ ØØ ØØ-ØØ ØØ ØØ ØØ ØØ ØØ ØØ ØØ    ................
Ø1DØ  ØØ ØØ ØØ ØØ ØØ ØØ ØØ ØØ-ØØ ØØ ØØ ØØ ØØ ØØ ØØ ØØ    ................
Ø1EØ  ØØ ØØ ØØ ØØ ØØ ØØ ØØ ØØ-ØØ ØØ ØØ ØØ ØØ ØØ ØØ ØØ    ................
Ø1FØ  ØØ ØØ ØØ ØØ ØØ ØØ ØØ ØØ-ØØ ØØ ØØ ØØ ØØ ØØ ØØ ØØ    ................
Ø2ØØ  B8 Ø2 ØØ 8E D8 BA ØØ ØØ-B4 Ø9 CD 21 BØ ØØ B4 4C    ...........!...L
Ø21Ø  CD 21 ØØ ØØ ØØ ØØ ØØ ØØ-ØØ ØØ ØØ ØØ ØØ ØØ ØØ ØØ    .!..............
Ø22Ø  44 4F 53 2Ø 5Ø 72 6F 67-72 61 6D 6D 65 72 27 73    DOS Programmer's
Ø23Ø  2Ø 52 65 66 65 72 65 6E-63 65 ØD ØA 24 ØØ ØØ ØØ    Reference..$...
Ø24Ø  73 74 61 63 6B 2Ø 2Ø 2Ø-73 74 61 63 6B 2Ø 2Ø 2Ø    stack   stack
Ø25Ø  73 74 61 63 6B 2Ø 2Ø 2Ø-73 74 61 63 6B 2Ø 2Ø 2Ø    stack   stack
Ø26Ø  73 74 61 63 6B 2Ø 2Ø 2Ø-73 74 61 63 6B 2Ø 2Ø 2Ø    stack   stack
Ø27Ø  73 74 61 63 6B 2Ø 2Ø 2Ø-73 74 61 63 6B 2Ø 2Ø 2Ø    stack   stack
Ø28Ø  73 74 61 63 6B 2Ø 2Ø 2Ø-73 74 61 63 6B 2Ø 2Ø 2Ø    stack   stack
Ø29Ø  73 74 61 63 6B 2Ø 2Ø 2Ø-73 74 61 63 6B 2Ø 2Ø 2Ø    stack   stack
Ø2AØ  73 74 61 63 6B 2Ø 2Ø 2Ø-73 74 61 63 6B 2Ø 2Ø 2Ø    stack   stack
Ø2BØ  73 74 61 63 6B 2Ø 2Ø 2Ø-73 74 61 63 6B 2Ø 2Ø 2Ø    stack   stack
Ø2CØ  73 74 61 63 6B 2Ø 2Ø 2Ø-73 74 61 63 6B 2Ø 2Ø 2Ø    stack   stack
Ø2DØ  73 74 61 63 6B 2Ø 2Ø 2Ø-73 74 61 63 6B 2Ø 2Ø 2Ø    stack   stack
Ø2EØ  ØØ ØØ ØØ ØØ ØØ ØØ ØØ ØØ-ØØ ØØ ØØ ØØ ØØ ØØ ØØ ØØ    ................
Ø2FØ  ØØ ØØ ØØ ØØ ØØ ØØ ØØ ØØ-ØØ ØØ ØØ ØØ ØØ ØØ ØØ ØØ    ................
Ø3ØØ  ØØ ØØ ØØ ØØ ØØ ØØ ØØ ØØ-ØØ ØØ ØØ ØØ ØØ ØØ ØØ ØØ    ................
Ø31Ø  ØØ ØØ ØØ ØØ ØØ ØØ ØØ ØØ-ØØ ØØ ØØ ØØ ØØ ØØ ØØ ØØ    ................
Ø32Ø  ØØ ØØ ØØ ØØ ØØ ØØ ØØ ØØ-ØØ ØØ ØØ ØØ ØØ ØØ ØØ ØØ    ................
Ø33Ø  ØØ ØØ ØØ ØØ ØØ ØØ ØØ ØØ-ØØ ØØ ØØ ØØ ØØ ØØ ØØ ØØ    ................
Ø34Ø  ØØ ØØ ØØ ØØ ØØ ØØ ØØ ØØ-ØØ ØØ ØØ ØØ ØØ ØØ ØØ ØØ    ................
Ø35Ø  ØØ ØØ ØØ ØØ ØØ ØØ ØØ ØØ-ØØ ØØ ØØ ØØ ØØ ØØ ØØ ØØ    ................
Ø36Ø  ØØ ØØ ØØ ØØ ØØ ØØ ØØ ØØ-ØØ ØØ ØØ ØØ ØØ ØØ ØØ ØØ    ................
Ø37Ø  ØØ ØØ ØØ ØØ ØØ ØØ ØØ ØØ-ØØ ØØ ØØ ØØ ØØ ØØ ØØ ØØ    ................
Ø38Ø  ØØ ØØ ØØ ØØ ØØ ØØ ØØ ØØ-ØØ ØØ ØØ ØØ ØØ ØØ ØØ ØØ    ................
```

Fig. 3.4. *continued*

```
Ø39Ø   ØØ ØØ ØØ ØØ ØØ ØØ ØØ ØØ-ØØ ØØ ØØ ØØ ØØ ØØ ØØ ØØ    ................
Ø3AØ   ØØ ØØ ØØ ØØ ØØ ØØ ØØ ØØ-ØØ ØØ ØØ ØØ ØØ ØØ ØØ ØØ    ................
Ø3BØ   ØØ ØØ ØØ ØØ ØØ ØØ ØØ ØØ-ØØ ØØ ØØ ØØ ØØ ØØ ØØ ØØ    ................
Ø3CØ   ØØ ØØ ØØ ØØ ØØ ØØ ØØ ØØ-ØØ ØØ ØØ ØØ ØØ ØØ ØØ ØØ    ................
Ø3DØ   ØØ ØØ ØØ ØØ ØØ ØØ ØØ ØØ-ØØ ØØ ØØ ØØ ØØ ØØ ØØ ØØ    ................
Ø3EØ   ØØ ØØ ØØ ØØ ØØ ØØ ØØ ØØ-ØØ ØØ ØØ ØØ ØØ ØØ ØØ ØØ    ................
Ø3FØ   ØØ ØØ ØØ ØØ ØØ ØØ ØØ ØØ-ØØ ØØ ØØ ØØ ØØ ØØ ØØ ØØ    ................
```

You can see from the dump that the stack initialization is stored as an image of the stack memory area. Table 3.1 decodes the EXE header shown in this dump. (All entries in the table are 2-byte words.) *Note:* Programs intended to run only with Microsoft Windows also are EXE files, but use a significantly different header scheme. Such programs are outside the scope of this book.

The EXE program header provides the information that the EXEC module needs to control the loading of the program and to assign its segments correctly. Each entry consists of a 2-byte data word stored low-order-byte first. Let's look at the meaning of each entry in table 3.1.

1. At offset 00h, a unique pair of bytes (4Dh 5Ah—ASCII codes 'MZ', which may stand for Mark Zbikowski, one of the principal designers of DOS) identify the file as an EXE file. Whenever the DOS EXEC function sees a file that starts with this byte sequence, the function automatically handles it as an EXE file. This is true no matter *what* extension (if any) the file name carries. Only the 'MZ' signature is used to determine the file type; any file not containing this signature is treated as a COM file.

2. At offset 02h, the length of the file (modulo 512) is stored. This value, along with the values at offsets 04h and 08h, is used to determine the size of the program.

3. At offset 04h, the length of the file (including the header) in 512-byte pages is stored. This value may be zero if the file occupies less than 512 bytes; Microsoft utilities never create EXE files shorter than 512 bytes, but those from some other vendors do.

4. Offset 06h has the number of items in the relocation table (the location of the relocation table is stored at offset 18h).

5. Offset 08h is the size, in paragraphs (16 bytes per paragraph), of the EXE program header.

6. Offset 0Ah is the minimum number of paragraphs needed to run the program (MINALLOC). If this much memory is not available, the program will not run. The linker sets this to zero unless overridden by a LINK command-line switch.

7. Offset 0Ch is the maximum number of paragraphs the program would like to get. The linker sets this to FFFFh (1M) unless overridden by a LINK command-line switch. If less than the amount specified here is available, the program will get all that can be assigned.

8. Offset 0Eh is the offset of the stack segment, in paragraphs, from the beginning of the program.

9. Offset 10h is the initial value of the SP register when the program is started.

10. Offset 12h is a checksum of the program for use by the EXEC function at runtime. (In most versions of DOS, it appears that no use is made of this checksum.)

11. Offset 14h is the initial value of the IP register when the program starts (the program's entry point).

12. Offset 16h is the segment displacement of the program's code segment.

13. Offset 18h is the offset (in the EXE file) of the relocation table's first entry.

14. Offset 1Ah is the overlay number. For a program, this value is zero.

Table 3.1. *Decoding an EXE Program Header*

Offset	Typical Values	Meaning
00h	4Dh	
	5Ah	Link program EXE file signature
02h	E0h	
	00h	Length of image
04h	02h	
	00h	Size of file in 512-byte pages (2)
06h	01h	
	00h	Number of relocation-table items (1)
08h	20h	
	00h	Size of header in paragraphs (32)

Typical Offset	Values	Meaning
0Ah	00h	
	00h	Minimum number of paragraphs above (MINALLOC)
0Ch	FFh	
	FFh	Maximum number of paragraphs above (65,535) (MAXALLOC)
0Eh	04h	
	00h	Displacement of stack segment in paragraphs
10h	A0h	
	00h	Offset in SP register
12h	9Ah	
	CFh	Word checksum
14h	00h	
	00h	IP register offset
16h	00h	
	00h	Code segment displacement
18h	1Eh	
	00h	Displacement of first relocation item
1Ah	00h	
	00h	Overlay number (Resident code = 0)

Immediately after the header, a small amount of reserved space is followed by the program's relocation table. Items in the relocation table are read, one at a time, into a work area. Each item's segment value is added to the program's start segment value, which the EXE loader calculates from the values at offsets 04h, 08h, and 02h in the EXE header. The resulting segment value and the item's offset value point to a word in the program; the calculated segment value is written to that location.

The relocation table is followed by another small amount of reserved space. (Either of the reserved spaces can vary in size.) Then comes the program itself, followed by the stack segment.

Figure 3.5 pulls together for comparison the dumps of the EXE and COM programs. The EXE program dump includes the stack area, initialized according to the instructions in the program source. Because the COM program does not have a defined stack area, no initialization is provided for one.

Fig. 3.5. *A comparison of the EXE and COM programs.*

```
ØØØØ  BA ØD Ø1 B4 Ø9 CD 21 BØ-ØØ B4 4C CD 21 44 4F 53    ......!...L.!DOS  ⎤
ØØ1Ø  20 50 72 6F 67 72 61 6D-6D 65 72 27 73 20 52 65    Programmer's Re   ⎥ COM
ØØ2Ø  66 65 72 65 6E 63 65 ØD-ØA 24                      ference..$        ⎦


ØØØØ  B8 Ø2 ØØ 8E D8 BA ØØ ØØ-B4 Ø9 CD 21 BØ ØØ B4 4C    ............!...L  ⎤
ØØ1Ø  CD 21 ØØ ØØ ØØ ØØ ØØ ØØ-ØØ ØØ ØØ ØØ ØØ ØØ ØØ ØØ    .!..............  ⎥
ØØ2Ø  44 4F 53 2Ø 5Ø 72 6F 67-72 61 6D 6D 65 72 27 73    DOS Programmer's  ⎥
ØØ3Ø  2Ø 52 65 66 65 72 65 6E-63 65 ØD ØA 24 ØØ ØØ ØØ    Reference..$...   ⎥
ØØ4Ø  73 74 61 63 6B 2Ø 2Ø 2Ø-73 74 61 63 6B 2Ø 2Ø 2Ø    stack   stack     ⎥
ØØ5Ø  73 74 61 63 6B 2Ø 2Ø 2Ø-73 74 61 63 6B 2Ø 2Ø 2Ø    stack   stack     ⎥
ØØ6Ø  73 74 61 63 6B 2Ø 2Ø 2Ø-73 74 61 63 6B 2Ø 2Ø 2Ø    stack   stack     ⎥
ØØ7Ø  73 74 61 63 6B 2Ø 2Ø 2Ø-73 74 61 63 6B 2Ø 2Ø 2Ø    stack   stack     ⎥ EXE
ØØ8Ø  73 74 61 63 6B 2Ø 2Ø 2Ø-73 74 61 63 6B 2Ø 2Ø 2Ø    stack   stack     ⎥
ØØ9Ø  73 74 61 63 6B 2Ø 2Ø 2Ø-73 74 61 63 6B 2Ø 2Ø 2Ø    stack   stack     ⎥
ØØAØ  73 74 61 63 6B 2Ø 2Ø 2Ø-73 74 61 63 6B 2Ø 2Ø 2Ø    stack   stack     ⎥
ØØBØ  73 74 61 63 6B 2Ø 2Ø 2Ø-73 74 61 63 6B 2Ø 2Ø 2Ø    stack   stack     ⎥
ØØCØ  73 74 61 63 6B 2Ø 2Ø 2Ø-73 74 61 63 6B 2Ø 2Ø 2Ø    stack   stack     ⎥
ØØDØ  73 74 61 63 6B 2Ø 2Ø 2Ø-73 74 61 63 6B 2Ø 2Ø 2Ø    stack   stack     ⎦
```

Although the two programs are nearly identical, the need for addressing modes that reach beyond a single segment creates slightly different instructions.

Some High-Level Language Examples

Having looked at assembly language programs as examples of COM and EXE programs, let's look at some examples that use high-level languages to do the same simple function. In a high-level language, the program source is *much* simpler to write. This is a significant advantage. As programs grow in complexity, program maintenance is easier if the source code is less complex.

Frequently, the high-level language version of the executable program is longer than the assembly language version for the same program. This happens because high-level languages must provide for many variations of use. For example, printf in C is loaded with special features not used in our simple example.

To provide a basis for comparison, we used several language compilers (in various high-level languages) to compile programs with the same function as the assembly language examples in the preceding section. As you will see, the high-level language versions have much larger executable files loaded and stored on disk.

Although it is difficult to detect differences in execution speed in programs this small, you can easily set up experiments to test their speed. We will focus on the simplicity of the programs, not on their speed or size.

Note: To keep this book to a reasonable size, comments have been omitted from sample listings when they duplicate text discussions. Obviously, this is not a practice we would encourage in your own programs.

A Turbo Pascal Program

Many people prefer working in BASIC to working in Turbo Pascal. To print just one line in Turbo Pascal, for example, you must deal with overhead on a program-language level. You must identify your program code as a program module and use a Begin-End pair to set off the program's executable code (see listing 3.3). Although this organizational detail may seem ridiculous at such a trivial level, you will find that as the program expands, your work also expands. The overhead then becomes more of a device for guarding against mistakes.

Listing 3.3

```
Program Demo;
{
    demotp.pas - Turbo Pascal version of simple print
    Prints 'DOS Programmer's Reference'
}
Begin
    writeln('DOS Programmer''s Reference');

End.
```

You will find that Pascal compilers control the computer's memory to a large extent. Because determinations about memory usage are made at compile time, the use of functions such as program execution and memory management requires a considerable amount of forethought.

A Compiled C Program

The C programming language was designed with systems-level programming in mind. Because access to system resources was originally much easier in C than in Pascal or BASIC, C generally is the language chosen for programs that have to make extensive use of DOS or BIOS functions. Later versions of Pascal have blurred the differences, but the trend has already been set.

The C version is shown in listing 3.4. As in the Pascal version, the overhead in C is minor in large, complex programs and is a major help in keeping the program understandable.

Listing 3.4

```
#include <stdio.h>

main()

/*
        demo.c - A C version of the simple print program
        Prints "Dos Programmer's Reference"
*/

{
        printf("DOS Programmer's Reference\n");

}
```

C compilers produce code that gives the programmer the most direct control of the underlying machine. This is intentional: the C programming language was designed to be used for writing operating systems.

The capability of providing tight control of a machine while still providing high-level language functions and control structures similar to those provided in Pascal make C the language of choice for most serious applications.

Most applications in this book are written in C. The examples in BASIC and Pascal are included to illustrate how you can use the same techniques in other languages. (Limited space precludes duplication of all examples in all languages.)

Comparing Different Versions of a Program

The results of a comparison of the compiled modules from each version of the program are shown in table 3.2. This table reflects neither an exhaustive test of one compiler versus another nor a performance test—it simply shows the comparative sizes (in bytes) of the compiled modules.

Keep in mind that any comparison of compilers depends on your perspective and your needs. Speed, the most frequently cited yardstick, is important in some programs but not in others. For example, if a program that transfers characters to a printer is already faster than the printer and has to wait, what difference does speed make?

This exercise *is* useful if you understand that your choice of a language influences the size and operation of your program and makes your conceptual work easier or more difficult. And remember—no matter what the benefits of a high-level language may be, nothing beats assembly language and hand coding if you need to squeeze the most from the available memory space and processor speed.

COM versus EXE Programs

Should you or shouldn't you? Is it worthwhile to write a program that you can convert to COM format, or should you leave it in EXE format? To decide, you should consider the following factors:

- A COM program is faster to load and start because it is a direct memory image.

- A COM program is limited to a maximum of 64K, including data and program code. (You can increase these limits, however, by manipulating the segment registers.)

- A COM program hogs all memory and has to release memory in order to EXEC other programs. (This item is important only if you are using concurrent programs. It is unimportant if the program will run on a single-user, single-task system.)

- A COM program uses less space on disk because it does not include the EXE program header or relocation table. In some cases, the difference is considerable, because the relocation table may be the largest part of the program.

- COM programs run faster because they cannot use FAR calls, which are a bit slower than NEAR calls. In most programs, the difference is imperceptible unless many such calls are executed per second.

Table 3.2. *Size (in Bytes) of Compiled Modules*

Language	Source File	Object File	Executable
Assembly (COM)	1367	144	42 (COM file)
Assembly (COM)	1367	144	810 (before EXE2BIN)
Assembly (EXE)	1361	233	736 (EXE file)
Turbo Pascal 6.0	178	N/A	1936 (EXE file)
Borland C++ 2.0	194	443	5584 (COM file)

COM programs are most useful when you need to squeeze as many programs as possible into a limited space. For example, if you wanted to take with you a floppy disk filled with simple utilities, COM files would be the answer. But for most programming, building a COM program makes no sense. An EXE program does as good a job and is likely to remain compatible with extensions to the DOS system well into the future. A well-designed EXE program can limit FAR calls to those needed for crossing segment boundaries. And, by using NEAR calls for most of the repetitive work, an EXE program can eliminate much of the overall speed advantage of a COM program.

If you work with a high-level language, you may not have a choice. Most compilers produce either COM or EXE programs; others produce both. Basically, the decision to convert an EXE program to a COM program will be determined in large part by your particular circumstances.

Now, having laid the groundwork, let's look at interrupts. Interrupts affect the way DOS, the BIOS—the whole system—work.

Interrupts

Old-style computer systems, which ran one program at a time to completion, were simple in theory, simple in design, and simple to operate. An early system that I worked on had punch-card input and a line printer for output. Large data sets were stored on one of five magnetic-tape drives (disks did not exist) and memory was 32K of magnetic core. When you programmed that system, you *knew* you had total control of your computer. When your program needed some data from a tape drive, the program simply waited. When it needed some input from the console (not even a keyboard—just switches!), it waited again. Working with that computer was extremely uncomplicated—but you waited much of the time.

Interrupts are a way to eliminate the waiting. When a computer requests a hardware service, such as a disk read, it waits for the results in one of three ways:

- It waits until the operation is completed.

- It continues with other tasks and checks periodically to see whether the operation is completed.

- It continues with other tasks and is notified by the operating system when the operation is completed.

Each method has its advantages and disadvantages. Consider serial communications, for example.

When your computer communicates with another computer over the telephone line, characters arrive at your serial port at random intervals. If all you had to do was read the characters from the line and dump them in a buffer, you could simply wait for a character to arrive, read it and write it to the buffer, then wait again. This type of tightly looping process is frequently called a *busy wait*.

This method would be acceptable if your computer were handling only communications between computers—nothing else. But you want your computer to pay attention to *you*. If you want the computer to pay attention to you and the serial line, you have to use a different method.

For example, you could write a program that checks repeatedly for something to do and, if it finds something to do, does it. You might write a simple program that performs the following steps:

1. If a character is at the keyboard, write it to the serial port.

2. If a character is at the serial port, write it to the screen.

3. Go to step 1.

(In Chapter 7, you will build a program just like this one to demonstrate basic serial communications.)

With communications at 1200 baud (1200 bits per second), however, about 120 characters arrive each second. A new character reaches the serial port every 8.33 milliseconds; if you are not ready to receive an incoming character, you lose it. How much can *you* do in 8.33 milliseconds? In computer terms, 8.33 milliseconds is a relatively long time, but not if you want to

- Place a character on the screen

- Scroll the screen up and blank the bottom line if the character was at the end of your screen

- Carry out a sequence if the character is part of a screen-control sequence

- Decide how to handle a nonprintable character

In addition to all this activity, you want to be ready to handle each character the moment it is typed on the keyboard. As you will discover, even if you work through the DOS and BIOS functions or read directly from the serial port, there is simply not enough time for you to do everything. In practice, this simple approach can lose as many as three incoming characters (at 1200 bps) each time the CRT has to scroll up one line!

Your only option is to use the interrupt system. Some people are afraid of interrupts, which have a reputation as an arcane technique known only to gurus and hackers. Nothing could be further from the truth. As soon as you understand basic interrupt operation, you can write an interrupt handler yourself. (You will write several in Chapter 11.)

Think of an interrupt as a doorbell. If you did not have a doorbell on your home, you would have to check periodically to see whether someone was at your door. This repeated checking, or *polling*, tends to be inefficient and wastes your time—as it would the computer's time in a computer environment. Going to the door only when the doorbell rings is much more efficient. An interrupt works like a doorbell for your computer.

When a program is running, events such as a character's arrival on the serial line cause an interrupt to occur. When an interrupt occurs, the system stops your program, saves the program's *state* (the CS, IP, and flags registers) on the stack, and branches to a handler for that interrupt. Basically, an interrupt handler is just another program, although (as you will discover in Chapter 11) interrupt handlers are somewhat restricted in what they can do.

Whether you realize it or not, the system you work with interrupts your work regularly. For example, the timer interrupt occurs about 18.2 times per second. Some programs tie in to this interrupt in order to display an on-screen clock.

Another important interrupt is generated whenever you press a key. This keyboard interrupt handles the keystroke. All you see is the character appearing on-screen. But interrupt control makes everything happen.

A PC has 256 interrupt routines. It accesses them through an interrupt vector table located at 0000:0000h through 0000:03FFh. (The addresses used are built into the CPU chip and cannot be changed by software.) Each four-byte entry in this table corresponds to an interrupt routine; the four bytes are the address of that routine's *entry point*. To understand the interrupts, you need to know how they are classified.

The 8086 processor family has four basic types of interrupts:

- Internal interrupts

- The non-maskable interrupt

- Hardware interrupts (also called *maskable* interrupts)

- Software interrupts

Let's look briefly at each type.

Internal Interrupts

The 8086 microprocessor family generates many interrupts that are sensed directly by the CPU. In the divide-by-zero interrupt, for example, the processor automatically issues the appropriate interrupt request when it detects a divide-by-zero error.

The Non-Maskable Interrupt

The non-maskable interrupt (NMI) is tied directly to a special NMI pin on the processor chip. The non-maskable interrupt forces the processor to deal immediately with some kind of catastrophic system failure. (You can think of the NMI as the "Now Move Immediately" interrupt.)

On the PC and compatibles, this interrupt is activated by a memory-parity error—an error indicating a major problem in the system's memory. The standard handler for this interrupt writes the message Memory Parity Error to the screen and then locks up the computer because there is no safe way to recover on a PC when a memory-parity error occurs.

Hardware (Maskable) Interrupts

Interrupts generated by external devices are called *maskable* interrupts. They come through a pin on the CPU that you can tell the processor to ignore temporarily. On a PC, interrupts come through the 8259 Programmable Interrupt Controller chip and can be masked individually. (You will learn more about the 8259 in Chapter 11.) The state of the interrupt flag in the flags register determines whether the processor pays attention to a maskable interrupt. To mask an interrupt, you use the clear interrupt instruction (CLI) to clear the flag. (See Chapter 2 for a detailed discussion of flags and the flags register.)

Maskable interrupts tend to be frequent and unpredictable. Because they come from external hardware, a program cannot predict when such interrupts will occur. Maskable interrupts need to be handled quickly so that the program can continue. Interrupt handlers should be optimized to perform only necessary operations.

Software Interrupts

Software interrupts are generated by programs, not by hardware. All DOS and BIOS functions are accessed through software interrupts. These interrupts do not have to "know" anything about the system in order to create a flexible method for programs to access system resources.

Ordinarily, software interrupts are synchronized to your program's operations. Handlers for these interrupts frequently provide special functions, such as mouse control and file handling. Although software interrupts are not as critical as hardware interrupts, they are called frequently and must be efficient.

As you will discover from the discussion of TSRs (terminate-and-stay-resident programs) in Chapter 11, some software interrupts trigger special programs that may take complete control of the computer. (Borland's Sidekick is a good example of this type of program.) Efficiency becomes more a matter of packing features into as little space as possible than of operating speed, although speed remains important. To keep the entire system from bogging down, other services (such as a handler for keyboard characters or a clock handler that updates a screen display) must be extremely speed efficient.

Interrupt service routines, or *handlers*, must be designed to minimize interaction with other programs, unless such interaction is a requirement for the specific handler. One example of a case in which such interaction *is* a requirement is Int 24h, the Critical Error handler. It is called only when DOS runs into an unpredictable problem while trying to perform input or output, and thus *must* interact with the running program.

To understand how Int 24h affects the stack, you need to examine how DOS uses the stack. When an Int 21h function is invoked, the Int 21h handler pushes all CPU registers on the stack. DOS then uses an internal stack for its own purposes. If a critical error occurs, the user stack is selected again but the register values pushed by Int 21h are left on the user stack. Then Int 24h is invoked and the resulting stack appears (see fig. 3.6).

With all of these registers available, you can easily determine where you were before the error occurred. The critical-error handler is extremely important. We all are familiar with its characteristic message:

```
Abort, Retry, Ignore?
```

(Note that in Version 3.3 it became the `Abort, Retry, Fail?` message.)

The error message usually tells you that a floppy disk drive is not ready. The default handler handles the situation in a straightforward, simple way. If you press *I* to ignore the error, control returns to the program and processing continues. If you press *R* (for Retry), the handler tries the function again to see whether the problem has been fixed. When you press *A* (for Abort), the handler aborts the process, returning to DOS. Beginning with Version 3.3, the Fail option, which forces DOS to return an error condition to the calling program, replaced the Ignore option.

Fig. 3.6. *A stack on entry to Int 24h (the critical-error handler).*

You must be wary of DOS critical errors. If a critical error occurs during execution of a program that creates its own general interrupt handlers (such as a terminal program that creates an interrupt handler for the serial port), the program may be terminated *without* restoring its interrupt handlers to their previous state. Chaos can result. If an interrupt for one of the affected handlers occurs after such a happening, the system probably will lock up, because no interrupt handler is available to deal with the data. The newer Fail option makes it possible to prevent such things, but cannot guarantee that they won't happen.

When you understand interrupts well enough to be able to add interrupt handlers for various conditions, you probably will want to write some of your own.

Interrupt handlers are not limited to dealing with an external event or processing a hardware function; they can do straight software work such as sorting and searching. There are several advantages to building a software package with standard utilities needed by a system. For example, you might be writing a system that needs standard menu displays, command input controls, or search procedures. If the system involves several independent programs, you might include all the standard functions in a package accessed through a system interrupt. All of the programs then have access to the same routines.

This approach has specific advantages. First, because the common routines are tied to an interrupt and not compiled into each program, the programs themselves are smaller. Second, because the functions are accessed through a common interrupt, you do not have to relink the individual programs when you change functions in the library.

A number of commercial programs, including Novell Netware and the Btrieve file-management system, use exactly this approach. Many of them actually tie into the standard DOS function interrupt (Int 21h) and add additional codes. Their codes are beyond the scope of this book, but if you run into any strange high-numbered functions for Int 21h while browsing through software, they are probably parts of such systems.

The DOS function interrupt (Int 21h) is a collection of standard functions that are available to all programs that need them. Mouse functions (Int 33h) and expanded memory functions (Int 67h) are other examples of such collections. With the functions provided in this form, people do not have to change their programs when newer versions of the functions become available—they can continue using the same programs.

With a standard run-time package loaded in memory, you can share its resources with all your programs. When you change the package, all programs receive the change without your having to relink them. You can include interrupt handlers in a resident package without having to worry about critical errors crashing the program. A handler always will be in the correct place. And because memory-resident run-time routines do not have to be added to a compiled module, your compiled programs will be smaller and simpler to work with. One drawback to such a package is that your library must be bug-free, because bugs in an interrupt library are hard to find.

Most programs do not use this technique. Rather, they build programs with overlays; the common routines are in the master overlay, which is always resident (even for programs that do not use it). If you have a mouse, you already have some experience with this. You cannot UNLOAD the mouse driver after it has been loaded—the memory has already been used.

All of these techniques are options. You can use them when appropriate, but you have to be aware of the trade-offs.

Finally, let's look at another important topic: memory management.

Memory Allocation and Management

After the operating system is loaded and you are running programs, memory allocation becomes extremely important. Unless enough memory is available, you cannot even load your program. You must understand how to manage memory before you can understand how memory management affects your programs.

DOS organizes available memory as a pool of blocks that are chained together from bottom to top. This chain, or *memory arena*, includes all available memory. Every *memory block* (or *arena entry*) is made up of a 16-byte (one paragraph) *memory control block* and the memory controlled by that block. Table 3.3 shows how the control block is organized.

Table 3.3. The Memory Control Block	
Byte	**Meaning**
00h	90h ('Z') if last block, 77h ('M') otherwise (Mark Zbikowski again?)
01h–02h	0 if the block is not allocated, Process ID of owning process otherwise
03h–04h	Size of the block in paragraphs
05h–07h	Not used (DOS V4; 05h–15h not used previously)
08h–0Fh	File name (no extension) of owning program (DOS V4, only for programs run through EXEC; otherwise unused)

Memory blocks are organized as a chain (or *linked list*) in which each memory control block represents a contiguous area of memory directly above the control block. Each control block points to the next control block in the chain (bytes 3–4 serve as this pointer). Figure 3.7 shows a conceptual picture of this memory-allocation chain. Starting from a DOS pointer to the first memory control block, each block gives the offset to the next block when it records the size of its own block. If two free blocks come together, DOS combines them into a single memory block. When they are separated by a block in use for some other reason (see fig. 3.7), no attempt is made to relocate the information and reassign the block locations.

A block can be as small as a single paragraph (16 bytes) or as large as all available memory. DOS uses the blocks to assign memory to programs, as necessary.

When DOS receives a request for memory, it looks through the chain of memory blocks to find a block large enough to fill the request. If DOS finds a break in the chain or some other anomaly, it returns an error. For example, if the calling program is COMMAND.COM trying to execute a program, DOS displays Memory allocation error and then halts the system. You must reboot to recover.

When a request for memory can be filled, DOS uses one of the following memory-allocation strategies to return a block:

- *First fit*: DOS allocates the first memory block on the chain big enough to fill the request.

- *Best fit*: DOS allocates the smallest memory block big enough to fill the request.

- *Last fit*: DOS allocates the highest memory block big enough to fill the request.

Fig. 3.7. *A chain of memory blocks.*

The first-fit strategy, which minimizes the time spent searching for a block of memory, is the fastest—but it may fragment memory. When a block is assigned, it is divided into two blocks: one that exactly matches the request, and the remainder (which is returned to the chain for later use).

No matter which allocation strategy is used, if more than one block is in use at any given time, memory will be fragmented into smaller and smaller blocks. A program that alternately grabs and frees blocks of memory can create free blocks surrounded by blocks in use. Requests for memory may fail when a program has created a large number of small blocks that cannot be recombined into a single block large enough to handle the request.

Suppose, for example, that a program grabs all of available memory in 16K blocks and then releases to the operating system ten of those blocks, none of which is next to another. Even though 160K of memory is available, a request for 32K of memory will fail because no single block is large enough to handle the request.

Memory fragmentation like this can be a serious problem in some systems. DOS does not do any special cleanup (often called *garbage collection*) to move allocated blocks around in order to recover space. If this sort of problem is important for one of your programs, look in any good book on algorithms or data structures for information on garbage collection techniques.

DOS provides access to the following three basic memory-allocation functions:

- *Allocate a memory block:* a function that requests assignment of a memory block to meet program requirements

- *Free memory block:* a function that returns a previously allocated memory block to the pool after the program has finished using it

- *Resize memory block:* a function that lets you make a previously allocated memory block larger or smaller, as needed; this function normally is called to shrink a program's memory block needed for a program to the smallest size possible

Beginning with DOS V3.2, you can use an additional function to determine the memory-allocation strategy. DOS defaults to the first-fit strategy, but the new function lets you override the default.

The most obvious use of the allocation functions is during program execution. When a program starts up, it receives memory for its operation. As you may recall from the discussion earlier in this chapter, a COM program gets all of memory and an EXE program gets the amount requested. Let's see how that arrangement works in terms of the memory-allocation scheme.

When a COM program is executed, it is allocated all of the available memory in the first block large enough to hold the program, the PSP, and the stack (at least two bytes). Although all of memory is not allocated directly to the COM program, it might as well be. Ordinarily only one block is in the chain at program execution time, and that block holds all of memory.

EXE programs, on the other hand, are allocated the amount of memory requested in the EXE program header's MAXALLOC field (maximum memory to allocate to the program), if that amount of memory is available. If the amount of memory specified in the MINALLOC field (minimum memory needed for the program to run) is not available, the program will not be executed.

When a program is linked, the linker automatically sets the MAXALLOC field to FFFFh (1M), unless it is overridden by command-line switches to request a smaller amount of memory. Therefore, an EXE program (like a COM program) is allocated all of memory on entry. You can override this allocation, however, and use command-line switches to request less than 1M of memory—you cannot do that with a COM program. Although most programmers do not bother with it, they should.

When you program in C, the program's start-up code (supplied with the compiler) ordinarily releases unused memory without your having to worry about it. Pascal and BASIC use all available memory for their data structures, but beginning with Version 4.0, Turbo Pascal offers an option that lets you specify how much memory to use.

When you work in Pascal, a portion of memory set aside by the compiler is used for an area called the *heap*. This area of memory is used by the compiler for allocation of dynamic variables (those created in specific program blocks) and for memory allocated with the standard Pascal routines. If you want memory available for running other programs when you are using Pascal or BASIC, you have to tell the compiler to leave the space available.

This overall management scheme works well. Because programs usually occupy the highest available memory (parents usually are at a lower memory address, although TSRs do not have to be), the allocation scheme ordinarily results in all of the available memory being held in a single block—the largest (and usually the only) block. But inherent in this scheme is the capability of allocating memory to multiple tasks that run concurrently.

Summary

This chapter has introduced the dynamics of DOS, showing how the hardware and software elements of the system interact dynamically in operations such as the boot sequence, command processing, and program execution. You have learned that the ROM bootstrap code is executed automatically when the PC's CPU is powered up. That code, in turn, loads and transfers control to the bootstrap record, which then loads IO.SYS and MSDOS.SYS (or their PC DOS analogues, IBMBIO.COM and IBMDOS.COM). Those programs perform other work needed to get the system up and running.

Command processing is a function of COMMAND.COM, the DOS shell. COMMAND.COM interprets user commands by searching its internal table for a command matching the user's command; if no match is found, COMMAND.COM then searches for an executable file with a name matching that of the user's command.

The differences between COM and EXE programs were also discussed in this chapter. Each has its advantages and disadvantages: COM programs are easier to code and faster to load but are limited in the code and data they can contain. EXE programs, on the other hand, are more complex and somewhat slower in loading but offer the programmer greater control over memory allocation and other parameters.

Interrupts, an important feature of the DOS landscape, were covered here also. Interrupt-driven control of the computer was compared with other methods, and its advantages were made clear. Interrupts are of four major types: internal interrupts, the non-maskable interrupt, hardware (or maskable interrupts), and software interrupts. Software interrupts are the principal programming interface to DOS.

And finally, you learned about DOS's memory-management functions. DOS manages memory as a series of blocks. Each memory block includes a memory-control block, which tells whether the memory block is allocated to a program and tells the location of the next block. DOS makes available three memory-allocation strategies; provides services for allocating, deallocating, and resizing memory blocks; and (in Version 3.2 and above) provides a function for determining the memory-allocation strategy.

Now you have learned the fundamentals of DOS as a system of dynamically interacting parts. In the next chapter, you will learn about exploiting DOS's capabilities in your own programs.

PROGRAMMING

The DOS and BIOS Interface

This chapter shows how your programs can access the services available from the DOS kernel and the BIOS. To access these services, you can invoke software interrupts from any language covered in this book. You will not learn everything about accessing system resources, but you will learn enough to get started.

This book focuses on four languages: assembly language, C, Pascal, and BASIC. The implementations described are Microsoft Macro Assembler, Microsoft C, Borland C++, Turbo Pascal Version 5.0 (with a few notes about earlier versions), Turbo BASIC, and Microsoft QuickBASIC. All four languages have features that let you directly access DOS and BIOS functions. But because not every necessary operation is provided by a built-in language feature, you have to code some operations yourself. In this chapter, you learn what is ready-made in the language you use, as well as what you need to do for yourself and how to do it.

4

CHAPTER

Accessing DOS and BIOS from Your Programs

To access DOS and BIOS resources, follow these simple steps:

1. Load the CPU's registers with appropriate values.

2. Generate a software interrupt to invoke the desired system resource.

3. Interpret the results (if any) returned in the CPU's registers.

Ordinarily, the values loaded into the registers are either 8- or 16-bit numeric parameters or the addresses of larger data structures. All the languages discussed in this book provide a convenient means for loading the CPU's registers, generating interrupts, and reading the returned results. If you need a quick overview of the CPU's registers and their uses, refer to Chapter 2, "The Structure of a DOS System."

Figure 4.1 is a diagram of the contents of the CPU'S registers immediately before and after a system call.

Fig. 4.1. *The contents of registers before and after a system call.*

BIOS
Printer Status Request

Invoked with Int 17h (BIOS Printer services interrupt)

AH =2 for Printer Status Request

DX =0 for LPT1

Result returned in AH

Before call   x =Not used in this system call   After call

Depending on which resource you want to invoke, you may need to do some additional work before you load the registers and generate the interrupt. Many file-oriented services, for example, require your program to load registers with the segment:offset address of a string or other data structure before the interrupt is generated. (If you are not familiar with the segment:offset form of address representation, refer to the "Memory Segmentation and the 8086" section in Chapter 2.)

First, your program must get the data item's address. Getting an item's address is a fairly simple procedure; any complexity is partly a function of the language you use. For each language covered in this book, a section later in this chapter demonstrates techniques for getting addresses of data items.

The string or other item must be in the appropriate form. Many DOS functions that take string arguments require strings in *ASCIIZ* (ASCII plus zero) format: characters are represented in their ASCII format, and the final character in the string is ASCII character zero ('\0' in C, CHR$(0) in BASIC, and Chr(0) in Pascal). Figure 4.2 shows the structure of an ASCIIZ string.

Fig. 4.2. *The structure of an ASCIIZ string.*

	Null character

Character:	M	Y	F	I	L	E	.	D	A	T	
ASCII code:	4D	59	46	49	4C	45	2E	44	41	54	00

If you program in C, you probably know that ASCIIZ is precisely the format in which the C language stores strings internally. In BASIC or Pascal, you have a little more work to do because neither language stores strings in the ASCIIZ format. The work is not complicated, however, and the examples later in this chapter show how it is done.

Because assembly language provides the most direct access to the CPU and to DOS and BIOS resources, the introductory examples in the following sections are in assembly language. For an introduction to the general principles of accessing DOS and BIOS resources, be sure to read the following subsections; the examples are clear, even if you are not fluent in assembly language.

Higher-level language resources for talking to the operating system are described later in this chapter. First, let's look at some simple assembly language examples that explore the DOS and BIOS interface.

A Simple Call to DOS

Each of the programming languages in this book has several services that provide access to the basic DOS and BIOS interrupts. The simplest of these languages is assembly language, which allows you to access the INT (interrupt) instruction directly to generate calls to BIOS or DOS functions.

The following code fragment, which uses Int 21h, Function 02h to output the character *X* to the console, is a typical call to DOS:

```
mov     ah,2       ; Character output function
mov     dl,'X'     ; Character X
int     21h        ; Execute DOS function interrupt
```

Int 21h, Function 02h is easy to use:

1. *Load registers with the appropriate values:* The value 2 is loaded immediately into AH to select DOS Function 2 (Console Character Output). The character *X* is loaded immediately into DL.

2. *Generate the interrupt:* The assembly language mnemonic INT is followed by the value 21h, the "generic" DOS interrupt number. (Because Microsoft's Macro Assembler [MASM] is the standard by which assembler compatibility is measured, the INT instruction should be available with any assembler you choose.)

Because Function 2 of Int 21h returns nothing, the third part of this DOS-call prototype is missing. The following example demonstrates the third step and illustrates basic techniques for obtaining and passing to DOS the addresses of data items "wider" than 16 bits.

Passing String Addresses to DOS

As mentioned, the CPU's registers often must be loaded with the segment and offset of data items "wider" than 16 bits. The following code fragment demonstrates one method for passing the address of a character string:

```
; PATH_NAME contains name of file to be opened
MOV     AX,SEG PATH_NAME         ; Segment address of path
MOV     DS,AX                    ;    in DS
MOV     DX,OFFSET PATH_NAME      ; Offset address of path
MOV     AL,C2h                   ; Mode for opening file
MOV     AH,3Dh                   ; Open the file
INT     21h                      ; DOS interrupt
JC      ERROR                    ; Carry set signals error
MOV     FILE_HANDLE,AX           ; Save file handle
```

This code fragment uses Int 21h, Function 3Dh to open a file. This function requires that DS and DX contain the segment and offset, respectively, of the file's path name. The first three lines of the code fragment load the registers accordingly. The next line puts C2h into AL; the value in AL specifies the mode in which the file is to be opened. (The encoding of modes in this value is explained in the "DOS Reference" section of this book.) With registers properly loaded, the DOS interrupt is then generated.

Like many DOS services, this one sets the carry flag if the service fails (that is, if the file could not be opened); the code therefore jumps to an error-handling routine if the carry flag is set (JC ERROR). But if the carry flag is clear, indicating success (that the file was opened), the file handle, returned in AX, is stored to a data word allocated for that purpose.

Note that the original DOS services (those which were provided in Version 1.0) do *not* use the carry flag to indicate an error. Like services in CP/M (the ancestor of DOS), they return their information in the AL register.

And not all the services added in Version 2.0 and subsequently indicate an error by means of the carry flag. Some (such as the Get PID service available in Version 3) are incapable of error because they merely return to the caller the content of a storage location used by DOS. These sometimes clear the carry flag, but some DOS versions just return with the flag in whatever state it had before DOS was called.

The point is that the carry flag should be considered to indicate an error *only* if the called function is documented as using it to do so. If the function is not officially documented, see the reference section of this book to learn whether it returns error indications and, if so, how.

High-Level Language Resources

High-level languages offer many different ways to call DOS and BIOS routines. Each language has a unique method that does not resemble that of any other language. Even within the same language, different implementations have different resources.

For example, compare Microsoft QuickBASIC Version 4.0 and its chief competitor, Turbo BASIC Version 1.0. QuickBASIC provides the function

```
CALL INTERRUPT (interrupt_number,
          registers_in,registers_out)
```

The equivalent function in Turbo BASIC is

```
CALL INTERRUPT interrupt_number
```

In Turbo BASIC, register values are global to the program and do not need to be passed explicitly in the CALL INTERRUPT statement. (Clearly, before using either of these instructions, you must load registers with the appropriate values.)

Variations between releases are common also. Turbo Pascal 3.0 provided no built-in means for accessing all files matching a wild-card file specification (such as C:\QTRLY\QTR?1988.DAT). To access such a group of files, you had to write two procedures: one that called DOS Int 21h, Function 4Eh to find the first file matching the specification, and another that called Function 4Fh to find any remaining matching files. When Turbo Pascal 4.0 was introduced, it not only allowed the user to create such routines and store them in a run-time library, but also provided the procedures FindFirst and FindNext for those purposes (along with many others in a run-time library "unit"). With the advent of Turbo Pascal 5.0, even the source code to these routines was made available (although at extra cost).

Each of the following subsections presents two sample programs. For each language, the first sample program (a simple one that illustrates the basic operations required for accessing operating system resources) uses BIOS Int 17h, Function 2 to check the printer's status. The second example is a slightly more complex program that illustrates the interpretation of results returned from a system call.

Avoiding Unnecessary Work

Many high-level languages have predefined functions, procedures, or variables that provide ready-made access to system resources. In most cases, these language elements access the same DOS and BIOS functions you would work with directly if you had to implement the system call yourself; the people who implemented the languages already have built the code for you. If you are considering the use of system resources in a language that is new to you—or in a new implementation of a familiar language—make sure that you are not reinventing the wheel. A principle we repeatedly return to in this book is that you should go to the system only when necessary. You should, therefore, use the built-in language resources unless your program has special needs that the language resources do not answer.

Always read your manual carefully. This basic advice is worth repeating: *Read your manual!* Many programmers, particularly those who are new to a language or operating system, have spent hours or days on unnecessary work. Had they read their language manuals more carefully, they would not have wasted their time in programming resources that are already available.

The more complex example differs according to the language. In accordance with our philosophy that you should not do unnecessary work, we have chosen programming examples that provide services you cannot get from the language. The BASIC examples show how to use DOS Int 21h, Functions 4Eh and 4Fh to retrieve file names matching a wild-card file specification. Because analogous functions are built into Turbo Pascal 4.0 (but not 3.0) and C, the sample programs in those languages perform different actions. The Pascal example uses DOS Int 21h, Function 57h to get the date and time of a specified file. The C example uses DOS Int 21h, Function 43h to get and set file attributes (archive, hidden, system, and read only). The examples use other functions as needed to perform necessary setup and cleanup work. Those ancillary function calls are described in the text and documented in the code.

The C Programming Language

For talking to an operating system, C is a programmer's delight. If you read the sections about other languages, you will see that the high-level character of Pascal and BASIC often gets in your way. The languages obscure or limit your access to system-level data structures and other information you have to get your hands on when you access DOS and BIOS resources.

The C programming language, with its handy blend of high-level and low-level resources, has been described as "high-level assembly language." C lets you "think like a microprocessor" while sparing you the drudgery of a detailed setup for operations in which you do not care about what happens at the level of bits and bytes.

C has a similar relationship to the operating system: many C functions are "DOS in C clothing." Those functions often take the same arguments as their DOS equivalents, and the same results are returned; indeed, the data structures accepted as input and returned as output often are identical to those used by their DOS equivalents.

Consequently, the more complex sample program in this section is presented in two versions: chmd.c calls DOS directly and chmc.c uses the equivalent C function. Only one version of the simpler example, called pronok.c, is presented; the program provides a capability not directly available from the Borland C++ library.

The C programs in this section were developed with the Borland C++ compiler. For information concerning the differences between Borland C++ and Microsoft C, be sure to read the comments in the listings and code fragments.

Accessing Registers and Generating Interrupts

The principal data structures for the interface between C and DOS are defined by the REGS union and the SREGS and REGPACK structures. These objects are declared in the header file DOS.H. Their declarations are shown in the following code fragment:

```
struct WORDREGS {
    unsigned int  ax, bx, cx, dx, si, di, cflag, flags;
};

/*Microsoft C lacks flags element */

struct BYTEREGS {
    unsigned char al, ah, bl, bh, cl, ch, dl, dh;
};
union REGS {
    struct WORDREGS x;
    struct BYTEREGS h;
};

struct SREGS {
    unsigned int es;
    unsigned int cs;
    unsigned int ss;
    unsigned int ds;
};

struct REGPACK {        /* Not defined in Microsoft C */
    unsigned r_ax, r_bx, r_cx, r_dx;
    unsigned r_bp, r_si, r_di, r_ds, r_es,  r_flags;
};
```

In addition, the contents of the CPU registers are available in Borland C++ through the pseudovariables _AX, _AL, _AH, and so on. Each of the 8086's general-purpose, offset, and segment registers (except IP) has a corresponding pseudovariable. Variables corresponding to the 16-bit and 8-bit registers are used (but not declared) as though they were of type unsigned int and unsigned char, respectively:

```
unsigned int _AX;
unsigned char _AL;
```

These declarations should *not* be included in your programs.

The pseudovariables described in the preceding paragraph are not available in Microsoft C. Their absence necessitates small changes in the programs at some points, so be sure to read the comments in the listings if you want to adapt the code for Microsoft's C compiler.

The DOS.H header file contains the following prototypes of the C functions for generating software interrupts:

```
int int86 (int intno, union REGS *inregs,
                      union REGS *outregs);
int int86x (int intno, union REGS *inregs,
                      union REGS *outregs,
                            struct SREGS *segregs);
```

```
int intdos (union REGS *inregs,
            union REGS *outregs);
int intdosx (union REGS *inregs,
             union REGS *outregs,
             struct SREGS *segregs);
```

```
void intr (int int_type, struct REGPACK *preg);
```

The `intdos()` function generates Int 21h, the principal DOS interrupt; `int86()` and `intr()` each generate the interrupt specified by the function's first argument (intno or `int_type`). Each `intdos` and `int86` has an *x* version that uses the segment registers as well as the general-purpose and offset registers. The `intr()` function is not available in Microsoft C.

The program in listing 4.1 demonstrates the use of the `int86()` function to verify that LPT1 is on-line.

Listing 4.1

```
/* prnok.c */
#include <conio.h>
#include <dos.h>

#define PRN_INT 0x17  /* Printer-services interrupt   */
#define STAT_RQ 0x02  /* Status-request service number */

int prnok(void)
{
    union REGS regs;

    regs.h.ah = STAT_RQ;   /* AH = 02 for printer status·*/
    regs.x.dx = 0;         /* DX = 00 for LPT1 */

    int86(PRN_INT, &regs, &regs);

    return( ((regs.h.ah & 0x80) == 0x80 ) ? 1 : 0 );

}

main()
{
    if (prnok())
        cputs("Ready to print!\n");
    else
        cputs("Please check the printer!\n");
}
```

A Note about the BIOS Printer-Status Request   *576*

The first sample program for each language uses BIOS Int 17h, Function 2 to verify that LPT1 is on-line. For this function, put 2 in AH and the printer number (0 for LPT1, 1 for LPT2, and so on) in DX. The function returns the printer's status, encoded in the bits of AH as follows:

Bit	Meaning (if set)
0	Time-out
1	Unused
2	Unused
3	I/O error
4	Printer is selected
5	Out of paper
6	Acknowledge
7	Printer not busy

The meanings of bit 0 and bits 3 through 7 are well defined, but the two hardware configurations we tested do not return the same result for the same condition. In every test case, the high bit of AH was set when the printer was powered up and on-line. However, on a Toshiba P351 printer connected to an IBM Personal System/2 Model 50, the program reports Ready to print when the printer is connected but not powered up. On an Epson RX-80 printer connected to a COMPAQ Portable Computer, the program responds Please check the printer! if the printer is connected but powered down. This is just a demo routine; a program with truly powerful status-checking capabilities needs more sophisticated logic.

Getting and Setting File Attributes

This section presents two sample C programs for changing the attributes of a specified file. These programs resemble the useful FA (file attribute) program included in the Norton Utilities; they differ from FA in that they accept only a literal file name, not a file specification containing wild-card characters. To keep the code as simple as possible, we have not included options for simply inquiring about the file's attributes or for changing more than one attribute at a time. The programs, which expect a command-line argument specifying an attribute to be set or cleared, terminate with an error message if an invalid argument is given.

If you are proficient in C programming, you should have no difficulty adding further options (such as "inquire") to the capabilities of this program. The information provided throughout this book makes it easy to add a capability for processing files specified by a wild card.

The two sample programs differ in that one calls the DOS interrupt directly, whereas the other uses a corresponding C library function to call the interrupt. The first example, shown in listing 4.2, makes a direct call to DOS Int 21h, Function 43h.

Listing 4.2

```
/* chmod().c */

#include <conio.h>
#include <stdio.h>
#include <ctype.h>
#include <process.h>
#include <dos.h>
#include "attrmask.h"                    /* Omit for Turbo C 2.0 */

#define GS_FATTR    0x43
#define GET_FATTR   0x00
#define SET_FATTR   0x01
/* For Turbo C 2.0, add these #define statements:
   define ARCHIVE_BIT   FA_ARCH
   define HIDDEN_BIT    FA_HIDDEN
   define RDONLY_BIT    FA_RDONLY
   define SYSTEM_BIT    FA_SYSTEM
*/

typedef enum { clr, set } clrorset;

void showattr(int attr);
int parsearg(char *thearg, clrorset *action, char *selection);

main( int argc, char *argv[] )
{
    extern char *sys_errlist[];    /* Provided by Turbo C */
    extern int errno;              /* Ditto                */

    union REGS regs;
    struct SREGS sregs;

    clrorset action;
    char selection;
```

continues

Listing 4.2 continued

```
    unsigned attrib, setting;
    int goahead;

    if (argc == 3) goahead = parsearg(argv[2], &action, &selection);
    else goahead = 0;

    if (!goahead)
        {
        if (argc == 3)
                {
                cputs("Can't parse ");
                cputs(argv[2]);
                }
        else
                cputs("No input");
        exit(1);
        }

    switch(selection) {
        case 'A': setting = ARCHIVE_BIT; break;
        case 'H': setting = HIDDEN_BIT;  break;
        case 'R': setting = RDONLY_BIT;  break;
        case 'S': setting = SYSTEM_BIT;  break;
        default:
            cputs("Bad input: "); cputs(argv[2]); cputs("\n\r");
            exit(1);
    }

    regs.h.ah = GS_FATTR;
    regs.h.al = GET_FATTR;
    regs.x.dx = (unsigned) argv[1];    /* Offset of first argument */
    sregs.ds  = _DS;
/* --------------------
   For Microsoft C, use the following in place of the
   preceding line:
   segread(&sregs);
*/

    intdosx(&regs,&regs,&sregs); /* Get the current attribute word */

    if (!regs.x.cflag) {          /* If carry is clear, success     */
        attrib = regs.x.cx;
        cputs("------------ Initial -----------\n\r");
        showattr(attrib);
```

```
        if (action == clr) {
            setting = ( (~setting)&attrib );
        } else {
            setting = (setting ¦ attrib);
        }

        regs.h.ah = GS_FATTR;
        regs.h.al = SET_FATTR;
        regs.x.cx = setting;
        regs.x.dx = (unsigned) argv[1];
        sregs.ds  = _DS;
/* ---------------------
   For Microsoft C, use the following in place of the
   preceding line:
   segread(&sregs);
*/

        intdosx(&regs,&regs,&sregs);  /* Set the attribute */

        attrib = regs.x.cx;
        cputs("------------ Final ------------\n\r");

        showattr(attrib);

    } else {        /* That is, if carry is not set */
        char *msg;
        cputs("function 0x43 failed: ");
        switch (regs.x.ax) {
            case 1:  msg = "Bad function code\n"; break;
            case 2:  msg = "Bad file name\n"; break;
            case 3:  msg = "Bad path\n"; break;
            case 5:  msg = "Can't change attribute\n"; break;
            default: msg = "Unknown cause\n";
        }
        cputs(msg);
    }

} /* End main */
```

Int 21h, Function 43h takes the following input:

Register	Value
AH	43h
AL	0 to get file attribute
	1 to set file attribute
DS:DX	Segment:offset address of the file path name

The program uses `#define` preprocessor directives to "name" the DOS function and the desired action (get or set). The file path name is provided as a command-line argument.

For a program compiled under the small memory model in Turbo C, you use the following statements to put the path name's segment and offset into DS and DX:

```
regs.x.dx = (unsigned) argv[1];
sregs.ds  = _DS;
```

Other methods of assignment may be necessary in other memory models. Because Microsoft C lacks register pseudovariables, the statement

```
segread(&sregs);
```

should be used instead.

If the operation is successful, the carry flag is clear and CX contains the file's attribute word. Bits of the attribute word and their corresponding attributes are

Bit	Meaning (if set)
0	Read only
1	Hidden
2	System
5	Archive

If the bit is set, the file has the corresponding attribute. (A set archive bit means that the file has not been backed up since the file was created or last modified.)

For convenience and legibility, `#define` directives are used also to create bit masks for the meaningful bits of the attribute word. (These definitions are in the ATTRMASK.H file; see the following code fragment.) The bit masks are used for changing and reading the file-attribute word.

```
/* attrmask.h */
#define ARCHIVE_BIT 0x20  /* Bit 5 of CX is the archive bit   */
#define SYSTEM_BIT  0x04  /* Bit 2 of CX is the system bit    */
#define HIDDEN_BIT  0x02  /* Bit 1 of CX is the hidden bit    */
#define RDONLY_BIT  0x01  /* Bit 0 of CX is the read-only bit */
```

Listings 4.3 and 4.4 show miscellaneous functions used by the two versions of the second sample program.

Listing 4.3

```
/* parsarg.c */

#include <conio.h>
#include <ctype.h>
```

```c
typedef enum { clr, set } clrorset;

int parsearg(char *thearg, clrorset *action, char *selection)
{

    if (*(thearg) == '/') {
        switch( *(thearg+2) ) {
            case '+':
                *action = set; break;
            case '-':
                *action = clr; break;
            default:
                cputs("Use '+' to set or '-' to clear\n\r");
                return(0);
        }
        *selection = toupper(*(thearg+1));
        return(1);
    } else {
        cputs("Usage: chmd filename /xy\n\r"
              "where x = A (archive) or H (hidden) or\n\r"
              "            R (read-only) or S (system),\n\r"
              "  and y = + (set) or - (clear)\n\r");
        return(0);
    }

}
```

Listing 4.4

```c
/* showatr1.c */

#include <conio.h>
#include "attrmask.h"

#define CLEAR 0
#define isclear(x,y) ((x&y)==CLEAR)      /* Parens around x, y ? */
#define putstat(x,y) cputs( isclear(x,y) ? "clear   " : "set     " )

void showattr(int attr)
{
    cputs("Archive System  Hidden  Read-only\n\r");

    putstat(attr,ARCHIVE_BIT);
    putstat(attr,SYSTEM_BIT);
    putstat(attr,HIDDEN_BIT);
    putstat(attr,RDONLY_BIT);
    cputs("\n\r");
}
```

If you compare listing 4.2 (the first version of this program) to listing 4.5 (the second version), you can see that error checking is slightly more sophisticated in a program that uses the interrupt rather than the C library function. Because of differences in the libraries, this program compiles under Turbo C only. Modifications are needed for Microsoft C, which lacks the chmod function.

Listing 4.5

```
/* chmc02.c */

#include <conio.h>
#include <stdio.h>
#include <io.h>
#include <ctype.h>
#include <process.h>
#include "attrmask.h"

#define GET_FATTR    0x00
#define SET_FATTR    0x01

typedef enum { clr, set } clrorset;

void showattr(int attr);            /* Show file attribute        */
int parsearg(char *thearg,          /* Parse command-line argument */
             clrorset *action,      /* Clear or set attribute     */
             char *selection);      /* Selected attribute         */

main( int argc, char *argv[] )
{
    extern char *sys_errlist[];   /* Provided by Turbo C  */
    extern int errno;             /* Ditto                */

    clrorset action;
    char selection;

    unsigned attrib, setting;
    int goahead;

    if (argc == 3) goahead = parsearg(argv[2], &action, &selection);

    if (!goahead)
        {
        if (argc == 3)
                {
                cputs("Can't parse ");
                cputs(argv[2]);
                }
```

```
        else
                cputs("No input");
        exit(1);
    }

    switch(selection) {
        case 'A': setting = ARCHIVE_BIT; break;
        case 'H': setting = HIDDEN_BIT;  break;
        case 'R': setting = RDONLY_BIT;  break;
        case 'S': setting = SYSTEM_BIT;  break;
        default:
            cputs("Bad input: "); cputs(argv[2]); cputs("\n\r");
            exit(1);
    }
    attrib = chmod(argv[1], GET_FATTR );

    if (attrib != 0xFFFF) {
        cputs("----------- Initial -----------\n\r");
        showattr(attrib);
        if (action == clr) {
            setting = ( (~setting)&attrib );
        } else {
            setting = (setting ¦ attrib);
        }
        attrib = chmod(argv[1], SET_FATTR, setting );
        cputs("----------- Final -----------\n\r");

        showattr(attrib);
    } else {
        cputs("function chmod failed:\n\r");
        cputs(sys_errlist[errno]); cputs("\n\r");
    }
} /* end main */
```

Notice that the chmod() C library function returns the file-attribute word as a functional return value (with –1 signaling an error), whereas Int 21h, Function 43h returns the attribute word in register CX and signals an error (as do most DOS functions) by setting the carry flag. Because the results returned by the C library function are the same as those returned in CX by the DOS function, you can use the showattr() function to decode the attribute word for both programs.

Turbo Pascal

Version 4.0 of Turbo Pascal improved on Version 3.0, which provided excellent support for calling DOS and BIOS functions. The subsequent step to Version 5.0 restored several useful features lost during the step from Version 3 to Version 4 and added for the first time a built-in debugger, which is a great help in complex programs. Version 5.5 added object-oriented programming capabilities to Turbo Pascal and support for math coprocessors. Version 6.0 added TurboVision, an object-oriented application framework for DOS programs, and an enhanced development environment.

The language has an extensive set of built-in facilities that provide access to system resources and minimize the need for programmers to write their own system-level code.

The file and console input/output functions meet almost any programming need; most common file and directory operations (get file size, get current directory, change directory, make directory, and so on) are fully supported. As mentioned earlier in this chapter, Versions 4.0 and 5.0 simplify the writing of programs that process a group of files selected by a wild-card file specification.

This collection of resources is so complete that you would have difficulty finding a DOS or BIOS service you would want to call directly from your program. Why call DOS or the BIOS for console input and output when Turbo Pascal has a full complement of functions and procedures for those operations?

But the time may come—if it hasn't already—when your program needs something that the language does not provide. Therefore, this section presents two sample programs that make direct calls to DOS and the BIOS. For tutorial purposes, the programs duplicate operations available on a higher level, in Turbo Pascal itself.

The first of these programs uses BIOS Int 17h, Function 2 to verify that the printer is on-line. (Similar results—with equally sophisticated error checking—are available through the language's built-in procedures and functions.) The second sample program, which also duplicates a function built into Turbo Pascal 4.0, gets a file's date and time of creation or most recent modification.

Accessing Registers and Generating Interrupts

Turbo Pascal's main data structure for accessing registers is the Registers record. The structure of this record, which is defined in the Dos unit of Turbo Pascal 4.0, is shown in the following lines of code. In Version 3.0, the record must be user-defined.

```
Type
{ Registers record used by Intr and MsDos }
    Registers = Record
        Case Integer of
            0: (AX,BX,CX,DX,BP,SI,DI,DS,ES,Flags : Word);
            1: (AL,AH,BL,BH,CL,CH,DL,DH : Byte)

        End;
```

Turbo Pascal has the following two procedures for generating interrupts:

```
MsDos(vars Regs :  Registers)
Intr(IntNo : Byte; vars Regs : Registers)
```

MsDos generates Int 21h, the "generic" DOS interrupt. Intr can generate *any* software interrupt, including 21h. (In Version 3.0, the first argument of Intr is an integer.)

The first sample Turbo Pascal program, in listing 4.6, demonstrates a simple call to the BIOS. The PrinterOnline function invokes BIOS Int 17h, Function 2 (Printer Status Request) to verify that the printer is on-line. Function 2 returns in AH a byte that indicates whether the printer is busy, selected, out of paper, and so on. (Be sure to see the note about this BIOS interrupt in the "High-Level Language Resources" section, earlier in this chapter.) This program, however, checks only bit 7 of AH; if the bit is set, the printer is selected.

Listing 4.6

```
Program PrinterDemo;
Uses Dos;

    Function PrinterOnline : Boolean;
        Const
            PrnStatusInt : Byte = $17;
            StatusRequest : Byte = $02;
            PrinterNum : Word = 0; { 0 for LPT1, 1 for LPT2, etc. }
        Var
            Regs : Registers;        { Type is defined in Dos unit. }
    Begin
    Regs.AH := StatusRequest;
    Regs.DX := PrinterNum;
    Intr(PrnStatusInt, Regs);
    PrinterOnline := (Regs.AH and $80) = $80
    End;

Begin                  { Program }
If PrinterOnline Then
    WriteLn('Ready to print!')
Else
    WriteLn('Please check the printer!')

End.
```

Reading a File's Date and Time Stamp

The date and time that you created or last modified a file are available through DOS Int 21h, Function 57h. The GetDateAndTime Pascal procedure demonstrates that DOS function's use (see listing 4.7).

Listing 4.7

```
{ ============================================ }
Procedure GetDateAndTime(Pathname : PathStr;
                         Var DateWord, TimeWord : Word);
    Const
        GetDateAndTime : Byte = $57;
        CloseFile : Byte = $3E;
    Var
        Regs : Registers;
        Handle : Word;

    Function CarryClear(Regs : Registers) : Boolean;
    Begin CarryClear := ((Regs.Flags and 1) = 0) End;

    { ============================================= }
    Function GetFileHandle(Pathname : PathStr) : Word;
        Const GetHandle : Byte = $3D; ReadAccess : Byte = 0;
        Var PathSeg, PathOfs : Word;
    Begin
    Pathname := Pathname + Chr(0);
    PathSeg := Seg(Pathname[1]);  PathOfs := Ofs(Pathname[1]);

    Regs.AH := GetHandle; Regs.AL := ReadAccess;
    Regs.DS := PathSeg;    Regs.DX := PathOfs;
    MsDos(Regs);
    If CarryClear(Regs) Then
        GetFileHandle := Regs.AX   { No semicolon before Else! }
    Else
        Begin
        WriteLn('Handle function failed!');
        Exit
        End; { If carry is clear }
    End;                    { Function GetFileHandle }


{ ===================================================== }
Begin                      { Procedure GetDateAndTime }

Handle := GetFileHandle(Pathname);

Regs.AH := GetDateAndTime; Regs.AL := 0;  Regs.BX := Handle;
MsDos(Regs);
If CarryClear(Regs) Then
    Begin  DateWord := Regs.DX;  TimeWord := Regs.CX  End
Else
    Begin
    DateWord := 0; TimeWord := 0; { Error flag for caller }
    End;
```

```
Regs.AH := CloseFile;    Regs.BX := Handle;
MsDos(Regs);
If NOT CarryClear(Regs) Then
    WriteLn(
        'Warning: Procedure GetDateAndTime did not close ',
        pathname)

End;              { Procedure GetDateAndTime }
```

The principal input item for Function 57h is a file handle. Turbo Pascal has a full complement of file-oriented procedures and functions, but the system-level details of Turbo's file management are concealed from the programmer. To use Function 57h, the GetDateAndTime procedure must "go around" Turbo's normal file-management routines. Thus, instead of using Pascal's procedures for opening a file (Assign and either Reset or Rewrite), the function calls DOS Int 21h, Function 3Dh. This system call is performed by the GetFileHandle function, which is nested in the GetDateAndTime procedure.

Function 3Dh requires the address of an ASCIIZ string that contains the file's path name. Because Turbo Pascal strings are not terminated by a zero byte, the function appends Chr(0) to the string Pathname. And because the length byte at the first position in the Turbo Pascal string must not be included in the string argument passed to Function 3Dh, the address of Pathname[1] is passed to the function. The Seg and Ofs functions give straightforward access to the components of the string's address.

Having obtained the file handle, the GetDateAndTime procedure passes it to DOS Function 57h. The AL register is set to 0, signaling that the DOS function should get (not set) the file's date and time. If Function 57h succeeds (as indicated by a clear carry flag), it returns the file's encoded time and date in CX and DX, respectively.

The FileDateAndTime program, shown in listing 4.8, demonstrates the use of the Turbo Pascal GetDateAndTime function.

Listing 4.8

```
{ TPEX0203.PAS }

Program FileDateAndTime;

    Uses Dos;
    Type
        PathNameType = String[64];
        String5 = String[5];
        { Max DOS path is 63; add 1 for the null. }
```

continues

Listing 4.8 continued

```
       Var
           Pathname : PathNameType;
           DateWord, TimeWord : Word;    { Use Integer in 3.0 }
           Hours, Mins, Secs, Year, Month, Day : Integer;

           Ch : Char;

{$i GETDTTM.PAS}
{ ========================================================= }
Begin                         { Program }

Write('Pathname? >');  ReadLn(Pathname);
GetDateAndTime(Pathname, DateWord, TimeWord);
If (DateWord <> 0) Then
    Begin
    { Decode date }
    Year  := ((DateWord AND $FE00) SHR  9) + 1980;
    Month := (DateWord AND $01E0) SHR  5;
    Day   := (DateWord AND $001F);

    { Decode time }
    Hours := (TimeWord AND $F800) SHR 11;
    Mins  := (TimeWord AND $07E0) SHR  5;
    Secs  := (TimeWord AND $001F) SHL  1; { Shift left to double }

    WriteLn('File Time: ', Hours:2,':', Mins:02,  ':', Secs:2);
    WriteLn('File Date: ', Year:4, '/', Month:02, '/', Day:2);

    End                       { No semicolon before Else }
Else
    WriteLn('GetDateAndTime has failed!');

End.
```

QuickBASIC

QuickBASIC shares the familiar file-oriented statements of its forerunners, BASICA and GW-BASIC. The KILL FileName$ statement deletes files, CHDIR changes the current directory, and so on. Input and output routines are flexible.

But BASIC's file-handling capabilities are lacking in some respects. For instance, the procedure for processing file names that match a wild-card file specification (with * or ?) is convoluted. You have to monkey around with passing a DOS command to the SHELL, directing the command's output to a file, and reading the output file into your program one line at a time, parsing file names (and skipping superfluous lines) as you go. Empty disk drives, write-protect tabs, and full disks can bring your program to an abrupt halt. And how do you *know* that the name you are using for SHELL's output is not the same as that of an existing file?

By programming at the DOS level, you can avoid all that hassle. The second sample program in this section shows how to call DOS Int 21h, Functions 4Eh and 4Fh to find the names of all files that match a file specification, which may contain one or more wild-card characters. (Some of the best uses of programming at the DOS level not only make programming convenient but also make running your programs more convenient for the user.)

First, let's look at a simple program that introduces the fundamentals of calling DOS from BASIC. This first QuickBASIC example (like those in the other languages) uses BIOS Int 17h, Function 2 to verify that the printer is on-line.

Accessing Registers and Generating Interrupts

QuickBASIC's principal data structure for the DOS and BIOS interface is the Registers record:

```
TYPE Registers
    AX AS INTEGER
    BX AS INTEGER
    CX AS INTEGER
    DX AS INTEGER
    BP AS INTEGER
    SI AS INTEGER
    DI AS INTEGER
    SI AS INTEGER
    FLAGS AS INTEGER
    DS AS INTEGER
    ES AS INTEGER
END TYPE
```

Register-type variables are declared by means of the DIM statement:

```
DIM InRegs AS Registers, OutRegs AS Registers
```

Because these variables obey the normal rules regarding scope, they can be declared as local to procedures.

QuickBASIC has two built-in procedures for generating interrupts:

```
CALL INTERRUPT(IntNumber, InRegs, OutRegs)
```

and

```
CALL INTERRUPTX(IntNumber, InRegs, OutRegs)
```

CALL INTERRUPT ignores the DS and ES registers (or the DS and ES fields of the Registers arguments), whereas CALL INTERRUPTX uses these registers or fields. If you want to leave DS and ES unchanged in a call to INTERRUPTX, assign the value −1 to the record's DS and ES fields.

Listing 4.9 demonstrates the use of the BIOS Printer Status Request function. Because the results of this function are not entirely consistent across hardware configurations, be sure to read "A Note about the BIOS Printer-Status Request" (in this chapter's section on C) if you want to use the function in a program.

Listing 4.9

```
'PRNOKQB.BAS
CONST PRN.Status.rq% = &H200          '2 in AH
CONST BIOS.PRN.INT% = &H17

TYPE Registers
    AX AS INTEGER
    BX AS INTEGER
    CX AS INTEGER
    DX AS INTEGER
    BP AS INTEGER
    SI AS INTEGER
    DI AS INTEGER
    FLAGS AS INTEGER
    DS AS INTEGER
    ES AS INTEGER
END TYPE

DIM InRegs AS Registers, OutRegs AS Registers

InRegs.AX = PRN.Status.rq%

CALL INTERRUPT(BIOS.PRN.INT%, InRegs, OutRegs)

IF ((OutRegs.AX AND &H8000) = &H8000) THEN
    PRINT "Printer OK"
ELSE
    PRINT "Please check the printer"
END IF

END        'PROGRAM
```

Finding Files That Match a File Specification

Frequently, sophisticated programs must process groups of files described by wild-card file specifications. QuickBASIC does not provide a built-in facility for finding the file names that match a user-supplied file specification; by building such a facility, you can make the language much more useful.

The DOS resources for using file specifications are Functions 4Eh (Find First) and 4Fh (Find Next) of Int 21h. These functions find, respectively, the first matching file name and any remaining matching names. Both place their output—the file names and other information—in the DTA (disk transfer area). By default, the DTA is a 128-byte buffer at offset 80h in the program segment prefix. But the sample program presented in this section uses DOS Function 1Ah to set a different DTA address, to avoid any possibility of interference with other DOS functions.

Most BASIC implementations, QuickBASIC included, do not store strings at a fixed location. A four-byte string descriptor keeps track of each string's location. The descriptor contains a 16-bit pointer to the string; this pointer contains the string's offset into the default data area. You do not have to bother with locating this descriptor and retrieving the address because the QuickBASIC function

```
SADD(TheString$)
```

returns the offset of the string supplied as an argument. (If you need to access the string descriptor, you can retrieve its segment and offset with the VARSEG and VARPTR functions.) SADD should be called immediately before your program accesses the string because a string can be "moved around" in memory during program execution, especially if your program changes the string's length.

The program in listing 4.10 demonstrates the use of Functions 4Eh and 4Fh to retrieve file names that match a file specification.

Listing 4.10

```
DECLARE SUB SetDTA (TheDTA$)
DECLARE SUB FindFirst (FileSpec$, FileName$)
DECLARE SUB FindNext (FileName$)
DECLARE SUB BuildName (TheName$)

TYPE Registers
    AX AS INTEGER
    BX AS INTEGER
    CX AS INTEGER
    DX AS INTEGER
    BP AS INTEGER
    SI AS INTEGER
    DI AS INTEGER
```

continues

Listing 4.10 continued

```
        FLAGS AS INTEGER
        DS AS INTEGER
        ES AS INTEGER
END TYPE

DTA$ = SPACE$(43)

INPUT "Filespec? >", FileSpec$

CALL SetDTA(DTA$)
' Get the first matching file name
CALL FindFirst((FileSpec$), FileName$)

IF FileName$ <> "" THEN
    PRINT "First match: "; FileName$
    DO
        CALL FindNext(FileName$)
        IF FileName$ <> "" THEN
            PRINT " Next match: "; FileName$
        END IF
    LOOP UNTIL FileName$ = ""
ELSE
    PRINT "No files match "; FileSpec$
END IF
END             ' PROGRAM
SUB BuildName (TheName$)
SHARED DTA$
    EndOfStr% = INSTR(31, DTA$, CHR$(0))
    TheName$ = MID$(DTA$, 31, EndOfStr% - 31)
END SUB


SUB FindFirst (FileSpec$, FileName$)
FileSpec$ = FileSpec$ + CHR$(0)    'make ASCIIZ
DIM InRegs AS Registers, OutRegs AS Registers
InRegs.AX = &H4E00                 'find first matching file
InRegs.DX = SADD(FileSpec$)        'offset of FileSpec$
InRegs.DS = VARSEG(FileSpec$)      'seg of FileSpec$
InRegs.CX = 0                      'normal files only--no dirs, etc.
CALL INTERRUPT(&H21, InRegs, OutRegs)
' Got a match? Yes, if CARRY FLAG (bit 0 of FLAGS) is clear.
IF (OutRegs.FLAGS AND 1) = 0 THEN
    CALL BuildName(FileName$):
ELSE
    FileName$ = ""
END IF
END SUB
```

```
SUB FindNext (FileName$)
    DIM InRegs AS Registers, OutRegs AS Registers
    InRegs.AX = &H4F00                  'find next matching file
    CALL INTERRUPT(&H21, InRegs, OutRegs)
    IF (OutRegs.FLAGS AND 1) = 0 THEN
        CALL BuildName(FileName$):
    ELSE
        FileName$ = ""
    END IF
END SUB

SUB SetDTA (DTA$)
DIM InRegs AS Registers, OutRegs AS Registers
' Set the Disk Transfer Area address
InRegs.DX = SADD(DTA$)          'offset of DTA
InRegs.DS = VARSEG(DTA$)        'segment of DTA
InRegs.AX = &H1A00              'DOS function for setting DTA addr
CALL INTERRUPT(&H21, InRegs, OutRegs)
' no return value for function &H1A
END SUB
```

The procedure

```
SetDTA(TheDTA$)
```

sets the disk transfer area address to the address of its string argument.

The procedures

```
FindFirst(FileSpec$, FileName$)
```

and

```
FindNext(FileName$)
```

locate the matching file names. If matching file names are found, both procedures assign the matching name to FileName$; if matching names are not found, they assign the empty string (" "). Although the sample program simply displays the file names, you can have your program do whatever you want with the returned values.

Summary

This chapter introduced the fundamentals of system-level programming in assembly language, C, Pascal, and BASIC, The procedure for accessing DOS and BIOS resources has three major components:

PROGRAMMING

- Loading registers with appropriate values

- Generating a software interrupt

- Interpreting the results returned in registers

Sometimes additional work is needed, as when your program must pass to the system the address of a string or other data item. Each language offers resources for getting the addresses of items; the simplicity of using addresses varies according to the language.

If you have read the sections about each language (not just about your language of choice), you probably have noticed that the languages differ greatly in the convenience and the amount of support they provide for accessing DOS and BIOS resources. You may want to consider these differences when you choose a language for your next programming project.

PROGRAMMING

Part II

Character Devices and Serial Devices

Output Devices

This chapter discusses the video display and the printer, the two fundamental output devices. They are perhaps the most important devices in computer programming because they serve as the interaction points between the program and the programmer.

Most computer books treat the auxiliary devices (the RS-232 ports) as character-output devices and describe them in chapters similar to this one. But in this book, RS-232 ports are treated separately in Chapter 7, "Serial Devices," because of their unique nature and diverse capabilities.

Like other chapters, this one emphasizes the utility of working with the highest available coding level to complete a task. Generally, you should use a service available directly from a high-level language. But in many situations, you must go lower, to either the DOS or BIOS level, to perform specific tasks. This chapter describes the DOS and BIOS services that control the video display and printer.

Basic Character Devices

Programming the video display and the printer can be a simple procedure or an extremely sophisticated one.

Beyond the level of simple character I/O, programming can quickly become a complex process, particularly when you work with graphics.

This book is not a comprehensive manual about graphics, but it does provide the basic principles for working with graphics. In this chapter, useful routines for system programming are developed and, most important, useful tools for working with output are constructed.

In C, services already available for working with the display and printer are adequate for typical programming chores. When you build a program, these services generally are the best ones to use for two reasons:

- By using standard library functions, you reduce your program's sensitivity to changes in DOS design.

- If standard calls are used properly, they can make your program compatible with UNIX or XENIX systems.

If you need to move beyond the level of standard library functions, you must balance carefully what might be lost against what might be gained. By moving from standard library functions to DOS services, you gain great control over output operations while preserving a fair amount of insensitivity to system design. You lose the convenience of the standard library functions, and you lose compatibility with UNIX or XENIX.

When are insensitivity and compatibility important considerations for programmers? Obviously, if you work with both DOS and UNIX or XENIX, having program code that successfully compiles without modification under the various operating systems can simplify program development and maintenance. These programs typically are simple utilities or simple interactive programs.

This dual-world approach does not work well with real-time interactive programs. Programs such as 1-2-3 and Microsoft Word would suffer from this approach. These types of programs are not acceptable unless they are written to utilize the fastest possible routines. In many instances, the hardware is programmed directly, thus eliminating compatibility.

How the Display System Works

The PC display system has evolved from simple beginnings to encompass the following variety of standards in use today:

- Monochrome Display Adapter (MDA)

- Color Graphics Adapter (CGA)

- Hercules Graphics Adapter (HGA)

- Enhanced Graphics Adapter (EGA)

- MultiColor Graphics Array (MCGA)

- Virtual Graphics Array (VGA)

All of the standards except the Hercules Graphics Adapter are endorsed and supported by IBM through standard BIOS and DOS services. The MDA, CGA, and EGA are used in the PC line of computers, and the MCGA and VGA are used in the Personal System/2 line. The HGA's popularity makes it the de facto standard for high-resolution monochrome graphics on the PC line, but a special driver is required to take advantage of its graphics capabilities. Neither the BIOS nor DOS has built-in services to take full advantage of the HGA. The HGA's unique nature and lack of support directly through BIOS or DOS services make an explanation of its programming beyond the scope of this book.

Types of Display Monitors

Many types of display monitors are available, and more are becoming available all the time. Not all types of display monitors can be mentioned in this chapter, but some of them are described in the following list:

Direct monochrome monitors display high-resolution text and character-level graphics. They can be driven by a monochrome display adapter (MDA), the Hercules adapter (HGA), or an EGA card set to emulate a monochrome adapter.

Composite monochrome monitors are inexpensive monochrome (often amber or green) monitors that can be driven from a CGA output. They can display CGA graphics but not color. Some of these monitors implement shading to indicate color differences.

Composite color monitors produce color and graphics output, but their resolution typically is poor on 80-column text displays. Television sets are at the low end of this range, but their poor resolution produces unsatisfactory results in text-display modes, except when you use 40-column lines.

RGB monitors produce clear, crisp color output in both text and graphics modes by using separate electrical lines for each primary color (red, green, and blue).

Enhanced RGB monitors provide color text and graphics that are superior to those provided by normal RGB monitors. They use the same technology (separate RGB lines) but use advanced display circuitry to provide a higher-quality image.

Multisync monitors currently provide the highest-quality text and graphics plus added flexibility. Using RGB connections, multisync monitors go beyond the capabilities of normal or enhanced RGB monitors. Multisync monitors can imitate any other type of monitor and provide enhanced display capabilities.

The video display can be accessed in one of three ways:

- *Through DOS function calls*. This method is the most compatible, but slowest, form of access. With DOS V2.0 and higher, the ANSI.SYS driver lets programs using this method of access have control of the screen through control-code sequences.

- *Through BIOS function calls*. This fairly compatible method of accessing the display is faster than DOS. Most systems, but not all of them, are compatible with this screen-access method. Through BIOS function calls, you can use graphics and other screen effects not available from the DOS level.

- *Directly at the hardware level*. This method is incompatible because wide hardware differences may exist among systems. Programs that use this method are generally not compatible with all systems considered PC-compatible. This method is not compatible in multiuser or multitasking systems. Both its advantage and the reason for its frequent use stem from the snappy displays and fast operations that occur at this level.

Programmers who decide to build sophisticated displays do not need to start at the hardware level (which, in fact, should be the "level of last resort"). Most good programs begin at the other end of the spectrum, with a high-level language. BASIC prototypes of major commercial programs frequently are a starting point for development. (VisiCalc, the original spreadsheet program, was first coded in BASIC.) After a program is working correctly, you can increase its speed and sophistication to make it as fast and tight as possible. Making a correct program fast is easier than making a fast program correct.

You *can* write sophisticated, useful programs using DOS and BIOS screen access. Programs that do sophisticated processing can work without direct access to the screen display. As you begin to work with multitasking environments such as Windows or DESQview, you start to appreciate this access level.

Storing and Displaying Video Data

The PC display system is based on the Motorola 6845 Cathode Ray Tube Controller (CRTC) chip. The EGA and VGA systems use custom chips based on this design. These chips manage many important display tasks so that programmers do not have to manage them:

- Detect light-pen signals
- Increment the video-buffer address counter
- Synchronize the display and timing

- Select the video buffer

- Determine the size and location of the hardware cursor

The system's design is conceptually simple. A PC display is a *memory-mapped* device, in which everything that appears on-screen reflects what is in the computer's memory (see fig. 5.1). A memory buffer stores information that appears on the display. The memory buffer's starting address and length vary, depending on the type of video display in use, the current display mode, and the amount of memory allocated to the display.

Fig. 5.1. *A display system that shows memory mapping.*

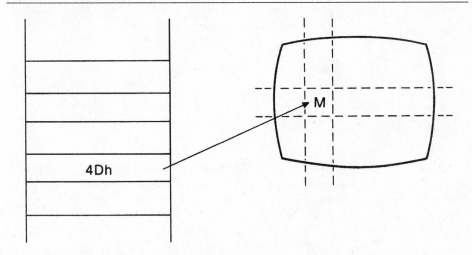

Display adapters generally contain from 4K to 256K of memory, and some of the new VGA adapters provide 512K of memory (for example, Designer VGA by Orchid Technology). Because the data needed to define a display screen may occupy significantly less space than this amount, some display adapters can control more than one display screen. Notice that we said display *screen* and not display *monitor*. Display screens, or *pages*, are the memory representation of what appears on your screen. Table 5.1 shows the beginning memory-buffer locations, the buffer lengths, and the number of display pages for the different display types.

For all display adapters, the number of display pages available for text modes is the result of two bytes per screen position. With 80 text characters per line, the result is 2×80×25, which equals 4000 bytes, or approximately 4K. If you use the adapter for 40 text characters per line (2×40×25), each screen occupies 2000 bytes, or about 2K of space. Using these calculations, you can easily see why the CGA can get eight display pages from 16K of buffer space.

Table 5.1. *Memory Configurations for Display Adapters*

Display Type	Mode	Buffer Segment Address	Buffer Length	Display Pages
MDA	Text	B000h	4K	1
CGA	Text	B800h	16K	4/8
	Graphics	B800h	16K	1
EGA	Mono	B000h	Varies	Varies
	Text	B800h	Varies	Varies
	Graphics	A000h	Varies	Varies
CGA	Graphics	B800h	Varies	Varies
MCG	Text	B800h	64K	8
	Graphics	A000h	64K	1
CGA	Graphics	B800h	64K	1
VGA	Mono	B000h	256K	8
	Text	B800h	256K	8
	Graphics	A000h	256K	1/2/4/8
CGA	Graphics	B800h	256K	1

The EGA card's buffer size varies because the EGA can have 64K, 128K, or 256K of memory. This RAM is a video buffer for the screen images and also holds patterns (fonts) for as many as 1024 display characters. The calculations from the preceding paragraph can help you determine the number of display pages available.

Table 5.1 shows that the EGA, MCGA, and VGA have two different graphics-buffer beginning addresses. These adapters can emulate the CGA (segment address B800h) as well as their native beginning segment address of A000h.

The CRTC chip, independent of a computer system's operation, scans the display memory area and, based on the information stored there, updates the video display. The actual screen display is produced by an electron beam that turns small screen dots (called picture elements, or *pixels*) on or off as each line of the screen is scanned. The beam traces a path from left to right and top to bottom over the entire screen.

To provide a steady image, the screen is refreshed (the electron beam makes one complete cycle of the entire screen) at a rate of 60 times per second. At the end of each line, the beam has to move from the right side of the screen back to the left side. This time period is called the *horizontal retrace interval* (HRI). Similarly, after the beam completes one cycle it must move from the lower right to the upper left corner of the screen to begin a new cycle. This movement is called the *vertical retrace interval* (VRI). During both the HRI and the VRI, the beam is turned off and nothing is written to the screen.

Programmers whose programs write directly to display memory should be aware of the HRI or VRI for some types of display adapters, because of the way that the adapters use the display memory. The memory used in some display adapters is actually a special *dual-ported* memory, in which the computer can write values into memory at the same time that the CRTC reads them. Because this type of memory is more costly than "ordinary" RAM, other display adapters omit the frill. If your computer happens to address a video memory location in a non-dual-ported adapter while the CRTC is reading the value at that same location, you may see a display-screen distortion called *snow*.

This snow problem is particularly important when you work with a genuine IBM CGA or with any clone that duplicates the CGA circuit. In such systems it has been so bad that users coined a special word to describe it: *chromablizzard*. To avoid snow on such a system, access the screen memory only during the HRI or VRI.

You can tell whether an HRI or VRI condition exists by polling the CRTC status register at I/O port 3DAh. Bit 0 indicates whether an HRI exists; bit 3 reflects the same information about the VRI. The respective bit is on when the retrace interval begins and off when it is complete. Because HRIs happen much more often than VRIs and are easier to detect when you are programming, most direct screen-memory routines test only for the HRI condition. When the bit goes on, you have time to put only one character in display memory (assuming standard 4.77 MHz system speed) without screen interference. And to get even this much time, you must disable all interrupts while polling; otherwise, some other action could steal the interval you were waiting for.

This guideline about screen interference applies both when you *write* to screen memory and when you *read* from screen memory. (Although it is not obvious why reading should interfere, experience shows that it does on many CGA boards.)

Video Display Formats

The display adapter's interpretation of video data depends on the display *mode*, which controls the way data appears on-screen. Table 5.2 details the display modes available with the different display adapters.

Table 5.2. *Video Modes*

Mode	Type	Colors	Resolution	MDA	CGA	EGA	MCGA	VGA	PCjr
00h	Text	16	40×25	X	X	X	X		
01h	Text	16	40×25	X	X	X	X		
02h	Text	16	80×25	X	X	X	X		
03h	Text	16	80×25	X	X	X	X		
04h	Graphics	4	320×200	X	X	X	X	X	
05h	Graphics	4	320×200	X	X	X	X	X	
06h	Graphics	2	640×200	X	X	X	X	X	
07h	Text	Mono	80×25	X	X	X	X		
08h	Graphics	16	160×200				X		
09h	Graphics	16	320×200				X		
0Ah	Graphics	4	640×200				X		
0Bh	——RESERVED——								
0Ch	——RESERVED——								
0Dh	Graphics	16	320×200		X	X			
0Eh	Graphics	16	640×200		X	X			
0Fh	Graphics	Mono	640×350		X	X			
10h	Graphics	16	640×35			X	X		
11h	Graphics	2	640×480		X	X			
12h	Graphics	16	640×480				X		
13h	Graphics	256	320×20			X	X		

The numbers in the resolution column represent rows and columns for text modes and represent pixels for graphics modes.

The MDA supports only 1 screen-display mode (mode 7), the CGA supports 7, and the EGA supports 12. The most sophisticated adapter is the VGA system, which supports 15 display modes. The VGA also supports graphics on a monochrome display, a display of 43 lines per screen, and a color palette of up to 256 colors.

The BIOS keeps track of the current display mode and stores the number at memory address 0040:0049. The number of columns per line is stored at 0040:004A. Although you can change these values directly, doing so is not wise because the BIOS not only changes the numbers at these memory locations but also performs other operations necessary for setting a video mode correctly.

Now let's look at the two major display-mode categories: text and graphics.

Text-Mode Display

Text mode is also called alphanumeric mode, as most IBM documentation refers to it. In text modes, two bytes of memory are assigned to each character position displayed on the screen: one byte to hold the character, one to hold its *attribute*. The character is in the byte at the even address, and the attribute is in the odd byte. Character attributes indicate to the display adapter how the character should be displayed. Table 5.3 shows the meaning of the character-attribute bits for monochrome text mode; table 5.4 shows the bit meanings for color text mode.

Table 5.3. *Monochrome Character Attributes*

Bits 76543210	Meaning
0.......	Normal character
1.......	Blinking character
.000....	Black background (normal)
.111....	White background (inverse)
....0...	Normal intensity
....1...	High intensity
.....000	White foreground (normal)
.....001	Underlined white foreground
.....111	Black foreground (inverse)

Table 5.4. *Color Character Attributes*

Bits 76543210	Meaning
0.......	Normal character
1.......	Blinking character
.xxx....	Background (see table 5.5)
....xxxx	Foreground (see table 5.5)

Notice in table 5.4 that only three bits are allowed for the background color and that four bits are allowed for the foreground. This is because the standard video display circuits provide the capability of making each character blink on and off by setting the high bit of the background field to 1. By modifying the value sent to the video adapter's mode display register, however, you can obtain the full range of brightness values for the background (at the expense of losing the blink capability).

To disable the blink feature and add intensity control to the background for a CGA, you must read the value stored by the BIOS at location 0040h:0065h, AND that byte with 0DFh to clear the blink bit, and OUT the result to port 03D8h (the CGA's MDR address). To do so for the HGA or MDA, you perform the same operation but send the result to port 03B8h.

Sample assembly language code to permit bright CGA backgrounds follows:

```
push  es                 ;save the register
mov   ax,40h             ;address BIOS work area
mov   es,ax
mov   al,es:65h          ;get last value sent to mode control
and   al,0DFh            ;clear blink control bit
mov   es:65h,al          ;save value for future reference
mov   dx,03D8h           ;get CGA mode control port address
out   dx,al              ;send to CGA mode control port
pop   es                 ;restore saved segment register
```

Note that this modification remains in effect *only* until the video mode is changed again by the BIOS; making it effective for all video modes requires alteration of the video tables pointed to by the Int 1Dh vector. Because the video tables normally reside in ROM, it is not a trivial task to copy them to RAM and be sure that they remain unchanged at all times; it is easier to just change the register as required.

For the EGA and later adapters, toggling the blink bit is much simpler. You use the BIOS interface at Int 10h, with AX set to 1303h:

```
mov   ax,1303h
int   10h
```

Table 5.5 lists the possible bit settings for each color. Be aware, however, that because the *normal* background is determined by three bits, only values up to 7 can be stored in the background unless the blink-enable bit has been toggled as described in the preceding paragraphs.

After the character's ASCII value is stored in the character's memory location and the attribute is set in the attribute byte, the adapter card's display circuitry creates the physical display of the character. Each character is converted on-screen to a dot pattern that corresponds to the character generated by the display adapter. The characters are converted from data contained in a ROM character generator on the adapter. The EGA and VGA cards also allow programmers to specify alternate user-defined character sets for character display.

In addition to monochrome and color text displays, two other types of text displays exist. The distinction between these displays lies in the number of characters displayed per line.

Some display adapters can display either 40 or 80 characters per line. The basic video-display format is the 80-by-25 display screen. Because the 40-column format generally is useful only when your video display is a composite television set, in which 40 characters per line is about right for readability, the major emphasis in this book is given to the 80-column format, which closely matches the standard 80-by-24 computer-terminal display.

Table 5.5. *Possible Bit Settings for Color Text Mode*

| Bit Value | | |
Binary	Decimal	Color
0000	0	Black
0001	1	Blue
0010	2	Green
0011	3	Cyan
0100	4	Red
0101	5	Magenta
0110	6	Brown
0111	7	White
1000	8	Gray
1001	9	Light blue
1010	10	Light green
1011	11	Light cyan
1100	12	Light red
1101	13	Light magenta
1110	14	Yellow
1111	15	High-intensity white

Graphics-Mode Display

IBM refers to the graphics display modes as the APA, or *all-points addressable,* modes. In graphics modes, each screen pixel is specified by a set number of memory bits. Each bit indicates whether the pixel is on or off and what color it is. The number of bits used for each pixel depends on the type of display adapter and the graphics mode being used. For example, the EGA system can display 16 colors from a palette of 64 available colors. To indicate which of the 16 colors a specific pixel should be, you need four bits. The number of bits required for each pixel can be represented by the following equation:

PROGRAMMING

$$BITS = \frac{\log(COLORS)}{\log(2)}$$

COLORS is the number of colors to be represented, and BITS is the number of bits required. With 16 colors available at any time for each EGA-screen pixel, the equation would look like the following:

$$BITS = \frac{\log(16)}{\log(2)} = \frac{1.20412}{0.30103} = 4 \text{ bits}$$

The resolution of a graphics display screen (refer to table 5.2) is expressed by pixels, with a horizontal and vertical resolution. For example, table 5.2 lists the resolution for mode 0Eh as 640-by-200, or 640 pixels wide by 200 scan lines (pixels) deep. This number represents a total of 128,000 pixels for the display screen. When you work with graphics, keep in mind the relationship between resolution, available colors, and memory requirements.

Identifying the Video Display Adapter

Although it is generally agreed that a well-behaved DOS application should use BIOS or, preferably, DOS functions to handle video, sometimes you have to throw the rule book out and program "down to the bare metal." You can write a paintbrush program, for example, using the BIOS video functions to read and write pixels to the screen. If you know which video adapter you are using, however, you can program the video controller directly, resulting in dramatic improvements in speed. The detailed programming of the individual video adapters is beyond the scope of this book, but determining which video adapter is present is not.

The listing in this section is a set of procedures that identify the following display adaptor types:

Monochrome Display Adaptor (MDA)

Hercules Graphics Card

Hercules Graphics Card Plus

Hercules InColor Card

Color Graphics Adaptor (CGA)

Enhanced Graphics Adaptor (EGA)

MultiColor Graphics Array (MCGA)

Video Graphics Array (VGA)

SuperVGA

Within the SuperVGA adapters, the manufacturer and the chip type are further identified.

The following display types are also identified:

MDA compatible (monochrome)

CGA compatible

EGA compatible

PS/2 compatible monochrome

PS/2 compatible color

Finally, the procedures detect up to two video hardware systems and differentiate between which is active and which is not.

Identification of the video adapter starts by attempting VGA- and EGA-specific Video BIOS calls. If these calls succeed, two tasks remain: identifying a CGA or MDA card that the EGA or VGA BIOS is unaware of, and identifying, in the case of a VGA adapter, a potential SuperVGA adapter.

You identify a CGA or MDA adapter by detecting the CRT controller (CTRC). The MDA's CRTC status port is usually found at I/O address 3B4h, and the CGA's is usually found at 3D4h. The program assumes that the address is correct, and an attempt is made to write to the cursor location low register. If, after a short delay, the value can be read back, you can assume that the CTRC status port has been found and that the CGA or MDA has been located.

If an MDA adapter is detected, it can be further identified as a plain MDA or a Hercules Graphics Adapter (HGA). This is done by exploiting a difference between the MDA and HGA: the vertical sync bit never changes on the MDA, but does on the HGA. The HGA can be further identified as a Hercules Graphics Card Plus, a Hercules InColor Card, or a Hercules Graphics Card by observing certain bits of the status port.

Detecting and identifying a SuperVGA adapter is an interesting problem. When vendors started cloning IBM's EGA and VGA, they produced adapters virtually indistinguishable from the original IBM adapters. Vendors went their own way, however, in developing the SuperVGA. Each adapter supports an 800×600 video mode (which is the usual criterion for deciding whether an adapter is VGA or SuperVGA), but each achieves it in a different, proprietary fashion. Each also supports resolutions or provides features that the others do not. Similarly, the method of identifying each SuperVGA adapter varies from vendor to vendor. The technique for identifying a particular vendor's adapter is described in the procedure for each. The technique of identifying a SuperVGA from a VGA is a matter of trying each SuperVGA identification technique; if they all fail, it is a simple VGA adapter.

Listing 5.1 identifies the video adapter. (Note that it is not a stand-alone program.)

Listing 5.1

```
page 55,132
name video_id
;
; Procedure for identifying the video system(s)
;


;
; Adapter types
;
UNKNOWN_ADAPTER       equu  000h
CGA                   equ  001h
MDA                   equ  002h
EGA                   equ  003h
MCGA                  equ  004h
VGA                   equ  005h
SVGA                  equ  006h
VESA_SVGA             equ  007h


ADAPTER_SYSTEM_MASK equ  007h
;
; Monitor types
;
UNKNOWN_MONITOR       equ  000h SHL 3
MDA_MONITOR           equ  001h SHL 3
CGA_MONITOR           equ  002h SHL 3
EGA_MONITOR           equ  003h SHL 3
VGA_MONO              equ  004h SHL 3
VGA_COLOR             equ  005h SHL 3


MONITOR_MASK          equ  007h SHL 3
;
; SVGA BIOS types
;
UNKNOWN_BIOS          equ  000h SHL 6
AHEAD                 equ  001h SHL 6
ATI                   equ  002h SHL 6
CIRRUS                equ  003h SHL 6
CTI_BASED             equ  004h SHL 6
GENOA                 equ  005h SHL 6
HEADLAND              equ  006h SHL 6
EVEREX                equ  007h SHL 6
PARADISE              equ  008h SHL 6
```

```
TSENG_BASED          equ   009h SHL 6
;
; Video chip types
;
UNKNOWN_CHIP         equ   000h SHL 10
HGC                  equ   001h SHL 10
HGCPLUS              equ   002h SHL 10
HERCULESINCOLOR      equ   003h SHL 10


AHEAD_VERSION_A      equ   001h SHL 10
AHEAD_VERSION_B      equ   002h SHL 10


ATI18800REV1         equ   001h SHL 10
ATI18800REV2         equ   002h SHL 10
ATI18800W18810       equ   003h SHL 10


CIRRUS_510_520       equ   001h SHL 10
CIRRUS_610_620       equ   002h SHL 10
CIRRUS_VSEVEN        equ   003h SHL 10


CTI82C451            equ   001h SHL 10
CTI82C452            equ   002h SHL 10
CTI82C453            equ   003h SHL 10


TRIDENT_8800BR       equ   001h SHL 10
TRIDENT_8800CS       equ   002h SHL 10


v_data           segment para 'V_DATA'

PrimarySystem        dw    (?)        ; Primary video system
SecondarySystem      dw    (?)        ; Secondary video system
adapter_table        db    UNKNOWN_ADAPTER OR UNKNOWN_MONITOR
                     db    MDA OR MDA_MONITOR
                     db    CGA OR CGA_MONITOR
                     db    UNKNOWN_ADAPTER OR UNKNOWN_MONITOR
                     db    EGA OR EGA_MONITOR
                     db    EGA OR MDA_MONITOR
                     db    UNKNOWN_ADAPTER OR UNKNOWN_MONITOR
                     db    VGA OR VGA_MONO
                     db    VGA OR VGA_COLOR
                     db    UNKNOWN_ADAPTER OR UNKNOWN_MONITOR
                     db    MCGA OR EGA_MONITOR
                     db    MCGA OR VGA_MONO
                     db    MCGA OR VGA_COLOR
                     db    (16 - 13) dup (0)
ega_table            db    EGA OR CGA_MONITOR
                     db    EGA OR EGA_MONITOR
                     db    EGA OR MDA_MONITOR
                     db    EGA OR CGA_MONITOR
```

continues

Listing 5.1 *continued*

```
                    db    EGA OR EGA_MONITOR
                    db    EGA OR MDA_MONITOR
                    db    (8 - 6) dup (EGA OR UNKNOWN_MONITOR)
AHEAD_BIOS_Signature      db    "AHEAD"
ATI_BIOS_Signature        db    "761295520"
ATI_BIOS_Sig2             db    "31"
CIRRUS_BIOS_Signature     db    "CL"
GENOA_BIOS_Signature      db    77h,11h,99h,66h
PARADISE_BIOS_Signature   db    "VGA="
VESA_BIOS_Signature       db    "VESA"
scratch_pad         db    256 dup (?)

v_data          ends

v_code          segment para 'V_CODE'

assume          cs:v_code
assume          ds:v_data


;
; Main procedure for identifying the video systems
;
_video_ident    proc far

        push bx
        push cx
        push ds         ; save caller's DS
        mov  ax,seg v_data  ;
        mov  ds,ax          ; get new DS
        ;
        ; Initialize structures
        ;
        mov  PrimarySystem,0
        mov  SecondarySystem,0
        ;
        ; Test for VGA presence
        ;
        mov  ax,01A00h      ; Read display codes function
        int  10h            ; Call video BIOS
        cmp  al,01Ah        ; Successful call?
        jne  no_vga_present ;
        ;
        ; we have VGA at least
        ;
        or   bh,bh          ; Secondary system detected?
        jz   no_secondary   ;
```

```
                ;
                ; We have a secondary system present
                ;
                push bx                ; Preserve bx
                mov  al,bh             ; Put secondary type in AL
                and  al,00Fh           ;
                mov  bx,offset adapter_table  ; Get lookup table
                xlat                   ;
                xor  ah,ah             ; Clear byte
                or   SecondarySystem,ax       ; Set flags
                pop  bx                ; Restore bx
                ;
                ; What is the primary system?
                ;
no_secondary:
                mov  al,bl             ; Put primary type in AL
                and  al,00Fh           ;
                mov  bx,offset adapter_table  ; Get lookup byte
                xlat                   ;
                xor  ah,ah             ; Clear byte
                or   PrimarySystem,ax         ; Set flags
                and  ax,ADAPTER_SYSTEM_MASK   ; What adapter?
                cmp  ax,VGA            ; Did we detect a VGA?
                je   pVGA_detected     ;
                mov  ax,SecondarySystem       ; How about the secondary?
                and  ax,ADAPTER_SYSTEM_MASK   ;
                cmp  ax,VGA            ;
                jne  noVGA_detected    ;
                mov  bx,offset SecondarySystem
                jmp  short detect_SVGA
pVGA_detected:
                mov  bx,offset PrimarySystem
                ;
                ; Attempt to detect SVGA systems
                ;
detect_SVGA:    call SVGA_detect
                ;
                ; Although the enhanced video BIOS call succeeded,
                ; no VGA was found
                ;
noVGA_detected:
                mov  ax,SecondarySystem ; Is secondary system MDA?
                and  ax,ADAPTER_SYSTEM_MASK
                cmp  ax,MDA            ; Is secondary system MDA?
                je   clarify_MDA       ; If it is, identify further
                mov  ax,PrimarySystem  ; How about the primary?
                and  ax,ADAPTER_SYSTEM_MASK
                cmp  ax,MDA            ; Is secondary system MDA?
```

continues

Listing 5.1 *continued*

```
            jne  swap_systems        ;
clarify_MDA:
            call Hercules_detect     ; Identify the specific MDA system
            jmp  short swap_systems
            ;
            ; The enhanced video BIOS call failed
            ;
no_vga_present:
            mov  bl,010h             ; Attempt to find EGA
            mov  ah,012h             ;
            int  10h                 ;
            cmp  bl,010h             ; Call failed?
            je   no_ega_present      ;
            mov  bx,offset ega_table ;
            mov  al,cl               ; Get switch settings
            shr  al,1                ;
            and  ax,7                ;
            xlat                     ;
            or   PrimarySystem,ax          ; Set values
            and  ax,ADAPTER_SYSTEM_MASK    ; What did we find?
            cmp  ax,MDA              ; MDA?
            je   seek_CGA            ; Then look for a CGA
            call MDA_detect          ; Else look for MDA
            jmp  short swap_systems
seek_CGA:
            call CGA_detect          ;
            jmp  short swap_systems  ;
            ;
            ; Efforts to find EGA failed too
            ;
no_ega_present:
            call CGA_detect          ; Seek CGA
            call MDA_detect          ; and MDA
            ;
            ; May need to swap primary/secondary systems
            ;
swap_systems:
            mov  ax,SecondarySystem  ; Get current mode
            and  ax,ADAPTER_SYSTEM_MASK
            cmp  ax,UNKNOWN_ADAPTER
            je   vid_exit            ;
            cmp  ax,MCGA             ;
            jae  vid_exit            ;
            mov  ax,PrimarySystem
            and  ax,ADAPTER_SYSTEM_MASK
            cmp  ax,MCGA             ;
```

```
              jae   vid_exit      ;
              mov   ah,00Fh       ; Get current video mode
              int   10h           ;
              and   al,7          ;
              cmp   al,7          ; Current mode is mono?
              jne   current_color ;
              mov   ax,PrimarySystem
              and   ax,MONITOR_MASK
              cmp   ax,MDA_MONITOR ;
              je    vid_exit      ;
do_swap:
              mov   ax,PrimarySystem
              xchg  ax,SecondarySystem
              mov   PrimarySystem,ax
              jmp short vid_exit
current_color:
              mov   ax,PrimarySystem
              and   ax,MONITOR_MASK
              cmp   ax,MDA_MONITOR
              je    do_swap
              ;
              ; Return to caller
              ;
vid_exit:
              mov   ax,PrimarySystem    ; Set return values
              mov   dx,SecondarySystem
              pop   ds              ; Restore caller's DS
              pop   cx              ;
              pop   bx              ;
              ret                   ; Return

_video_ident    endp
;
;    Attempt to detect SVGA
;
;    On entry, BX is a pointer to the VGA system word
;
SVGA_detect     proc near

              ;
              ; First, let's try to identify the BIOS itself
              ;
              ; We'll start with AHEAD
              ;

assume        es:nothing

              push ax               ; Save registers
              push cx               ;
```

continues

Listing 5.1 continued

```
                push di             ;
                push dx             ;
                push si             ;
                push es             ;
                mov   ax,0C000h     ; Point to ROM
                mov   es,ax         ;
                mov   di,00025h     ; Signature is at C000:0025
                mov   si,offset AHEAD_BIOS_Signature
                mov   cx,5          ; Length of signature
                cld                 ;
        repe cmpsb                  ;
                jne   not_ahead_bios ;
                ;
                ; It's an AHEAD BIOS--now identify which chip version
                ;
                and   word ptr [bx],NOT ADAPTER_SYSTEM_MASK
                or    word ptr [bx],SVGA OR AHEAD
                mov   dx,003CEh     ; Get i/o address
                mov   al,00Fh       ; Get index of enable register
                out   dx,al         ;
                inc   dx            ; Get I/O address of data
                mov   al,020h       ; Get enable value
                out   dx,al         ;
                jmp   $+2           ;
                in    al,dx         ; Get value
                cmp   al,020h       ; Version A?
                je    ahead_a       ;
                cmp   al,021h       ; Version B?
                jne   test_vesa_isle ;
                or    word ptr [bx],AHEAD_VERSION_B
                jmp   short test_vesa_isle      ;
ahead_a:
                or    word ptr [bx],AHEAD_VERSION_A
test_vesa_isle:
                jmp   test_vesa     ;
                ;
                ; Wasn't AHEAD. Test for ATI
                ;
not_ahead_bios:
                mov   di,00031h     ; ATI signature at C000:0031
                mov   si,offset ATI_BIOS_Signature
                mo    cx,9          ;
        repe cmpsb                  ;
                jne   not_ati_bios  ;
                ;
                ; So far, so good...
```

```
                ;
        mov  di,00040h       ; "31" at C000:0040
        mov  si,offset ATI_BIOS_Sig2  ;
        mov  cx,2            ;
   repe cmpsb               ;
        jne  not_ati_bios    ;
                ;
        ; It's an ATI BIOS--now identify the chipset
                ;
        and  word ptr [bx],NOT ADAPTER_SYSTEM_MASK
        or   word ptr [bx],SVGA OR ATI
        mov  al,es:043h      ;
        cmp  al,'1'          ; Which chipset?
        je   ati_1           ;
        cmp  al,'2'          ;
        je   ati_2           ;
        cmp  al,'3'          ;
        jne  test_vesa_isle  ;
        or   word ptr [bx],ATI18800W18810
        jmp  test_vesa       ;
ati_1:
        or   word ptr [bx],ATI18800REV1
        jmp  test_vesa       ;
ati_2:
        or   word ptr [bx],ATI18800REV2
        jmp  test_vesa       ;
                ;
        ; Now check for Cirrus
                ;
not_ati_bios:
        mov  di,6            ;
        mov  si,offset CIRRUS_BIOS_Signatur
        mov  cx,2            ;
   repe cmpsb               ;
        jne  not_cirrus_bios ;
                ;
        ; It's a Cirrus BIOS--now identify the chip
                ;
        and  word ptr [bx],NOT ADAPTER_SYSTEM_MASK
        or   word ptr [bx],SVGA OR CIRRUS
        xor  ax,ax           ; Find CRTC
        mov  es,ax           ;
        mov  dx,es:00463h    ;
        push dx              ;
        mov  al,00Ch         ; Get start address
        out  dx,al           ;
        inc  dx              ;
        in   al,dx           ; Read register
        mov  ah,al           ; Save what we read
```

continues

Listing 5.1 *continued*

```
        mov  al,00Ch        ;
        push ax             ;
        xor  al,al          ; Clear register
        out  dx,al          ;
        dec  dx             ;
        mov  al,01Fh        ; Get ID register
        out  dx,al          ;
        inc  dx             ;
        in   al,dx          ; Read unlock password
        mov  ch,al          ; Save it--it's the key to the chip ID
        mov  dx,003C4h      ; Address of sequencer
        mov  al,006h        ; Extension control reg
        out  dx,al          ;
        inc  dx             ;
        mov  al,ch          ; Get unlock password
        out  dx,al          ;
        in   al,dx          ; Read it back
        cmp  al,1           ; Unlocked?
        jne  not_cirrus_chip
        mov  al,ch          ;
        mov  cl,4           ;
        ror  al,cl          ;
        out  dx,al          ;
        in   al,dx          ;
        or   al,al          ; Locked?
        jnz  not_cirrus_chip
        cmp  ch,0ECh        ; 510/520?
        jne  not_cirrus_510 ;
        or   word ptr [bx],CIRRUS_510_520
        jmp  short not_cirrus_chip
not_cirrus_510:
        cmp  ch,0CAh        ; 610/620?
        jne  not_cirrus_610
        or   word ptr [bx],CIRRUS_610_620
        jmp  short not_cirrus_chip
not_cirrus_610:
        cmp  ch,0EAh        ; Video seven?
        jne  not_cirrus_chip
        or   word ptr [bx],CIRRUS_VSEVEN
not_cirrus_chip:
        pop  ax             ; Restore CRTC
        pop  dx             ;
        out  dx,ax          ;
        jmp  test_vesa      ;
        ;
        ; Check for CTI
```

```
        ;
not_cirrus_bios:
        cli                     ; Disable interrupts
        mov  dx,046E8h          ; Put chip in setup mode
        in   al,dx              ;
        or   al,010h            ;
        out  dx,al              ;
        mov  dx,00103h          ; Read extended enable register
        in   al,dx              ;
        or   al,080h            ; Turn enable on
        out  dx,al              ;
        inc  dx                 ; Read global ID
        in   al,dx              ;
        mov  ah,al              ; Save it
        mov  dx,046E8h          ; Turn setup back off
        in   al,dx              ;
        and  al,0EFh            ;
        out  dx,al              ;
        sti                     ; Reenable interrupts
        mov  dx,003D6h          ; Read version
        xor  al,al              ;
        out  dx,al              ;
        inc  dx                 ;
        in   al,dx              ;
        cmp  ah,0A5h            ; Right global ID?
        jne  not_cti_bios       ;
        ;
        ; Seems to be a CTI chip. Which version?
        ;
        and  al,0F0h            ; Check version
        cmp  al,000h            ;
        jne  not_cti82C451      ;
        and  word ptr [bx],NOT ADAPTER_SYSTEM_MASK
        or   word ptr [bx],CTI82C451 OR SVGA OR CTI_BASED
        jmp  test_vesa          ;
not_cti82C451:
        cmp  al,010h            ;
        jne  not_cti82C452      ;
        and  word ptr [bx],NOT ADAPTER_SYSTEM_MASK
        or   word ptr [bx],CTI82C452 OR SVGA OR CTI_BASED
        jmp  test_vesa          ;
not_cti82C452:
        cmp  al,030h            ;
        jne  not_cti_bios       ;
        and  word ptr [bx],NOT ADAPTER_SYSTEM_MASK
        or   word ptr [bx],CTI82C453 OR SVGA OR CTI_BASED
        jmp  test_vesa          ;
        ;
        ; Check for Genoa
```

continues

Listing 5.1 continued

```
                ;
    not_cti_bios:
                mov  di,0037h       ; Read pointer
                les  di,es:[di]     ; Dereference it
                mov  si,offset GENOA_BIOS_Signature
                mov  cx,4           ;
            repe cmpsb              ;
                jne  not_genoa_bios ;
                and  word ptr [bx],NOT ADAPTER_SYSTEM_MASK
                or   word ptr [bx],GENOA OR SVGA
                jmp  test_vesa      ;
                ;
                ; Try Headland
                ;
    not_genoa_bios:
                push bx             ;
                xor  bx,bx          ; Special Headland BIOS call
                mov  ax,06F00h      ;
                int  10h            ;
                cmp  bx,'V7'        ;
                jne  not_headland   ;
                mov  ax,06F07h      ;
                int  10h            ;
                cmp  bl,070h        ;
                jb   not_headland   ;
                cmp  bl,07Fh        ;
                ja   not_headland   ;
                pop  bx             ;
                and  word ptr [bx],NOT ADAPTER_SYSTEM_MASK
                or   word ptr [bx],HEADLAND OR SVGA
                jmp  short test_vesa
    not_headland:
                pop  bx             ; Restore pointer
                ;
                ; Try Trident/Everex
                ;
                push bx             ; Save pointer
                mov  ax,07000h      ; Extended BIOS call
                xor  bx,bx          ;
                int  10h            ;
                cmp  al,070h        ; Okay?
                jne  not_everex_bios
                and  dx,0FFF0h      ; Get board number
                cmp  dx,06780h      ;
                jne  not_everex_bios
                pop  bx             ;
```

```
            and   word ptr [bx],NOT ADAPTER_SYSTEM_MASK
            or    word ptr [bx],EVEREX OR SVGA
            jmp   short test_trident
not_everex_bios:
            po    bx                ;
test_trident:
            ;
            ; Identify the chip itself
            ;
            mov   dx,003C4h         ;
            mov   al,00Bh           ;
            out   dx,al             ;
            inc   dx                ;
            in    al,dx             ;
            and   al,00Fh           ;
            cmp   al,1              ;
            je    found_8800BR      ;
            cmp   al,2              ;
            jne   not_trident       ;
            and   word ptr [bx],NOT ADAPTER_SYSTEM_MASK
            or    word ptr [bx],TRIDENT_8800CS OR SVGA
            jmp   short test_vesa
found_8800BR:
            and   word ptr [bx],NOT ADAPTER_SYSTEM_MASK
            or    word ptr [bx],TRIDENT_8800BR OR SVGA
            jmp   short test_vesa
            ;
            ; Try Paradise
            ;
not_trident:
            mov   ax,0C000h         ;
            mov   es,ax             ;
            mov   di,0007Dh         ;
            mov   si,offset PARADISE_BIOS_Signature
            mov   cx,4              ;
       repe cmpsb                   ;
            jne   not_paradise      ;
            and   word ptr [bx],NOT ADAPTER_SYSTEM_MASK
            or    word ptr [bx],SVGA OR PARADISE
            jmp   short test_vesa
            ;
            ; Try Tseng
            ;
not_paradise:
            mov   dx,003CDh         ;
            in    al,dx             ;
            mov   ah,al             ;
            and   al,0C0h           ;
            or    al,055h           ;
```

continues

Listing 5.1 continued

```
                out   dx,al        ;
                in    al,dx        ;
                cmp   al,055h      ;
                jne   test_vesa    ;
                mov   al,0AAh      ;
                out   dx,al        ;
                in    al,dx        ;
                cmp   al,0AAh      ;
                jne   test_vesa    ;
                and   word ptr [bx],NOT ADAPTER_SYSTEM_MASK
                or    word ptr [bx],SVGA OR TSENG_BASED
                ;
                ; Test for VESA BIOS
                ;
test_vesa:      mov   ax,04F00h ;
                mov   di,offset scratch_pad
                push  ds          ;
                pop   es          ;
                int   10h         ;
                cmp   ax,0004Fh    ;
                jne   svga_exit    ;
                cld               ;
                mov   si,offset VESA_BIOS_Signature
                mov   cx,4        ;
          repe  cmpsb             ;
                jne   svga_exit    ;
                and   word ptr [bx],NOT ADAPTER_SYSTEM_MASK
                or    word ptr [bx],VESA_SVGA
svga_exit:
                pop   es          ;
                pop   si          ;
                pop   dx          ;
                pop   di          ;
                pop   cx          ;
                pop   ax          ;
                ret               ; Return

SVGA_detect     endp
;
; Attempt to detect Hercules MDA card
;
Hercules_detect      proc near

                push  si          ;
                push  dx          ;
                push  cx          ;
```

```
            push bx               ;
            push ax               ;
            mo   si,offset PrimarySystem
            mov  ax,[si]          ;
            and  ax,ADAPTER_SYSTEM_MASK   ;
            cmp  ax,MDA           ;
            je   test_Hercules    ;
            mov si,offset SecondarySystem
test_Hercules:
            mov  dx,003BAh        ; Get status port
            in   al,dx            ;
            and  al,080h          ; Save VSYNC bit
            mov  bl,al            ; Save it
            xor  cx,cx            ;
VSYNC:
            in   al,dx            ; Read port
            mov  ah,al            ;
            and  ah,080h          ; Isolate VSYNC
            cmp  ah,bl            ;
            jne  found_Hercules   ;
            loop VSYNC            ;
            jmp  short Herc_exit
found_Hercules:
            ;
            ; Now that we found it, try to identify which board
            ;
            and  al,070h          ;
            cmp  al,010h          ; HGCPlus?
            jne  not_HGCPlus      ;
            or   word ptr [si],HGCPLUS     ;
            jmp  short Herc_exit
not_HGCPlus:
            cmp  al,050h;
            jne  is_HGC           ;
            or   word ptr [si],HERCULESINCOLOR
            jmp  short Herc_exit
is_HGC:
            or   word ptr [si],HGC
1
            pop  ax               ;
            pop  bx               ;
            pop  cx               ;
            pop  dx               ;
            pop  si               ; .
            ret                   ; Return

Hercules_detect      endp
;
; Attempt to detect MDA card
;
```

continues

Listing 5.1 continued

```
MDA_detect     proc near

        mov  dx,003B4h       ; If MDA, CRTC is 3B4h
        call CRTC_detect     ;
        jne  no_MDA          ;
        mov  ax,PrimarySystem     ; Found MDA; primary or secondary?
        and  ax,ADAPTER_SYSTEM_MASK   ;
        cmp  ax,UNKNOWN_ADAPTER       ;
        je   MDA_primary              ;
        or   SecondarySystem,MDA OR MDA_MONITOR
        jmp  short found_MDA
MDA_primary:
        or   PrimarySystem,MDA OR MDA_MONITOR
found_MDA:
        call Hercules_detect      ; See if it's a Hercules board
no_MDA:
        ret                  ; Return

MDA_detect     endp
;
; Attempt to detect CGA card
;
CGA_detect     proc near

        mov  dx,003D4h       ; If CGA, CRTC is 3D4h
        call CRTC_detect     ;
        jne  CGA_exit        ;
        mov  ax,PrimarySystem     ; Found CGA; primary or secondary?
        and  ax,ADAPTER_SYSTEM_MASK   ;
        cmp  ax,UNKNOWN_ADAPTER       ;
        je   CGA_primary              ;
        or   SecondarySystem,CGA OR CGA_MONITOR
        jmp  short CGA_exit
CGA_primary:
        or   PrimarySystem,CGA OR CGA_MONITOR
CGA_exit:
        ret                  ; Return

CGA_detect     endp
;
; Attempt to detect the CRT controller
;
; On entry, DX is the alleged CRTC port
;
; If detected, returns Z set; else Z reset
;
```

```
CRTC_detect     proc near

        push dx                 ; Save registers
        push cx                 ;
        push bx                 ;
        push ax                 ;
        mov  al,00Fh            ; Select (alleged) cursor low
        out  dx,al              ;   register
        inc  dx                 ; Select register
        in   al,dx              ; Read old value
        mov  bl,al              ; Save it in BL
        mov  al,066h            ; Write new value
        out  dx,al              ;
        xor  cx,cx              ; Loop a while
CRTC_Delay:
        nop                     ;
        loop CRTC_Delay         ;
        in   al,dx              ; Get new value
        mov  bh,al              ; Save it
        mov  al,bl              ; Get old value
        out  dx,al              ; Write it out
        cmp  bh,066h            ; Is new value correct?
        pop  ax                 ; Restore registers
        pop  bx                 ;
        pop  cx                 ;
        pop  dx                 ;
        ret                     ; Return

CRTC_detect     endp

public          _video_ident

v_code          ends

        end
```

Video Functions

Now that you know how screen displays work, you can try some simple
functions to see how they work. Like most of the topics discussed in this book, the
video functions are available in two categories: DOS and BIOS. Unlike other
programming areas, however, the preponderance of video functions are relegated
to BIOS. No DOS services are available for controlling the screen; only a few DOS
services are available for displaying information on the screen.

The DOS services are simplest to use. Each DOS service provides a simple output mechanism that is redirectable and compatible with all system operations.

The BIOS services generally are the functions of choice for serious programming in which you do not directly access video memory. These services not only provide extensive control of a video system but also are faster and much more flexible than the DOS services. The BIOS services provide access to the cursor, to attributes for display, and to other controls.

An undocumented function of DOS—Int 29h—may prove handy when you want the fastest possible output to the CRT, but want to avoid using BIOS in order to maintain as much compatibility with generic MS-DOS systems as possible. Int 29h (which DOS itself has used for most of its display output since Version 2.0) is fast because, unlike the documented DOS output functions, it does not check for Ctrl-C each time it puts a character on the screen.

To use Int 29h, put the character to be displayed into the AL register, and then invoke the interrupt:

```
mov   al,'A'
int   29h
```

Unlike other services, Int 29h uses whatever screen attributes are already in place and recognizes only the bell, CR, and LF characters as control actions; all other "control" characters are displayed on the screen. When a character is put on the last column of the last row, or when an LF is sent while the cursor is anywhere on the last row, the screen automatically scrolls up one line.

Because Int 29h is not documented, it could be taken away in a future version of DOS; but this is unlikely because Int 29h is the method that DOS itself uses most (in Versions 2.0 through 4.01) and it is an integral part of the ANSI.SYS alternate display driver system. However, the risks involved in its use (like the use of any other undocumented feature) should be evaluated before reaching a decision.

Remember that DOS and BIOS simply provide the building blocks for creating screens. A programmer's imagination and skill provide much of the "glitz" that makes a program perform well or look snappy. If your abilities in creating displays are not on a par with your programming techniques, your displays may look shoddy.

Programming with DOS and BIOS Video Functions

In this section we build some simple window functions to see how easy using the BIOS and DOS functions can be. The purpose of this chapter is not to build a complete windowing system—such an endeavor is beyond the scope of this book. We investigate screen operations in terms of some simple window display functions that illustrate the use of the BIOS and DOS functions.

The first program, testscn.c, is a simple test that fills the screen with data and then clears a window in the middle of the screen. You will write more data to the screen and then put the original window data back into place and scroll it. Listing 5.2 shows the testscn.c program.

Listing 5.2

```
#include <stdio.h>

main()
{
    int i;

    /*
        Display a screen full of lines
    */
    cls();
    for (i=0; i<50; i++)
        printf("DOS Programmer's Reference        ");

    /*
        Save the data in the rectangle (5,5) to (12,40),
        then clear that area and put a border around it.
    */
    savewin(5,5,12,40);
    clearwin(5,5,12,40);
    border(5,5,12,40);

    /*
        Wait 5 seconds and then scroll the screen again.
        (Note: Everything scrolls, including the window.)
    */
    sleep(5);
    gotoxy(24,0);
    for (i=0; i<50; i++)
        printf("This is the Second Screen of the Demo   ");

    /*
        Wait 5 seconds, then clear the window and fill it.
    */
    sleep(5);
    clearwin(5,5,12,40);
    putwin(5,5,12,40);

    /*
        Scroll the inside of the window up one line every
        2 seconds for 10 steps.
    */
```

continues

Listing 5.2 *continued*

```
for (i=0; i<10; i++) {
    sleep(2);
    upwin(1,6,6,11,39);
}

/*
    Finally, clear the screen again and then end the
    program.
*/
cls();

}
```

Testscn.c is built on three simple function collections contained in the files window.c, screen.c, and chario.c. Window.c (see listing 5.3) handles the window functions called by testscn.c. With the functions in window.c, you can do the following:

savewin()   Save the current data in the window
clearwin()   Clear the window
putwin()   Put data into a window
border()   Put a border around a window
upwin()   Scroll the window up

This small collection of functions makes no attempt to be super sophisticated. It just handles single, nonoverlapping windows such as those you might use to display help information and so forth. Because it uses nothing lower than the BIOS functions, it is compatible with other environments such as DESQview.

Listing 5.3

```
#include <stdio.h>
#include <dos.h>

#define VIDEO 0x10

/*   Basic screen size definitions */

#define    LINES    24
#define    COLS     80

/*
    Structure for each character position--character and
    attribute.
*/
```

```c
struct  charpos {
    char ch;
    char att;
};

/*  The screen is made up of LINES*COLS character positions */
struct charpos screen[LINES][COLS];

/*
    Function: savewin()
*/
savewin(lr,lc,rr,rc)

int  lr,  lc,  rr,  rc;
{
    int i, j;
    for (i=lr; i<=rr; i++)
        for (j=lc; j<=rc; j++) {
            gotoxy(i,j);
            rch(&screen[i][j].ch,&screen[i][j].att);
        }
}

/*
    Function: clearwin()
*/
clearwin(lr,lc,rr,rc)

int  lr,  lc,  rr,  rc;

{
    union REGS regs;

    regs.h.ah = 0x06;
    regs.h.al = 0;
    regs.h.bh = 7;
    regs.h.ch = lr;
    regs.h.cl = lc;
    regs.h.dh = rr;
    regs.h.dl = rc;
    int86(VIDEO,&regs,&regs);
}

/*
    Function: putwin()
*/
putwin(lr,lc,rr,rc)

int lr, lc, rr, rc;
```

continues

Listing 5.3 *continued*

```c
{
    int  i,   j;

    for (i=lr; i<=rr; i++)
        for (j=lc; j<=rc; j++) {
            gotoxy(i,j);
            wch(screen[i][j].ch,screen[i][j].att);
        }
    border(lr,lc,rr,rc);
}

#define VERTLINE     186
#define UPPERRIGHT   187
#define LOWERRIGHT   188
#define LOWERLEFT    200
#define UPPERLEFT    201
#define HORIZLINE    205

/*
    Function: border()
*/
border(lr,lc,rr,rc)

int lr, lc, rr, rc;

{
    int  i, j;

    for (i=lr; i<=rr; i++) {
        gotoxy(i,lc); wch(VERTLINE,7);
        gotoxy(i,rc); wch(VERTLINE,7);
        if (i==lr || i==rr) {
            for (j=lc; j<=rc; j++) {
                gotoxy(i,j);
                wch(HORIZLINE,7);
            }
            if (i==lr) {
                gotoxy(lr,lc); wch(UPPERLEFT,7);
                gotoxy(lr,rc); wch(UPPERRIGHT,7);
            }
            if (i==rr) {
                gotoxy(rr,lc); wch(LOWERLEFT,7);
                gotoxy(rr,rc); wch(LOWERRIGHT,7);
            }
        }
```

```
        }
}
/*
      Function: upwin()
*/
upwin(n,lr,lc,rr,rc)

int n;
int lr, lc, rr, rc;

{
    union REGS regs;

    regs.h.ah = 0x06;
    regs.h.al = n;
    regs.h.bh = 7;
    regs.h.ch = lr;
    regs.h.cl = lc;
    regs.h.dh = rr;
    regs.h.dl = rc;
    int86(VIDEO,&regs,&regs);

}
```

The functions in the screen.c file handle screen-related functions such as positioning the cursor and clearing the screen (the gotoxy() and cls() functions, respectively). Note that cls() is just clearwin() with set values for the upper left and lower right corners corresponding to the whole screen.

The screen.c functions (see listing 5.4) are global to the whole screen display. They act on a screen-wide basis. Window.c functions work within a single window. Additional functions could be added to handle working within a window.

Listing 5.4

```
Screen.c:

#include <stdio.h>
#include <dos.h>

#define    VIDEO  0x10

/*
      Function: gotoxy()
*/
gotoxy(r,c)

int r, c;
```

continues

Listing 5.4 *continued*

```
{
    union REGS regs;

    regs.h.ah = 0x02;
    regs.h.bh = 0;
    regs.h.dh = r;
    regs.h.dl = c;
    int86(VIDEO,&regs,&regs);
}

/*
    Function: cls()
*/
cls()
{
    union REGS regs;

    regs.h.ah = 0x06;
    regs.h.al = 0;
    regs.h.bh = 7;
    regs.h.ch = 0;
    regs.h.cl = 0;
    regs.h.dh = 25;
    regs.h.dl = 80;
    int86(VIDEO,&regs,&regs);

}
```

At the lowest level of the program, screen-character functions allow us to look at a single screen position or to change it by using the BIOS screen-display functions (see listing 5.5).

Listing 5.5

```
Chario.c:

#include <stdio.h>
#include <dos.h>

#define VIDEO 0x10

union REGS regs;

/*
    Function: wch()
```

```
*/
wch(ch, attr)

char ch,  attr;

{
    regs.h.ah = 0x09;
    regs.h.bh = 0;
    regs.h.bl = attr;
    regs.h.al = ch;
    regs.x.cx = 1;
    int86(VIDEO,&regs,&regs);
}

rch(ch, attr)
/*
     Function: rch()
*/

char *ch, *attr;

{
    regs.h.ah = 0x08;
    regs.h.bh = 0;
    int86(VIDEO,&regs,&regs);
    *ch = regs.h.al;
    *attr = regs.h.ah;

}
```

If you are using Microsoft C, you do not have a sleep() function as of Version 4.0. The following function will wait until a specified number of seconds have passed:

```
#include <stdio.h>
sleep(n)
/*
     Function: sleep()
*/
int  n;
{
    long timeval,  time();
    timeval = time(NULL);
    while(time(NULL)  < timeval + n);

}
```

Using Multiple Display Pages

All of the display functions used for this simple windowing system deal specifically with only one screen page (page zero), so they are independent of the type of monitor system you are using. You could add screen-page control, but not all functions allow it. For example, the scrolling functions have no page assignment among their arguments. Thus, you cannot use these facilities for paging the display. (If you write your own window functions to access display memory directly, you are not bound by this limitation.) Also, Function 0Eh does not work with all pages on all BIOS ROMs. In all non-IBM ROMs that we were able to test, this function worked only on the currently displayed page and not on a nondisplayed page.

One way to add screen-page control is to change the routines to include a current screen-page number and a way to set it. For example, you could change screen.c to include a setpage command (see listing 5.6).

Listing 5.6

```
#include <stdio.h>
#include <dos.h>

#define     BOOL    int
#define     VIDEO   0x10

static int cpage = 0;              /* Current display page */

/*
     Function: gotoxy()
*/
gotoxy(r,c)

int   r,   c;

{
     union REGS regs;

     regs.h.ah = 0x02;
     regs.h.bh = cpage;
     regs.h.dh = r;
     regs.h.dl = c;
     int86(VIDEO,&regs,&regs);
}

/*
     Function: cls()
*/
cls()

{
     union REGS regs;
```

```
        regs.h.ah = 0x06;
        regs.h.al = 0;
        regs.h.bh = 7;
        regs.h.ch = 0;
        regs.h.cl = 0;
        regs.h.dh = 25;
        regs.h.dl = 80;
        int86(VIDEO,&regs,&regs);

}

/*
    Function: setpage()
*/
setpage(n,clrflg)

int  n;
BOOL clrflg;

{
    union REGS regs;

    cpage = n;
    regs.h.ah = 0x05;
    regs.h.al = n;
    int86(VIDEO,&regs,&regs);
    if(clrflg)
        cls();
}

/*
    Function: pgprint()
*/
pgprint(str)

char *str;

{
    union REGS regs;

    regs.h.ah = 0x0e;
    regs.h.bh = cpage;
    while (*str) {
        regs.h.al = *str;
        int86(VIDEO,&regs,&regs);
        str++;

    }

}
```

In listing 5.6, the `pgprint()` function has been added to let you print strings to the current page. By adding page control to your screen functions, you can build programs in which you use the window and page functions together to preserve displays that can be recovered rapidly simply by shifting the display page. The `testpage.c` sample program (see listing 5.7) lets you try the new `setpage()` and `pgprint()` functions.

Listing 5.7

```c
#include <stdio.h>

#define FALSE 0
#define TRUE  !FALSE

main()

{
    int    i;

    setpage(1,TRUE);
    for (i=0; i<50; i++)
        pgprint("DOS Programmer's Reference            ");
    sleep(5);
    setpage(0,FALSE);

}
```

If you have a monochrome monitor system, you will not be able to see anything. In fact, when the `setpage()` function is executed, your screen will not change; you will simply see everything remain static for a few seconds and then return to the next action. But if you have a CGA or EGA monitor or better, the screen will change and display the test line, then return to the same display you had on the screen when you executed the program.

Using a current display page for all functions is not as impressive as working with undisplayed pages. By including the display page in the function arguments, you can apply a function such as `gotoxy()` to pages that are not yet displayed. You then can build a complete display and, when you make it the current display, the user will see it displayed instantaneously.

Printer Functions

The printer is the only other major output device over which we have direct control in the system. Printer functions are much simpler than screen functions because they deal only with character output and minimally with input from the printer.

The simplest way to write to the printer is to use the DOS-level printer-output function (Int 21h, Function 05h), as shown in listing 5.8. This function allows you to send characters to the printer device. DOS will handle error conditions by invoking the critical-error handler if there is a problem using the function.

Listing 5.8

```c
#include <stdio.h>
#include <dos.h>

main()

{
    outprt("This is a line to the printer\012\015");
}
outprt(str)

char    *str;


{
    union REGS regs;

    regs.h.ah = 0x05;
    while (*str) {
        regs.h.dl = *str;
        intdos(&regs,&regs);
        str++;
    }

}
```

At a lower level, you can invoke the BIOS print functions (Int 17h) to get greater control over the print function. At this level, you can check the printer's status directly and respond to printer errors in your program as needed. Listing 5.9 shows an example of how you might use the BIOS functions to handle printer interfacing.

Listing 5.9

```
#include <stdio.h>
#include <dos.h>
main()

{
    int     i;

    for (i=0; i<10; i++) {
        if(!prtrdy())
            exit(1);
        outprt("This is a line to the printer\012\015");
    }
}
#define PRINTER 0x17

outprt(str)

char    *str;

{
    union REGS regs;

    regs.x.dx = 0;
    while (*str) {
        regs.h.ah = 0x00;
        regs.h.al = *str;
        int86(PRINTER,&regs,&regs);
        putchar(*str);
        str++;
    }
}
prtrdy()

{
    union REGS regs;

    regs.h.ah = 2;
    regs.x.dx = 0;
    int86(PRINTER,&regs,&regs);
    printf("Printer Status: %x\n",regs.h.ah);
    if (regs.h.ah & 0x20)
        printf("Printer out of paper\n");
    if (regs.h.ah & 0x08)
        printf("Printer I/O error\n");
    return((regs.h.ah&0x20)==0 && (regs.h.ah&0x08)==0);

}
```

As these examples show, you can perform printer output directly from your programs and recognize what is happening with the printer at the same time.

Sophisticated printer-control functions such as graphics and font control are specific to the printer you are using. Neither the BIOS nor DOS has any built-in functions for handling printers beyond simply sending characters to them. Specialized printer-control functions are beyond the scope of this book.

Summary

This chapter covered a wide range of functions for output, primarily related to the video display. You learned about the various screen modes available and the various screen displays you can use.

In DOS, screen control is limited to a few simple functions that allow basic output to the screen and little else. More sophisticated control requires access to the BIOS functions to allow cursor positioning, character-attribute control, and so forth. At the BIOS level, you can do graphical displays, screen positioning, and even window functions. Programs that create sophisticated screens almost always have to work at the BIOS level or below, using direct access to the screen-display memory.

Printer functions are even more limited than screen functions. There are no primitive functions for anything other than outputting characters to the printer and checking the printer's status. We cannot call BIOS or DOS functions to do printer graphics or special printer functions such as font changing. Any special control must be performed by your programs.

In the next chapter, you move on to input functions, which are a complement to the output functions just discussed.

PROGRAMMING

Input Devices

Input and output are so tied together in most people's minds that we normally think in terms of "I/O" or "input/output" and rarely deal only with one or the other. In this chapter, which complements Chapter 5's discussion of output devices, you learn about input devices.

This chapter focuses on the two most popular input devices: the keyboard and the mouse. The keyboard is handled by DOS and BIOS functions included in the system, whereas a driver must be added to the system to make the mouse's functions available.

Keyboards are much more sophisticated than most people realize. The keyboard itself is an intricate piece of engineering. It works with low-level functions in the BIOS and makes keyboard operations almost invisible to programs by buffering character input and providing interrupts to allow the BIOS to handle keyboard characters as they are typed.

Because interrupts are not covered until Chapter 11, "Interrupt Handlers," this chapter deals with the mouse in a simplistic manner. But even that makes for an interesting program. By using the mouse functions (when they are present), you can build mouse-control functions into a variety of programs.

Both keyboard and mouse functions can be made much more interesting by combining them with interrupt-handling functions. Terminate-and-stay-resident programs that use hot keys to start or mouse-driven programs that interrupt on mouse input provide for immediate response to the user's needs. Chapter 11 discusses interrupts in greater detail. At this point, however, you need to learn the basic input functions.

6

CHAPTER

Keyboards

You can always count on the PC to have a keyboard as an input device—every PC has one, and most programs use them. Although alternative input devices such as the mouse have gained popularity for some types of programs, few programs can operate without some keyboard input.

In this section, you look at the use of BIOS and DOS functions for keyboard input. These functions, when used instead of the normal input functions of a high-level language, result in the following advantages:

- Maximum control over your input. You can add user-oriented editing features, special help functions, and so forth.

- Smaller programs than those possible when using the keyboard input routines provided with high-level languages. These routines, which are written to provide for virtually every possible input situation and condition, carry a great deal of "overhead code."

- Snappier, more responsive input because you can make the program react however you choose.

Before we discuss programming, let's look at how the keyboard works.

How the Keyboard Works

To programmers, the keyboard probably is the most familiar but least understood device on a computer. Most of us understand file systems and disk operations because we have read books about them. But the lowly keyboard is discussed minimally and is well known to only a few specialists.

Instead of trying to describe the hardware that makes keyboards work, this book concentrates on the sequence of events you must understand if you want to use the keyboard-related DOS and BIOS services.

First, imagine that you are looking from your computer through the cable that connects your computer and the keyboard. As you press keys, you can see numbers (the keyboard "scan codes") coming from the keyboard through the cable to the computer.

Each time a key is pressed, it generates a unique 8-bit number (the most significant bit is always 0, to tell the difference between a keypress and its later release), with even the left and right Shift keys represented by different numbers. These scan codes indicate exactly which keys were pressed.

Whenever a key is released, another scan code is generated. This code is the same as that for the keystroke, except that the high-order bit is set (which adds 128 to the scan code). In this way, the scan code signals to the ROM BIOS that the key has been released.

IBM has sold three different keyboard designs for the PC, identified as the PC (83-key) keyboard, the Personal Computer AT (84-key) keyboard, and the enhanced (101-key) keyboard. Although most of the scan codes remain the same for all three designs, there are differences. Figures 6.1, 6.2, and 6.3 show the scan codes (hexadecimal) on the PC, Personal Computer AT, and enhanced keyboards, respectively. Note that the enhanced keyboard uses multiple scan codes to identify some of its added keys.

Fig. 6.1. *Hexadecimal scan codes for a PC keyboard.*

Fig. 6.2. *Hexadecimal scan codes for an AT keyboard.*

Fig. 6.3. Hexadecimal scan codes for an enhanced keyboard.

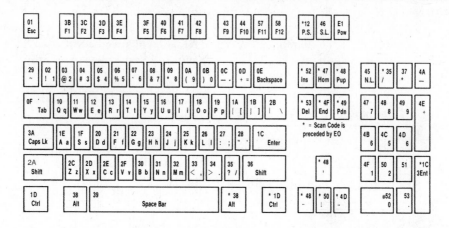

When you hold down a key for more than half a second, the keyboard generates a sequence of scan codes that corresponds to the keystroke, repeated at a specified rate. The BIOS can tell that a key is being held down (not pressed repeatedly) because the keyboard does not generate any key-release codes in this sequence.

The keyboard recognizes only the *key* (not the character) that you press, and supplies only the scan code that corresponds to the key. (The scan code simply indicates that a specific key has been pressed.) The BIOS interprets the scan code to determine which ASCII character corresponds to the keystroke. BIOS ROMs designed for the older 83-key and 84-key designs simply ignore the extra keys of the 101-key keyboard; for this reason many programs make no use of these added keys.

Whenever you press a key, the keyboard generates not only the scan code but also Int 09h, which tells the ROM BIOS that a key has been pressed. Control of the system is transferred momentarily to the interrupt handler for Int 09h, which reads port 96 (60h) to determine which key was pressed. The service routine reads the scan code and converts it to a 16-bit code that represents the keystroke. The code's lower byte is the keystroke's ASCII value; its upper byte is the scan code. See table 6.1 for a list of these codes.

Table 6.1. *ASCII and Scan Codes*

Key	PC Scan Code	AT Scan Code	Enhanced Scan Code
Esc	01	01	01
! 1	02	02	02
@ 2	03	03	03
# 3	04	04	04
$ 4	05	05	05
% 5	06	06	06
^ 6	07	07	07
& 7	08	08	08
* 8	09	09	09
(9	0A	0A	0A
) 0	0B	0B	0B
_ -	0C	0C	0C
+ =	0D	0D	0D
Backspace	0E	0E	0E
Tab	0F	0F	0F
Q q	10	10	10
W w	11	11	11
E e	12	12	12
R r	13	13	13
T t	14	14	14
Y y	15	15	15
U u	16	16	16
I i	17	17	17
O o	18	18	18
P p	19	19	19
{ [	1A	1A	1A
}]	1B	1B	1B
Enter	1C	1C	1C
Left Ctrl (L on 101)	1D	1D	1D
A a	1E	1E	1E
S s	1F	1F	1F
D d	20	20	20
F f	21	21	21

continues

Table 6.1. *continued*

Key	PC Scan Code	AT Scan Code	Enhanced Scan Code
G g	22	22	22
H h	23	23	23
J j	24	24	24
K k	25	25	25
L l	26	26	26
: ;	27	27	27
" '	28	28	28
~ `	29	29	29
Left Shift	2A	2A	2A
| \	2B	2B	2B
Z z	2C	2C	2C
X x	2D	2D	2D
C c	2E	2E	2E
V v	2F	2F	2F
B b	30	30	30
N n	31	31	31
M m	32	32	32
< ,	33	33	33
> .	34	34	34
? /	35	35	35
Right Shift	36	36	36
PrtSc *	37	37	E0 12
Left Alt (L on 101)	38	38	38
Space bar	39	39	39
Caps Lock	3A	3A	3A
F1	3B	3B	3B
F2	3C	3C	3C
F3	3D	3D	3D
F4	3E	3E	3E
F5	3F	3F	3F
F6	40	40	40
F7	41	41	41
F8	42	42	42
F9	43	43	43
F10	44	44	44
Num Lock	45	45	45
Scroll Lock	46	46	46
7 Home	47	47	47

Key	PC Scan Code	AT Scan Code	Enhanced Scan Code
8 Cursor Up	48	48	48
9 PgUp	49	49	49
Gray –	4A	4A	4A
4 Cursor Left	4B	4B	4B
5	4C	4C	4C
6 Cursor Right	4D	4D	4D
Gray +	4E	4E	4E
1 End	4F	4F	4F
2 Cursor Down	50	50	50
3 PgDn	51	51	51
0 Ins	52	52	52
. Del	53	53	53

The following is on personal computer AT keyboard only:

Key	PC Scan Code	AT Scan Code	Enhanced Scan Code
SysRq	n/a	54	n/a

The following are on enhanced keyboard only:

Key	PC Scan Code	AT Scan Code	Enhanced Scan Code
Gray Enter	n/a	n/a	E0 1C
Right Ctrl	n/a	n/a	E0 1D
Gray /	n/a	n/a	E0 35
Gray *	n/a	n/a	37
Right Alt	n/a	n/a	E0 38
Gray Home	n/a	n/a	E0 47
Gray C Up	n/a	n/a	E0 48
Gray PgUp	n/a	n/a	E0 49
Gray C Left	n/a	n/a	E0 4B
Gray C Right	n/a	n/a	E0 4D
Gray End	n/a	n/a	E0 4F
Gray C Down	n/a	n/a	E0 50
Gray PgDn	n/a	n/a	E0 51
Gray Ins	n/a	n/a	E0 52
Gray Del	n/a	n/a	E0 53
F11	n/a	n/a	57
F12	n/a	n/a	58
Pause/Break	n/a	n/a	E1

Special keys, such as the function keys and numeric keypad keys, have a zero in their lower byte to indicate that the keystroke is not a standard ASCII character and must be specially processed.

When the BIOS keyboard interrupt handler finishes processing a keystroke, it places the code in the keyboard buffer, where it remains until a program requests it. Two very special keystrokes, Ctrl-Break and Shift-PrintScreen, are *not* processed in this manner; rather, they generate interrupt requests that are processed immediately by other portions of the BIOS. Ctrl-Break invokes Int 1Bh, which DOS sets up to force a Ctrl-C into the buffer for later "normal" processing. Shift-PrintScreen invokes Int 05h, which performs the screen printing actions.

We will not write any programs that access keyboard data at this level. Rather, we will rely on the BIOS or DOS to preprocess all keyboard input data so that we have to deal only with the ASCII codes for normal keys and the scan codes for special keys.

Reading the Keyboard from BASIC

Before you start using DOS and BIOS calls to read the keyboard, let's look at a BASIC program that uses standard BASIC functions for keyboard input. The KEYBD.BAS program (see listing 6.1) uses functions available in the BASIC interpreter.

Listing 6.1

```
10 REM --- KEYBD.BAS     Basic keyboard demonstration
20 C$=INKEY$:IF C$="" THEN 20
30 GOSUB 100:GOTO 20
100 REM --- Display keyboard input
110 IF LEN(C$)>1 THEN GOSUB 200 ELSE GOSUB 300
120 PRINT USING "Character: ! ### ###";CH$;C;SC
130 RETURN
200 REM --- Keystroke has scan code included
210 CH$=".":C=ASC(MID$(C$,1,1)):SC=ASC(MID$(C$,2,1))
220 RETURN
300 REM --- Keystroke is character only
310 CH$=C$:C=ASC(C$):SC=0

320 RETURN
```

For compatibility with the BASIC interpreter, this program is written with line numbers. The simple structure of this program follows:

1. Wait for a keystroke.

2. Print the keystroke character, ASCII code, and scan code.

3. Repeat from step 1.

INKEY$ (which is put into a tight loop in line 20 of listing 6.1) gives you a way to read the keyboard without having to wait for a keystroke. Subroutine 100 translates the return from INKEY$ according to whether the string is more than one character long. In BASIC, if the string returned by INKEY$ is more than one character long, the first character is the character's ASCII value and the second one is the scan code. (The subroutine beginning at line 200 deals with such a case.) Usually, the string is one character long. The subroutine at line 300 is used to decode the string.

If you run the program in listing 6.1, you will notice that the scan codes correspond only to a limited extent to individual keys (refer to figs. 6.1 and 6.2). The KEYBD.BAS program has the following limitations:

- INKEY$ returns only "meaningful" characters (in this case, characters that are "meaningful" only to the BASIC interpreter).

- Scan codes are returned only for completed keystrokes that are *not* ASCII characters. (You do not see the Shift keys, the Ctrl key, or the Alt key.)

From now on, instead of continuing with an interpreter-compatible BASIC program, we will work with a BASIC compiler: either QuickBASIC or Turbo BASIC. Listing 6.2 shows the program modified for QuickBASIC to take advantage of the features of the compiler.

Listing 6.2

```
' KEYBD2.BAS

'QuickBASIC Keyboard Demonstration

Start:
    C$ = INKEY$: IF C$ = "" THEN GOTO Start
    GOSUB Display: GOTO Start

Display:
    'Display Keyboard Input
    IF LEN(C$) > 1 THEN GOSUB Scan ELSE GOSUB Char
    PRINT USING "Character: ! ### ###"; CH$; C; SC
    RETURN

Scan:
    'Keystroke includes scan code
    CH$ = ".": C = ASC(MID$(C$, 1, 1)): SC = ASC(MID$(C$, 2, 1))
    RETURN

Char:
    'Keystroke is character only
    CH$ = C$: C = ASC(C$): SC = 0

    RETURN
```

Starting from the sample program in listing 6.2, we will substitute BIOS function calls to perform input. As we do, we will be able to see more of the keystrokes on the keyboard.

Accessing the Keyboard Using Int 16h

When you get ready to use the BIOS functions, the first thing you notice is that Int 16h, Function 0 (the BIOS keyboard input function) waits for a keystroke. This is shown in listing 6.3.

Listing 6.3

```
/* Borland C++ Keyboard Demonstration */

#include  <stdio.h>
#include  <dos.h>

main()
    {
    unsigned char  scancode;
    unsigned char  charcode;
    union REGS     regs;

    while (1)
        {
        regs.h.ah = 0;
        int86(0x16, &regs, &regs);
        scancode = regs.h.ah;
        charcode = regs.h.al;
        printf("%.3d %.3d [%c]\n", scancode, charcode, charcode);
        }
    }
```

Instead of waiting for a keystroke, you can read a keystroke only when one is available. Int 16h, Function 1 indicates whether a keystroke is waiting. If no key is waiting, the zero flag is set in the processor's flags register. You can test that register as shown in listing 6.4.

Listing 6.4

```
/* Borland C++ Keyboard Demonstration, take 2 */

#include  <stdio.h>
#include  <dos.h>

main()
    {
    unsigned char  scancode;
    unsigned char  charcode;
    union REGS     regs;

    puts("Input Test");
    while (1)
        {
        while (1)
            {
            putchar('.');
            regs.h.ah = 1;
            int86(0x16, &regs, &regs);
            if ((regs.x.flags & 0x40) == 0)
                break;
            }
        regs.h.ah = 0;
        int86(0x16, &regs, &regs);
        scancode = regs.h.ah;
        charcode = regs.h.al;
        printf("%.3d %.3d [%c]\n", scancode, charcode, charcode);
        }

    }
```

Before getting the key from the keyboard, the program first looks to see whether a key is ready. If no key is ready, it simply prints a dot on the screen. Whenever a key is pressed, the program stops printing dots and displays information that tells you which key was pressed. Then the program resumes printing dots.

Instead of "idling" while they wait for a keystroke, programs that have a way to check for keyboard input can do other tasks. For example, you might use such a routine to move data on the screen and terminate the operation when a key is pressed.

Int 16h, Function 2 lets you determine the state of keys that you cannot "see": the Ins, Caps Lock, Num Lock, Scroll Lock, Alt, Ctrl, and left and right Shift keys. The next version of the keyboard input program lets you check the status of these keys (see listing 6.5).

Listing 6.5

```c
/* Borland C++ Keyboard Demonstration, take 3 */

#include  <stdio.h>
#include  <dos.h>

main()
    {
    unsigned char   scancode;
    unsigned char   charcode;
    union REGS      regs;
    int  ins;
    int  caps;
    int  num;
    int  scroll;
    int  alt;
    int  ctrl;
    int  left;
    int  right;

    while (1)
        {
        while (1)
            {
            regs.h.ah = 2;
            int86(0x16, &regs, &regs);
            ins = regs.h.al & 0x80;
            caps = regs.h.al & 0x40;
            num = regs.h.al & 0x20;
            scroll = regs.h.al & 0x10;
            alt = regs.h.al & 0x08;
            ctrl = regs.h.al & 0x04;
            left = regs.h.al & 0x02;
            right = regs.h.al & 0x01;
            gotoxy(10, 12);
            puts(" INS CAPS  NUM SCRL  ALT CTRL LEFT RGHT");
            gotoxy(10, 13);
            printf("%s %s %s %s %s %s %s %s\n",
                ins ? " ON " : " OFF",
                caps ? " ON " : " OFF",
                num ? " ON " : " OFF",
                scroll ? " ON " : " OFF",
                alt ? " ON " : " OFF",
                ctrl ? " ON " : " OFF",
                left ? " ON " : " OFF",
                right ? " ON " : " OFF"
                );
```

```
                regs.h.ah = 1;
                int86(0x16, &regs, &regs);
                if ((regs.x.flags & 0x40) == 0)
                        break;
                }
        regs.h.ah = 0;
        int86(0x16, &regs, &regs);
        scancode = regs.h.ah;
        charcode = regs.h.al;
        printf("%.3d %.3d [%c]\n", scancode, charcode, charcode);
        }

    }
```

In the program in listing 6.5, `putchar('.')` has been replaced by code that checks the status of the special keys and prints their status in the center of the screen. This status information gives you a complete picture of what is happening on the keyboard. If you want your program to check for a trigger event such as both the left and right Shift keys being pressed, Int 16h, Function 2 can tell when that event occurs.

Int 16h, Function 2 returns a single byte in the AL register. Every bit corresponds to a specific keystroke. Table 6.2 shows the bit assignments for this function.

Table 6.2. *Keyboard Flag Byte*

Bit 76543210	*Meaning*
.......0	Right Shift key not pressed
.......1	Right Shift key pressed
......0.	Left Shift key not pressed
......1.	Left Shift key pressed
.....0..	Ctrl key not pressed
.....1..	Ctrl key pressed
....0...	Alt key not pressed
....1...	Alt key pressed
...0....	Scroll Lock off
...1....	Scroll Lock on
..0.....	Num Lock off
..1.....	Num Lock on
.0......	Caps Lock off
.1......	Caps Lock on
0.......	Insert off
1.......	Insert on

BIOS functions for keyboard input represent the most primitive level of access short of going to the machine. The BIOS level is the lowest level you can use and still be guaranteed that a program is portable to compatible PCs.

Accessing the Keyboard Using Int 21h

When you go to the DOS level to get keyboard input in the conventional way, you lose immediate access to every possible keystroke. DOS input functions indicate whether special keys have been pressed (if the first byte returned is a zero, the next byte is the scan code). But DOS functions do not give you the scan code for any key that has an ASCII code, nor does DOS report on the status of Alt, Shift, and so on. In addition, the most often used DOS input functions wait for a keystroke, which may force use of the BIOS interface in some programs. Later, we look at one DOS input function that overcomes this limitation.

Int 21h, Function 1 (Character Input with Echo) is the most basic DOS character input function you might want to use (see listing 6.6).

Listing 6.6

```
/* Keyin.c */
#include <stdio.h>
#include <dos.h>

#define CTRL_D    0x04
#define LF        0x0a
#define ENTER     0x0d

main()

{
    int c;

    printf("Testing Int 21h Input Functions\n");
    while ((c = keyin())!=CTRL_D)
        if (c >= 256)
            printf("SPECIAL: %d\n",c - 256);
        else if (c==ENTER)
            putchar(LF);
}

keyin()
{
    union REGS regs;
    int offset;
```

```
        offset = 0;
        regs.h.ah = 0x01;
        intdos(&regs,&regs);
        if (regs.h.al == 0) {
            offset = 256;
            regs.h.ah = 0x01;
            intdos(&regs,&regs);
        }
        return(regs.h.al + offset);

}
```

The `keyin.c` program takes the following approach:

1. Wait for a character from the keyboard.

2. If that character is a special character (a function key or a cursor key, for example), print SPECIAL and the key's scan code.

3. If the character is the Enter key, the character input function outputs a Return without a line feed; you have to output a line feed to the screen.

4. Repeat from step 1.

If you try to run the program without the special portion that prints the line-feed character to the screen, you will see the characters echoed by the DOS function as you type them; but when you press Enter, the cursor will not move to the next line. Remember that the function echoes the *characters you type* and that the Enter key represents only the carriage return—not the line-feed character.

One of the program's interesting features is its special coding that differentiates function keys from regular keys. Because ASCII characters are always less than or equal to 255, this feature creates an extended character set by adding 256 to the scan value of a key that returns a 0 ASCII code. In practice, this method often simplifies the process of decoding the keystrokes and causes no problems. Many programmers do not use this method because they associate the keystrokes with character variables. By associating the returned characters with integers, you have a larger range of special codes for representing special keystrokes.

A problem with this approach to reading in characters when you expect special keys (function keys and arrows, for example) is that when you make the second call to get the special key's scan code, the DOS function prints the scan code's ASCII equivalent as though you were retrieving the ASCII code rather than the scan code. To prevent this situation from occurring, you can use Int 21h, Function 8 and echo the characters yourself (see listing 6.7).

Listing 6.7

```
/* Keyin2.c */
#include <stdio.h>
#include <dos.h>

#define CTRL_D  0x04
#define LF      0x0a
#define ENTER   0x0d

main()
{
    int c;
    printf("Testing Int 21h Input Functions\n");
    while ((c = keyin())!=CTRL_D)
        if (c >= 256) {
            printf("SPECIAL: %d\n",c - 256);
        } else {
            putchar(c);
            if (c == ENTER)
                putchar(LF);
        }
}

keyin()

{
    union REGS regs;
    int offset;

    offset = 0;
    regs.h.ah = 0x08;
    intdos(&regs,&regs);
    if (regs.h.al == 0) {
        offset = 256;
        regs.h.ah = 0x08;
        intdos(&regs,&regs);
    }
    return(regs.h.al + offset);

}
```

The differences between this program and the one in listing 6.6 are so subtle that you can miss them if you do not look closely. First, in the keyin() function, you set up to call Int 21h, Function 8 rather than Function 1. Your main routine must echo every character to the screen as it is typed (because the DOS kernel is not echoing characters for you). Because the special keys are handled separately, you are not plagued by the echo of bogus function-key codes—only the keys you type are echoed.

Every DOS function used so far in this chapter waits for a keystroke but, as with the BIOS functions, you can check periodically to see whether a character is waiting (this process is called *polling*). Interrupt 21h, Function 0Bh indicates whether a character is waiting to be read. Listing 6.8 shows how to use this function to perform a task while you wait for a keystroke.

Listing 6.8

```
/* Keyin3.c */
#include <stdio.h>
#include <dos.h>

#define CTRL_D 0x04
#define LF     0x0a
#define ENTER  0x0d

main()

{
    int c;

    printf("Testing Int 21h Input Functions\n");
    while ((c = keyin())!=CTRL_D)
        if (c >= 256) {
            printf("SPECIAL: %d\n",c - 256);
        } else {
            putchar(c);
            if (c == ENTER)
                putchar(LF);
        }
}

keyin()
{
    union REGS regs;
    int offset;

    while (!charwait())
        putchar('.');
    offset = 0;
    regs.h.ah = 0x08;
    intdos(&regs,&regs);
    if (regs.h.al == 0) {
        offset = 256;
        regs.h.ah = 0x08;
        intdos(&regs,&regs);
    }
```

continues

Listing 6.8 continued

```
        return(regs.h.al + offset);
    }

charwait()
{
    union REGS regs;

    regs.h.ah = 0x0b;
    intdos(&regs,&regs);
    return(regs.h.al);

}
```

This program introduces a new function, charwait(), which watches for a character at the keyboard. If a character is waiting, charwait() returns TRUE; otherwise, it returns FALSE.

The charwait() function is based on Int 21h, Function 0Bh, which sets the AL register to FFh (255) if a character is waiting and to 0 otherwise. By returning the value of the AL register, the charwait() function indicates whether a character is waiting (FALSE is a zero value, and TRUE is a nonzero value).

To gauge how quickly the program checks for characters, run it and watch the periods march across the screen while the program waits for you to type a character. This program is fairly responsive to input. You can make it extremely sluggish by substituting a long, complicated operation for the simple putchar('.').

Earlier in this chapter we mentioned a special DOS input function that overcomes many of the limitations of conventional DOS input: the general I/O function Int 21h, Function 06h.

If the DL register contains 0FFh when Int 21h, Function 06h is invoked, the function obtains input from the keyboard buffer (returning with the zero flag set if no character is available). If anything else is in the DL register, it is output to the CRT with no checks being performed. Thus, this single function provides most of the capability you would get using direct BIOS input and output, while retaining full DOS compatibility. Because it is one of the original "CP/M legacy" functions, it is not as popular as it might be, which is unfortunate.

Listing 6.9 is a translation of listing 6.8 from C to Turbo Pascal, modified to use Int 21h, Function 06h for both input and output. Function and procedure names remain the same, and the action is identical. Instead of using Int 21h, Function 0Bh to check for key-ready status, however, this program simply tests the zero flag using the ZFlag constant provided by the DOS unit of Turbo Pascal, thus eliminating the charwait function, and instead of using putchar for single-byte output, this program adds the putch function to perform output through Function 06h.

Listing 6.9

```
program keyin4;
uses DOS;                  { run-time DOS library  }

const
  CTRL_D  = $04;
  LF      = $0a;
  ENTER   = $0d;

var
  c   : integer;
  reg : registers;         { declared in DOS unit }

procedure putch( i : integer );
  begin
    reg.ah := $06;         { general I/O function }
    reg.dl := byte(i);     { OUTPUT the character }
    MsDos(reg);
  end;

function keyin : integer;
  var
    i      : integer;
    offset : integer;

  begin
    repeat                 { wait for keystroke   }
      putch( $2E );        { put '.' on CRT       }
      reg.ah := $06;       { general I/O function }
      reg.dl := $FF;       { flag for INPUT use   }
      MsDos(reg);
      i := reg.flags AND FZero;
    until i <> FZero;      { declared in DOS unit }

    if (reg.al = 0) then   { flag as extended key }
      begin
        offset := 256;
        reg.ah := $06;     { and go get scan code }
        reg.dl := $FF;
        MsDos(reg);
      end
    else                   { set as normal key    }
      offset := 0;

    keyin := reg.al + offset;
  end;
```

continues

Listing 6.9 *continued*

```
begin
  writeln('Testing Int 21h Input Function 06h');
  c := keyin;
  while (keyin <> CTRL_D) do
    begin
      if (c >= 256) then
        begin
          writeln('SPECIAL: ',c - 256,' decimal');
        end
      else
        begin
          putch(c);
            if (c = ENTER) then
                putch(LF);
        end;
      c := keyin;
    end;
end.
```

If you are willing to relinquish control over the input until Enter is pressed, you can call the buffered input function (Int 21h, Function 0Ah) and let it get your input, echo it, and allow line editing. Some books on DOS programming indicate that the function will return function keys, arrows, and other special keys by returning a 2-byte sequence (including a zero byte and the scan code). The keyin5.c program (see listing 6.10) was written to show these special keys if they are returned—but they aren't. The *IBM Technical Reference* manual states that the 2-byte key codes are not included.

Listing 6.10

```
/* Keyin5.c */
#include <stdio.h>
#include <dos.h>
#define CTRL_D   0x04
#define LF       0x0a
#define ENTER    0x0d
main()
{
    char buffer[11];
    printf("Testing Int 21h Input Functions\n");
    while ( getline(buffer,10) > 0 ) {
        printf("<<%s>>\n",buffer);
    }
```

```
}
getline(buffer,n)
char *buffer;
int n;
{
    union REGS regs;
    char locbuf[514];
    int i, j;
    locbuf[0] = n;
    locbuf[1] = 0;
    regs.h.ah = 0x0a;
    regs.x.dx = (int)&locbuf;
    intdos(&regs,&regs);
    for(i=0, j=0; i<locbuf[1]; i++, j++)
        if (locbuf[i+2]==0) {
            i++;
            buffer[j] = 'X';
        } else {
            buffer[j] = locbuf[i+2];
        }
    buffer[j] = NULL;
    return(locbuf[1]);

}
```

The requirements of the buffered input function make it special. Because of its layout, the buffer does not fit naturally with the way strings are handled in BASIC, C, or Pascal. When the function is invoked, you must pass it a buffer large enough to handle the input characters plus two extra characters. The first character in the buffer is the *maximum* number of characters to input; the second, which is filled in by DOS, represents the number of characters read.

Identifying the Level of Keyboard Support

If the BIOS supports the enhanced keyboard, two sets of BIOS functions access the keyboard: Functions 00h, 01h, and 02h support the older keyboards, and Functions 10h, 11h, and 12h support the newer keyboards. How can a program tell whether it can use the enhanced keyboard functions?

You can use Function 05h, Write to Keyboard Buffer, to test for the presence of enhanced keyboard functions. When you write a value of FFFFh to the buffer, you should find AL set to either 00h or 01h. If this is the case, use Function 10h, Get Keystroke, to read the buffer. If the enhanced keyboard functions are present, you will read the FFFFh value in at most 16 calls (because there are 16 words in the keyboard buffer).

With DOS 5.0, detection of the enhanced keyboard is automatic; Functions 01h, 06h, 07h, 08h, 0Ah, 0Bh, and 0Ch all use the enhanced keyboard functions if present.

Listing 6.11

```
        page 55,132

comseg      segment

        assume      cs:comseg
        assume      ds:comseg
        assume      es:comseg
        assume      ss:comseg

Forg  0100h
;
;       Determine whether the BIOS enhanced keyboard functions are
;       present. Prints the level supported and returns an errorlevel
;       of 0 (no enhanced keyboard) or 1 (enhanced keyboard).
;
;       Assembled with MASM 5.10a, linked with LINK 3.05.
;
;       MASM /M1 /n /p /w2 /Zd KEYBOARD;
;       LINK KEYBOARD;
;       EXE2BIN KEYBOARD Keyboard.COM
;
check       proc near
        ;
        ;       clear keyboard buffer
        ;
clear:
        mov  ah,1           ; check for keystroke present
        int  16h            ;
        jz   buffer_clear   ; if none, proceed...
        mov  ah,0           ; read the keystroke and discard it
        int  16h            ;
        jmp  clear          ; check again
        ;
        ;       stuff 0FFFFh into buffer
        ;
buffer_clear:
        mov  ax,5FFh        ; stuff FFFF in
        mov  cx,0FFFFh      ;
        int  16h            ;
        cmp  al,1           ; success?
        ja   no_enhanced    ; no, BIOS plainly doesn't support it
        ;
        ;       try to read 0FFFFh
```

```
        ;
        mov  cx,1              ; 16 entries in the standard buffer
tryit:
        mov  ah,11h            ; use enhanced check for keystroke present
        int  16h              ;
        jz   no_enhanced      ; nothing there, it didn't work
        mov  ah,10h            ; use enhanced function to read keystroke
        int  16h              ;
        cmp  ax,0FFFFh         ; our keystroke?
        je   enhanced
        loop tryit
        ;
        ;    no enhanced keyboard
        ;
no_enhanced:
        mov  dx,offset no      ; print negative message
        mov  al,1              ; set error code to 1
printit:
        push ax               ; save error code
        mov  ah,9              ; print string
        int  21h              ;
        pop  ax               ; restore error code
        mov  ah,04CH           ; exit with error code
        int  21h              ; exit
        ;
        ;    enhanced keyboard
        ;
enhanced:
        mov  dx,offset yes     ; print positive message
        xor  al,al             ; zero error code
        jmp  printit
check   endp

no   db   "NO "
yes  db   "ENHANCED KEYBOARD FUNCTIONS SUPPORTED$"

comseg  ends

        end  check
```

The Mouse

Use of a mouse (or some equivalent device, such as a trackball) as part of computer systems is increasing. Furthermore, software products that depend on a mouse for their effective use are increasing. Microsoft Windows can be used with only the keyboard, but the full convenience of the graphics interface can be obtained only with a mouse. And although programs such as Microsoft's Paint (which runs under Windows) can be used with a keyboard, doing so easily is impossible. Guide (Owl International's Hypertext system) simply cannot be used without a mouse.

DOS does not include a mouse driver.

For protection in case of a wrong guess, Microsoft allows new drivers to be added easily to the system. One of these drivers, Microsoft's MOUSE.SYS, is added to the operating system when you boot the system. (MOUSE.SYS is provided by Microsoft if you purchase one of their mice.) In this section, we see how the mouse software works.

How the Mouse Works

The mouse is one of the truly simple pieces of equipment that can be attached to a computer. It consists of virtually nothing more than a little ball inside a "mouse" that rolls on a flat surface. As the ball rotates, circuitry in the mouse reports the movement to the computer, which interprets and translates that movement into mouse cursor movement on the screen. In addition to the ball, the mouse contains two or three buttons (pressure switches) that you can use to signal the computer in various ways.

Initializing the Mouse Driver

Depending on which software you have, you may have one of several ways to set up the mouse driver. Some packages create a TSR to handle the mouse; others have a driver. If you have a driver, you install it on the system by including in your CONFIG.SYS file a line that tells the system to load the driver when it boots. Use the following line:

```
DEVICE=C:\MOUSE.SYS
```

if you have Microsoft's mouse driver stored in the root directory on drive C.

Where Is the Mouse?

First, your program must determine whether a mouse is installed. Int 33h, Function 0 tells you that a mouse is available if AX is nonzero on return. (With DOS versions earlier than 3.0, the vector for Int 33h is not initialized to point to an IRET; before using the Function 0 test, you should verify that the vector does not point to location 0000:0000.)

If you know that a mouse is available, you can use it by either periodically polling it for changes in position and key clicks or by setting up an interrupt service routine to act whenever the mouse moves or a button is clicked. For simplicity, we discuss only the polling technique here.

Because the mouse driver takes care of the mouse cursor's on-screen position, your program does not have to do so. You simply need to know that the mouse is positioned where users want something done. The sample program Mouse.c, which is based on Keyin3.c, shows how you can the check the mouse while you wait for other input (see listing 6.12).

Listing 6.12

```c
/* mouse.c */
#include <stdio.h>
#include <dos.h>

#define CTRL_D  0x04
#define LF      0x0a
#define ENTER   0x0d

main()
{
    int c;

    printf("Testing Mouse Input\n");
    chk_mouse();
    while ((c = keyin())!=CTRL_D)
        if (c >= 256) {
            printf("SPECIAL: %d\n",c - 256);
        } else {
            putchar(c);
            if (c == ENTER)
                putchar(LF);
        }
}

keyin()
{
    union REGS regs;
    int offset;

    while (!charwait())
        mousepos();
    offset = 0;
    regs.h.ah = 0x08;
    intdos(&regs,&regs);
    if (regs.h.al == 0) {
        offset = 256;
        regs.h.ah = 0x08;
        intdos(&regs,&regs);
    }
```

continues

Listing 6.12 continued

```c
        return(regs.h.al + offset);
}

charwait()

{
    union REGS regs;

    regs.h.ah = 0x0b;
    intdos(&regs,&regs);
    return(regs.h.al);
}

#define MOUSE 0x33

static int mouse = 0;

chk_mouse()

{
    union REGS regs;

    struct SREGS sregs;
    regs.x.ax = 0x3533;
    intdosx(&regs,&regs,&sregs);
    if ((regs.x.bx | sregs.es) == 0) {
        printf("No Driver Present\n");
        exit(255);
    }
    regs.x.ax = 0;
    int86(MOUSE,&regs,&regs);
    if (regs.x.ax != 0) {
        mouse = regs.x.bx;
        regs.x.ax = 0x01;
        int86(MOUSE,&regs,&regs);
    }
}

mousepos()
 {
    union REGS regs;
    char buttons[6];

    gotoxy(12,10);
    if (mouse) {
        regs.x.ax = 0x03;
        int86(MOUSE,&regs,&regs);
```

```
        switch(regs.x.bx & 0x03) {
            case 0:    /* no buttons */
                strcpy(buttons,"NONE ");
                break;
            case 1:    /* left button */
                strcpy(buttons,"LEFT ");
                break;
            case 2:    /* right button */
                strcpy(buttons,"RIGHT");
                break;
            case 3:    /* both buttons */
                strcpy(buttons,"BOTH ");
                break;
        }
        printf("X = %4.4d Y = %4.4d %s",
            regs.x.cx,regs.x.dx,buttons);
    } else {
        printf("NO MOUSE");
    }
}

#define VIDEO 0x10

gotoxy(row,col)

int row, col;

{
    union REGS regs;

    if (row<0 || row > 24) return;
    if (col<0 || col > 79) return;

    regs.h.ah = 2;
    regs.h.bh = 0;
    regs.h.dh = row;
    regs.h.dl = col;
    int86(VIDEO,&regs,&regs);

}
```

Mouse.c includes the chk_mouse() function, which checks for the existence of a mouse driver and, if the driver is present, for the mouse. Instead of printing periods as it waits for input, the program moves the cursor to the center of the screen and displays information about the mouse's position and buttons.

If you have a mouse installed, move it around and watch the mouse status change to reflect the mouse's movement. Within these basic functions is a minimum level of operability for mouse functions. The gotoxy() function, which uses the BIOS screen-addressing routines to position the cursor on-screen, also has been added to the Mouse.c program. (Chapter 5, "Output Devices," explains how this function operates.)

The sample program includes only three basic mouse functions. The first, which determines whether a mouse is installed and how many buttons it has, sets the number of buttons in a global variable. When other mouse functions are called, they can check this variable to determine whether they have anything to do.

If a mouse *is* installed, you call the second function (Int 33h, Function 1) to display the mouse cursor on-screen. With the mouse available, you call Int 33h, Function 3 to check for the mouse status (position and button status) whenever you check for (but do not find) a character. This function returns the status of the buttons coded into the bottom two bits of the BX register. If bit 0 is set, the left button has been pressed; if bit 1 is set, the right button has been pressed.

The mouse's position on-screen is always given in the range 0 to 639 across the screen (x-coordinate) and 0 to 199 down the screen (y-coordinate). Depending on the current display mode, you can determine from table 6.3 the mouse's position in terms of columns or coordinates.

Table 6.3. Mouse Coordinates

Screen Mode	Coordinates
0 to 1	row = DX/8, column = CX/16
2 to 3	row = DX/8, column = DX/8
4 to 5	x = CX/2, y = DX
6	x = CX, y = DX
7	row = DX/8, column = CX/8
14 to 16	x = CX, y = DX

Additional mouse functions (described in the "Interrupt 33h: Mouse Functions" section at the end of this book) help you control the size, shape, and on-screen boundaries of the mouse cursor, as well as the speed of on-screen movement in response to that of the mouse. You also can set a function to be called whenever a mouse event (such as a key press or release) occurs. You will learn about this type of routine, called an interrupt handler, in Chapter 11.

Summary

In this chapter, you looked at keyboard and mouse functions and learned some basic operations that can be used to implement input functions. By using the keyboard functions available through the BIOS, you can tell which keys are pressed on the keyboard and keep track of operations. You can see not only the ASCII codes for character input (like those returned from high-level language input functions) but also the scan codes, which are returned only for some keys. And you can monitor the position of the Shift, Alt, Ctrl, Scroll Lock, Num Lock, and Caps Lock keys.

Using the mouse functions on DOS Int 33h, you can monitor the position of the buttons on the mouse as well as the position of the mouse on the screen. You can even set interrupts for mouse functions that execute special handlers whenever mouse events (such as a key click) occur.

PROGRAMMING

Serial Devices

The modern computing world's serial devices are fascinating. Thanks to serial devices we can communicate with different people around the world through such services as CompuServe or MCI Mail. Why serial devices work the way they do and how you can exploit their properties are the subjects of this chapter.

Throughout this chapter, you will be working with serial devices in terms of communications with other computers—the most visible use of such communications today. Serial communications can be used also with printers, sensors, and many other devices, and the communications need not be two-way. Communications with printers, for example, are predominantly one-way: from computer to printer. Or you might build a program to read the Associated Press news wire (a 1200 bps [bits per second] one-way data feed) or the NOAA weather wire (50 bps, one-way).

This chapter concentrates on a simple two-way terminal communications program, which embodies all aspects of serial communications. Before you write a terminal program, however, you should understand how the serial interface works. After defining some basic terminology, we provide specifics about the way the IBM PC's serial interface chip (the 8250) works. Then the discussion progresses to the hardware level so that you learn how to control the chip directly.

7

CHAPTER

With the groundwork laid, we will write two terminal programs. The first one uses the BIOS functions to access the serial port. You will find that such a program is too slow for serious communications. You can gain some speed and control by working directly with the 8250 chip. The second terminal program illustrates this technique, but even this program is too slow for practical communications at 1200 bps. For a truly practical communications program, you will have to wait for Chapter 11, "Interrupt Handlers," which introduces interrupt processing.

Serial Interfaces

Fundamentally, a serial interface transforms the computer's internal, parallel format of data (an 8-bit byte) into a serial format (1 bit) that can be transmitted over a single data line. This transformation can be done by software; in a PC, however, it is done more effectively by hardware.

Figure 7.1 illustrates the basic purpose of a serial interface: to convert information from parallel to serial format or from serial to parallel format. Data enters one side of the interface and emerges, translated, from the other side. The interface converts data to a serial format by converting each character into a "packet" of information that can be transmitted in a way agreed upon by both the sender and the receiver. (Serial format will be discussed shortly in greater detail.) Computers can communicate successfully with one another only if each end of the *serial link* (the serial connection between two computers or between a computer and another device) uses the same format for the data and the same transmission speed.

Fig. 7.1. *A serial interface converts the format of data from parallel (in) to serial (out).*

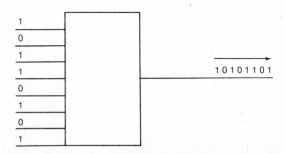

Two methods of transmitting serial information are generally accepted. Both are named for the timing method that paces the information transmitted and received over the serial link. The first method, called *synchronous communication*, maintains rigid control of transmission and reception of data through the link. In this process, data is transmitted at precisely timed intervals. The clocking information is transmitted with the data so that the receiving computer can be synchronized with the information received. This type of communications, generally used in mini-computer or mainframe applications, is beyond the scope of this book.

In the second method, called *asynchronous communication*, individual information packets are placed on the communications line with no precisely defined timing between them. These data packets can be transmitted quickly, one after another, or with varying time delays between each transmission. The asynchronous method is native to most microcomputers, including the IBM family.

Although you can buy hardware interfaces for other types of serial communication (such as the previously mentioned synchronous method), asynchronous communication should suffice for most general-purpose needs.

Figure 7.2 shows a serial information packet (as a function of time for asynchronous communications) on a communications line. The line usually is kept in a *mark state* (high voltage). The start of a character (the start bit) is signaled by a drop to the *space state* (low voltage). To determine whether the next bit is high or low, the line is sampled at precisely timed intervals based on the bit rate. The data bits are followed by one or more stop bits, in the mark state, which allow sufficient time for the character to be processed and for the system to get ready for the next character.

Fig. 7.2. *Serial transmission.*

In preparation for a more detailed discussion of asynchronous communications, you should understand basic communications terminology. As you will recall, a serial interface converts parallel data into packets of information that can be transmitted easily through a serial communications link. These packets are made up of a specific number of bits of information, each with a specific purpose: start bits, data bits, stop bits, and parity. Definitions of these and a few other critical terms follow:

• **Start bit:** A bit sent before the actual character data to alert the receiving computer that a character is coming. Start bits are sent automatically by the serial device.

- **Data bits:** The bits representing the individual character being transmitted. (The number of data bits is often referred to as the *word length*.) Normal communications to serial devices use a word length of either seven bits if parity is computed (see the following definition) or eight bits if no parity is computed. The serial communications chip on an IBM PC can handle from five to eight data bits.

- **Parity:** A simple character-level check the receiver can use to see whether the character was received correctly. Parity is computed by counting the number of bits set to 1 in the data portion of the information packet being transmitted and then appending a parity bit representative of the type of parity you want. For EVEN parity, the total number of data bits set to 1 plus the parity bit must result in an even number. Conversely, for ODD parity, the number of data bits set to 1 plus the parity bit must result in an odd number. Other possible settings for the parity bit include MARK (always set to 1), SPACE (always set to 0), or NONE (always ignored).

- **Stop bits:** The bits sent at the end of the information packet to give the receiver time to process a character before the next one arrives. One stop bit is normal for all communications you are likely to handle. (Two stop bits are needed only when communications occur at extremely slow speeds, such as 110 bps).

- **Baud rate:** An electrical term that represents the signaling (or transfer) rate of a communications line. This term is frequently (albeit incorrectly) used to refer to the bit rate.

- **Bit rate:** The transmission speed, expressed as bits per second, and frequently (albeit incorrectly) referred to as the baud rate. Bit rate, the more accurate term, is used in this book.

- **Full duplex:** A means of communication in which the information displayed on your screen is an echo of the character you have transmitted to a remote computer.

- **Half duplex:** A means of communication in which the information sent to a remote computer is not echoed back to your computer.

When one computer communicates with another, both machines must operate by a set of predefined parameters that define the format in which information is transferred. If both computers are not set to the same values, communications between them will not be reliable. One reason that communications between computers are less widespread than they might be is that those of us who work with computers have been unable to agree on a standard for communications between computers (without involving users in specialized, frustrating terminology).

Several configurations, however, are fairly standard. Generally, either eight data bits, no parity, and one stop bit or seven data bits, EVEN or ODD parity, and one stop bit will work. The bit rate for most on-line computer systems is fairly well established at 300, 1200, or 2400 bps.

If you try one of these configurations, you almost always can match one of the on-line computer systems. But some systems are not always what they seem to be. For example, a computer system advertising seven bits, EVEN parity was best accessed with seven bits, ODD parity. In this case, the results of determining the cause of the problem were not worth the cost of the equipment needed to determine it. If a configuration works, use it.

A Tale of Swapped Bits

A possible cause of the EVEN/ODD parity swap mentioned in the main text is an error on some copies of the specification sheet for the National Semiconductor type 8250 UART chip, which forms the heart of the standard serial interface card used in DOS machines. The error transposed the descriptions of EVEN and ODD actions; thus, following the sheet's information for EVEN parity made the chip react for ODD, and vice versa.

Although the error was quickly corrected, not all bad copies could be removed from circulation. As a result, some commercial packages (including at least one expensive developers' diagnostic toolbox) give the wrong result based on that bad spec sheet. This fact earned Jim Kyle a significant consulting fee from an owner of said toolbox (who was quite happy to pay the fee to get his program working).

This is neither the first nor the worst such mistake in the history of microcomputing. An even more serious example of the same type of error was a bit reversal between the original Western Digital series of floppy disk controllers (the 1771 series) and the accepted standard for Address Mark encoding. For compatibility, the error had to be carried on to the upgrade design (the 1793 series) as well, but software authors were advised to correct their use of the bit! As a result, Radio Shack's TRS-80 line's Model 3 (which used the 1793) was unable to write diskettes that could be read on the Model 1 (which used the 1771) although the disks were, in all other respects, compatible.

After an information packet has been transmitted, timing is critical. The communications line is idle until the start bit is received. After the start bit arrives, the line has to be sampled at precise intervals in order to receive the individual bits that make up the character. The parity bit, which is used to calculate the correctness of the transmitted character, follows the data. Finally, the stop bits are received and discarded, and the receiver again waits for a start bit.

If this background information has confused you, relax. IBM microcomputers are equipped with hardware that manages the low-level details of serial communication. After you have determined which communications parameters to use and have entered that information, the serial-conversion hardware ensures that you get what you want.

PC Serial Conversion: The 8250 UART

IBM microcomputers (and most compatibles) use a hardware chip based on the 8250 Asynchronous Communications Controller, also known as UART (Universal Asynchronous Receiver Transmitter). Compared to some systems that rely on software to manage their communications properly, the UART is a wonder. By attending to the details of receiving and transmitting bits of information, the UART frees the programmer for other tasks.

Suppose that you want to send data across a series of wires while the voltage level on the line changes. If you were to write a program to manage the line, you could control the line directly and signal anything you wanted. Sound difficult? In concept, it isn't. But the process is tedious and subject to subtle errors. Some systems (the original TRS-80 Color Computer, for example) can handle serial communications only in this way.

With the 8250 UART, you do not have to go to the trouble of programming a software controller to get data on and off a communications line. For much less effort than you would spend writing and testing a software UART, the UART chip gives you an enormous amount of control and allows rapid, standard communications with other devices.

Each 8250 has 10 programmable 1-byte registers that control and monitor the serial port. Most of these registers are for initialization, and only a few are used regularly. All of the registers are accessed through seven I/O port addresses. These addresses are calculated as an offset from a base address that varies according to which communications port is used. The base addresses for COM1: through COM4: are shown in table 7.1; the offsets from these addresses, which control each UART register, are listed in table 7.2.

Table 7.1. *Base Addresses for the IBM Communications Ports*

Communications Port	Base Address
COM1:	03F8h
COM2:	02F8h
COM3:	03E8h
COM4:	02E8h

Table 7.2. *8250 Registers: Offset from Base Address*

Offset	LSR Bit 7	Meaning
0	0	Transmitter holding register (THR) and receiver data register (RDR)
0	1	Baud rate divisor, low byte (BRDL)
1	0	Interrupt enable register (IER)
1	1	Baud rate divisor, high byte (BRDH)
2	x	Interrupt identification register (IIR)
3	x	Line control register (LCR)
4	x	Modem control register (MCR)
5	x	Line status register (LSR)
6	x	Modem status register (MSR)

Although the 8250 UART has ten registers to control its operation, there are only seven port addresses for these ten registers. Three of the seven addresses serve more than one register. At offset 0, the THR is accessed whenever you *write* to the port, and the RDR is accessed whenever you *read* from the port. Because neither register requires both read and write access, this combination makes sense.

Register offsets 0 and 1 serve another function when bit 7 of the LSR is set to 1. When this happens, these two ports access the BRD registers. (Because the BRD registers are accessed only during initialization of the chip, they can be kept safely out of the way during normal operations.)

Let's look at what each 8250 register does.

The Transmitter Holding Register (THR)

The transmitter holding register (THR) holds the byte of data that is about to be sent. You write data to this register when bit 5 of the line status register (LSR) indicates that the register is empty.

The Receiver Data Register (RDR)

The receiver data register (RDR) holds the byte of data most recently received from the communications line. You read this register when LSR bit 0 indicates that a byte has been received.

The Baud Rate Divisor (BRD)

The baud rate divisor (BRD) is a 16-bit number that specifies the bit transfer rate (*not* the baud rate, despite the official name given by the UART designers) used by the UART. It is divided between two 8-bit ports (BRDL and BRDH). To determine the bit transfer rate, you divide the UART's internal clock rate (1.8432 MHz) by the BRD, as in the following formula:

$$BRD = \frac{\text{clock speed}}{16 \times \text{desired bps}}$$

If you use this formula, determining the settings for different bit speeds is easy. For example, you can calculate the BRD for 1,200 bps as follows:

$$BRD = \frac{1843200}{16 \times 1200} = \frac{1843200}{19200} = 96 = 0060h$$

Thus, BRDH must be set to 0, and BRDL must be set to 60h.

You can use the equation to construct the BRD for the typical bit rates listed in table 7.3.

Table *7.3. Baud Rate Divisors*

Bit Rate	BRDH	BRDL
50	09h	00h
110	04h	17h
300	01h	80h
1200	00h	60h
2400	00h	30h
4800	00h	18h
9600	00h	0Ch
19200	00h	06h

Note: IBM cautions users of its early versions of BIOS not to set the rate higher than 9600 bps, but you can safely drive the UART at rates of 19,200 bps (or even higher).

To set the BRD, you first must set bit 7 of the line control register (LCR) to 1. Then you can safely output the required divisors to their I/O locations (refer to table 7.2). After you have set the BRD, good practice dictates that you immediately clear bit 7 of the LCR.

The Interrupt Enable Register (IER)

The interrupt enable register (IER) controls the type of interrupts generated by the UART. You can enable one or more interrupts at a time, depending on how you have written your interrupt handler. Note that whenever an interrupt is enabled, a specific action must be taken to clear it. Table 7.4 shows the assignments of interrupts to bits in the register and the appropriate action needed to clear each interrupt.

Table *7.4. Interrupt Enable Register*

Bit	Activates	Action
0	Data received	Read RDR
1	THR empty	Output to THR
2	Data error or break	Read LSR
3	MSR change	Read MSR
4–7	Unused; always set to zero	

Interrupts are generated when one of the activating conditions shown in table 7.4 occurs and the corresponding IER bit is set to 1. You will learn more about the interrupt enable register in Chapter 11, "Interrupt Handlers," when you develop an interrupt-driven communications program.

The Interrupt Identification Register (IIR)

When an interrupt occurs, a communications program can identify it from the bit settings of the interrupt identification register (IIR). Table 7.5 lists the meanings of these bits.

Table 7.5. *Interrupt Identification Register*

Bit	Meaning
0	More than one interrupt has occurred
1–2	Interrupt ID
	00 = Change in modem status register (MSR)
	01 = Transmitter holding register (THR) empty
	10 = Data received
	11 = Data reception error or break

If your software is interrupt driven, you first must specify the type of interrupts you want to generate (refer to table 7.4). Then, after an interrupt request is received, you must examine the IIR to see what type of interrupt occurred. Again, this process is described in greater detail in Chapter 11.

The Line Control Register (LCR)

The line control register (LCR) is the primary control register for the serial line. Table 7.6 details the bit assignments for this register.

The Modem Control Register (MCR)

The modem control register (MCR) sets control lines to the modem and, through these lines, tells the modem that the computer is ready to send characters, receive characters, or both. Table 7.7 gives the bit assignments for this register.

Table 7.6. *Line Control Register*

Bit	Meaning	Settings	Notes
0-1	Character Length		
	5 bits	00	
	6 bits	01	
	7 bits	10	
	8 bits	11	
2	Stop Bits		
	1 bit	0	
	1.5 bits	1	If using 5-bit characters
	2 bits	1	If using 6-, 7-, or 8-bit characters
3-5	Parity		
	IGNORE	000	
	ODD	100	
	EVEN	110	
	MARK	101	
	SPACE	111	
6	Break Condition		
	Disabled	0	
	Enabled	1	
7	Port Toggle		
	Normal	0	Use THR/RDR and IER registers
	Alternate	1	Use BRDL and BRDH registers

Table 7.7. *Modem Control Register*

Bit	Meaning
0	Set DTR line active
1	Set RTS line active
2	User output #1 (Hayes Reset)
3	User output #2 (Enable Ints)
4	UART loopback
5–7	Unused; set to zero

The data terminal ready (DTR) line tells the modem that the computer is powered on and ready to receive information from the modem. The request to send (RTS) line tells the modem that the computer is ready to send something to the line. Ordinarily, you can safely set both DTR and RTS to 1 to turn on these lines. Some modems ignore (or can be set to ignore) these signals, but older modems cannot be set to ignore them. Bit 2 (user output #1) is used only by specialized hardware (such as the Hayes Smartmodem internal board, which uses bit 2 to reset the modem) and should be initialized to 0. Bit 3 (user output #2), which is tied to the interrupt servicing for the 8250, blocks interrupt handling if *not* set to 1. (Bit 3 is discussed in greater detail in Chapter 11.) Bit 4 allows testing of a communications program without any over-the-line communications. In this *loopback* state, data that you send out the port reappears as input.

The Line Status Register (LSR)

The line status register (LSR) gives you the status of the communications line (see table 7.8). From this register, you can diagnose common line problems.

Table **7.8.** *Line Status Register*

Bit	Meaning
0	Data received; byte in RDR
1	Overrun error occurred because the previous byte was not read before the next byte arrived
2	Parity error
3	Framing error occurred because the transmission was not in sync (no stop bit was found after the character had been read)
4	Break detect
5	THR is empty; okay to output a character to the line
6	Transmitter shift register (TSR) is empty; the TSR takes the character from the THR and places it on the line, one bit at a time
7	Time out

The Modem Status Register (MSR)

The modem's status depends on whether a certain status line is high or low and whether the status on a specified line has changed since the last register read. Table 7.9 shows how the bits are assigned in the modem status register.

Table *7.9. Modem Status Register*

Bit	Meaning
0	Change in clear to send (CTS)
1	Change in data set ready (DSR)
2	Change in ring indicator (RI)
3	Change in data carrier detect (DCD)
4	Clear to send (CTS) set high
5	Data set ready (DSR) set high
6	Ring indicator (RI) set high
7	Data carrier detect (DCD) set high

The modem signals correspond to changes in the status of an electrical signal line connecting the computer and the serial device. Depending on the device, these hardware signals may or may not be used. Some modems make no use of them and rely solely on the Hayes command set to handle communications. Because your modem (or other serial device) may use modem signals, their meaning is described in table 7.10.

Table *7.10. Modem Signals*

Signal	Meaning
CTS	Clear to send: The modem is ready to receive characters from the computer.
DSR	Data set ready: The modem is powered on and ready to operate.
RI	Ring indicator: The telephone line is ringing. As the line rings, RI is held high (electrically) so that your computer can detect the rings.
DCD	Data carrier detect: The modem is connected to another modem.

Initializing the Communications Port

Working directly with the 8250 serial controller is not as easy as it may seem. Even initialization can become a complex operation that depends on sequencing registers in the correct order to produce a specific effect. For many programs (even those that intend to access the 8250 directly), you do not have to initialize the UART directly. You can control initialization through a BIOS function designed to simplify the task. In this area of programming (as elsewhere), never make more work for yourself than necessary.

To access the BIOS function that initializes a serial port, load the AH register with 0 and the DX register with a zero-based number that represents the communications port to be initialized (thus, 0=COM1:, 1=COM2:, 2=COM3:, and 3=COM4:). Because some versions of the IBM BIOS do not intrinsically support four communications ports, you may be limited to a DX setting of either 0 or 1. All of the PS/2 series of computers support four communications ports.

Finally, you load AL with the initialization parameters you want; each bit is significant. Table 7.11 lists the possible AL settings.

Table 7.11. BIOS Communications Port Initialization Settings for AL

Bit	Meaning	Settings
0–1	Word length	
	Not used	00
	Not used	01
	7 bits	10
	8 bits	11
2	Stop bits	
	1 bit	0
	2 bits	1
3–4	Parity	
	NONE	00
	ODD	01
	NONE	10
	EVEN	11
5–7	Bit rate	
	110 bps	000
	150 bps	001
	300 bps	010
	600 bps	011
	1200 bps	100
	2400 bps	101
	4800 bps	110
	9600 bps	111

After you have loaded AH, AL, and DX with the necessary values, issue an Int 14h; the communications port will be set according to your specifications. (For a summary of the register settings necessary for this BIOS function, see table 7.14. Further information on this function is available in the "BIOS Function Reference" section in Part V.)

As you can see from table 7.11, you cannot set a data length of 5 or 6 bits, nor can you set a bit rate below 110 bps or above 9600 bps. Your initialization options are quite limited for certain applications. For example, when you try to tie in to a specialized application such as the NOAA weather wire, which is 50 bps with a 5-bit word length, your only option is to initialize the communications port through direct manipulation of the UART registers.

The IBM PS/2 series computers have another BIOS function that provides an additional degree of control over your communications interface. You access this function by loading the AH register with 4 and, as in the normal BIOS function, loading the DX register with a zero-based number that represents the communications port to be initialized. Next, AL is set to either 0 or 1, depending on whether you want a break condition on the line. Ordinarily, AL is set to 0 (no break). BH must be set to the desired parity, as outlined in table 7.12.

Table 7.12. *Parity Settings for BH (Function 14/4)*

Setting	Parity Meaning
0	NONE
1	ODD
2	EVEN
3	MARK
4	SPACE

BL must be set to the number of stop bits you want: 0 represents 1 stop bit, and 1 represents either 1.5 (for a 5-bit data length) or 2 (for 6-, 7-, and 8-bit data lengths) stop bits.

The data length is specified in CH, with the value in CH equaling five less than the number of data bits required. Thus, a value of 0 represents five data bits, and a value of 3 equals eight data bits.

Finally, CL is loaded with the bit rate you want. This value is determined by the settings detailed in table 7.13.

Table 7.13. *Bit Rate Settings for CL (Function 14/4)*

Setting	Bit Rate
0	110 bps
1	150 bps
2	300 bps
3	600 bps
4	1200 bps
5	2400 bps
6	4800 bps
7	9600 bps
8	19200 bps

After you have loaded all the registers (AH, AL, BH, BL, CH, CL, and DX), issue an Int 14h to set the communications port as specified. Table 7.14 summarizes the register settings needed for the two BIOS functions presented in this section. Further information about these functions is available in the "BIOS Function Reference" section in Part V.

Table 7.14. *Summary of BIOS Communications Port Initialization Functions*

Function	Parameter	Notes and Possible Settings
AH=0	AL	Set according to information in table 7.11
	DX	Communications port desired: 0 (COM1:) through 3 (COM4:)
AH=4		Works only on PS/2 series
	AL	Break condition setting
	BH	Parity
	BL	Stop bits
	CH	Word length
	CL	Bit rate
	DX	Communications port desired: 0 (COM1:) through 3 (COM4:)

Despite the BIOS's capabilities for initializing communications ports, you may have to access the UART directly if you cannot set a certain register (through the BIOS function) to a value you need. Before you make the assumption that "BIOS can't do it," try to work with the BIOS initialization functions—you may find them more than adequate.

If the thought of doing all the setup for the UART seems frightening, remember that you can change any part of the setup at any time. This means that you can use the BIOS routine to set all the parameters in its range, then go directly to the UART hardware to modify the speed, word size, or parity.

By using direct UART initialization, you can set any speed up to 115.2 K bps. The secret to achieving this speed is implied in the speed equations shown a few pages back; they are a bit simpler, though, when you reduce the format to

$$\text{Divisor} = \frac{115,200}{\text{desired bps rate}}$$

The major difference here is that the clock speed and 16-time multiplier have been combined into the single numeric constant. You can see that the 115.2K bps rate achieved by some laptop computer data-transfer programs is the maximum possible from the serial interface (a divisor of 0001).

Tables 7.1 through 7.10 give all the information you need to do this; the only caution is to avoid attempting to *IN*put from a port immediately after doing an *OUT* to it because the UART is significantly slower in reacting than many modern CPUs. The BIOS code includes the `JMP $+2` command after every OUT command, specifically to introduce enough delay to be certain that no problems result at high clock speeds; this is a good rule to copy if you add your own initialization procedures.

Modems

Modem is a contraction of the term *m*odulator-*dem*odulator. Although detailed instructions about using a specific modem are beyond the scope of this book, some general observations should be made.

First, most modems are advertised as Hayes compatible, which means that all modem control is in the command sequences (character strings) sent to the modem rather than in the modem control lines. Many sophisticated terminal programs use these Hayes command sequences to communicate with the modem; these programs can control the modem's many functions directly. All you have to do is tell the program what you want.

If your modem uses the modem control lines rather than a string command set, you will be able to control the modem only by manipulating the modem control lines directly at the BIOS or hardware level. The BIOS and DOS functions generally do a good job of hiding these control lines from your program, which means that you have to go directly to the 8250 UART to control them.

You do not need a modem for all serial communications. In most offices with serial connections to a central computer, for example, the connections can be wired directly to a PC if the central computer and the PC are fairly close to each other. Technically, they should be no more than 150 feet apart, although runs of up to 400 feet can work if there is no outside interference. And you also can run printers and serial devices without a modem if they meet the cable-length requirements.

To communicate through a telephone line you *must* use a modem. The bandwidth of most telephone systems is relatively limited (300 to 3000 Hz). The output from the 8250 UART is a series of square waves that will be distorted beyond recognition if you try to send them, unaltered, through a telephone line. The result would be no communication at all. A modem translates the square wave output from an 8250 UART into a series of tones that fall within the telephone line's bandwidth.

Older, slower modems translated the output simply: one tone corresponded to 0, another to 1. Newer, faster modems use not only tones but also multiplexing, phasing, and other electrical-signal components to pass a greater volume of information through a line.

Writing a Terminal Program

Now that you have seen how the 8250 UART functions and how modems work, you are almost ready to design a simple terminal program. But before you begin, you should be aware of several other considerations.

A communications program can be implemented in two ways. The first uses a polling method: your program periodically checks the serial port to determine whether an incoming character is available. If a character is available, you can process it and continue. The second method, which is more efficient in terms of computer time, is based on interrupts: you and the computer work until interrupted by the UART when an incoming character is available. You process the character and then return to the task you were working on before the interruption.

Only the polling method of serial interfacing is described in this chapter. The method, however, has problems. Although your computer can communicate with other computers, you may lose some incoming characters at speeds greater than 300 bps, especially when the screen fills and has to scroll up a line. These polling-based programs are for learning rather than general use. The interrupt method is discussed in greater detail in Chapter 11, "Interrupt Handlers."

Duplex Considerations

Before you can use the polling method of serial control, you must decide whether you want your communications to be full duplex or half duplex. You may recall from the terms introduced earlier in this chapter that in full-duplex communications, every character sent over the communications link is echoed back from the remote computer. A character that you see on-screen is the character received by the other computer, echoed back (or retransmitted) by the other computer. These characters travel in both directions simultaneously—you can send characters to the remote computer while it sends others back. Therefore, the outline for a full-duplex implementation of a simple terminal program is as follows:

1. If a character is at the keyboard, send it.
2. If a character is at the serial port, display it.
3. Go to step 1.

Although most computers use full-duplex communications, some use half-duplex (characters travel in only one direction at a time). Because the remote computer does not echo back (retransmit) the characters it receives, the concept of a half-duplex terminal program differs from that of the full-duplex version in only one minor point:

1. If a character is at the keyboard, send *and* display it.
2. If a character is at the serial port, display it.
3. Go to step 1.

The differences in implementation rest in the coding section that handles getting a character from the keyboard. In the next section, you will see how your coding is affected.

The Controlling Program: Term.c

At the highest conceptual level, the communications program is quite simple. The program in listing 7.1, written in C, implements the basic concepts discussed so far in this chapter.

Listing 7.1

```
/* Term.c */
#include <stdio.h>

#define FALSE 0
#define TRUE !FALSE

main()
{
```

continues

Listing 7.1 continued

```
        clrscr();
        printf("Simple Terminal Program\n\n\n");
        setup();
        while(TRUE){
            if(!keybd())
                exit(0);
            serial();
        }
    }
```

Except for clearing the terminal screen (accomplished by the cls() function) and setting up the port (through the setup() function), this is a simple application of the terminal procedure. It repeats forever, retrieving characters alternately from the keyboard (with the keybd() function) or from the serial port (with the serial() function).

Notice that, as all reasonable programs should, this program provides a way to end the program: if the keyboard-handling routine ever returns FALSE, the program ends. (As you will see in listing 7.4, the keyboard function has been programmed to return FALSE whenever the Shift-F1 key combination is pressed.)

Supporting Functions

Let's look at each of the supporting functions. Two versions of the keybd() function are provided: one handles full-duplex operation and the other handles half-duplex. Use whichever fits your needs.

Initialization: Setup( ) Function

Setup(), the first user-developed function, initializes the serial port. As presented here, the function uses a simplified, hard-coded setup for 1200 bps, 8 bits, no parity, and 1 stop bit. Listing 7.2 shows how this setup is implemented.

Listing 7.2

```
/* Setup.c */
#include <stdio.h>
#include <dos.h>

#define   COM1      0
#define   RS232     0x14
#define   SETUP     0x83   /* 1200 baud, 8 bits, no parity, */
                           /*   1 stop bit */
```

```
setup()

{
    union REGS regs;
    printf("Setup the serial port\n");
    regs.h.ah = 0;
    regs.x.dx = COM1;
    regs.h.al = SETUP;
    int86(RS232, &regs, &regs);
}
```

As the program comments state, setup() initializes COM1: to 1200 bps, an 8-bit word length, no parity, and 1 stop bit. Setup() uses the basic BIOS communications-port initialization function presented earlier in this chapter.

Setup() initializes COM1 using the basic BIOS communications-port initialization function presented earlier in this chapter.

An Initialization Alternative

The setup() function in listing 7.2 is not flexible—it can be used only to set the serial port to one specific bit rate and data format. As an alternative, you can create a more flexible setup() function to handle multiple initialization parameters (see listing 7.3).

Listing 7.3

```
/* Setup.c, version 2 */
#include <stdio.h>
#include <dos.h>

#define    RS232      0x14

#define    B300       0x40
#define    B1200      0x80
#define    B2400      0xa0

#define    NOPARITY   0x00
#define    EVEN       0x18
#define    ODD        0x08

#define    WORD7      0x02
#define    WORD8      0x03

#define    STOP1      0x00
#define    STOP2      0x40
```

continues

Listing 7.3 continued

```
setup(port,bps,word,parity,stop)

int   port,                   /* COM port, 0=COM1, 1=COM2, etc.*/
      bps,                    /* bps rate */
      word,                   /* word length */
      parity,                 /* 0 = off, 1 = EVEN, 2 = ODD */
      stop;                   /* number of stop bits */

{
      union REGS regs;
      unsigned char setup;

      setup = 0;
      printf("Set up the serial port\n");

      if(port!=0 && port!=1)
            return(-1);             /* bad COM port */

      switch(bps){
            case 300:
                  setup |= B300;
                  break;
            case 1200:
                  setup |= B1200;
                  break;
            case 2400:
                  setup |= B2400;
                  break;
            default:
                  return(-2);       /* not 300/1200/2400 bps */
      }

      if(word==7)
            setup |= WORD7;
      else if(word==8)
            setup |= WORD8;
      else
            return(-3);             /* not 7 or 8 bits */

      if(parity==0)
            setup |= NOPARITY;
      else if(parity==1)
            setup |= EVEN;
      else if(parity==2)
            setup |= ODD;
      else
            return(-4);             /* bad parity code */

      if(stop==1)
            setup |= STOP1;
```

```
        else if(stop==2)
            setup |= STOP2;
        else
            return(-5);              /* not 1 or 2 bits */

        regs.h.ah = 0;
        regs.x.dx = port;
        regs.h.al = setup;
        int86(RS232, &regs, &regs);  /* set up the port */
        return(0);
}
```

This longer version of setup() allows you to error-check each parameter and gives you greater flexibility in setting parameters. The version of term.c in listing 7.1 cannot use this alternate setup() function. It is written on the assumption that the setup values are built into the program. You can add it if you want to, but then you also must provide a means of setting the proper initialization parameters, either from the command line or as inputs to the program.

If you initialize a port other than COM1, you also must change the other supporting functions—xmit(), chrdy(), rch(), and loopback()—to support other communications ports. For testing, and until you feel comfortable with basic serial-port programming, you may want to use the limited version of setup() shown in listing 7.2, then experiment later with the version in listing 7.3.

Keyboard Control: Keybd( ) Function

Through the keybd() function, which manages the keyboard, you can determine whether a character has been entered at the keyboard and then, if it has, transmit the character (see listing 7.4).

Listing 7.4

```
/* Keybd.c */
#include <stdio.h>
#include <dos.h>

#define    FALSE     0
#define    TRUE      !FALSE
#define    SF1       84

keybd()

{
    char c;
```

continues

Listing 7.4 continued

```
        if((c=get_ch())>=0){
            /* There has been a keystroke */
            if(c == 0){
            /* The first character was zero */
                if((c = get_ch())==SF1)
                    return(FALSE);
                return(TRUE);
            }
            xmit(c);
        }
        return(TRUE);
    }
```

Operation of the get_ch() function, which is integral to keybd() operation, is discussed in the following section. What you need to understand now is that if get_ch() returns a 0, a special character or key combination has been entered from the keyboard. In this case, get_ch() must be called again to retrieve the keyboard scan code of the key pressed.

Keybd() specifically looks for this special character value (a zero); if keybd() finds the value, it looks for a second character. If the second character is Shift-F1, that character returns FALSE to the calling routine; if it is not Shift-F1 (for example, if you pressed another special key combination or non-ASCII character), the value TRUE is returned and the character entry is ignored.

If you enter a normal ASCII value from the keyboard, the get_ch() function does not return a 0; the character is transmitted (as entered, without alteration) through the xmit() function.

Keybd( ) for Half-Duplex Communications

Only one additional line is necessary to make the keybd() function compatible with half-duplex operations. Insert the following line immediately after the line containing the xmit() function:

```
putscrn(c);
```

Basically, this function displays a character to the screen. (You will learn about the exact development and usage of putscrn(c) later in this chapter.)

I/O Control: Get_ch( ) and Xmit( ) Functions

Two functions support the basic keybd() function: get_ch(), shown in listing 7.5, retrieves a character from the keyboard (if a character is available), and xmit() transmits a character through the serial port.

Listing 7.5

```
/* Get_ch.c */
#include <stdio.h>
#include <dos.h>

#define   MASK      0x7f
#define   ZFLAG     0x40

get_ch()

{
    union REGS regs;
    regs.h.ah = 6;
    regs.h.dl = 0xff;
    intdos(&regs,&regs);
    if(regs.x.flags & ZFLAG)
        return(-1);
    return(regs.h.al & MASK);
}
```

Get_ch() uses the DOS direct console I/O function (see Chapter 6) to input characters. You may recall that this DOS function sets the zero flag (ZFLAG) to indicate whether a character is available. Get_ch() tests the ZFLAG to see whether a character is available. If a character is available, it is in AL; the function returns it to the calling routine with the high-order bit set to 0. (The high-order bit is stripped by ANDing it with the MASK value. This masking process eliminates any possible problems with transmitting 8-bit characters.)

Xmit.c(), the other routine needed for the successful completion of keybd(), is shown in listing 7.6.

Listing 7.6

```
/* Xmit.c */
#include <stdio.h>
#include <dos.h>

#define   RS232     0x14
#define   WRITECH   1
#define   COM1      0

xmit(ch)

char ch;
{
    union REGS regs;
```

continues

Listing 7.6 continued

```
        regs.h.ah = WRITECH;
        regs.x.dx = COM1;
        regs.h.al = ch;
        int86(RS232, &regs, &regs);
}
```

The xmit() function simply writes the character to the serial port handler in the BIOS. As you can see from listing 7.6, this BIOS function requires the use of only three registers: AH contains the desired function number (1), AL is the character value to transmit (passed to xmit() by the calling routine), and DX is the communications port to use for the transmission (0, designating COM1). For additional information about this BIOS function, see the "BIOS Function Reference" section in Part V.

Receiving Characters: Serial( ) Function

Now that you understand keybd(), get_ch(), and xmit(), you are ready to examine the other major part of your terminal program—the part that receives and displays any incoming characters. Listing 7.7 shows this function, called serial().

Listing 7.7

```
/* Serial.c */
#include <stdio.h>
#include <dos.h>

serial()

{
    char c;

    if(chrdy()){
        c = rch();
        putscrn(c);
    }
}
```

Let's examine each of the three functions necessary for the successful completion of serial(): chrdy(), rch(), and putscrn().

Serial Port Status: Chrdy( ) Function

The chrdy() function checks whether an incoming character is available at the serial port. It uses BIOS Int 14h, Function 03h, which returns the communications port status. (For details about this BIOS function, see the "BIOS Function Reference" section in Part V.) Listing 7.8 shows how chrdy() is implemented.

Listing 7.8

```
/* Chrdy.c */
#include <stdio.h>
#include <dos.h>

#define    RS232      0x14
#define    STATUS     3
#define    COM1       0
#define    DTARDY     0x100

chrdy()

{
    union REGS regs;

    regs.h.ah = STATUS;
    regs.x.dx = COM1;
    int86(RS232, &regs, &regs);
    return(regs.x.ax & DTARDY);
}
```

Accessing Received Characters: Rch( ) Function

When chrdy() returns TRUE, informing you that a character is waiting, the rch() function is used to retrieve the character (see listing 7.9).

Listing 7.9

```
/* Rch.c */
#include <stdio.h>
#include <dos.h>

#define    COM1      0
#define    RS232     0x14
#define    READCH    2
#define    MASK      0x7f

rch()


{
    union REGS regs;

    regs.h.ah = READCH;
    regs.x.dx = COM1;
    int86(RS232, &regs, &regs);
    return(regs.h.al & MASK);            /* strip parity bit */
}
```

The high-order bit of the incoming character is stripped here, as it was in get_ch(), by ANDing the value in AL with the MASK value.

Screen Display: Putscrn( ) and Put_ch( ) Functions

The final portion of serial() is the routine for displaying a character on-screen. Because only printable characters can be displayed, putscrn(), shown in listing 7.10, is designed to ignore all control characters except a carriage return and a line feed.

Listing 7.10

```
/* Putscrn.c */
#include <stdio.h>
#include <dos.h>

#define    CR    0x0d
#define    LF    0x0a

putscrn(c)

char c;

{
    if(c>=' ' || c==CR || c==LF)
        put_ch(c);
}
```

Putscrn() calls put_ch() to write the character to the display, using the basic character-out DOS function. (For a detailed description of this function, see the "DOS Reference" section in Part V.) Listing 7.11 shows how put_ch() works.

Listing 7.11

```
/* Put_ch.c */
#include <stdio.h>
#include <dos.h>

#define   CHAROUT    2

put_ch(c)

char c;

{
    union REGS regs;
    regs.h.ah = CHAROUT;
    regs.h.dl = c;
    intdos(&regs,&regs);
}
```

Using Term.c

Now that you have learned about each of the functions needed for term.c, enter them and try using term.c. You will discover that, although your computer can communicate with other computers, you may lose some of the incoming characters if more than a few arrive in quick succession. A short message of only one or two lines probably will overload the program. What's wrong?

Several problems exist:

- Because the terminal program has not been programmed for efficiency, it includes many subroutine calls—each of which uses time. You could speed up the program by coding it with fewer individual functions.

- DOS function calls were used to handle the keyboard and screen. Although you are not likely to type faster than the characters can be read, the time spent on DOS function calls is time taken away from the needs of the serial channel.

- The BIOS function calls used are not spectacularly efficient.

Despite these problems, we will not change the program's basic design—its primary purpose is to show *how* to use the BIOS and DOS functions in the program. But you *can* speed up the program by changing it so that it can work directly with the 8250 chip. This may reduce, but will not eliminate, the loss of incoming characters at speeds above 300 bps; the loss is due largely to the time the BIOS routines require to scroll the screen, and nothing can be done (short of switching to interrupt-driven input as we do in Chapter 11) to get around that problem.

Directly Accessing the 8250 UART

Direct UART access is one way to make the program tighter and faster, but you need to know when direct access is suitable and justifiable. You should be aware of some important trade-offs when you go directly to the UART.

Working directly at the hardware level

- Results in the greatest speed increases you can get from the computer

- Provides the greatest programming flexibility

- Is the most machine-dependent type of programming and is most susceptible to compatibility problems when you transfer the program to another type of computer

IBM's promise to maintain serial-interface compatibility with the 8250 UART may be a great comfort if you work with computers produced by IBM. However, this promise is not a guarantee. Nor is it a safe bet when you work with other computers that use DOS. Although most of these computers currently use the 8250, be on the lookout for subtle differences in some models that use different UARTs.

As we mentioned in the preceding section, the version of term.c in listing 7.1 causes loss of incoming characters because that version cannot keep up with a steady stream of characters. Many programmers cannot get the required performance from the DOS or BIOS serial-interface functions; they have solved this dilemma by always working directly with the 8250. To do this, you must access it through I/O ports. Although some languages do not provide ways to access the I/O ports, every language used in this book does.

Assembly

In assembly language, you access the ports with the IN and OUT instructions: IN reads a word or byte into the AL or AX register; OUT writes a word or byte from the AL or AX register to the port. Variations of the OUT instruction include OUTS (BL or CX registers), OUTSB (byte from DS:[SI]), and OUTSW (word from DS:[SI]).

C

In Microsoft and Borland C++, the `inport` and `outport` functions input or output words to a port. `Inportb` and `outportb` do the same for bytes.

BASIC

Basic functions INP and OUT read bytes from or write bytes to a port.

Pascal

Unlike the other languages, Pascal has no function for accessing the ports. Instead, Turbo Pascal treats the ports as an array (`Port` for bytes, `Portw` for words). Input and output to the port is accomplished by reading and writing to the array.

Modifying Term.c

To modify the terminal program, you simply change the three serial-port routines: `chrdy()`, `xmit()`, and `rch()`. You can (and will) safely leave control of the setup to the BIOS function.

When you access the 8250 directly, `chrdy()` is simplified considerably (see listing 7.12).

Listing 7.12

```
/* Chrdy.c */
#include <stdio.h>

#define    COM1      0x3f8
#define    LSR       5
#define    DTARDY    0x01

chrdy()

{
    return(inportb(COM1+LSR) & DTARDY);
}
```

The `rch()` function for reading a character also is simplified considerably (see listing 7.13).

Listing 7.13

```c
/* Rch.c, version 2 */
#include <stdio.h>

#define   COM1      0x3f8
#define   RDR       0
#define   MASK      0x7f

rch()

{
     return(inportb(COM1+RDR) & MASK);
}
```

The modified `xmit()` function takes the form shown in listing 7.14.

Listing 7.14

```c
/* Xmit.c, version 2 */
#include <stdio.h>

#define   COM1      0x3f8
#define   LSR       5
#define   THR       0
#define   THRRDY    0x20

xmit(ch)

char ch;

{
     register int cnt;

     cnt = 0;
     while(!(inportb(COM1+LSR) & THRRDY) && cnt < 10000) cnt++;
     if(cnt>=10000)
          return(-1);
     outportb(COM1+THR,ch);
     return(0);
}
```

The modified version of `xmit()` is slightly more complicated than the earlier version because you need to be sure that the transmitter holding register (THR) is ready for a character before you write one to it. A maximum-retry counter is set to prevent the system from locking into an infinite loop.

The other `term.c` functions do not need to be modified to make the program work. My comments about the BIOS version of `term.c` and why it is slow still apply here. Even when you access the 8250 UART directly, you will not have enough speed to handle 1200 bps without problems.

In this instance, the problems are caused by the method used for handling the incoming serial characters. As you may recall, a polling method is used in the examples in this chapter. In other words, the program sequentially checks the keyboard, then the serial interface, ad infinitum. If more than one character arrives at the serial port while the program's attention is focused on the keyboard or, more usually, the screen, those incoming characters may be lost before the program has a chance to record them. Chapter 11, "Interrupt Handlers," shows you a more reliable method of serial programming, using interrupts.

Loopback Testing

When you use the modified version of `term.c`, you can also add a function that allows loopback testing. In other words, the UART will "think" that it is talking to a remote computer; what really happens is a local echo (in the UART) of what is being sent to the serial interface. The process is implemented as shown in listing 7.15.

Listing 7.15

```
#include <stdio.h>
#define    MCR        0x3fc
#define    LOOPBACK   0x10
loopback()
{
    int  mcr_value;
    printf("Toggling Loopback\n");
    inportb(MCR,mcr_value);
    mcr_value = mcr_value ^ LOOPBACK;
    outportb(MCR,mcr_value);
    mcr_value = mcr_value & LOOPBACK;
    printf("Loopback ");
    if(mcr_value == 0)
        printf("cleared");
    else
        printf("set");
    printf(" ... continuing\n");
}
```

DOS
PROGRAMMING

Invoking loopback() from term.c (immediately after the setup() function is called) causes all characters you type to be echoed back instead of transmitted over the serial communications link. Why use loopback()? It is helpful for testing to make sure that communications software functions properly before you test the software on-line with another computer.

Note also that this routine directly accesses the modem control register (MCR) for COM1. After your computer has been set in loopback mode with this function, the only way to turn off loopback is to turn off your computer and then turn it on again, or to invoke loopback() a second time. (The best place to add this second loopback() to the term.c program is immediately preceding the final closing brace.)

Evaluation of the Serial I/O Services

The basic serial I/O services are wholly inadequate for the job of high-performance communications applications. In high-speed (greater than 1200 bps), error-free file transfers or multihost, real-time terminal operations, speed is essential and should not be sacrificed (not lightly, at any rate) to achieve compatibility. To achieve throughput and responsiveness, direct access to hardware is often more justifiable in communications than in other applications.

The basic term.c terminal program is adequate but cannot handle high speeds. Before you can improve its capability, you need to learn about interrupts and interrupt handlers. In Chapter 11 you will learn how to build a significant terminal program: an interrupt-driven communications program with which you can do (without problems) most of the tasks you need to do.

We do not mean that a noninterrupt-driven program is useless. If you can put together a program in which the PC's undivided attention is devoted to the communications link, you can manage safely without interrupts. A package created on exactly this basis is used nationwide as a master control system; it provides control of a PC from a UNIX-based system. All communications to the PC are in packets and are either file transfers or commands to be executed. This program, which was built in a few hours by programmers using only the simplest techniques, has been in use for several years. It runs at speeds as high as 19,200 bps. Simple, direct programming can sometimes be the best solution to problems. But note that this package does not display received data on the screen and does not process packets too large to fit entirely in RAM.

Summary

This chapter has focused on the use and control of the IBM microcomputer family's serial interface. This interface, based on the 8250 UART, offers programmers a good deal of hands-off control over a serial communications link.

Despite the capabilities and freedom presented by the 8250, the task of programming serial-communications software can be tedious and frustrating. Although BIOS and DOS services can be used to simplify the task somewhat, their value is diminished because they offer only limited access to the 8250's power. Furthermore, they introduce overhead that can seriously degrade the performance of time-critical software.

PROGRAMMING

PROGRAMMING

Part III

Disks, Directories, and Files

Disks

When you learn a programming language, you usually start by learning about basic input and output (as you did by reading Chapters 5, 6, and 7). You learn how to get data into and out of a computer, and you play with it.

Before you can begin to write serious programs, you need to learn about files (and you will, in Chapter 9, "Directories and Files") because most programs work with different types of files. Some programs work directly with the disk and directory structure. To lay the groundwork for Chapter 9, let's examine disks.

First you will learn how basic magnetic-disk technology works. Floppy disks and hard disks differ in capacity but are alike in the way they can be accessed through the DOS functions. The function calls used to open or close files, read or write files, or access directories are the same on any disk. As you work through this chapter, you will learn about tracks, sectors, and clusters and the role they play when you build a program.

Then, by applying your newfound knowledge about how disks work, you will produce a basic track-formatting function to reformat disks with. Using this function requires special caution, however; you can easily make a mistake that may destroy critical disks.

Disk Internals

Anyone who uses a PC works with disks. No matter what kind of system you have, you most likely store information on disks. Given the importance of disks in the operation of personal computers, you would expect people to know how disks work—but they don't. If you plan to work on the disks themselves (even if only to examine their structure or the data stored on them), you should understand how they work.

You can think of a disk as a collection of files—not unlike a drawer in a file cabinet. Each disk holds many files, and you can access any file "folder" directly.

During the formatting process, the operating system imposes the familiar file structure on your disks. DOS creates an index to the files (the directory) as well as a way to determine the files' locations on the disk (the file allocation table, or FAT). DOS records information about the disk's layout (the boot record), which—even on disks without the system files—includes a start-up program.

Basically, each side of a disk is a magnetically coated surface. This surface is magnetized by a read/write head that passes over the rotating disk. Double-sided disks have two recording surfaces; single-sided disks have only one (although both sides are coated, only one side is certified to meet quality standards). Hard disks typically have two to four platters, or disks, with recording surfaces on both sides.

On any disk drive, the read/write head or heads are moved across the disk surface by a special *stepper motor*. This motor has precisely defined stops (called *steps*) at which the head comes to rest. Each of these resting points defines a *track* on which data can be recorded. Most hard disks have a multiple-platter system in which the heads move together on all platters. The tracks (on all platters) corresponding to one step of the stepper motor are referred to as a *cylinder*.

The FORMAT program divides the tracks into 512-byte sectors to create more manageable disk segments: 8 or 9 sectors per track on a floppy disk; 17 sectors per track on a hard disk.

DOS allocates space to a file in units called *clusters*. Each cluster consists of two to eight sectors, depending on the type of disk. When a file needs additional disk space, the operating system allocates one or more additional clusters to that file. Figure 8.1 shows a typical disk platter layout.

The disk is divided into the following five important areas:

- Partition table

- Boot record

- File allocation table (FAT)

- Directory

- Data space

All of these are discussed in the following sections.

Fig. 8.1. *A disk platter (showing a track, sector, and cluster).*

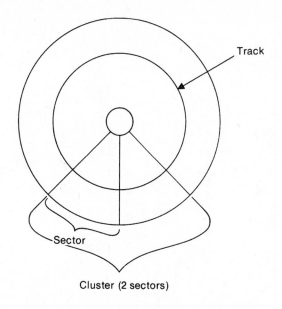

Cluster (2 sectors)

The Partition Table

Almost every hard disk has a master record that resides at cylinder (track) 0, head (side) 0, sector 1. (The few which do not are eligible for museum status; it is unlikely that you will run into one in use.) This master record is responsible for reading and deciphering the disk partition table contained at the end of the master record. Control then passes to the boot record of the currently bootable hard disk partition, as indicated in the partition table. If a disk has no such master record, its place is taken by the *boot record*, which is discussed in the next section.

The partition table describes how the hard disk is divided. To be recognizable by programs such as FDISK, this partition table must conform to a standard layout. As many as four partitions can be on a hard disk, each with a corresponding entry in the partition table. Figure 8.2 shows a memory dump of the master boot record from a COMPAQ Deskpro 286. Notice the partition table information stored at the end of the sector. Entries begin at offset 01BEh for partition 1, 01CEh for partition 2, 01DEh for partition 3, and 01EEh for partition 4. The last two bytes of the sector (those immediately following the partition table at offset 01FEh) are a signature word for the sector, in this case AA55h.

Fig. 8.2. *Hard disk master boot record, disk partition table.*

```
0000  33 C0 8E D8 8E C0 FA 8E-D0 BC 00 7C FB 8B F4 BF   3..........|....
0010  00 06 B9 00 01 FC F3 A5-50 B8 1E 06 50 CB B9 04   ........P...P...
0020  00 BE BE 07 80 3C 80 74-2C 83 C6 10 E2 F6 B4 0F   .....<.t,.......
0030  CD 10 B3 07 BE 97 06 B9-78 00 AC B4 0E CD 10 E2   ........x.......
0040  F9 C7 06 72 04 34 12 B8-FF FF 50 1E B4 0F CD 10   ...r.4....P.....
0050  32 E4 CD 16 CB B2 80 8B-DC 8A 74 01 BD 05 00 8B   2.........t.....
0060  4C 02 B8 01 02 CD 13 73-1E 80 FC 11 75 10 1E B8   L......s....u...
0070  00 F0 8E D8 33 FF 81 7D-EA 43 4F 1F 74 09 32 E4   ....3..}.CO.t.2.
0080  CD 13 4D 75 DD EB A7 81-BF FE 01 55 AA 75 9F 8B   ..Mu.......U.u..
0090  EE 1E 53 CB 43 52 4A 0D-0A 45 72 72 6F 72 20 6C   ..S.CRJ..Error 1
00A0  6F 61 64 69 6E 67 20 6F-70 65 72 61 74 69 6E 67   oading operating
00B0  20 73 79 73 74 65 6D 20-66 72 6F 6D 20 66 69 78    system from fix
00C0  65 64 20 64 69 73 6B 2E-0D 0A 0D 0A 49 6E 73 65   ed disk.....Inse
00D0  72 74 20 43 4F 4D 50 41-51 20 44 4F 53 20 64 69   rt COMPAQ DOS di
00E0  73 6B 65 74 74 65 20 69-6E 20 64 72 69 76 65 20   skette in drive
00F0  41 2E 0D 0A 50 72 65 73-73 20 61 6E 79 20 6B 65   A...Press any ke
0100  79 20 77 68 65 6E 20 72-65 61 64 79 3A 20 07 00   y when ready: ..
0110  00 00 00 00 00 00 00 00-00 00 00 00 00 00 00 00   ................
0120  00 00 00 00 00 00 00 00-00 00 00 00 00 00 00 00   ................
0130  00 00 00 00 00 00 00 00-00 00 00 00 00 00 00 00   ................
0140  00 00 00 00 00 00 00 00-00 00 00 00 00 00 00 00   ................
0150  00 00 00 00 00 00 00 00-00 00 00 00 00 00 00 00   ................
0160  00 00 00 00 00 00 00 00-00 00 00 00 00 00 00 00   ................
0170  00 00 00 00 00 00 00 00-00 00 00 00 00 00 00 00   ................
0180  00 00 00 00 00 00 00 00-00 00 00 00 00 00 00 00   ................
0190  00 00 00 00 00 00 00 00-00 00 00 00 00 00 00 00   ................
01A0  00 00 00 00 00 00 00 00-00 00 00 00 00 00 00 00   ................
01B0  00 00 00 00 00 00 00 00-00 00 00 00 00 00 80 01   ................
01C0  01 00 04 04 51 E9 11 00-00 00 A1 A2 00 00 00 00   ....Q...........
01D0  41 EA 05 04 D1 D2 B2 A2-00 00 5D A2 00 00 00 00   A.........].....
01E0  00 00 00 00 00 00 00 00-00 00 00 00 00 00 00 00   ................
01F0  00 00 00 00 00 00 00 00-00 00 00 00 00 00 55 AA   ..............U.
```

— Partition table

Notice that the partition table information shown in figure 8.2 has only two entries filled in—there are only two partitions on this hard disk. Each entry in the partition table is 16 bytes long. Table 8.1 details the layout for each partition table entry, using sample values taken from the partition table shown in figure 8.2.

Notice the information stored in the partition table. Most of this information describes boundaries for each partition, but two fields, the boot indicator and the system ID, are of particular interest. The boot indicator signals whether the partition is bootable. Only one of the four possible partitions can be labeled as bootable. The system ID is used to designate the partition type. Table 8.1 indicates several possible system ID values, but various other operating systems (such as XENIX, UNIX, and Pick) will necessarily expand the possible system ID list.

Because this table must be recognized not only by DOS but also by other operating systems, its format is not subject to change from one DOS version to another (or from one operating system to another); any tampering with the partition table format would destroy all chance of selling the software commercially.

Table 8.1. *Hard Disk Partition Table Entry Layout*

Byte Offset	Field Length	Sample Value	Meaning
00h	Byte	80h	Boot indicator 00h = Nonbootable 80h = Bootable
01h	Byte	01h	Starting head
02h	Byte	01h	Starting sector (bits 0-5; bits 6-7 are bits "8 and 9" for cylinder)
03h	Byte	00h	Starting cylinder (low 8)
04h	Byte	04h	System ID 00h = Unknown 01h = DOS, 12-bit FAT 04h = DOS, 16-bit FAT 05h = DOS, extended disk, 16-bit FAT
05h	Byte	04h	Ending head
06h	Byte	51h (11)	Ending sector (bits 0-5; bits 6-7 are bits "8 and 9" for cylinder)
07h	Byte	E9h (1E9)	Ending cylinder (low 8)
08h	Double word	00000011	First partition sector
0Ch	Double word	0000A2A1	Sectors in partition

During the system boot, the BIOS consults the first sector on the disk to continue with the booting process. With a floppy disk, this is the boot sector (see the following section). With a hard disk, this first sector is the master record described earlier. Within this master record, the partition table is located and the BIOS determines (by the boot-indicator fields) which partition is bootable. After the bootable partition has been located, control is passed to the boot sector of that partition and booting continues as it would for a floppy disk.

Disk partitioning establishes a set of logical disks on the hard disk. Each logical disk acts like a smaller disk drive (and is assigned a drive letter by the disk driver). A single hard disk can use all logical drives for one operating system, or each logical drive can hold a different one. Systems often have MS-DOS in one partition and XENIX in another—not unlike having two computers for the price of one.

Partitioning is often necessary when you use hard disks with a capacity greater than 32M. Most versions of DOS before 4.x are limited to 32M or less in a single partition. By using multiple partitions, you can make use of disks as large as 160M. Commercial utilities are available to eliminate the 32M limit with special disk drivers. But because the disks frequently cannot be used without the drivers, this can lead to problems if you try to run other operating systems or boot from floppy disks.

One of the major features of DOS Version 4 is that it removes the 32M limit on the size of a hard disk. By permitting sector numbers to be as large as 32 bits and permitting the file allocation table to grow to 64K sectors, the disk capacity limit was pushed into the gigabyte region.

Because of this, you are not *required* to do partitioning when you use a large hard disk and DOS Version 4. But you can do so if you prefer to organize your system in the traditional manner or you maintain multiple operating systems.

The Boot Record

When the system has determined where to locate the boot record for the bootable disk partition, the BIOS loads the boot record into memory. Typical boot sectors for a floppy disk are shown in figure 8.3; note how they differ from one DOS version to another.

Fig. 8.3. *Boot sector for a floppy disk.*

A) Boot sector layout for V2 disk.

```
            Jump instruction      System name        BPB

0000   E9 8D 00 00 00 00 00 00-00 00 00 00 02 02 01 00   ................
0010   02 70 00 D0 02 FD 02 00-09 00 02 00 00 00 00 00   .p..............
0020   00 DF 02 25 02 0F 2A FF-50 F6 00 02 0D 0A 4E 6F   ...%..*.P.....No
0030   6E 2D 53 79 73 74 65 6D-20 64 69 73 6B 20 6F 72   n-System disk or
0040   20 64 69 73 6B 20 65 72-72 6F 72 2E 0D 0A 52 65    disk error...Re
0050   70 6C 61 63 65 20 61 6E-64 20 70 72 65 73 73 20   place and press
0060   61 6E 79 20 6B 65 79 20-77 68 65 6E 20 72 65 61   any key when rea
0070   64 79 0D 0A 07 00 49 4F-20 20 20 20 20 20 53 59   dy....IO     SY
0080   53 4D 53 44 4F 53 20 20-20 53 59 53 00 00 00 00   SMSDOS   SYS....
0090   FC 33 C0 8E D8 8E C0 FA-8E D0 BC 00 7C FB A1 78   .3..........|..x
00A0   00 A3 8C 7C A1 7A 00 A3-8E 7C 8D 06 21 7C A3 78   ...|.z...|..!|.x
00B0   00 8C 1E 7A 00 E8 38 00-A1 8E 7C A3 7A 00 A1 8C   ...z..8...|.z...
00C0   7C A3 78 00 8A 16 20 7C-EA 00 00 70 00 A1 8E 7C   |.x... |...p...|
00D0   A3 7A 00 A1 8C 7C A3 78-00 BE 2C 7C AC 0A C0 74   .z...|.x..,|...t
00E0   09 B4 0E BB 07 00 CD 10-EB F2 B4 00 CD 16 CD 19   ................
00F0   33 C0 CD 13 72 D7 8B 36-0E 7C A0 10 7C B4 00 F7   3...r..6.|..|...
0100   26 16 7C 03 F0 8B EE BB-20 00 A1 11 7C F7 E3 B1   &.|...... ...|...
0110   09 05 FF 01 D3 E8 03 E8-8D 1E 00 05 B8 01 00 E8   ................
0120   3B 00 BE 76 7C BF 00 05-B9 0B 00 F3 A6 74 02 EB   ;..v|........t..
0130   9C BF 20 05 B9 0B 00 F3-A6 74 02 EB 90 BB 00 07   .. ......t......
0140   8B F5 A1 1C 05 B1 09 05-FF 01 D3 E8 E8 0E 00 8B   ................
0150   1E 1C 7C 03 DD 8B 0E 1E-7C 83 D1 00 C3 96 03 06   ..|.....|.......
0160   1C 7C 8B 16 1E 7C 83 D2-00 F7 36 18 7C 8B CA 41   .|...|....6.|..A
0170   BA 00 00 F7 36 1A 7C 8A-E8 B0 00 D1 E8 D1 E8 8A   ....6.|.........
0180   E1 0A C8 8A F2 8A 16 20-7C A0 18 7C 2A C4 FE C0   ....... |..|*...
0190   B4 00 3B F0 73 02 8B C6-BF 03 00 50 B4 02 CD 13   ..;.s......P....
01A0   58 73 06 4F 75 F5 E9 24-FF 2B F0 74 26 8A E0 B0   Xs.Ou..$.+.t&...
01B0   00 D1 E0 03 D8 80 E1 C0-80 C9 01 80 C6 01 3A 36   ..............:6
01C0   1A 7C 75 0A B6 00 80 C5-01 73 03 80 C1 40 A1 18   .|u......s...@..
01D0   7C EB BF C3 00 00 00 00-00 00 00 00 00 00 00 00   |...............
01E0   00 00 00 00 00 00 00 00-00 00 00 00 00 00 00 00   ................
01F0   00 00 00 00 00 00 00 00-00 00 00 00 00 00 55 AA   ..............U.
```

Loader routine

B) Boot sector layout for MS-DOS 3.2

Jump instruction   System name   BPB

```
0000 EB 34 90 4D 53 44 4F 53-33 2E 32 00 02 04 01 00   k4.MSDOS 3.2.....
0010 02 00 02 BC CB F8 33 00-11 00 09 00 11 00 80 00   ...<Kx3. ........
0020 00 00 00 00 00 00 00 00-00 00 00 00 00 00 00 0F   ........ ........
0030 00 00 00 00 01 00 FA 33-C0 8E D0 BC 00 7C 16 07   ......z3 @.P<.|..
0040 BB 78 00 36 C5 37 1E 56-16 53 BF 2B 7C B9 0B 00   ;x.6E7.V .S?+|9..
0050 FC AC 26 80 3D 00 74 03-26 8A 05 AA 8A C4 E2 F1   |,&.=.t. &..*.Dbq
0060 06 1F 89 47 02 C7 07 2B-7C FB 8A 16 FD 7D CD 13   ...G.G.+ |{.}}M.
0070 72 66 A0 10 7C 98 F7 26-16 7C 03 06 1C 7C 03 06   rf .|.w& .|...|..
0080 0E 7C A3 3F 7C A3 37 7C-B8 20 00 F7 26 11 7C 8B   .|#?|#7| 8 .w&.|.
0090 1E 0B 7C 03 C3 48 F7 F3-01 06 37 7C BB 00 05 A1   ..|.CHws ..7|;..!
00A0 3F 7C E8 94 00 B0 01 E8-A9 00 72 19 8B FB B9 0B   ?|h..O.h ).r..{9.
00B0 00 BE D5 7D F3 A6 75 0D-8D 7F 20 BE E0 7D B9 0B   .>U}s&u. .: >'}9.
00C0 00 F3 A6 74 18 BE 76 7D-E8 61 00 32 E4 CD 16 5E   .s&t.>v} ha.2dM.^
00D0 1F 8F 04 8F 44 02 CD 19-BE BF 7D EB EB A1 1C 05   ....D.M. >?}kk!..
00E0 33 D2 F7 36 0B 7C FE C0-A2 3C 7C A1 37 7C A3 3D   3Rw6.|\@ "<|!7|#=
00F0 7C BB 00 07 A1 37 7C E8-3F 00 A1 18 7C 2A 06 3B   |;..!7|h ?.!.|*.;
0100 7C 40 50 E8 4D 00 58 72-CF 28 06 3C 7C 76 0C 01   |@PhM.Xr O(.<|v..
0110 06 37 7C F7 26 0B 7C 03-D8 EB D9 8A 2E 15 7C 8A   .7|w&.|. XkY...|.
0120 16 FD 7D 8B 1E 3D 7C EA-00 00 70 00 AC 0A C0 74   .}}..=|j ..p.,.@t
0130 21 B4 0E B3 FF C0 10 EB-F3 33 D2 F7 36 18 7C FE   !4.3:M.k s3Rw6.|.
0140 C2 88 16 3B 7C 33 D2 F7-36 1A 7C 88 16 2A 7C A3   B..;|3Rw 6.|..*|#
0150 39 7C C3 B4 02 8B 16 39-7C 8A EA D0 CE D0 CE 80   9|C4...9 |.jPNPN.
0160 E6 C0 8A 0E 3B 7C 80 E1-3F 0A CE 8A 36 2A 7C 8A   f@..;|.a ?.N.6*|.
0170 16 FD 7D CD 13 C3 0D 0A-4E 6F 6E 2D 53 79 73 74   .}}M.C.. Non-Syst
0180 65 6D 20 64 69 73 6B 20-6F 72 20 64 69 73 6B 20   em disk  or disk
0190 65 72 72 6F 72 0D 0A 52-65 70 6C 61 63 65 20 61   error..R eplace a
01A0 6E 64 20 73 74 72 69 6B-65 20 61 6E 79 20 6B 65   nd strik e any ke
01B0 79 20 77 68 65 6E 20 72-65 61 64 79 0D 0A 00 0D   y when r eady....
01C0 0A 44 69 73 6B 20 42 6F-6F 74 20 66 61 69 6C 75   .Disk Bo ot failu
01D0 72 65 0D 0A 00 49 4F 20-20 20 20 20 20 53 59 53   re...IO     SYS
01E0 4D 53 44 4F 53 20 20 20-53 59 53 00 00 00 00 00   MSDOS   SYS.....
01F0 00 00 00 00 00 00 00 00-00 00 00 00 00 80 55 AA   ........ ......U*
```

Loader routine

C) Boot sector layout for IBM DOS 4.01

Jump instruction   System name   BPB

```
0000 EB 3C 90 49 42 4D 20 20-34 2E 30 00 02 01 01 00   k<.IBM  4.0.....
0010 02 70 00 D0 02 FD 03 00-09 00 02 00 00 00 00 00   .p.P.}.. ........
0020 00 00 00 00 00 00 29 CC-10 3D 20 4E 4F 20 4E 41   ......)L .= NO NA
0030 4D 45 20 20 20 20 46 41-54 31 32 20 20 20 FA 33   ME    FA T12   z3
0040 C0 8E D0 BC 00 7C 16 07-BB 78 00 36 C5 37 1E 56   @.P<.|.. ;x.6E7.V
0050 16 53 BF 3E 7C B9 0B 00-FC F3 A4 06 1F C6 45 FE   .S?>|9.. |s$..FE\
0060 0F 8B 0E 18 7C 88 4D F9-89 47 02 C7 07 3E 7C FB   ....|.My .G.G.>|{
0070 CD 13 72 7C 33 C0 39 06-13 7C 74 08 8B 0E 13 7C   M.r|3a9. .|t....|
0080 89 0E 20 7C A0 10 7C F7-26 16 7C 03 06 1C 7C 13   .. | .|w &.|....|.
0090 16 1E 7C 03 06 0E 7C 83-D2 00 A3 50 7C 89 16 52   ..|...|. R.#P|..R
00A0 7C A3 49 7C 89 16 4B 7C-B8 20 00 F7 26 11 7C 8B   |#I|..K| 8 .w&.|.
00B0 1E 0B 7C 03 C3 48 F7 F3-01 06 49 7C 83 16 4B 7C   ..|.CHws ..I|..K|
00C0 00 BB 00 05 8B 16 52 7C-A1 50 7C E8 87 00 72 20   .;...R| !P|h..r
00D0 B0 01 E8 A1 00 72 19 8B-FB B9 0B 00 BE DB 7D F3   O.h!.r.. {9.>[}s
00E0 A6 75 0D 8D 7F 20 BE E6-7D B9 0B 00 F3 A6 74 18   &u..: >f }9..s&t.
00F0 BE 93 7D E8 51 00 32 E4-CD 16 5E 1F 8F 04 8F 44   >.}hQ.2d M.#....D
0100 02 CD 19 58 58 58 EB E8-BB 00 07 B9 03 00 A1 49   .M.XXXkh ;..9..!I
0110 7C 8B 16 4B 7C 50 52 51-E8 3A 00 72 E6 B0 01 E8   |..K|PRQ h:.rf0.h
0120 54 00 59 5A 58 72 C9 05-01 00 83 D2 00 03 1E 0B   T.YZXrI. ...R....
0130 7C E2 E2 8A 2E 15 7C 8A-16 24 7C 8B 1E 49 7C A1   |bb...|. .$|..I|!
0140 4B 7C EA 00 00 70 00 AC-0A C0 74 29 B4 0E BB 07   K|j..p., .@t)4.;.
0150 00 CD 10 EB F2 3B 16 18-7C 73 19 F7 36 18 7C FE   .M.kr;.. |s.w6.|\
0160 C2 88 16 4F 7C 33 D2 F7-36 1A 7C 88 16 25 7C A3   B..O|3Rw 6.|..%|#
0170 4D 7C F8 C3 F9 C3 B4 02-8B 16 4D 7C B1 06 D2 E6   M|xCyC4. ..M|1.Rf
0180 0A 36 4F 7C 8B CA 86 E9-8A 16 24 7C 8A 36 25 7C   .6O|.J.i ..$|.6¥|
0190 CD 13 C3 0D 0A 4E 6F 6E-2D 53 79 73 74 65 6D 20   M.C..Non -System
01A0 64 69 73 6B 20 6F 72 20-64 69 73 6B 20 65 72 72   disk or  disk err
01B0 6F 72 0D 0A 52 65 70 6C-61 63 65 20 61 6E 64 20   or..Repl ace and
01C0 70 72 65 73 73 20 61 6E-79 20 6B 65 79 20 77 68   press an y key wh
01D0 65 6E 20 72 65 61 64 79-0D 0A 00 49 42 4D 42 49   en ready ...IBMBI
01E0 4F 20 20 43 4F 4D 49 42-4D 44 4F 53 20 20 43 4F   O  COMIB MDOS  CO
01F0 4D 00 00 00 00 00 00 00-00 00 00 00 00 00 55 AA   M....... ......U*
```

Loader routine

D) Boot sector layout for MS-DOS DOS 5.0

Jump instruction   System name   BPB

```
0000  EB 3C 90 4D 53 44 4F 53 35 2E 30 00 02 04 01 00   k<.MSDOS5.O.....
0010  02 00 02 77 FF F8 40 00 11 00 08 00 11 00 00 00   ...w.x@.........
0020  00 00 00 00 80 00 29 E0 7D EF 16 20 20 20 20 20   ......)'}o.
0030  20 20 20 20 20 20 46 41 54 31 36 20 20 20 FA 33        FAT16   z3
0040  C0 8E D0 BC 00 7C 16 07 BB 78 00 36 C5 37 1E 56   @.P<.|..;x.6E7.V
0050  16 53 BF 3E 7C B9 0B 00 FC F3 A4 06 1F C6 45 FE   .S?>|9..|s$..FE~
0060  0F 8B 0E 18 7C 88 4D F9 89 47 02 C7 07 3E 7C FB   ....|.My.G.G.>|{
0070  CD 13 72 79 33 C0 39 06 13 7C 74 08 8B 0E 13 7C   M.ry3@9..|t....|
0080  89 0E 20 7C A0 10 7C F7 26 16 7C 03 06 1C 7C 13   .. | .|w&.|...|.
0090  16 1E 7C 03 06 0E 7C 83 D2 00 A3 50 7C 89 16 52   ..|...|.R.#P|..R
00A0  7C A3 49 7C 89 16 4B 7C B8 20 00 F7 26 11 7C 8B   |#I|..K|8 .w&.|.
00B0  1E 0B 7C 03 C3 48 F7 F3 01 06 49 7C 83 16 4B 7C   ..|.CHws..I|..K|
00C0  00 BB 00 05 8B 16 52 7C A1 50 7C E8 92 00 72 1D   .;....R|!P|h..r.
00D0  B0 01 E8 AC 00 72 16 8B FB B9 0B 00 BE E6 7D F3   0.h,.r..{9..>f}s
00E0  A6 75 0A 8D 7F 20 B9 0B 00 F3 A6 74 18 BE 9E 7D   &u... 9..s&t.>.}
00F0  E8 5F 00 33 C0 CD 16 5E 1F 8F 04 8F 44 02 CD 19   h_.3@M.^...D.M.
0100  58 58 58 EB E8 8B 47 1A 48 48 8A 1E 0D 7C 32 FF   XXXkh.G.HH...|2.
0110  F7 E3 03 06 49 7C 13 16 4B 7C BB 00 07 B9 03 00   wc..I|..K|;..9..
0120  50 52 51 E8 3A 00 72 D8 B0 01 E8 54 00 59 5A 58   PRQh:.rX0.hT.YZX
0130  72 BB 05 01 00 83 D2 00 03 1E 0B 7C E2 E2 8A 2E   r;....R....|bb..
0140  15 7C 8A 16 24 7C 8B 1E 49 7C A1 4B 7C EA 00 00   .|..$|.I|!K|j..
0150  70 00 AC 0A C0 74 29 B4 0E BB 07 00 CD 10 1B F2   p.,.@t)4.;..M..r
0160  3B 16 18 7C 73 19 F7 36 18 7C FE C2 88 16 4F 7C   ;..|s.w6.|~B..0|
0170  33 D2 F7 36 1A 7C 88 16 25 7C A3 4D 7C F8 C3 F9   3Rw6.|..%|#M|xCy
0180  C3 B4 02 8B 16 4D 7C B1 06 D2 E6 0A 36 4F 7C 8B   C4...M|1.Rf.60|.
0190  CA 86 E9 8A 16 24 7C 8A 36 25 7C CD 13 C3 0D 0A   J.i..$|.6%|M.C..
01A0  4E 6F 6E 2D 53 79 73 74 65 6D 20 64 69 73 6B 20   Non-System disk
01B0  6F 72 20 64 69 73 6B 20 65 72 72 6F 72 0D 0A 52   or disk error..R
01C0  65 70 6C 61 63 65 20 61 6E 64 20 70 72 65 73 73   eplace and press
01D0  20 61 6E 79 20 6B 65 79 20 77 68 65 6E 20 72 65    any key when re
01E0  61 64 79 0D 0A 00 49 4F 20 20 20 20 20 20 53 59   ady...IO      SY
01F0  53 4D 53 44 4F 53 20 20 20 53 59 53 00 00 55 AA   SMSDOS   SYS U*
```

Loader routine

In all four versions, the boot sector begins with a jump to the start of the bootstrap loader routine, which "bootstraps" the system into operation. The small bootstrap program is loaded and, in turn, loads the larger operating system. (See Chapter 3, "The Dynamics of DOS," for a more detailed discussion of DOS loading procedures.)

The 3-byte jump instruction is followed by an 8-byte system-name field that identifies the manufacturer whose system formatted the disk (some manufacturers do not put a name here). This is followed by the BIOS parameter block (BPB), which provides the information listed in table 8.2. The format and content of the BPB account for most of the differences between the different boot sectors; at each major step, more data was added to it. The sample values shown in table 8.2 are taken from the boot sectors in figure 8.3. (These values are all from 360K DSDD floppy disks.)

Note particularly in table 8.2 how the spec has, at each change, attempted to maintain compatibility with older versions, even going to the extreme of providing two different fields for the Total Number of Sectors data when it became possible to have more than 65,535 sectors on a single disk. Unfortunately, not all manufacturers left the reserved areas alone in older versions, which may cause disks formatted with those versions to be unreadable when one of the newer versions is installed.

Table 8.2. *BIOS Parameter Block (BPB) Layout*

Byte Offset	Field Length	Sample Value	Meaning
00h	Word	0200	Number of bytes per sector
02h	Byte	02	Number of sectors per cluster
03h	Word	0001	Number of reserved sectors starting at sector 0
05h	Byte	02	Number of FATs
06h	Word	0070	Maximum number of root directory entries
08h	Word	02D0	Total number of sectors (or 0 in V3 if > 65,535)
0Ah	Byte	FD	Media descriptor
0Bh	Word	0002	Number of sectors per FAT
0Dh	Word	0009	Number of sectors per track
0Fh	Word	0002	Number of heads
11h	Double word	00000000	Number of hidden sectors
15h	11 bytes	——	Reserved (before V3)
—V3 BPB Extension—			
15h	Double word	00000000	Total number of sectors if word at 08h = 0
19h	7 bytes	——	Reserved (BPB outside boot record area)
—V4 Boot Record Extensions—			
19h	Byte	00	Physical drive number
1Ah	Byte	00	Reserved
1Bh	Byte	29	Signature byte for extended boot record
1Ch	Double word	203D10CC	Volume serial number (made from date/time)
20h	11 bytes	NO NAME	Volume label
2Bh	8 bytes	FAT12	Reserved

In all versions of DOS above V2, the BPB is critical to the operation of the bootstrap program because the program must know these parameters to find and load the operating system BIOS and kernel.

Before V3, the loaders assumed that the ROM BIOS version of the BPB was applicable at boot time and that the media code would apply after DOS had been loaded; thus, they made no use of the data in the boot sector. As a result, some firms (notably Tandy and Heath-Zenith) omitted the BPB data from diskettes formatted using DOS 2.

These diskettes worked nicely until Version 3, at which point they turned out to be unreadable because the new DOS was reading the bootstrap program's code as being the actual disk parameters. Because IBM's V2 produced diskettes that *did* follow the published rules for the BPB, those could be read satisfactorily, giving rise to a widespread belief that the new version looked for the "magic initials" *IBM* in bytes 3, 4, and 5 of the boot sector; what it actually looked for was the data following that 8-byte OEM name region.

A similar situation occurred with the step from Version 3 to Version 4. In this case, however, the IBM version of DOS does look for the magic initials at the start of the BPB; if anything but the letters *IBM* are in that location (even if it finds MSDOS), it reports an unknown media error. No reason is known for this action; changing bytes 3 through 10 to "IBM V2.0" or "IBM V3.0" makes the disk acceptable to the system.

The File Allocation Table (FAT)

DOS uses the file allocation table (or FAT) to manage the disk's data area. The FAT indicates to DOS which portions of the disk belong to each file. Because of the FAT's critical nature, DOS usually maintains two copies that reside, one after the other, on the disk. As changes are made to the original FAT, DOS meticulously updates the second copy.

The FAT follows the boot record on the disk. Because the boot record is only one sector long (sector 0), the FAT starts with sector 1. The length of the FAT (in sectors) is specified in the boot record BPB itself, as is the number of FAT copies.

It is interesting to note that no native DOS commands use the second FAT copy. If the original FAT is somehow damaged, a separate utility program (not supplied with DOS or even available from Microsoft or IBM) must be used with the second FAT copy to recover disk files. In practice, however, virtually every disaster that can affect one copy also destroys the other at the same time or immediately thereafter, making the usefulness of the second FAT copy questionable at best.

Each FAT consists of a series of entries, either 12 or 16 bits long, which record the status of each *cluster* on the disk drive. If 12-bit entries are used, two of them are packed into three consecutive bytes of the table (24 bits). This minimizes the amount of space required for each FAT.

The *cluster* is the smallest unit of disk space that can be allocated for use; it always consists of one or more consecutive logical sectors (which need not necessarily be on the same surface or track; the first sector of the first surface of the first track is logical sector 0, and numbering then proceeds sector by sector, surface by surface, track by track, in ever increasing sequence).

The number of sectors in a cluster is always a power of 2, to simplify conversion between cluster number and logical sector number. Floppy disks usually use a cluster size of two sectors (1024 bytes); the first hard disks used 8-sector clusters, but users found the minimum allocation of 4096 bytes wasteful when many small files were stored. With the introduction of V3, the cluster size for large hard disks was reduced to 4 sectors. For each disk, the cluster size is one of the key items found in the BPB (see table 8.2).

Within the FAT, each entry exactly corresponds to one cluster on the disk. The entry corresponding to cluster 0 holds the disk media code, and that for cluster 1 is always filled with 1 bits (hex FFF or FFFF). The first cluster usable for data is numbered as cluster 2.

When any cluster is available for allocation, the value of its corresponding entry in the FAT is 0. When the first cluster is allocated to a file, its entry in the FAT is changed to FFFh or FFFFh to indicate that this is the *last* cluster in the file. The cluster number is also recorded in the file's directory entry, which we will examine in Chapter 9, "Directories and Files." As each new cluster is allocated, the FFFh/FFFFh entry moves to the new cluster's entry in the FAT, and the cluster number of the new entry replaces the FFFh/FFFFh value in the previous one.

In this manner, the FAT links all the clusters assigned to each file, regardless of where on the disk the clusters happen to be with respect to each other.

Special codes indicate whether the cluster is damaged, and if so, in what way. The values FF7h through FFEh (FFF7 through FFFEh for 16-bit tables) are used for this purpose.

The "32M barrier" has long been a notorious feature of DOS; it vanished in V4. Before we look at the impact of these changes on FAT coding and other disk parameters, let's see where the barrier was created.

Although one of the first barriers was established by the size originally chosen for FAT entries, the real barrier was a result of the 512-byte sector size and the limit of 16-bit values for sector numbers used in all I/O routines. Because a 16-bit number cannot exceed 65,535, that became the maximum possible sector number in a volume. And with 512-byte sectors, the resulting maximum volume size became 33,553,920 bytes, or 32M.

Versions of DOS before V3 were limited to 12-bit FAT entries; the largest number of clusters a disk could contain was 2^{12} (or 4096). Because 9 of the 4096 possible FAT entry values are used to represent cluster status, only 4087 clusters can actually be represented. That maximum-sized FAT occupies 6144 bytes itself, or twelve 512-byte sectors.

Note that the actual maximum disk size that these 4087 clusters can represent depends entirely on the cluster size chosen. For a single-sector cluster size, the limit is 2,092,544 (4087×512) bytes. This suffices for all popular floppy disks. (There is no explaining how the 2-sector cluster became standard.) It is unusable, though, for even the smallest hard disk.

Increasing the cluster size to 8 sectors brings the size limit up to 16,740,352 bytes, adequate for the 10-megabyte drive of the original XT model. Doubling the cluster size to 16 sectors, with its resulting 8192-byte minimum allocation size (for even a 1-byte file) brought the FAT capacity up to the 32M limit. This waste of space irritated users.

Additional increases in cluster size could have extended the limit in the FAT, but not in the volume itself. Only an increase in sector size (or an apparent increase, which is how third-party drivers actually did it) could break the volume size limit. The sector size was limited also by the available controller hardware.

The waste problem was circumvented in Version 3 by allowing DOS to use a FAT that is encoded differently. If the disk drive was large enough to produce more than 4087 clusters with an 8-sector cluster size (bigger than 17 megabytes), DOS V3 switches to a 4-sector cluster size and uses a 16-bit FAT entry. The 16-bit FAT allows a maximum of 65,527 clusters. With that many clusters available in the FAT, two-sector clusters could be used without exceeding 32M.

However, a FAT that large would require 131,072 bytes for each copy, or 512 sectors at the 512-byte standard sector size for the usual pair of FATs. To keep overhead as low as possible, the DOS designers chose to limit the number of FAT entries to 16,384, thus keeping the 32-megabyte limit and 4-sector clusters and cutting the FAT space down to 128 sectors.

Times change, and many disks now run headlong into the 32M barrier. (This text is being written on a system with an 80M hard disk, partitioned into three 26M logical drives.) So with Version 4, the sector number can be either 16 or 32 bits, and the number of bytes in the FATs can grow to its maximum value with 16-bit entries, which raise the disk capacity limit to 128M with 4-sector clusters or 256M with the old 8-sector cluster size. But 300M plus drives are already advertised; who knows what the future will bring?

When a disk is formatted, the FORMAT program determines which coding scheme to use. If the size of the disk indicates that it can be represented adequately with a 12-bit FAT, that scheme is used; otherwise, a 16-bit FAT is used. If the volume's size exceeds 32M, 32-bit sector numbers are used also. (If not, the older 16-bit sector number size is retained.) Let's take a look at each type of FAT.

The 12-Bit FAT

The 12-bit FAT results in a table 25 percent smaller than the 16-bit FAT. This fact was probably responsible for the adoption of the 12-bit FAT. Two 12-bit numbers are held in three bytes. Figure 8.4 shows a sample sector from a 12-bit FAT.

Notice the composition of the file allocation table. In this example, the first two FAT entries (the first three bytes) contain system information. Thus, clusters 0 and 1 of the data area are inaccessible by the FAT. The following one and one half bytes (12 bits, the FAT entry for cluster 2) are followed by the entry for cluster 3, and so on. Notice the three bytes at offset 0103h, which are the FAT entries for clusters 2 and 3. You can divide 03 40 00 into two separate FAT entries by using the following formulas (all values are hexadecimal):

Entry 1 = ((Byte2 AND 0F) × 1000) + Byte1
Entry 2 = (Byte3 × 10) + ((Byte2 AND F0) / 10)

Thus, the FAT entry for cluster 2 is

FAT Entry 2
$$= ((40 \text{ AND } 0F) \times 1000) + 03$$
$$= ((0) \times 1000) + 03$$
$$= 03$$

and the FAT entry for cluster 3 is

FAT Entry 3
$$= 00 \times 10 + ((40 \text{ AND } F0) / 10)$$
$$= 0 + (40 / 10)$$
$$= 04$$

Fig. 8.4. *A sample 12-bit FAT.*

```
2D14:0100   FD FF FF 03 40 00 05 60-00 07 80 00 09 A0 00 0B    ....a..:........
2D14:0110   C0 00 0D E0 00 0F 00 01-11 20 01 13 40 01 15 60    ......... ..a..:
2D14:0120   01 17 F0 FF 19 A0 01 1B-C0 01 1D E0 01 1F 00 02    ................
2D14:0130   21 20 02 23 40 02 25 60-02 27 80 02 29 A0 02 2B    ! .#a.%:.'..)..+
2D14:0140   C0 02 2D E0 02 2F 00 03-31 20 03 33 40 03 35 F0    ..-../..1 .3a.5.
2D14:0150   FF 37 80 03 39 A0 03 3B-C0 03 3D E0 03 3F 00 04    .7..9..;..=..?..
2D14:0160   41 20 04 43 40 04 45 60-04 47 80 04 49 A0 04 4B    A .Ca.E:.G..I..K
2D14:0170   C0 04 4D E0 04 FF 0F 00-00 00 00 00 00 00 00 00    ..M............
2D14:0180   00 00 00 00 00 00 00 00-00 00 00 00 00 00 00 00    ................
2D14:0190   00 00 00 00 00 00 00 00-00 00 00 00 00 00 00 00    ................
2D14:01A0   00 00 00 00 00 00 00 00-00 00 00 00 00 00 00 00    ................
2D14:01B0   00 00 00 00 00 00 00 00-00 00 00 00 00 00 00 00    ................
2D14:01C0   00 00 00 00 00 00 00 00-00 00 00 00 00 00 00 00    ................
2D14:01D0   00 00 00 00 00 00 00 00-00 00 00 00 00 00 00 00    ................
2D14:01E0   00 00 00 00 00 00 00 00-00 00 00 00 00 00 00 00    ................
2D14:01F0   00 00 00 00 00 00 00 00-00 00 00 00 00 00 00 00    ................
2D14:0200   00 00 00 00 00 00 00 00-00 00 00 00 00 00 00 00    ................
2D14:0210   00 00 00 00 00 00 00 00-00 00 00 00 00 00 00 00    ................
2D14:0220   00 00 00 00 00 00 00 00-00 00 00 00 00 00 00 00    ................
2D14:0230   00 00 00 00 00 00 00 00-00 00 00 00 00 00 00 00    ................
2D14:0240   00 00 00 00 00 00 00 00-00 00 00 00 00 00 00 00    ................
2D14:0250   00 00 00 00 00 00 00 00-00 00 00 00 00 00 00 00    ................
2D14:0260   00 00 00 00 00 00 00 00-00 00 00 00 00 00 00 00    ................
2D14:0270   00 00 00 00 00 00 00 00-00 00 00 00 00 00 00 00    ................
2D14:0280   00 00 00 00 00 00 00 00-00 00 00 00 00 00 00 00    ................
2D14:0290   00 00 00 00 00 00 00 00-00 00 00 00 00 00 00 00    ................
2D14:02A0   00 00 00 00 00 00 00 00-00 00 00 00 00 00 00 00    ................
2D14:02B0   00 00 00 00 00 00 00 00-00 00 00 00 00 00 00 00    ................
2D14:02C0   00 00 00 00 00 00 00 00-00 00 00 00 00 00 00 00    ................
2D14:02D0   00 00 00 00 00 00 00 00-00 00 00 00 00 00 00 00    ................
2D14:02E0   00 00 00 00 00 00 00 00-00 00 00 00 00 00 00 00    ................
2D14:02F0   00 00 00 00 00 00 00 00-00 00 00 00 00 00 00 00    ................
```

Each FAT entry points to the next cluster occupied by the file. Thus, the FAT entries form a chain; when all the "links" in this chain are put together, the chain signifies the clusters occupied by a specific file.

Some values for FAT entries, however, do not represent a subsequent cluster number; rather, these values represent a status of the cluster. Table 8.3 summarizes the possible codes for a FAT entry.

Table 8.3. *12-Bit FAT Assignment Bytes*

Category	Codes
Free for assignment	0
Part of a file (pointer to next cluster)	2–FF6
Bad cluster	FF7
End of cluster chain	FF8–FFF

Using the 12-bit FAT shown in figure 8.3, let's follow a cluster chain. A file's directory entry points to the first cluster occupied by a file (directory entries are discussed in Chapter 9). In this illustration, the directory entry for IBMBIO.COM (22,100 bytes in length) points to a beginning cluster number of 2. If you look at the entry for cluster 2, you will see a pointer to cluster 3—and cluster 3 points to cluster 4 (remember, we just worked out the math for this). Cluster 4 then points to 5, which points to 6, and so on until cluster 18h is reached. Here the FAT entry is FFFh, which indicates that the end of the cluster chain has been reached.

Using cluster 2 as the starting cluster, you can find the next cluster as follows:

1. Multiply the cluster number by 2 and round down the result.

2. Get the word at the resulting offset.

3. If the original cluster number (2, in this case) was even, take the low 12 bits of the word; otherwise, take the high 12 bits.

The 16-Bit FAT

The release of DOS V3 brought support for larger hard disks and a FAT that uses 16 bits (2 bytes) per entry. Figure 8.5 shows a sample sector from a 16-bit FAT.

Translation is much more straightforward with this file allocation table than with the 12-bit FAT. The first two entries (four bytes) are used for system information; each subsequent entry occupies two bytes. Notice the two bytes at offset 0104h (the FAT entry for cluster 2). The value here (0003h) points to the entry for cluster 3.

Fig. 8.5. *A sample 16-bit FAT.*

```
2D14:0100  F8 FF FF FF 03 00 04 00-05 00 06 00 07 00 08 00   ................
2D14:0110  09 00 0A 00 0B 00 0C 00-FF FF 0E 00 0F 00 10 00   ................
2D14:0120  11 00 12 00 13 00 14 00-15 00 16 00 17 00 18 00   ................
2D14:0130  19 00 1A 00 1B 00 FF FF-78 0A FF FF 20 00 FF FF   ........x... ...
2D14:0140  FF FF FF FF FF FF 6D 04-26 00 FF FF 27 00 28 00   ......m.&...'.(.
2D14:0150  29 00 2A 00 2B 00 2C 00-2D 00 2F 00 FF FF 32 00   ).*.+.,.-./...2.
2D14:0160  FF FF 00 00 33 00 51 00-42 00 36 00 37 00 38 00   ....3.Q.B.6.7.8.
2D14:0170  FF FF 3A 00 3B 00 3C 00-3D 00 3E 00 3F 00 41 00   ..:.;.<.=.>.?.A.
2D14:0180  FF FF FF FF 43 00 44 00-45 00 48 00 FF FF FF FF   ....C.D.E.H.....
2D14:0190  49 00 4A 00 4B 00 4C 00-4F 00 FF FF FF FF 50 00   I.J.K.L.O.....P.
2D14:01A0  FF FF 52 00 53 00 54 00-55 00 57 00 FF FF 81 00   ..R.S.T.U.W.....
2D14:01B0  59 00 5A 00 5B 00 5C 00-61 00 72 00 FF FF 60 00   Y.Z.[.\.a.r...`.
2D14:01C0  FF FF 62 00 6B 00 FF FF-FF FF 66 00 FF FF FF FF   ..b.k.....f.....
2D14:01D0  FF FF 6A 00 FF FF 6C 00-6D 00 78 00 6F 00 FF FF   ..j...l.m.x.o...
2D14:01E0  71 00 FF FF 83 00 FF FF-FF FF 76 00 77 00 FF FF   q.........v.w...
2D14:01F0  7B 00 FF FF FF FF 7C 00-7D 00 7E 00 7F 00 80 00   {.....|.}.~.....
2D14:0200  FF FF 82 00 D0 00 84 00-85 00 86 00 87 00 88 00   ................
2D14:0210  8C 00 8A 00 8B 00 FF FF-8D 00 8E 00 FF FF 00 00   ................
2D14:0220  00 00 00 00 93 00 94 00-95 00 96 00 97 00 98 00   ................
2D14:0230  99 00 9A 00 9B 00 9C 00-9D 00 C3 00 FF FF A0 00   ................
2D14:0240  A1 00 A2 00 A3 00 A4 00-A5 00 A6 00 A7 00 A8 00   ................
2D14:0250  A9 00 AA 00 AB 00 AC 00-AD 00 AE 00 AF 00 B0 00   ................
2D14:0260  B1 00 B2 00 B3 00 B4 00-C2 00 B6 00 B7 00 B8 00   ................
2D14:0270  B9 00 BA 00 BB 00 BC 00-BD 00 BE 00 BF 00 C0 00   ................
2D14:0280  C1 00 FF FF FF FF C4 00-C5 00 C7 00 FF FF C8 00   ................
2D14:0290  CF 00 CA 00 CB 00 CC 00-CD 00 CE 00 FF FF FC 01   ................
2D14:02A0  D1 00 D2 00 D3 00 D9 00-D5 00 D6 00 D7 00 D8 00   ................
2D14:02B0  FF FF DA 00 DB 00 DC 00-DD 00 DE 00 DF 00 E0 00   ................
2D14:02C0  E1 00 E2 00 E3 00 E4 00-E5 00 E6 00 E7 00 E8 00   ................
2D14:02D0  E9 00 EA 00 EB 00 EC 00-ED 00 EE 00 EF 00 F0 00   ................
2D14:02E0  F1 00 F2 00 F3 00 F4 00-F5 00 F6 00 F7 00 F8 00   ................
2D14:02F0  F9 00 FA 00 FB 00 FC 00-FD 00 FE 00 FF 00 00 01   ................
```

Just as with the 12-bit version, each FAT entry points to the next cluster occupied by the file. Thus, the FAT entries form a chain that signifies, when all its "links" are put together, the clusters occupied by a specific file. As with the 12-bit FAT, other values for FAT entries do not represent a subsequent cluster number; rather, these values represent the status of the cluster. Table 8.4 summarizes the possible codes for a FAT entry.

Table 8.4. *16-Bit FAT Assignment Bytes*

Category	Codes
Free for assignment	0
Part of a file (pointer to next cluster)	2–FFF6
Bad cluster	FFF7
End of cluster chain	FFF8–FFFF

Let's follow a cluster chain, using the 16-bit FAT shown in figure 8.5. A file's directory entry points to the first cluster occupied by a file; in figure 8.5, the directory entry for IBMBIO.COM (22,100 bytes in length) points to a beginning cluster number of 2. The entry for cluster 2 points to cluster 3. Cluster 3 points to cluster 4, which points to 5, which points to 6, and so on until cluster 0Ch is reached. The FAT entry at cluster 0Ch is FFFFh, which indicates that the end of the cluster chain has been reached.

The larger disk capacity made available in V4 was obtained by permitting the FAT to grow to full size rather than cutting it short. This is the only difference in the FAT strategies of V3 and V4, although the sector-number size may vary.

More FAT Information

When DOS requests space for a file, that space is assigned to the file in units of one or more clusters. As you have seen from the discussions of the 12- and 16-bit FATs, the clusters in a file are chained, with each FAT entry giving the cluster number of the next entry (see fig. 8.6).

Fig. 8.6. *FAT cluster chaining.*

The FAT reserves, but does not use, the space for entries 0 and 1. The first byte of the FAT is used for a disk identification (ID) byte that helps identify the disk format (see table 8.5). Because clusters 0 and 1 are reserved for the system, cluster 2 is the first cluster that can be assigned.

Table 8.5. *Some Possible FAT ID Byte Values*

Value	Disk Characteristics
F0	Not identifiable
F8	Fixed disk
F9	Double sided, 15 sectors/track
F9	Double sided, 9 sectors/track (720K)
FC	Single sided, 9 sectors/track
FD	Double sided, 9 sectors/track (360K)
FE	Single sided, 8 sectors/track
FF	Double sided, 8 sectors/track

Remember from our FAT discussion that DOS allocates the space for files by complete clusters. Thus, regardless of the actual size of the file, the minimum disk usage for a file is one cluster. A 1-byte file may occupy 512, 1024, 2048, 4096, or more bytes of disk space, depending on the number of sectors per cluster.

As you learned from decoding the floppy disk BPB, the sample disk had two FAT tables. Whenever disk operations allocate or deallocate space on the disk, both FATs are updated automatically. When a disk is first accessed, DOS compares the FATs to see whether they are consistent. Although there can be more than two FATs, in which case they will be stored sequentially on the disk, most disks have two.

After the last FAT comes the root directory, with 32 bytes for each entry. The BPB gives the size of the directory so that you can determine where the file area begins (immediately after the root directory).

Now that you know where to find things on the disk, let's see what functions DOS provides to manipulate them.

Using Disk Functions

There are no BIOS functions for dealing with a DOS file system because the file system (including all the tables just discussed) is a construction of DOS. To the BIOS, the disk is just a series of sectors, starting at sector number 0 and proceeding sequentially to the highest numbered sector. The BIOS knows about tracks, sectors, and disk heads, but not about files, FATs, or directories. All of the functions you will use are DOS-oriented functions.

Drive Information

You can use DOS function calls to get information about the disk drive. The drvinfo.c program illustrates how you can get and display this information (see listing 8.1). Note that this program does not take the new 32-bit sector number possibility of V4 into account; the V4 *Technical Reference Manual* does not indicate that the drive information functions are even aware of the change.

Listing 8.1

```c
/* drvinfo.c */
#include <stdio.h>
#include "drvinfo.h"

main(argc,argv)

int  argc;
char *argv[];

{
    int  drive;

    drive = get_drive();
    printf("Current Drive Code = %d\n",drive);
    printf("Drive is %c:\n",'A'+drive);

    get_drvinfo('A'+drive,&info);
    printf("Drive Information for drive %c:\n",'A'+drive);
    printf("    Number of Sectors per cluster = %d\n",info.spc);
    printf("    Size of Physical Sector = %d\n",info.secsize);
    printf("    Number of Clusters = %d\n",info.clusters);
    printf("\n");
    printf("    Drive size is = %uK\n",
        info.clusters * ((info.spc * info.secsize)/1024));
    printf("\n\n");

    get_drvspace('A'+drive,&info);
    printf("Drive Information for drive %c:\n",*argv[1]);
    printf("    Number of Sectors per cluster = %d\n",info.spc);
    printf("    Size of Physical Sector = %d\n",info.secsize);
    printf("    Number of Clusters = %d\n",info.clusters);
    printf("    Number of Available Clusters = %d\n",info.avail);
    printf("\n");
    printf("    Drive size is = %uK\n",
        info.clusters * ((info.spc * info.secsize)/1024));
    printf("    Available Space is = %dK\n",
        info.avail * ((info.spc * info.secsize)/1024));
}
```

To get information about the drive, drvinfo.c calls three subroutines:

get_drive(), to get the current drive number

get_drvinfo(), to get general information about the drive

get_drvspace(), to get other information

All of this information is entered into the drvinfo structure (in the drvinfo.h file) as follows:

```
struct drvinfo {
     int  spc;           /* Sectors per cluster */
     int  avail;         /* Available clusters  */
     int  fatseg;        /* FAT segment of ID byte */
     int  fatoff;        /* FAT offset of ID byte  */
     int  secsize;       /* Physical sector size */
     int  clusters;      /* Number of clusters   */
     char fatid;         /* FAT ID byte */
} info;
```

By defining a structure to hold related information about the disk, you can keep the information organized logically as you work with it.

Notice that the drvinfo.c program (see listing 8.1) includes two subroutine calls; these calls illustrate that the same information can be obtained in more than one way.

Getting the drive information is a simple procedure—you call the DOS services interrupt (Int 21h). This call is performed in C by the intdos function and in Pascal by the Msdos function. The DOS service returns the drive code in the AL register.

The get_drive() function does not interpret the drive code; it simply returns the code to drvinfo.c in the following manner:

```
#include <stdio.h>
#include <dos.h>

get_drive()

{
     union REGS regs;
     regs.h.ah = 0x19;
     intdos(&regs,&regs);

     return(regs.h.al);
}
```

But the process of requesting drive information is more complex than a simple request for the drive number. Information is returned in segment registers as well as in the general-purpose registers. To access the segment registers, you must use the intdosx function (see listing 8.2).

Listing 8.2

```
/* drvinfo */
#include <stdio.h>
#include <dos.h>
#include "drvinfo.h"

get_drvinfo(drv,info)

char drv;
struct drvinfo *info;

{
    union REGS regs;
    struct SREGS segs;
    int dn;

    /* Converts drive letter to internal representation */
    drv = toupper(drv);
    dn = drv - 'A' + 1;

    /* Set up and call DOS */
    regs.h.ah = 0x1c;
    regs.h.dl = dn;
    intdosx(&regs,&regs,&segs);
    info->spc = regs.h.al;
    info->fatseg = segs.ds;
    info->fatoff = regs.x.bx;
    info->secsize = regs.x.cx;
    info->clusters = regs.x.dx;
}
```

The get_drvinfo() and get_drvspace() functions are examples of a good programming practice—that of hiding implementation details inside the functions. In this case, the functions determine the correct drive code from the standard user-oriented designation for the drives (A, B, C, and so forth). Allowing the drive name to be passed as a letter is a way to hide the fact that the drive designations in DOS and BIOS routines are not always consistent. Some routines use *0* to designate drive A, whereas some use *0* to designate the default drive.

Functions (such as get_drvinfo() and get_drvspace) that will be included in a library for many programmers to use should hide as many implementation details as possible. This type of "programmer friendly" library routine helps programmers build programs without having to worry about the details of the machine.

The get_drvinfo() function in listing 8.2 is ready for use with DOS versions before V4 and with V4 if the volume is below the 32M limit. (It has not been tested using V4, V5, or a volume larger than 32M.) It is written for inclusion in a library of functions and can be compiled alone as an object module.

After the function calls DOS (the `intdosx` function call), it saves the returned information from the registers in the `info` structure that was passed by the function call. Putting the information in this structure allows someone with no knowledge of registers and DOS calls to access it from the program that calls the function. The function can be included in a library for programmers who do not know how to deal with DOS.

DOS function 36h provides another, more complete way of getting disk information. The `get_drvspace()` function, shown in listing 8.3, not only loads disk information into the `info` structure but also returns the available space on the disk. Clearly, this function is useful for programs that work with large disk files or with many files.

Listing 8.3

```
/* get_drvspace() */
#include <stdio.h>
#include <dos.h>
#include "drvinfo.h"

get_drvspace(drv,info)

char drv;
struct drvinfo *info;

{
    union REGS regs;
    struct SREGS segs;
    int  dn;

    /* Converts drive letter to internal representation */
    drv = toupper(drv);
    dn = drv - 'A' + 1;

    /* Set up and make the DOS call */
    regs.h.ah = 0x36;
    regs.h.dl = dn;
    intdosx(&regs,&regs,&segs);
    info->spc = regs.x.ax;
    info->avail = regs.x.bx;
    info->secsize = regs.x.cx;
    info->clusters = regs.x.dx;
}
```

To determine how much free space is available on the disk, you use the following information (returned by DOS function 36h):

Register	Contains
AX	Number of sectors per cluster
BX	Number of available sectors
CX	Bytes per sector
DX	Clusters per drive

To calculate the free space on the drive, use the following formula:

$BX \times AX \times CX$

The total drive capacity is calculated by the following formula:

$DX \times AX \times CX$

If you want to find out only how much free space is on the disk, you can write a function (get_free()) to return only this information. The free.c program in listing 8.4 gets this information by calling get_free() with the drive name and pointers to integers for both the available and total disk space.

Listing 8.4

```
/* free.c */
#include <stdio.h>

main(argc,argv)

int   argc;
char *argv[];

{
    int  avail, total;

    get_free(*argv[1],&avail,&total);
    if(*argv[1])
        printf("Disk Free Space on drive %c: is %dK of %dK\n",
            *argv[1],avail,total);
    else
        printf("Disk Free Space on default drive is %dK of %dK\n",
            avail,total);
}
```

The program is written to check the first command-line argument for the drive name. If *no* first argument is supplied, the program assumes that it should find the information for the default drive.

The get_free() function determines which drive it should check, then sets up and makes the call to DOS (see listing 8.5). Function 36h is used again to determine the free space, but most of the disk information is thrown away because it is not needed for the limited purpose of the function.

Listing 8.5

```
/* get_free() */
#include <stdio.h>
#include <dos.h>

get_free(drv,avail,total)

char drv;
int  *avail,
     *total;

{
    union REGS regs;
    struct SREGS segs;
    int  dn;

    /* Determines the drive and sets the drive number */
    if(drv){
        drv = toupper(drv);
        dn = drv - 'A' + 1;
    } else {
        dn = 0;
    }

    /* Sets up and makes the DOS function call */
    regs.h.ah = 0x36;
    regs.h.dl = dn;
    intdosx(&regs,&regs,&segs);
    *avail = ((regs.x.ax * regs.x.cx)/1024) * regs.x.bx;
    *total = ((regs.x.ax * regs.x.cx)/1024) * regs.x.dx;
}
```

The same operations can be performed in BASIC, as you can see from the free.bas program in listing 8.6.

Listing 8.6

```
'free.bas
$include "REGNAMES.INC"

def fnchkspc(drv)
```

```
'determine the free space from Int 21h, Function 36
    reg %ax, &h3600
    reg %dx, drv
    call interrupt &h21

    fnchkspc = reg(%bx) * (reg(%ax) * reg(%cx)/1024)
end def

def fnsize(drv)
'determine the space from Int 21h, Function 36h
    reg %ax, &h3600
    reg %dx, drv
    call interrupt &h21
    fnsize = reg(%dx) * (reg(%ax) * reg(%cx)/1024)
end def

'MAIN PROGRAM

    input "Drive: ",dv$
    dv$ = left$(dv$,1)
    drive = int((instr("AaBbCcDdEeFfGg",dv$)+1)/2)
    print "Free Space on Drive ";dv$;" Is " ;fnchkspc(drive);"K"
    print "Drive Capacity Is ";fnsize(drive);"K"
end
```

If you want to build a truly useful utility for yourself, why not build one that copies a group of files to a floppy disk or to a series of floppies. Such a utility checks the size of the next file that you want to copy. If sufficient space is available on the disk, the utility copies the file; if not, the utility prompts for another floppy. Such a program might look like this:

```
FOR i=1 TO number_of_arguments
    TOP:
    size = size of file i
    space = get space on target drive
    IF size>space THEN
        ask for another floppy disk
        wait for user to press a key
        GOTO TOP:
    ELSE
        copy file i to floppy
    ENDIF
NEXT i
```

Although you do not yet know how to do everything needed to make this program practical, you will learn about file sizes and executing other programs in Chapter 9, "Directories and Files," and Chapter 10, "Program and Memory Management." Then you will be able to build the program.

Formatting Disks

Disk formatting is a simple yet dangerous task most people do not need to do for themselves. The basic FORMAT program distributed with DOS is one of several adequate disk-formatting programs available. Special formatters are available (often as part of utility packages such as PCTOOLS) for those who want faster or more sophisticated formatting.

Beginners should plan carefully before they try to write disk-formatting programs because these programs, if handled incorrectly, can wipe out critical disk systems and destroy months of work. This section describes some basic formatting techniques and shows a few examples of ways to access the formatting routines present in the system. But remember: *You put your system at risk if you make a mistake here!* When you test a formatting program, follow these simple precautions:

- Whenever possible, test a formatting program on a "floppy disk only" system (no fixed disk). Use system disks that you can afford to lose if something goes wrong.

- If you must make test runs on a system that includes a hard disk, disable the hard disk if you can (by pulling the hard disk controller, for example).

- Be sure to have a current backup of your system. (*You should always have a current backup!*)

Good programming practice dictates that you must recognize the inevitability of mistakes and that your testing must attempt to foresee and provide for all possible errors. If you are careful, nothing is likely to happen to your system when you test your programs.

BIOS provides Int 13h, Function 05h to format disk tracks. The concept is simple and the function is easy to use. Let's look at how you use this function to format a disk.

If you start with an unformatted disk (or if you want to clear an old one), you must use Int 13h, Function 05h to format the disk, track-by-track, as follows:

> *For each track from 0 to the last track*
> > *Set up the call for the track*
> > *Call the track-formatting routine*

The disk will be formatted correctly and BIOS routines will be able to read it—but it is *not* a DOS disk. As you may recall from the discussion earlier in this chapter, DOS requires that a disk have certain structures: the boot sector, FAT, and root directory. The format procedure provides none of these.

To produce a disk acceptable to DOS, you must not only give a disk its basic format but also initialize the disk structure as follows:

For each track from 0 to the last track
  Set up the call for the track
  Call the track formatting routine
Write the boot sector to the disk
Write FAT information to the disk
Write root directory information to the disk

You can handle the last two steps by simply writing zeros into the FAT and disk-directory areas. Zero entries in the FAT table indicate that the clusters are free and ready for reassignment. Zeros in the disk directory indicate that the directory entries have never been used. Except for the boot sector, then, the formatting process can be fairly simple: format the tracks, write the boot sector, then zero the FAT and root-directory areas.

Let's write a routine for formatting a disk track. After you know how to format one track, you can format a disk simply by "stepping through" all the tracks.

You call BIOS Int 13h, Function 05h with the register settings shown in table 8.6.

Table 8.6. *Register Settings for BIOS Int 13h, Function 05h*

Register	Meaning
AH	05h (the function code)
ES:BX	Pointer to track-address field table
CH	Track number
DH	Head number
DL	Drive number

The track-address table is the heart of the formatting operation. It specifies the order of logical disk sectors on the physical disk track. Each disk sector is represented in the table by a 4-byte entry that gives the label for each sector on the track. You can use the table to assign logical sector numbers in a different order than the physical sectors on the disk (a process known as *interleaving*).

The number of tracks varies according to the type of disk you use: 5¼-inch disks (360K, double sided, double density) have 40 tracks per side; 3½-inch disks (720K, double sided, double density) have 80 tracks per side. The head number (for floppy disks) should be 0 or 1.

The drive number (DL) indicates which physical drive you want to work on. (Floppy drives are specified by counting from zero: drive A is number 0, drive B is 1, and so on. Hard disks, though, are identified a bit differently: drive C is usually 80h.)

On an unformatted disk, a track is an unstructured blank section of the magnetic surface. The formatting procedure imposes a structure on the disk by magnetically creating "storage bins" on the track (see fig. 8.7). Information can be stored in these bins, which are called sectors.

Fig. 8.7. *Disk track.*

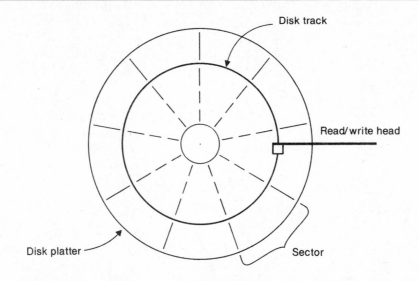

You can place the bins around the track in the physical order in which they occur, but this method can have drawbacks.

Think about reading from a set of disk sectors. Suppose that you copy a disk sector into memory, then come back immediately to read the next sector. This is no problem: simply tell the disk controller which sector you want, and the controller gets the right one. But if the two sectors are one after another on the disk, your request for the second sector will occur after the beginning of that sector has passed the read/write head. To get the sector, you must wait while the disk makes a full revolution (about a fifth of a second for a floppy at 300 rpm).

If you try to read an entire disk, one sector after another, those fifths of a second add up to more than two minutes that the program spends waiting for a specific sector to rotate into position under the read/write head! In applications that do a great deal of disk I/O, the time overhead adds up quickly. By doing something to eliminate the problem, you can significantly improve such applications.

One way to avoid the wait for disk sectors is to interleave them so that one physical sector separates consecutive logical sectors. In other words, you alternate the sector numbers around the track. Figure 8.8 shows how nine sector-sized pieces of a file can be interleaved on a nine-sector track.

Fig. 8.8. *Storing file sectors.*

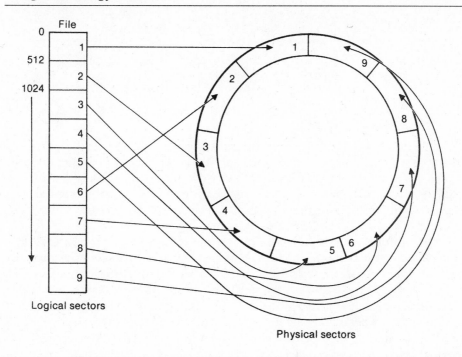

The interleave factor has achieved considerable significance for hard disks, after IBM's default settings were reported to be inappropriate for modern equipment. For most systems, a factor of 3 or below gives the best results on a hard drive. A number of shareware programs test the factor on your system, recommend the best to use, and then, in some cases, change it for you upon request.

The track-address table lets you specify (to the BIOS function) what the logical sector numbers will be for each physical sector on the track. By specifying the size of each sector, you can change the sector size around the track. The information from the track address table is stored on the disk so that the disk controller can find a specific sector without having to consult special tables and figure out the disk's layout. When you use the track-address table to establish the layout, you create the track interleaving as a permanent part of the disk's logical structure.

The track-address table is a series of 4-byte entries (one for each sector on the track) that represent the track, the head, the logical sector number, and the code size. Table 8.7 lists the allowable code sizes.

Table 8.7. *Size Codes*

Code	Sector Size (in Bytes)
0	128
1	256
2	512
3	1024

The information from the track-address table goes into the header written for each sector by the controller. When the controller reads the disk, it uses these sector headers to locate the desired data. Each entry in the table provides data for one header, which is written immediately prior to the data area for that sector. Both the beginning and end of the header are identified by special codes called *address marks*; the controller handles these automatically.

The entries in the track-address table are always arranged on the disk by physical sector number. Each physical sector can have a logical sector number (in any order you want) so that interleaving can be implemented. The track-address table sets the access order of the sectors on a track; PCs read the disk by accessing the sector header to determine which sector has been requested. To write more or less than nine sectors per track, you must change both the number of entries in the table and the size code so that the total number of bytes specified by adding all sectors together does not exceed 4608. Larger sectors can get by with a few bytes more, and smaller sectors will permit less; the sector headers take space too.

The track-address table for track 3 of a 360K, double-sided, double-density disk with nine sectors per track might look like the one in figure 8.8. The logical sector numbers in figure 8.8 correspond to the following physical sectors:

Physical Sector   1 2 3 4 5 6 7 8 9
Logical Sector   1 6 2 7 3 8 4 9 5

To indicate an error during formatting, the carry flag is set on return from the BIOS function. If the flag is set, AH contains an error code. The meanings of the individual bits of this error code are shown in table 8.8. If an error occurs, your program should immediately call BIOS Int 13h, Function 00h (which resets the disk), then handle the error appropriately.

The fmt_trk() function is an example of the track-formatting procedure implemented in C (see listing 8.7). This function assumes that you are formatting a 360K, DSDD disk in a standard PC drive. The function provides only for simple error recovery; it also assumes that the calling routine handles all interaction with the user. If successful, it returns 0; any other value indicates an error.

Table 8.8. *Disk-Error Status Bits*

—Error Code— Hex Value	Binary Value	Meaning
	76543210	
01	1	Bad command
02	......1.	Bad sector address mark
03	11	Write-protect error
04	.....1..	Bad sector/sector not found
08	....1...	DMA overrun
09	....1..1	DMA error
10	...1....	Bad CRC on disk read
20	..1.....	Controller malfunction
40	.1......	Seek failure
80	1.......	Time out

Listing 8.7

```c
/* fmt_trk() */
#include <stdio.h>
#include <dos.h>

#define DISK    0x13

fmt_trk(dsk,trk,head)

int  dsk;
int  trk;
int  head;

{

    union REGS regs;
    struct SREGS sregs;
    char trktbl[36];
    int  i;

    for(i=0; i< 9; i++){
        trktbl[ i*4]   = trk;
        trktbl[ i*4+1] = head;
        trktbl[ i*4+2] = i;
        trktbl[ i*4+3] = 2;
    }
```

continues

Listing 8.7 *continued*

```
        regs.h.ah = 0x05;
        regs.h.ch = trk;
        regs.h.dh = head;
        regs.h.dl = dsk;
        regs.x.bx = FP_OFF(trktbl);
        sregs.es = FP_SEG(trktbl);
        int86x(DISK,&regs,&regs,&sregs);
        if(regs.x.cflag)
                return(fmt_error(regs.h.ah));
        return(0);
}

fmt_error(code)

/*
This routine returns an error code of 1 to indicate that a
write-protect error (which can be recoverable) occurred.
All other errors are assumed to be nonrecoverable and thus
are lumped together.
*/

char code;

{
    union REGS regs;

    regs.h.ah = 0;
    int86(DISK,&regs,&regs);
    return((code==3)?1:2);
}
```

Summary

In this chapter, you learned about the basic structure of disks and how they are formatted. And you learned that the BIOS knows only about tracks, sectors, and disk heads, not about files and directories. The BIOS knows how to locate the disk's partition table and the boot record for the disk, but its knowledge stops there.

All file-related disk operations are DOS-level functions. DOS maintains the disk's directories, files, and file allocation tables (FATs). The structure and location of these tables are given in the BIOS parameter block (BPB) stored in the boot record (the first sector of the bootable partition).

After you have the basic information about the disk, you can access information about the disk (free space, disk capacity, and so forth) from standard DOS calls. Armed with what you have learned from this chapter, you are ready to tackle Chapter 9.

PROGRAMMING

Directories and Files

Nothing is more basic to programming than disk files. As programmers, we have to deal with disk files no matter which audience (business, development, entertainment, or scientific) we program for. Most programming languages, therefore, provide a wealth of easy ways to create, open, read, write, close, and delete files.

Dealing with files from a high-level language is so easy that you generally do not have to think about file operations on a DOS level. With the file-handling functions provided by C, BASIC, and Pascal, you can do your job safely without much fuss. But if you work in assembly language, you need to become familiar with DOS's file-manipulation functions.

Even if you do not program in assembly language, some functions are not readily available from C, BASIC, or Pascal libraries; you cannot do certain types of operations effectively unless you use the DOS functions.

You may be wondering why we refer only to DOS file functions—not to the BIOS. The answer is that files and directories are beyond the realm of BIOS. The BIOS "knows" nothing about files. It assigns no structure (other than tracks and sectors) to disks. Disk file structure is under the direct control of DOS, which contains all the functions necessary for accessing disk files and directories.

9

CHAPTER

This chapter begins with a look at the structure of directories and proceeds by discussing disk files and file functions. Finally, we show you how you can use your newly acquired knowledge of directories and files to build a program that allows you to locate a specific file anywhere in the directory system.

Disk Directories

Directories represent a major advance in the way disk operating systems handle disk files. The early operating systems (CP/M, TRSDOS, Apple DOS, and a myriad of others) all treated files in much the same way. In these *flat file* systems, all of the disk files were available through a single directory. DOS treated files this way until the advent of DOS V2.

Beginning with DOS V2, a file-ordering concept was borrowed from UNIX and XENIX. This *hierarchical directory* scheme allows easy ordering and manipulation of a large number of disk files (usually, but not always, stored on a hard disk). In a system with hierarchical directories, every disk has a predefined, fixed-size *root directory* stored at a known location on the disk. Like the flat-file concept described in the preceding paragraph, the root directory can contain a specific number of equally accessible files.

If we were to stay in the confines of the single root directory, we would be no better off than before. The root directory of a V2 disk is indistinguishable from the only directory of a V1 disk. But the hierarchical directory system lets you create special entries in the root directory (called *subdirectories*) that are similar to files except that their file space contains additional directory entries. Like the root directory, subdirectories are directories in their own right.

Unlike the root directory, subdirectories are not limited by arbitrary size restrictions. They can grow, as necessary, to accommodate additional files. Furthermore, you can create subdirectory entries within subdirectories, with each entry containing references to individual groups of files. The only limit to this nesting process is the 65-character maximum size of a pathspec (the full path from root to file, listing all directories that must be traversed), which does not permit more than 32 levels of nesting. Let's look at the way DOS keeps track of the individual files and directories on a disk.

The Root Directory

The root directory is located in a fixed position on the disk and has a fixed size, which is determined by the FORMAT program when it formats the disk. The root directory's size and disk location are recorded in the BIOS parameter block of the disk's boot sector (see Chapter 8, "Disks").

In DOS V1, the root directory was the only directory on a disk. Support for subdirectories began with DOS V2. As you now know, a subdirectory is simply a special type of file that contains other directory entries rather than ordinary data.

The first two entries in a root directory are reserved for the BIOS and DOS-kernel system file entries. The disk bootstrap program uses these entries during system start-up (see Chapter 3, "The Dynamics of DOS"). Figure 9.1 shows the first sector of a typical root directory that includes the operating system.

Fig. 9.1. *A root-directory dump.*

A) Nonbootable disk (first sector only)

```
00  53 52 43 20 20 20 20 20-20 20 20 10 00 00 00 00   SRC        .....
10  00 00 00 00 00 00 6E 00-9B 10 02 00 00 00 00 00   ......n.........
20  44 45 4D 4F 43 4D 20 20-41 53 4D 20 00 00 00 00   DEMOCM  ASM ....
30  00 00 00 00 00 00 D7 83-4F 0F 09 00 79 04 00 00   ........O...y...
40  44 45 4D 4F 43 4D 20 20-4F 42 4A 20 00 00 00 00   DEMOCM  OBJ ....
50  00 00 00 00 00 00 7B BD-9B 10 0B 00 6C 00 00 00   ......{.....l...
60  44 45 4D 4F 43 4D 20 20-45 58 45 20 00 00 00 00   DEMOCM  EXE ....
70  00 00 00 00 00 00 81 BD-9B 10 0C 00 2B 03 00 00   ............+...
80  44 45 4D 4F 43 4D 20 20-43 4F 4D 20 00 00 00 00   DEMOCM  COM ....
90  00 00 00 00 00 00 84 BD-9B 10 0D 00 2B 00 00 00   ............+...
A0  44 45 4D 4F 43 4D 20 20-44 4D 50 20 00 00 00 00   DEMOCM  DMP ....
B0  00 00 00 00 00 00 2A BE-9B 10 0E 00 29 05 00 00   ......*.....)...
C0  00 00 00 00 00 00 00 00-00 00 00 00 00 00 00 00   ................
D0  00 00 00 00 00 00 00 00-00 00 00 00 00 00 00 00   ................
E0  00 00 00 00 00 00 00 00-00 00 00 00 00 00 00 00   ................
F0  00 00 00 00 00 00 00 00-00 00 00 00 00 00 00 00   ................
```

B) Bootable disk (system files included, first sector only)

```
00  49 4F 20 20 20 20 20 20-53 59 53 07 00 00 00 00   IO      SYS.....
10  00 00 00 00 00 00 00 66-EA 0C 02 00 3C 1F 00 00   .......f....<...
20  4D 53 44 4F 53 20 20 20-53 59 53 07 00 00 00 00   MSDOS   SYS.....
30  00 00 00 00 00 00 75 6B-06 0B 0A 00 E0 6C 00 00   ......uk.....1..
40  43 4F 4D 4D 41 4E 44 20-20 43 4F 4D 00 00 00 00   COMMAND COM.....
50  00 00 00 00 00 00 1A 00-AF 0A 26 00 95 58 00 00   ........&..X..
60  53 52 43 20 20 20 20 20-20 20 20 10 00 00 00 00   SRC        .....
70  00 00 00 00 00 00 80 01-9B 10 3D 00 00 00 00 00   ..........=...
80  44 45 4D 4F 43 4D 20 20-41 53 4D 20 00 00 00 00   DEMOCM  ASM ....
90  00 00 00 00 00 00 D7 83-4F 0F 44 00 79 04 00 00   ........O.D.y...
A0  44 45 4D 4F 43 4D 20 20-4F 42 4A 20 00 00 00 00   DEMOCM  OBJ ....
B0  00 00 00 00 00 00 7B BD-9B 10 46 00 6C 00 00 00   ......{...F.1...
C0  44 45 4D 4F 43 4D 20 20-45 58 45 20 00 00 00 00   DEMOCM  EXE ....
D0  00 00 00 00 00 00 81 BD-9B 10 47 00 2B 03 00 00   ..........G.+...
E0  44 45 4D 4F 43 4D 20 20-43 4F 4D 20 00 00 00 00   DEMOCM  COM ....
F0  00 00 00 00 00 00 84 BD-9B 10 48 00 2B 00 00 00   ..........H.+...
```

The root directory must start at a clearly defined point so that it can be found by programs that know nothing about the file system. The kernel and BIOS files must be the very first ones stored on disk so that they can be located without having to provide a search routine during the process of booting the disk. The bootstrap loader program assumes that these files are the first ones in the root directory and that at least the BIOS file (both files in V1) is stored contiguously on the disk.

Directory Entries

Understanding the structure of directory entries is imperative if you are to understand how DOS keeps track of files and directories. After you learn the structure of directory entries, interpreting them is easy.

Each directory entry (32 bytes of data) contains identifying information about the file: the file's name, extension, attribute, size, and starting location on the disk, as well as the date and time of the directory entry's most recent update. Table 9.1 shows the basic structure of a 32-byte directory entry.

Table 9.1. *Structure of the Directory Entry*

Offset	Size	Meaning
00h	8 bytes	File name
08h	3 bytes	File extension
0Bh	Byte	File attribute
0Ch	10 bytes	Reserved (not used)
16h	Word	Time of last update
18h	Word	Date of last update
1Ah	Word	Beginning disk cluster
1Ch	Double word	File size

Every directory entry is formatted in this way; each piece of information about the file is stored at a fixed offset within the 32-byte entry. Each field in the directory entry tells you something unique about the file. With the exception of the 10 bytes reserved by DOS (offset 0Ch), we will take a fairly detailed look at each field in the directory entry.

File Name (Offset 00h)

The first eight bytes of the entry are the file's root name (stored as ASCII text). Now you can see why file names in DOS are limited to eight characters—only that amount of space is available in the directory entry.

In many DOS programs, you can use file names longer than eight characters, but DOS will truncate them to fit in its eight-character limit. If the root file name is less than eight characters long, it is left-justified in the field and padded with spaces. DOS stores all file names as uppercase ASCII characters.

The first byte of the file-name field has several special meanings (see table 9.2).

Table 9.2. *Special Meanings of File Name's First Byte*

Value of First Byte	Meaning
00h	Entry has never been used; no further entries follow this one.
05h	First character of the file name is actually E5h.
2Eh	Entry is an alias for the current subdirectory. If the next byte is 2Eh, the directory entry's beginning disk cluster field contains the cluster number of the parent of the current directory.
E5h	File erased.

The 00h code saves DOS from fruitless searches of unused directory entries. When this code is encountered during a search for a file name, it is interpreted as "end of directory" and the search ends instantly.

The E5h character (displayed on an IBM as the Greek *sigma* character) can be used as the first character of a file name but is stored in the directory entry as 05h. (Why anyone would want to use it in a file name is left as a question for the reader; the automatic translation, however, makes it possible.)

An E5h as the first character marks files that have been erased; DOS ignores such entries when searching or reuses them when a new file is created. Only the first byte changes to mark an entry as deleted; the rest of the directory entry remains unaltered. Theoretically, you can resurrect an erased file by changing the first character to a valid ASCII character. But if another file has already overwritten the disk space previously occupied by the erased file, you cannot unerase the file.

The 2Eh entry is a period. Found only in subdirectories, it marks a directory entry for the current directory. If the next byte is also a period, the entry points to the parent of the current directory. You see these dot (.) and dot-dot (..) entries at the beginning of every subdirectory whenever you use the DOS DIR command; they are created automatically when the subdirectory is brought into existence and cannot be removed.

Any attempt to ERASE . is interpreted as ERASE *.* for the subdirectory, and ERASE .. becomes ERASE *.* for the parent! The standard DOS query Are you sure (Y/N)? offers little protection because it does not indicate that mass file destruction will result. In V4, the message was expanded to explicitly tell you that the entire directory would be erased.

File Extension (Offset 08h)

The three characters that begin at offset 08h are the file type or extension (also stored as ASCII characters). If the file has no extension, or if the extension is shorter than three characters, the extension is left-justified in the field and the name is padded with spaces. Notice that the period, which generally is used as a delimiter between the root file name and the extension, is not stored with the file name in the directory entry. DOS assumes the presence of a period between the eighth and ninth bytes of the directory entry.

File Attribute (Offset 0Bh)

The file's attribute (the byte at offset 0Bh) indicates both the type of file represented by the directory entry and its accessibility. Each bit of the attribute marks one of the file's characteristics or features (see table 9.3).

Table 9.3. *An Attribute Byte*

Bit 76543210	Meaning
.......x	Read only
......x.	Hidden
.....x..	System
....x...	Volume label
...x....	Subdirectory
..x.....	Archive
xx......	Reserved (unused)

The read-only characteristic means exactly what it says—the file can only be read, not written to. If this bit is set, the file cannot be deleted. Although this precaution provides some security to the file, the file can be renamed and then modified.

What about the other attributes? Hidden files are not available to DIR, COPY, or many other DOS commands. Although DOS does not provide the tools to do so, many third-party utilities permit you to set the hidden bit on a directory entry, which makes the directory entry itself invisible to DIR. However, you can use the CD command to enter it, and the files inside will be visible.

The term *system* refers specifically to the DOS kernel and BIOS files but can also be used for other files. (For example, you could flag COMMAND.COM and the other system utilities as both system and hidden files on systems that are used primarily by nontechnical personnel; this saves having to restore files deleted by users during attempts to "clean house" on the disks.)

The *volume label* identifies a directory entry that contains the label (or name) for a given disk. Although each disk should have a label, until Version 4 DOS did not check for a label during most disk functions. Volume labels are discussed more fully later in this chapter.

The subdirectory bit marks the file as a special file containing other directory entries. A subdirectory is another directory subordinate to the current one. (We will come back to directories and subdirectories later in this chapter.)

The archive bit (a status bit for the file) is set whenever the file is updated. Typically, hard disk backup programs use the archive bit to indicate which files need to be backed up.

Time of Last Update (Offset 16h)

The word (two bytes) beginning at offset 16h is the time of the file's last update. Sometimes called the file's *time stamp*, it is stored least-significant byte first.

The file's time field is set when you create the file and updated thereafter whenever you close the file, but *only* if information has been written to the file. This field is not updated if the file is merely read, copied (with the DOS COPY command), or renamed (with the DOS REN command). When the time field is updated, the new time is retrieved from the system clock.

Table 9.4 shows the meaning of each bit in the time field. The hour is contained in five bits (24-hour clock) and the minutes in six. Because this leaves only five bits in which to store the seconds, they are divided by 2.

Table 9.4. *Encoding of the Time Field*

Bits FEDCBA98 76543210	Meaning
XXXXX...	Hours
.....XXX XXX.....	Minutes
....XXXXX	Two-second increments

Note that because the seconds are divided by 2, the time stamp is accurate only to an even number of seconds. (This limitation is not significant in most applications.)

A little-known fact about the file time field is that if *all* bits in both bytes are 0, the DIR command will not show any time. If the seconds field contains a 1 and all other bits are 0, however, the file time displays as 12:00a (midnight). Some software publishers use this quirk to help identify revision levels for their distribution disks.

Date of Last Update (Offset 18h)

The word (two bytes) beginning at offset 18h is the date of the file's last update, sometimes referred to as a file's *date stamp*. It is stored least-significant byte first.

The date field is similar to the time field—it is set when you create the file and updated thereafter whenever you close the file, but *only* if information has been written to the file. The date field is not updated if the file is read, copied (with the DOS COPY command), or renamed (with the DOS REN command). When the date field is updated, it encodes (from the system clock) the date of the file's most recent modification.

Table 9.5 shows the layout of the date field. The year is stored in seven bits, the month in four, and the day in five.

***Table 9.5.** Encoding of the Date Field*

Bits FEDCBA98 76543210	Meaning
xxxxxxx.	Year count (relative to 1980)
.......x xxx.....	Month
....xxxxx	Day

Notice that the year entry is relative to 1980. In other words, it is an offset from 1980, not an absolute value (such as 1988). The year 1988, for example, is stored as 8. To identify the absolute year, you simply add the offset to 1980. Seven bits are allocated for the year; because 127 is the largest value that can be represented in 7 bits, the year can range from 1980 (offset 0) to 2107 (offset 127).

Beginning Disk Cluster (Offset 1Ah)

The word (two bytes) beginning at offset 1Ah is the file's beginning disk cluster. This word is stored with its least significant byte first.

This word gives only the starting point of the file. To locate the second cluster and succeeding clusters, the value of this field is also used to calculate the offset to the file allocation table (FAT). From the FAT, any additional clusters used by the file can be located. (See Chapter 8 for a detailed discussion of the FAT.)

File Size (Offset 1Ch)

The four-byte file size field contains the exact length of the file, in bytes. Thus, the largest size DOS can handle is 4,294,967,295 bytes. Because this is 13 times bigger than today's largest MS-DOS hard disk, we have a few years to go before reaching this limit.

Some high-level languages (early versions of BASIC, in particular) were notorious for setting this value equal to the total number of bytes in the sectors occupied by the file. If the file contained 520 bytes and occupied two 512-byte sectors, the file size would be set to a clearly misleading 1024. Normally, however, this entry will reflect accurately the file's size in bytes.

Subdirectories

We have already mentioned that each directory entry contains an attribute byte for the file. Bit 4 of this attribute byte marks a directory entry as a pointer to a subdirectory.

A subdirectory is a file, like all the others on the system. The subdirectory entry points to the number of the directory file's beginning cluster, which can contain 16 entries; you "step through" subsequent file clusters to find subsequent entries. Figure 9.2 shows a dump of a typical subdirectory.

Fig. 9.2. *A subdirectory dump.*

```
00   2E 20 20 20 20 20 20 20-20 20 20 10 00 00 00 00 00   .          .....
10   00 00 00 00 00 00 6E 00-9B 10 02 00 00 00 00 00   ......n.........
20   2E 2E 20 20 20 20 20 20-20 20 20 10 00 00 00 00 00   ..         .....
30   00 00 00 00 00 00 6E 00-9B 10 00 00 00 00 00 00   ......n.........
40   44 45 4D 4F 45 58 20 20-41 53 4D 20 00 00 00 00   DEMOEX  ASM ....
50   00 00 00 00 00 00 DC 8B-4F 0F 03 00 0D 05 00 00   ........O.......
60   44 45 4D 4F 45 58 20 20-4F 42 4A 20 00 00 00 00   DEMOEX  OBJ ....
70   00 00 00 00 00 00 91 BD-9B 10 05 00 B7 00 00 00   ................
80   44 45 4D 4F 45 58 20 20-45 58 45 20 00 00 00 00   DEMOEX  EXE ....
90   00 00 00 00 00 00 94 BD-9B 10 06 00 E0 02 00 00   ................
A0   44 45 4D 4F 45 58 20 20-44 4D 50 20 00 00 00 00   DEMOEX  DMP ....
B0   00 00 00 00 00 00 5A BE-9B 10 07 00 2A 05 00 00   ......Z.....*...
C0   00 00 00 00 00 00 00 00-00 00 00 00 00 00 00 00   ................
D0   00 00 00 00 00 00 00 00-00 00 00 00 00 00 00 00   ................
E0   00 00 00 00 00 00 00 00-00 00 00 00 00 00 00 00   ................
F0   00 00 00 00 00 00 00 00-00 00 00 00 00 00 00 00   ................
```

The structure of a subdirectory is exactly like that of the root directory, with one exception: At the beginning of each subdirectory are two special entries bearing the . and .. file names.

The first of these entries (.) points to the current directory; the beginning cluster field in this directory entry points to the first cluster of the current subdirectory. The second entry (..) does the same for the parent directory; the beginning cluster field in this file entry points to the parent directory's first cluster. If this cluster number is 0, the parent directory is the root directory. Neither of these two special directory entries can be deleted. Any attempt to do so will, instead, delete *all* files in the corresponding directory!

You cannot handle subdirectories as you would normal files. DOS Function 43h cannot set a subdirectory's attribute bit. The subdirectory's system and hidden bits can be set to exclude the directory from normal directory listings, but its accessibility cannot be changed. CHDIR can still reach it.

Volume Labels

A volume label is a directory entry in which bit 3 of the file attribute byte is set. To interpret the entry, all you need to do is locate it—the file name is the volume label.

Although generally not used by most software before V4, volume labels can be extremely useful if software is written to take advantage of them. A program can use unique volume labels as disk identifiers. By remembering which disks are in use, a program can prompt for a specific disk by name rather than by a general title. The Macintosh, for example, does this when you use more than one disk on a single drive system. On the Macintosh desktop, the names of disks that have been identified to the system are shown and, if one of these disks is needed, it is requested by name. The system, which can tell whether you have inserted the wrong disk, will continue to ask for the proper disk by name.

Although most PC programs do not handle disks this way, they could—thanks to the volume label. The only way to create a disk label is through the extended FCB functions, which are described in this chapter's "Extended File Control Blocks" section. (For a list of DOS functions for all FCB operations, see the "DOS Reference" section at the end of this book.)

With the introduction of DOS Version 4, the volume label moved up in the world. It is now copied into the boot sector, as well as being in the root directory, and DOS makes some use of it to determine quickly whether a disk has been changed (if the label has not changed, more detailed checks are still made).

Because there is no way to guarantee that two different disks do not bear the same label, though, something new was added to increase the likelihood that identities would be unique: the *volume serial number*. This number is created when a disk is formatted, based on the time and date stamps derived from the system clock at that time, and is stored in the boot sector together with the label. The volume label and serial number together provide a highly reliable indicator of disk changes because the serial number generated will change every two seconds.

What Is a File?

We use files for all sorts of things. Simply speaking, a file is an organized place in which to store information. The term *files* is used also to refer to devices. Following the lead of UNIX, DOS V2 introduced the concept of the *file handle*. The file system can assign unique numbers, called *handles*, to devices such as the printer, the RS-232 port, the keyboard, and the video screen. Many of us were accustomed to treating these devices as special objects, but file handles have changed that.

The concept of using file handles is more powerful than many people realize. With a file handle, you can use the same techniques to access both files and devices. For example, in a program written to deal with the keyboard and the video screen (using STDIN and STDOUT), you can redirect not only the input so that it comes from a file but also the output to a file. The *same program* works in each case—you change only the handle used for input or output.

How Files Are Handled Through DOS

DOS provides two basic ways to deal with files: the FCB method or the handle-function method.

Before DOS V2 was introduced, the file control block (FCB) method (an outgrowth of the old CP/M system) was the only way to access files. FCB functions are built around the presence of a file control block that the programmer controls directly.

You do not need to have all the details of the file at your fingertips for most operations, such as opening, closing, reading, writing, or maintaining a file (renaming or deleting it). For these types of file operations, you use the other method: the handle functions.

Handle functions give programmers only limited access to file information; DOS controls the files internally. Programmers request file operations either by a specific file name (to open or create files) or by using a file handle (to read, write, or close files). DOS uses the handle to look up information about the file.

Handle functions have several advantages over FCB functions:

- Because handle functions are simpler to use, it is easier to prevent or correct mistakes.

- Handle functions are likely to remain compatible with changes in DOS and, later, in OS/2.

- Handle functions can take advantage of DOS's hierarchical directory structure.

- Handle functions relieve programmers of a great deal of bookkeeping. (The bookkeeping—file location and everything stored in an FCB—is done inside the DOS kernel.)

We recommend that, whenever you can, you use the handle functions for accessing files. You have to use FCB functions to create disk volume labels but, for any other file operation, handles are a better way to work with files.

Regardless of whether you use FCB or handle functions, DOS is quite adept at informing you of any errors it may detect. For a comprehensive list of DOS error codes, see the "DOS Reference" section at the end of this book (see particularly Int 21h, Function 59).

Standard File Control Blocks

The standard FCB used by all FCB functions comes almost directly from the original CP/M environment. Its 36 bytes make up 11 fields, as you can see from the layout of the standard FCB shown in table 9.6.

The file control block is made up of information supplied by DOS, some of which comes directly from the values in a file's directory entry. Notice that no allowance is made for using path names with FCBs. All FCB functions operate in the confines of the current directory.

The file name, extension, file size, and date and time of last update are all reflections of the file's directory entry. The other fields are either initialized by the individual FCB functions or modified by the programmer to indicate to DOS what he or she wants.

Extended File Control Blocks

Extended FCBs allow additional file information to be included in the FCB. The extended portion of the FCB is composed of seven bytes (three fields) added to the beginning of the traditional FCB.

Table 9.6. *The Standard File Control Block*

Offset	Length	Meaning	Notes
00h	1	Drive specification	0=default, 1=A, 2=B, and so on
01h	8	File name	Left-justified ASCII; padded with blanks
09h	3	Extension	Left-justified ASCII; padded with blanks
0Ch	2	Current block number	
0Eh	2	Record size	Default of 80h bytes with DOS OPEN or CREATE functions
10h	4	File size	
14h	2	Date created/updated	Same format as directory entry
16h	2	Time created/updated	Same format as directory entry
18h	8	Reserved	
20h	1	Current record number	
21h	4	Random record number	Only 3 bytes used if record size is less than 64 bytes

By examining the FCB's first byte, DOS can tell which type of FCB you are using. If the first byte is FFh, DOS assumes that you are using an extended FCB. (The first byte in a standard FCB represents the disk drive designator. FFh is an illegal value as a disk drive number.)

All DOS FCB functions can use extended FCBs. If you decide to use FCB functions, use extended FCBs so that you will have to keep track of only one structured FCB area.

Most of the information in an extended FCB is identical to that in a standard FCB. If you compare table 9.6 with table 9.7, which details the layout of an extended FCB, you can see that (beginning with byte offset 07h) the two layouts are identical.

Basic FCB File Handling

To work successfully with FCBs, follow these basic steps:

1. Set all the bytes of the FCB to 0.

2. Get the file name information. To do so, you may need to use the DOS parse function (29h).

3. OPEN (Function 0Fh) or CREATE (Function 16h) the file.

4. If the record-size field should not be 80h, change it.

DOS
PROGRAMMING

5. Set the record-number field if you are doing random-access operations.

6. Set the DTA address (if it has not been set).

7. Execute the appropriate function.

8. After you have finished, close the file.

Table 9.7. *An Extended File Control Block*

Offset	Length	Meaning	Notes
00h	1	FFh	Signals DOS that this is an extended FCB
01h	5	Reserved	Used by DOS; normally 0s
06h	1	Attribute byte	Same meaning as directory entry
07h	1	Drive specification	0=default, 1=A, 2=B, and so on
08h	8	File name	Left-justified ASCII; padded with blanks
10h	3	Extension	Left-justified ASCII; padded with blanks
13h	2	Current block number	
15h	2	Record size	Default of 80h bytes with DOS OPEN or CREATE functions
17h	4	File size	
1Bh	2	Date created/updated	Same format as directory entry
1Dh	2	Time created/updated	Same format as directory entry
1Fh	8	Reserved	
27h	1	Current record number	
28h	4	Random record number	Only 3 bytes used if record size is less than 64 bytes

When To Use FCB Functions

Even in DOS V4, the use of FCB functions is justified for the following reasons:

- When you use FCBs, you can have an unlimited number of open files.

- FCBs provide the only way to create a volume label for a disk.

- FCBs ensure that methods of accessing files are compatible with DOS V1.

The first point is true because you have total control of the "housekeeping" associated with file I/O. (In the most recent versions of DOS, users can specify in the CONFIG.SYS file how many files can be open simultaneously.)

The second point is important, no matter which version of the operating system you use. If your program creates a volume label for a disk, you *must* use FCBs.

The third reason may be the most important: FCBs are the only way to verify compatibility with systems that use DOS V1. If you are sure that the software will be used on a system with DOS V2 or later, or if you can sacrifice the compatibility of earlier systems, you always should choose handle functions.

Handle Functions

As we mentioned earlier in this chapter, the handle functions are an advance in programming technique. Their introduction to DOS provides file control similar to that found in UNIX. In fact, you can port UNIX applications (written in C) to DOS. These applications will run just like their UNIX counterparts.

You should recognize the two basic features of handle functions:

- Under the handle functions, no distinction is made between sequential and random-access files. All files are seen as a string of bytes, much like an array. This view of a file is standard for UNIX files.

- Handles are kept internally by DOS. The only information a program needs is the file name and handle number.

Not all programmers agree that these features are advantages. Some programmers object to having to give up the control provided by FCBs; others insist that by not providing random-access record structures, the system becomes less powerful.

Which group is right? Neither. For simple programming, nothing beats the handle functions for ease of use. Despite the objections of some programmers, programs seldom need to do their own file bookkeeping. Random file access still is available, but you must approach it differently.

A handle is simply a pointer into an internal DOS table that maintains all relevant information about an open file. Programmers do not have to maintain a detailed accounting of information, as they do when they use the FCB functions; rather, the handle functions relinquish all bookkeeping functions to DOS. For most programming applications, this feature significantly eases the programmer's burden. Because you do not have to manipulate or worry about special file control blocks, your programs, conceptually, are simpler, easier to debug, and easier to keep compatible with future DOS releases.

DOS
PROGRAMMING

Basic Handle File Handling

The basic technique for using handles is much simpler than that for using the corresponding FCB functions. Because the system handles the basic details, you simply identify the file you want and let DOS do the rest. In the handle file-handling method, you follow these steps:

1. Create an ASCIIZ file name string.

2. OPEN (Int 21h, Function 3Dh) or CREATE (Int 21h, Function 3Ch) the file. (V3 and V4 provide additional OPEN/CREATE functions; see the reference section.)

3. Set the file pointer into the file (Int 21h, Function 42h).

4. Complete the required operations.

5. Close the file.

An ASCIIZ string is simply an ASCII text string that ends in a NUL character (ASCII 0). In high-level languages, such as C, strings generally are stored as ASCIIZ strings.

To set a file's size, set the file pointer where the end is to be, then do a write of 0 bytes. Space will be added or removed as required to make the file exactly that size.

When To Use Handle Functions

In certain instances, which arise because of advanced functions provided by DOS V2 and later versions, you *must* use file handles rather than FCBs. For example, use file handles

- Whenever you use path names

- Whenever I/O redirection and piping are important

- To support file sharing and locking

- To support networked environments

- To use enhanced error reporting

- For easy access to arbitrary locations in the file

- To set file size under program control

We recommend that you use file handle functions whenever and wherever you can. (But be sure to use FCBs to create volume labels.) By using file handles for all your programs, you instantly gain portability for future environments in which FCBs will not exist. More important, you simplify your programming task.

Ordinarily, when you work with a high-level language such as C or BASIC, you will not want to come down to the level of detail covered in this chapter. High-level languages, after all, offer significant file-manipulation operations. But you will want to use compatible functions—handles. The latest C, BASIC, and Pascal releases all use handle functions for their file-access routines.

Directory Searching: A Practical Example

To illustrate the use of the DOS directory functions, let's develop a simple application that will tell us where a file resides in the hierarchical directory system. All we have to know is the file's name. The program described in the remainder of this chapter was developed to find a file (given its name) anywhere in the file system.

The program, called find.c, searches through the file structure. (C's recursive nature allows descent through the file system without making the program overly complicated.) This program illustrates how file handle functions can be used to access information quickly and naturally.

The basic technique for this simple program is

For each argument on the command line, search the file system for all files that have that name.

The program is implemented as shown in listing 9.1.

Listing 9.1

```
/* Find.c */
#include <stdio.h>
main(argc,argv)
/*
    find.c
    This search program locates file names in the directory
    structure of a hard disk. It illustrates the use of the DOS
    directory functions from a high-level language.
    Use the link switch
        /STACK:30000
    with Microsoft C.
*/
int  argc;
```

continues

Listing 9.1 *continued*

```
char *argv[];
{
    int  i;
    for(i=1; i<argc; i++)
        depth_search("", argv[i]);
}
```

Using file-search procedures that match the requirements of the file name, the search routine (depth_search) checks for files in each directory in the file system. The basic algorithm follows:

Check the current directory for any files that match the desired file name.

Locate every subdirectory in the current directory and search all of them.

Whenever you enter this recursive routine, a new disk transfer area (DTA) is created. Whenever the function returns, the previous DTA is again made current. You do not have to work with only one DTA: you can have as many as you want, depending on what you need to solve your problem. In this case, the problem was best solved by the program in listing 9.2.

Listing 9.2

```
/* depth_search() */
#include <stdio.h>
/* FIRST or NEXT search flags */
#define   FIRST     0
#define   NEXT      1
/* File attribute for search */
#define   FILE      0
#define   DIR       16
depth_search(dir,name)
char *dir,
     *name;
{
    char filename[256];   /* File name to search for  */
    char dirname[256];    /* Directory name to search */
    char dta[43];         /* Disk transfer area       */
    int  flag;            /* Search type flag         */
    sprintf(filename,"%s\\%s",dir,name);
    /* Set the DTA to the local DTA buffer */
    set_dta(dta);
    flag = FIRST;
    while(search(filename,flag,FILE)){
        printf("DEPTH:FOUND: %s\\%s\n",dir,dta+30);
        flag = NEXT;
```

```
        }

    sprintf(filename,"%s\\*.",dir);
    flag = FIRST;
    while(search(filename,flag,DIR)){
        flag = NEXT;

        /* Specifically exclude "." and ".." from searching */

        if(!streql(".",dta+30) && !streql("..",dta+30)){
            sprintf(dirname,"%s\\%s",dir,dta+30);
            depth_search(dirname,name);
        }
        /* Return to local DTA buffer for next directory */
        set_dta(dta);
    }
}
```

This routine controls the search through the directory structure but uses the DOS *find first file* function (4Eh) to locate files according to the specified search criteria. Whenever a file is found, DOS updates the DTA with information about that file. This information, which is derived from the file's directory entry, is used in depth_search() to print the file name (or to access the directory).

Search(), the routine that interfaces with the DOS functions, is shown in listing 9.3.

Listing 9.3

```
/* search() */
include <stdio.h>
#include <dos.h>
#define    FALSE       0
#define    TRUE ! FALSE
search(fname,flag,type)
char *fname;
int  flag;
int  type;
{
    union REGS regs;
    regs.h.ah = 0x4e + flag;
    regs.x.cx = type;
    regs.x.dx = (int)fname;
    intdos(&regs,&regs);
    if(regs.x.cflag==1)
        return(FALSE);
    return(TRUE);
}
```

Notice in the search() routine that the same registers are set for each function call, whether you are looking for the first occurrence of the file or for any successive occurrences. The only difference is the setting in AH (4Eh for find first, 4Fh for find next). Although all the set information is required only for the Find First File function (4Eh), it does not deter the operation of the Find Next File function (4Fh). For more detailed information about these functions, refer to the "DOS Reference" section at the end of this book.

When a search goes to another level in the hierarchical system, you must retain the DTA from the previous level or levels to continue searching. The following routine, set_dta(), lets you designate a buffer area as the current DTA:

```
#include <stdio.h>
#include <dos.h>
set_dta(ptr)
char *ptr;
{
    union REGS regs;
    regs.h.ah = 26;
    regs.x.dx = (int)ptr;
    intdos(&regs,&regs);
}
```

The remaining routine, streql(), illustrates the convenience of programming with C functions. In this routine, strcmp() (the standard C library function used for comparing two strings) returns 0 if the strings are the same. But sometimes, especially in the early development stages of building a program, you will find it convenient to create functions that serve as mnemonic reminders of what you *really* want them to do. For example, streql() returns either TRUE or FALSE, depending on whether the two strings are equal. By using the streql() function, we clarify our logic a little and can concentrate more on the problems that need to be solved. You can squeeze a little speed out of the routine by defining a streql() macro such as the following:

```
#define streql(x,y)        (strcmp(x,y)==0)
```

By using the macro, you eliminate the overhead of a function call. Why not do it then? You can—depending on your intentions. By defining streql() as a function, you can include it in a library and the linker will make sure it is there when you need it. If you define it as a macro, you must define the macro in the program or in an include file to make it available. One way is simpler for development; one eliminates some overhead.

For most programs, the choice of which form to use depends on the programmer. Some programmers favor functions; others favor macros. The only critical factor during program development is clarity. You want to make everything as clear as possible to minimize development problems.

The code listing for the streql() routine follows:

```
#include <stdio.h>
streql(str1,str2)
char *str1,
     *str2;
{
     return(strcmp(str1,str2)==0);
}
```

Now that all the pieces of find.c have been described in detail, let's take the program for a test drive. The following test run searches for all occurrences of the autoexec.* file:

```
C>find autoexec.*
DEPTH:FOUND: \AUTOEXEC.BAT
DEPTH:FOUND: \AUTOEXEC.DV
DEPTH:FOUND: \AUTOEXEC.BAK
DEPTH:FOUND: \AUTOEXEC.WIN
DEPTH:FOUND: \BIN\LOTUS\INSTALL\AUTOEXEC.BAT
DEPTH:FOUND: \SYS\AUTOEXEC.DV
DEPTH:FOUND: \SYS\AUTOEXEC.OLD
DEPTH:FOUND: \SYS\AUTOEXEC.BAT
```

Summary

In this chapter, you learned that file access is handled through one of two methods: file control blocks (FCBs) or file handles. FCBs are the older form of file access, compatible all the way back to DOS V1. Disk volume labels can be written only with FCBs, but every other kind of file access can be done with handle functions.

Handle functions can work in and with the hierarchical directory structure introduced in DOS V2. They also make programming much simpler because they let the operating system do the bookkeeping for a file.

Building, as always, on what you have learned, you are ready to move on to the next chapter, "Program and Memory Management," which deals with program execution.

PROGRAMMING

Part IV

Memory Management and Miscellaneous Topics

Program and Memory Management

To "get the job done," programmers have developed several dodges and devices for getting more into a program than could be contained in memory. Program chaining, overlays, and other techniques have long been staples of the programmer's art. The first system we worked on, for example, was an IBM 7040 with only 32K of memory; some programs simply could not be done without overlays (see the brief explanation of overlays at the end of this section).

Specialized techniques can turn into debugging nightmares that make programs highly nonportable. Because of the increased memory and processor speed of large systems, computer programmers have developed techniques for handling programs from within other programs. Command shells, such as COMMAND.COM, use these techniques to execute programs on demand.

On a DOS system, you can control the execution of a program from within another program by using the same functions used by COMMAND.COM. (This is similar to facilities provided on UNIX systems.) This is a relatively clean method of handling program functions. Major modules of the system can exist as stand-alone programs. Each such program can be thoroughly tested and debugged as an independent entity. UNIX programmers have found this technique to be extremely effective for program development.

This chapter begins by describing how memory works, how you can get more memory when you need it, and how to let DOS keep the memory you do not need. When you work in a high-level language, the compiler manages this process. In assembly language, however, you should be explicit about what you want to do with memory. The chapter also takes a closer look at extended memory and expanded memory and examines what can be done with them.

The discussion then moves to program execution—how one process, the *parent*, executes another process, the *child*, and then regains control. A simple example is presented to show how this works.

Finally, a preliminary examination is made of a special kind of program, the TSR (terminate and stay resident). TSRs are different in many ways from "normal" programs (applications such as word processors and spreadsheets). The most obvious difference is that, after they stop, TSRs stay in memory and are not overwritten. A TSR can get control from another program in several ways, the most important of which involves connecting to an interrupt (see Chapter 11, "Interrupt Handlers"). This chapter lays the groundwork for procedures to follow after you understand interrupts.

Let's go on, then, to memory management.

Program Overlays

A program overlay is a section of code or data that is not kept permanently in memory. The program may exist as several binary images, each of which handles some specific functions. The master segment handles overall coordination and usually has functions needed by all overlays.

In a typical program with overlays, the main menu and common functions are in the primary overlay, which is kept in memory at all times. Whenever the program needs a submenu, its overlay is loaded into an area in memory that holds the overlay code. The main module then transfers control to the overlay, and the submenu and its functions are operable.

When the user is finished with the submenu and returns to the program's main menu, control is transferred back to the primary overlay. Because the submenu's overlay in memory is no longer needed, the memory space can be used by another overlay (the submenu's program code is "overlaid" by the new code).

How Memory Works

The basic PC or compatible has an address space that holds as much as 1M of memory. (Remember that a megabyte is 1024K.) As pointed out in Chapter 3, "The Dynamics of DOS," only 640K of this memory is available for program use. The remaining 384K is assigned to the ROM BIOS, display adapters, and cartridges.

The lower 640K of memory is not for user programs only, however. In this space, 1024 bytes of interrupt vectors are reserved by the processor. Only interrupt vectors go in these locations, which, as hardware engineers like to say, are *hardwired* into the processor (see Chapter 11). Next come BIOS and DOS tables, the DOS kernel, system drivers, and finally the resident portion of the command processor. All of this memory comes from the user area of memory.

Calculating how much memory you lose is difficult because it depends on which system you use and which drivers you have loaded. The first user programs generally loaded (in the memory map) are TSRs such as Borland's SideKick. (Figure 10.1 is a graphic representation of memory use with TSRs loaded.) You must subtract their memory use from the available space. If you add a window package similar to DESQview, only about 350K of memory may remain from a starting point of 640K—and all without really starting a program to *do* something!

The space that remains after start-up (usually about 500K to 550K with SideKick loaded) is free and available for use. This space is called the transient program area (TPA), a name used also for the equivalent area on CP/M systems. The name is appropriate because user programs are transient in this area—they come and go as users working on the system need them.

The machine's 640K limit on memory for a working area seemed virtually infinite when PCs were introduced. At that time, a PC with 64K of memory was considered standard; people who had 128K and the rich few who had machines with 256K were envied, although not much software was capable of using the extra memory. As needs grew, the 640K limit became more than an interesting sidelight—it became a major system limitation. Applied to computer memory, the corollary of Murphy's law "No matter how much you have, you will need more" became more than a joke.

After the introduction of the 80286 chip, as much as 16M of memory became possible with the PC system. ("Hallelujah," some said. "Now we have a serious system," said others.) But DOS cannot utilize that memory in regular operation. The memory over the 1M limit, known as *extended memory*, is available on the 80286 processor and later models. DOS cannot use it, however; to access such memory, the 80286 chip must operate in protected mode, which DOS cannot do. Under DOS, only specially written programs capable of switching the CPU mode can use extended memory.

Fig. 10.1. *Memory use with TSRs loaded.*

Protected Mode

The protected-mode feature on the 80286 and 80386 processors gives access to special processor functions that control multitasking operations. *Real mode* provides essentially the same environment as that of the 8088/8086 processors with access to only 1M of memory. When the processor is shifted to *protected mode* (generally done inside an operating system), the system can control the operation of multiple programs in memory and shift from one task to another.

This chapter does not describe the features of protected mode in great detail because DOS does not use that mode. To learn more about protected mode, consult any of the many books about 80286/80386 assembly language programming.

DOS runs everything in the processor's real mode; memory above 1M, therefore, is not accessible to programs that work through the normal DOS functions. Even when a system has the extra memory, you cannot use it effectively.

Although programs such as DESQview can tuck some of their operating code into RAM-disk drivers that use 80286 extended memory like a disk, the memory is not accessible to most programs. (Programs must shift the processor to protected mode before they access the memory and back to real mode upon completion.) Even RAM disks are not necessarily fast when they operate in extended memory because the processor shifts from real mode to protected mode and back again to get to the data—a process that can be relatively slow. On an 80286 processor, going to the hard disk may be faster.

Since the introduction of the Personal Computer AT, BIOS provides two functions to help programs determine how much memory is available (Int 15h, Function 88h) and move data blocks to and from extended memory above the 1M mark (Int 15h, Function 87h). But using these routines causes a serious problem because there is no management for this extended memory space. One program can easily write over data that another program (or a RAM-disk driver) is keeping in the extended memory space; nothing senses the problem or reports the error.

Expanded memory, first introduced as a joint effort by Lotus and Intel at the 1985 spring COMDEX show (version 3.0), provides a way to allow access to as much as 8M of memory without requiring a special shift in processor mode. Expanded memory gives the processor access to extra memory through 16K *pages*, which can be mapped into an unused area in the memory space between 640K and 1M. Four 16K pages are mapped into a 64K *page frame* at a location determined by users of the system when the board is installed. (See Chapter 3, "The Dynamics of DOS," for a more extensive discussion of expanded memory.)

The expanded memory manager (EMM) causes expanded memory to act like a file with a handle. When your program asks for space in expanded memory, the EMM sets aside the space and returns a unique "handle" that can be used to get access to the space.

When you want to get to any 16K page from expanded memory, you use Int 67h to call the EMM and tell it to bring the page into the page frame. Then you can address the memory directly from your program. Figure 10.2 shows what happens.

You install EMM.SYS (the expanded memory manager driver) by adding the following line to your CONFIG.SYS file:

```
DRIVER=EMM.SYS
```

The expanded memory manager driver works only partially like a true driver. (*True* drivers are described in Chapter 12, "Device Drivers"; for now, accept that it does not work normally.) Instead of accessing EMM.SYS like a file, as you would any other driver, you access its functions through Int 67h. See the "DOS Reference" section for a detailed listing of the functions available through Int 67h.

Fig. 10.2. *Expanded memory access.*

The functions available through EMM.SYS include

- Reporting the status of expanded memory
- Allocating pages in expanded memory
- Deallocating pages in expanded memory
- Diagnostics
- Multitasking support
- Mapping physical pages in expanded memory to logical pages assigned to programs

This paged-memory technique has been used in computers for a long time. There is no reason why your programs cannot take advantage of expanded memory when it is available.

Shortly after expanded memory was introduced, Microsoft announced its support for Version 3.2 of the standard, which included facilities useful for multitasking operating systems. Version 3.2 became known as LIM EMS (Lotus-Intel-Microsoft Expanded Memory Specification). Ashton-Tate, AST Research, and Quadram noticed a limitation in the standard: you could map only a 16K page into an unused area of memory. Why not, therefore, map a large area of memory from the TPA? These circumstances led to the development of the Enhanced Expanded Memory Specification (EEMS).

With enhanced expanded memory, you can move one whole program to the expanded memory area and substitute another program. This capability means that a PC can become multitasking in a real sense. LIM 4.0, introduced in 1988, includes EEMS as well as the old LIM 3.2 standard in its specification. All the companies that have been involved in expanded memory technology support this new standard to at least some degree, although not all firms have implemented all the features called for in the standard.

As long as we use the basic PC machines, we have to learn to live with the 640K area of space assigned to us. Newer machines lift these 640K restrictions.

Memory Management

Memory management under DOS concerns the free area in the TPA. To maintain compatibility between programs and future releases of the operating system, DOS calls should be used for all memory allocation and deallocation requests.

Although we currently can perform all kinds of tricks in memory, tricky programs will cease to work as we move toward multitasking. By learning to work with the limitations of DOS, you will be able to write more portable programs. Unfortunately, some of these tricks (such as direct access to video-display memory) are the staples of DOS programming. Without them, the system is not responsive enough to give users the kind of "feel" necessary for a professional program. Although these tricks make programs that use them less portable, some loss of portability is necessary at times to make good programs.

There are no tricks, however, in memory allocation. Even a tiny error causes the system to lock up. Let's look next at how DOS controls memory in the TPA.

The TPA is organized into a structure called the *memory arena*. DOS maintains a chained list of memory blocks called arena entries, each with its own special control block called an arena header (we examined these in Chapter 3, and table 3.3 shows the header layout). Three DOS functions (Int 21h, Functions 48h, 49h, and 4Ah) request or release memory. The "DOS Reference" section describes each function in detail.

The arena chain (see fig. 10.3) connects each memory block into a list of memory blocks. Whenever two free memory blocks come in contact, they are combined into a single, larger block with only one arena header in the chain.

Fig. 10.3. *Memory-allocation chain.*

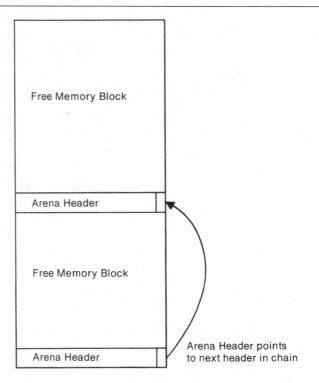

When a request is made for memory, DOS searches through the arena chain to locate a block big enough to fill the request. To assign the blocks, DOS employs a *first-fit* strategy, in which it uses the first block big enough to meet the requirements. If the block contains more memory than was requested, the block is split in two and the excess memory is put back in the list as a separate memory block.

DOS uses this first-fit strategy because it is the most efficient one in general use. Beginning with DOS V3, you can change the allocation strategy to either of the following alternative methods:

- *Best Fit*: In this strategy, the whole memory is searched and the memory block that most closely matches the request fills it.

- *Last Fit*: The last block on the chain (the block with the highest memory address) that fits the allocation request is used.

The memory-allocation strategy does not need to be changed because the most efficient method is already in use. (Very limited testing with DOS V3 seems to indicate that DOS continues to use first fit when loading any program, no matter what method is set. This is not conclusive—because of the number of variables involved, much more testing is required to provide definite answers. One problem is that the DOS loader *always* starts by attempting to get all remaining RAM.) Whenever DOS gets an allocation request, it checks the arena list to see whether any problems exist there. If you write over arena headers and otherwise destroy the list, your program is aborted and you see this message: `Memory Allocation Error.`

Shrinking Program Memory

When a COM program starts, it is assigned all memory because DOS is inherently a single-user system that runs only one program at a time. The loader starts by asking for 65,535 paragraphs (more than possibly can be available) to find how many actually are available, and then asks for exactly that many.

EXE programs also are usually assigned all memory, but in this case you can reduce the assignment if you desire. The EXE program's header has two parameters: MINALLOC and MAXALLOC. MINALLOC is the minimum memory allocation that the program needs to run. If a block with at least the minimum amount of memory needed is available, the program can run.

But DOS always tries to assign a block with MAXALLOC bytes of memory in it, if possible. The Microsoft linker always sets MINALLOC to 0 and MAXALLOC to FFFFh (1,048,560 bytes), unless you tell it other values to use. Thus, whenever you link an EXE program without specifying these values, you guarantee that it gets all available memory.

Note that both Turbo C and Microsoft C automatically release excess memory when they start. Turbo Pascal, however, like the Microsoft linker, does not do so automatically. In Turbo Pascal Versions 4 and 5, which generate EXE files, all available memory is used by default, with the highest area managed as a heap. But a compiler directive can set the size if you want to control it yourself. In addition, internal variables (well documented in the manual) tell you exactly how memory is used.

With older Turbo Pascal versions, which generated COM files, the only way to limit the amount of memory used by a program was to set a maximum size for the heap during compilation. Because of the way its memory is allocated, with the stack and the heap above the program, no effective method exists for determining where a Pascal COM program will end.

BASIC also poses problems for programmers because there is no effective way to determine where the program ends in memory, nor is there a way to start a program except by accessing the EXEC function. A special MEMSET function lets the program set its upper memory limit, but this function is intended to allow a BASIC program to load assembly-language support routines rather than to provide for execution of other programs. CHAIN and RUN (BASIC statements for executing other BASIC programs) replace the existing program in memory with a new program instead of maintaining the present program's status.

Among high-level languages, both C and the newer versions of Turbo Pascal are suitable for dynamic memory-allocation work. C provides good functions for memory allocation and deallocation; you never have to access the DOS functions for this purpose. The latest Turbo Pascal versions incorporate many extensions of conventional (or "standard") Pascal and offer the same functions as C, under slightly different names.

Only programs written in assembly language must explicitly return memory to the memory pool on start-up. Listing 10.1 shows how this is done.

Listing 10.1

```
        mov     sp,offset stack     ;Move stack to safe area
        mov     ah,4Ah              ;Set block
        mov     bx,280h             ;Retain 10K of space
        int     21h
        jc      alloc_error         ;Allocation error

        [MORE PROGRAM CODE]

        dw      64 dup (?)
stack   equ     $
```

Getting More Memory

If a program needs more memory, it can call for additional memory using the Modify Memory Allocation function (Int 21h, Function 4Ah). Upon return, if the memory is available, the carry flag is clear and the AX register has the segment address of the base of the memory. If not enough memory is available to fill the request, the carry flag is set, AX has an error flag (7 = memory control blocks destroyed, 8 = insufficient memory), and register BX has the size of the largest available block.

Both C and the newer versions of Turbo Pascal provide useful functions for obtaining additional memory and for deallocating memory. The capability of older versions of Turbo Pascal (before Version 4.0) for calling for additional memory is minimal or nonexistent unless you use special compiler switches. BASIC provides no way to change allocation of memory to the BASIC program and no way to determine where to go in memory to restrict memory use.

Sometimes, tricky programming can be used in an attempt to free up memory. But Turbo BASIC, for example, while running in the interactive programming environment, stores a symbol table in high memory. This table would be overwritten by another program if you tried to use the memory to load programs.

Again, only in assembly language do we need to access the DOS allocation function directly. In C and the newer Turbo Pascal versions, the library allocation routines access the DOS functions for us. Listing 10.2 provides a way to get memory and determine how much memory is left if the first attempt is denied.

Listing 10.2

```
getmem:
        mov     ah,48h          ;Allocate memory
        mov     bx,bufsize      ;16K memory
        int     21h
        jc      nomem           ;Cannot allocate
        mov     bufseg,ax       ;Save pointer
        jmp     pgm             ;Continue program
nomem:
        cmp     ax,8
        jnz     quit            ;Major alloc error
        mov     bufsize,bx      ;Save buffer size
        mov     ah,48h          ;Allocate memory
        int     21h
        jc      quit            ;Still cannot allocate
pgm:


                [MAIN PART OF PROGRAM]


done:
        mov     ah,49h          ;Deallocate memory
        mov     es,bufseg       ;Point to buffer segment
        int     21h
bufsize dw      400h

bufseg  dw      0
```

Several allocation and deallocation functions are available to programs written in either C or the newer versions of Turbo Pascal, without access to the DOS calls for memory allocation. Using these available functions makes sense because they significantly simplify the operation and keep it under control of the language system. Versions of Turbo Pascal before 4.0 own all available memory in the heap and, as needed, provide for allocation and deallocation of this space to the program. These Pascal allocation and deallocation routines do not get or return space from the arena. BASIC requests and returns nothing.

Programmers of BASIC and Pascal (before Turbo Pascal 4.0) can limit memory artificially with compiler switches, then use DOS function calls to request and free additional memory. But this exercise leads to confusion and poor memory handling. Programs that must have dynamic memory handling should be written in C, the new Turbo Pascal, or assembly language.

Expanded Memory

Sooner or later (when you run out of memory on your PC and have added all the chips needed to take your system to the 640K limit), you probably will buy an expanded memory board. Expanded memory allows quick, effective access to huge amounts of data storage (EMS) or regions for multitasking (EEMS).

Determining Expanded Memory's Availability

To determine whether expanded memory has been installed, use one of the following methods:

- Attempt to open the file EMMXXXX0 (the device driver's guaranteed name). If the open succeeds, either the driver is there or a file with the same name exists. To see whether the driver is there, use the IOCTL function to make a "get output status" request. The driver returns FFh; a file returns 00h. Close the file so that the handle can be reused.

- Inspect the address at the Int 67h vector location. This address is the interrupt entry point for the driver. If EMM.SYS (or an alternate driver) is present, the segment address given is the base of the driver; at offset 000Ah in that segment, the driver name appears as part of the driver's header. Although this process is faster than opening a file (open and close overhead is significant), the method relies on the program to access memory outside its normal memory range.

Listings 10.3 and 10.4 give two separate routines in C to check for the presence of the EMS driver.

Listing 10.3.

```
/* emmtest() */
#include <dos.h>

emmtest()

{
        union REGS regs;
        struct SREGS sregs;
        short int result;
        unsigned int handle;

        regs.h.ah = 0x3d;                /* Open file */
        regs.h.al = 0;                   /* Read mode only */
        regs.x.dx = FP_OFF("EMMXXXX0"); /* File name */
        sregs.ds = FP_SEG("EMMXXXX0");  /* Set the DS register */
        intdosx(&regs,&regs,&sregs);

        handle = regs.x.ax;              /* File handle */
        /* If opened OK, then close the file */
        if(result = (regs.x.cflag == 0)){
                regs.h.ah = 0x3e;
                regs.x.bx = handle;
                intdos(&regs,&regs);
        }
        return(result);
}
```

Listing 10.3, which uses the opening-the-file method to determine whether the EMM is installed, does not bother to check the IOCTL call to see whether the open returned a file or a driver. In most cases this is not a problem. But to be safe you should add a check of the IOCTL call to the function.

Note that compiling this function with Borland C++ yields a warning in the `if()` statement that sets `result`. This warning can be safely ignored because the desired effect is to set the function return value to either TRUE or FALSE, depending on the result of the test. The compiler complains but handles it.

Listing 10.4 turned out to be a real problem for some C programmers who were unaccustomed to dealing with far pointers. When you work on a PC, you must realize the difference between pointers that point within a segment (near pointers); pointers that can point anywhere in memory, given the segment and offset address (far pointers); and pointers that can point anywhere in memory as though memory were not segmented (huge pointers). Whenever pointer arguments are used, you must be precise and always match them; otherwise, unexpected results prevent your program from running.

Listing 10.4

```
/* emmchk() */
#include <dos.h>
#include <malloc.h>                  /* Note: See new include file */

emmchk()

{
        union REGS regs;
        struct SREGS sregs;
        char far *emptr, far *nameptr;
        nameptr = "EMMXXXX0";

        regs.h.ah = 0x35;        /* Get interrupt vector */
        regs.h.al = 0x67;        /* Get it for the EMM */
        intdosx(&regs,&regs,&sregs);

        /* Make a FAR pointer to access the driver */
        emptr = MK_FP(sregs.es,0);   /* Not in Microsoft C 6.0 */
        if (emptr = _fmalloc(sregs.es,9))==NULL)
            {
            printf("Unable to allocate far pointer.\n");
            exit(0);
            }

        /* Return TRUE if they are the same for eight characters */
        return(farcmp(emptr+10,nameptr,8));
}

#define        FALSE    0
#define        TRUE     !FALSE

farcmp(str1,str2,n)

char    far *str1,
        far *str2;
int     n;

{
        while(*str2 && n>0){
                if(*str1 != *str2)
                        return(FALSE);
                n--;
                str1++; str2++;
        }
        return(TRUE);
}
```

A more serious error stems from the way some books describe expanded memory. This error occurs because many expanded-memory discussions mistakenly explain that the pointer at Int 67h points to the beginning of the driver and that 10 bytes from the memory location given in the Int 67h vector is the name EMMXXXX0. A moment's reflection tells you that this statement cannot be true; the interrupt vector points to the location at which control is transferred when the interrupt is called, but the first byte of the driver is part of the driver header and cannot be executable code. (You will learn more about this in Chapter 12, "Device Drivers.")

The vector provides the segment portion of the address, but the name is found at absolute offset 000Ah within that segment because the driver's memory is always allocated to it on paragraph boundaries (only multiples of paragraphs can be allocated). The segment address of any installed driver base is *normalized*—a fancy way of saying that the segment address is adjusted until the offset is zero.

Listing 10.5 is a small program that tests for the presence of expanded memory by both methods and shows you what each one returns.

Listing 10.5

```
#include <stdio.h>

main()

{
        if(emmchk())
                printf("MEM: Expanded memory is present\n");
        else
                printf("MEM: Expanded memory is NOT present\n");
        if(emmtest())
                printf("OPEN: Expanded memory is present\n");
        else
                printf("OPEN: Expanded memory is NOT present\n");
}
```

Using Expanded Memory

When you know that expanded memory is available, you can use the expanded memory functions tied to Int 67h to get and use memory. (The EMS reference section describes the expanded memory functions.) Listings 10.6 and 10.7 show a simple example of the memory functions tied to Int 67.

Listing 10.6

```c
#include <stdio.h>

unsigned int emmalloc();

main()

{
        unsigned int emmhandle;
        char    teststr[80];
        int     i;

        /* Is there any expanded memory? */
        if(!emmtest()){
                printf("Expanded memory is NOT present\n");
                printf("   cannot run this program\n");
                exit(0);
        }

        /* Is the expanded memory manager functional? */
        if(!emmok()){
                printf("Expanded memory manager NOT available\n");
                printf("   cannot run this program\n");
                exit(0);
        }

        /* Get 10 pages of expanded memory for the demo. */
        if((emmhandle = emmalloc(10)) < 0){
                printf("There are not enough pages available\n");
                printf("   cannot run this program\n");
                exit(0);
        }

        /* Write the test string into each of the 10 pages. */
        for(i=0; i<10; i++){
                sprintf(teststr,"%2d: Terry was here\n",i);
                emmmap(emmhandle,i,0);
                emmmove(0,teststr,strlen(teststr)+1);
        }

        /* Now read them back in and recover the test string. */
        for(i=0; i<10; i++){
                emmmap(emmhandle,i,0);
                emmget(0,teststr,strlen(teststr)+1);
                printf("READING FROM BLOCK %d: %s\n",i,teststr);
```

```
        }

        /* Finally, release the expanded memory. */
        emmclose(emmhandle);
}
```

Listing 10.7

```
#include <dos.h>

#define      FALSE    0
#define      TRUE     !FALSE

#define      EMM      0x67

char far *emmbase;

emmtest()

{
        union REGS regs;
        struct SREGS sregs;
        short int result;
        unsigned int handle;

        regs.h.ah = 0x3d;              /* Open file */
        regs.h.al = 0;                 /* Read mode only */
        regs.x.dx = (int)"EMMXXXX0";   /* File name */
        sregs.ds = _DS;                /* Set the DS register */
        intdosx(&regs,&regs,&sregs);

        handle = regs.x.ax;            /* File handle */
        if(result = (regs.x.cflag == 0)){
                regs.h.ah = 0x3e;
                regs.x.bx = handle;
                intdos(&regs,&regs);
        }
        return(result);

}

emmok()

{
        union REGS regs;

        regs.h.ah = 0x40;                    /* Get manager status */
```

continues

Listing 10.7 *continued*

```
                int86(EMM,&regs,&regs);
                if(regs.h.ah != 0)
                        return(FALSE);

                regs.h.ah = 0x41;                    /* Get page frame segment */
                int86(EMM,&regs,&regs);
                if(regs.h.ah != 0)
                        return(FALSE);

                emmbase = MK_FP(regs.x.bx,0);
                return(TRUE);
        }

unsigned int emmalloc(n)

int     n;

{
        union REGS regs;

        regs.h.ah = 0x43;         /* Get handle and allocate memory */
        regs.x.bx = n;
        int86(EMM,&regs,&regs);
        if(regs.h.ah != 0)
                return(-1);
        return(regs.x.dx);
}

emmmap(handle,phys,page)

unsigned int    handle;
int     phys;
int     page;

{
        union REGS regs;

        regs.h.ah = 0x44;              /* Map memory */
        regs.h.al = page;
        regs.x.bx = phys;
        regs.x.dx = handle;
        int86(EMM,&regs,&regs);
        return(regs.h.ah == 0);
}

emmmove(page,str,n)
```

```
int     page;
char    *str;
int     n;

{
        char far *ptr;

        ptr = emmbase + page*16384;
        while(n-- > 0)
                *ptr++ = *str++;
}

emmget(page,str,n)

int     page;
char    *str;
int     n;

{
        char far *ptr;

        ptr = emmbase + page*16384;
        while(n-- > 0)
                *str++ = *ptr++;
}

emmclose(handle)

unsigned int    handle;

{
        union REGS regs;

        regs.h.ah = 0x45;               /* Release handle */
        regs.x.dx = handle;
        int86(EMM,&regs,&regs);
        return(regs.h.ah == 0);
}
```

The program in listing 10.6 demonstrates basic operation of expanded memory. The program does the following:

- Tests to see whether expanded memory is there

- Rests to see whether the expanded memory manager is working properly

- Attempts to allocate 10 pages of expanded memory

- Maps the pages one at a time into the page frame and writes a test string into each page

- Maps the pages back into the page frame, then reads out and prints the test string

These are the most basic operations on expanded memory. They allow you to use the memory area in a wide variety of programs. You can use this type of technique to put a spreadsheet or database in expanded memory: to do so, you define an array of values in the page frame and fill them by their pointers. Remember to use far or huge pointers to access the page because the area certainly will be out of the current segment.

Listing 10.7 is a small library of the expanded memory functions used in listing 10.6. In combination, these functions cover the expanded memory operations, although you might want to add to them by including error checking.

The functions included in the library are

emmtest	Tests for the presence in memory of the expanded memory manager
emmok	Tests the functionality of the expanded memory manager and determines the base address of the page frame
emmalloc	Requests a designated number of pages from the expanded memory manager
emmmap	Maps an expanded memory page into the page frame
emmmove	Moves data into a designated page in the page frame
emmget	Gets data from a designated page in the page frame
emmclose	Returns control of the expanded memory handle to the expanded memory manager

Simple applications of expanded memory can start with these basic functions and then grow as error checking and new features are added.

Extended Memory

Extended memory refers to the memory above the 8086's 1M address limitations. In the confines of the Extended Memory Specification (XMS), extended memory refers also to the high memory area (HMA) and the upper memory blocks (UMBs).

UMBs are areas of usable memory between the 640K boundary of DOS memory and the 1M boundary of the 8086. These areas are usually not contiguous to the 640K available and, until DOS 5.0, they were unavailable to the programmer except through the XMS driver. Beginning with DOS 5.0, UMBs may be accessed through DOS's memory services; the DOS memory services access the XMS driver for you.

The HMA is an oddity in which the 21st address line (line A20) is activated while the CPU is in real mode, adding 65,520 bytes to the amount of memory available for direct access by the CPU in real mode. The way this works follows. Consider the mapping of a segment value plus an offset to physical memory. The physical address accessed may be found by multiplying the segment value by 16 and adding the offset. If this value exceeds 20 bits, the higher bits are truncated, keeping the physical address in the range 000000H through 0FFFFFH. Thus, an address of 0FFFF:0010H describes the physical address 000000H, unless the A20 line is activated. When it is, the address 0FFFF:0010H describes the physical address 0100000H. This is where the extra 65,520 bytes of memory come from; the addresses 0FFFF:0010H through 0FFFF:FFFFH, which are normally mapped to the physical addresses 000000H through 00FFEFH, are mapped to the physical addresses 0100000H through 010FFEFH.

Five groups of services are provided by the XMS driver: driver information functions, HMA management functions, A20 management functions, extended memory management functions, and upper memory management functions. Two additional services find out whether the XMS driver is present and get the address of the XMS driver's control function.

Determining Extended Memory's Availability

To find out whether the XMS driver is present, you can execute the following code:

```
;
;
;
mov  AX,04300H
int  02FH
cmp  AL,080H
jne  XMS_NotPresent
;
; XMS is present
;
```

If the XMS is present, it is necessary to get the address of the XMS driver's control function. This is accomplished through the following code fragment:

```
code segment
```

```
        ;
        ;
        ;
        mov  AX,04310H
        int  02FH
        mov  word ptr [XMS_Control],BX
        mov  word ptr [XMS_Control],ES
        ;
        ;
        ;
        code ends
        data segment
        ;
        ;
        ;
        XMS_Control    dd    (?)
        ;
        ;
        ;
        data ends
```

Using Extended Memory

When you know that extended memory is available, you can use the extended memory functions to get and use memory. (The XMS reference section in Part V describes the expanded memory functions.) The two listings in this section are simple examples of the extended memory functions.

The program in listing 10.8 demonstrates the basic operation of extended memory. The program does the following:

- Tests to see whether extended memory is present

- Gets the XMS version number, checks to see whether the HMA exists, and gets the size of the largest free block of extended memory

- Attempts to allocate an extended memory block

- Writes data to the extended memory block

- Reads data back from the extended memory block

- Frees the extended memory block

- Attempts to allocate an upper memory block

- Frees the upper memory block

These are the most basic operations on expanded memory. They allow you to use the memory area in a wide variety of programs. You can use this type of technique to put data in extended memory.

Listing 10.8

```c
#include  <ctype.h>
#include  <dos.h>
#include  <stdio.h>

struct    XMS_status
    {
    unsigned short version;
    unsigned short revision;
    unsigned short HMA_existence;
    };

struct    XMS_memory_status
    {
    unsigned short largest_block;
    unsigned short total_free_memory;
    unsigned short error_status;
    };

struct bstat
    {
    unsigned short lock_count;
    unsigned short free_handle_count;
    };

union     memory_address
    {
    unsigned long  long_offset;
    struct conventional_address
        {
        unsigned short conventional_offset;
        unsigned short conventional_segment;
        }       c_a;
    };

struct    XMS_move_data
    {
    unsigned long          transfer_size;
    unsigned short         source_handle;
    union memory_address   source_offset;
    unsigned short         destination_handle;
    union memory_address   destination_offset;
    };
```

continues

Listing 10.8 continued

```
struct umb_data
    {
    unsigned short segment_number;
    unsigned short segment_size;
    };

extern unsigned short far
    a20_stat(void);
extern unsigned short far
    alter_a20(unsigned short change_code);
extern unsigned short far
    hma_alloc(unsigned short size_in_bytes);
extern unsigned short far
    hma_free(void);
extern void far
    hma_move(unsigned short count, unsigned short direction,
                             unsigned short hma_offset,
                             void far *data);
extern unsigned short far
    umb_alloc(unsigned short size, struct umb_data far *ptr);
extern unsigned short far
    umb_free(unsigned short segment);
extern unsigned short far
    xms_alloc(unsigned short size, unsigned short far *handle);
extern void far
    xms_avail(struct XMS_memory_status far *ptr);
extern unsigned short far
    xms_bstat(unsigned short handle, struct bstat far *ptr);
extern unsigned short far
    xms_free(unsigned short handle);
extern unsigned short far
    xms_lock(unsigned short handle,
              unsigned long *linear_address);
extern unsigned short far
    xms_move(struct XMS_move_data far *ptr);
extern unsigned short far
    xms_realloc(unsigned short handle, unsigned short size);
extern void far
    xms_stat(struct XMS_status far *ptr);
extern unsigned short far
    xms_test(void);
extern unsigned short far
    xms_unlock(unsigned short handle);
```

```
/*    Return codes   */

#define    A20_DISABLED                       (0x0000)
#define    A20_ENABLED                        (0x0001)
#define    FAILURE                            (0x0000)
#define    SUCCESS                            (0x0001)
#define    FUNCTION_NOT_IMPLEMENTED           (0x0080)
#define    VDISK_DEVICE_DETECTED              (0x0081)
#define    A20_ERROR_OCCURRED                 (0x0082)
#define    HMA_DOES_NOT_EXIST                 (0x0090)
#define    HMA_ALREADY_IN_USE                 (0x0091)
#define    NOT_ENOUGH_BYTES_TO_ALLOC_HMA      (0x0092)
#define    HMA_NOT_ALLOCATED                  (0x0093)
#define    A20_LINE_STILL_ENABLED             (0x0094)
#define    ALL_EXTENDED_MEMORY_ALLOCATED      (0x00A0)
#define    ALL_EXTENDED_MEMORY_HANDLES_USED   (0x00A1)
#define    INVALID_HANDLE                     (0x00A2)
#define    INVALID_SOURCE_HANDLE              (0x00A3)
#define    INVALID_SOURCE_OFFSET              (0x00A4)
#define    INVALID_DESTINATION_HANDLE         (0x00A5)
#define    INVALID_DESTINATION_OFFSET         (0x00A6)
#define    INVALID_LENGTH                     (0x00A7)
#define    INVALID_OVERLAP                    (0x00A8)
#define    PARITY_ERROR                       (0x00A9)
#define    BLOCK_NOT_LOCKED                   (0x00AA)
#define    HANDLE_IS_LOCKED                   (0x00AB)
#define    LOCK_COUNT_OVERFLOW                (0x00AC)
#define    LOCK_FAILED                        (0x00AD)
#define    SMALLER_UMB_AVAILABLE              (0x00B0)
#define    NO_UMBS_AVAILABLE                  (0x00B1)
#define    INVALID_UMB_SEGMENT                (0x00B2)
#define    ILLEGAL_PARAMETER                  (0xFFFF)


/*    Codes for alter_a20()    */

#define    GLOBAL_A20_LINE     (0)
#define    LOCAL_A20_LINE      (2)
#define    ENABLE_A20_LINE     (0)
#define    DISABLE_A20_LINE    (1)


/*    Codes for hma_move()     */

#define    COPY_FROM_HMA   (1)
#define    COPY_TO_HMA     (0)


#define    KILOBYTE   (1024)

unsigned char   test_buffer[ KILOBYTE ];
```

continues

DOS
PROGRAMMING

Listing 10.8 *continued*

```c
void test_hma(void)
    {
    int             HMA_allocated;
    int             A20_status;
    int             original_A20_status;
    unsigned short result;

    HMA_allocated = 0;
    result = hma_alloc(0xFFF0);
    switch (result)
        {
        case SUCCESS:
            printf("HMA successfully allocated to current process\n");
            HMA_allocated++;
            break;
        case FUNCTION_NOT_IMPLEMENTED:
            printf("HMA allocate not implemented by XMS\n");
            break;
        case VDISK_DEVICE_DETECTED:
            printf("VDISK device detected; couldn't allocate HMA\n");
            break;
        case HMA_DOES_NOT_EXIST:
            printf("HMA cannot be allocated; doesn't exist\n");
            return;
        case HMA_ALREADY_IN_USE:
            printf("HMA cannot be allocated; already in use\n");
            break;
        case NOT_ENOUGH_BYTES_TO_ALLOC_HMA:
            printf("Not enough bytes to allocate HMA were specified\n");
            return;
        default:
            printf("Invalid result of hma_alloc(): 0x%.4X\n", result);
            return;
        }
    if (HMA_allocated)
        {
        original_A20_status = A20_status = -1;
        result = a20_stat();
        switch (result)
            {
            case A20_DISABLED:
                original_A20_status = A20_status = 0;
                break;
            case A20_ENABLED:
                original_A20_status = A20_status = 1;
                break;
            case FUNCTION_NOT_IMPLEMENTED:
                printf("Can't get A20 line status; function not implemented\n");
```

```
                    break;
              case VDISK_DEVICE_DETECTED:
                    printf("Can't get A20 line status; VDISK device detected\n");
                    break;
              default:
                    printf("Can't get A20 line status; unexpected result 0x%.4X \n",
                        result);
                    break;
              }
      if (A20_status == 0)      /* Disabled */
          {
          result = alter_a20(GLOBAL_A20_LINE ¦ ENABLE_A20_LINE);
          switch (result)
              {
              case SUCCESS:
                    printf("A20 line globally enabled\n");
                    A20_status = 1;
                    break;
              case FUNCTION_NOT_IMPLEMENTED:
                    printf("Function not implemented; couldn't enable A20 line\n");
                    break;
              case VDISK_DEVICE_DETECTED:
                    printf("VDISK device detected; couldn't enable A20 line\n");
                    break;
              case A20_ERROR_OCCURRED:
                    printf("Error occurred while attempting to enable A20 line\n");
                    break;
              case ILLEGAL_PARAMETER:
                    printf("Illegal argument to alter_a20()\n");
                    break;
              default:
                    printf("Unexpected result 0x%.4X from alter_a20()\n", result);
                    break;
              }
          }
      if (A20_status == 1)
          {
          int  k;

          memset(test_buffer, 0x55, KILOBYTE);
          hma_move(KILOBYTE, COPY_TO_HMA, 0, test_buffer);
          memset(test_buffer, 0xAA, KILOBYTE);
          hma_move(KILOBYTE, COPY_FROM_HMA, 0, test_buffer);
          result = 1;
          for (k = 0; k < KILOBYTE; k++)
              {
              if (test_buffer[ k ] != 0x55)
```

continues

Listing 10.8 continued

```c
                    {
                    printf("Error transferring data to/from HMA\n");
                    result = 0;
                    break;
                    }
                }
        if (result)
            {
            memset(test_buffer, 0xAA, KILOBYTE);
            hma_move(KILOBYTE, COPY_TO_HMA, 0, test_buffer);
            memset(test_buffer, 0x55, KILOBYTE);
            hma_move(KILOBYTE, COPY_FROM_HMA, 0, test_buffer);
            for (k = 0; k < KILOBYTE; k++)
                {
                if (test_buffer[ k ] != 0xAA)
                    {
                    printf("Error transferring data to/from HMA\n");
                    result = 0;
                    break;
                    }
                }
            }
        if (result)
            printf("Transfer of data to/from HMA test successful\n");
        if (original_A20_status == 0)
            {
            result = alter_a20(GLOBAL_A20_LINE | DISABLE_A20_LINE);
            switch (result)
                {
                case SUCCESS:
                    printf("A20 line globally disabled\n");
                    break;
                case FUNCTION_NOT_IMPLEMENTED:
                    printf("Function not implemented; disable A20 line\n");
                    break;
                case VDISK_DEVICE_DETECTED:
                    printf("VDISK device detected; disable A20 line\n");
                    break;
                case A20_ERROR_OCCURRED:
                    printf("Error while attempting to disable A20 line\n");
                    break;
                case ILLEGAL_PARAMETER:
                    printf("Illegal argument to alter_a20()\n");
                    break;
                case A20_LINE_STILL_ENABLED:
                    printf("A20 line still enabled\n");
                    break;
```

```
                                    default:
                                        printf("Unexpected result 0x%.4X from alter_a20()\n",
                                            result);
                                        break;
                                }
                        }
                }
            result = hma_free();
            switch (result)
                {
                case SUCCESS:
                    printf("HMA successfully freed\n");
                    break;
                case FUNCTION_NOT_IMPLEMENTED:
                    printf("HMA free not implemented by XMS\n");
                    break;
                case VDISK_DEVICE_DETECTED:
                    printf("VDISK device detected; couldn't free HMA\n");
                    break;
                case HMA_DOES_NOT_EXIST:
                    printf("HMA does not exist\n");
                    return;
                case HMA_NOT_ALLOCATED:
                    printf("HMA was not allocated\n");
                    return;
                default:
                    printf("Invalid result of hma_free(): 0x%.4X\n", result);
                    return;
                }
            }
    else
        {
        original_A20_status = A20_status = -1;
        result = a20_stat();
        switch (result)
            {
            case A20_DISABLED:
                original_A20_status = A20_status = 0;
                break;
            case A20_ENABLED:
                original_A20_status = A20_status = 1;
                break;
            case FUNCTION_NOT_IMPLEMENTED:
                printf("Can't get A20 line status; function not implemented\n");
                break;
            case VDISK_DEVICE_DETECTED:
                printf("Can't get A20 line status; VDISK device detected\n");
                break;
```

continues

Listing 10.8 continued

```
            default:
                printf("Can't get A20 line status; unexpected result 0x%.4X\n",
                    result);
                break;
            }
    if (A20_status == 0)      /* Disabled */
        {
        result = alter_a20(GLOBAL_A20_LINE | ENABLE_A20_LINE);
        switch (result)
            {
            case SUCCESS:
                printf("A20 line globally enabled\n");
                A20_status = 1;
                break;
            case FUNCTION_NOT_IMPLEMENTED:
                printf("Function not implemented; couldn't enable A20 line\n");
                break;
            case VDISK_DEVICE_DETECTED:
                printf("VDISK device detected; couldn't enable A20 line\n");
                break;
            case A20_ERROR_OCCURRED:
                printf("Error occurred while attempting to enable A20 line\n");
                break;
            case ILLEGAL_PARAMETER:
                printf("Illegal argument to alter_a20()\n");
                break;
            default:
                printf("Unexpected result 0x%.4X from alter_a20()\n", result);
                break;
            }
        }
    if (A20_status == 1)      /* Enabled */
        {
        int  k;
        int  m;

        memset(test_buffer, 0, KILOBYTE);
        hma_move(KILOBYTE, COPY_FROM_HMA, 0, test_buffer);
        for (k = 0; k < (KILOBYTE / 16); k++)
            {
            printf("HMA:%.3X0 ", k);
            for (m = 0; m < 16; m++)
                printf("%.2X ", test_buffer[ (k << 4) + m ]);
            for (m = 0; m < 16; m++)
                {
                if (isprint(test_buffer[ (k << 4) + m ]))
                    printf("%c", test_buffer[ (k << 4) + m ]);
```

```
                        else
                            printf(".");
                    }
                printf("\n");
                    }
            if (original_A20_status == 0)
                {
                result = alter_a20(GLOBAL_A20_LINE | DISABLE_A20_LINE);
                switch (result)
                    {
                    case SUCCESS:
                        printf("A20 line globally disabled\n");
                        break;
                    case FUNCTION_NOT_IMPLEMENTED:
                        printf("Function not implemented; disable A20 line\n");
                        break;
                    case VDISK_DEVICE_DETECTED:
                        printf("VDISK device detected; disable A20 line\n");
                        break;
                    case A20_ERROR_OCCURRED:
                        printf("Error while attempting to disable A20 line\n");
                        break;
                    case ILLEGAL_PARAMETER:
                        printf("Illegal argument to alter_a20()\n");
                        break;
                    case A20_LINE_STILL_ENABLED:
                        printf("A20 line still enabled\n");
                        break;
                    default:
                        printf("Unexpected result 0x%.4X from alter_a20()\n",
                            result);
                        break;
                    }
                }
            }
        }
    }

void test_xms(void)
    {
    struct XMS_memory_status status;
    struct bstat            block_status;
    struct XMS_move_data    move_block;
    unsigned short          handle;
    unsigned short          result;
    unsigned long           address;
    int                     move_ok;
```

continues

Listing 10.8 continued

```
xms_avail(&status);
printf("Largest block of XMS memory available = %.4X Kbytes\n",
    status.largest_block);
printf("Total free memory =                    %.4X Kbytes\n",
    status.total_free_memory);
printf("Error status =                         %.4X\n", status.error_status);
if (status.error_status)
    return;
result = xms_alloc(status.largest_block, &handle);
switch (result)
    {
    case SUCCESS:
        printf("Memory allocated; handle = %.4X\n", handle);
        break;
    case FUNCTION_NOT_IMPLEMENTED:
        printf("Function not implemented: xms_alloc\n");
        return;
    case VDISK_DEVICE_DETECTED:
        printf("VDISK device detected: xms_alloc\n");
        return;
    case ALL_EXTENDED_MEMORY_ALLOCATED:
        printf("All memory allocated: xms_alloc\n");
        return;
    case ALL_EXTENDED_MEMORY_HANDLES_USED:
        printf("All memory handles in use: xms_alloc\n");
        return;
    default:
        printf("Unexpected result from xms_alloc: %.4X\n", result);
        return;
    }
result = xms_realloc(handle, status.largest_block / 2);
switch (result)
    {
    case SUCCESS:
        printf("Block successfully reallocated in half\n");
        break;
    case FUNCTION_NOT_IMPLEMENTED:
        printf("xms_realloc not implemented\n");
        break;
    case VDISK_DEVICE_DETECTED:
        printf("VDISK device detected: xms_realloc\n");
        break;
    case ALL_EXTENDED_MEMORY_ALLOCATED:
        printf("xms_realloc failed: all extended memory allocated\n");
        break;
    case ALL_EXTENDED_MEMORY_HANDLES_USED:
        printf("xms_realloc failed: all extended memory handles in use\n");
```

```
                break;
        case INVALID_HANDLE:
                printf("xms_realloc failed: invalid handle\n");
                break;
        case HANDLE_IS_LOCKED:
                printf("xms_realloc failed: handle is locked\n");
                break;
        default:
                printf("Unexpected result from xms_realloc: 0x%.4X\n", result);
                break;
        }
memset(test_buffer, 0x55, KILOBYTE);
move_block.transfer_size = KILOBYTE;
move_block.source_handle = 0;
move_block.source_offset.c_a.conventional_offset = FP_OFF((void far *)test_buffer);
move_block.source_offset.c_a.conventional_segment = FP_SEG((void far *)test_buffer);
move_block.destination_handle = handle;
move_block.destination_offset.long_offset = 0L;
result = xms_move(&move_block);
move_ok = 0;
switch (result)
        {
        case SUCCESS:
                printf("Data successfully written to XMS\n");
                move_ok = 1;
                break;
        case FUNCTION_NOT_IMPLEMENTED:
                printf("xms_move not implemented\n");
                break;
        case VDISK_DEVICE_DETECTED:
                printf("VDISK device detected: xms_alloc\n");
                break;
        case INVALID_SOURCE_HANDLE:
                printf("Invalid source handle\n");
                break;
        case INVALID_SOURCE_OFFSET:
                printf("Invalid source offset\n");
                break;
        case INVALID_DESTINATION_HANDLE:
                printf("Invalid destination handle\n");
                break;
        case INVALID_DESTINATION_OFFSET:
                printf("Invalid destination offset\n");
                break;
        case INVALID_LENGTH:
                printf("Invalid offset\n");
                break;
        case INVALID_OVERLAP:
                printf("Invalid overlap\n");
```

continues

Listing 10.8 continued

```
                break;
        case PARITY_ERROR:
                printf("Parity Error\n");
                break;
        default:
                printf("Unexpected result from xms_move(): 0x%.4X\n");
                break;
        }
    if (move_ok)
        {
        memset(test_buffer, 0xAA, KILOBYTE);
        move_block.transfer_size = KILOBYTE;
        move_block.source_handle = handle;
        move_block.source_offset.long_offset = 0L;
        move_block.destination_handle = 0;
        move_block.destination_offset.c_a.conventional_offset =
            FP_OFF((void far *)test_buffer);
        move_block.destination_offset.c_a.conventional_segment =
            FP_SEG((void far *)test_buffer);
        result = xms_move(&move_block);
        move_ok = 0;
        switch (result)
            {
            case SUCCESS:
                printf("Data successfully read from XMS\n");
                move_ok = 1;
                break;
            case FUNCTION_NOT_IMPLEMENTED:
                printf("xms_move not implemented\n");
                break;
            case VDISK_DEVICE_DETECTED:
                printf("VDISK device detected: xms_alloc\n");
                break;
            case INVALID_SOURCE_HANDLE:
                printf("Invalid source handle\n");
                break;
            case INVALID_SOURCE_OFFSET:
                printf("Invalid source offset\n");
                break;
            case INVALID_DESTINATION_HANDLE:
                printf("Invalid destination handle\n");
                break;
            case INVALID_DESTINATION_OFFSET:
                printf("Invalid destination offset\n");
                break;
            caseINVALID_LENGTH:
                printf("Invalid offset\n");
```

```
                        break;
              case INVALID_OVERLAP:
                  printf("Invalid overlap\n");
                  break;
              case PARITY_ERROR:
                  printf("Parity Error\n");
                  break;
              default:
                  printf("Unexpected result from xms_move(): 0x%.4X\n");
                  break;
              }
      if (move_ok)
              {
              int   k;

              for (k = 0; k < KILOBYTE; k++)
                  {
                  if (test_buffer[ k ] != 0x55)
                      {
                      printf("Error: corrupted data at offset 0x%.4X; data = %.2X\n",
                          k, test_buffer[ k ]);
                      move_ok = 0;
                      }
                  }
              if (move_ok)
                  printf("Data read from XMS verified OK\n");
              }
          }
result = xms_lock(handle, &address);
switch (result)
      {
      case SUCCESS:
          printf("Block locked; linear address = %.8lX\n", address);
          break;
      case FUNCTION_NOT_IMPLEMENTED:
          printf("Function not implemented: xms_lock\n");
          break;
      case VDISK_DEVICE_DETECTED:
          printf("VDISK device detected: xms_lock\n");
          break;
      case INVALID_HANDLE:
          printf("Handle is invalid\n");
          break;
      case LOCK_COUNT_OVERFLOW:
          printf("Lock count overflowed\n");
          break;
      case LOCK_FAILED:
          printf("Lock failed\n");
```

continues

Listing 10.8 continued

```
                    break;
            default:
    printf("Unexpected result from xms_lock: %.4X\n", result);
                break;
        }
    result = xms_free(handle);
    switch (result)
        {
        case SUCCESS:
            printf("XMS memory freed\n");
            break;
        case FUNCTION_NOT_IMPLEMENTED:
            printf("Function not implemented: xms_free\n");
            break;
        case VDISK_DEVICE_DETECTED:
            printf("VDISK device detected: xms_free\n");
            break;
        case INVALID_HANDLE:
            printf("Handle is invalid\n");
            break;
        case HANDLE_IS_LOCKED:
            printf("Handle is locked\n");
            break;
        default:
            printf("Unexpected result from xms_free: %.4X\n", result);
            break;
        }
    result = xms_bstat(handle, &block_status);
    switch (result)
        {
        case SUCCESS:
            printf("Lock count =        %d\n", block_status.lock_count);
            printf("Free handle count = %d\n", block_status.free_handle_count);
            break;
        case FUNCTION_NOT_IMPLEMENTED:
            printf("Function not implemented: xms_bstat\n");
            break;
        case VDISK_DEVICE_DETECTED:
            printf("VDISK device detected: xms_bstat\n");
            break;
        case INVALID_HANDLE:
            printf("Handle is invalid\n");
            break;
        default:
            printf("Unexpected result from xms_bstat: %.4X\n", result);
            break;
```

```
        }
    result = xms_lock(handle, &address);
    switch (result)
        {
        case SUCCESS:
            printf("Block locked; linear address = %.8lX\n", address);
            break;
        case FUNCTION_NOT_IMPLEMENTED:
            printf("Function not implemented: xms_lock\n");
            break;
        case VDISK_DEVICE_DETECTED:
            printf("VDISK device detected: xms_lock\n");
            break;
        case INVALID_HANDLE:
            printf("Handle is invalid\n");
            break;
        case LOCK_COUNT_OVERFLOW:
            printf("Lock count overflowed\n");
            break;
        case LOCK_FAILED:
            printf("Lock failed\n");
            break;
        default:
            printf("Unexpected result from xms_lock: %.4X\n", result);
            break;
        }
    result = xms_bstat(handle, &block_status);
    switch (result)
        {
        case SUCCESS:
            printf("Lock count =        %d\n", block_status.lock_count);
            printf("Free handle count = %d\n", block_status.free_handle_count);
            break;
        case FUNCTION_NOT_IMPLEMENTED:
            printf("Function not implemented: xms_bstat\n");
            break;
        case VDISK_DEVICE_DETECTED:
            printf("VDISK device detected: xms_bstat\n");
            break;
        case INVALID_HANDLE:
            printf("Handle is invalid\n");
            break;
        default:
            printf("Unexpected result from xms_bstat: %.4X\n", result);
            break;
        }
    result = xms_unlock(handle);
    switch (result)
```

continues

Listing 10.8 *continued*

```
        {
    case SUCCESS:
        printf("Block unlocked\n");
        break;
    case FUNCTION_NOT_IMPLEMENTED:
        printf("Function not implemented: xms_unlock\n");
        break;
    case VDISK_DEVICE_DETECTED:
        printf("VDISK device detected: xms_unlock\n");
        break;
    case INVALID_HANDLE:
        printf("Handle is invalid\n");
        break;
    case BLOCK_NOT_LOCKED:
        printf("Block was not locked\n");
        break;
    default:
        printf("Unexpected result from xms_unlock: %.4X\n", result);
        break;
    }
result = xms_free(handle);
switch (result)
        {
    case SUCCESS:
        printf("XMS memory freed\n");
        break;
    case FUNCTION_NOT_IMPLEMENTED:
        printf("Function not implemented: xms_free\n");
        break;
    case VDISK_DEVICE_DETECTED:
        printf("VDISK device detected: xms_free\n");
        break;
    case INVALID_HANDLE:
        printf("Handle is invalid\n");
        break;
    case HANDLE_IS_LOCKED:
        printf("Handle is locked\n");
        break;
    default:
        printf("Unexpected result from xms_free: %.4X\n", result);
        break;
    }
result = xms_bstat(handle, &block_status);
switch (result)
        {
    case SUCCESS:
        printf("Lock count =        %d\n", block_status.lock_count);
        printf("Free handle count = %d\n", block_status.free_handle_count);
        break;
```

```
        case FUNCTION_NOT_IMPLEMENTED:
            printf("Function not implemented: xms_bstat\n");
            break;
        case VDISK_DEVICE_DETECTED:
            printf("VDISK device detected: xms_bstat\n");
            break;
        case INVALID_HANDLE:
            printf("Handle is invalid\n");
            break;
        default:
            printf("Unexpected result from xms_bstat: %.4X\n", result);
            break;
    }
result = xms_unlock(handle);
switch (result)
    {
    case SUCCESS:
        printf("Block unlocked\n");
        break;
    case FUNCTION_NOT_IMPLEMENTED:
        printf("Function not implemented: xms_unlock\n");
        break;
    case VDISK_DEVICE_DETECTED:
        printf("VDISK device detected: xms_unlock\n");
        break;
    case INVALID_HANDLE:
        printf("Handle is invalid\n");
        break;
    case BLOCK_NOT_LOCKED:
        printf("Block was not locked\n");
        break;
    default:
        printf("Unexpected result from xms_unlock: %.4X\n", result);
        break;
    }
result = xms_bstat(handle, &block_status);
switch (result)
    {
    case SUCCESS:
        printf("Lock count =        %d\n", block_status.lock_count);
        printf("Free handle count = %d\n", block_status.free_handle_count);
        break;
    case FUNCTION_NOT_IMPLEMENTED:
        printf("Function not implemented: xms_bstat\n");
        break;
    case VDISK_DEVICE_DETECTED:
        printf("VDISK device detected: xms_bstat\n");
        break;
```

continues

Listing 10.8 *continued*

```
                case INVALID_HANDLE:
                    printf("Handle is invalid\n");
                    break;
            default:
                printf("Unexpected result from xms_bstat: %.4X\n", result);
                break;
        }
    result = xms_free(handle);
    switch (result)
        {
        case SUCCESS:
            printf("XMS memory freed\n");
            break;
        case FUNCTION_NOT_IMPLEMENTED:
            printf("Function not implemented: xms_free\n");
            break;
        case VDISK_DEVICE_DETECTED:
            printf("VDISK device detected: xms_free\n");
            break;
        case INVALID_HANDLE:
            printf("Handle is invalid\n");
            break;
        case HANDLE_IS_LOCKED:
            printf("Handle is locked\n");
            break;
        default:
            printf("Unexpected result from xms_free: %.4X\n", result);
            break;
        }
    }


void test_umb(void)
    {
    unsigned short     status;
    unsigned short     size;
    struct umb_data    umb;

    status = umb_alloc(0xFFFF, &umb);
    switch (status)
        {
        case SUCCESS:
            printf("We somehow allocated 1Mb of UMBs!\n");
            return;
        case FUNCTION_NOT_IMPLEMENTED:
            printf("UMB alloc not implemented...\n");
            return;
        case SMALLER_UMB_AVAILABLE:
```

```
                  size = umb.segment_size;
                  printf("Smaller UMB available: 0x%.4X paragraphs\n", size);
                  break;
          case NO_UMBS_AVAILABLE:
                  printf("Sorry, no UMBs available\n");
                  return;
          default:
                  printf("Unexpected result from umb_alloc(): 0x%.4X\n", status);
                  return;
          }
  status = umb_alloc(size, &umb);
  switch (status)
          {
          case SUCCESS:
                  printf("0x%.4X paragraphs allocated at %.4X:0000\n", umb.segment_size,
                         umb.segment_number);
                  break;
          case FUNCTION_NOT_IMPLEMENTED:
                  printf("UMB alloc not implemented...\n");
                  return;
          case SMALLER_UMB_AVAILABLE:
                  size = umb.segment_size;
                  printf("Smaller UMB available: 0x%.4X paragraphs\n", size);
                  return;
          case NO_UMBS_AVAILABLE:
                  printf("Sorry, no UMBs available\n");
                  return;
          default:
                  printf("Unexpected result from umb_alloc(): 0x%.4X\n", status);
                  return;
          }
  status = umb_free(umb.segment_number);
  switch (status)
          {
          case SUCCESS:
                  printf("UMB successfully freed\n");
                  break;
          case FUNCTION_NOT_IMPLEMENTED:
                  printf("umb_free not implemented...\n");
                  break;
          case INVALID_UMB_SEGMENT:
                  printf("Invalid segment\n");
                  break;
          default:
                  printf("Unexpected result from umb_free: 0x%.4X\n", status);
                  break;
          }
  }
```

continues

Listing 10.8 *continued*

```c
int main()
    {
    unsigned short     result;
    struct XMS_status  status;
    int                k;
    int                m;

    result = xms_test();
    switch (result)
        {
        case SUCCESS:
        printf("XMS Detected\n");
            break;
        case FAILURE:
            printf("XMS Not Detected\n");
            return 1;
        default:
            printf("Invalid result of xms_test(): 0x%.4X\n",
                result);
            return 1;
        }
    xms_stat(&status);
    printf("XMS Version:        %.2X.%.2X\n", status.version >> 8,
        status.version & 0x00FF);
    printf("XMS Driver Revision: %.2X.%.2X\n", status.revision >> 8,
        status.revision & 0x00FF);
    printf("HMA existence:      %.4X\n", status.HMA_existence);
    if (status.HMA_existence == 1)
        test_hma();
    test_xms();
    test_umb();
    return 0;
    }
```

Listing 10.9 is a small library of the extended memory functions used in listing 10.8. In combination, these functions cover the extended memory operations. The following functions are included in the library:

_xms_test   Tests for the presence of the extended memory manager

_xms_stat   Gets the version number of the extended memory manager and checks for the existence of the HMA

_xms_avail   Gets the size of the largest free block of extended memory

_xms_alloc   Requests an extended memory block from the extended memory manager

_xms_realloc	Reallocates an extended memory block, changing its size
_xms_lock	Locks a block of extended memory
_xms_unlock	Unlocks a block of extended memory
_xms_bstat	Gets the status of an extended memory block
_xms_move	Moves data into or out of an extended memory block
_xms_free	Returns an extended memory block to the extended memory manager
_hma_alloc	Allocates the HMA
_hma_free	Releases the HMA
_hma_move	Moves data into or out of the HMA
_alter_a20	Enables or disables the A20 line
_a20_stat	Gets the status of the A20 line
_umb_alloc	Allocates a UMB
_umb_free	Frees a UMB

Simple applications of extended memory can start with these basic functions and then grow as error checking and new features are added.

Listing 10.9

```
page 55,132
;
; XMS library functions
;

XMS_CODE  SEGMENT    'CODE'

public    _xms_test
public    _xms_stat
public    _xms_avail
public    _xms_alloc
public    _xms_realloc
public    _xms_lock
public    _xms_unlock
public    _xms_bstat
public    _xms_move
public    _xms_free
public    _hma_alloc
public    _hma_free
public    _hma_move
```

continues

Listing 10.9 continued

```
        public  _alter_a20
        public  _a20_stat
        public  _umb_alloc
        public  _umb_free

        ASSUME  CS:XMS_CODE
        ASSUME  DS:NOTHING
        ASSUME  ES:NOTHING
        ASSUME  SS:NOTHING


        ;
        ; Storage for XMS call address
        ;
        XMS_Control         LABEL    DWORD

        XMS_Control_Offset  dw   (?)
        XMS_Control_Segment dw   (?)


        ;
        ; Test for the presence of the XMS driver and, if present,
        ; get the address of the XMS function call
        ;
        ; Returns AX = 1 if XMS found; otherwise AX = 0
        ;
        ; Borland C++ prototype: unsigned short far xms_test(void);
        ;


                ALIGN   16

_xms_test PROC FAR

                push ES             ; Save ES
                mov  AX,04300H      ; See if XMS is present
                int  2FH            ;
                cmp  AL,080H        ; If it is, AL = 80H
                jne  __x_t2
                ;
                ; XMS is present; get the function address
                ;
                mov  AX,04310H      ;
                int  2FH            ;
                mov  CS:[XMS_Control_Offset],BX
                mov  CS:[XMS_Control_Segment],ES

                ASSUME    DS:NOTHING
```

```
              mov  AX,1              ; Return 1
              ;
              ; Return...
              ;
__x_t1:
              pop  ES               ; Restore ES
              ret                   ;
              ;
              ; Return error
              ;
__x_t2:
              xor  AX,AX            ; Return 0
              jmp  __x_t1

_xms_test ENDP
;
; Get XMS status
;
; Stores the XMS version number, driver revision number,
; and HMA existence flag at the address on the stack
;
; Borland C prototype:
:     void far xms_stat(struct XMS_status far *ptr);
;
; Data structure:     struct   XMS_status
;                     {
;                     unsigned short version;
;                     unsigned short revision;
;                     unsigned short HMA_existence;
;                     };
;


              ALIGN     16


_xms_stat PROC FAR

              push SI               ; Save registers
              push DS               ;
              push BP               ;
              mov  BP,SP            ; Set argument pointer
              mov  AH,0             ; call XMS
              call CS:[XMS_Control]
              lds  SI,[BP + 10]     ; Get address of pointer
              mov  [SI],AX          ; Store XMS version number
              mov  [SI + 2],BX      ; Store driver revision number
              mov  [SI + 4],DX      ; Store HMA existence flag
              pop  BP               ; Restore registers
```

continues

Listing 10.9 continued

```
        pop  DS           ;
        pop  SI           ;
        ret               ; Return

_xms_stat ENDP
;
; Get XMS memory status
;
; Stores the size of the largest free XMS block and the total
; amount of free XMS memory at the address on the stack
;
; Borland C++ prototype:
:    void far xms_avail(struct XMS_memory_status far *ptr);
;
; Data structure:    struct   XMS_memory_status
;                    {
;                    unsigned short largest_block;
;                    unsigned short total_free_memory;
;                    unsigned short error_status;
;                    };
;
; Note: the block size and the amount of free memory are in K bytes
;


        ALIGN    16


_xms_avail    PROC FAR

        push SI           ; Save registers
        push DS           ;
        push BP           ;
        mov  BP,SP        ; Set argument pointer
        xor  BX,BX        ;
        mov  AH,8         ; Call XMS
        call CS:[XMS_Control]
        lds  SI,[BP + 10] ; Get address of pointer
        mov  [SI],AX      ; Store largest block size
        mov  [SI + 2],DX  ; Store total memory available
        xor  BH,BH        ;
        mov  [SI + 4],BX  ; Store error status
        pop  BP           ; Restore registers
        pop  DS           ;
        pop  SI           ;
        ret               ; Return

_xms_avail    ENDP
;
```

```
; Allocate a block of extended memory
;
; Returns status in AX:   0001 Success
;                         0080 Function not implemented
;                         0081 VDISK device detected
;                         00A0 All extended memory is allocated
;                         00A1 All extended memory handles are in use
;
; Borland C++ prototype:
;    unsigned short far xms_alloc(unsigned short size,
;    unsigned short far *handle);
;

            ALIGN    16

_xms_alloc      PROC FAR

            push SI              ; Save registers
            push DS              ;
            push BP              ; Make pointer to arguments
            mov  BP,SP           ;
            mov  DX,[BP + 10]    ; Get size in K bytes
            mov  AH,9            ; Request memory
            call CS:[XMS_Control
            or   AX,AX           ; Error?
            jz   __x_a2          ;
            ;
            ; Set handle and return
            ;
__x_a1:
            lds  SI,[BP + 12]    ; Store handle
            mov  [SI],DX         ;
            pop  BP              ; Restore registers
            pop  DS              ;
            pop  SI              ;
            ret                  ; Return
            ;
            ; Return error
            ;
__x_a2:
            mov  AL,BL           ; Get return code
            xor  DX,DX           ; Create NULL handle
            jmp  __x_a1          ;

_xms_alloc      ENDP
;
; Resize an XMS block
;
; Returns status in AX:   0001 Success
```

continues

Listing 10.9 *continued*

```
;                          0080 Function not implemented
;                          0081 VDISK device detected
;                          00A0 All extended memory is allocated
;                          00A1 All extended memory handles in use
;                          00A2 Invalid handle
;                          00AB Block is locked
;
; Borland C++ prototype:
;    unsigned short far xms_realloc(unsigned short handle,
;    unsigned short size);
;

          ALIGN     16

_xms_realloc    PROC FAR

          push BP              ; Point to arguments
          mov  BP,SP           ;
          mov  DX,[BP + 6]     ; Get handle
          mov  BX,[BP + 8]     ; Get size
          mov  AH,0FH          ;
          call CS:[XMS_Control]
          or   AX,AX           ; Error?
          jz   __x_r2          ;
          ;
          ; return
          ;
__x_r1:
          pop  BP              ; Restore BP
          ret                  ; Return
          ;
          ; return error
          ;
__x_r2:
          mov  AL,BL           ; Get error code
          jmp  __x_r1          ;

_xms_realloc    ENDP
;
; Lock a block of XMS memory
;
; Returns status in AX:  0001 Success
;                        0080 Function not implemented
;                        0081 VDISK device detected
;                        00A2 Invalid handle
;                        00AC Lock count overflow
;                        00AD Lock failed
```

```
;
; Borland C++ prototype:
;     unsigned short far xms_lock(unsigned short handle,
;     unsigned long *linear_address);
;


            ALIGN    16

_xms_lock PROC FAR

            push BP                 ; Save registers
            push DS                 ;
            push SI                 ;
            mov  DX,[BP + 10]       ; Get handle
            mov  AH,0CH             ;
            call CS:[XMS_Control]
            or   AX,AX              ; Error?
            jz   __x_12            ;
            lds  SI,[BP + 12]       ; Get address of pointer
            mov  [SI],BX            ; Store linear address
            mov  [SI + 2],DX        ;
            ;
            ; Return
            ;
__x_11:
            pop  SI                 ; Restore registers
            pop  DS                 ;
            pop  BP                 ;
            ret                     ; Return
            ;
            ; Return error
            ;
__x_12:
            mov  AL,BL              ; Get error code
            jmp  __x_11            ;


_xms_lock ENDP
;
; Unlock a block of XMS memory
;
; Returns status in AX:   0001 Success
;                         0080 Function not implemented
;                         0081 VDISK device detected
;                         00A2 Invalid handle
;                         00AA Block was not locked
;
;
; Borland C++ prototype:
;     unsigned short far xms_unlock(unsigned short handle);
;
```

continues

Listing 10.9 continued

```
                ALIGN    16

_xms_unlock    PROC FAR

        push BP              ; Get pointer to argument
        mov  BP,SP           ;
        mov  DX,[BP + 6]     ; Get handle
        mov  AH,0DH          ;
        call CS:[XMS_Control]
        or   AX,AX           ; Error?
        jz   __x_u2          ;
        ;
        ; Return
        ;
__x_u1:
        pop  BP              ; Restore BP
        ret                  ; Return
__x_u2:
        mov  AL,BL           ; Get error code
        jmp  __x_u1          ;

_xms_unlock    ENDP
;
; Get status of an XMS block
;
; Returns status in AX:  0001 Success
;                        0080 Function not implemented
;                        0081 VDISK device detected
;                        00A2 Invalid handle
;
; Borland C++ prototype:
;    unsigned short far xms_bstat(unsigned short handle,
;    struct bstat far *ptr);
;
; Data structure:   struct bstat
;                   {
;                   unsigned short lock_count;
;                   unsigned short free_handle_count;
;                   };
;

                ALIGN    16

_xms_bstat     PROC FAR

        push BP              ; Save registers
        push DS              ;
```

```
                push SI              ;
                mov  BP,SP           ; Point to arguments
                mov  DX,[BP + 10]    ; Get handle
                mov  AH,0EH          ;
                call CS:[XMS_Control]
                or   AX,AX           ; Error?
                jz   __x_b2          ;
                lds  SI,[BP + 12]    ; Get pointer to structure
                xor  DX,DX           ; Clear DX
                mov  DL,BH           ; Get lock count
                mov  [SI],DX         ; Store it
                mov  DL,BL           ; Get number of free handles
                mov  [SI + 2],DX     ; Store it
                ;
                ; Return
                ;
__x_b1:
                pop  SI              ; Restore registers
                pop  DS              ;
                pop  BP              ;
                ret                  ; Return
__x_b2:
                mov  AL,BL           ; Get error code
                jmp  __x_b1          ;

_xms_bstat      ENDP
;
; Move data to or from an extended memory block
;
; Returns status in AX:    0001 Success
;                          0080 Function not implemented
;                          0081 VDISK device detected
;                          0082 A20 error occurred
;                          00A3 Invalid source handle
;                          00A4 Invalid source offset
;                          00A5 Invalid destination handle
;                          00A6 Invalid destination offset
;                          00A7 Invalid length
;                          00A8 Invalid overlap on move
;                          00A9 Parity error occurred
;
; Borland C++ prototype:
;    unsigned short far xms_move(struct XMS_move_data far *ptr);
;
; Data structure:     struct    XMS_move_data
;                     {
;                     unsigned long  transfer_size;
;                     unsigned short source_handle;
;                     unsigned long  source_offset;
```

continues

Listing 10.9 *continued*

```
;                       unsigned short destination_handle;
;                       unsigned long  destination_offset;
;                       };
;

             ALIGN   16

_xms_move PROC FAR

          push BP             ; Save registers
          push DS             ;
          push SI             ;
          mov  BP,SP          ; Get argument pointer
          lds  SI,[BP + 10]   ; Get address
          mov  AH,0BH         ;
          call CS:[XMS_Control]
          or   AX,AX          ; Error
          jz   __x_m2         ;
          ;
          ; Return
          ;
__x_m1:
          pop  SI             ; Restore registers
          pop  DS             ;
          pop  BP             ;
          ret                 ; Return
          ;
          ; Return error
          ;
__x_m2:
          mov  AL,BL          ; Get error code
          jmp  __x_m2         ;

_xms_move ENDP
;
; Free a block of extended memory
;
; Returns status in AX:   0001 Success
;                         0080 Function not implemented
;                         0081 VDISK device detected
;                         00A2 Invalid handle
;                         00A4 Handle is locked
;
; Borland C++ prototype:
;    unsigned short far xms_free(unsigned short handle);
;
```

```
          ALIGN    16

_xms_free PROC FAR

          push BP                ; Make pointer to argument
          mov  BP,SP             ;
          mov  DX,[BP + 6]       ; Get handle
          mov  AH,0AH            ; Free it
          call CS:[XMS_Control]
          or   AX,AX             ; Error?
          jz   __x_f2            ;
          ;
          ; Return
          ;
__x_f1:
          pop  BP                ; Restore BP
          ret                    ; Return
          ;
          ; Return error
          ;
__x_f2:
          mov  AL,BL             ; Get error code
          jmp  __x_f1            ;

_xms_free ENDP
;
; Allocate the HMA
;
; Returns status in AX:  0001 Success
;                        0080 Function not implemented
;                        0081 VDISK device detected
;                        0090 HMA does not exist
;                        0091 HMA already in use
;                        0092 Not enough bytes requested
;
; Borland C++ prototype:
;    unsigned short far hma_alloc(unsigned short size_in_bytes);
;

          ALIGN    16

_hma_alloc     PROC FAR

          push BP                ; Get pointer to arguments
          mov  BP,SP             ;
          mov  DX,[BP + 6]       ; Get number of bytes
          mov  AH,1              ; Request HMA
          call CS:[XMS_Control]
          or   AX,AX             ; Failure?
```

continues

Listing 10.9 *continued*

```
                jz   __h_a2          ; If so, get return code
                ;
                ; Return
                ;
__h_a1:
                pop  BP              ; Restore BP
                ret                  ; Return
                ;
                ; Set error code
                ;
__h_a2:
                mov  AL,BL           ; Return error code
                jmp  __h_a1          ;

_hma_alloc      ENDP
;
; Free the HMA
;
; Returns status in AX:  0001 Success
;                        0080 Function not implemented
;                        0081 VDISK device detected
;                        0090 HMA does not exist
;                        0093 HMA not allocated
;
; Borland C++ prototype:
;    unsigned short far hma_free(void);
;


                ALIGN    16

_hma_free PROC FAR

                mov  AH,2            ; Release HMA
                call CS:[XMS_Control]
                or   AX,AX           ; Error?
                jz   __h_f2          ; If so, get code
                ;
                ; Return
                ;
__h_f1:
                ret                  ; Return
                ;
                ; Return error
                ;
__h_f2:
                mov  AL,BL           ; Store error code
                jmp  __h_f1          ;
```

```
_hma_free ENDP
;
; Move data into or out of the HMA
;
; Borland C++ prototype:
;    void far hma_move(unsigned short count, unsigned short
direction,
;           unsigned short hma_offset, void far *data);
;
; Note: if the direction is zero, data is copied to HMA; otherwise,
;       it is copied from the HMA
;


        LIGN 16

_hma_move PROC FAR

        push BP              ; Get pointer to arguments
        mov  BP,SP           ;
        push DS              ; Save registers
        push ES              ;
        push DI              ;
        push SI              ;
        mov  CX,[BP + 6]     ; Get byte count
        mov  AL,[BP + 8]     ; Get direction flag
        or   AL,AL           ; If set, copy from HMA
        mov  AX,0FFFFH       ; Set HMA segment
        jz   __h_m2          ; If clear, copy to HMA
        ;
        ; Copy data from HMA
        ;
        mov  DS,AX           ; Set source = HMA
        mov  SI,[BP + 10]    ; Get offset
        add  SI,10H          ; Add 10H to offset
        les  DI,[BP + 12]    ; Get destination address
        ;
        ; Do move and return
        ;
__h_m1:
        cld                  ; Clear direction flag
        shr  CX,1            ; Convert bytes to words
    rep movsw                ; Copy data
        adc  CX,0            ; Add carry
    rep movsb                ; Copy data
        pop  SI              ; Restore data
        pop  DI              ;
        pop  ES              ;
        pop  DS              ;
```

continues

Listing 10.9 continued

```
            pop   BP              ;
            ret                   ; Return
            ;
            ; Copy data to HMA
            ;
    __h_m2:
            mov   ES,AX           ; Set destination = HMA
            mov   DI,[BP + 10]    ; Get offset
            add   DI,10H          ; Add 10H to offset
            lds   SI,[BP + 12]    ; Get source address
            jmp   __h_m1          ;

_hma_move ENDP
;
; Alter the A20 line status
;
; Valid arguments are (GLOBAL_A20_LINE ¦ ENABLE_A20_LINE)  == 0
;                     (GLOBAL_A20_LINE ¦ DISABLE_A20_LINE) == 1
;                     (LOCAL_A20_LINE  ¦ ENABLE_A20_LINE)  == 2
;                     (LOCAL_A20_LINE  ¦ DISABLE_A20_LINE) == 3
;
; Returns status in AX:  0001 Success
;                        0080 Function not implented
;                        0081 VDISK device detected
;                        0082 A20 error occurred
;                        0094 A20 line still enabled (args 1 and 3)
;                        FFFF Illegal argument
;
; Borland C++ prototype:
;    unsigned short far alter_a20(unsigned short change_code);
;


            ALIGN    16

_alter_a20      PROC FAR

            push  BP              ; Get pointer to argument
            mov   BP,SP           ;
            mov   AX,[BP + 6]     ; Get argument
            cmp   AX,3            ; Check range
            ja    __a_a2          ;
            mov   AH,AL           ; Create function code
            add   AH,3            ;
            call  CS:[XMS_Control]
            or    AX,AX           ; Failure?
            jz    __a_a3          ;
            ; Return
```

```
          ;
__a_a1:
          pop  BP              ; Restore BP
          ret                  ; Return
          ;
          ; Illegal argument
          ;
__a_a2:
          mov  AX,-1           ; Return ILLEGAL_ARGUMENT
          jmp  __a_a1          ;
          ;
          ; Bad result
          ;
__a_a3:
          mov  AL,BL           ; Return error code
          jmp  __a_a1          ;

_alter_a20      ENDP
;
; Get A20 line status
;
; Returns status in AX:   0000 A20 disabled
;                         0001 A20 enabled
;                         0080 Function not implemented
;                         0081 VDISK device detected
;
; Borland C++ prototype:
;    unsigned short far a20_stat(void);
;

          ALIGN    16

_a20_stat PROC FAR

          xor  BX,BX
          mov  AH,7            ; Get line status
          call CS:[XMS_Control]
          or   BL,BL           ; Error?
          jnz  __a_s2          ;
          ;
          ; Return
          ;
__a_s1:
          ret
          ;
          ; Return error
          ;
__a_s2:
          xor  AX,AX           ; Clear AX
```

continues

Listing 10.9 continued

```
                mov   AL,BL           ; Get error code
                jmp   _ _a_s1         ;

_a20_stat ENDP
;
; Allocate an upper memory block
;
; Returns status in AX:   0001 Success
;                         0080 Function not implemented
;                         00B0 A smaller UMB is available
;                         00B1 No UMBs are available
;
; Borland C++ prototype:
;    unsigned short far umb_alloc(unsigned short size,
;    struct umb_data far *ptr);
;
; Data structure:    struct umb_data
;                    {
;                    unsigned short segment_number;
;                    unsigned short segment_size;
;                    };
;

                ALIGN    16

_umb_alloc      PROC FAR

                push  BP              ; Save registers
                push  DS              ;
                push  SI              ;
                mov   BP,SP           ; Point to arguments
                mov   DX,[BP + 10]    ; Get size
                mov   AH,10H          ;
                call  CS:[XMS_Control]
                or    AX,AX           ; Error
                jz    _ _u_a2         ;
                lds   SI,[BP + 12]    ; Get address of data structure
                mov   [SI],BX         ; Store segment number
                ;
                ; Return
                ;
_ _u_a1:
                mov   [SI + 2],DX     ; Store size in paragraphs
                pop   SI              ; Restore registers
                pop   DS              ;
                pop   BP              ;
                ret                   ; Return
```

```
                ;
                ; Return error
                ;
__u_a2:
                mov  AL,BL          ; Store error code
                lds  SI,[BP + 12]   ; Point to data structure
                jmp  __u_a1         ;

_umb_alloc      ENDP
;
; Free UMB
;
; Returns status in AX:  0001 Success
;                        0080 Function not implemented
;                        00B2 Invalid segment number
;
; Borland C++ prototype:
;    unsigned short far umb_free(unsigned short segment);
;


                ALIGN    16

_umb_free PROC FAR

                push BP             ; Get pointer to argument
                mov  BP,SP          ;
                mov  DX,[BP + 6]    ; Get segment number
                mov  AH,011H        ;
                call CS:[XMS_Control]
                or   AX,AX          ; Error?
                jz   __u_f2         ;
                ;
                ; Return
                ;
__u_f1:
                pop  BP             ; Restore BP
                ret                 ; Return
                ;
                ; Return error
                ;
__u_f2:
                mov  AL,BL          ; Get error code
                jmp  __u_f1         ;

_umb_free ENDP

XMS_CODE  ENDS

                END
```

Program Execution

One of DOS's most useful features is its capability to run a program, the child, from within another program, the parent, without losing the original or parent program's current state. On a UNIX system, the function can spin off parallel processes. DOS is similar, but the parent process sleeps (stops functioning) while the new one runs.

Some of the EXEC function's basic features let programs perform the following tasks:

- Spin off a child in the system's free memory

- Wait for the completion of the child's operations

- Receive from the child a return code that can be used for indicating normal completion, error terminations, or status codes

You may have heard that EXEC is hard to use or dangerous. Nothing could be further from the truth. The V2 edition of EXEC did have a few "growing pains" problems, which we discuss later (along with how to avoid them), but all subsequent versions perform exactly as specified. The function does require that you follow all the rules, but we make those clear as we go.

To use the EXEC function, enough memory must be available to run the new program. (See the earlier discussion to learn how to release memory.)

The EXEC Function

When enough program memory is available, you can execute another program with the EXEC function. When you call the EXEC function (Int 21h, Function 4Bh), the registers must be set up like this:

Register	Purpose
AL=0	Load and execute program
DS:DX	Pointer to full path name
ES:BX	Pointer to parameter block

AL can be set to 03h to tell the EXEC function to load into memory an overlay that the parent process already owns. Because overlays are not a factor at this point, you can concentrate on executing programs.

The DS:DX register pair points to the path name of the executable file. The path name can be one of the following:

- The file name of the program to execute, including the .EXE or .COM extension. (In this case, the program must be in the present directory.)

- A relative path name to the file, starting with a dot (.) and giving the directories in the path from the current working directory to the program

- A full path name to the file, which starts at the root directory (\) and goes to the file, and which may include the drive letter and colon

Suppose, for example, that you want to execute the DEMO.EXE program in the \UTIL directory. If you are already in the \UTIL directory, you can refer to the program as

```
DEMO.EXE
```

If you are in the \APPL directory, you can refer to the program by its relative path name:

```
.\..\UTIL\DEMO.EXE
```

In this case, you can simplify the path name by starting with the "dot-dot" directory:

```
..\UTIL\DEMO.EXE
```

Finally, from any location, you can always refer to the program as

```
\UTIL\DEMO.EXE
```

A path name must include everything needed to find the file; it cannot contain wild-card characters. The file name must be spelled out in full and must include the .EXE or .COM extension. Batch files (.BAT extension) cannot be executed directly with the EXEC function, but you can EXEC a copy of COMMAND.COM and pass both the \C option switch and the batch file's name to it as part of the parameter block, which will achieve the same result.

Features you may be accustomed to using, such as wild cards in file names or path searches for the file, are functions of COMMAND.COM, not of the EXEC function. COMMAND.COM looks for files by searching the path environment variable. It also executes batch files using internal batch-file execution procedures. None of this can be done directly with the EXEC function.

The same principle applies to COMMAND.COM internal commands. Commands such as DIR that are internal to COMMAND.COM cannot be executed separately. The trick of copying COMMAND.COM itself with the EXEC command, however, provides a way around these limitations. The one thing the trick will *not* let you do is modify the environment; as we shall see, each program copied with the EXEC command gets its own copy of the environment, and changes made there cannot affect the original copy, which is the one used by any subsequent command.

The ES:BX register pair points to a parameter block that contains four additional addresses:

- Environment block (two bytes, segment address)

- Command tail (four bytes, offset then segment)

- File control block 1 (four bytes, offset then segment)

- File control block 2 (four bytes, offset then segment)

The environment block is the collection of program environment variables of the form VARIABLE=VALUE set by DOS or added by your SET instructions. For example, the TMP variable could be set equal to \TMP, a temporary directory area, so that some programs that create temporary files will create them there. The AUTOEXEC.BAT file would have the following line:

```
SET TMP=C:\TMP
```

All such variables together are what you point at with the environment block. For most circumstances, you simply want to retain the environment in which your present program works. Setting the environment block to zero causes EXEC to pass a *copy* of the parent program's environment to the child. This copy will be just large enough to contain the data; it will have no room for you to add more (doing so would be wasted effort because the copy is released when the child process terminates— the parent never sees it).

The command-tail pointer locates the portion of the command line that follows the command itself. For example, if you type the command

```
\BIN\COMMAND /C DIR
```

the command tail is /C DIR.

The command tail is stored as a count byte that gives the command-tail length, the command tail itself, and a carriage return (Function 0Dh). This command tail, fully laid out for use, would look like this:

```
1   2 3 4 5 6 7 8
06h / C   D I R C/R
```

Note that the carriage return is not included in the count.

The last two parameters are initial settings for the file control blocks (FCBs) included in the program segment prefix (PSP). Unless you use FCB functions, either to maintain compatibility with DOS V1 or to permit use of EXEC with other programs that use FCBs, you can safely let them point almost anywhere because you will ignore them. If you do intend to use FCBs, they should be set up as described in Chapter 9, "Directories and Files." These FCBs will be copied into the PSP by EXEC.

The program in listing 10.10 shows the use of the COMMAND.COM trick mentioned a few paragraphs back; it executes the COMMAND.COM program with the /C DIR command tail. There are some special features to note here:

- The stack pointer has not been saved explicitly, even though this function destroys it. intdos restores it automatically.

- The segment registers had to be retrieved in order to properly set all the pointers.

- The program simply assumes that COMMAND.COM is located in the root directory of the current drive; it would be advisable, for general use, to add code that searches the environment for the COMSPEC= string and then copies all characters following the equal sign. The program then would be able to run when the current drive did not contain COMMAND.COM.

Listing 10.10

```
#include <stdio.h>
#include <dos.h>

main()

{
        union REGS regs;
        struct SREGS segs;
        struct {
                int     envblk;     /* Environment block */
                int     ocmd;       /* Command tail */
                int     scmd;
                int     ofcb;       /* FCB #1 */
                int     sfcb;
                int     ofcb2;      /* FCB #2 */
                int     sfcb2;
        } pblock;
        char    buffer[256];
        char    name[128];

        segread(&segs);

        strcpy(name,"\\command.com");
        printf("Executing program %s\n",name);

        /* Set up the command tail */
        buffer[0] = 6;                      /* Number of characters */
        strcpy(buffer+1,"/c dir\015");   /* Command tail */
        pblock.ocmd = (int)buffer;
        pblock.scmd = segs.ds;

        /* Use parent's environment */
        pblock.envblk = 0;
```

continues

Listing 10.10 continued

```
/* Set up FCBs #1 and #2 */
pblock.ofcb = (int)buffer;
pblock.sfcb = segs.ds;
pblock.ofcb2 = (int)buffer;
pblock.sfcb2 = segs.ds;

/*
        Execute the designated program using the
        EXEC function 4Bh
*/
regs.h.ah = 0x4b;
regs.h.al = 0;
regs.x.dx = (int)name;
segs.es = segs.ds;
regs.x.bx = (int)&pblock;
intdosx(&regs,&regs,&segs);

/*
        If the carry flag is set, an error code is
        in the AX register
*/
if(regs.x.cflag==1)
        printf("Error Code = %d\n",regs.x.ax);
}
```

After the program knows the segment register values, it sets up each parameter for the EXEC function call, command tail, environment (the default), and FCBs. Then it executes the function and checks whether any error codes are returned.

C's perfectly good exec() function for running children is preferred in all but the most unusual cases. Turbo Pascal versions 4.0 and later also provide exec(), though the usage is slightly different. As mentioned earlier, neither BASIC nor pre-4.0 versions of Turbo Pascal have such facilities.

Program Exits

One of DOS EXEC's powerful features is its capability to have a program pass back a final status to the program that spawned it. By using Int 21h, Function 4Ch (the preferred exit function), a program can pass back an exit status that can be used for further decision making. UNIX systems use this capability all the time to manage the execution of systems of programs.

One recent example from our experience is a program that sequenced a series of other programs through a succession of operations. Depending on how certain programs ended, the main program could provide branches to alternative processing. In this case, the complicated process included interfacing with an IBM mainframe and making intelligent decisions about a database. If the IBM mainframe data transfer did not take place, the "add records to database" step was skipped and the database was processed for use.

The return code from a program is available inside a batch file as the ERRORLEVEL variable, which can be used to branch the logic in the file. If you are executing the program from another program, the parent can get the return code from the child by calling Int 21h, Function 4Dh after the EXEC function returns. Register AH has one of the following exit types:

Exit code	Meaning
00	Normal termination
01	Terminated by a Ctrl-C command
02	Critical device error
03	TSR return (Int 21h, Function 31h)

Register AL has the return code from the child process.

Possible EXEC Problems

Several pages back, we hinted that the DOS V2 edition of EXEC had potential problems and promised to provide you a way to avoid them. Here is the information.

The problem usually is apparent only when you work in assembly language; high-level languages seem to provide the solution as part of their normal DOS interfacing. The problem stems from the fact that the V2 DOS routines that perform the EXEC function begin by using block-move instructions to transfer all the blocks of data into DOS's own workspace. Block moves are controlled by a *direction* flag in the CPU chip. If this flag is set, the address passed is assumed to be the *end* of the block; thus, the block of data ending at that address is moved. If the flag is clear, the address is taken to be the *start*, and a different block of data is moved.

The EXEC function assumed that the flag was clear but never did anything to guarantee that this was the case. Consequently, if the flag was set when EXEC was invoked, what happened next was not at all what the DOS designers intended. Most often, the system would simply lock up because it was using a set of binary machine instructions as a file name and thus was trying to load and execute a nonexistent file.

This problem was corrected in V3 by adding a CLD instruction at the beginning of the EXEC code to make sure that the flag was properly clear. The cure for V2 is to issue the CLD instruction yourself, immediately before the Int 21h that calls the EXEC function.

The only other potential pitfall, which applies to all versions and is fully documented, is that no registers except CS and IP will be preserved across the call. This means that you *must* save both SS and SP in locations that you can address with CS when you come back, or you will lose control of your program.

Entering a Command to DOS

When you enter a command, DOS first separates the command name from the command parameters. DOS then checks whether the command is an internal command. The code required to execute internal commands (such as CLS or DIR) is in the DOS command-line interpreter. Because these commands are checked first, you cannot write your own program named DIR and have it execute from the DOS command line. There are methods, however, for superseding and adding to the DOS internal commands, depending on the version of DOS you are running.

Assuming the command was not found to be an internal command, the disk system is searched for an appropriate file. The current working directory is searched for the file name, with the .COM, .EXE, then .BAT extension, in that order. If no exact match is found in the current working directory, each directory in the PATH string of the environment variables is searched for the three names. If no file is found after exhausting the PATH, the Bad filename or command message is displayed and DOS returns to the prompt.

If a batch file (.BAT extension) is found, the DOS batch file interpreter is given control of the file. Otherwise, the DOS EXEC function (Function 04BH, Subfunction 000H) is invoked. If the first two bytes of the file are MZ, the file is treated as an EXE-type file, regardless of the extension. Thus, you can guarantee that an EXE file will be loaded first by renaming it with the .COM extension. A new program segment prefix (PSP) is created, the COM file is copied verbatim into memory, the segment registers are set to the paragraph in memory where the program is written, and control is passed to CS:00100H. What happens to the EXE file is a bit more complex (see fig. 10.4).

As with the COM file, a PSP is created; the EXE file, less the EXE header, is loaded into memory above the PSP, at an address we will call the load address. The DS and ES registers are set to point to the PSP. The CS:IP and SS:SP registers are set from the values in the EXE header, with the load address segment added to the CS and SS registers.

Finally, the relocation table in the EXE header is used to modify segment references in the image. The relocation table consists of segment:offset pointers. These pointers are addresses of words in the image; the addresses are relative to the load address. The words pointed to, in turn, are segment values in the program. The word pointed to has the load address segment added to it. In this way, the program's segment references are modified to compensate for the address in memory where the program is loaded.

Fig. 10.4. *EXE file header.*

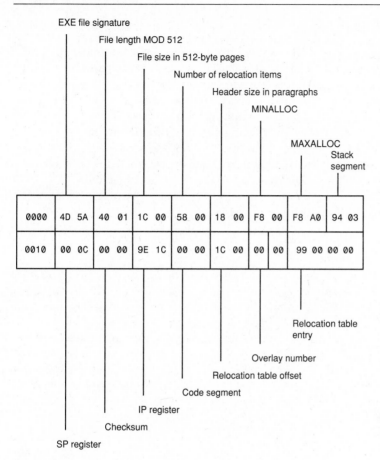

EXE file signature
File length MOD 512
File size in 512-byte pages
Number of relocation items
Header size in paragraphs
MINALLOC
MAXALLOC
Stack segment

| 0000 | 4D 5A | 40 01 | 1C 00 | 58 00 | 18 00 | F8 00 | F8 A0 | 94 03 |
| 0010 | 00 0C | 00 00 | 9E 1C | 00 00 | 1C 00 | 00 | 00 | 99 00 00 00 |

Relocation table entry
Overlay number
Relocation table offset
Code segment
IP register
Checksum
SP register

| 0180 | 55 89 E5 FA FF 76 06 FF 76 04 8A 46 08 30 E4 B9 | CODE |

0200	8B 46 FA 0B 46 FC 74 36 83 6E FA 0E C4 7E FA 06
0210	57 C4 7E F6 06 57 9A CE 06	3E 02	75 1F 83 46 FA
0220	0F C4 7E FA 26 C4 05 8C C2 A3 11 00 89 16 13 00

Note: The boxed entry is at CODE +00000099. The current code
       segment value will be added to 023E and written to
       CODE +00000099.

Superseding DOS's Internal Commands

There are three main techniques for superseding DOS's internal commands. The first, and the one guaranteed to work for all versions of DOS, is to directly modify COMMAND.COM with DEBUG or the third-party file editing utility of your choice and change the name of the command. This is not too difficult, because the list of names in COMMAND.COM is easy to pinpoint. You can retain the utility of the original internal command's name by changing one of the letters in the name to another uppercase letter, such as changing *COPY* to *KOPY*. If you want to abolish the internal command, change one of the letters to lowercase, such as *COPY* to *cOPY*. The *cOPY* command will never be matched to the command typed in.

The second method, which works with DOS Version 3.00 and later, is to specify the full path for your name-alike. For example:

```
C:\DOSCLONE\COPY *.*
```

will invoke your version of COPY.

The third method, which works with DOS Version 3.3 and later, is to create a TSR that chains to DOS Interrupt 2F, intercepting Function 0AEH, Subfunctions 000H and 001H. These interrupt functions are called by DOS before it checks its own internal list of commands.

The first call, to Function 0AEH, Subfunction 000H, is made with DS and ES pointing to DOS's transient area, BX pointing to a buffer containing two count bytes and an exact copy of the DOS command line, and SI pointing to a buffer containing the command word from the command line, converted to uppercase and preceded by its character count. If your command (or one of your commands) *exactly* matches the SI buffer, it should set AL to 0FFH and return. Otherwise, it should chain to the previous interrupt handler.

In the second call, to Function 0AEH, Subfunction 001H, the registers are set as before. The data pointed to by BX, however, may have changed in the interim. Therefore, it is a good idea to copy the command-line parameters to an internal buffer while servicing the 000H Subfunction call. After executing your code, you should clear the character count in the DS:SI command buffer so that DOS will know you executed your code.

The code you execute does not need to do anything except clear the character count. Although the code has done nothing useful, DOS is satisfied that useful work has been done. This is a convenient way to eliminate troublesome DOS internal commands, such as DEL or ERASE.

Why Some EXE Files Cannot Be Converted to COM Files

EXE2BIN will not convert an EXE file into a COM file if it fails to meet some simple criteria:

- The EXE file must have the MZ signature in its header

- The SS:SP reference in the header must be 0000:0000

- The CS:IP reference must be either 0000:0100 or 0000:0000 (for device drivers)

- The number of items in the relocation table must be zero

The Program Segment Prefix

The program segment prefix (PSP) is a 256-byte block of data that DOS constructs for each program it runs. The PSP contains information for the program to use, as well as information DOS needs to maintain. Table 10.1 shows the structure of the PSP.

Table 10.1. *PSP Structure*

Offset	Contents	Meaning
000H–001H	CD 20	Call to the DOS terminate routine
002H–003H	Varies	Segment address of the top of the program's allocated memory block
004H	00	Filler
005H–009H	Varies	FAR CALL to INT 21H dispatcher
00AH–00DH	Varies	INT 22H vector
00EH–011H	Varies	INT 23H vector
012H–015H	Varies	INT 24H vector
016H–017H	Varies	Segment of the parent process PSP
018H–02BH	01 01 01 00 02 FF FF FF FF FF FF FF FF FF FF FF FF FF FF FF	Indices to the system file table

continues

Table 10.1. *continued*

Offset	Contents	Meaning
02CH–02DH	aries	Segment address of the environment copy
02EH–031H	00 00 00 00	SS:SP storage
032H–033H	14 00	Number of file handles available
034H–037H	Varies	Pointer to the file handle table
038H–03BH	Varies	SHARE's previous PSP
03CH–04FH	00 00 00 00 00 00 00 00 00 00 00 00 00 00 00 00 00 00 00 00	Unused
050H–052H	CD 21 CB	Call to INT 21H and RETF
053H–05BH	00 00 00 00 00 00 00 00 00	Unused
05CH–06BH	Varies	Default FCB 1
06CH–07FH	Varies	Default FCB 2
080H	Varies	Command tail count
081H–0FFH	Varies	Command tail

The code at PSP:0000 and PSP:0005 are remnants of the early days of DOS when compatibility with CP/M was an issue; they function the same as CP/M CALL 0000 and CALL 0005.

The segment address at PSP:0002 can be used by the program to determine whether enough memory is allocated to it.

The vector addresses at PSP:000A, PSP:000E, and PSP:0012 will be restored by MS-DOS on exit. Programmers are warned not to amend any values below PSP:005C, but PSP:000E and PSP:0012 (the CTRL-C and critical error handler vectors, respectively) can be modified without harm. The vector at PSP:000A is actually the return address of the parent process, immediately following the DOS EXEC call. This address can be modified to point to a user-defined procedure that can unhook any special handlers the program may have installed. The procedure must then return to the original vector at PSP:000A. When the procedure is invoked, all program memory has been freed, files have been closed, and the PSP is set to that of the parent process. No file access or other I/O should be attempted.

The parent process PSP can be used to trace the PSP chain back to the parent COMMAND.COM, whose PSP shows itself as its own parent. This COMMAND.COM may not be the master COMMAND.COM; it can be a shell.

The indices to the system file table refer to open handles for stdin, stdout, stderr, stdaux, and stdprn. The value FF refers to unopened handles. The value at PSP:0032 and the pointer at PSP:0034 can be changed to reflect a different handle table; the value at PSP:0034 is initialized as PSP:0018.

The environment segment address can be used to access the program's copy of the environment. You can trace back the parent's PSP to access and modify the parent's environment. Again, there is no guarantee that this is the master environment.

DOS uses the SS:SP storage at PSP:002E to store the program's SS:SP on entry to INT 21H. This allows DOS to perform multitasking, but this capability has not been exploited yet.

The pointer at PSP:0038H is used to store the parent PSP when SHARE is in use under DOS 3.3 and later. Prior to DOS 3.3, the pointer at PSP:0038H is set to FFFF:FFFF.

The code at PSP:0050H provides another mechanism to access INT 21H, this time with a far call.

The FCBs are for use by programs using FCB-style file I/O. They are loaded with the first two parameters in the command tail, under the assumption that these parameters are file names. This is another holdover from CP/M days.

The command tail count is the length of the command tail. The command tail is the remainder of the command, from after the command name to the carriage return at the end. The command tail count does not count the carriage return. If a command has no parameters, its command tail count is 0, and the carriage return code (0DH) is found at PSP:0081.

The command tail and command tail count are also set up by DOS as the default disk transfer area (DTA). This is of use if you use FCB file handling, and is another holdover from CP/M.

Memory-Resident Programming

The TSR utility is a hot item for programming PCs. Borland's introduction of SideKick caused a major upheaval in the PC software market. So many TSR utilities are available now that if you used them all, there would not be room for executable programs. We always seem to want more TSRs than we can possibly accommodate.

Most people do not realize that what they consider to be a TSR is only one of two types of TSRs that can be set up and used. The TSR utility (like SideKick and others) was not the TSR function's intended purpose. TSRs originally were seen as extensions of the operating system.

The two types of TSRs are

- *Active TSRs:* These pop-up utilities, such as SideKick, are the most common type of TSRs. They usually are operated by responding to a specified keystroke called the hot key. When these utilities are activated, they take over the computer and perform their function before they return control to the program that originally controlled the machine.

- *Inactive TSRs:* These TSRs respond when a calling program calls a designated interrupt. When called, they perform a defined function, similar to a subroutine, then return control to the calling program.

Active TSRs give users the impression of multitasking on a PC. TSRs do not actually multitask, but you get the impression that more than one operation is happening simultaneously. To give this illusion of operation, active TSRs are complex. As you know, DOS is not reentrant (you cannot break out of the middle of an internal DOS routine and restart it from somewhere else). If DOS is processing something (a disk access, for example) when a TSR activates to write something to the disk, you can cause serious problems and possibly mess up your disk.

Active TSRs have to watch what both DOS and users do. You will see some of these tricks in Chapter 11's discussion of TSRs as interrupt service routines.

Inactive TSRs work in a benign environment. An inactive TSR starts nothing until it is called by a program. Because DOS is a single-tasking environment, only one operation can be in progress at a time and we know that no DOS operation can be in progress when the TSR is called. Therefore, we are safe using DOS calls from an inactive TSR.

The TSR concept has undergone some major changes since DOS was introduced. The original TSR function (Int 27h) has been superseded by Int 21h, Function 31h. This function is more convenient to use because it allows a return code to be passed and lets the TSR use more than 64K of memory. Both of these factors justify using the preferred TSR call: Int 21h, Function 31h.

When a TSR runs, it sets up its memory tables and prepares for execution by connecting to a DOS interrupt. When everything is ready, the program determines how much memory it needs to keep; then it sets AH to 31h, AL to the return code, and DX to the number of paragraphs (16-byte blocks) to allocate to the TSR. When the program exits, the amount of memory available for executing programs is reduced by the amount assigned to the TSR, and the exit code passes back to the parent.

Sounds simple, doesn't it? It can be—for extremely simple TSRs. But if you are writing the next SideKick utility, you will find that much more is involved than simply executing the TSR.

First, you must have a way to trigger the TSR's action. You can attach the TSR to the timer interrupt and activate the TSR's operation every specified number of seconds. More often, you attach the TSR to the keyboard service interrupt and look for a certain keystroke. With a proliferation of TSRs, collisions will occur because most keystrokes are used somewhere.

No matter how you attach a TSR to a system, the TSR must recognize the possible presence of other TSRs in the system. To allow other operations to occur on the trigger, a TSR must call the interrupt service routine that originally handled the interrupt before the start of the TSR. Furthermore, to prevent overlap with other functions, you should be able to change the keystrokes that trigger the TSR.

When you deal with DOS functions, TSRs and interrupt service routines (ISRs) are in the same danger. The MS-DOS system was always intended to be a single-user, single-task system and so is not reentrant. Because an active TSR or ISR responds to events that may not be synchronized to the operation of DOS functions, it is possible for a TSR or ISR to get control of the computer while an internal DOS function is in progress. Several undocumented DOS functions help us to determine when using DOS functions is safe and when it is not. These undocumented functions are discussed in Chapter 11, "Interrupt Handlers."

Writing a successful TSR can be a major project, well worth a book of its own. A sophisticated TSR that includes many subfunctions, windows, and other features can take a team of sophisticated programmers a long time to implement. We will build a simple TSR in Chapter 11 after you have learned enough about interrupts to make them work for you.

Summary

This chapter has covered memory management, expanded memory, and program execution. You have learned that TPA (transient program area) memory is allocated by DOS to fill requests from programs that need memory. When programs start, they normally get all available memory to work in and should release any memory that they will not use.

Assembly language programmers must explicitly release memory. Programmers who use C or the latest versions of Turbo Pascal have it done by the start-up code for their programs. BASIC and other Pascal programmers cannot release memory except at compile time.

Expanded memory gives us access to additional memory by paging a large amount of memory into the addressable 1M of PC memory. We can use this memory in 16K pages to store and retrieve data. To do so, we use the Int 67h function calls, which are detailed in the EMS reference section at the end of this book.

Extended memory gives us access to additional memory by taking advantage of the 80286, 80386 and 80486's capability to address more than the conventional 1M of PC memory. We can use this memory in arbitrary units of 1K to store and retrieve data. To do so, we use the XMS function calls, which are detailed in the XMS reference section at the end of this book.

When we have enough memory available, DOS lets us run programs from within other programs (just as COMMAND.COM does). We can use this memory to tie individual programs together into a software system. TSRs (terminate and stay resident programs) allow us to create programs that coexist in memory while other programs are operating. With the techniques discussed in the next chapter, "Interrupt Handlers," we can create TSRs that can be invoked from the keyboard to give the impression of multitasking.

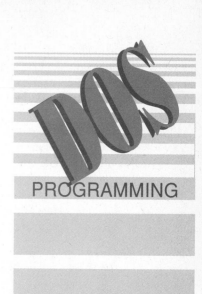

Interrupt Handlers

In this chapter, we look deep into the DOS system to discuss something that has a reputation for obscurity unlike anything else in computer programming—interrupt handlers. Interrupt handlers are programs that respond to the activation of an interrupt.

You may find that interrupt handling is really not so bad. At some levels, in fact, it is easily managed. But there are still a few "black holes" that you can drop into and never escape. The information in this chapter can keep you from getting lost.

Interrupts have been around for years. Part of their unsavory reputation was gained when they were first introduced as a major part of system design. On early computer systems, interrupts were often a major headache because programmers had no experience working with them and took unjustified shortcuts.

Interrupts have been the domain of systems programmers and hardware engineers for so long that many programmers are afraid to touch them. Luckily, a PC is a relatively benign place to work with interrupts. The problems you may have are managed simply if you write your interrupt handlers according to some general guidelines. As you gain experience, you will be able to control interrupts without thinking about it.

11

CHAPTER

This chapter starts with a description of interrupts. There is a discussion of interrupts generated by internal and external hardware as well as those generated in software. As the discussion proceeds, you should begin to develop a feel for how interrupts can serve you. Some practical examples round out the interrupt-handling discussion.

After you learn about interrupts, the chapter returns to a discussion that was started in the last chapter—the discussion of terminate-and-stay-resident (TSR) utilities. Nearly every TSR attaches itself in some way to an interrupt and responds to it as an interrupt service routine (ISR). This chapter describes what makes a good TSR and discusses instances when using one does not make sense.

Let's start at the most basic level by trying to find out what an interrupt is.

What Is an Interrupt?

An interrupt is a signal to the processor that an event needing special attention has happened. It is used to catch the processor's attention for something important. If you did not have interrupts, you would have to *poll* each device periodically and check whether it had something for you.

If you have 60 devices on a polled system and checking a device takes one second, each device is checked one time per minute. If you need a faster response to a condition in this example, polling is just not suitable. That is why interrupts were invented: to eliminate the need for polling and the resulting slow service for external events.

An interrupt may occur, for example, when a disk drive signals that it has a sector of information ready to transfer to main memory. If the processor is slow in responding to the interrupt, the block is lost, so the processor is forced to put whatever it is doing "on hold" and immediately pick up the interrupt.

Interrupts like the one in the preceding example are caused by external events. They can be caused also by internal events, such as a divide-by-zero error in a calculation or a program's specific request to execute a software interrupt.

Whenever your computer senses an interrupt condition, it saves whatever it is doing, "marks its place" in the program, and transfers control to an interrupt handler, which is expected to service the condition and then return. Some processors provide only restricted interrupt identification and depend on the interrupt handler to identify the interrupt and take appropriate action.

Interrupts are handled more efficiently on the 8086 family of processors by using *interrupt vectors* to speed you on your way to a specific interrupt handler. An interrupt vector is a far pointer (32 bits, in *offset:segment* form) to the actual handler routine; in the 8086 family, the first 1024 bytes of RAM are dedicated to providing 256 such vectors for the interrupts that the processor can recognize.

Programming interrupt handlers has been a somewhat arcane art, known to only an enlightened few, especially on some older computer systems. Interrupt handling on some systems involved issues of precise timing and a knowledge of the intricacies of processor and computer design that went far beyond what typical programmers ever encountered. On systems in which interrupts can occur, multi-level interrupt errors are the bane of all programmers' existence because the path to an error may be random at best and nearly impossible to find.

Interrupts on PCs, however, are relatively well behaved both because PCs are single-user, single-process systems and because the interrupt structure is much more sophisticated. You still have to be careful, but you can use this standard interrupt structure to handle the following situations:

1. Save anything that the processor did not save automatically when the interrupt occurred. (On a PC, this means all registers that might be changed during the handler's operation; it is safest to just save all of them, except CS, IP, SS, and SP, by pushing them onto the stack.)

2. Block any interrupts that might interfere with the handler's operation.

3. Enable interrupts that can occur safely during the handler's operation.

4. Handle the interrupt.

5. Restore the processor registers saved in step 1.

6. Reenable interrupts.

7. Return to normal processing.

This prescription does not guarantee good interrupt handling but it does guide you through this nest of vipers with your eyes open.

You already have encountered one situation, serial I/O, that cannot be handled effectively unless you tie an interrupt handler to the serial port. Microsoft BASIC provides an internal interrupt handler for communications that allows you to do serial I/O. In C, Pascal, or assembly language, you have to write your own handler.

The Ctrl-Break/Ctrl-C handler is another useful interrupt handler. For many programs, Ctrl-Break leaves the program in a bad state—with files not updated and so forth. To close down the program in an orderly manner, a Ctrl-Break handler lets your program control the exit.

How Interrupts Work

When an interrupt occurs, the processor can be in any state. A processor is designed so that it always completes any step in progress before it responds to an interrupt. When the processor recognizes an interrupt, it responds by pushing the flag register (the program status word), the instruction pointer (IP), and the code segment register (CS) on the stack and disabling interrupts.

After this critical machine-state information is saved, the processor looks to the system bus for an 8-bit number, the *interrupt request level* (IRQ). This level identifies exactly which device has issued the interrupt and lets the processor know which vector to use in response. As we already explained, interrupt vectors are pointers to the actual handler routines for specific functions.

In the PC (and its successors), a fixed offset of 8 is added to the number supplied by the interrupting device to determine the interrupt that is signaled. For example, IRQ level 0 generates Int 08h, and IRQ level 7 generates Int 0Fh. (This process is modified somewhat in the AT and PS/2 designs, which recognize more than eight levels of interrupt request, but the principle remains the same.)

The processor multiplies the Int number by 4 to obtain the offset into the *interrupt vector table* and then looks in segment 0000h to find the vector. The contents of the vector are put into CS:IP, and control automatically transfers to the first instruction of the program that processes the interrupt (the interrupt handler).

After the processor is in the interrupt handler, the handler controls the processor. Most handlers first reenable interrupts so that higher-priority interrupts can be serviced. They also save any other registers that they use and then carry out their own operations as quickly as possible. For some devices a special acknowledgment signal must be passed so that the device knows it has been serviced. The handler must provide this where necessary.

Interrupt handlers generally must be written to be as tight and as fast as possible. Most of them are written in assembly language to eliminate all possible overhead and to ensure that the routine runs as quickly as possible. You can write handlers in C (there are C examples in this chapter) but time-critical interrupts should be handled with as little overhead as possible.

Interrupts triggered through the 8259A Programmable Interrupt Controller (PIC)—the hardware interrupts generated by IRQ levels—must send an end-of-interrupt signal to the PIC when the processing is finished. All interrupts must restore the machine state by first restoring any registers saved and then executing an interrupt return (IRET) instruction that restores the flag register, CS, and IP to the values that existed before the interrupt occurred.

The Intel 8086 Family Interrupts

Interrupts on the 8086 microprocessor family come in three basic classes:

- Internal hardware
- External hardware
- Software

This section describes all three of these types of interrupts.

Internal Hardware Interrupts

Internal hardware interrupts are designed into a processor to handle special cases, such as a divide-by-zero error or other conditions in which a processor has recognized an error. These conditions are listed in table 11.1.

Table 11.1. *Internal Hardware Interrupts*

Interrupt Level	Vector Offset Address	Meaning
—8086 Processor Hardware Interrupts—		
00h	00h	Divide by zero
01h	04h	Single step
02h	08h	Nonmaskable interrupt
03h	0Ch	Break point
04h	10h	Overflow
—80286 Processor Hardware Interrupts—		
05h	14h	Bound range exceeded
06h	18h	Invalid opcode
07h	1Ch	Processor extension not available
08h	20h	Double exception
09h	24h	Segment overrun
0Ah	28h	Invalid task-state segment
0Bh	2Ch	Segment not present
0Ch	30h	Stack segment overrun
0Dh	34h	General protection fault

We do not program directly with any of these interrupts. In the basic PC design, IBM reassigned some of these interrupts (which were not used by the original 8086/8088 design but were reserved for future expansion) to deal with other conditions. When the next generation chip (80186) appeared, a conflict arose, and remains to this day, between what is designed into the 8086 family chips and what IBM has used the interrupt vectors for. This is not a good situation, but we have to deal with it. Table 11.2 lists the IBM-assigned interrupt vectors. Compare tables 11.1 and 11.2 to see the conflicts.

Table 11.2. *Interrupt Vectors*

Vector	Action
00h	Divide by zero
01h	Single step
02h	Nonmaskable interrupt
03h	Break point
04h	Overflow
05h	Print screen
06h	Unused
07h	Unused
08h	Hardware IRQ0 (timer tick)
09h	Keyboard input interrupt
0Ah	Reserved
0Bh	Asynchronous port controller 1 (COM2)
0Ch	Asynchronous port controller 0 (COM1)
0Dh	Fixed disk controller
0Eh	Floppy disk controller
0Fh	Printer controller
10h	Video driver
11h	Equipment-configuration check
12h	Memory-size check
13h	Floppy disk/fixed disk (PC/XT)
14h	Comm port driver
15h	Cassette/network service
16h	Keyboard driver
17h	Printer driver
18h	ROM BASIC
19h	Restart system
1Ah	Set/read real-time clock
1Bh	Ctrl-Break handler
1Ch	Timer tick (user defined)
1Dh	Video parameter table
1Eh	Disk parameter table
1Fh	Graphics character table (characters 80h–FFh)
20h	Program terminate
21h	DOS function dispatcher
22h	Terminate vector

Vector	Action
23h	Ctrl-C vector
24h	Critical-error vector
25h	Absolute disk read
26h	Absolute disk write
27h	Terminate and stay resident
28h	DOS OK interrupt
2Fh	Multiplex interrupt (see reference section)
40h	Floppy disk driver (PC/XT)
41h	Fixed disk parameter table
43h	Graphics character table

External Hardware Interrupts

External hardware can be tied to the processor to allow the device to signal an interrupt. Most early microcomputer systems that used interrupts were built this way. Two connections are available: the nonmaskable interrupt (NMI) and the maskable interrupt (INTR). As the names imply, you can turn off the INTR but you cannot turn off the NMI.

NMI interrupts are used for problems in which you do not want the interrupt turned off for any reason. On some systems, a physical reset switch wired to an NMI interrupt lets operators get the processor's attention—no matter what.

INTR interrupts are wired through the 8259A PIC to take advantage of the chip's capability to prioritize and control interrupts under software control. Processor instructions can directly enable or disable interrupts, and instructions to the PIC can selectively enable and disable interrupts.

The interrupts, however, are set at the hardware level. In some cases, manufacturers set the interrupt levels, and nothing can change them. Some devices provide switches or jumpers that can reset the interrupt level within a limited range of values.

Software Interrupts

Software interrupts are caused by a program issuing the software interrupt instruction to make the processor act as though it received a hardware interrupt. This method is convenient for accessing DOS and BIOS services independent of any one program. The services can be linked to specific interrupts and changed at will without affecting applications programs that call them.

Interrupt Vectors

The interrupt vector table is stored in the lowest 1024 bytes of system memory with 4 bytes per interrupt, for a total of 256 distinct interrupt vectors. Each 4-byte entry is composed of the segment number and offset of the interrupt handler for that function. In several cases, a vector contains the address of a table of data values rather than the address of a routine—such as the graphics-character table pointed to by Int 1Fh.

Getting and Setting Interrupt Vectors

All the cautions about interrupt vectors should warn you that anything affecting the interrupt vectors can have damaging side effects. Imagine that you are two bytes into changing an interrupt vector four bytes long and you are interrupted by another process that needs the vector you are changing; the CPU jumps to an incomplete vector address and can end up virtually anywhere in memory. This situation most often results in "hanging" your computer, but it *could* erase your hard disk.

How realistic is this scenario? DOS is a single-task system, in which only one operation can happen at a time. But another interrupt service routine, responding to a hardware interrupt, simply takes control and leaves your program halfway through it. Many a TSR takes control of interrupts when the TSR is activated, then returns the interrupts to their original settings when the TSR is finished. This situation *can* happen. And in programming, anything that *can* happen eventually *will*; the only question is whether it will happen sooner or later.

More important is the upward-compatibility issue. Modifying an interrupt vector directly is not compatible with future DOS upgrades (including OS/2, if you want to view it as an upgrade). Although direct modification works now, it is guaranteed not to work on a multitasking system. DOS, however, provides a safe way to change the interrupt vectors by using Int 21h, Functions 25h (Set Interrupt Vector) and 35h (Get Interrupt Vector).

To set an interrupt vector, follow these steps:

1. Use Function 35h to get the current vector value and store it for later use in chaining to any routine already using the interrupt and in restoring the interrupt.

2. Use Function 25h to set the new vector.

This process is simple in assembly language (see listing 11.1).

Listing 11.1

```
;------------ Get the Ctrl-C vector  ----------
      mov       ah,35h          ;Get vector
      mov       al,23h          ;Ctrl-C
      int       21h
      mov       oldseg,es       ;Store old vector
      mov       oldoff,bx

;------------ Set the Ctrl-C vector  ----------
      mov       ah,25h              ;Set vector
      mov       al,23h              ;Ctrl-C
      mov       dx, seg c_hand
      mov       ds,dx
      mov       dx, offset c_hand
      int       21h
```

You do not need to go down to the DOS level to set the interrupts. The available high-level language services help set them cleanly and eliminate concern over encountering a problem. These high-level language routines are more convenient ways of performing the Int 21h, Functions 25h and 35h services.

Turbo C provides two functions, getvect and setvect, that do the same thing as DOS Functions 35h and 25h without actually calling the DOS functions. In Microsoft C Compiler Version 5.0, the new _dos_getvect and _dos_setvect functions perform the same actions. In Turbo Pascal 4.0 and above, the GetIntVec and SetIntVec functions perform the same actions.

When Should You Write an Interrupt Handler?

Creating an interrupt handler of your own makes sense in the following situations:

- *When you have to trap an interrupt to keep your program from failing in unusual cases.* When you write commercial programs, you should never let users "bomb out" of your program on a divide-by-zero error or on some other error. Your program should handle the error. Furthermore, if your program performs any "fancy" operations, you should trap Ctrl-C and Ctrl-Break events and handle them, rather than let the system cut you off.

- *When you have to link into an interrupt chain*. Here are two examples: writing a TSR that executes on certain keystrokes and writing a special timing routine that you want to do in a program.

- *When you have to control the serial port*. As we have mentioned, DOS does not provide adequate service for the serial ports. If you want to write a real terminal program, it must have an interrupt-driven, serial-port servicing routine.

In cases other than the ones just described, you should attempt to make your code as high-level as possible. If you can code the interrupt handler in a high-level language, by all means do so, unless the interrupt handler simply does not run fast enough in your program. Debugging is much easier in a high-level language than in assembly language. You can always recode the handler if it is not fast enough.

Wherever possible, take advantage of the high-level language facilities for interrupt handling. Turbo C provides the `ctrlbrk()` function for setting a Ctrl-C interrupt handler from a high-level code module. Microsoft C provides the UNIX-compatible `signal()` function for handling signal traps. Turbo BASIC and QuickBASIC provide handlers similar to ON KEY, TIMER, and so on for handling events. Turbo Pascal can handle interrupts that have in-line assembly code or the new `Interrupt` directive defined in Turbo Pascal 4.0. Choose the highest level that can do the job.

When you write an interrupt handler, do not use DOS-type functions unless special care is taken. DOS is not reentrant: if it is interrupted while it is doing something, you could easily cause the system to lock up by calling DOS functions again.

One way not to invoke DOS functions is to have the interrupt handler do some setup processing (copy data to a memory buffer, for example). It can set a flag that can be recognized by the program currently using the system to do some additional processing, which might involve DOS calls. More to the point, DOS has some hidden ways to find out when DOS calls are safe. Hackers who spend their time trying to find out how other people perform computer techniques discovered and published some ways to learn what DOS does.

First, an Int 21h function (Function 34h) returns a pointer in the ES:BX registers. This pointer points to a DOS busy flag, called the *InDOS flag*. The flag is a single byte buried in the operating system kernel. Whenever an Int 21h function starts, the flag is incremented by one. When the function ends, the flag is decremented by one. Whenever the flag is zero, no DOS functions are executing.

TSRs check for this flag whenever their hot key is pressed. If the flag is nonzero, the TSR sets a hot-key flag in the TSR. TSRs that do this tie into the clock interrupt and check the status of InDOS 18.2 times per second until the flag clears. When InDOS is clear and the hot-key flag is set, the TSR starts its operations.

That is good, but it leaves you hanging when the command processor is waiting for you to type a command line. Because the command processor uses DOS functions for command-line input, the InDOS flag is set while DOS waits for characters. Clearly, DOS is in a safe position and can be interrupted for other operations provided you do not use the DOS functions to do any console I/O. To allow console I/O to occur, DOS has another interrupt, 28h, which is called repeatedly by the console input routines while they are waiting. This is the DOS Idle (or DOSOK) interrupt.

The DOS Idle interrupt normally does an IRET, which returns control to the console input routine. If a TSR is tied to the interrupt and notices that the hot-key flag is on, the body of the TSR can be executed immediately.

When you work with interrupts, be sure to follow a simple rule: *always* assume that other programs may be involved. For example, you should never set interrupt vectors directly. Int 21h, Function 25h is provided for this purpose and prevents any mix-ups between programs setting the vectors. Unless you write something such as a Ctrl-C handler, you should preserve the original handler vector and branch to it when you complete your processing. You also can install another handler, which needs to be activated. If you do not observe this simple rule, you can get into trouble.

When your program ends, it must clear any interrupt handlers it has set (the system automatically takes care of Fatal-Error and Ctrl-C handlers). If you write a terminal program, for example, you should restore the original interrupt handlers before you leave the program, thus preventing an interrupt from branching to where your handler *used* to be. If your program is setting up a resident handler, you should use the TSR exit so that the handler will be permanently allocated the memory it needs and will not be overwritten.

Writing a Ctrl-C Handler

A simple Ctrl-C handler serves as an example of interrupt handling. This handler is presented in several stages to show you several methods for handling the interrupt problem.

In the first example, handler.c, we have used the ctrlbrk() function in Turbo C to create a handler totally in C (see listing 11.2). Handler.c allows you to interrupt the process in progress and determine whether to leave. Because the ctrlbrk() function handles aborts, you return the appropriate code to the routine depending on the answer to the question. This method of writing the routine is particularly convenient because it is high level, works the first time, and involves no arcane programming. Furthermore, Turbo C indicates that this routine may use longjmp and other functions to interact directly with the program at a high level.

Listing 11.2

```
/* handler.c */
#include <stdio.h>
#define     CR    0x0D
#define     LF    0x0A
int   handler();
main()
{
    int   c;
    int   i;
    if(getcbrk()==0)
       printf("BREAK checking is OFF\n");
    else
       printf("BREAK checking is ON\n");
    ctrlbrk(handler);
    for(i=0; i<100; i++){
       printf("%4.4d:TESTING CTRL BREAK\n",i);
    }
    printf("CHARACTER INPUT\n");
    while((c=getche())!=0)
       if(c==CR || c==LF)
          putchar(LF);
}
handler()
{
    int   c;
    printf("\nCTRL BREAK HANDLER\n");
    printf("Do you want to quit? ");
    while((c = getch())!='y' && c!='Y' && c!='n' && c!='N');
    printf("\n");
    return(((c=='Y'||c=='y')?0:1));
}
```

Handler.c does two things to allow you to test the Ctrl-C handling:

1. It displays on the screen 100 lines that you can break into with Ctrl-C or Ctrl-Break.

2. It accepts characters from the keyboard so that you can try Ctrl-C or Ctrl-Break during keyboard input.

You also can code directly, in assembly language, a function that works much the same as ctrlbrk(), although the assembly language function is greatly simplified. You must work in assembly language because you have to complete your handler with a return from interrupt (IRET) rather than the normal function return. The handler could be in-line code, but producing something that can be assembled is more instructive.

A good assembly language programmer can produce an interrupt handler directly, but you may be unsure about how to put one together. To build this assembly language routine, start with an empty C routine and compile it to assembly language source code (the -S switch on the Microsoft C compiler):

```
set_brk()
{
}
brk()
{
    handler();
}
```

You compile the code like this:

```
C>CL /Fa set_brk.c;
```

to get the assembly language source code in listing 11.3 (Microsoft C).

Listing 11.3

```
; set_brk.asm
            name        set_brk
_text       segment     byte public 'code'
dgroup      group       _data,_bss
            assume      cs:_text,ds:dgroup,ss:dgroup
_text       ends
_data       segment     word public 'data'
_d@         label       byte
_data       ends
_bss        segment     word public 'bss'
_b@         label       byte
_bss        ends
_text       segment     byte public 'code'
_set_brk    proc        near
            ret
_set_brk    endp
_brk        proc        near
            call        near ptr _handler
            ret
_brk        endp
_text       ends
_data       segment     word public 'data'
_s@         label       byte
_data       ends
_text       segment     byte public 'code'
```

continues

Listing 11.3 *continued*

```
        extrn    _handler:near
        public   _brk
        public   _set_brk
_text   ends
        end
```

This empty C program (sometimes called a NULL program) produces a kind of fill-in-the-blank routine with which you can build an interrupt handler. Some assembly language "hot shots" may laugh at this type of approach, but professional programmers have been using the method for years to learn how a compiler generates code or to provide a way for recoding a function in assembly language to save processing time.

Building an Assembly Language Routine

Serious assembly language programmers may cringe at the thought, but you can prepare an assembly language routine by first writing it in a high-level language such as C and then compiling with an option that produces assembly language source code. In the example from listing 11.3, development time has been reduced significantly because the skeleton of the routine was produced from the compiler.

This technique is good to remember if you have to produce an assembly language program or if you want to optimize a program already in a high-level language. Converting the program to assembly code and editing the resulting file gives you a working program in a minimum amount of time.

To create the working interrupt handler in listing 11.4 for TASM 2.5, follow these steps:

1. Let the _set_brk() function set up the interrupt handler, using Int 21h, Function 25h.

2. Save all registers in the _brk function before calling the C function, then restore them when it returns.

3. Change RET to IRET.

In Turbo Pascal 4.0 and beyond, you can declare a procedure with the interrupt directive to be an interrupt handler. The compiler automatically handles the registers and the IRET instruction. The resulting procedure saves all registers; if you need to save only a few, inline code still may be more efficient.

Listing 11.4

```
; set_brk.asm
        name    set_brk
_text   segment byte public 'code'
dgroup  group   _data,_bss
        assume  cs:_text,ds:dgroup,ss:dgroup
_text   ends
_data   segment word public 'data'
_d@     label   byte
_data   ends
_bss    segment word public 'bss'
_b@     label   byte
_bss    ends
_text   segment byte public 'code'
_set_brk proc   near
        push    bp              ;Save the registers
        push    ds
        push    di
        push    si
        mov     dx,cs
        mov     ds,dx
        mov     dx,offset _brk
        mov     ah,25h          ;Set interrupt vector
        mov     al,23h          ;Ctrl-C handler
        int     21h
        pop     si              ;Retrieve the registers
        pop     di
        pop     ds
        pop     bp
        ret
_set_brk endp
_brk    proc    near
        push    ax              ;Save the registers
        push    bx
        push    cx
        push    dx
        push    di
        push    si
        push    bp
        call    near ptr _handler
        pop     bp              ;Retrieve the registers
        pop     si
        pop     di
        pop     dx
        pop     cx
        pop     bx
        pop     ax
        iret
```

continues

Listing 11.4 continued

```
        _brk     endp
        _text    ends
_data   segment  word public 'data'
_s@     label    byte
_data   ends
_text   segment  byte public 'code'
        extrn    _handler:near
        public   _brk
        public   _set_brk
_text   ends
        end
```

Notice that no effort has been made to clean up the code beyond what was provided by the compiler. Some of the chaff could have been cleaned out (hot-shot assembly language programmers will do so), but it is not necessary. The only requirement is that the code works. It does.

Finally, the revision is added to the handler.c program (see listing 11.5).

Listing 11.5

```
/* handler2.c */
#include <stdio.h>
#define    CR    0x0D
#define    LF    0x0A
main()
{
   int   c;
   int   i;
   if(getcbrk()==0)
      printf("BREAK checking is OFF\n");
   else
      printf("BREAK checking is ON\n");
   SET_BRK();
   for(i=0; i<100; i++){
      printf("%4.4d:TESTING CTRL BREAK\n",i);
   }
      printf("CHARACTER INPUT\n");
      while((c=getche())!=0)
         if(c==CR || c==LF)
            putchar(LF);
}
HANDLER()
{
   int   c;
   printf("\nCTRL BREAK HANDLER\n");
```

```
        printf("Do you want to quit? ");
        while((c = getch())!='y' && c!='Y' && c!='n' && c!='N');
        printf("\n");
        if(c=='Y'||c=='y')
            exit(0);
        return(0);
}
```

Compiling the program and linking it to the assembly language routine yields a working Ctrl-C handler.

Writing a Critical Error Handler

A critical error handler is perhaps one of the most involved interrupt handlers you can write. The critical error handler is invoked by DOS when an error occurs and DOS gives the user the ability to decide whether to go gamely on past the problem or to stop the program. The standard DOS manifestation is the famous "Abort, Retry, Fail?" prompt. For a programmer, this message is a catastrophe; it pays no attention to your carefully crafted screens, and it only pays a small amount of attention to exactly what happened. DOS provides the critical error handler with a great deal of information about just what happened. The code in listing 11.6 is a module that can be incorporated into a complete application; it takes advantage of this wealth of information.

Listing 11.6

```
page 55,132
;
; functions for creating a pop-up critical error handler
;
criterr_data    segment
MAXLINES  equ  19
    OldCritErrOffset            dw   (?)  ; Old critical error address
    OldCritErrSegment           dw   (?)  ;
    DeviceDriverHeaderOffset    dw   (?)  ; Device driver address
    DeviceDriverHeaderSegment   dw   (?)
    ErrorCode                   dw   (?)  ; Error code on entry
    Line                        dw MAXLINES dup (?) ; Pointers to menu lines
    DOS_MajorVersion            db   (?)  ; DOS major version
    IO_Type                     db   (?)  ; I/O type of error
```

continues

Listing 11.6 continued

```
            DriveNumber              db    (?)   ; Which drive had error
            MenuLines                db    (?)   ; Number of lines on screen - 1
            CurrentOption            db    (?)   ; Currently selected option
            MaximumOption            db    (?)   ; Number of valid options - 1
            ReturnCodes              dw    (?)   ; Pointer to list of valid return codes
            TopLine                  db    (?)   ; Top line of window
            BottomLine               db    (?)   ; Bottom line of window
            LeftRow                  db    (?)   ; Left line of window
            RightRow                 db    (?)   ; Right line of window
            ActiveDisplayPage        db    (?)   ; Active display video page
            OriginalRow              db    (?)   ; Where cursor was
            OriginalColumn           db    (?)   ;
Set__2_      db    2
Set__23      db    2,3
Set_12_      db    1,2
Set_123      db    1,2,3
Set0_2_      db    0,2
Set0_23      db    0,2,3
Set012_      db    0,1,2
Set0123      db    0,1,2,3
ATTRIBUTE equ  17H  ; WHITE ON BLUE
TopMenu                   db    "╔═══════════════╡Critical Error╞═══════════════════╗"
UnknownFunction           db    "║Unknown DOS Function                              ║"
Fn_00                     db    "║Terminate Program Line                            ║"
Fn_01                     db    "║Keyboard Input With Echo                          ║"
Fn_02                     db    "║Display Output                                    ║"
Fn_03                     db    "║Auxiliary Input                                   ║"
Fn_04                     db    "║Auxiliary Output                                  ║"
Fn_05                     db    "║Printer Output                                    ║"
Fn_06                     db    "║Direct Console I/O                                ║"
Fn_07                     db    "║Direct STDIN Input                                ║"
Fn_08                     db    "║STDIN Input                                       ║"
Fn_09                     db    "║Display String                                    ║"
Fn_0A                     db    "║Buffered STDIN Input                              ║"
Fn_0B                     db    "║Check STDIN Status                                ║"
Fn_0C                     db    "║Clear Buffer And Input                            ║"
Fn_0D                     db    "║Reset Disk                                        ║"
Fn_0E                     db    "║Select Disk                                       ║"
Fn_0F                     db    "║Open File (FCB)                                   ║"
Fn_10                     db    "║Close File (FCB)                                  ║"
Fn_11                     db    "║Search For First Entry (FCB)                      ║"
Fn_12                     db    "║Search For Next Entry (FCB)                       ║"
Fn_13                     db    "║Delete File (FCB)                                 ║"
Fn_14                     db    "║Read Sequential File (FCB)                        ║"
Fn_15                     db    "║Write Sequential File (FCB)                       ║"
Fn_16                     db    "║Create File (FCB)                                 ║"
Fn_17                     db    "║Rename File (FCB)                                 ║"
Fn_19                     db    "║Get Default Drive                                 ║"
```

```
Fn_1A          db    "‖Set DTA Address                                      ‖"
Fn_1B          db    "‖Get Allocation Table Information                      ‖"
Fn_1C          db    "‖Get Allocation Table Information For Specific Drive‖"
Fn_1F          db    "‖Get Default Disk Parameter Block                      ‖"
Fn_21          db    "‖Random File Read (FCB)                                ‖"
Fn_22          db    "‖Random File Write (FCB)                               ‖"
Fn_23          db    "‖Get File Size (FCB)                                   ‖"
Fn_24          db    "‖Set Random Record Field (FCB)                         ‖"
Fn_25          db    "‖Set Interrupt Vector                                  ‖"
Fn_26          db    "‖Create PSP                                            ‖"
Fn_27          db    "‖Random Block Read (FCB)                               ‖"
Fn_28          db    "‖Random Block Write (FCB)                              ‖"
Fn_29          db    "‖Parse File Name                                       ‖"
Fn_2A          db    "‖Get System Date                                       ‖"
Fn_2B          db    "‖Set System Date                                       ‖"
Fn_2C          db    "‖Get System Time                                       ‖"
Fn_2D          db    "‖Set System Time                                       ‖"
Fn_2E          db    "‖Set Verify Flag                                       ‖"
Fn_2F          db    "‖Get DTA Address                                       ‖"
Fn_30          db    "‖Get DOS Version Number                                ‖"
Fn_31          db    "‖Terminate And Stay Resident                           ‖"
Fn_32          db    "‖Get Drive Parameter Block                             ‖"
Fn_3300        db    "‖Get Ctrl-Break Flag                                   ‖"
Fn_3301        db    "‖Set Ctrl-Break Flag                                   ‖"
Fn_3305        db    "‖Get Boot Drive Code                                   ‖"
Fn_34          db    "‖Return Address Of InDOS Flag                          ‖"
Fn_35          db    "‖Get Interrupt Vector                                  ‖"
Fn_36          db    "‖Get Free Disk Space                                   ‖"
Fn_3700        db    "‖Get Switchchar                                        ‖"
Fn_3701        db    "‖Set Switchchar                                        ‖"
Fn_3702        db    "‖Read Device Availability                              ‖"
Fn_3703        db    "‖Set Device Availability                               ‖"
Fn_38          db    "‖Get Set Country Information                           ‖"
Fn_39          db    "‖Create Subdirectory                                   ‖"
Fn_3A          db    "‖Remove Subdirectory                                   ‖"
Fn_3B          db    "‖Set Directory                                         ‖"
Fn_3C          db    "‖Create Truncate File Handle                           ‖"
Fn_3D          db    "‖Open File Handle                                      ‖"
Fn_3E          db    "‖Close File Handle                                     ‖"
Fn_3F          db    "‖Read File Or Device Handle                            ‖"
Fn_40          db    "‖Write To File Or Device Handle                        ‖"
Fn_41          db    "‖Delete File                                           ‖"
Fn_42          db    "‖Move File Pointer                                     ‖"
Fn_4300        db    "‖Get File Attributes                                   ‖"
Fn_4301        db    "‖Set File Attributes                                   ‖"
Fn_4400        db    "‖Get Device Information                                ‖"
Fn_4401        db    "‖Set Device Information                                ‖"
Fn_4402        db    "‖Device IOCTL Read                                     ‖"
Fn_4403        db    "‖Device IOCTL Write                                    ‖"
```

continues

Listing 11.6 *continued*

```
Fn_4404        db      "‖Block Driver IOCTL Read              ‖"
Fn_4405        db      "‖Block Driver IOCTL Write             ‖"
Fn_4406        db      "‖Get Input Status                     ‖"
Fn_4407        db      "‖Get Output Status                    ‖"
Fn_4408        db      "‖Block Device Removable               ‖"
Fn_4409        db      "‖Block Device Local                   ‖"
Fn_440A        db      "‖Handle Local                         ‖"
Fn_440B        db      "‖Set Sharing Retry Count              ‖"
Fn_440C        db      "‖Generic IOCTL Handles                ‖"
Fn_440D        db      "‖Generic IOCTL Block Devices          ‖"
Fn_440E        db      "‖Get Logical Drive Map                ‖"
Fn_440F        db      "‖Set Logical Drive Map                ‖"
Fn_4410        db      "‖Query IOCTL Handle                   ‖"
Fn_4411        db      "‖Query IOCTL Device                   ‖"
Fn_45          db      "‖Duplicate Handle                     ‖"
Fn_46          db      "‖Force Duplicate Handle               ‖"
Fn_47          db      "‖Get Current Directory                ‖"
Fn_48          db      "‖Allocate Memory                      ‖"
Fn_49          db      "‖Release Memory                       ‖"
Fn_4A          db      "‖Modify Memory Allocation             ‖"
Fn_4B00        db      "‖Execute Program                      ‖"
Fn_4B01        db      "‖Load Program                         ‖"
Fn_4B03        db      "‖Load Overlay                         ‖"
Fn_4B05        db      "‖Enter Exec State                     ‖"
Fn_4C          db      "‖Terminate With Return Code           ‖"
Fn_4D          db      "‖Get Return Code                      ‖"
Fn_4E          db      "‖Search For First Match               ‖"
Fn_4F          db      "‖Search For Next Match                ‖"
Fn_50          db      "‖Set PSP Segment                      ‖"
Fn_51          db      "‖Get PSP Segment                      ‖"
Fn_52          db      "‖Get Disk List                        ‖"
Fn_53          db      "‖Translate BPB To DPB                 ‖"
Fn_54          db      "‖Get Verify Flag                      ‖"
Fn_55          db      "‖Create PSP                           ‖"
Fn_56          db      "‖Rename File                          ‖"
Fn_5700        db      "‖Get File Date And Time               ‖"
Fn_5701        db      "‖Set File Date And Time               ‖"
Fn_5800        db      "‖Get Allocation Strategy              ‖"
Fn_5801        db      "‖Set Allocation Strategy              ‖"
Fn_5802        db      "‖Get UMB Link Status                  ‖"
Fn_5803        db      "‖Set UMB Link                         ‖"
Fn_59          db      "‖Get Extended Error Information        ‖"
Fn_5A          db      "‖Create Uniquely Named File           ‖"
Fn_5B          db      "‖Create New File                      ‖"
Fn_5C00        db      "‖Set File Access Locks                ‖"
Fn_5C01        db      "‖Clear File Access Locks              ‖"
Fn_5D00        db      "‖Copy Data To DOS Save Area           ‖"
```

```
Fn_5D06            db      "‖Get Critical Error Flag Address         ‖"
Fn_5D0A            db      "‖Set Error Data Values                   ‖"
Fn_5E00            db      "‖Get Machine Name                        ‖"
Fn_5E01            db      "‖Set Machine Name                        ‖"
Fn_5E02            db      "‖Set Network Printer Setup               ‖"
Fn_5E03            db      "‖Get Network Printer Setup               ‖"
Fn_5F02            db      "‖Get Redirection List Entry              ‖"
Fn_5F03            db      "‖Set Redirection List Entry              ‖"
Fn_5F04            db      "‖Cancel Redirection List Entry           ‖"
Fn_60              db      "‖Expand Path Name String                 ‖"
Fn_62              db      "‖Get PSP Address                         ‖"
Fn_6300            db      "‖Get System Lead Byte Table              ‖"
Fn_6301            db      "‖Set/Clear Interim Console Flag          ‖"
Fn_6302            db      "‖Get Value Of Interim Console Flag       ‖"
Fn_64              db      "‖Set Current Country Byte                ‖"
Fn_65              db      "‖Set Extended Country Information         ‖"
Fn_6600            db      "‖Get Global Code Page                    ‖"
Fn_6602            db      "‖Set Global Code Page                    ‖"
Fn_67              db      "‖Set Handle Count                        ‖"
Fn_68              db      "‖Flush Buffer                            ‖"
Fn_6A              db      "‖Allocate Memory                         ‖"
Fn_6C              db      "‖Extended Open Create                    ‖"
UnknownErrorCode   db      "‖Error Code: Unknown                     ‖"
ErrorCode00        db      "‖Error Code: Write Protect Error         ‖"
ErrorCode01        db      "‖Error Code: Unknown Unit                ‖"
ErrorCode02        db      "‖Error Code: Drive Not Ready             ‖"
ErrorCode03        db      "‖Error Code: Unknown Command             ‖"
ErrorCode04        db      "‖Error Code: Data Error                  ‖"
ErrorCode05        db      "‖Error Code: Bad Request Structure Length ‖"
ErrorCode06        db      "‖Error Code: Seek Error                  ‖"
ErrorCode07        db      "‖Error Code: Unknown Media Type          ‖"
ErrorCode08        db      "‖Error Code: Sector Not Found            ‖"
ErrorCode09        db      "‖Error Code: Printer Out Of Paper        ‖"
ErrorCode0A        db      "‖Error Code: Write Fault                 ‖"
ErrorCode0B        db      "‖Error Code: Read Fault                  ‖"
ErrorCode0C        db      "‖Error Code: General Failure             ‖"
ErrorCode0F        db      "‖Error Code: Invalid Disk Change         ‖"
L2                 db      "‖      AX = "
L2AX               db      "0000 BX = "
L2BX               db      "0000 CX = "
L2CX               db      "0000 DX = "
L2DX               db      "0000        ‖"
L3                 db      "‖      DI = "
L3DI               db      "0000 SI = "
L3SI               db      "0000 BP = "
L3BP               db      "0000 SP = "
L3SP               db      "0000        ‖"
L4                 db      "‖            DS = "
```

continues

Listing 11.6 *continued*

```
L4DS            db      "0000 ES = "
L4ES            db      "0000 SS = "
L4SS            db      "0000           ‖"
L5              db      "‖         CS:IP = "
L5CS            db      "0000:"
L5IP            db      "0000 Flags = "
L5Flags         db      "--------        ‖"
L7_Char         db      "‖Device: "
L7_Device       db      "                                                ‖"
L7_UnknownChar  db      "‖Unknown Character (?) Device                    ‖"
DiskError0      db      "‖Drive  : Error Reading MS-DOS Area              ‖"
DiskError1      db      "‖Drive  : Error Writing MS-DOS Area              ‖"
DiskError2      db      "‖Drive  : Error Reading FAT                      ‖"
DiskError3      db      "‖Drive  : Error Writing FAT                      ‖"
DiskError4      db      "‖Drive  : Error Reading Root Directory           ‖"
DiskError5      db      "‖Drive  : Error Writing Root Directory           ‖"
DiskError6      db      "‖Drive  : Error Reading Files Area               ‖"
DiskError7      db      "‖Drive  : Error Writing Files Area               ‖"
DRIVE_OFFSET    equ     7
Bridge2Line     db      "‖------------------------------------------------‖"
EEC_01          db      "‖Extended Error Code|Invalid Function Number     ‖"
EEC_02          db      "‖Extended Error Code|File Not Found              ‖"
EEC_03          db      "‖Extended Error Code|Path Not Found              ‖"
EEC_04          db      "‖Extended Error Code|No Handles Available        ‖"
EEC_05          db      "‖Extended Error Code|Access Denied               ‖"
EEC_06          db      "‖Extended Error Code|Invalid Handle              ‖"
EEC_07          db      "‖Extended Error Code|Memory Ctrl Blocks Destroyed‖"
EEC_08          db      "‖Extended Error Code|Insufficient Memory         ‖"
EEC_09          db      "‖Extended Error Code|Invalid Memory Block Address ‖"
EEC_0A          db      "‖Extended Error Code|Invalid Environment         ‖"
EEC_0B          db      "‖Extended Error Code|Invalid Format              ‖"
EEC_0C          db      "‖Extended Error Code|Invalid Access Code         ‖"
EEC_0D          db      "‖Extended Error Code|Invalid Data                ‖"
EEC_0F          db      "‖Extended Error Code|Invalid Drive               ‖"
EEC_10          db      "‖Extended Error Code|Remove Current Directory    ‖"
EEC_11          db      "‖Extended Error Code|Not the Same Device         ‖"
EEC_12          db      "‖Extended Error Code|No More Files               ‖"
EEC_13          db      "‖Extended Error Code|Disk Write-Protected        ‖"
EEC_14          db      "‖Extended Error Code|Unknown Unit                ‖"
EEC_15          db      "‖Extended Error Code|Drive Not Ready             ‖"
EEC_16          db      "‖Extended Error Code|Unknown Command             ‖"
EEC_17          db      "‖Extended Error Code|CRC Error                   ‖"
EEC_18          db      "‖Extended Error Code|Bad Request Structure Length‖"
EEC_19          db      "‖Extended Error Code|Seek Error                  ‖"
EEC_1A          db      "‖Extended Error Code|Unknown Media Type          ‖"
EEC_1B          db      "‖Extended Error Code|Sector Not Found            ‖"
EEC_1C          db      "‖Extended Error Code|Out of Paper                ‖"
```

```
EEC_1D               db      "‖Extended Error Code|Write Fault                 ‖"
EEC_1E               db      "‖Extended Error Code|Read Fault                  ‖"
EEC_1F               db      "‖Extended Error Code|General Failure             ‖"
EEC_20               db      "‖Extended Error Code|Sharing Violation           ‖"
EEC_21               db      "‖Extended Error Code|Lock Violation              ‖"
EEC_22               db      "‖Extended Error Code|Invalid Disk Change         ‖"
EEC_23               db      "‖Extended Error Code|FCB Unavailable             ‖"
EEC_24               db      "‖Extended Error Code|Sharing Buffer overflow     ‖"
EEC_26               db      "‖Extended Error Code|Can't Complete File Operation ‖"
EEC_32               db      "‖Extended Error Code|Network Request Not Supported ‖"
EEC_33               db      "‖Extended Error Code|Remote Computer Not Listening ‖"
EEC_34               db      "‖Extended Error Code|Duplicate Name on Network   ‖"
EEC_35               db      "‖Extended Error Code|Network Name Not Found       ‖"
EEC_36               db      "‖Extended Error Code|Network Busy                ‖"
EEC_37               db      "‖Extended Error Code|Netwrk Device No Longer Exists ‖"
EEC_38               db      "‖Extended Error Code|NetBIOS Command Limit Exceeded ‖"
EEC_39               db      "‖Extended Error Code|Network Adapter Error       ‖"
EEC_3A               db      "‖Extended Error Code|Incorrect Network Response  ‖"
EEC_3B               db      "‖Extended Error Code|Unexpected Network Error    ‖"
EEC_3C               db      "‖Extended Error Code|Incompatible Remote Adapter ‖"
EEC_3D               db      "‖Extended Error Code|Print Queue Full            ‖"
EEC_3E               db      "‖Extended Error Code|Not Enough Room For Print File ‖"
EEC_3F               db      "‖Extended Error Code|Print File Deleted          ‖"
EEC_40               db      "‖Extended Error Code|Network Name Deleted        ‖"
EEC_41               db      "‖Extended Error Code|Access Denied               ‖"
EEC_42               db      "‖Extended Error Code|Network Device Type Incorrect ‖"
EEC_43               db      "‖Extended Error Code|Network Name Not Found       ‖"
EEC_44               db      "‖Extended Error Code|Network Name Limit Exceeded ‖"
EEC_45               db      "‖Extended Error Code|NetBIOS Session Limit Exceeded ‖"
EEC_46               db      "‖Extended Error Code|Sharing Temporarily Paused  ‖"
EEC_47               db      "‖Extended Error Code|Network Request Not Accepted ‖"
EEC_48               db      "‖Extended Error Code|Print/Disk Redirection Paused ‖"
EEC_50               db      "‖Extended Error Code|File Already Exists         ‖"
EEC_52               db      "‖Extended Error Code|Cannot Make Directory Entry ‖"
EEC_53               db      "‖Extended Error Code|Fail on Int 24              ‖"
EEC_54               db      "‖Extended Error Code|Too Many Redirections       ‖"
EEC_55               db      "‖Extended Error Code|Duplicate Redirection       ‖"
EEC_56               db      "‖Extended Error Code|Invalid Password            ‖"
EEC_57               db      "‖Extended Error Code|Invalid Parameter           ‖"
EEC_58               db      "‖Extended Error Code|Network Data Fault          ‖"
EEC_59               db      "‖Extended Error Code|Fn Not Supported By Network ‖"
EEC_5A               db      "‖Extended Error Code|Req'd Sys. Comp. Not Installed ‖"
EEC_Unknown          db      "‖Extended Error Code|Unknown                     ‖"
ECC_01               db      "‖   Error Class Code|Out Of Resource            ‖"
ECC_02               db      "‖   Error Class Code|Temporary Situation        ‖"
ECC_03               db      "‖   Error Class Code|Authorization              ‖"
ECC_04               db      "‖   Error Class Code|Internal                   ‖"
ECC_05               db      "‖   Error Class Code|Hardware Failure           ‖"
ECC_06               db      "‖   Error Class Code|System Failure             ‖"
```

continues

Listing 11.6 *continued*

```
ECC_07          db    "||    Error Class Code|Application Program Error        ||"
ECC_08          db    "||    Error Class Code|Not Found                        ||"
ECC_09          db    "||    Error Class Code|Bad Format                       ||"
ECC_0A          db    "||    Error Class Code|Locked                           ||"
ECC_0B          db    "||    Error Class Code|Media                            ||"
ECC_0C          db    "||    Error Class Code|Already Exists                   ||"
ECC_Unknown     db    "||    Error Class Code|Unknown                          ||"
RAC_1           db    "|| Recommended Action|Retry Then Abort/Ignore           ||"
RAC_2           db    "|| Recommended Action|Delay & Retry Then Abort/Ignore||"
RAC_3           db    "|| Recommended Action|Get Correct Data From User        ||"
RAC_4           db    "|| Recommended Action|Abort Application With Cleanup    ||"
RAC_5           db    "|| Recommended Action|Abort Without Cleanup Attempt     ||"
RAC_6           db    "|| Recommended Action|Ignore Error                      ||"
RAC_7           db    "|| Recommended Action|Correct Error Then Retry          ||"
RAC_Unknown     db    "|| Recommended Action|Unknown                           ||"
Locus_2         db    "||              Locus|Block Device                      ||"
Locus_3         db    "||              Locus|Network                           ||"
Locus_4         db    "||              Locus|Serial Device                     ||"
Locus_5         db    "||              Locus|Memory Related                    ||"
Locus_Unknown   db    "||              Locus|Unknown                           ||"
BridgeLine      db    "||-------------------------------------------------||"
IgnoreOption    db    "||  |Ignore Error                                       ||"
RetryOption     db    "||  |Retry Function Call                                ||"
TerminateOption db    "||  |Terminate Program                                  ||"
FailCallOption  db    "||  |Fail Function Call                                 ||"
BottomMenu      db    "||_____||"
LINEWIDTH       equ   $-BottomMenu
ScreenSave      db    (LINEWIDTH * MAXLINES * 2) dup (?)
MainTable dw    Fn_00
          dw    Fn_01
          dw    Fn_02
          dw    Fn_03
          dw    Fn_04
          dw    Fn_05
          dw    Fn_06
          dw    Fn_07
          dw    Fn_08
          dw    Fn_09
          dw    Fn_0A
          dw    Fn_0B
          dw    Fn_0C
          dw    Fn_0D
          dw    Fn_0E
          dw    Fn_0F
          dw    Fn_10
          dw    Fn_11
          dw    Fn_12
```

```
            dw    Fn_13
            dw    Fn_14
            dw    Fn_15
            dw    Fn_16
            dw    Fn_17
            dw    UnknownFunction
            dw    Fn_19
            dw    Fn_1A
            dw    Fn_1B
            dw    Fn_1C
            dw    UnknownFunction
            dw    UnknownFunction
            dw    Fn_1F
            dw    UnknownFunction
            dw    Fn_21
            dw    Fn_22
            dw    Fn_23
            dw    Fn_24
            dw    Fn_25
            dw    Fn_26
            dw    Fn_27
            dw    Fn_28
            dw    Fn_29
            dw    Fn_2A
            dw    Fn_2B
            dw    Fn_2C
            dw    Fn_2D
            dw    Fn_2E
            dw    Fn_2F
            dw    Fn_30
            dw    Fn_31
            dw    Fn_32
            dw    -1
            dw    Fn_34
            dw    Fn_35
            dw    Fn_36
            dw    -1
            dw    Fn_38
            dw    Fn_39
            dw    Fn_3A
            dw    Fn_3B
            dw    Fn_3C
            dw    Fn_3D
            dw    Fn_3E
            dw    Fn_3F
            dw    Fn_40
            dw    Fn_41
            dw    Fn_42
```

continues

Listing 11.6 continued

```
              dw    -1
              dw    -1
              dw    Fn_45
              dw    Fn_46
              dw    Fn_47
              dw    Fn_48
              dw    Fn_49
              dw    Fn_4A
              dw    -1
              dw    Fn_4C
              dw    Fn_4D
              dw    Fn_4E
              dw    Fn_4F
              dw    Fn_50
              dw    Fn_51
              dw    Fn_52
              dw    Fn_53
              dw    Fn_54
              dw    Fn_55
              dw    Fn_56
              dw    -1
              dw    -1
              dw    Fn_59
              dw    Fn_5A
              dw    Fn_5B
              dw    -1
              dw    -1
              dw    -1
              dw    -1
              dw    Fn_60
              dw    UnknownFunction
              dw    Fn_62
              dw    -1
              dw    Fn_64
              dw    Fn_65
              dw    -1
              dw    Fn_67
              dw    Fn_68
              dw    UnknownFunction
              dw    Fn_6A
              dw    UnknownFunction
              dw    Fn_6C
Table33       dw    Fn_3300
              dw    Fn_3301
              dw    UnknownFunction
              dw    UnknownFunction
              dw    UnknownFunction
              dw    Fn_3305
```

```
Table37    dw    Fn_3700
           dw    Fn_3701
           dw    Fn_3702
           dw    Fn_3703
Table43    dw    Fn_4300
           dw    Fn_4301
Table44    dw    Fn_4400
           dw    Fn_4401
           dw    Fn_4402
           dw    Fn_4403
           dw    Fn_4404
           dw    Fn_4405
           dw    Fn_4406
           dw    Fn_4407
           dw    Fn_4408
           dw    Fn_4409
           dw    Fn_440A
           dw    Fn_440B
           dw    Fn_440C
           dw    Fn_440D
           dw    Fn_440E
           dw    Fn_440F
           dw    Fn_4410
           dw    Fn_4411
Table4B    dw    Fn_4B00
           dw    Fn_4B01
           dw    UnknownFunction
           dw    Fn_4B03
           dw    UnknownFunction
           dw    Fn_4B05
Table57    dw    Fn_5700
           dw    Fn_5701
Table58    dw    Fn_5800
           dw    Fn_5801
           dw    Fn_5802
           dw    Fn_5803
Table5C    dw    Fn_5C00
           dw    Fn_5C01
Table5D    dw    Fn_5D00
           dw    UnknownFunction
           dw    UnknownFunction
           dw    UnknownFunction
           dw    UnknownFunction
           dw    UnknownFunction
           dw    Fn_5D06
           dw    UnknownFunction
           dw    UnknownFunction
           dw    UnknownFunction
```

continues

Listing 11.6 *continued*

```
                dw      Fn_5D0A
    Table5E     dw      Fn_5E00
                dw      Fn_5E01
                dw      Fn_5E02
                dw      Fn_5E03
    Table5F     dw      UnknownFunction
                dw      UnknownFunction
                dw      Fn_5F02
                dw      Fn_5F03
                dw      Fn_5F04
    Table63     dw      Fn_6300
                dw      Fn_6301
                dw      Fn_6302
    Table66     dw      Fn_6600
                dw      UnknownFunction
                dw      Fn_6602
    ECTable     dw      ErrorCode00
                dw      ErrorCode01
                dw      ErrorCode02
                dw      ErrorCode03
                dw      ErrorCode04
                dw      ErrorCode05
                dw      ErrorCode06
                dw      ErrorCode07
                dw      ErrorCode08
                dw      ErrorCode09
                dw      ErrorCode0A
                dw      ErrorCode0B
                dw      ErrorCode0C
                dw      UnknownErrorCode
                dw      UnknownErrorCode
                dw      ErrorCode0F
    DiskErrorTable dw    DiskError0
                dw       DiskError1
                dw       DiskError2
                dw       DiskError3
                dw       DiskError4
                dw       DiskError5
                dw       DiskError6
                dw       DiskError7
    EEC_Table   dw      EEC_Unknown
                dw      EEC_01
                dw      EEC_02
                dw      EEC_03
                dw      EEC_04
                dw      EEC_05
                dw      EEC_06
```

```
dw    EEC_07
dw    EEC_08
dw    EEC_09
dw    EEC_0A
dw    EEC_0B
dw    EEC_0C
dw    EEC_0D
dw    EEC_Unknown
dw    EEC_0F
dw    EEC_10
dw    EEC_11
dw    EEC_12
dw    EEC_13
dw    EEC_14
dw    EEC_15
dw    EEC_16
dw    EEC_17
dw    EEC_18
dw    EEC_19
dw    EEC_1A
dw    EEC_1B
dw    EEC_1C
dw    EEC_1D
dw    EEC_1E
dw    EEC_1F
dw    EEC_20
dw    EEC_21
dw    EEC_22
dw    EEC_23
dw    EEC_24
dw    EEC_Unknown
dw    EEC_26
dw    EEC_Unknown
dw    EEC_Unknown
dw    EEC_Unknown
dw    EEC_Unknown
dw    EEC_Unknown
dw    EEC_Unknown
dw    EEC_Unknown
dw    EEC_Unknown
dw    EEC_Unknown
dw    EEC_Unknown
dw    EEC_Unknown
dw    EEC_32
dw    EEC_33
dw    EEC_34
dw    EEC_35
dw    EEC_36
dw    EEC_37
```

continues

Listing 11.6 continued

```
                dw    EEC_38
                dw    EEC_39
                dw    EEC_3A
                dw    EEC_3B
                dw    EEC_3C
                dw    EEC_3D
                dw    EEC_3E
                dw    EEC_3F
                dw    EEC_40
                dw    EEC_41
                dw    EEC_42
                dw    EEC_43
                dw    EEC_44
                dw    EEC_45
                dw    EEC_46
                dw    EEC_47
                dw    EEC_48
                dw    EEC_Unknown
                dw    EEC_Unknown
                dw    EEC_Unknown
                dw    EEC_Unknown
                dw    EEC_Unknown
                dw    EEC_Unknown
                dw    EEC_Unknown
                dw    EEC_50
                dw    EEC_Unknown
                dw    EEC_52
                dw    EEC_53
                dw    EEC_54
                dw    EEC_55
                dw    EEC_56
                dw    EEC_57
                dw    EEC_58
                dw    EEC_59
                dw    EEC_5A
ECC_Table       dw    EEC_Unknown
                dw    ECC_01
                dw    ECC_02
                dw    ECC_03
                dw    ECC_04
                dw    ECC_05
                dw    ECC_06
                dw    ECC_07
                dw    ECC_08
                dw    ECC_09
                dw    ECC_0A
                dw    ECC_0B
```

```
                  dw    CC_0C
RAC_Table  dw    RAC_Unknown
                  dw    RAC_1
                  dw    RAC_2
                  dw    RAC_3
                  dw    RAC_4
                  dw    RAC_5
                  dw    RAC_6
                  dw    RAC_7
Locus_Table      dw    Locus_Unknown
                  dw    Locus_Unknown
                  dw    Locus_2
                  dw    Locus_3
                  dw    Locus_4
                  dw    Locus_5
criterr_data     ends
;
;  Stack structure in CritErr
;
CE_CallerStack struc
     OldDS            dw    (?)   ; DS on entry
     OldES            dw    (?)   ; ES on entry
     OldBP            dw    (?)   ; BP on entry
     OldSI            dw    (?)   ; SI on entry
     OldDI            dw    (?)   ; DI on entry
     OldBX            dw    (?)   ; BX on entry
     OldCX            dw    (?)   ; CX on entry
     OldDX            dw    (?)   ; DX on entry
     Int21IP          dw    (?)   ; Int 21 IP
     Int21CS          dw    (?)   ; Int 21 CS
     Int21Flags       dw    (?)   ; Int 21 Flags
     UsersAX          dw    (?)   ; Caller's AX
     UsersBX          dw    (?)   ; Caller's BX
     UsersCX          dw    (?)   ; Caller's CX
     UsersDX          dw    (?)   ; Caller's DX
     UsersSI          dw    (?)   ; Caller's SI
     UsersDI          dw    (?)   ; Caller's DI
     UsersBP          dw    (?)   ; Caller's BP
     UsersDS          dw    (?)   ; Caller's DS
     UsersES          dw    (?)   ; Caller's ES
     UsersIP          dw    (?)   ; Caller's IP
     UsersCS          dw    (?)   ; Caller's CS
     UsersFlags       dw    (?)   ; Caller's Flags
CE_CallerStack ends
criterr_code     segment
assume    CS:criterr_code
assume    DS:nothing
assume    ES:nothing
```

continues

Listing 11.6 *continued*

```
        assume    SS:nothing
        CritErr   proc
                  push DX          ; Save registers
                  push CX          ;
                  push BX          ;
                  push DI          ;
                  push SI          ;
                  push BP          ;
                  push ES          ;
                  push DS          ;
                  mov  BX,seg criterr_data       ; Set DS to local data
                  mov  DS,BX
                  assume    DS:criterr_data
                  mov  IO_Type,AH              ; Save special values
                  mov  DriveNumber,AL
                  mov  ErrorCode,DI
                  mov  DeviceDriverHeaderSegment,BP
                  mov  DeviceDriverHeaderOffset,SI
                  mov  BP,SP                   ; Let BP point to stack structure
                  mov  Line,offset DS:TopMenu
                  mov  Line + 2,offset DS:UnknownFunction
                  mov  AX,[BP.UsersAX]    ; Get caller's AX value
                  cmp  AH,6CH             ; Out of known range?
                  jbe  ValidFunction
                  jmp  DumpRegistersIsle
        ValidFunction:
                  cmp  AH,33H             ; Identify subfunction?
                  jne  Not_Fn33
                  jmp  Fn33
        Not_Fn33:
                  cmp  AH,37H
                  jne  Not_Fn37
                  jmp  Fn37
        Not_Fn37:
                  cmp  AH,43H
                  jne  Not_Fn43
                  jmp  Fn43
        Not_Fn43:
                  cmp  AH,44H
                  jne  Not_Fn44
                  jmp  Fn44
        Not_Fn44:
                  cmp  AH,4BH
                  jne  Not_Fn4B
                  jmp  Fn4B
        Not_Fn4B:
                  cmp  AH,57H
```

```
                    jne    Not_Fn57
                    jmp    Fn57
Not_Fn57:
                    cmp    AH,58H
                    jne    Not_Fn58
                    jmp    Fn58
Not_Fn58:
                    cmp    AH,5CH
                    je     Fn5C
                    cmp    AH,5DH
                    je     Fn5D
                    cmp    AH,5EH
                    je     Fn5E
                    cmp    AH,5FH
                    je     Fn5F
                    cmp    AH,63H
                    je     Fn63
                    cmp    AH,66H
                    je     Fn66
                    shl    AH,1        ; Double the index
                    mov    BL,AH       ; Put in BX
                    xor    BH,BH
                    mov    AX,MainTable[ BX ]
                    jmp    SetFunction
Fn66:
                    cmp    AL,02H      ; Undefined?
                    ja     DumpRegistersIsle
                    shl    AL,1
                    mov    BL,AL
                    xor    BH,BH
                    mov    AX,Table66[ BX ]
                    jmp    SetFunction
Fn63:
                    cmp    AL,02H      ; Undefined?
                    ja     DumpRegistersIsle
                    shl    AL,1
                    mov    BL,AL
                    xor    BH,BH
                    mov    AX,Table63[ BX ]
                    jmp    SetFunction
Fn5F:
                    cmp    AL,04H      ; Undefined?
                    ja     DumpRegistersIsle
                    shl    AL,1
                    mov    BL,AL
                    xor    BH,BH
                    mov    AX,Table5F[ BX ]
                    jmp    SetFunction
```

continues

Listing 11.6 continued

```
Fn5E:
                cmp   AL,03H    ; Undefined?
                ja    DumpRegistersIsle
                shl   AL,1
                mov   BL,AL
                xor   BH,BH
                mov   AX,Table5E[ BX ]
                jmp   SetFunction
Fn5D:
                cmp   AL,0AH    ; Undefined?
                jbe   Fn5D_1
DumpRegistersIsle:
                jmp   DumpRegisters
Fn5D_1:
                shl   AL,1
                mov   BL,AL
                xor   BH,BH
                mov   AX,Table5D[ BX ]
                jmp   short SetFunction
Fn5C:
                cmp   AL,01H    ; Undefined?
                ja    DumpRegisters
                shl   AL,1
                mov   BL,AL
                xor   BH,BH
                mov   AX,Table5C[ BX ]
                jmp   short SetFunction
Fn58:
                cmp   AL,03H    ; Undefined?
                ja    DumpRegisters
                shl   AL,1
                mov   BL,AL
                xor   BH,BH
                mov   AX,Table58[ BX ]
                jmp   short SetFunction
Fn57:
                cmp   AL,01H    ; Undefined?
                ja    DumpRegisters
                shl   AL,1
                mov   BL,AL
                xor   BH,BH
                mov   AX,Table57[ BX ]
                jmp   short SetFunction
Fn4B:
                cmp   AL,05H    ; Undefined?
                ja    DumpRegisters
                shl   AL,1
```

```
                   mov   BL,AL
                   xor   BH,BH
                   mov   AX,Table4B[ BX ]
                   jmp   short SetFunction
           Fn44:
                   cmp   AL,11H    ; Undefined?
                   ja    DumpRegisters
                   shl   AL,1
                   mov   BL,AL
                   xor   BH,BH
                   mov   AX,Table44[ BX ]
                   jmp   short SetFunction
           Fn43:
                   cmp   AL,01H    ; Undefined?
                   ja    DumpRegisters
                   shl   AL,1
                   mov   BL,AL
                   xor   BH,BH
                   mov   AX,Table43[ BX ]
                   jmp   short SetFunction
           Fn37:
                   cmp   AL,03H    ; Undefined?
                   ja    DumpRegisters
                   shl   AL,1
                   mov   BL,AL
                   xor   BH,BH
                   mov   AX,Table37[ BX ]
                   jmp   short SetFunction
           Fn33:
                   cmp   AL,05H    ; Undefined?
                   ja    DumpRegisters
                   shl   AL,1
                   mov   BL,AL
                   xor   BH,BH
                   mov   AX,Table33[ BX ]
           SetFunction:
                   mov   Line + 2,AX
           DumpRegisters:
                   mov   BX,offset L2AX
                   mov   AX,[ BP.UsersAX ]
                   call  FillWord
                   mov   BX,offset L2BX
                   mov   AX,[ BP.UsersBX ]
                   call  FillWord
                   mov   BX,offset L2CX
                   mov   AX,[ BP.UsersCX ]
                   call  FillWord
                   mov   BX,offset L2DX
```

continues

Listing 11.6 continued

```
                mov   AX,[ BP.UsersDX ]
                call  FillWord
                mov   Line + 4,offset L2
                mov   BX,offset L3DI
                mov   AX,[ BP.UsersDI ]
                call  FillWord
                mov   BX,offset L3SI
                mov   AX,[ BP.UsersSI ]
                call  FillWord
                mov   BX,offset L3BP
                mov   AX,[ BP.UsersBP ]
                call  FillWord
                mov   BX,offset L3SP
                mov   AX,BP
                add   AX,size CE_CallerStack
                call  FillWord
                mov   Line + 6,offset L3
                mov   BX,offset L4DS
                mov   AX,[ BP.UsersDS ]
                call  FillWord
                mov   BX,offset L4ES
                mov   AX,[ BP.UsersES ]
                call  FillWord
                mov   BX,offset L4SS
                mov   AX,SS
                call  FillWord
                mov   Line + 8,offset L4
                mov   BX,offset L5CS
                mov   AX,[ BP.UsersCS ]
                call  FillWord
                mov   BX,offset L5IP
                mov   AX,[ BP.UsersIP ]
                call  FillWord
                mov   BX,offset L5Flags
                mov   AX,[ BP.UsersFlags ]
                test  AX,0800H
                jz    OF_Clear
                mov   byte ptr [ BX ],'O'
OF_Clear:
                inc   BX
                test  AX,0400H
                jz    DF_Clear
                mov   byte ptr [ BX ],'D'
DF_Clear:
                inc   BX
                test  AX,0200H
                jz    IF_Clear
                mov   byte ptr [ BX ],'I'
```

```
IF_Clear:
        inc  BX
        test AX,0100H
        jz   TF_Clear
        mov  byte ptr [ BX ],'T'
TF_Clear:
        inc  BX
        test AX,0080H
        jz   SF_Clear
        mov  byte ptr [ BX ], 'S'
SF_Clear:
        inc  BX
        test AX,0040H
        jz   ZF_Clear
        mov  byte ptr [ BX ],'Z'
ZF_Clear:
        inc  BX
        test AX,0010H
        jz   AF_Clear
        mov  byte ptr [ BX ],'A'
AF_Clear:
        inc  BX
        test AX,0004H
        jz   PF_Clear
        mov  byte ptr [ BX ],'P'
PF_Clear:
        inc  BX
        test AX,0001H
        jz   CF_Clear
        mov  byte ptr [ BX ],'C'
CF_Clear:
        mov  Line + 10,offset L5
        mov  AX,offset UnknownErrorCode
        mov  BX,ErrorCode
        xor  BH,BH
        cmp  BX,0FH
        ja   SetErrorCode
        shl  BX,1
        mov  AX,ECTable[ BX ]
SetErrorCode:
        mov  Line + 12,AX
        test IO_Type,80H
        jz   DiskError
        mov  AX,DeviceDriverHeaderSegment
        mov  ES,AX
        mov  BX,DeviceDriverHeaderOffset
        test word ptr ES:[ BX + 4 ],8000H
        jz   UnknownDevice
        push DS
```

continues

Listing 11.6 continued

```
                push   ES
                mov    DS,AX
                lea    SI,[ BX + 10 ]
                mov    AX,seg criterr_data
                mov    ES,AX
                mov    DI,offset criterr_data:L7_Device
                mov    CX,8
                cld
        rep     movsb
                pop    ES
                pop    DS
                mov    Line + 14,offset L7_Char
                jmp    short SetBridge
    UnknownDevice:
                mov    Line + 14,offset L7_UnknownChar
                jmp    short SetBridge
    DiskError:
                mov    BL,IO_Type
                and    BL,7
                xor    BH,BH
                shl    BX,1
                mov    BX,DiskErrorTable[ BX ]
                mov    Line + 14,BX
                mov    AL,DriveNumber
                add    AL,'A'
                mov    [ BX + DRIVE_OFFSET ],AL
    SetBridge:
                mov    Line + 16,offset Bridge2Line
                push   DS
                mov    AH,59H
                xor    BX,BX
                int    21H
                pop    DS
                mov    Line + 18,offset EEC_Unknown
                cmp    AX,5AH
                ja     No_EEC
                push   BX
                mov    BX,AX
                shl    BX,1
                mov    AX,EEC_Table[ BX ]
                pop    BX
                mov    Line + 18,AX
    No_EEC:
                mov    Line + 20,offset ECC_Unknown
                cmp    BH,0CH
                ja     No_ECC
                push   BX
```

```
                    mov   BL,BH
                    xor   BH,BH
                    shl   BX,1
                    mov   AX,ECC_Table[ BX ]
                    mov   Line + 20,AX
                    pop   BX
No_ECC:
                    mov   Line + 22,offset RAC_Unknown
                    cmp   BL,7
                    ja    No_RAC
                    xor   BH,BH
                    shl   BX,1
                    mov   AX,RAC_Table[ BX ]
                    mov   Line + 22,AX
No_RAC:
                    mov   Line + 24,offset Locus_Unknown
                    cmp   CH,5
                    ja    No_Locus
                    mov   BL,CH
                    xor   BH,BH
                    shl   BX,1
                    mov   AX,Locus_Table[ BX ]
                    mov   Line + 24,AX
No_Locus:
                    mov   Line + 26,offset BridgeLine
                    cmp   DOS_MajorVersion,2
                    ja    NotARF
                    jmp   SetARF
NotARF:
                    mov   AL,IO_Type
                    and   AL,38H
                    cmp   AL,00H
                    jne   NotOption0
                    mov   Line + 28,offset TerminateOption
                    mov   Line + 30,offset BottomMenu
                    mov   MenuLines,15
                    mov   MaximumOption,0
                    mov   ReturnCodes,offset Set__2_
                    jmp   DrawScreen
NotOption0:
                    cmp   AL,08H
                    jne   NotOption1
                    mov   Line + 28,offset TerminateOption
                    mov   Line + 30,offset FailCallOption
                    mov   Line + 32,offset BottomMenu
                    mov   MenuLines,16
                    mov   MaximumOption,1
                    mov   ReturnCodes,offset Set__23
                    jmp   DrawScreen
```

continues

Listing 11.6 continued

```
NotOption1:
        cmp    AL,10H
        jne    NotOption2
        mov    Line + 28,offset RetryOption
        mov    Line + 30,offset TerminateOption
        mov    Line + 32,offset BottomMenu
        mov    MenuLines,16
        mov    MaximumOption,1
        mov    ReturnCodes,offset Set_12_
        jmp    DrawScreen
NotOption2:
        cmp    AL,18H
        jne    NotOption3
        mov    Line + 28,offset RetryOption
        mov    Line + 30,offset TerminateOption
        mov    Line + 32,offset FailCallOption
        mov    Line + 34,offset BottomMenu
        mov    MenuLines,17
        mov    MaximumOption,2
        mov    ReturnCodes,offset Set_123
        jmp    DrawScreen
NotOption3:
        cmp    AL,20H
        jne    NotOption4
        mov    Line + 28,offset IgnoreOption
        mov    Line + 30,offset TerminateOption
        mov    Line + 32,offset BottomMenu
        mov    MenuLines,16
        mov    MaximumOption,1
        mov    ReturnCodes,offset Set0_2_
        jmp    DrawScreen
NotOption4:
        cmp    AL,28H
        jne    NotOption5
        mov    Line + 28,offset IgnoreOption
        mov    Line + 30,offset TerminateOption
        mov    Line + 32,offset FailCallOption
        mov    Line + 34,offset BottomMenu
        mov    MenuLines,17
        mov    MaximumOption,2
        mov    ReturnCodes,offset Set0_23
        jmp    short DrawScreen
NotOption5:
        cmp    AL,30H
        jne    NotOption6
```

```
SetARF:
        mov   Line + 28,offset IgnoreOption
        mov   Line + 30,offset RetryOption
        mov   Line + 32,offset TerminateOption
        mov   Line + 34,offset BottomMenu
        mov   MenuLines,17
        mov   MaximumOption,2
        mov   ReturnCodes,offset Set012_
        jmp   short DrawScreen
NotOption6:
        mov   Line + 28,offset IgnoreOption
        mov   Line + 30,offset RetryOption
        mov   Line + 32,offset TerminateOption
        mov   Line + 34,offset FailCallOption
        mov   Line + 36,offset BottomMenu
        mov   MenuLines,18
        mov   MaximumOption,3
        mov   ReturnCodes,offset Set0123
DrawScreen:
        mov   AX,0040H
        mov   ES,AX
        mov   AL,ES:84H
        sub   AL,MenuLines
        shr   AL,1
        mov   TopLine,AL
        add   AL,MenuLines
        mov   BottomLine,AL
        mov   AL,ES:4AH
        sub   AL,LINEWIDTH
        shr   AL,1
        mov   LeftRow,AL
        add   AL,LINEWIDTH - 1
        mov   RightRow,AL
        mov   AH,0FH     ; Get current display mode
        int   10H
        mov   ActiveDisplayPage,BH
        mov   AH,3       ; Read cursor position and configuration
        int   10
        mov   OriginalRow,DH
        mov   OriginalColumn,DL
        mov   SI,offset ScreenSave
        mov   DI,offset Line
        mov   DH,TopLine
OuterLoop:
        mov   DL,LeftRow
InnerLoop:
        mov   AH,2       ; Set cursor position
        int   10H
```

continues

Listing 11.6 *continued*

```
            mov   AH,8       ; Read character and attribute
            int   10H
            mov   [ SI ],AH
            inc   SI
            mov   [ SI ],AL
            inc   SI
            mov   AH,9       ; Write character and attribute
            push  SI
            mov   SI,DS:[ DI ]
            mov   AL,[ SI ]
            inc   SI
            mov   DS:[ DI ],SI
            pop   SI
            mov   BL,ATTRIBUTE
            mov   CX,1
            int   10H
            inc   DL          ; Next row
            cmp   DL,RightRow
            jbe   InnerLoop
            inc   DI
            inc   DI
            inc   DH          ; Next line
            cmp   DH,BottomLine
            jbe   OuterLoop
            mov   CurrentOption,0
            mov   AH,2       ; Set cursor position
            mov   DH,TopLine
            add   DH,14
            mov   DL,LeftRow
            inc   DL
            int   10H
            mov   AH,9       ; Write character and attribute
            mov   AL,10H
            mov   BL,ATTRIBUTE
            mov   CX,1
            int   10H
GetKey:
            xor   AH,AH       ; Get keyboard character
            int   16H
            or    AL,AL       ; Character code 0?
            jz    CheckScanCode
            cmp   AL,13       ; Return?
            jne   GetKey
            jmp   Return
CheckScanCode:
            cmp   AH,47H      ; Home?
            je    GoHome
```

```
                cmp   AH,48H     ; CursorUp?
                je    GoUp
                cmp   AH,49H     ; PageUp?
                je    GoUp
                cmp   AH,4BH     ; CursorLeft?
                je    GoUp
                cmp   AH,4DH     ; CursorRight?
                je    GoDown
                cmp   AH,4FH     ; End?
                je    GoEnd
                cmp   AH,50H     ; CursorDown?
                je    GoDown
                cmp   AH,51H     ; PageDown?
                jne   GetKey
        GoDown:
                mov   AH,9        ; Write character and attribute
                mov   AL,' '
                mov   BL,ATTRIBUTE
                mov   CX,1
                int   10H
                mov   AL,CurrentOption
                cmp   AL,MaximumOption
                jne   MoveDown
                xor   AL,AL
        MoveCursor:
                mov   CurrentOption,AL
                mov   AH,2
                mov   BH,ActiveDisplayPage
                mov   DH,TopLine
                add   DH,14
                add   DH,AL
                mov   DL,LeftRow
                inc   DL
                int   10H
                mov   AH,9        ; Write character and attribute
                mov   AL,10H
                mov   BL,ATTRIBUTE
                mov   CX,1
                int   10H
                jmp   GetKey
        MoveDown:
                inc   AL
                jmp   MoveCursor
        GoHome:
                cmp   CurrentOption,0
                je    GetKey
                mov   AH,9        ; Write character and attribute
                mov   AL,' '
                mov   BL,ATTRIBUTE
```

continues

Listing 11.6 *continued*

```
                mov   CX,1
                int   10H
                xor   AL,Al
                jmp   MoveCursor
        GoUp:
                mov   AH,9       ; Write character and attribute
                mov   AL,' '
                mov   BL,ATTRIBUTE
                mov   CX,1
                int   10H
                mov   AL,CurrentOption
                or    AL,AL
                jnz   MoveUp
                mov   AL,MaximumOption
                jmp   MoveCursor
        MoveUp:
                dec   AL
                jmp   MoveCursor
        GoEnd:
                mov   AL,MaximumOption
                cmp   AL,CurrentOption
                jne   EraseOption
                jmp   GetKey
        EraseOption:
                mov   AH,9       ; Write character and attribute
                mov   AL,' '
                mov   BL,ATTRIBUTE
                mov   CX,1
                int   10H
                mov   AL,MaximumOption
                jmp   MoveCursor
        Return:
                mov   SI,offset ScreenSave
                mov   DH,TopLine
        OuterLoop2:
                mov   DL,LeftRow
        InnerLoop2:
                mov   AH,2       ; Set cursor position
                int   10H
                mov   AH,9       ; Write character and attribute
                mov   BH,ActiveDisplayPage
                mov   BL,[ SI ]
                inc   SI
                mov   AL,[ SI ]
                inc   SI
                mov   CX,1
                int   10H
```

```
                inc   DL          ; Next row
                cmp   DL,RightRow
                jbe   InnerLoop2
                inc   DI
                inc   DI
                inc   DH          ; Next line
                cmp   DH,BottomLine
                jbe   OuterLoop2
                mov   AH,2
                mov   BH,ActiveDisplayPage
                mov   DH,OriginalRow
                mov   DL,OriginalColumn
                int   10H
                mov   AL,CurrentOption
                xor   AH,AH
                mov   BX,ReturnCodes
                add   BX,AX
                mov   AL,[ BX ]
                pop   DS          ; Restore registers
                pop   ES          ;
                pop   BP          ;
                pop   SI          ;
                pop   DI          ;
                pop   BX          ;
                pop   CX          ;
                pop   DX          ;
                iret              ; Interrupt return
CritErr         endp
assume          DS:criterr_data
FillWord  proc near
                xchg  AH,AL
                call  FillByte
                xchg  AH,AL
                call  FillByte
                ret
FillWord  endp
FillByte  proc near
                push  CX
                push  AX
                mov   CL,4
                shr   AL,CL
                call  FillNibble
                pop   AX
                call  FillNibble
                pop   CX
                ret
FillByte  endp
FillNibble    proc    near
                push  AX
```

continues

Listing 11.6 continued

```
                and   AL,0FH
                cmp   AL,9
                jbe   FillNibble_1
                add   AL,7
FillNibble_1:
                add   AL,'0'
                mov   [ BX ],AL
                inc   BX
                pop   AX
                ret
FillNibble      endp
assume      DS:nothing
assume      ES:nothing
assume      SS:nothing
;
;     Install the new critical error handler
;
_CritErrInit    proc far
                push DS         ; Save old registers
                push ES         ;
                push AX         ;
                push BX         ;
                push CX         ;
                push DX         ;
                mov   AX,seg criterr_data
                mov   DS,AX      ; Set DS to local data
                assume     DS:criterr_data
                mov   AH,30H     ; Get DOS version
                int   21H        ;
                mov   DOS_MajorVersion,AL
                mov   AH,35H     ; Get old critical error handler address
                mov   AL,24H     ;
                int   21H        ;
                mov   OldCritErrOffset,BX
                mov   OldCritErrSegment,ES
                mov   AH,25H     ; Set new critical error handler address
                mov   AL,24H     ;
                mov   DX,seg criterr_code
                mov   DS,DX      ;
                mov   DX,offset CS:CritErr
                int   21H        ;
                pop   DX         ; Restore old registers
                pop   CX         ;
                pop   BX         ;
                pop   AX         ;
                pop   ES         ;
                pop   DS         ;
                ret              ; Return to caller
```

```
_CritErrInit    endp
assume    DS:nothing
;
;    Reinstall the critical error handler (as after returning from
;    a DOS shell)
;
_CritErrReInit    proc    far
        push DS       ; Save old registers
        push AX       ;
        push DX       ;
        mov  AH,25H   ; Set new critical error handler address
        mov  AL,24H   ;
        mov  DX,seg criterr_code
        mov  DS,DX    ;
        mov  DX,offset CS:CritErr
        int  21H      ;
        pop  DX       ; Restore old registers
        pop  AX       ;
        pop  DS       ;
        ret           ; Return to caller
_CritErrReInit    endp
;
;    Uninstall the critical error handler (as before invoking
;    a DOS shell)
;
_CritErrUnInit    proc    far
        push DS       ; Save old registers
        push AX       ;
        push DX       ;
        mov  AX,seg criterr_data
        mov  DS,AX    ; Set DS to local data
        assume    DS:criterr_data
        mov  AX,OldCritErrOffset
        mov  DX,OldCritErrSegment
        mov  DS,DX    ;
        assume    DS:nothing
        mov  AH,25H   ; Set old critical error handler address
        mov  AL,24H   ;
        int  21H      ;
        pop  DX       ; Restore old registers
        pop  AX       ;
        pop  DS       ;
        ret           ; Return to caller
_CritErrUnInit    endp
public    _CritErrInit
public    _CritErrReInit
public    _CritErrUnInit
criterr_code    ends
        end
```

Now that you have learned something about interrupts and about how TSRs are activated, let's see how TSRs work.

Revisiting TSRs

TSRs originally were intended to be a convenient way to add ISRs to DOS by allowing programs to initialize themselves and link into the system-interrupt structure. Service routines that sort, search, and perform other utility functions were envisioned as normal uses for this function—and with good reason.

When DOS first entered the market, operating systems such as CP/M and TRSDOS had no TSR facility. But programmers had discovered how to build utilities and stash them in memory for other programs to use. Several popular packages with sorting utilities, display-handling utilities, and programmers' tools were available then; it seems likely that the designers of MS-DOS were aware of them and wanted to make building such utilities an easier process.

As users gained experience with DOS they learned that they could tie an interrupt service routine into the keyboard interrupt and see what was happening. Early copies of the PC's *Technical Reference Manual* included a ROM BIOS listing, so it was easy to see how things worked and what the effect would be of linking into the keyboard interrupt. On PCs, no effect would be visible to users; but for the TSR, it was another story.

When the TSR was linked to the keyboard interrupt, it no longer was a *passive* TSR. It became *active* because it could decide on its own when to do something; an active TSR took on an existence of its own.

A passive TSR would sit quietly in memory and respond only when a program passed a specific request for service. This type of TSR is easy to write because it needs no special coding tricks. When the TSR is called, you know that DOS is not active because the application program that invoked the interrupt had to have control of the machine. In this situation, anything the machine could do was legal. But that stopped with active TSRs.

An active TSR could interrupt the machine at any time. Knowing what the machine was executing when the TSR got control was impossible. Because DOS and PCs were designed as single-user, single-task systems, no provision had ever been made for the possibility that someone might run more than one program at the same time. BIOS and DOS, therefore, store large amounts of information in global tables. Intermediate results of data entry and calculations all use the same buffers. When you interrupt the system, the implication is that control *might* be inside DOS at the time of the interrupt. If you then call DOS again, you lose what DOS is doing and probably crash the system.

Early TSRs continually caused system crashes. They interfered not only with DOS but also with each other. Some were as tenacious as bulldogs in taking control of the machine. Hard-won experience has led to the following unofficial rules for writing TSRs:

- Never call DOS functions unless you have no other way to get what you want. (File system access is the major reason for having to call DOS.)

- If you *have* to do I/O, you can do the following:

  Use something other than DOS console I/O functions (Int 21h, Functions 01h–0Ch). Better ways of getting to the console are available.

  Monitor the InDOS flag. When this flag is nonzero, DOS is executing an Int 21h function. Do not run your process when this flag is nonzero. (See the discussion of Int 21h, Function 34h in the "DOS Reference" section for information about how to access this flag.)

  Monitor Int 28h. This interrupt tells you that even though DOS is doing Int 21h functions, it is in a "busy wait" for console I/O. If you do your own console I/O below DOS, you can safely execute anything else. (See Int 28h in the "DOS Reference" section for more information.)

  Provide a check function that lets your TSR indicate whether it is already installed. Linking to an unused interrupt vector lets the TSR check for the presence of an earlier copy in memory, but is rife with danger because the machine has only a limited number of vectors available. You can link into the Multiplex interrupt chain provided by DOS for its *own* TSRs (PRINT, APPEND, SHARE, and so on) to use, and that will be much safer. Refer to Appendix D, "A Standard TSR-Identification Technique," for a standardized method of using Multiplex interrupt 2Fh to identify TSRs.

  Put a signature inside the executable code to tell whether the TSR is present.

  Always assume that other TSRs are present. Chain any interrupts used by your TSR by passing control to the interrupt vector your TSR found when it started.

  Use your own stack rather than the one controlled by the interrupted program. You have no way of knowing what might be on that stack, nor do you know the *size* of the stack or the amount of space that is left before you crash into something.

Because of all the conflicts, a group of leading independent TSR authors banded together in early 1986 to try to develop a standard for TSRs. Although the original goal (providing a total Application Package Interface that could be accepted by all commercial vendors in addition to independent authors) could not be met, some members of the group persisted. In 1988, they released a set of library functions—compatible with C, Turbo Pascal 4.0 and above, and assembler—that handles the difficult parts of TSR design for you.

This package, TesSeRact, is available as a shareware package on CompuServe and from many local bulletin-board systems. An overview, including the means by which it standardizes conflict resolution, is included as Appendix D. It is only fair to point out, though, that Jim Kyle was a charter member of the team and one of the two still participating in the project.

A number of commercial developers have accepted this interface standard even though they write their own internal routines rather than use the library. This is encouraged by the team; the idea is to avoid conflicts by agreeing on a standard, rather than promote the use of any single code package to the exclusion of all others.

Interrupts Essential to TSRs

Some of the many interrupts are documented. Interrupts are important to anyone who writes a TSR. The "DOS Reference" section gives as much detail as we know about each of them. This section introduces you to the interrupts so that you can see the kinds of assistance they can provide.

The Keyboard Interrupt

The keyboard interrupt (Int 09h) is the way an active TSR takes control. By monitoring what happens at the keyboard, the TSR can tell when the hot key is pressed and activated. Here is the basic method:

```
Int 09h activates on keystroke
Handler activates and reads keystroke
if(hot key has been found){
   throw away the keystroke
   check DOS
   if(in DOS){
      set a hot key flag
      return from the interrupt
   } else {
      activate the TSR
      when the TSR is done, return
         from the interrupt
   }
} else {
   chain to the next handler on Int 09h
}
```

What's this about "check DOS"? Remember that DOS is not reentrant. If you call DOS for anything, you might crash the system. To check DOS, use Int 21h, Function 34h, which is described in the next section.

The InDOS Flag, DOSOK Interrupt, and Timer Interrupt

Calling Int 21h, Function 34h returns a pointer to the InDOS flag (DOS busy flag). If this flag is nonzero, DOS was interrupted to execute a function. If your TSR did interrupt DOS, the function usually will return in a fraction of a second. The preceding pseudocode for Int 09h shows where you would check the InDOS flag. After you set the hot-key flag, you must have a way to pick it up. For this purpose, you have the DOSOK interrupt and the timer interrupt.

When you start up, you initialize for Int 28h a special interrupt handler such as the following:

```
Int 28h activates
check hot key flag
if(hot key flag is set){
  turn hot key flag off
  activate the TSR
}
call the next Int 28h service routine
return from the interrupt
```

Int 28h (the DOSOK interrupt) activates when DOS is waiting for console input in Int 21h, Functions 01h–0Ch. If you see this interrupt, you know that you can safely use other DOS functions. (Two exceptions to this statement when you run under DOS V2 are the undocumented functions 50h and 51h; see the reference section for details and how you can use them safely at this point.)

If DOS is not waiting for input, you use the timer interrupt. The timer interrupt (1Ch) ticks 18.2 times per second. You can attach to this interrupt the following service routine that checks the hot-key flag as well:

```
Timer Interrupt activates
call next timer interrupt service
check hot key flag
if(hot key flag is set){
  turn hot key flag off
  activate the TSR
}
return from the interrupt
```

After you get control, you have other problems. Your TSR wants to work as simply as possible, but you do not know the state of the machine you are interrupting. How deep is the stack? How much space below the stack pointer is free for growth? More important, you do not want the TSR to be grabbed by a system error.

To make your TSR as robust as possible, you want to have it take control of the Critical-Error interrupt (Int 24h) and the Ctrl-Break interrupt (Int 23h). The TSR can also insert itself into the interrupt chain of the BIOS disk driver (Int 13h) and any other routines that might cause problems. Then, if a problem occurs, the TSR can correct it and you can shift to an internal stack and execute your functions.

Some programmers advocate *context switching*, where the DOS pointer to the active process's PSP is changed to point to the TSR's PSP. You use Int 21h, Function 51h to get the segment address of the interrupted program, save that address, then use Int 21h, Function 50h to tell DOS that the TSR's program segment prefix (PSP) is the current active process. Under V2, this process is fraught with danger if executed during service of Int 28h because 50h and 51h use the same DOS stack space as 28h and, as a result, the system will hang.

Context switching is a useful technique if you do file I/O or otherwise want to have total control. The danger in V2 can be avoided by setting the DOS *critical error* flag before calling either function (thus causing DOS to use an alternate stack area), then clearing the flag upon return from the function so that DOS will act normally. Unfortunately, this in turn creates more problems because the location of the critical error flag differs from one version of DOS to another. The best solution is to avoid context switching unless it is absolutely necessary (as for handle-based file I/O); if you must use it, see Functions 50h and 51h in the reference section for details.

When the TSR finishes with its main business, it must "clean itself up," restore the interrupts, and reset the stack to normal. Then it can return to the interrupted program.

To demonstrate basic TSR operation, we have put some of the concepts to work in a simple clock program (`clock.c`) that sets itself up and then waits for a clock tick to activate (see listing 11.7).

Listing 11.7

```
/* clock.c */
#include <stdio.h>
#include <dos.h>
/*   Define needed constants */
#define      BOOL        int
#define      FALSE       0
#define      TRUE        !FALSE
/*   Define program size for the system */
#define      PGMSIZE     3000
/*   Define base address for video display */
#define      MONOBASE    0xb000
```

```
#define         COLORBASE   0xb800
/*   Define interrupt vectors for BIOS and DOS needed by program */
#define         GOTOXY      0x02
#define         GETXY       0x03
#define         TELETYPE    0x0e
#define         VIDEO       0x10
#define         CLOCK       0x1a
#define         TIMER       0x1c
#define         DOS         0x21
#define         TSR         0x31
#define         TEST        0x66
void interrupt (*orig_clock)();     /* Original clock vector */
void interrupt clock();             /* Declare clock() */
void interrupt test();              /* Declare test()  */
BOOL inclock = FALSE;               /* Clock processing flag */
BOOL extra = FALSE;                 /* Extra tick flag */
int count = 0;                      /* Clock tick counter */
char buf[20];                       /* Time buffer */
char far *clkptr;                   /* Pointer to screen location */
int  sp;                            /* Stack pointer */
int  ss;                            /* Stack segment */
int  hr, min, sec;                  /* Current time */
main(argc,argv)
int  argc;
char *argv[];
{
    union REGS regs;
    int  mode;
/*   Initialize clock output buffer with a string for printing */
strcpy(buf," TEST  ");
orig_clock = getvect(TEST);
if(streql(argv[1],"-u") && orig_clock!=0){
    printf("UPDATING THE CLOCK\n");
    int86(TEST,&regs,&regs);
    exit(0);
}
if(orig_clock != 0){
    printf("ALREADY INSTALLED ... EXITING\n");
    exit(0);
}
setvect(TEST,test);
/*   Read the initial value of the clock at startup,
     then set the clock pointer to the screen address
*/
orig_clock = getvect(CLOCK);
setvect(CLOCK,clock);
readclock(&hr,&min,&sec);
mode = getmode();
printf("DISPLAY MODE IS %d\n",mode);
```

continues

Listing 11.7 *continued*

```
    if(mode==7)
        clkptr = MK_FP(MONOBASE,120);
    else
        clkptr = MK_FP(COLORBASE,120);
    /*  TSR exit to save the memory for the program */
    tsrexit();
    }
    void interrupt clock()
    {
    (*orig_clock)();
    count++;
    if(sec%5==0 && count%18==0 && !extra){
        extra=TRUE;
        count--;
    } else {
        extra=FALSE;
    }
    if(count%18 == 0){
        disable();
        sp = _SP;
        ss = _SS;
        _SS = _CS;
        _SP = PGMSIZE;
        enable();
        sec++;
        if(sec>=60){
            sec=0; min++;
        }
        if(min>=60){
            min=0;hr++;
        }
        if(hr>=24) hr = 0;
        if(!inclock){
            inclock = TRUE;
            sprintf(buf+6,"%02.2d:%02.2d:%02.2d ",hr,min,sec);
            displayclk(buf);
            inclock = FALSE;
        }
        disable();
        _SP = sp;
        _SS = ss;
        enable();
        }
    }
    tsrexit()
    {
        union REGS regs;
```

```
        regs.h.ah = TSR;
        regs.h.al = 0;
        regs.x.dx = PGMSIZE;
        int86(DOS,&regs,&regs);
}
displayclk(str)
char      *str;
{
        char far     *ptr;
        ptr = clkptr;
        while(*str){
                *ptr++ = *str++;
                ptr++;
        }
}
readclock(hr,min,sec)
int  *hr, *min, *sec;
{
        union REGS regs;
        unsigned long  clock;
        unsigned long  remain;
        unsigned long  x1, x2;
        regs.h.ah = 0;
        int86(CLOCK,&regs,&regs);
        x1 = regs.x.cx * 65536L; x2 = regs.x.dx;
        clock = x1 + x2;
        *hr = (int) (clock / 65543L);
        remain = clock % 65543L;
        *min = (int) (remain / 1092);
        remain = remain % 1092;
        *sec = remain / 18.21;
}
void interrupt test()
{
        register int ds;
        disable();
        sp = _SP;
        ss = _SS;
        _SS = _CS;
        _SP = PGMSIZE;
        ds = _DS;
        _DS = _CS;
        readclock(&hr,&min,&sec);
        _DS = ds;
        _SP = sp;
        _SS = ss;
        enable();
}
streql(str1,str2)
```

continues

Listing 11.7 continued

```
char *str1, *str2;
{
    return(strcmp(str1,str2)==0);
}
getmode()
{
    union REGS regs;
    regs.h.ah = 0x0f;
    int86(VIDEO,&regs,&regs);
    return(regs.h.al);
}
```

Let's go over the program to see how it works.

Notice that part of the setup involves putting the word TEST at the beginning of the clock output buffer so that it will be displayed when the clock is updated. (This is just a convenience for the demonstration program.)

Standard Turbo C functions are used to access the interrupt vector table (instead of making the calls directly). But first we have to see whether the TSR is already installed. We chose a simple way to do this: we used Int 66h as a marker because it is unused by most TSRs and its value normally is zero. If Int 66h is non-zero, the program assumes that the TSR has set it. If the value is zero, you know that it has not been set.

Int 66h is used also to force the clock program to reset its current time from the system. Rather than write a new program to do that, simply start the TSR with a -u flag. If the first argument is -u, reset the clock and leave.

The Turbo C getvect() function is used to get the value of the vector. Next, the program checks for the -u flag if the Int 66h vector has been set. If it finds the -u flag and if the vector is nonzero, an Int 66h is issued to reset the clock and exit.

If there is no -u flag, the program checks whether the vector is nonzero. If it is, the program assumes that the clock program has already started. If another TSR that uses Int 66h is active, you will not be able to start the clock program (because of the Int 66h vector).

If after all your checks you find that the vector is zero, you set the vector to point to the test() interrupt function (which forces the TSR to read the BIOS clock) and proceed to set up the clock function.

To set up the clock function, you first get the original clock vector, save it for future use, and reset the vector to point to the clock() interrupt function. Then you read the initial clock time from the BIOS clock function, get the current display mode to identify a monochrome versus a color monitor, and establish a pointer (clkptr) to point to the screen location at which you will write the clock. To eliminate the use of BIOS or DOS functions while the TSR is operating, you put the clock directly to the screen display buffer. *This will work only in text modes; programs that shift the display to graphics modes will show garbage from the clock.*

After everything is set up, the TSR exit is called and the program is resident. The clock interrupt handler, clock(), is the heart of the TSR. Let's go over it step by step to see how it operates.

First, we call the original clock timer so that it does whatever is required on each clock tick. Then we can proceed. The count variable keeps track of timer ticks (which occur at a rate of 18.2 per second). The clock advances one second every 18 ticks. Every five seconds, one extra tick is allowed to bring the average over five-second periods to 18.2 ticks per second. After advancing the count, check whether you are at a five-second interval. If you are, you decrease the count by one to force a wait of one extra tick (giving you 19 ticks on this second). The extra flag tells you that you are doing the extra tick and prevents you from decrementing the count whenever you come back at the fifth second.

With the period between seconds covered, you now check for every 18th tick. When you find it, you reset the stack to your internal stack and advance the timer by one second (sec++). Then, to keep the clock running correctly, you check for 60 seconds, 60 minutes, and 24 hours. After everything else is finished, you display the clock.

If you are not already in the clock display section (inclock is set to FALSE), you enter that portion of the program, set inclock to TRUE, and set up and display the clock. Finally, you reset the stack to its status when the clock() function was called.

The clock display is simple. You write directly to the screen memory, advancing the screen buffer pointer by 2 to get past the attribute byte for each byte of the clock that you write to the screen. The rest of the clock program is made up of some simple, self-explanatory functions.

The program is compiled with the Turbo C compiler, using the MAKE utility provided with Version 1.5 of the software. The makefile that compiles the program correctly is shown in listing 11.8.

Listing 11.8

```
# clock.mak
clock.exe:      clock.obj
    tlink /x lib\c0t clock, clock,, lib\emu lib\maths lib\cs
clock.obj:      clock.c
    tcc -c -mt -f clock.c
```

The MAKE utility recompiles the program only when necessary. Such a utility, although of minimal use here, is especially useful on large projects.

The important thing about the compilation is that the program is compiled with the TINY memory model (the same as a COM program, so that Code, Data, and Stack segments are all the same). Consult your *Borland C++ User's Guide* for details on how to use the compiler switches.

If you are using Microsoft C, you can modify the program to handle segment registers within the limits of the Microsoft system and establish similar compilation switches for control of the program compilation.

Summary

This chapter showed you how to work with interrupts. By using utilities provided as part of DOS Int 21h, you can change an interrupt vector to point to a function that you design. You have written a sample handler in C with an assembly language front end to handle the interfacing. Turbo Pascal 4.0 provides a specific way for you to create interrupt handlers as Pascal functions.

Terminate-and-stay-resident utilities can be written to trigger on interrupts (the keyboard and clock interrupts, for example). These utilities can be extremely dangerous to programs, however, because DOS was never intended to handle multitasking operations. DOS is a purely nonreentrant system and can fail when a TSR calls functions that were in progress when the TSR got control of the computer.

You learned several ways to minimize problems with TSRs. You know not to call DOS functions unless absolutely necessary and to use BIOS or direct calls for keyboard and screen I/O. You know about monitoring the InDOS flag to see when performing DOS functions is safe, and you know about monitoring Int 28h to determine when the system is waiting for keyboard input. You learned to provide a check function that lets the TSR check to see whether it is already loaded and to always assume that another TSR is present. And you know that using an internal stack is a good way to prevent problems in stack operations.

PROGRAMMING

Device Drivers

In the early days of computing, programmers wrote all types of programs directly at the hardware level. Each program had to deal directly with the intricacies of card readers, printers, tape drives, and other equipment connected to computers. Programmers, therefore, had to master all kinds of arcane information about handling each type of error, processing correct input and output, and so on.

As computers developed, programmers saw that their time for this sort of repetitive work was at a premium. Handlers for external devices gradually became standard items that programmers added to their programs. Before long, these handlers were collected into a primitive operating system in which *all* programs could use the same set of device handlers, or *drivers*.

In the earliest operating systems, the different *device drivers* were coded as integral parts of the system and interacted in intricate ways with the rest of the system. As a result of attempts to make device drivers more independent, systems programmers are able to install device drivers as needed during start-up.

Although most significant operating systems have some such flexibility, DOS provides the most flexibility for *users* to install drivers. Many microcomputer operating systems required tedious patching to accomplish what can be done with a prewritten driver and the system configuration file.

12

CHAPTER

For most people who work with DOS, their only contact with drivers is to load them from distribution disks and make the required entry in the CONFIG.SYS file. (These entries are described later in this chapter.) Users follow written instructions that tell them, line for line, how to make the changes. In some systems, you do not have even this much contact because an installation program makes the changes for you.

Most programmers eventually begin to feel rather confident about their skills and decide to write a device driver. Experienced assembly language programmers find this a relatively easy task—they just have to follow a formula. If you follow the formula correctly, your driver will work correctly. Many programmers fail because they do not stick to the rigid outline of what a driver has to do and how it has to be laid out. In this chapter we hope to show you how to write good device drivers.

For maximum speed and coding convenience, device drivers usually are written in assembly language on PCs. Although parts of a device driver can be written in a language such as C, problems would occur in getting the correct structure and in minimizing overhead. Because of a device driver's rigid structure, modules compiled in C can provide only functional services to the driver. If you use C to build functions for a driver, you must start with an assembly language section that gets initial control and then calls C routines as needed. You *cannot* call C library functions because many of them refer to DOS functions. (A driver is not allowed to call DOS services. You will read more about this subject in this chapter's "Driver Initialization" section.)

Here are three good reasons for using assembly language to code the entire driver:

- Because a device driver is at the heart of all access to a device, it must be coded as tightly as possible to save execution time and memory space.

- The driver layout is rigidly defined; only assembly language gives you the required layout control.

- You must manipulate specified CPU registers at specific times. This is hard to do from C.

Coding device drivers in C is common in the UNIX world, but the interface requirements are different. An assembly language front end that you do not see links and controls the operating system. Coding a driver in C can be fun, if you want to try it.

Before you learn how to build a device driver, you should understand how a device driver is laid out and how it works. Implementation will flow naturally from what you learn.

As you learn about drivers, you will build a driver shell into which you can drop additional code to make real drivers for real devices. You will start by learning about types of drivers and how they work.

Driver Types

The two basic types of device drivers—character devices and block devices—are fundamentally different. You should understand how they differ before you continue.

Character Device Drivers

Character devices are byte-oriented devices such as printer ports or serial ports. All communication with the device occurs on a character-by-character basis.

I/O from a character device occurs in one of two basic modes: cooked and raw. In *cooked mode*, DOS requests one character at a time from the driver and buffers the input internally. Special keystrokes such as Ctrl-C and the carriage return are processed by DOS. In *raw mode*, DOS does not buffer the data nor does it look for and respond to Ctrl-C or the carriage return. Rather, requests for input of a fixed number of characters are passed directly to the driver; the return is made up of the characters read by the driver.

Character devices are given names (CON, AUX, LPT, and so on) that can be up to eight characters (like file names). The eight-character limitation arises because the driver's name held in the device header is only eight characters. (The header is discussed in the "Device Header" section later in this chapter.) This limitation was deliberately designed into DOS to make it possible to deal with both named files and named devices using the same I/O routines. It also makes it impossible to access a file that has the same name as any driver present in the system; the routines will access the driver, instead.

Block Device Drivers

Block devices process blocks of data such as those on tapes and disks. Each access to a block device *always* transfers data in the appropriate block sizes. With block devices, there is no equivalent to the character device drivers' cooked and raw modes.

Block devices are assigned drive letters and become one or more of the system's logical drives (A, B, C, and so on). A single block device driver can handle more than one hardware unit or map one hardware unit into multiple logical devices. Each logical device is structured with a base-file system that includes a FAT (file allocation table) and root directory (for additional information about these structures, see Chapter 2, "The Structure of a DOS System," and Chapter 8, "Disks").

How Device Drivers Work

When an applications program calls DOS Int 21h to perform any I/O function, device drivers get involved in almost every case (except for system functions like extended error processing). Consider an example in which you try to write to a file on the disk.

Whether you explicitly code the file-writing operation as a call to DOS or use a library function, the applications program sets up the registers and makes a call to Int 21h (DOS service routines) to handle the disk I/O. When the service routine gets control, it in turn sets up and makes a call to Int 26h (Absolute Disk Write). Int 26h sets up a request header (a command buffer for the driver) in a reserved area of memory and calls the strategy routine for the device driver that handles the disk. The strategy routine simply saves the address of the request header and returns control to the interrupt handler.

Next, DOS calls the interrupt portion of the driver. (Its name, like that of the strategy routine, does not reflect its function.) The interrupt portion of the driver reads the request header and determines what is requested. The interrupt portion then transfers control to the appropriate internal routine and executes the disk write by calling the BIOS disk write function, Int 13h. When the disk write is completed, control returns through the chain to the applications program, and status codes are adjusted to reflect what each calling routine expects.

Figure 12.1 shows the sequence of events. Each step of the operation involves a transfer of control to successively lower-level routines until the disk write occurs.

All of these steps take place for each individual operation of the disk; there may be many such calls to the driver. If you use high-level language resources in the file call, you may need additional access to the disk to read the FAT, allocate space, and update parameters on the disk. Drivers can be extremely busy.

Although this example of a disk write is complicated, you can handle it with a call to the BIOS. You do not have to worry about the "down and dirty" interfacing details (the hardware operation itself). On each PC and compatible, the BIOS is supposed to make all devices look like a set of standard devices. But what if you add a custom piece of equipment? Figure 12.2 shows what happens. The driver has to manipulate the new hardware directly. There will be no BIOS to handle the interfacing details.

When you add a board that adds a new capability to the system, you must add a new device driver. When you add a CD-ROM drive, a mouse, a local area network, or a music synthesizer, you add hardware that the PC system software was never designed to handle. MS-DOS has no software to handle a mouse device. The driver that comes with the mouse has to work directly with the hardware. This is where the complexity begins. To interface this hardware to the system, you need a driver.

Fig. 12.1. *Calling for a disk write.*

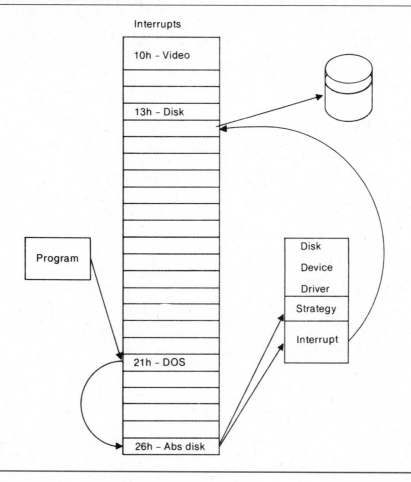

The example of disk access through the driver (refer to fig. 12.1) hides one important fact: the BIOS already has taken care of the hardware details. All the timing details, bit manipulations, and so on are handled by the BIOS. For a custom add-on, your driver must handle the hardware details directly.

When you add a piece of hardware to the system and write the driver for it, *you* must complete all of the interfacing details. If you add an analog-digital converter so that you can read some instrumentation, you must service the chips on the hardware level. If you have to observe timing restrictions or deal with other problems, *you* must know about them.

Demonstration of a working interface to a special board is beyond the scope of this book. To perform a successful interface, you must have an intimate knowledge of the hardware you want to run. Nothing less is acceptable. This book tries to give you a framework in which to make your driver work, whether you are writing a driver for a new piece of hardware to be added to a system or for some existing hardware.

Fig. 12.2. *A custom device driver.*

Device Driver Structure

A device driver is made up of three parts: the device header, the strategy routine, and the interrupt routine. In DOS V2, the driver had to be a memory image (or a COM program) with no origin (ORG 0, or no statement at all). And it had to be coded as a FAR procedure. The EXE2BIN program converts the assembled driver to an image file, and the system loads the image during the boot operation. By convention, drivers usually have the extension .SYS (or sometimes .BIN). The file extension is changed to .SYS to prevent someone from accidentally executing the driver as a program.

In DOS V3.0 and later versions, drivers can be object files in EXE format. The operating system will load them correctly. But to maintain backward compatibility with DOS V2, most people who write drivers work with the COM format. (DOS V1 had no provision for loadable drivers.) The examples in this chapter are COM-type drivers.

This section examines the structure of the driver. We will look first at the device header—the first important part of a working driver.

Device Header

The device header is an 18-byte area divided into five fields (see fig. 12.3).

Fig. 12.3. *The device header.*

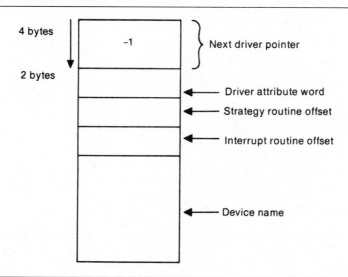

Here are the five fields:

- *Next driver pointer*: four bytes are initialized to –1 (FFFFFFFFh). DOS uses this field to load a pointer to the next driver in the list of drivers. The last driver in the list is marked with –1. (Actually, only the *offset* half of this pointer must be –1; the *segment* half may be zero.)

- *Driver attribute word*: two bytes that specify the driver characteristics (see table 12.1).

- *Strategy routine offset*: a two-byte offset to the strategy routine within the driver.

- *Interrupt routine offset*: a two-byte offset to the interrupt routine within the driver.

- *Device name*: If the device is a character device, an eight-character, left-justified, blank-filled device name appears next. If the name is the same as that of an existing device, the new driver replaces the existing device. If the device is a block device, the first byte in this field is the number of logical devices associated with the driver; the other bytes are ignored (some versions of DOS include special information about the boot block device here).

Table 12.1. *Driver Attribute Word*

Bits FEDCBA98 76543210	Meaning
....1	Standard input device
....0	Not standard input device
....1.	Character device: Standard output device
	Block device: Can handle 32-bit sector numbers (V4 only)
....0.	Character device: Not standard output device
	Block device: Cannot handle 32-bit sector numbers (V4 only)
....1..	NUL device
....0..	Not NUL device
....1...	Clock device
....0...	Not clock device
....1....	Driver services Int 29h
.....000 000.....	Reserved before V3.2 (set to zero)
....0.....	Reserved in V3.2 and up (set to zero)
.... .1......	Driver supports generic IOCTL (V3.2 and up)
.... .0......	Driver does not support generic IOCTL (V3.2 and up)
.....000 0.......	Reserved in V3.2 and up (set to zero)
....0...	OPEN/CLOSE/Removable media supported (V3 and up)
....1...	OPEN/CLOSE/Removable media not supported (V3 and up)
...0....	Reserved (set to zero)
..1.....	Character device: Device does not support output-till-busy operation
	Block device: IBM block format
..0.....	Character device: Device supports output-till-busy operation
	Block device: Not IBM block format
.1......	IOCTL supported
.0......	IOCTL not supported
1.......	Character device
0.......	Block device

As DOS initializes itself, it establishes a chain of the standard device drivers; the next driver pointer in each driver gives the address of the next driver in the chain (see fig. 12.4). The last driver in the chain has a pointer of –1 to indicate the end of the chain.

Fig. 12.4. *The driver chain.*

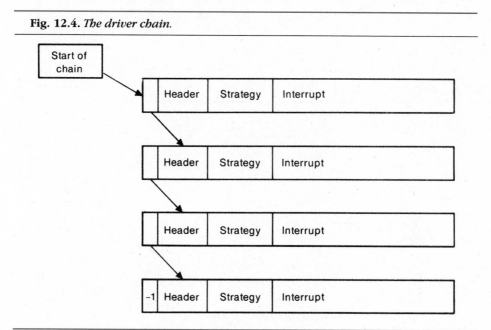

When DOS finally reads the CONFIG.SYS file, a driver chain already has been set up. New drivers are added at the head of the chain (see fig. 12.5).

DOS looks for a character device driver by searching through the chain of drivers for a driver name that matches the name called for. Starting at the beginning of the driver list, DOS checks the name of the first driver to see whether it matches the requested name. If not, the Next Driver Pointer field is consulted to find the next driver in the list and DOS checks there. DOS checks each driver in the chain (skipping over block device drivers) until it finds either the requested driver or the end of the list (marked by a –1 in the Next Driver Pointer field).

A new driver is always added to the beginning of the chain (refer to fig. 12.5). Then, when DOS searches for a driver, it will check the new driver first. If you add a driver with the same name as an existing driver (for example, you add a new driver with the name PRN—the same name as that of the printer driver), the new driver will "replace" the existing one because a search always results in the new driver being used, never the old one.

Fig. 12.5. Adding a new driver to the driver chain.

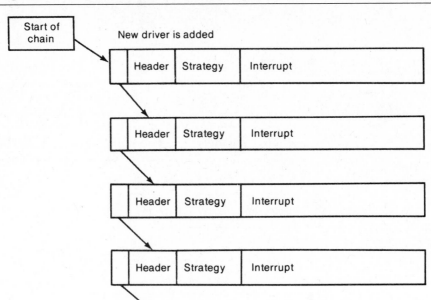

The ANSI.SYS driver works this way when it is included in the CONFIG.SYS file. It has the same name (CON) as the console driver; when it is added to the driver chain, it will be found first whenever a console operation occurs. All console operations then work through the ANSI.SYS driver rather than the normal DOS console driver.

To illustrate how you set up and work with a driver, let's create a practical example (or at least a *working* shell for a real driver). Listing 12.1 is the header for a real driver called drvr.asm. Later in this chapter this driver is assembled into one that does not actually do anything. The driver is a shell to which more code for actual applications can be added.

Listing 12.1

```
;      Header and assembler directives for drvr.asm

CR        EQU    0Dh            ;Carriage return
LF        EQU    0Ah            ;Line feed
MAXCMD    EQU    16             ;DOS V3.0, 12 in DOS V2.0
ERROR     EQU    8000h          ;Set error bit
BUSY      EQU    0200h          ;Set busy bit
DONE      EQU    0100h          ;Set done bit
```

```
UNKNOWN    EQU   8003h          ;Set unknown status
cseg segment    public 'code'   ;Start the code segment
     org        0               ;Zero origin
     assume     cs:cseg,ds:cseg,es:cseg
drvr       proc     far         ;FAR procedure
           dd       -1          ;Next driver pointer
           dw       8000h       ;Attribute
           dw       strategy    ;Pointer to strategy
           dw       interrupt   ;Pointer to interrupt
           db       'DRVR    '  ;Device name
;
```

The first part of the driver is made up of instructions to the assembler. First, for convenience during the program, define several constants such as CR (carriage return), LF (line feed), MAXCMD (the maximum command number: 16 for DOS V3.0 and V3.1, 12 for V2.X), and so on. These definitions simplify your programming as you continue.

As mentioned earlier in this chapter, listing 12.1 has been defined as a code segment with a 0 origin (ORG 0). All of the segment registers are set the same as the code segment so that you can assemble the driver as a binary image (COM format) file.

The first part of the driver that affects memory starts with the label drvr, where you declare that this is a FAR procedure. This is necessary because all drivers will be called by DOS with a FAR subroutine call. A FAR subroutine call is one that can go across segment boundaries—it pushes the return address (both segment and offset) on the stack as part of the call. By declaring this to be a FAR procedure, you ensure that the assembler will use a FAR return (which gets both segment and offset off the stack) to return control to DOS.

The first field in the header (a double word, or eight bytes) initially is declared to be –1. DOS sets this word to the address of the next driver in the chain. You then set the attribute word to 8000h to indicate that this character driver has no special capabilities (refer to table 12.1). This step is followed by the pointers (offsets only) to the driver's strategy and interrupt procedures, then by this driver's eight-character name.

The header is critical to proper driver operation. When DOS needs to refer to the driver, it checks the attribute word to see what the driver can do and then uses the strategy and interrupt pointers to locate the routines. If the header is not right, the driver fails before it starts. Because the header is all bookkeeping and the assembler does the bookkeeping for you, let's move on to the strategy routine.

Strategy Routine

A strategy routine has little to do with what usually is considered "strategy"—it does not try to devise the best way to drive the device or anything of that sort. You can write the strategy routine in as little as five lines; its purpose is to "remember" where in memory the operating system has assigned the location of the device's *request header* (RH). The RH serves the following two functions:

- It is a data area for DOS's internal operations.

- It is a communication area in which DOS tells the driver what to do and the driver responds with the result of the operation.

When a driver is asked to output data, the data address comes by way of the RH. The driver responds by performing its output task and then setting a flag or status byte in the request header to indicate completion.

When a driver is about to be called by DOS, the request header is built in a reserved area of memory and its address is passed to the strategy routine in ES:BX. Although each call to the driver can have a new address, in practice the address generally is the same. The strategy routine saves this value for future use by the driver's interrupt routine.

Request headers vary in length but always have a fixed 13-byte header (sometimes called the "static portion" of the request header). The structure of the request header is shown in table 12.2.

Table 12.2. *Request Header Leading Bytes*

Byte Offset	Field Length	Meaning
00h	Byte	Length of the request header
01h	Byte	Unit code: the device number for block devices
02h	Byte	Command code: the number of the most recent command sent to the driver
03h	Word	Status: status code set by the driver after each call. If bit 15 is set, an error code is in the low-order eight bits. A status code of 0 means a successful completion.
05h	8 bytes	Reserved for use by DOS
0Dh	Variable	Data required by the driver

Most of the fields in the request header are self-explanatory. The status word (bytes 03-04h), however, needs clarification.

The status word passes the completion status of a request back to DOS in the format shown in table 12.3.

Table 12.3. *Request Header Status Word*

Bits FEDCBA98 76543210	Meaning
1....... 00000000	Write-protect violation error
1....... 00000001	Unknown unit error
1....... 00000010	Drive not ready error
1....... 00000011	Unknown
1....... 00000100	CRC error
1....... 00000101	Bad drive request structure length error
1....... 00000110	Seek error
1....... 00000111	Unknown media error
1....... 00001000	Sector not found error
1....... 00001001	Printer out of paper error
1....... 00001010	Write fault
1....... 00001011	Read fault
1....... 00001100	General failure
1....... 00001101	Reserved
1....... 00001110	Reserved
1....... 00001111	Invalid disk change
......X	Done
.....X.	Busy
.XXXXX..	Reserved
0.......	No error

The error bit in the status word is set to indicate that an error occurred in the operation of the driver. The error code is returned in the lower eight bits of the status word. When the error bit is not set, the error code should be set to zero to indicate satisfactory completion of the operation.

The busy bit is set to indicate that the device was busy when called. The done bit is set when the driver has completed the operation. The driver sets the bits to indicate the status of whatever operation is requested. All functions should set the done bit to indicate completion.

The strategy routine for the sample driver (drvr.asm) looks like listing 12.2.

Listing 12.2

```
rh_seg    dw    ?            ;RH segment address
rh_off    dw    ?            ;RH offset address
strategy:
          mov   cs:rh_seg,es
          mov   cs:rh_off,bx
          ret
```

Listing 12.2 allocates space in which to store the segment and the offset of the request header. The whole strategy routine consists of saving the request header pointer (the segment address in the ES register and the offset address in the BX register). Why doesn't it do more? A more pointed question might be "Why have two entry points?" Why not pass the pointer to the interrupt routine in ES:BX and be done with it?

The answer involves the operating system's compatibility and internal mechanisms. The driver structure was designed to be compatible with a future extension that was intended to convert DOS into a multitasking structure. When the operating system runs multiple tasks, more than one request may be sent to a specific driver before a single request can be handled. In other words, the requests may have to be queued.

If you make requests for disk-sector reads, for example, multiple requests may arrive before the first request can be satisfied, especially if the requested sector is far from the present location on the disk. You also can add intelligence to the strategy routine and let it try to optimize access to a disk device by sequencing multiple requests to minimize head movement. None of this, however, is applicable to DOS up through V4.01.

Because DOS is a single-user, single-task system, the potential capability for multiple processes accessing any driver does not exist. But the structure is in place to allow an extension in that direction (should such an extension ever be deemed necessary).

After the request header's address is stored safely, you can return to DOS and await the call to the interrupt routine: it occurs immediately in a single-task system.

Interrupt Routine

The major portion of the driver, called the interrupt routine, does all the work. It is poorly named because it does not act like an interrupt and it ends with RET rather than IRET. The name reflects plans that have not materialized; it was intended that the queued requests would be serviced by interrupt handlers. Each device would interrupt DOS when it could take care of its next task, then the handler would direct control to the interrupt routine. But like the strategy design, this does not yet apply to DOS.

The interrupt routine contains code for as many as 20 functions required by the DOS system (13 on DOS V2, 17 on DOS V3, and 20 on DOS V3.2). Whenever the device driver is called, it gets the address of the request header and looks at the byte at offset 02h of the header to find the command code that indicates which function the driver will perform.

Most drivers create a table with pointers to the driver's functions. The command code is used as an index into the table to locate the desired function. Listing 12.3 shows such a dispatch table for the sample driver.

Listing 12.3

```
d_tbl:
      dw    s_init         ;Initialization
      dw    s_mchk         ;Media check
      dw    s_bpb          ;BIOS parameter block
      dw    s_ird          ;IOCTL read
      dw    s_read         ;Read
      dw    s_nrd          ;Nondestructive read
      dw    s_inst         ;Current input status
      dw    s_infl         ;Flush input buffer
      dw    s_write        ;Write
      dw    s_vwrite       ;Write with verify
      dw    s_ostat        ;Current output status
      dw    s_oflush       ;Flush output buffers
      dw    s_iwrt         ;IOCTL write
      dw    s_open         ;Open
      dw    s_close        ;Close
      dw    s_media        ;Removable media
      dw    s_busy         ;Output until busy
```

The table is particularly easy to lay out because the assembler keeps track of the functions and automatically inserts the correct offset addresses in the table. This driver (as written) does not support the special functions introduced in DOS V3.2: Generic IOCTL and Get/Set Logical Device. This is not a problem because the Get/Set Logical Device functions are for block drivers only (remember that this is a character device) and most programs, to run with older versions of DOS, do not use the calls that depend on these functions.

The body of the interrupt routine determines the nature of the request to be served. It branches from the dispatch table to the appropriate function. Listing 12.4 shows the rest of the body of the interrupt routine.

Listing 12.4

```
interrupt:
            cld              ;Save machine state
            push es          ;Save all registers
            push ds
            push ax
            push bx
            push cx
            push dx
            push si
            push di
            push bp
```

continues

Listing 12.4 continued

```
                mov     dx,cs:rh_seg
                mov     es,dx
                mov     bx,cs:rh_off
                mov     al,es:[bx]+2     ;Command code
                xor     ah,ah
                cmp     ax,MAXCMD        ;Legal command?
                jbe     ok               ;Jump if okay
                mov     ax,UNKNOWN       ;Unknown command
                jmp     finish

ok:
                shl     ax,1             ;Multiply by 2
                mov     bx,ax
                jmp     word ptr [bx + d_tbl]

finish:
                mov     dx,cs:rh_seg
                mov     es,dx
                mov     bx,cs:rh_off
                or      ax,DONE          ;Set the DONE bit
                mov     es:[bx]+3,ax

                pop     bp               ;Restore the registers
                pop     di
                pop     si
                pop     dx
                pop     cx
                pop     bx
                pop     ax
                pop     ds
                pop     es
                ret                      ;Back to DOS
```

The interrupt routine starts by saving the present machine state on the stack. Then it gets the pointer to the request header from the location at which the strategy routine stored it. The interrupt routine determines what it is supposed to do by looking at offset 02h in the request header. The routine then checks to make sure that the command is legal: if it is, the routine branches to the location at which it handles the function. An illegal command (one that is larger than the maximum command number) results in the driver returning an error flag set to indicate that the command was unknown.

When the command number is determined to be less than MAXCMD (the number of commands the driver supports), the driver multiplies the command number by two (by means of a left shift, which is the same as multiplying by two) to obtain the offset of the command code within the dispatch table. The shift is necessary because two bytes are stored for each table entry in the dispatch table. Then the offset is added to the dispatch table's base address and the driver jumps to the designated routine.

When the function finishes, the driver retrieves the pointer to the request header and sets the done bit in the status word to reflect the operation's completion. The registers saved at the beginning of the driver are restored and control is returned to the DOS kernel.

Before we look at each separate driver function, let's look at the sample driver's remaining code. As in any driver, only some functions need to be implemented. In cases in which a function is not needed, the driver can simply return a status code and do nothing. Some people advocate returning a zero code that indicates successful operation; others suggest returning an error code 3 (Command Unknown). If you write your own driver to use with your own software, you can make your own choice. But if you write a driver to replace an existing one, the new return codes should be consistent with those returned by the original driver.

Listing 12.5 gives the remainder of `drvr.asm`.

Listing 12.5

```
s_mchk:                        ;Media check
s_bpb:                         ;BIOS parameter block
s_ird:                         ;IOCTL read
s_read:                        ;Read
s_nrd:                         ;Nondestructive read
s_inst:                        ;Current input status
s_infl:                        ;Flush input buffers
s_vwrite:                      ;Current output status
s_ostat:                       ;Current output status
s_oflush:                      ;Flush output buffers
s_iwrt:                        ;IOCTL write
s_open:                        ;Open
s_close:                       ;Close
s_media:                       ;Removable media
s_busy:                        ;Output until busy
        MOV AX, UNKNOWN        ;Set error bits
        jmp  finish
ident:
        db   CR,LF
        db   'Sample Device Driver -- Version '
        db   '0.0'
        db   CR,LF,LF,'$'

s_init:
        mov  ah,9              ;Print string
        mov  dx, offset ident
        int  21h
        mov  dx,cs:rh_seg
        mov  es,dx
        mov  bx,cs:rh_off
        lea  ax,end_driver    ;Get end of driver address
        mov  es:[bx]+14,ax
```

continues

Listing 12.5 *continued*

```
                mov   es:[bx]+16,cs
                xor   ax,ax          ;Zero the AX register
                jmp   finish

        s_write:
                xor   ax,ax          ;Zero the AX register
                jmp   finish

        end_driver:
        drvr endp
        cseg ends
             end
```

When you write a driver, you can ignore all the functions that you do not need to do something with. In drvr.asm, for example, only the initialization function and the write function will do anything. All the remaining functions are handled with a single section that returns a code that tells DOS that the requested function was unknown. A driver that needs only read and write could provide only those functions.

The only function that *must* be included in all drivers is the initialization function: it must put the address of the end of the driver into the request header at offset 0Eh for use by the operating system's initialization code. If this address is zero, for a block device driver, the entire driver header will be removed from memory during installation. This might be advisable if a fatal error was encountered while initializing; one enterprising developer used this feature to create a driver that merely displayed data on the screen and then vanished. A character device driver, however, cannot do this; its "end" address *must* leave the entire header, at least, in place. If it does not, all subsequent character devices will be disabled.

To ignore the functions, you simply return a code that says you do not know what DOS is requesting. Then you jump to the part of the interrupt routine that closes out the operation and sets the done bit (bit 8) in the request header's status word (offset 03h).

Initialization is next. You print a string to the screen (so that you know the driver is there), then determine the address of the end of the driver. (The label end_driver is the end of this routine.) This address must be stored in the request header so that DOS knows where to load the next driver. Because drivers are loaded from low to high memory, the next driver will be loaded after the ending address of the current driver (see fig. 12.6).

Finally, the write routine sets the AX register to zero (the function return status for the driver) to indicate no errors in the operation of the driver. This type of simple function setup is typical of most drivers. Most drivers require only a few of the functions to do anything. As you will learn when we go over the functions individually, some of them make sense for only one type of driver. For example, the BIOS Parameter Block function is meaningless for a driver that deals with the keyboard.

Fig. 12.6. *The next driver is loaded after the ending address of the current driver.*

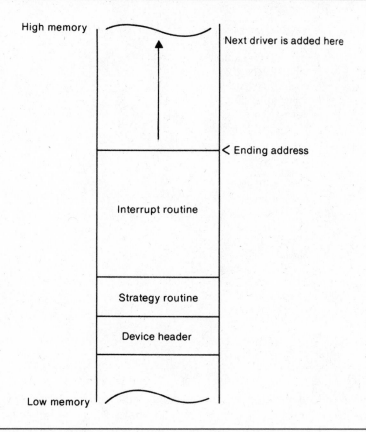

Table 12.4 lists the device driver functions and indicates which are applicable to specific versions of DOS. We will examine each function in detail to see how it works.

Driver Initialization

The initialization function is the one function that *must* be present in all drivers. It performs any needed setup for the driver. One task of the initialization function is essential to DOS: it must set the address of the end of the driver into byte offset 0Eh of the request header. If your driver were driving a hard disk system, the initialization section would have to check for the presence and proper operation of the disk, initialize the disk parameters, and so forth. For a serial port, it should initialize the port and establish default settings.

Table 12.4. *Device Driver Functions*

Function	Meaning	DOS Version(s)
00h	Driver initialization	2, 3, 4, 5
01h	Media check	2, 3, 4, 5
02h	Build BIOS parameter block	2, 3, 4, 5
03h	I/O control read	2, 3, 4, 5
04h	Read	2, 3, 4, 5
05h	Nondestructive read	2, 3, 4
06h	Input status	2, 3, 4
07h	Flush input buffers	2, 3, 4
08h	Write	2, 3, 4, 5
09h	Write with verify	2, 3, 4, 5
0Ah	Output status	2, 3, 4
0Bh	Flush output buffers	2, 3, 4
0Ch	I/O control write	2, 3, 4, 5
0Dh	Open	3, 4, 5
0Eh	Device close	3, 4, 5
0Fh	Removable media	3, 4, 5
10h	Output until busy	3
11h	Generic IOCTL	3.2, 3.3
13h	Generic IOCTL	4, 5
17h	Get logical device	3.2, 3.3, 4, 5
18h	Set logical device	3.2, 3.3, 4, 5
19h	IOCTL query	5.0

The driver's initialization section is the only section that can call DOS functions legally. No other part of the driver is allowed to call DOS. (Remember that DOS is not reentrant. While your program is inside the driver, it *is* DOS!) Only Functions 01h–0Ch (Limited Console I/O) and 30h (Get DOS Version) are available for use. Because other parts of DOS have not been initialized when driver initialization occurs, calls to disk drives (and so on) fail and lock up the system.

To permit parameters to be passed to the driver by means of the CONFIG.SYS command line, a pointer to the command line is passed to the driver in the RH. This pointer points to the first character after the equal sign in the "DEVICE=" line; the initialization code is permitted to only read the data, not change it.

In keeping with the improved error reporting throughout DOS V4, a flag was added to the initialization function's RH format to permit display of the Error in CONFIG.SYS message. If you want the message displayed should installation fail, pass any nonzero value in this 16-bit field; a zero value prevents the display, and operation is the same as in earlier DOS versions.

The initialization process must update the request header by adding the following information:

Byte Offset	Contents
03h	Return status
0Dh	Number of units (for block devices)
0Eh	Address of first free memory above driver
12h	BIOS parameter block pointer (block devices)

Figure 12.7 shows the request header as it enters the initialization function; figure 12.8 shows the request header coming out of the function.

Fig. 12.7. *The request header on entry to the initialization function.*

Request header Offset		Contents
00h	00	Length
01h	01	Unit number
02h	02	Command code
03h	03	
04h	04	Return status
05h	05	
06h	06	
07h	07	
08h	08	Reserved for DOS
09h	09	
0Ah	10	
0Bh	11	
0Ch	12	
0Dh	13	
0Eh	14	
0Fh	15	
10h	16	
11h	17	
12h	18	Offset of CONFIG.SYS command line
13h	19	
14h	20	Segment of CONFIG.SYS command line
15h	21	
16h	22	First unit #
17h	23	CONFIG.SYS Error Msg control Flag word (V4 only)
18h	24	
19h	25	
1Ah	26	
1Bh	27	
1Ch	28	
1Dh	29	
1Eh	30	
1Fh	31	

Fig. 12.8. *The request header on return from initialization.*

Request header

Offset		Contents
00h	00	Length
01h	01	Unit number
02h	02	Command code
03h	03	
04h	04	Return status
05h	05	
06h	06	
07h	07	
08h	08	Reserved for DOS
09h	09	
0Ah	10	
0Bh	11	
0Ch	12	
0Dh	13	# units
0Eh	14	Offset of free memory
0Fh	15	
10h	16	Segment of free memory
11h	17	
12h	18	Offset of BPB
13h	19	
14h	20	Segment of BPB
15h	21	
16h	22	
17h	23	
18h	24	
19h	25	
1Ah	26	
1Bh	27	
1Ch	28	
1Dh	29	
1Eh	30	
1Fh	31	

Because the initialization code is called only once, many programmers save memory by placing it at the end of the driver module, then setting the first free memory address to the start of the initialization code. Big drivers with large initialization sections can gain a great deal of space this way. But the example is not that sophisticated. We simply used a defined address at the end of the code segment to define the end of the driver.

Media Check

DOS gives the media check function the following information in the request header:

Byte Offset	Contents
01h	Unit code
02h	Command code (1 for media check)
0Dh	Media descriptor byte

The media check function is supposed to check whether the disk medium on a block device has been changed since the last access. For a character device, the routine should always return DONE (the request header status word is set to 0100h; the done bit, bit 8, is set; all other bits are zero). This means "complete" (see listing 12.1 for a definition). For a fixed block device (such as a hard disk) the routine should always indicate that the medium has not changed by placing a 1 at byte offset 0Eh in the request header. But how can you tell whether a removable disk has been changed?

Many programmers have wrestled with this problem. But because the DOS world never had standards (before V4) for insisting on volume labels and so on, no one has been able to come up with a truly reliable answer. Here are some ideas that have been tried:

- Go back so fast for another disk access that the disk could not have been removed. So far, no one has figured out how fast is fast enough (as soon as someone does, the Olympics will have a new event—opening disk drive doors); the IBM manuals for V4 specify 2 seconds as the time to use.

- If opening of the drive door can be sensed, and it *has* been opened, you could assume that the medium has been changed. (But what if the door opened accidentally and was simply reclosed?)

- If the volume ID has changed since the last disk access, you know that the medium is not the same. Unfortunately, the inverse of this statement is not true. (How many disks do you have with the same volume ID?)

- If you are using DOS V4 and the volume serial number has changed, the medium has changed. This is the most reliable method, but works only in V4; earlier versions do not have volume serial numbers.

Clearly, no foolproof ways to determine that the disk has not been changed work across all versions of DOS. On the Macintosh, disks cannot be changed except through the operating system itself. There is no way (other than by a series of manipulations with a paper clip) to remove the disk without the operating system being involved. Because the PC is not this restrictive, the DOS programmer is left holding the proverbial "bag." In general, we can never really be sure whether the disk we write to is the one intended.

DOS's reaction depends on the return code placed in byte offset 0Eh of the request header. If the value is 1, DOS assumes that the device has not been changed and proceeds to write without rereading the FAT from the disk. A code of –1 tells DOS that the disk has been changed and forces DOS to dump any write buffers and then reread the FAT and directory from the device. When DOS dumps its buffers, the information in them is simply thrown away.

A code of 0 means "maybe" (the driver cannot tell whether the media has been changed). In this case, DOS assumes that everything is okay and flushes any buffers directly to the disk. If the buffers are empty, DOS rereads the FAT and the directory to be sure that the buffers are empty. Generally, this is the safest response. If there is any doubt, DOS will at least try to save the information (if the disk has been changed, this usually will result in disk sectors being overwritten).

Beginning with DOS V3, this function also returns a pointer to the last volume-ID read from the disk. Figure 12.9 shows the request header on entry to the media check function; figure 12.10 shows the request header on return.

Fig. 12.9. *The request header on entry to the media check function.*

Request header

Offset		Contents
00h	00	Length
01h	01	Unit number
02h	02	Command code
03h	03	Return status
04h	04	
05h	05	
06h	06	
07h	07	
08h	08	Reserved for DOS
09h	09	
0Ah	10	
0Bh	11	
0Ch	12	
0Dh	13	Media ID
0Eh	14	
0Fh	15	
10h	16	
11h	17	
12h	18	
13h	19	
14h	20	
15h	21	
16h	22	
17h	23	
18h	24	
19h	25	
1Ah	26	
1Bh	27	
1Ch	28	
1Dh	29	
1Eh	30	
1Fh	31	

The safe course of action for a disk driver is to always return NOT CHANGED (a value of 1 at byte offset 0Eh in the request header) for a hard disk and DON'T KNOW (a value of 0 at byte offset 0Eh in the request header) for a floppy disk.

Fig. 12.10. *The request header on return from the media check function.*

Request header

Offset	Contents	
00h	00	Length
01h	01	Unit number
02h	02	Command code
03h	03	
04h	04	Return status
05h	05	
06h	06	
07h	07	
08h	08	Reserved for DOS
09h	09	
0Ah	10	
0Bh	11	
0Ch	12	
0Dh	13	
0Eh	14	Media change code
0Fh	15	Offset of volume label
10h	16	
11h	17	Segment of volume label
12h	18	
13h	19	
14h	20	
15h	21	
16h	22	
17h	23	
18h	24	
19h	25	
1Ah	26	
1Bh	27	
1Ch	28	
1Dh	29	
1Eh	30	
1Fh	31	

DOS V3 & later

Build BIOS Parameter Block

For block devices only, build BIOS parameter block (BPB) functions build a BIOS parameter block and return a pointer to it at offset 12h in the request header. Character devices should just return DONE. In DOS V3 and later systems, this routine should also read and store the device volume ID for later use by the media check function, which must return a pointer to the volume label in DOS V3 and later (refer to fig. 12.10).

On entry to the build BPB function, the request header contains the following information:

Byte Offset	Meaning
01h	Unit code
02h	Command code (2)
0Dh	Media descriptor byte
0Eh	Buffer address

A one-sector buffer is passed to this routine. If the non-IBM format bit in the device attribute word is zero, the buffer contains the first sector of the FAT and should not be changed. If the bit is set, the buffer can be used as a scratch area in which to build the BPB.

Whenever the media check detects a disk change or "thinks" that the disk may have been changed, DOS calls the BPB routine to rebuild its BPB from the disk. The BPB's layout is shown in table 12.5. The original BPB structure was extended in V3.2 to permit use of sector numbers requiring 32-bit storage, but the extended structure did not come into general use until V4. V4 uses the original BPB for drives with less than 64K sectors and the extended one for those exceeding this size.

Table 12.5. *BIOS Parameter Block (BPB) Layout*

Byte Offset	Field Length	Meaning
00h	Word	Number of bytes per sector
02h	Byte	Number of sectors per cluster
03h	Word	Number of reserved sectors that start at sector 0
05h	Byte	Number of FATs
06h	Word	Maximum number of root-directory entries
08h	Word	Total number of sectors (0 in V3 and above if > 65,535)
0Ah	Byte	Media descriptor
0Bh	Word	Number of sectors per FAT
0Dh	Word	Number of sectors per track (DOS V3)
0Fh	Word	Number of heads (DOS V3)
11h	Double word	Number of hidden sectors (DOS V3)
15h	Double word	Total sectors if word at 08h is zero (DOS V3 and above)
19h	Seven bytes	Reserved

The request header on entry to the function is shown in figure 12.11; figure 12.12 shows it on return.

Fig. 12.11. *The request header on entry to the build BPB function.*

Request header

Offset		Contents
00h	00	Length
01h	01	Unit number
02h	02	Command code
03h	03	
04h	04	Return status
05h	05	
06h	06	
07h	07	
08h	08	Reserved for DOS
09h	09	
0Ah	10	
0Bh	11	
0Ch	12	
0Dh	13	Media ID
0Eh	14	Offset of FAT buffer
0Fh	15	
10h	16	Segment of FAT buffer
11h	17	
12h	18	
13h	19	
14h	20	
15h	21	
16h	22	
17h	23	
18h	24	
19h	25	
1Ah	26	
1Bh	27	
1Ch	28	
1Dh	29	
1Eh	30	
1Fh	31	

I/O Control Read

The I/O control (IOCTL) read function allows a program to access the device directly by means of the IOCTL call. This function is called *only* when the IOCTL bit is set in the attribute word of the device header. The request header includes the following information:

Byte Offset	Meaning
01h	Unit code
02h	Command code (3)
0Dh	Media descriptor byte
0Eh	Transfer address
12h	Byte/sector count

Fig. 12.12. *The request header on return from the build BPB function.*

Request header

Offset		Contents
00h	00	Length
01h	01	Unit number
02h	02	Command code
03h	03	
04h	04	Return status
05h	05	
06h	06	
07h	07	
08h	08	Reserved for DOS
09h	09	
0Ah	10	
0Bh	11	
0Ch	12	
0Dh	13	
0Eh	14	
0Fh	15	
10h	16	
11h	17	
12h	18	Offset of BPB
13h	19	
14h	20	Segment of BPB
15h	21	
16h	22	
17h	23	
18h	24	
19h	25	
1Ah	26	
1Bh	27	
1Ch	28	
1Dh	29	
1Eh	30	
1Fh	31	

The routine should return the status word at offset 03h and the actual number of bytes transferred at offset 12h. DOS does no error checking on the call.

All IOCTL calls (read, write, and the generic call added in DOS V3.2) communicate with the *driver,* not with the device. Programs use these calls to tell the driver what to do or how to configure itself. With a serial driver, for example, you might use an IOCTL write to set the baud rate, word length, stop bits, and parity; you could use an IOCTL read to determine the current settings. The problem is that IOCTL calls are extremely specific to the driver.

An IOCTL command has no DOS-defined structure. The command (in any form in which the application puts it) is stored at the transfer address. If a program wants to configure a serial port, it might place the string

```
WORD=8,BAUD=1200,STOP=1,PARITY=N
```

at the transfer address to indicate eight bits, 1200 baud, one stop bit, and no parity (for a discussion of the meaning of these terms, see Chapter 7, "Serial Devices"). But *there is no guarantee that the driver will understand the control string.*

If you were to try an IOCTL call to our sample driver (refer to listing 12.5), the driver would ignore any information passed and the IOCTL call would be unsuccessful. The IOCTL call would never reach the driver because the IOCTL-supported bit (bit 14 in the device attribute word in table 12.1) has not been set. Furthermore, even if the driver is reached, the unknown function error from the IOCTL read and write functions is returned. Our sample driver has not been written to respond to IOCTL calls.

In most books, information about IOCTL is vague or undefined. IOCTL information that is defined is included in the "DOS Reference" section of this book.

Read

The read function reads data from the device and returns the data to a designated buffer. The function also returns a completion code and the number of bytes or sectors transferred. All of these *must* be passed, even if an error occurs. In DOS V3 (and later versions), the driver must also return a pointer to the volume ID if error 0Fh is returned.

The read function communicates with the device by reading from it and making what it reads available to the program that called the device driver. On entry to the function, the request header contains the following information:

Byte Offset	Meaning
01h	Unit code
02h	Command code (3)
0Dh	Media descriptor byte
0Eh	Transfer address
12h	Byte/sector count
14h	Starting sector number (block devices). If −1 with DOS V4, use value at 16h instead if the driver can deal with 32-bit sector numbers
16h	32-bit starting sector number (V4 only)

The read function is called to read both character and block devices. When a single character read is supposed to take place, the driver is given a byte count of 1. Parameters that have no meaning for the driver are simply ignored. (The same principle applies also in the write calls.)

Nondestructive Read

A nondestructive read is a look-ahead read for character devices only. This command is meaningless for block drivers; they should return DONE. On entry, the request header contains only the command code (05h) at position 02h (see fig. 12.13). The driver should read the next character but leave it in the input buffer to be used by the read function when it is called. The character should be returned in the request header at position 0Dh, as shown in figure 12.14.

Fig. 12.13. *The request header on entry to the nondestructive read function.*

Request header Offset		Contents
00h	00	Length
01h	01	Unit number
02h	02	Command code
03h	03	
04h	04	Return status
05h	05	
06h	06	
07h	07	
08h	08	Reserved for DOS
09h	09	
0Ah	10	
0Bh	11	
0Ch	12	
0Dh	13	
0Eh	14	
0Fh	15	
10h	16	
11h	17	
12h	18	
13h	19	
14h	20	
15h	21	
16h	22	
17h	23	
18h	24	
19h	25	
1Ah	26	
1Bh	27	
1Ch	28	
1Dh	29	
1Eh	30	
1Fh	31	

DOS uses the nondestructive read function for a look-ahead read during keyboard operations. This is the function DOS uses to look for a Ctrl-C character in the input stream from the keyboard.

Input Status

DOS uses the input status function to check whether characters are waiting in the input buffer on a character device. Block devices automatically return DONE for this routine. Character devices return their status at position 03h of the request header. This function, unlike a nondestructive read, does not read any characters; it simply returns the busy status of the device.

When this function is available, DOS uses it to check whether the device is busy before attempting to read. On entry, the request header contains only the command code (06h) at position 02h.

Fig. 12.14. *The request header on return from the nondestructive read function.*

Request header Offset		Contents
00h	00	Length
01h	01	Unit number
02h	02	Command code
03h	03	
04h	04	Return status
05h	05	
06h	06	
07h	07	
08h	08	Reserved for DOS
09h	09	
0Ah	10	
0Bh	11	
0Ch	12	
0Dh	13	Character
0Eh	14	
0Fh	15	
10h	16	
11h	17	
12h	18	
13h	19	
14h	20	
15h	21	
16h	22	
17h	23	
18h	24	
19h	25	
1Ah	26	
1Bh	27	
1Ch	28	
1Dh	29	
1Eh	30	
1Fh	31	

Flush Input Buffers

The flush input buffers command code (07h, at position 02h in the request header on entry to the function) tells the driver to dump any characters waiting to be input from the device. The function should return the return status code at position 03h in the request header. Block drivers should always return DONE.

Write

The write function (command code 08h at position 02h in the request header) takes characters out of the buffer passed with the request header and outputs them to the device. The function returns the return status (at position 03h), the number of bytes or sectors transferred (at position 12h), and (with DOS V3.0 and later versions) a pointer to the volume ID (at position 16h) if the 0Fh error code is returned. The error status and number of bytes transferred *must* be returned.

The layout of the request header is identical to that of the read function (and the write with verify function).

Write with Verify

The write with verify function (command code 09h at position 02h in the request header), the format of which is identical to that of the write function, should also verify the completed write. Verification can consist of anything from an outright lie (that is, no verification at all, as the normal CON drivers do) to performing a complete byte-by-byte comparison of the data that was written to the data read back after writing. The standard block device driver performs only a CRC (cyclic redundancy check) of data written in response to this command.

Any device unable to perform verification should respond to this request with the nonverifying write action. If the DOS verify flag is ON, all write requests are converted automatically to write with verify; thus, it is essential that the function be supported.

Output Status

The output status function (command code 0Ah at position 02h in the request header) returns the status of a character device. To determine whether a device is busy, DOS calls this function before outputting to the device. When data to be printed is passed to the printer driver, the driver sees this call. The return status word (bytes 03h–04h in the request header) is used to return the device status. If the lower eight bits are zero, the device is ready. If the device is not ready, its status is coded from the standard code in table 12.3.

Flush Output Buffers

The flush output buffers function (command code 0Bh at position 02h in the segment header) dumps the contents of the output buffers. Like the flush-input function, it is for character devices only. Block devices should return DONE.

I/O Control Write

Like the I/O control read function, the I/O control (IOCTL) write function (command code 0Ch at position 02h in the request header) accesses the device directly. It is called only if the IOCTL bit is set in the device header's attribute word. Everything (except the command code) said about the IOCTL read function applies here, but in reverse—IOCTL write passes information *to* the driver, for example. As with the read function, the driver *and* the application must agree on what should be sent and its format.

Functions 0Dh through 14h are supported *only* on DOS V3 and later.

Open

If the OPEN/CLOSE/RM bit is set in the device attribute word, the open function (command code 0Dh at position 02h in the request header) is called when an open is attempted on the device. For block devices, the call can be used to keep track of the number of open files on the device. Unfortunately, FCB function calls can leave this count hanging because files opened with the FCB may not be closed. When you deal with handles, DOS automatically closes the files when a process ends. With FCB functions, however, there is no call to the FCB CLOSE function unless the process closes it. On character devices, the situation is easier because we commonly use this call to pass special start-up strings (such as printer-initialization strings) to the device, or to deny simultaneous access to more than one process.

On entry to the function, the request header contains the unit code (at position 01h) and the command code (0Dh, at position 02h). On return from the function, you pass the status word at position 03h.

Device Close

The device close function (command code 0Eh at position 02h in the request header) can help keep track of whether the device is currently open to one or more processes. If the open function (command code 0Dh) increments an internal counter whenever it is called, the close function can decrement the count and flush buffers when the count reaches zero. But the problems with FCB open functions remain. Termination strings (such as final form feeds) can be sent to character devices. The entry parameters for this function are like those of the open functions: the unit code at position 01h and the command code (0Eh) at position 02h.

Removable Media

If the OPEN/CLOSE/RM bit is set in the device header, the removable media call (command code 0Fh at position 02h of the request header) is used in DOS V3 and later versions to determine whether the device has removable media. If not, DOS can optimize its strategy for dealing with the device by loading disk tables into memory for faster access. Character devices should simply return DONE. Status codes are selected from table 12.3 to return in the status word at position 03h of the request header.

If the device has removable media, this call returns a 0 in the BUSY bit of the status word; a 1 indicates nonremovable media.

Output until Busy

The output until busy function (command code 10h at position 02h in the request header) was provided primarily for print spooling. Some types of devices, most notably printers with large internal buffers or separate printer buffers, can accept characters at an extremely high rate—higher than the computer can feed them. The driver, if allowed to do so, could transfer continuously a large number of bytes to the device without the device becoming busy. That is the purpose of this function.

When called, this function transfers bytes to the device as fast as it can. It will transfer as many bytes as it can, either until the device becomes busy or until all the bytes it was given to transfer have been transferred. On entry to the function, the request header has the command code at position 02h, the transfer address (where the bytes to write to the device are located) at position 0Eh, and the byte count to be transferred at position 12h.

On return from the function, the request header must have the return status at position 03h and the number of bytes transferred at position 12h. If the number of bytes transferred is less than the number to be transferred, there is no error. Block devices should return DONE for this function.

Functions above 11h are available only on DOS V3.2 and later. Several command code numbering conflicts appear to exist between V3 and V4 in this area.

Generic IOCTL

Like the IOCTL read and IOCTL write functions, the generic IOCTL function (command code 11h at position 02h in the request header with V3, and command code 13h at the same position for V4) depends on the use of an agreed upon set of signals between the driver and the applications program. Because there are no rules, this function usually works best for programmers who write their own drivers. Generic IOCTL supports some of the new IOCTL functions in DOS V3.3. (These functions are described in detail in the "DOS Reference" section.)

Figure 12.15 shows the layout of the request header on entry to the function; the layout on return is shown in figure 12.16.

Get and Set Logical Device

The get and set logical device functions (command codes 12h and 13h in V3 or 17h and 18h in V4, at position 02h in the request header) support the operation of Int 21h, Function 44h (Subfunctions 0Eh and 0Fh). They determine which block device name was last used to refer to a given device, and they tell the driver which device name will be used next. For additional information about these functions, see the "DOS Reference" section.

The get and set logical device functions are called with the unit number at position 01h of the request header and the command code at position 02h. On return, the last device unit code is returned at position 01h and the device status is returned at position 03h.

Fig. 12.15. *The request header on entry to the generic IOCTL.*

Request header

Offset		Contents
00h	00	Length
01h	01	Unit number
02h	02	Command code
03h	03	Return status
04h	04	Return status
05h	05	Reserved for DOS
06h	06	
07h	07	
08h	08	Reserved for DOS
09h	09	
0Ah	10	
0Bh	11	
0Ch	12	
0Dh	13	Category (major) code
0Eh	14	Function (minor) code
0Fh	15	SI register
10h	16	
11h	17	DI register
12h	18	
13h	19	Offset of IOCTL
14h	20	data packet
15h	21	Segment of IOCTL
16h	22	data packet
17h	23	
18h	24	
19h	25	
1Ah	26	
1Bh	27	
1Ch	28	
1Dh	29	
1Eh	30	
1Fh	31	

The Whole Driver

The sample driver (drvr.asm) is listed in full in listing 12.6. You can produce a working driver by typing in this listing and assembling it according to the directions in the next section. (Although this driver does not do much, it is a beginning.) But be careful: Although this driver has been tested, you can mess up your system if you mistype something, if a smudge in your book hides an important step, or if a step does not complete properly (and you miss it). Whenever you test drivers, be sure to work on a floppy rather than on your main system. And be sure to follow the precautions listed in the following section.

Fig. 12.16. *The request header on return from the generic IOCTL.*

Request header Offset		Contents
00h	00	Length
01h	01	Unit number
02h	02	Command code
03h	03	
04h	04	Return status
05h	05	
06h	06	
07h	07	
08h	08	Reserved for DOS
09h	09	
0Ah	10	
0Bh	11	
0Ch	12	
0Dh	13	
0Eh	14	
0Fh	15	
10h	16	
11h	17	
12h	18	
13h	19	
14h	20	
15h	21	
16h	22	
17h	23	
18h	24	
19h	25	
1Ah	26	
1Bh	27	
1Ch	28	
1Dh	29	
1Eh	30	
1Fh	31	

Listing 12.6

```
CR        EQU    0Dh              ;Carriage return
LF        EQU    0Ah              ;Line feed
MAXCMD    EQU    16               ;DOS 3.0, 12 DOS 2.0
ERROR     EQU    8000h            ;Set error bit
BUSY      EQU    0200h            ;Set busy bit
DONE      EQU    0100h            ;Set completion bit
UNKNOWN   EQU    8003h            ;Set unknown status
;
cseg segment    public 'code'    ;Start the code segment
     org        0                ;Zero origin
```

```
        assume    cs:cseg,ds:cseg,es:cseg
;
;=======================================================
drvr       proc      far        ;FAR procedure
           dd        -1         ;Next driver pointer
           dw        8000h      ;Attribute
           dw        strategy   ;Pointer to strategy
           dw        interrupt  ;Pointer to interrupt
           db        'DRVR    ' ;Device name
;
;=======================================================
;
rh_seg    dw   ?                ;RH segment address
rh_off    dw   ?                ;RH offset address
strategy:
           mov   cs:rh_seg,es
           mov   cs:rh_off,bx
           ret
;
;=======================================================
;
d_tbl:
      dw   s_init              ;Initialization
      dw   s_mchk              ;Media check
      dw   s_bpb               ;BIOS parameter block
      dw   s_ird               ;IOCTL read
      dw   s_read              ;Read
      dw   s_nrd               ;Nondestructive read
      dw   s_inst              ;Current input status
      dw   s_infl              ;Flush input buffer
      dw   s_write             ;Write
      dw   s_vwrite            ;Write with verify
      dw   s_ostat             ;Current output status
      dw   s_oflush            ;Flush output buffers
      dw   s_iwrt              ;IOCTL write
      dw   s_open              ;Open
      dw   s_close             ;Close
      dw   s_media             ;Removable media
      dw   s_busy              ;Output until busy
;
interrupt:
      cld                      ;Save machine state
      push es                  ;Save all registers
      push ds
      push ax
      push bx
      push cx
      push dx
      push si
```

continues

Listing 12.6 continued

```
        push di
        push bp
;
        mov   dx,cs:rh_seg
        mov   es,dx
        mov   bx,cs:rh_off
;
        mov   al,es:[bx]+2        ;Command code
        xor   ah,ah
        cmp   ax,MAXCMD           ;Legal command?
        jle   ok                  ;Jump if okay
        mov   ax,UNKNOWN          ;Unknown command
        jmp   finish
;
;
ok:
        shl   ax,1               ;Multiply by 2
        mov   bx,ax
        jmp   word ptr [bx + d_tbl]
;
finish:
;
        mov   dx,cs:rh_seg
        mov   es,dx
        mov   bx,cs:rh_off
;
        or    ax,DONE            ;Set the DONE bit
        mov   es:[bx]+3,ax
;
        pop   bp                 ;Restore the registers
        pop   di
        pop   si
        pop   dx
        pop   cx
        pop   bx
        pop   ax
        pop   ds
        pop   es
        ret                      ;Back to DOS
;
s_mchk:                          ;Media check
s_bpb:                           ;BIOS parameter block
s_ird:                           ;IOCTL read
s_read:                          ;Read
s_nrd:                           ;Nondestructive read
s_inst:                          ;Current input status
s_infl:                          ;Flush input buffers
```

```
s_vwrite:                        ;Current output status
s_ostat:                         ;Current output status
s_oflush:                        ;Flush output buffers
s_iwrt:                          ;IOCTL write
s_open:                          ;Open
s_close:                         ;Close
s_media:                         ;Removable media
s_busy:                          ;Output until busy
        MOV  AX, UNKNOWN         ;Set error bits
        jmp  finish
;
ident:
    db  CR,LF
    db  'Sample Device Driver -- Version '
    db  '0.0'
    db  CR,LF,LF,'$'
s_init:
    mov  ah,9                    ;Print string
    mov  dx, offset ident
    int  21h
;
;   Retrieve the rh pointer
;
    mov  dx,cs:rh_seg
    mov  es,dx
    mov  bx,cs:rh_off
;
    lea  ax,end_driver          ;Get end of driver address
    mov  es:[bx]+14,ax
    mov  es:[bx]+16,cs
;
xor ax,ax                        ;Zero the AX register
    jmp  finish
;
s_write:
    xor  ax,ax                   ;Zero the AX register
    jmp  finish
;
end_driver:
drvr endp
cseg ends
    end
;=========================================================
```

Assembling the Driver

To assemble the driver, you need to run the macro assembler, the linker, and then the EXE2BIN program to create the driver as a binary image. These steps have been combined into a standard batch file that also copies the driver to drive A (just in case you forget to do so). Listing 12.7 is the MAKEDRVR.BAT file.

Listing 12.7

```
;==========================================================
echo off
masm %1;
if errorlevel 1 goto mfail
link %1;
if errorlevel 1 goto lfail
exe2bin %1 %1.sys
if errorlevel 1 goto efail
copy %1.sys a:
goto done
:mfail
echo *** Assembly Failed ***
goto done
:lfail
echo *** Link Failed ***
goto done
:efail
echo *** Conversion to .sys failed ***
goto done
:done
echo on
```

The batch file first assembles the driver. If the driver assembles properly, it gets linked. If the link is successful, EXE2BIN is executed to convert the driver to a memory-image format. When the program ends, the driver is copied to drive A. (Note that EXE2BIN is not provided with the standard DOS distribution disks in V3.3 and later, but must be purchased separately as part of the *Technical Reference Manual*.)

When most programmers work on a driver, they repeatedly reassemble. The batch file helps ease the tension that surrounds repeated failures with *nothing* visible and no clear way to get an output. If you write a driver, expect to lock up the system a few times before you get it right.

To use the batch file, you must give it the name of the driver's source file (without the extension). To execute the drvr.asm program, you type:

```
C:> makedrvr drvr
```

The batch file will see automatically that the output is a file (called DRVR.SYS) that can be added to the CONFIG.SYS file.

Installing the Driver

The operating system installs device drivers when it processes the CONFIG.SYS file during the system boot procedure. If DRVR.SYS (your driver) is stored in the root directory on drive A, you can add it to the system by editing the CONFIG.SYS file to include the following line:

```
DEVICE=A:DRVR.SYS
```

Debugging the Driver

If your driver works the first time you run it, you are better than most programmers. Even the best programmers must test and retest the driver until they "get it right." Sometimes the problem is not something the programmer did wrong; it may be something he or she did not understand (or know) about the device.

To debug a device driver, you need to do a great deal of intensive head-scratching. A minor error in address modes during initialization can lock up a DOS system if the pointers it is looking for are somewhere else in memory. A call to a driver can disappear down a black hole, never to return again. Applications programs can be given incorrect responses to a function call because the driver returned the wrong count.

Because printing from inside a driver is not easy, getting information on an error is a nightmare. Sometimes, when an error is time-critical, just putting in the debugging code causes the driver to work perfectly. One driver that we worked on for a UNIX system would not work unless a certain amount of undetermined time was eaten up in the middle of the driver. Although many systems programmers have worked on the function, the delay is still there. DOS can get you the same way.

To debug a driver, remember the following guidelines:

- *Never test a new driver on your hard disk.* Make a bootable floppy disk and copy the driver and the CONFIG.SYS file to the floppy for testing. If you test on the hard disk and the driver fails on initialization, you cannot boot the hard disk directly. You will have to boot to a floppy to change CONFIG.SYS on the hard disk.

- *If you have a system without a hard disk, do the testing there.* Even a simple problem can have damaging consequences at the driver level. (What if your driver scrambles your hard disk's FAT?)

- *Use BIOS calls to print the driver's status at critical points.* If you want to understand the output, be careful not to include so many debugging outputs that you cannot read them as they go by.

- *Anything that records the screen display during testing and can be played back at slow speed can help.* Small computers, the system printer, or even a videotape can help if they can be configured to record what is happening.

Making a Practical Driver

You can make the sample driver more concrete by adding some substance to it. We will add a write function to make the driver capable of writing to the printer as it gets characters. If you want this driver to replace the default printer driver, you can change its name (to PRN) in the device header.

Everything in drvr.asm remains the same, but we expand the write function (see listing 12.8).

Listing 12.8

```
        mov   cx,es:[bx]+12h        ;Number of bytes to print
        mov   di,es:[bx]+0eh        ;Offset of data buffer
        mov   ax,es:[bx]+10h        ;Segment address of data buffer
        mov   es,ax
;
        mov   dl,0                  ;Printer 0
        mov   bx,0                  ;Count 0 bytes printed
;
s_prt1:
        cmp   bx,cx                 ;Printed all characters yet?
        je    s_done                ;All done
;
        mov   al,es:[di]            ;Get a character
        inc   di                    ;Point to the next one
;
        mov   ah,2                  ;Check printer status
        int   17h
        test  ah,80h               ;Busy?
        jne   s_prtch              ;Print it
        jmp   s_err                ;Busy device, exit
s_prtch:
        cmp   al,LF                 ;Is the character a line feed?
        je    s_bxinc              ;Skip it
        mov   ah,0                  ;Print character
        int   17h
        test  ah,09h               ;I/O error?
        jne   s_err                ;Handle it
s_bxinc:
        inc   bx                    ;Count one printed
```

```
        jmp   s_prt1
s_err:
        mov   ax,800ch              ;General failure error
        jmp   s_end
s_done:
        mov   ax,bx                 ;Save count
        mov   bx,cs:rh_off          ;Get req.hdr
        mov   es:[bx]+12h,ax        ;Store byte count
        xor   ax,ax                 ;Zero AX register
s_end:
        jmp   finish
```

The new code prints characters to the printer and ignores line feed characters on their way out. This function is useful if you want to use one of the older printers that interprets carriage returns or line feeds as a "carriage return and line feed" pair.

The function is simple. It begins by locating the request header pointer to the data buffer (offset 0Eh and 10h) and the number of bytes to transfer (offset 12h). Then it checks the printer status and, if the printer is busy, returns an error. If the printer is not busy, it prints the character. In this simplistic routine, any error that prevents you from writing the characters to the device causes the function to set an error code in the AX register (the device return status).

You could expand the entire function to do more sophisticated error processing—such as recognizing which errors are which and returning appropriate codes—but the basic function is sound.

Using the Device Driver

To test the device driver, you have to use it. There are several simple ways to use it from a program or directly from the command-line prompt.

Our sample driver is named DRVR (refer to listing 12.6). Like all other devices, this driver is activated when called by name. If you wanted to redirect something to the printer with the normal driver (PRN), you could type:

```
C>type autoexec.bat >prn:
```

This would direct a copy of the AUTOEXEC.BAT file out to the printer. To use the driver, you can type:

```
C>type autoexec.bat >drvr:
```

When you attempt to write to drvr, DOS checks the driver chain to locate the name DRVR and then uses the driver to print the data.

You also can access the driver from a program by opening the device as you would a file. You could use a handle function call to open the device (see listing 12.9).

Listing 12.9

```
union REGS regs;
regs.h.ah = 0x3d;       /* Open-file function     */
regs.h.al = 0x01;       /* Write access           */
regs.x.dx = (int)"drvr"; /* Creates pointer to string */
intdos(&regs,&regs);    /* Call DOS function int  */
handle = regs.x.ax;     /* Save the file handle   */
```

Either way you choose to access the driver, you can test its operation according to its design. In the case of drvr, you want to be able to test whether it prints characters to the printer and whether it eliminates line feeds from the character stream.

Summary

This chapter has dealt with what most programmers find the hardest part of programming in DOS: creating device drivers. You have learned that you can create device drivers by following a standard "mold" for a driver.

All drivers are built in three primary sections:

- The device header

- The strategy routine

- The interrupt routine

Each has its own structure. The device header contains the name of the driver and the pointer to the next driver in the chain of system drivers. The strategy routine provides only for remembering where the system request header will be stored for communication between the driver and the operating system kernel.

Most of the driver is contained in the individual functions (as many as 20 of them) that make up the interrupt routine. Any given driver may implement only a few of these functions and ignore the rest, returning a suitable completion code if such a request is made to the driver.

Miscellaneous Functions

This chapter focuses on three basic types of functions: DOS information functions, date and time functions, and extended error processing. The first two types are simple and do not require extensive treatment. The third type of function is an extremely powerful extension to DOS's error-processing capabilities. Because this type of function tends to be extremely program dependent, this chapter does not include a practical example of its usefulness.

DOS Version Information

A function was added in DOS V2.0 to let you retrieve the DOS version number. This information can be essential to knowing what functions to use in running a system. Fortunately, because DOS versions earlier than V2.0 (in other words, V1.x) reliably return a 0, any return value less than 2 indicates a DOS V1.x system. You cannot tell V1.0 from V1.1, but at least you know that the major change point at which full DOS came into existence has not been reached.

If detecting the DOS version does not seem important, remember that many people have never upgraded from DOS V1.0 or V1.1. For example, a couple stopped at a Seattle computer store to buy extra hardware so that they could expand their two-disk, *original* IBM PC to a hard disk system. They were still running DOS V1.1 and had to be told that it would not run the equipment they were buying. They walked out of the store with their hardware and DOS V3.2.

To maintain perfect compatibility across the various versions of DOS, you would have to restrict your programming to only those functions that were available in DOS V1—a laudable but silly goal. Most programming these days requires *at least* DOS V2.0; with earlier versions, such features as directories cannot even be used.

We recommend that you use the DOS version number in one of two ways:

1. Check for the proper DOS level and tell the user if it is not high enough to support the program.

2. Check for the DOS level and compensate as necessary.

The second approach will create considerable overhead, unless you are limiting DOS-specific code to overlays (with a separate overlay for each DOS version) or doing an installation that will patch in the correct code version for the DOS level in use.

The lines of code following this paragraph check for minimum functionality (at least DOS V2). The function returns two numbers: AL is the major version number (02h is DOS V2, 03h is DOS V3) and AH is the minor version number (10 is .10, 20 is .20, and so forth). Save registers BX and CX if you will need them after the call—the interrupt will destroy them.

Int 21h, Function 30h: Get DOS Version Number

```
mov      ah,30h      ; DOS version
int      21h
cmp      al,2        ; Check for greater than or equal to V2
jl       wrong       ; Wrong version
```

You can create (and use as a library function) a C subroutine that gives you the DOS version number. For example, if you simply want to check for a minimum version of DOS, you can use the chkver() subroutine in listing 13.1.

Listing 13.1

```
/* C version of chkver() */

#include <stdio.h>

main()

{
```

```
        int  ver;

        if((ver = chkver()) < 3){
            printf("ERROR -- Version MUST be at least 3.0\n");
            printf("        Yours is only version %d\n",ver);
            exit(0);
        }
        printf("Thanks ... you have version %d of DOS\n",ver);
}

#include <dos.h>

chkver()

{

        union REGS regs;

        regs.h.ah = 0x30;
        intdos(&regs,&regs);
        if(regs.h.al == 0) regs.h.al = 1;

        return(regs.h.al);
}
```

Because of the way this program is written, you can pull out the `chkver()` subroutine, place it in a subroutine library, and use it with other C programs. At the beginning of the program, be sure to add the statement

```
#include <stdio.h>
```

so that standard I/O functions are declared for the subroutine.

The subroutine itself simply calls Function 30h. Although the function returns both the major and minor numbers of the version (in registers AL and AH, respectively), only the major number is important.

Listing 13.2 is a BASIC version of the same program.

Listing 13.2

```
' chkver

$include "REGNAMES.INC"

def fnchkver
'Determine the DOS version from Int 21h, Function 30h
    reg %ax, &h3000
    call interrupt &h21
```

continues

Listing 13.2 continued

```
        if reg(%ax) and &h00ff = 0 then reg %ax,&h0001
        fnchkver = reg(%ax) and &h00ff
end def

'MAIN PROGRAM
'
'Use the check version function to print the
'system's version number

        if fnchkver<3 then
            print "OOPS -- You have an operating system version"
            print "Earlier than 3.0, You need to upgrade."
        else
            print "Operating System version 3 or above"
        end if
end
```

If you want to print the DOS version number, you can use the `getversion()` subroutine shown in listing 13.3.

Listing 13.3

```
/* getversion() */
<dos.h>

char *getversion()

{
    static char buffer[5];
    union REGS regs;

    regs.h.ah = 0x30;
    intdos(&regs,&regs);
    if(regs.h.al == 0) regs.h.al = 1;
    sprintf(buffer,"%d.%d",regs.h.al,regs.h.ah);

    return(buffer);
}
```

The `getversion()` subroutine, which uses the DOS version's major and minor numbers, is more complex than the `chkver()` subroutine. To make the version numbers accessible for printing, you create a static character buffer into which the version string is written in the proper format. Be careful, because the static buffer is only five characters (the last of which *must* be a NULL character). A five-character buffer will work until versions of DOS have three-digit minor numbers or two-digit major numbers; if version numbers get too high, you will have to make the buffer larger. (Note that programs running in the DOS compatibility box of OS/2 now return a DOS version number of 10!)

Because you return a pointer to the static character buffer, your main routine can simply print the return value and—voilà—you have the DOS version. You can include this getversion() subroutine in a library and use it, as needed, for other programs.

Listing 13.4 is a BASIC version of the subroutine. The BASIC function is substantially the same as the C routine but (because of the way BASIC works) seems quite different.

Listing 13.4

```
' getver
$include "REGNAMES.INC"

def fngetver
'Determine the DOS version from Int 21h, Function 30h
'     vn = version number
'     rn = revision number

      reg %ax, &h3000
      call interrupt &h21

      if reg(%ax) and &h00ff = 0 then reg %ax,&h0001
      vn = (reg(%ax) and &h00ff)

      rn = (reg(%ax) and &hff00)/256
      fngetver = vn + rn/100
end def

'MAIN PROGRAM
'
'Use the get version function to print the
'system's version number
'NOTE: You must use PRINT USING to get the
'      proper number of decimal places

      cls
      print using "Version Number: #.##" ;fngetver

end
```

Equipment Information

You may want to know what equipment is included on your system as well as the DOS version number. BIOS Int 11h returns a code in register AX that indicates the equipment installed on the computer. Table 13.1 shows how the information is coded.

Table 13.1. *BIOS Int 11h Return Code*

Bit(s)	Meaning
0	Set if disk drives installed (bits 6–7 significant)
1	Set if math coprocessor installed (AT only)
2–3	Memory configuration (not meaningful for AT)
	0 = 16K system board RAM
	1 = 32K system board RAM
	2 = 48K system board RAM
	3 = 64K system board RAM
4–5	Initial video mode
	1 = 40 × 25, text, color
	2 = 80 × 25, text, color
	3 = 80 × 25, text, mono
6–7	Number of disk drives minus 1
	(Valid only if bit 0 is 1)
8	Not used
9–11	Number of RS232 ports
12	Set if game adapter installed (PC only)
13	Set if internal modem installed (AT only)
14–15	Number of printers attached

To determine the equipment in a computer, you simply invoke Int 11h and then interpret the return code. The C program in listing 13.5 uses the interrupt in a subroutine. (Note, though, that the video information returned by this routine is not adequate to determine the exact type of video system in use; if that is essential to your program, this is only a starting point that can eliminate certain possibilities.)

Listing 13.5

```c
#include <stdio.h>

#define    BOOL      int
#define    FALSE     0
#define    TRUE      !FALSE

main()

{
    int  eqpt;
```

```
        eqpt = equipment(TRUE);
        printf("Equipment Value is %x\n",eqpt);
}

#include <dos.h>

#define    EQUIPMENT 0x11

equipment(print)

BOOL print;

{
    union REGS regs;
    int  eqpt;

    int86(EQUIPMENT,&regs,&regs);
    if(print){
        eqpt = regs.x.ax;
        if(eqpt & 0x01)
            printf("Floppy Drives are attached\n");
        if((eqpt>>1) & 0x01)
            printf("Math Coprocessor installed (AT only)\n");
        switch((eqpt>>4) & 0x03){
            case 1:
                printf("Initial video mode 40X25 color\n");
                break;
            case 2:
                printf("Initial video mode 80X25 color\n");
                break;
            case 3:
                printf("Initial video mode 80X25 mono\n");
                break;
        }
        if((eqpt>>6) & 0x01)
            printf("Number of disk drives is %d\n",
                ((eqpt>>6) & 0x03) + 1);
        printf("Number of RS-232 ports is %d\n",
            (eqpt>>9) & 0x07);
        if((eqpt>>12) & 0x01)
            printf("Game adapter installed\n");
        if((eqpt>>13) & 0x01)
            printf("Internal modem installed (AT only)\n");
        printf("Number of printers is %d\n",
            (eqpt>>14) & 0x03);
    }
    return(regs.x.ax);
}
```

The `equipment()` function can be pulled from this program and added to a function library of useful routines.

Notice the use of the `EQUIPMENT` definition in the interrupt call. By defining constants such as `EQUIPMENT (0x11)`, you can simplify program maintenance and make your code much more readable.

Listing 13.6 shows the equipment program written in BASIC.

Listing 13.6

```
' eqpt.bas
$include "REGNAMES.INC"

def fngeteqpt

    call interrupt &h11
    fngeteqpt = reg(%ax)

end def

'MAIN PROGRAM
'
'Get the installed equipment with the function
'geteqpt and interpret it with the subroutine
'printeqpt
    cls
    print "System Equipment Installed"
    eq% = fngeteqpt
    print "   Equipment code = ";HEX$(eq%)
    call printeqpt(eq%)
end

sub printeqpt(n%)
'
'This procedure prints the installed equipment list
'given the equipment code number

    if n% and &h01 then print "FLOPPY DRIVES ATTACHED"
    if n% and &h02 then print "MATH COPROCESSOR INSTALLED"
    if n% and &h1000 then print "GAME ADAPTER INSTALLED"
    vm = (n% and &h30)/16
    select case vm
        case 1
            print "40X25 text, color"
        case 2
            print "80X25 text, color"
        case 3
            print "80X25 text, mono"
    end select
```

```
dd = (n% and &hC0)/64 + 1
print "Number of disk drives: ";dd
rs = (n% and &hE00)/512
print "Number of RS-232 ports: ";rs
pr = (n% and &hC000)/16384
print "Number of printer ports: "'

end sub
```

Date and Time Functions

During system start-up, the date and time are initialized to their default values. If your system does not have an internal hardware clock, the default date is 1/1/80 and the default time is 00:00:00.00 (midnight). If your computer has an internal clock, the date and time are set from the values in the internal clock. From this point, the time is kept in the BIOS data area and the date is kept in COMMAND.COM. If your computer does not have an internal clock, the system date and time are reset with the DOS commands DATE and TIME.

In some versions of DOS V3, a bug prevents the date from changing when midnight rolls around. The bug was present in early versions, then was fixed, but reappeared later. In MS-DOS V3.2, the BIOS code returned the "passed-midnight" flag to DOS when called, but the DOS code ignored the result.

The only reliable correction is to use one of the public domain replacement CLOCK$ device drivers, such as CLKFIX.SYS, available from commercial services or BBSs. These drivers essentially replace the faulty code with a corrected version and reroute all affected interrupt vectors to the new code.

Even with the correction, though, a design flaw in the date routines can cause entire days to be skipped. For example, if a computer is left running over the weekend and nobody uses it for more than 24 hours, including two midnight passages, only one of the passages will be recognized.

The passing of midnight sets a flag, rather than a counter; thus, DOS does not know when more than one midnight has gone by since the last time it asked. Unlike the other bug, this one has no simple correction. The most direct cure is to reboot the computer every Monday morning to reset the calendar.

The best way to access the time and date is to use the DOS functions provided for that purpose. In DOS V1.1 and later versions, the system date function gets the day, month, year, and day of the week as follows:

Int 21h, Function 2Ah: Get System Date

```
mov         ah,2ah        ; Get date
int         21h
mov         dow,al        ; Day of week
mov         mo,dh         ; Month
mov         dy,dl         ; Day
mov         yr,cx         ; Year
```

The returned values are in the following ranges:

Day   1–31

Month   1–12

Year   1980–2099

Day of week   0–6 (0=Sunday, 1=Monday, and so on)

These ranges are used when you set the system date with DOS Int 21h, Function 2Bh. DOS returns AL=0 if the date is set successfully, or FFh if the date is not valid.

You can also set the system date under program control through the use of the following DOS function:

Int 21h, Function 2Bh: Set System Date

```
mov         ah,2bh        ; Set date
mov         cx,yr         ; Year
mov         dh,mo         ; Month
mov         dl,dy         ; Day
int         21h
or          al,al         ; Test for invalid
jnz         error         ; Jump on error
```

In addition to the functions provided for getting and setting the system date, DOS includes functions for getting and setting the system time. When it gets the system time, DOS returns values in the following ranges:

Hours (CH)   0–23

Minutes (CL)   0–59

Seconds (DH)   0–59

Hundredths of seconds (DL) 0–99

Because of the relatively slow speed of some computer systems, the real-time clock may not have an accurate resolution of 100ths of seconds. On these systems, the DL value should not be used for accurate or critical timing.

You get the system time by executing the following DOS interrupt and function:

Int 21h, Function 2Ch: Get System Time

```
mov     ah,2ch      ; Get time
int     21h
mov     hr,ch       ; Hours
mov     mn,cl       ; Minutes
mov     sc,dh       ; Seconds
mov     hn,dl       ; Hundredths of seconds
```

The range restrictions for setting the time are the same as those for getting the time. To set the time, use DOS Int 21h, Function 2Dh. The system will return AL=0 if the time is set successfully, or AL=FFh if the time set is not valid.

Int 21h, Function 2Dh: Set System Time

```
mov     ah,2dh      ; Set time
mov     ch,hr       ; Hour
mov     cl,mn       ; Minutes
mov     dx,0        ; Seconds = 0
int     21h
or      al,al       ; Error?
jnz     error
```

Listing 13.7 includes a set of C functions for getting the time and date. The cdate() and ctime() subroutines can be pulled out of the listing and added to your library of functions. Each will return a string pointer to a static buffer inside the function, with the date or time formatted appropriately in this buffer.

Listing 13.7

```
/* Date and time functions */

#include <stdio.h>

char *cdate(), *ctime();

main()

{
    printf("Date: %s Time: %s\n",cdate(), ctime());
}

#include <dos.h>

char *cdate()

{
    static char buffer[9];
    union REGS regs;
```

continues

Listing 13.7 continued

```
        regs.h.ah = 0x2a;
        intdos(&regs,&regs);

        sprintf(buffer,"%02.2d/%02.2d/%02.2d",
            regs.h.dh, regs.h.dl, regs.x.cx-1900);
        return(buffer);
}

char *ctime()

{

        static char    buffer[9];
        union REGS regs;

        regs.h.ah = 0x2c;
        intdos(&regs,&regs);


        sprintf(buffer,"%02.2d:%02.2d:%02.2d",
            regs.h.ch, regs.h.cl, regs.h.dh);
        return(buffer);

}
```

Each function is put together to hold the string representation of the date or time until you can use the string. Such static variables are permanently allocated and can take up a great deal of memory that will be used only infrequently. Be careful not to use too many of them.

Listing 13.8, the Pascal program clock.pas, is another example of the use of the date and time functions. This program displays an on-screen clock until you press the Escape key (Esc).

Listing 13.8

```
{ clock.pas }

{ Turbo Pascal 4.0 and greater. For 3.0, omit next code line }
{ and declare the Registers record type.              }

uses crt, Dos;

const    cr:  char = ^M;
```

```
var hour,min,sec,month,day,year : byte;
    ch : char;

Procedure get_time( var hr,mi,se : byte );

var
    I: Integer;
    Regs: Registers;

begin { get_time }
    With Regs Do
        begin
            AH:=$2C;
            Flags:=0;
            MsDos(Regs);    {execute software interrupt}
            hr:=CH;
            mi:=CL;
            se:=DH;
        end; { With Regs }
end; { end get_time }


Procedure get_date( var mo, da, yr : byte);

var
    I: Integer;
    Regs: Registers;

begin { get_date }
    With Regs Do
        begin
            AH:=$2A;
            Flags:=0;
            MsDos(Dos.Registers(Regs)); {execute software interrupt}
            yr:=(CX mod 100);
            da:=DL;
            mo:=DH;
        end; { With Regs }
end; { end get_date }

procedure print_time( hr,mi,se,mo,dy,yr : byte);

begin { procedure print_time }
    write(mo:2,'/',dy:2,'/',yr:2);
    write(' ',hr:2,':',mi:2,':',se:2);
    write(cr);
end; { end print_time }
```

continues

Listing 13.8 *continued*

```
begin { Main Routine }
    repeat
        get_time(hour,min,sec);
        get_date(month,day,year);
        print_time(hour,min,sec,month,day,year);
        delay(10);
    until keypressed;
    { flush the input buffer }
    while keypressed do ch := readkey;
    { for version 3.0, replace preceding line with }
    {     while keypressed do read(kbd,ch); }
end. { end Main Routine }
```

Clock.pas is a simplistic program. The main part of the program occurs at the end, between the begin-end pair marked as Main Routine. This main routine sets up a continuous loop (repeat-until) that gets the date and time and prints them every 10 seconds until a key is pressed. (Whenever a key is pressed, keypressed is set to TRUE so that Turbo Pascal can recognize it.)

After the clock loop ends, the program clears any keystrokes in the input buffer simply by reading characters as long as keypressed remains TRUE. Then the program ends.

Extended Error Processing

A DOS function, introduced with DOS V3, lets you determine extended error information. *Extended error information* provides detailed information about an error that has just occurred (after a DOS service call) and suggests action to remedy the error. Although this function is most useful at the assembly language level, you also can get suggested recovery actions by using the routine from a high-level language.

If you are working in assembly language, you should save any essential registers before you call Function 59h because this special function destroys most of your register setups while it is processing. (If you are working in a high-level language, you do not need to save the registers.)

The following DOS function saves the registers, then gets the extended error information:

Int 21h, Function 59h: Get Extended Error Information
```
push        ax          ; Save registers before call
push        bx
push        cx
```

```
push       dx
push       si
push       di
push       bp
push       ds
push       es
mov        ah,59h       ; Extended error info
mov        bx,0
int        21h
```

The routine returns the following codes:

AX = Extended error code

BH = Error class

BL = Recommended action

CH = Error locus

The meaning of these codes is detailed in the following tables. The codes are self-explanatory; how you respond to them depends on the program and the nature of the call that generated the problem.

Table 13.2 lists the error codes with the primary error indication—in other words, the "what happened?" This type of error indication is familiar to programmers accustomed to working with operating system calls. Informational messages (maybe we should call them "semi-informational") give us something to tell the user but are not of much help to us unless only one thing could possibly be wrong. If there is more than one possible cause for an error, the informational message is only marginally helpful. In most cases, if you can expect the error, you should have programmed around it in the first place.

Table 13.2. *Extended Error Codes Returned in AX*

Code	Meaning
1	Invalid function
2	File not found
3	Path not found
4	No handles available
5	Access denied
6	Invalid handle
7	Memory control blocks destroyed
8	Insufficient memory
9	Invalid memory block address
10	Invalid environment
11	Invalid format
12	Invalid access code

continues

Table 13.2. *continued*

Code	Meaning
13	Invalid data
14	Reserved
15	Invalid drive
16	Attempt to remove current directory
17	Not the same device
18	No more files
19	Disk write-protected
20	Unknown unit
21	Drive not ready
22	Unknown command
23	CRC error
24	Bad request structure length
25	Seek error
26	Unknown media type
27	Sector not found
28	Out of paper
29	Write fault
30	Read fault
31	General failure
32	Sharing violation
33	Lock violation
34	Invalid disk change
35	FCB unavailable
36	Sharing buffer overflow
37	Code page mismatch
38	Error handling EOF
39	Handle disk full
40–49	Reserved
50	Network request not supported
51	Remote computer not listening
52	Duplicate name on network
53	Network name not found
54	Network busy
55	Network device no longer exists
56	Net BIOS command limit exceeded
57	Network adapter error
58	Incorrect network response
59	Unexpected network error
60	Incompatible remote adapter
61	Print queue full
62	Not enough space for print file
63	Print file deleted
64	Network name deleted
65	Access denied
66	Network device type incorrect

Code	Meaning
67	Network name not found
68	Network name limit exceeded
69	Net BIOS session limit exceeded
70	Temporarily paused
71	Network request not accepted
72	Print or disk redirection is paused
73–79	Reserved
80	File already exists
81	Reserved
82	Cannot make directory entry
83	Fail on INT 24
84	Too many redirections
85	Duplicate redirection
86	Invalid password
87	Invalid parameter
88	Network data fault

The error class codes in table 13.3 go one step beyond the error codes themselves. Error class codes classify the error, based on internal knowledge of the operating system.

Table 13.3. *Error Class Codes Returned in BH*

Class	Meaning
1	Out of resource
2	Temporary situation
3	Authorization
4	Internal
5	Hardware failure
6	System failure
7	Application program error
8	Not found
9	Bad format
10	Locked
11	Media
12	Already exists
13	Unknown

With most systems, an operating system error can arise from so many causes that the program must be extremely sophisticated in its error handling if it is to shield the user from problems. All experienced programmers have thought "it must be an operating system bug" as they have butted heads against a seemingly intractable problem. DOS will try to tell you if there seems to be such an error—but do you trust

DOS to admit its own mistakes? If, when you are running a program intended for commercial use, you do get an indication of an error that cannot be corrected by the software, you can help minimize your own support problems if you make sure that the program clearly tells the user the source of the error. If you can point out a hardware failure, your customer service group will thank you for every call they did *not* have to take.

Most experienced programmers have wondered what to do if certain errors occur. The recommended action codes shown in table 13.4 are meant to help but are not a total solution. By suggesting possible actions to the programmer, the designers of DOS have applied their knowledge of the system to your problems. You can take reasonable action based on the action codes.

Table 13.4. *Recommended Action Codes Returned in BL*

Action Code	Meaning
1	Retry; if not cleared in a reasonable number of attempts, prompt user to Abort or Ignore
2	Delay then retry; if not cleared in reasonable number of attempts, prompt user to Abort or Ignore
3	Get corrected information from user (bad file name or disk drive)
4	Abort application with cleanup
5	Abort application without cleanup (cleanup may increase problems)
6	Ignore error
7	Prompt user to correct error and then retry

Errors that involve the user are especially prone to difficulties in error correction, particularly if the user does not understand your error message and prompts (Abort or Ignore error, for example). Suggested actions do not eliminate the programmer's responsibility for making the program as user-friendly as possible.

Action codes should be used as the basis for error recovery when an error condition is recognized. In most situations, only one or two of the recommended actions will make sense—you can ignore the others. But be careful—provide a graceful way to exit a program if an error (that cannot be corrected by software) occurs. If the user has to reboot the system to get out of an error-correction loop, the error has not been corrected. Always include an override to allow frustrated users to get out.

The error locus codes shown in table 13.5 expand information about an error and attempt to tell you something about the origin of the error—in other words, which device caused the error. (We can know the area of DOS from which an error originated because these values are stored internally by DOS, as each functional area of the DOS code is entered. In this way, a common error detection routine can process errors with different locus codes.)

Table 13.5. *Error Locus Codes Returned in CH*

Locus Code	Meaning
1	Unknown
2	Block device (disk or disk emulator)
3	Network
4	Serial device
5	Memory related

On a single-user system, error locus code information is marginally useful because, in most cases, the original error code has told you what caused the error. This type of error information becomes useful in situations that deal with the possibilities inherent in redirection and device independence.

For example, if you write a program that works with the standard input and output devices, a user can redirect the output to a disk drive, a network, or the RS-232 port without the program being aware of the change. The error locus code can give you the key to interpreting and correcting the error.

Some programmers have reported that the Extended Error function has returned inappropriate information when called after errors occur on a character (rather than block) device using DOS V3. Study of the actual code used in V4 shows that three of the four items returned (the class, action, and locus) are set at entry to other DOS functions so that they can be used later in case of error and are never explicitly returned to zero if no error occurs. Not all are set by every function; some functions set only one or two.

The remaining item, the extended error code itself, is mapped by a straight table-lookup procedure from the older error codes, but only when an error is detected. This item *is* set to zero at the start of each DOS function to indicate that no error has yet occurred.

When the Extended Error function is called, it merely gets the four values stored earlier and returns them to the caller. No analysis is performed on these values. Thus it is possible, though unlikely, that a call to the function might return values stored by DOS functions that are different from the one reporting an error. If so, it would be a significant bug in DOS; with the exception of a few scattered reports that might have been due to errors in the calling programs, no such bug has been reported. Still, if you find inconsistent results, be aware that others have reported problems.

DOS PROGRAMMING

Undocumented Features

No discussion of the miscellaneous functions of DOS can be complete without touching on the famed "undocumented features" that Microsoft and IBM tenaciously show in the official reference manuals as "reserved." Such features have been a significant part of DOS from the start. Most authorities tell you to avoid them because they are never guaranteed to stay the same from one version to the next or to be present in any specific OEM version of DOS.

These features span a wide range. Some are so intimately connected with the internals of how DOS does its job that they are essentially useless outside of DOS itself. Others provide hooks for things that are not yet fully implemented. A few have moved into the twilight zone of semi-respectability (we discussed them previously, in connection with TSR programming).

In the reference section of this book, we tell you all that we have been able to learn about these intriguing bits of mystery. In every case, we provide a disclaimer that the feature may behave differently, or even be absent, on your machine. This was more true of V2 than it has been since the introduction of network support in V3, because at that time Microsoft changed their OEM contracts to require that certain areas (including many of the "reserved" functions) not be changed; they are necessary now for network support.

Note, though, that the use of these functions is still risky. Despite literally years of study by some of the best analytical minds in the industry, nobody outside Microsoft and IBM knows exactly what all of them are supposed to do. This means that any of them could have serious hidden side effects under relatively rare circumstances; when we know of such side effects, we tell you, but we do not know everything.

Still, experimenting with these things is fun, and the risk can be minimized by following the rules set forth for testing device drivers: limit your exposure and keep a good set of backups in case things go wrong.

Rather than provide examples of the use of such features in this chapter, we have added them as Appendix E. You can use the programs described there to do your own snooping inside DOS.

Summary

This chapter has discussed a group of special functions that do not fit neatly into a single category: the DOS version functions, BIOS equipment function, DOS date and time functions, and DOS error-handling function. All of these standard functions are valuable additions to a personal function library. You have learned how to build a few sample routines (in C, BASIC, and Pascal) for each of these functions.

Finally, we looked briefly at the subject of the "reserved" functions listed in all official reference manuals. At this point, you are ready to start using the rest of this book and what you have learned so far to design and build your own programs.

PROGRAMMING

Part V

Reference

BIOS Function Reference

BIOS (basic input/output system) functions are the fundamental level of any PC or compatible computer. BIOS functions embody the basic operations needed for successful use of the computer's hardware resources. These functions also are used by DOS to carry out its own operations. Most programming on PCs or compatibles is done above the BIOS level. Programmers who need special functions call BIOS functions directly when no other method will work. In some cases, even the BIOS does not provide the services needed, and programmers will go below it to the hardware itself.

The BIOS in a PC or compatible is largely contained in ROM (thus, the term ROM BIOS) as part of the hardware system. Ordinarily, the BIOS is provided by the manufacturer of a system, according to Microsoft's specifications for MS-DOS. Extensions of the ROM BIOS for EGA monitors or other devices can be added easily to the system. These extensions serve as one of the foundations of the PC environment's extendable nature. Some parts of the BIOS are loaded from disk when the system boots (a hidden system file, typically called either IO.SYS or IBMBIO.COM). See Chapter 3, "The Dynamics of DOS," for a detailed description of how DOS is booted.

The ROM release date is located in the eight bytes starting at F000:FFF5h. Some important BIOS release dates include:

Date	Machine Type
04/24/81	PC
10/19/81	Revised PC with bug fixes
08/16/82	PC XT
10/27/82	PC to XT upgrade
11/08/82	Portable PC
06/01/83	PC*jr*
01/10/84	Personal Computer AT
09/13/85	Convertible PC
04/21/86	PC XT 286
09/02/86	PS/2 line

These dates, which cover only the IBM ROM BIOS, are meaningful only if you are working with an IBM PC. Systems that do not have the true IBM ROM are likely to have different dates. The table does not cover *all* releases of the BIOS ROM. From time to time, notes in magazines or on bulletin boards (mostly reporting bugs) refer to other dates for ROM, but it seems that no comprehensive list of dates exists.

A model-identification byte (located at F000:FFFEh) can be used to differentiate between models (see table BIOS.1). The PS/2 family continues to support this model-identification byte. For non-IBM machines, however, this byte cannot be relied on; no standard set of values has ever been established.

Table BIOS.1. *Model Identification Bytes*

Byte	System
9Ah	COMPAQ Plus
FFh	IBM PC
FEh	PC XT, Portable PC
FDh	PC*jr*
FCh	Personal Computer AT, PS/2 Models 50 and 60
FBh	PC XT (after 1/10/86)
FAh	PS/2 Model 30
F9h	Convertible PC
F8h	PS/2 Model 80

For additional information on the BIOS release dates and model identification, refer to the description of Int 15, Function C0h, later in this section.

On the PS/2, no BIOS stands between OS/2 and the hardware. All hardware interfacing is done through device drivers. (See Chapter 12, "Device Drivers," for a discussion of device drivers.) The BIOS remains in the PS/2 system for three reasons: to bootstrap the operating system, to support DOS (if DOS is being used), and to support the Compatibility Box for running DOS programs.

Device drivers are direct interfaces linked into the operating system to control access to hardware. In a multitasking operating system such as UNIX or OS/2, these drivers can handle multiple requests from processes (programs) and keep everything in order. Access through drivers is essential in a multitasking environment such as OS/2 because any program with direct access to the hardware or to an all-encompassing BIOS could destroy what other programs are trying to do.

A BIOS originally written to support DOS V3 would have trouble running under OS/2 because the BIOS will not run in protected mode. Some processor instructions are not allowed in protected mode, and programs are prevented from accessing portions of memory assigned to other programs. Protected mode makes multitasking operations possible because you can write a program without worrying about its effect on other programs. The IBM PS/2 includes an advanced BIOS (ABIOS) that can work with a device driver in real and protected modes, support multitasking, and address up to 16M of memory.

On the PS/2, BIOS calls are supported for programs running in the Compatibility Box. Even Borland's SideKick (which uses undocumented system calls) will run on the PS/2, although the official position of Microsoft and IBM is to support only *documented* DOS calls. Under OS/2, however, DOS programs that must run in the background will be suspended. The OS/2 developers made the worst-case assumption that DOS programs are not compatible with multitasking because they directly access memory (writing directly to the screen, for example).

Readers moving into the OS/2 environment will find that this section indicates (wherever possible) the PS/2 aspects of interrupt processing in the BIOS. Keep in mind that IBM is not publishing the BIOS listing for the PS/2 as they did for the original PC. Instead, they are publishing only the entry points, which are almost entirely compatible with the old PC BIOS. Programs built on a BIOS foundation will continue to work with the PS/2. Programs whose timing depends on the speed of the BIOS will work much faster on the PS/2 family than they do on a PC.

The major changes in the PS/2 BIOS are shown in table BIOS.2.

Except for communications programs that customarily take control of interrupts 0Bh and 0Ch, these changes should have no effect on most programs.

The BIOS Functions

The BIOS functions in this section are arranged in ascending numerical order by interrupt and function, from 00h through 1Fh. Interrupts or functions that are considered reserved are not detailed here unless they were detailed for earlier versions of the BIOS and are now marked as reserved in recent BIOS releases.

Table BIOS.2. *Personal System/2 Differences*

Interrupt	Meaning
0Bh	Reserved, no longer communications
0Ch	Reserved, no longer communications
0Dh	Reserved
0Fh	Reserved
15h	System services (cassette I/O)
40h	Diskette BIOS revector
41h	Fixed disk parameters
46h	Fixed disk parameters
4Ah	User alarm
71h–74h	Reserved
76h–77h	Reserved
F1h–FFh	User program interrupts

Each BIOS interrupt or function is presented in the following manner:

Int 21h   Function 66h
Get global code page

The first line for each function lists the interrupt number and the function number (if any). The second line lists the purpose of the function. Additional information includes a quick description, calling registers, return registers, and comments.

This section is intended as a reference to BIOS functions and their use. Because all BIOS function calls have the same form, this section does not include examples of how individual BIOS calls are used.

The information in this section was compiled from the widest available range of sources. Every effort was made to ensure the technical accuracy and timeliness of this information; if you find discrepancies, Que Corporation would be interested in your comments.

BIOS Function Quick Reference

Int	Function	Purpose	Page
00h		Divide-by-Zero Interrupt	493
01h		Single Step Interrupt	493
02h		Non-Maskable Interrupt	494
03h		Breakpoint Interrupt	495
04h		Arithmetic Overflow Interrupt	495
05h		Print Screen	496
06h		Reserved	
07h		Reserved	
08h		System Timer	496
09h		Keyboard Interrupt	497
0Ah		Reserved	
0Bh		Communications	499
0Ch		Communications	499
0Dh		Hard Disk Management	500
0Eh		Floppy Disk Management	500
0Fh		Printer Management	501
10h		Video	501
	00h	Set Video Mode	501
	01h	Set Cursor Type	503
	02h	Set Cursor Position	503
	03h	Read Cursor Position and Configuration	505
	04h	Read Light Pen Position	505
	05h	Select Active Display Page	506
	06h	Scroll Window Up	507
	07h	Scroll Window Down	508
	08h	Read Character and Attribute	509
	09h	Write Character and Attribute	509
	0Ah	Write Character at Cursor	510
	0Bh	Set Color Palette	511
	0Ch	Write Graphics Pixel	512
	0Dh	Read Graphics Pixel	513
	0Eh	Write Text in Teletype Mode	513
	0Fh	Get Current Display Mode	514
	10h	Set Palette Registers	515
	11h	Character Generator	517
	12h	Alternate Select	519
	13h	Write String	520
	1Ah	Read/Write Display Codes	521
	1Bh	Get Display State	522

Int	Function	Purpose	Page
	1Ch	Save/Restore Display State	522
11h		Get Equipment Status	523
12h		Get Memory Size	524
13h		Diskette	525
	00h	Reset Disk System	525
	01h	Get Disk System Status	526
	02h	Read Disk Sectors	527
	03h	Write Disk Sectors	527
	04h	Verify Disk Sectors	528
	05h	Format Disk Track	529
	06h	Format Cylinder and Set Bad Sector Flags	530
	07h	Format Drive from Specified Cylinder	531
	08h	Return Disk Drive Parameters	531
	09h	Initialize Fixed Disk Table	533
	0Ah	Read Long Sector	533
	0Bh	Write Long Sector	534
	0Ch	Seek Cylinder	536
	0Dh	Alternate Disk Reset	536
	0Eh	Read Sector Buffer	537
	0Fh	Write Sector Buffer	537
	10h	Test Fixed Disk System Status	538
	11h	Recalibrate Fixed Disk Drive	538
	12h	Diagnose Controller RAM	539
	13h	Diagnose Drive	539
	14h	Diagnose Controller	539
	15h	Return DASD Type	540
	16h	Read Disk Change Line Status	541
	17h	Set DASD Type for Disk Format	541
	18h	Set Media Type for Format	542
	19h	Park Heads	543
	1Ah	Format ESDI Unit	543
14h		Asynchronous Communications	544
	00h	Initialize Communications Port	544
	01h	Write Character to Communications Port	546
	02h	Read Character from Communications Port	546
	03h	Request Communications Port Status	547
	04h	Extended Initialization (PS/2)	548
	05h	Extended Communications Port Control	549
15h		System Services	550
	00h	Turn On Cassette Motor	550
	01h	Turn Off Cassette Motor	550
	02h	Read Data Blocks from Cassette Drive	551
	03h	Write Data Blocks to Cassette Drive	551
	0Fh	ESDI Unit Format Periodic Interrupt	552
	21h	Power-On Self-Test Error Log	552

Int	Function	Purpose	Page
	4Fh	Keyboard Intercept	553
	80h	Device Open	554
	81h	Device Close	554
	82h	Program Termination	555
	83h	Event Wait	555
	84h	Joystick Support	556
	85h	System Request Key Pressed	557
	86h	Delay	557
	87h	Move Block	558
	88h	Extended Memory Size Determination	559
	89h	Switch Processor to Protected Mode	560
	90h	Device Wait	561
	91h	Interrupt Complete	562
	C0h	Return System Configuration Parameters	563
	C1h	Return Extended BIOS Data Area Segment Address	564
	C2h	Pointing Device BIOS Interface	565
	C3h	Enable/Disable Watchdog Timeout	567
	C4h	Programmable Option Select	568
16h		Keyboard	568
	00h	Read Keyboard Character	568
	01h	Read Keyboard Status	569
	02h	Return Keyboard Flags	570
	03h	Adjust Keyboard Repeat Rate	571
	04h	Key-Click On/Off	572
	05h	Write to Keyboard Buffer	572
	10h	Get Keystroke	572
	11h	Check Keyboard	573
	12h	Get Keyboard Status Flags	573
17h		Printer	574
	00h	Write Character to Printer	574
	01h	Initialize Printer Port	575
	02h	Request Printer Port Status	576
18h		Execute ROM BASIC	576
19h		System Warm Boot	576
1Ah		System Timer/Real-Time Clock Services	577
	00h	Get Clock Counter	577
	01h	Set Clock Counter	577
	02h	Read Real-Time Clock	578
	03h	Set Real-Time Clock	579
	04h	Read Date from Real-Time Clock	580
	05h	Set Date of Real-Time Clock	580
	06h	Set System Alarm	581
	07h	Disable Real-Time Clock Alarm	581
	09h	Read Real-Time Clock Alarm	582

DOS PROGRAMMING

Int	Function	Purpose	Page
	0Ah	Get Day Count	582
	0Bh	Set Day Count	582
	80h	Set Sound Source	583
1Bh		Ctrl-Break Address	583
1Ch		Timer Tick Interrupt	584
1Dh		Video-Initialization Parameter Table	584
1Eh		Disk-Initialization Parameter Table	585
1Fh		Graphics Display Character Bit-Map Table	585
70h		Real-Time Clock Interrupt	586
4Fh		VESA BIOS Services	586
	00h	Return SuperVGA Information	587
	01h	Return SuperVGA Mode Information	588
	02h	Set SuperVGA Display Mode	589
	03h	Return SuperVGA Display Mode	590
	04h	Save/Restore SuperVGA Video State	590
	05h	Display Memory Window Control	591

Int 00h

Divide-by-Zero Interrupt
(Hardware Error)

Called by the CPU if an attempt is made to divide by a zero value

Calling Registers: None

Return Registers: Nothing

Comments: The divide-by-zero interrupt is invoked automatically when the processor attempts to perform the illegal operation divide by zero. Because the division process in the computer can never end if the divisor is zero, the operation is always treated as an error on any computer. The interrupt handler automatically deals with this error.

At start-up, the BIOS sets this interrupt to point to an IRET instruction. But DOS resets the interrupt to point to a handler that generates the message Divide by Zero and then aborts the program that caused the error. This is handled at the DOS level because a corresponding handler does not exist at the BIOS level. A divide-by-zero error can leave the operating system unstable, resulting in other errors. If a divide-by-zero error occurs, the best course is to restart the system manually or to create a better handler (like the one for DOS Int 24h).

If you are writing a program in which user input may cause this type of error, you should trap the interrupt and handle it in a routine of your own. It is good programming practice to write your programs so that they screen user input and never allow this error trap to occur. Sometimes, however, your program can generate the divide by zero in ways you hadn't thought of.

A divide-by-zero error can occur unexpectedly during operation of a program in which a stack problem results in attempts by the processor to execute Int 00h. Occasionally, a divide-by-zero error occurs when particularly intricate stack manipulation takes place during the process of debugging a program.

In addition to these causes, some versions of DOS generate a divide-by-zero error when an attempt is made to access a file that does not exist; the error apparently occurs in the calculations DOS performs to convert a cluster number to the track/head/sector address format required by all disk controllers. This error is especially mystifying because there is no *apparent* relation between the user's actions and the error message.

Int 01h

Single Step Interrupt

Called by the CPU if the trap flag is set

Calling Registers: None

Return Registers: Nothing

Comments: Whenever the trap flag (TF) is set, Int 01h will be called after each instruction has been executed. The debugger uses this interrupt to handle program single stepping. (Other types of programs should not call this interrupt.)

If you are writing a debugger, you need to take special care with the STI (Set Interrupt Flag) instruction to prevent trapping your own interrupt handler. When you enter your handler, interrupts are off and the trap flag is set. If you re-enable interrupts before you turn off the trap flag, your interrupt handler will be single stepped. You will have to reboot to regain control.

Int 02h
Non-Maskable Interrupt (NMI)

Called by the CPU on a memory parity error

Calling Registers: None

Return Registers: Nothing

Comments: From the programmer's standpoint, the non-maskable interrupt (NMI) is one of the least useful interrupts because it represents a major system failure in progress. When an NMI occurs, you probably will not have time to recover. The NMI cannot be blocked or turned off—it simply must be accepted.

On the PC family of computers (including the PS/2 Model 30), this interrupt reports parity errors. When a memory parity error occurs on the system board, ROM BIOS displays PARITY CHECK 1 and then locks up the machine. PARITY CHECK 2 indicates an I/O channel parity error. A display of ????? indicates an intermittent-read problem with memory.

Although you could trap the interrupt to shut down the system in an orderly manner, the interrupt handler may not be in good memory because this interrupt arises from a memory parity error. More important, any attempt to flush disk buffers or update your files may damage an otherwise good file. However, several public domain and shareware programs are available to trap the interrupt and give you a choice of action rather than force a reboot.

This interrupt is used for parity checks on the PS/2 family (except the Model 30) but the error messages are numeric codes taken from the following table:

Code	Meaning
110	System-board memory failure
111	I/O channel-check activated
112	Watchdog timeout
113	Direct memory access bus timeout

A fault in I/O channel memory causes error 111. The watchdog timeout is used to detect a missed IRQ0 (system timer) interrupt. When such an interrupt occurs with the watchdog timeout enabled, NMI error 112 is generated. On systems driven by direct memory access (DMA), error 113 is generated if a DMA device is given control of the system bus for more than 7.8 microseconds.

Int 03h

Breakpoint Interrupt

Used by debuggers to trap program breakpoints

Calling Registers: None

Return Registers: Nothing

Comments: Debugging programs put a vector that points to their breakpoint-handling routines at this interrupt. Debuggers place an Int 03h (using the special single-byte synonym opcode 0CCh) at the desired breakpoint and allow the program to run. When the program reaches the breakpoint, the interrupt handler returns control to the debugger.

Such a special single-byte opcode may sound foreign to some programmers, but Intel provided this alternative to 0CDh 03h (the normal coding for INT 03h) to facilitate the easy placing of breakpoints in executable code.

Interrupts 03h and 01h are the primary hardware tools available for debugging assembly language programs.

Int 04h

Arithmetic Overflow Interrupt

Called by the CPU when an arithmetic operation overflows

Calling Registers: None

Return Registers: Nothing

Comments: When arithmetic operations generate results larger than the data type allows, you can call this interrupt by executing the INTO (Interrupt on Overflow) instruction. To enable the instruction, the overflow bit (bit 11) in the flag register must be set before the arithmetic instruction (such as MUL or IMUL) is executed.

Because arithmetic overflow is not much of a problem for most programs, no action is usually taken. The default for the interrupt is to point to an IRET instruction and return immediately from the interrupt. No special handler is used to deal with overflow because the Intel microprocessor instruction set includes the JO and JNO (Jump if Overflow and Jump if Not Overflow) instructions, which are ordinarily used for handling overflow.

Int 05h
Print Screen

Prints the text screen to the printer

Calling Registers: None

Return Registers: Nothing

Comments: To trigger this function, which prints the current screen display to the printer, you press the PrtSc key (usually Shift-PrtSc). Function 05h transfers to a routine that sends to the printer the ASCII contents of the video screen buffer. Notice that we said *ASCII contents*—if you are working with a graphics screen, this interrupt will cause printing to occur, but what is printed will be unpredictable.

Most versions of DOS include the GRAPHICS.COM utility, which installs a substitute print-screen interrupt handler capable of dealing with graphics. Versions before V4 worked properly only with IBM (Epson-compatible) graphics printers; with V4, support was extended to all current IBM printer models.

Several other alternative Int 05h routines are widely distributed. Intel, for example, provides a replacement handler as part of the software supplied with the Above Board Plus EMS-memory board, which gives you control of their software print buffering facility while retaining the print-screen feature.

You can call Int 05h from your own programs if you want to provide a way to print the screen display. Printing the screen display can be particularly useful in database programs, for example—you can print the contents of the screen instead of having to print records.

In some cases, you may need to replace the interrupt vector with a special handler that deals with special screen conditions or performs a completely different function. The standard function saves the cursor position, then prints the screen to printer 1 on the system. It runs with interrupts enabled so that any interrupt (except another print screen) can take control of the system.

This function, which does not modify any registers, maintains a status byte at memory location 0050:0000h. If this status byte is 1, printing is in progress. If the value is 0, a successful print operation has occurred; FFh indicates that the last print operation was unsuccessful.

Int 08h
System Timer

Called by the system clock approximately 18.2 times per second (65,536 times per hour)

Calling Registers: None

Return Registers: Nothing

Comments: Int 08h, which is called 18.2 times per second to advance the time-of-day counter, is tied directly to channel 0 of the system timer chip. People who write TSRs with utilities such as SideKick, for example, find Int 08h particularly useful for time-related triggering (as with a clock or alarm). This interrupt calls Int 1Ch (Timer Tick). Most TSRs should connect to Int 1Ch rather than to Int 08h.

Because this interrupt is called every 55 milliseconds, all handlers for it must execute as quickly as possible. Interrupt processing should be a small part of the normal use of the processor system. And because the timer is attached as IRQ0 (the highest priority hardware interrupt), servicing this interrupt takes precedence over all other interrupts on the system. If this interrupt is poorly handled, it could lead to problems servicing other important interrupts such as disk servicing.

Note that because Int 1Ch (the user hook for the timer) is called *before* the Int 08h handler completes its processing, all actions performed in a handler for it will *also* take precedence over any other hardware interrupt requests. This fact is often overlooked, even by experienced software designers.

Address 0040:006Ch is a 32-bit time-of-day indicator, counting the number of ticks since power-up. Position 0040:0070h is set to 1 each time the count reaches 24 hours and is cleared to 0 when the BIOS reads it. Should another 24 hours elapse with no intervening read action, an entire day will vanish from the computer's time system.

This interrupt also provides an automatic motor-off function for disks by decrementing location 0040:0040h. When location 0040:0040h reaches zero, the motor-running flag in the motor status at 0040:003Fh is reset to turn off the disk motor.

The reason for the odd frequency with which the timer calls Int 08h (18.2 times per second) is that the designers attempted to simplify their time-display chores by setting things up so that the high word of the 32-bit value at 0040:006Ch would increment exactly once per hour, permitting a simple comparison to 24 (decimal) to detect the midnight rollover.

Dividing 65,536 (the count at which the low word rolls over) by 3600 (the number of seconds in one hour) gives 18.20 exactly, which was the target frequency. Unfortunately, the timer chip's countdown frequency was actually slightly lower, and the actual number of counts detected in the BIOS is 11 more than the goal would indicate. In practice, the frequency varies slightly from one system to another, so the clocks must be reset from time to time; this normally happens each time the system is booted, but on some systems with separate real-time clocks, those clocks also gain or lose several seconds per week.

Int 09h
Keyboard Interrupt

The primary keystroke interrupt, called whenever a key is pressed or released

PROGRAMMING

Calling Registers: None

Return Registers: Nothing

Comments: Whenever a key is pressed or released, the keyboard sends a signal (IRQ1) that triggers this interrupt. The handler for this interrupt reads the key information from the keyboard port (port 60h) and processes that information into character and scan code information, which it then puts into the 32-byte input character queue (normally stored at 0040:001Eh). The two codes are placed at the location pointed to by 0040:001Ch (keyboard buffer tail pointer) and the pointer is incremented by 2. If the buffer is already full, the pointer is recycled to the beginning of the buffer. Instead of accessing the keyboard directly, the BIOS console-input routines access this input queue, thereby allowing programmers considerable flexibility in keyboard handling.

Special keystrokes are interpreted by the handler as follows:

Keystroke	Handling
Ctrl	0040:0017h and 0040:0018h (keyboard control bytes) are updated and 0040:0096h (keyboard mode flags) are updated
Alt	Same as Ctrl
Shift	Same as Ctrl
Ctrl-Alt-Del	0040:0072h (reset flag) is set to 1234h, and system control is transferred to the POST (Power-On Self Test) routines; POST bypasses the normal start-up memory tests when this flag is set
Pause	Causes the handler to loop until it gets a valid character
Print Screen	Issues Int 05h to call the print-screen routine
Ctrl-Break	Issues Int 1Bh to call the Control-Break processor
System Request	PC XT BIOS (dates after 1/10/86), Personal Computer AT, PC XT 286, PC Convertibles, and PS/2 systems issue an Int 15h, Function 85h (SysReq key pressed)

If you are using a PC XT with a BIOS release date after 1/10/86, or if you are using a Personal Computer AT, a PC XT 286, PC Convertible, or PS/2 system, this interrupt also issues an Int 15h, Function 91h (Interrupt Complete) with AL set to 02h after the keystroke has been processed. (See Int 15h, Function 91h for more information.)

TSRs (terminate-and-stay-resident utilities) that provide immediate response to keypresses frequently intercept and act upon this interrupt. Because the keyboard routines have to do a great deal of processing, intercepting keyboard requests from the normal BIOS keyboard routines is preferable to intercepting operations at this interrupt. If immediate responsiveness is essential, Int 09h is the best one to use.

Int 0Bh

COM1 and COM3 Interrupt Service
(PC, PC XT)
COM2 and COM4 Interrupt Service
(Personal Computer AT)
Reserved (PS/2)

Called when the serial port hardware issues an interrupt on IRQ3

Calling Registers: None

Return Registers: Nothing

Comments: Telecommunications programs generally intercept this interrupt vector. All other methods of accessing the serial port (BIOS or DOS functions) are not fast enough to handle speeds greater than 1200 bps. (See Chapter 7, "Serial Devices," and Chapter 11, "Interrupt Handlers," for a more detailed discussion.) By tying a custom interrupt handler here, the programmer can handle speeds up to the capacity of the machine (about 38.4K bits per second) if the interrupt handler is programmed carefully.

   Int 0Ch handles the COM ports not handled by this interrupt.

   Unfortunately, this interrupt is listed as reserved on the PS/2. Communications programs that rely on this interrupt for speed will have to be rewritten on the PS/2.

Int 0Ch

COM2 and COM4 Interrupt Service
(PC, PC XT)
COM1 and COM3 Interrupt Service
(Personal Computer AT)
Reserved (PS/2)

Called when the serial port hardware issues an interrupt on IRQ4

Calling Registers: None

Return Registers: Nothing

Comments: Telecommunications programs generally intercept this interrupt vector. All other methods of accessing the serial port (BIOS or DOS functions) are not fast enough to handle speeds greater than 1200 bps. (See Chapter 7, "Serial Devices," and Chapter 11, "Interrupt Handlers," for a more detailed discussion.) By tying a custom interrupt handler here, the programmer can handle speeds up to the capacity of the machine (about 38.4K bits per second) if the interrupt handler is programmed carefully.

   Int 0Bh handles the COM ports not handled by this handler.

Unfortunately, this interrupt is marked as reserved on the PS/2. Communications programs that rely on this interrupt for speed will have to be rewritten on the PS/2.

Int 0Dh

Hard Disk Management (Disk Controller)
(PC XT)
LPT2 Control (Personal Computer AT)
Reserved (PS/2)

Called by the designated hardware controllers using hardware-interrupt request line IRQ5

Calling Registers: None

Return Registers: Nothing

Comments: This interrupt handler was added only in later versions of the ROM BIOS. It represents a function that is available beginning with the PC XT.

On the Personal Computer AT, Int 0Dh is used for LPT2 handling. (See Int 0Fh for a discussion of printer services.)

On the PS/2, Int 0Dh is reserved; its functions are redistributed elsewhere. Because few (if any) programs make direct use of this interrupt, this change will not affect most programmers.

Int 0Eh

Floppy Disk Management

Called by the floppy disk controller (hardware) using hardware request line IRQ6

Calling Registers: None

Return Registers: Nothing

Comments: Int 0Eh is used by the floppy disk controller to detect disk transfer completions. Typically, because the operations available through this interrupt are attainable through other BIOS functions, this interrupt can be ignored. Most programmers do not use this interrupt.

Int 0Fh

Printer Management (LPT1)
Reserved (PS/2)

Internal printer-control interrupt using hardware request line IRQ7

Calling Registers: None

Return Registers: Nothing

Comments: On the PC, Int 0Fh was assigned to the printer controller to detect printer errors and print completion. Programmers typically do not use it because many printer controllers do not generate it reliably. Generally, you can ignore this interrupt.

The IRQ7 request (because it is the lowest priority level request) also can be generated as a default by the 8259 Priority Interrupt Controller, if the controller is unable to determine which device requested service. Thus, it is never safe to assume that an interrupt reaching this handler was originated by the printer; it could have originated anywhere.

On the PS/2, Int 0Fh is marked as reserved; its functions are allocated elsewhere.

Int 10h

Function 00h
Set Video Mode

Sets the display mode used by the video adapter

Calling Registers: AH   00h
                         AL   Display mode (see table BIOS.3)

Return Registers: Nothing

Comments: This function sets the video mode, clears the screen, and selects the video adapter (if more than one is present). To prevent the screen-clear on EGA, MCGA, and VGA systems, set bit 7 of AL to 1.

Table BIOS.3. *Video Display Modes*

Video Mode	Mode Type	Display Adapter	Pixel Resolution	Box Size	Characters	Colors
00h	Text	CGA	320×200	8×8	40×25	16 (gray)
		EGA(2)	320×350	8×14	40×25	16 (gray)
		MCGA	320×400	8×16	40×25	16
		VGA(1)	360×400	9×16	40×25	16
01h	Text	CGA	320×200	8×8	40×25	16
		EGA(2)	320×350	8×14	40×25	16
		MCGA	320×400	8×16	40×25	16
		VGA(1)	360×400	9×16	40×25	16
02h	Text	CGA	640×200	8×8	80×25	16 (gray)
		EGA(2)	640×350	8×14	80×25	16 (gray)
		MCGA	640×400	8×16	80×25	16
		VGA(1)	720×400	9×16	80×25	16
03h	Text	CGA	640×200	8×8	80×25	16
		EGA(2)	640×350	8×14	80×25	16
		MCGA	640×400	8×16	80×25	16
		VGA(1)	720×400	9×16	80×25	16
04h	Graph	CGA/EGA/ MCGA/VGA	320×200	8×8	40×25	4
05h	Graph	CGA/EGA/ MCGA/VGA	320×200	8×8	40×25	4 (gray)
			320×200	8×8	40×25	4
06h	Graph	CGA/EGA/ MCGA/VGA	640×200	8×8	80×25	2
07h	Text	MDA/EGA	720×350	9×14	80×25	Mono
		VGA(1)	720×400	9×16	80×25	Mono
08h	Graph PC*jr*		160×200	8×8	20×25	16
09h	Graph PC*jr*		320×200	8×8	40×25	16
0Ah	Graph PC*jr*		640×200	8×8	80×25	4
0Bh		—— R E S E R V E D ——				
0Ch		—— R E S E R V E D ——				
0Dh	Graph	EGA/VGA	320×200	8×8	40×25	16
0Eh	Graph	EGA/VGA	640×200	8×8	80×25	16
0Fh	Graph	EGA/VGA	640×350	8×14	80×25	Mono
10h	Graph	EGA/VGA	640×350	8×14	80×25	16
11h	Graph	MCGA/VGA	640×480	8×16	80×30	2
12h	Graph	VGA	640×480	8×16	80×30	16
13h	Graph	MCGA/VGA	320×200	8×8	40×25	256

Notes: (1) Enhanced VGA mode; otherwise, the VGA can emulate either the CGA or the EGA characteristics for this mode.
(2) EGA mode when connected to an enhanced color display; otherwise, emulates the CGA characteristics for this mode.

Int 10h

Function 01h
Set Cursor Type

Used to set the height of the video cursor

Calling Registers: AH   01h
                                CH   Starting (top) scan line for cursor in bits 0–4
                                CL   Ending (bottom) scan line for cursor in bits 0–4

Return Registers: Nothing

Comments: This function sets the type of the text-mode cursor by specifying the cursor's starting and ending scan lines. The video-display system displays a blinking cursor by turning scan lines on and off. A character cell has 8 scan lines in the CGA and 14 in the EGA. To specify the cursor size, the scan lines are numbered from the top, beginning with 0.

Cursor size in text mode is controlled by specifying the start and end scan line numbers of the character box, starting with line 0. The starting scan line is specified in CH; the ending scan line, in CL. On a CGA-equipped machine, for example, if you want to produce a two-line cursor that occupies the lower two lines of the character cell, you would set CX to 0607h.

Many programmers do not realize that the cursor will wrap around inside the character cell on many video adapters. If CH is less than CL, a normal one-piece cursor is displayed. By setting CH greater than CL, you can create a two-piece cursor. On some adapters, attempting such a wraparound disables the cursor display. To disable the cursor on those systems that permit wraparound, set CH=20h (the value for CL need not be changed). On other adapters, you may need to position the cursor to a nondisplayable address such as line 25, column 0.

There is only one cursor type for all video pages. When a program uses different cursors on different video pages, it has to do the bookkeeping itself and explicitly change the cursor when it changes screen pages.

For monochrome video modes, the default starting cursor scan line is 0Bh and the ending scan line is 0Ch. For color video modes, the default starting scan line is 06h and the ending scan line is 07h. These values provide an underline cursor two scan lines high; for a full block cursor, change the starting line number in both cases to 0.

Int 10h

Function 02h
Set Cursor Position

Used to specify the cursor coordinates for the video display

Calling Registers: AH   02h
                                BH   Page number (0 for graphics modes)

DH	Row (zero based)
DL	Column (zero based)

Return Registers: Nothing

Comments: This function positions the cursor for the specified page at a specific location on the text screen. The system permits tracking separate cursor locations for each possible display page, up to a maximum of eight pages in text mode.

Positions are defined relative to the upper left corner (position 0,0) when the screen is in text mode. The lower left corner is position 79,24 in 80×25 text mode and position 39,24 in 40×25 modes. Depending on the video mode, valid ranges for DL and DH are

80-column Text Mode	*40-column Text Mode*
DL = 0 to 79	DL = 0 to 39
DH = 0 to 24	DH = 0 to 24

You can usually turn off the cursor by placing it off the screen (position 0,25 is often used). Be careful about using this trick if you expect to run your programs on an EGA-equipped system in 43-line mode or on a VGA's 50-line display; it might backfire.

You can position the cursor on any page to allow a program to do extensive work on a page that is not displayed on the screen. Then, when the completed screen is ready, you can present it almost instantaneously to the user. Table BIOS.4 shows the valid page numbers for different display types. You can display only those pages for which a specific video adapter has adequate memory. For example, the MDA has only one display page; other display adapters (depending on their mode) can have as many as seven display pages.

Table BIOS.4. *Valid Page Numbers*

Page Numbers	Modes	Adapters
0–7	00–01h	CGA, EGA, MCGA, VGA
0–3	02–03h	CGA
0–7	02–03h	EGA, MCGA, VGA
0	07h	MDA
0–7	07h	EGA, VGA

If you are working in graphics modes, you should set the page number to 0. Use Function 05h to set the currently displayed page.

Int 10h

Function 03h
Read Cursor Position and Configuration

Returns the cursor coordinates and type

| **Calling Registers:** | AH | 03h |
| | BH | Page number |

Return Registers:	BH	Video page number
	CH	Starting line for cursor
	CL	Ending line for cursor
	DH	Row
	DL	Column

Comments: This function gets the current cursor position and returns the same values that were used to position the cursor with Function 02h. In 80×25 mode, position 0,0 is the upper left corner and position 79,24 is the lower right corner; in 40×25 mode, position 39,24 is the lower right corner.

This function also returns the starting and ending rows for the cursor (see Function 01h for information on setting these values). You can use this function to determine the exact cursor type before you change it, so that you can restore it after your program has completed its work. If your program has to coexist in a mixed program environment, restoring the cursor type to what it was when your program started is good programming practice.

Not all programs use the BIOS to handle their cursor positioning. TSR pop-up programs are prone to bypass BIOS and go directly to the video controller chip; when this is done, the information you get back using this BIOS call will be meaningless. There is little you can do to make other programs behave, but at least you can keep your own program from adding to the chaos. *Always* do cursor positioning through the BIOS, at least for the last character written at each operation, so that other programs will be able to restore your position and type properly.

Int 10h

Function 04h
Read Light Pen Position

Returns the coordinates of the light pen

| **Calling Registers:** | AH | 04h |

Return Registers:	AH	0, light pen not down/not triggered
		1, light pen down/triggered
	BX	Pixel column (0–319 or 0–639, depending on mode)

CH	Pixel row (0–199)
CX	Pixel row (0–nnn, depending on mode)
DH	Character row (0–24)
DL	Character column (0–79 or 0–39, depending on mode)

Comments: This function reads the light pen's status and position. Although the mouse is more widely used than the light pen on the PC system, some applications use the light pen (and others could use it). Before using the light pen, you must check to see whether it has been triggered (AH=1). If the light pen has been triggered, its location is given in the other registers; if it has not been triggered, the information contained in the other return registers has no meaning and should be ignored.

The light pen returns a vertical position accurate to only two scan lines. Horizontal accuracy of the light pen is no better than 2 pixels (320 pixels per scan line) or 4 pixels (640 pixels per scan line). Because of this, the light pen is not suitable for high-resolution graphics control. On most monochrome monitors, use of the light pen is not effective because of the long image-retention time of the display phosphors.

The vertical resolution of some video modes is greater than 200 pixels. In such modes, the pixel row will be returned in CX, rather than in CH. Be sure to check the video mode to ascertain which register (CH or CX) will contain the value you should use.

PS/2 systems (MCGA or VGA) do not support the light pen (AH will always return 00h).

Int 10h

Function 05h
Select Active Display Page

Used to select the video display page to be viewed

Calling Registers:

	AH	05h
	AL	Page number selected (see table BIOS.5)

Return Registers: Nothing

Comments: This function, which selects the active (displayed) video page, works with the CGA, MCGA, EGA, and VGA. It cannot be used with monochrome adapters, which have only one display page of memory. Table BIOS.5 shows the valid page numbers.

Note that this function operates differently with the PC*jr* than it does with all other models; the AL register contains a subfunction code rather than a page number, and BX contains CRT and CPU page numbers. The differences are major, and reliable information is absent from most PC reference manuals. See the PC*jr* Technical Reference Manual if you need to do animation on that machine, and don't worry about it otherwise.

Table BIOS.5. Valid Page Numbers

Page Numbers	Modes	Adapters
0–7	00h, 01h	CGA, EGA, MCGA, VGA
0–3	02h, 03h	CGA
0–7	02h, 03h	EGA, MCGA, VGA
0–7	07h, 0Dh	EGA, VGA
0–3	0Eh	EGA, VGA
0–1	0Fh, 10h	EGA, VGA

This function is particularly useful for building spectacular text-screen displays. By building a screen in a nondisplayed page and then calling this function to display it, you can create an instantaneous screen change that gives your program an impressive, snappy look. Most of the important output functions can write to any page.

Int 10h   Function 06h
Scroll Window Up

Used to blank the screen or scroll the text screen up by a specified number of lines in a defined area of the screen

Calling Registers:	AH	06h
	AL	Number of lines to scroll (if zero, entire window is blanked)
	BH	Attribute used for blanked area
	CH	Row, upper left corner
	CL	Column, upper left corner
	DH	Row, lower right corner
	DL	Column, lower right corner

Return Registers: Nothing

Comments: This function (which is the opposite of Int 10h, Function 07h) initializes a window to blank with a specified attribute or scrolls the window up a specified number of lines. The scroll function moves all lines in the window up one line, adds a blank line (with the designated attribute) at the bottom of the window, and eliminates the line that previously was at the top of the window. (If the new line is to be filled with text, your program must do the work.)

You can use this window-oriented function to define rectangular areas to clear (or scroll) on the screen and to set attribute values for the cleared line or lines within a window.

To clear the window, set AL either to 0 or to a value greater than the number of lines in the window. The BIOS listing in early versions of the *IBM Technical Reference Manual* shows this function implemented as a "clear a line, decrement the counter" function until the counter reaches zero. (IBM does not include BIOS listings in the current editions of the technical reference manuals.) Given this algorithm, a "clear window" performed by setting AL to 0 will take longer than if you set AL to 25 (or some other value greater than the height of the rectangle being cleared). Unless your application is extremely screen-intensive, the time differential introduced by setting AL to 0 will not be noticeable. In any event, a simpler, faster way to clear the entire screen is to set the screen mode (Function 00h).

This function affects only the currently active display page.

Int 10h

Function 07h
Scroll Window Down

Used to scroll the text screen down by a specified number of lines in a defined area of the screen

Calling Registers:	AH	07h
	AL	Number of lines to scroll (if zero, entire window is blanked)
	BH	Attribute used for blanked area
	CH	Row, upper left corner
	CL	Column, upper left corner
	DH	Row, lower right corner
	DL	Column, lower right corner

Return Registers: Nothing

Comments: This function initializes a window to blank with a specified attribute or scrolls the window down a specified number of lines. Use this function (which is the opposite of Int 10h, Function 06h) to scroll down the screen. The scroll function moves all lines in the window down one line, adds a blank line (with the designated attribute) at the top of the window, and eliminates the line that previously was at the bottom. (If the new line is to be filled with text, your program must do the work.)

You can use this window-oriented function to define rectangular areas to clear (or scroll) on the screen and to set attribute values for the cleared line or lines within the window.

To clear the window, set AL either to 0 or to a value greater than the number of lines in the window. The BIOS listing in earlier versions of the *IBM Technical Reference Manual* shows this function implemented as a "clear a line, decrement the counter" function until the counter reaches zero. (IBM does not include BIOS listings in the current editions of the technical reference manuals.) Given this algorithm, a "clear window" performed by setting AL to 0 will take longer than if you set AL to 25 (or some other value greater than the height of the rectangle being cleared). Unless your application is extremely screen-intensive, the time differential introduced by setting AL to 0 will not be noticeable. In any event, a simpler, faster way to clear the entire screen is to set the screen mode (Function 00h).

This function affects only the currently active display page.

Int 10h

Function 08h
Read Character and Attribute

Returns the character and attribute at the current cursor position

Calling Registers: AH   08h
                         BH   Display page

Return Registers: AH   Attribute byte
                         AL   ASCII character

Comments: This function reads the character and attribute bytes (for a specified display page) at the cursor's current position. Because you can get this information directly from the screen, you do not have to store information about the screen in your program, nor do you need tricky techniques to pass the screen display from one program to the next. The screen is in the screen memory.

TSR spelling and thesaurus utilities use this function to read the screen, so that they can determine which word to check. But if you are writing this type of utility, be careful. Because some programs access screen memory directly, without updating the screen cursor, the cursor mentioned in the descriptions of Functions 01h through 03h may *not* indicate the word you want.

Int 10h

Function 09h
Write Character and Attribute

Stores a specific number of copies of a single character with a defined attribute, starting at the cursor position

Calling Registers: AH   09h
                         AL   Character
                         BH   Display page
                         BL   Attribute byte of character in AL
                         CX   Number of characters to write

Return Registers: Nothing

Comments: This function writes character and attribute bytes to the display, starting at the cursor's current position on a specified display page. Use it to write many characters quickly to the screen (the characters and attribute must all be the same).

In text mode, the function will write as many as 65,536 characters to the screen. (The largest normal text-mode display, 132 columns by 50 rows, can hold only 6600 characters on one display page; the rest overflow onto following display pages if they exist.) As the function writes characters, it wraps lines — continuing from the end of one line to the beginning of the next without stopping. In graphics mode, the function goes only to the end of the line it was on at the start. While each character appears on the screen, the cursor position does not change.

An interesting way to use this function is to clear an area on-screen for text entry just before you call the input character function. You can set this area with a different color attribute to make it stand out. Because this function can clear an area much larger than the screen, the area can be as large as needed for data entry. Because the cursor does not move, you do not need to reposition it before you enter data.

In graphics modes, use the video attribute byte in BL to determine the color of the character written. But if bit 7 is set, the value in BL is XORed with the background color when the character is displayed (which can be extremely useful). You can erase a character from the screen by writing it to the display in graphics mode and then rewriting it with bit 7 on.

In graphics modes, the characters for codes 80–FFh come from a bit-map table whose address is stored in interrupt vector 1Fh. By resetting this pointer to a table of your own, you can create your own table of characters. (See Function 1Fh for a discussion of the bit-map character table.) The characters for codes 00–7Fh are generated from a ROM character table that cannot be reset (EGA and VGA users *can* reset normal display fonts; see Int 10h Function 11h).

Int 10h
Function 0Ah
Write Character at Cursor

Stores a specific number of copies of a single character, starting at the cursor position

Calling Registers:

	AH	0Ah
	AL	Character
	BH	Display page number
	BL	Color of character in AL (in graphics modes only)
	CX	Number of characters/attribute words to write

Return Registers: Nothing

Comments: This function (which is identical to Function 09h, except that you cannot set the attribute byte for the character in text mode) writes a number of characters at the cursor's current position on a specified display page. The attribute at the position where each character is written remains unchanged.

Use this function when you want to write many characters quickly to the screen. In text mode, the function will write as many as 65,536 characters to the screen. As the function writes characters, it wraps lines (continuing from the end of one line to the beginning of the next without stopping). In graphics modes, the function will go only to the end of the line on which it started. The cursor position remains unchanged throughout the operation.

In graphics modes, BL determines the color of the character written. If bit 7 is set, however, the value in BL is XORed with the background color when the character is displayed. This feature can be extremely useful for erasing a character from the screen—you simply write a character to the display in graphics mode and then rewrite it with bit 7 on.

In graphics modes, the characters for codes 80–FFh come from a bit-map table whose address is stored in interrupt vector 1Fh. By resetting this pointer to a table of your own, you can create your own table of characters. (See Function 1Fh for a discussion of the bit-map character table.) The characters for codes 00–7Fh are generated from a ROM character table that cannot be reset (EGA/VGA users *can* reset normal display fonts; see Int 10h Function 11h).

Int 10h

Function 0Bh
Set Color Palette

Selects colors for the graphics display

Calling Registers: AH   0Bh
                          BH   Color palette ID being set
                                    0, BL has background and border color
                                    1, BL has palette color
                          BL   Color value to be used for that color ID

Return Registers: Nothing

Comments: This function, when BH=1, selects or sets the contents of the color palette for medium-resolution (4-color) graphics displays such as mode 4. The function has no direct effect on memory. Rather, by interpreting the codes and changing the colors, this function affects the way that the 6845 CRT controller interprets the video memory. By using this function to rapidly change the palette, you can produce a flashing display. Function 10h provides additional palette control for the PC*jr*, EGA, VGA, and MCGA.

In text mode (BH=0), this function sets the screen's border color.

Table BIOS.6 lists the valid color palettes the function can set.

Table BIOS.6. *Color Palettes*

Palette	Pixel	Color
0	0	Same as background
	1	Green
	2	Red
	3	Brown
1	0	Same as background
	1	Cyan
	2	Magenta
	3	White

Int 10h   Function 0Ch
Write Graphics Pixel

Writes a single pixel to the screen at the current cursor position

Calling Registers:	AH	0Ch
	AL	Color value
	BH	Page number
	CX	Pixel column number
	DX	Pixel row number

Return Registers: Nothing

Comments: This function, which writes a single pixel to the screen at a specified graphics coordinate, is the most basic graphics-plotting service. Complex graphics-handling functions are built up by collections of operations that set the value of screen pixels.

In medium-resolution modes, the exact effect of the function depends on the palette in use. High-resolution CGA (mode 6) can show only black and white colors for pixels; mode 4 or 5 allows the pixels to be set from a four-color palette. With this function, if bit 7 of AL is set to 1, the new color is XORed with the current pixel; you can erase that pixel by writing it a second time.

The limits on the screen position that this function can address are 0–199 or 0–349 in the vertical and 0–319 or 0–639 in the horizontal, depending on the graphics mode. Refer to table BIOS.3 for details on screen limits by mode. Table BIOS.7 gives the valid page numbers (BH register) used by this function.

Table BIOS.7. Valid Page Numbers		
Page Numbers	**Modes**	**Adapters**
0–7	0Dh	EGA, VGA
0–3	0Eh	EGA, VGA
0–1	0Fh, 10h	EGA, VGA

Int 10h   Function 0Dh
Read Graphics Pixel

Returns the color of the pixel at a specific screen coordinate

Calling Registers: AH   0Dh
                          BH   Page number
                          CX   Pixel column number
                          DX   Pixel row number

Return Registers: AL Color value

Comments: This function, which gets the value of the pixel at the specified graphics coordinates, is often used in video games and advanced graphics applications. In video games, it is useful for collision detection. When advanced graphics programs move a graphic object on the screen, they can use this function to detect boundaries.

The limits for addressing are 0–199 or 0–349 in the vertical and 0–319 or 0–639 in the horizontal, depending on the video mode. Refer to table BIOS.3 for details on the addressing limits of the various video modes. Refer to table BIOS.7 for the valid page numbers that can be set in BH.

Int 10h   Function 0Eh
Write Text in Teletype Mode

Outputs characters with limited control processing

Calling Registers: AH   0Eh
                          AL   Character
                          BH   Display page (alpha modes)
                          BL   Foreground color (graphics modes)

Return Registers: Nothing

Comments: This function writes text to the screen as though the screen were an old-fashioned teletype machine. The function interprets the ASCII character codes for the bell (07h), backspace (08h), carriage return (0Dh), and line feed (0Ah) in order to ring the console bell, backspace the cursor, move the cursor to the beginning of the line, or move to the next line, respectively. All other control characters, including the tab and form-feed characters, are displayed (smiley faces, pointing arrows, and so on) rather than acted upon. After the write, the cursor moves to the next character position.

Despite its somewhat archaic designation (which may make you think of the old teletypewriter machines), this function is useful. DOS uses it in the console driver to put operating-system text and messages on the screen.

For Function 0Eh to work on PC BIOS ROMs dated 4/24/81 and 10/19/81, the BH register *must* point to the currently displayed page. With later ROMs, this function works on either displayed or nondisplayed pages.

The significant difference between this and other display functions is that Function 0Eh automatically handles the normal control functions of the bell, backspace, line feed, and carriage return, as well as line wrap and scrolling. Although it does not allow you to change the video attributes of what you write, this is the best function for simple output.

Even if you are working on a nondisplayed page, the bell character will sound the system bell to call attention to any background operations. Unfortunately, this function does *not* expand tab characters to spaces.

Int 10h   Function 0Fh
Get Current Display Mode

Returns the video display mode, screen width, and active page

Calling Registers: AH   0Fh

Return Registers: AH   Number of columns on the screen
                       AL   Display mode (refer to table BIOS.3)
                       BH   Active display page

Comments: This function, which gets the video controller's display mode, including the number of character columns and the current display page, is most useful during program initialization. You use it to determine the present setting of the display system so that when your program is finished, it can return the display system to its original display mode.

Knowing the current display mode is especially important if you are writing TSR (terminate and stay resident) utilities that will pop up on the screen during another application. Your utility may be working with a character screen, but the program that had control when your utility started may have been using a mode that is not what you need to use. Early TSRs failed to handle the screen display properly—in many cases, the resulting display looked as though a bomb had exploded inside the computer.

Although you can use Function 0Fh to determine the width of the screen, we recommend that you set the mode you want instead of trying to work out what is already there.

Int 10h **Function 10h**
Set Palette Registers

Controls operations on the color-palette registers in PC*jr*, EGA, VGA, and MCGA video controllers

Calling Registers:	AH	10h
	AL	00h, set palette register
	BX	0712h is only allowable value (MCGA only)
	BH	Color value
	BL	Palette register to set
	AL	01h, set border color register (not on MCGA)
	BH	Color value
	AL	02h, set all registers and border (not on MCGA)
	ES:DX	Pointer to 17-byte color list
	AL	03h, toggle blink/intensity
	BL	Blink/intensity bit
		00h Enable intensity
		01h Enable blinking
	AL	07h, read palette register (VGA only)
	BL	Palette register to read (0–15)
	AL	08h, read overscan (border) register (VGA only)
	AL	09h, read palette registers and border (VGA only)
	ES:DX	Pointer to 17-byte table for values
	AL	10h, set individual color register (MCGA and VGA only)
	BX	Color register to set
	CH	Green value to set
	CL	Blue value to set
	DH	Red value to set
	AL	12h, set block of color registers (MCGA and VGA only)
	BX	First color register to set
	CX	Number of color registers to set
	ES:DX	Pointer to color values

AL	13h, select color page (VGA only)
BL	00h, select paging mode
BH	Paging mode
	00h 4 register blocks of 64 registers
	01h 16 register blocks of 16 registers

AL	13h, select color page (VGA only)
BL	01h, select page
BH	Page number
	00–03h for 64 register blocks
	00–0Fh for 16 register blocks

AL	15h, read color register (MCGA and VGA only)
BX	Color register to read

AL	17h, read block of color registers (MCGA and VGA only)
BX	First color register to read
CX	Number of color registers to read
ES:DX	Pointer to buffer to hold color register values

AL	18h, update video DAC mask register (MCGA and VGA only)
BL	DAC mask register value

AL	19h, read video DAC mask register (MCGA and VGA only)

AL	1Ah, read color page state (VGA only)

AL	1Bh, sum color values to gray shades (MCGA and VGA only)
BX	First color register to sum
CX	Number of color registers to sum

Return Registers: Subfunctions 07h–08h
BH	Value read

Subfunction 09h
ES:DX	Pointer to 17-byte table

Subfunction 15h
CH	Green value read
CL	Blue value read
DH	Red value read

Subfunction 17h
ES:DX	Pointer to color table

Subfunction 19h
BL   Value read

Subfunction 1Ah
BL   Current paging mode
CX   Current page

Comments: On the PC*jr*, MCGA, EGA, and VGA display systems, this function, with its 17 subfunctions, controls the correspondence of colors to pixel values. Although listed as reserved in the IBM Personal Computer AT BIOS, this function is an extension to the BIOS, applicable to EGA and VGA display systems.

A detailed explanation of this function is beyond the scope of this book. If you are interested in programming display systems directly, refer to the bibliography for further guidance.

Some subfunctions (as designated by the contents of AL when calling this function) are not available on the PS/2 Model 30 system. These subfunctions are 01h, 02h, 07h, 08h, 09h, 13h, and 1Ah.

| **Int 10h** | **Function 11h** |
| | *Character Generator* |

Supports the graphics character-generator functions, allowing a program to set up its own character-generator tables

Calling Registers:	AL	00h, user alpha load (EGA, VGA, and MCGA)
	BH	Number of bytes per character
	BL	Block to load
	CX	Count to store
	DX	Character offset into table
	ES:BP	Pointer to user table
	AL	01h, ROM monochrome set (EGA and VGA)
	BL	Block to load
	AL	02h, ROM 8 × 8 double dot (EGA, VGA, and MCGA)
	BL	Block to load
	AL	03h, set block specifier (PC*jr*, EGA, VGA, and MCGA)
	BL	Character-generator block selection
	AL	04h, load 8 × 16 ROM (VGA and MCGA)

AL	10h, user alpha load (EGA, VGA, and MCGA)
BH	Number of bytes per character
BL	Block to load
CX	Count to store
DX	Character offset into table
ES:BP	Pointer to user table
AL	11h, ROM monochrome set (EGA and VGA)
BL	Block to load
AL	12h, ROM 8 × 8 double dot (EGA, VGA, and MCGA)
BL	Block to load
AL	14h, load 8 × 16 ROM (VGA and MCGA)
AL	20h, set user graphics character pointer at 1Fh (EGA, VGA, and MCGA)
ES:BP	Pointer to user table
AL	21h, set user graphics character pointer at 43h (EGA, VGA, and MCGA)
BL	Row specifier
CX	Bytes per character
ES:BP	Pointer to user table
AL	22h, ROM 8 × 14 set (EGA, VGA, and MCGA)
BL	Row specifier
AL	23h, ROM 8 × 8 double dot (EGA, VGA, and MCGA)
BL	Row specifier
AL	30h, font information (EGA, VGA, and MCGA)
BH	Font pointer

Return Registers: Varies by subfunction

Comments: Although listed as reserved in the IBM Personal Computer AT BIOS, this function is an extension to the BIOS, applicable to EGA and VGA display systems.

A detailed explanation of this function is beyond the scope of this book. If you are interested in programming display systems directly, refer to the bibliography for further guidance.

Some subfunctions (as designated by the contents of AL when calling this function) are not available on the PS/2 Model 30 system. These subfunctions are 01h, 10h, 11h, 12h, and 22h.

Int 10h   Function 12h
Alternate Select

Provides additional control of EGA (and PS/2 emulations of EGA)

Calling Registers:	AH	12h
	AL	00h, enable subfunctions 31h–34h and 36h
		01h, disable subfunctions 31h–34h and 36h
	BL	10h, return EGA information
	BL	20h, select alternate print-screen routine
	BL	30h, select scan lines for A/N modes
	AL	Number of scan lines
		00h 200 scan lines
		01h 350 scan lines
		02h 400 scan lines
	BL	31h, control palette loading during set mode command operation
	BL	32h, video on/off
	BL	33h, summing to gray shades on/off
	BL	34h, cursor emulation
	BL	35h, video display switching
	AL	00h, initial adapter video off
		01h, initial planar video on
		02h, switch active video off
		03h, switch inactive video on
	ES:DX	Pointer to 128-byte save area (for AL = 00h, 02h, or 03h)
	BL	36h, video refresh control
Return Registers:	Subfunction 10h	
	BH	Default BIOS video mode
		00h Color
		01h Monochrome
	BL	Amount of EGA video RAM
		00h 64K
		01h 128K
		02h 192K
		03h 256K

CH	Feature bits
CL	Configuration switch setting

Subfunctions 30h–36h

AL	12h

Comments: Although listed as reserved in the IBM Personal Computer AT BIOS, this function is an extension to the BIOS, applicable to EGA/VGA display systems.

A detailed explanation of this function is beyond the scope of this book. If you are interested in programming display systems directly, refer to the bibliography for further guidance.

Int 10h   Function 13h
Write String

Writes an ASCII string to the display

Calling Registers:

AH	13h
AL	Write mode (see table BIOS.8)
BH	Video page
BL	Attribute (write modes 0 and 1)
CX	Length of string
DH	Row at which to write string
DL	Column at which to write string
ES:BP	Pointer to string

Return Registers: Nothing

Table BIOS.8. Write String Modes

Mode	Comments
0	Attribute in BL. String is characters only. Cursor not updated.
1	Attribute in BL. String is characters only. Cursor updated.
2	String alternates characters and attributes. Cursor not updated.
3	String alternates characters and attributes. Cursor updated.

Comments: This function, *which is available only on PC XTs with BIOS dates of 1/10/86 or later, on the Personal Computer AT, and on machines in the PS/2 family,* writes a string of characters to the currently active display.

Use this function to designate a string (with embedded or global attributes for the characters) and then write it to the screen. Because it relies on other BIOS functions to actually write the string, this function is not particularly fast.

Because this function uses the Teletype interrupt (Int 10h, Function 0Eh) for output, it responds to the backspace (ASCII 08h), bell (ASCII 07h), line feed (ASCII 0Ah), and carriage return (ASCII 0Dh) characters by moving the cursor back one space, ringing the console bell, moving down one line, or moving the cursor to the beginning of the current line, respectively. It also performs line wrap and scrolling.

Int 10h

Function 1Ah
Read/Write Display Codes

Reads or writes display codes

Calling Registers:	AH	1Ah
	AL	00h, read display codes
	BH	Alternate display code
	AL	01h, write display codes
	BL	Active display code

Return Registers:	If reading display codes:	
	BH	Alternate display code
	BL	Active display code
	If writing display codes:	
	AL	1Ah, codes were changed

Comments: This function, supported only on the PS/2 models, permits the display codes to be read or written. The codes used are

Value	Meaning
00h	No display
01h	Mono with mono monitor
02h	CGA with color monitor
03h	Reserved
04h	EGA with color monitor
05h	EGA with mono monitor
06h	Professional Graphics System with color monitor
07h	VGA with analog mono monitor (not on Model 30)
08h	VGA with analog color monitor (not on Model 30)
09h	Reserved
0Ah	Reserved
0Bh	MCGA with analog mono monitor (Model 30)
0Ch	MCGA with analog color monitor (Model 30)
0Dh–FEh	Reserved for expansion
FFh	Unknown type of monitor

These codes are most useful in determining the type of monitor connected to a system.

Int 10h   Function 1Bh
Get Display State

Provides 51 bytes of detailed information concerning the video system

Calling Registers: AH   1Bh
                         ES:DI   Point to 64-byte buffer to receive video state
                                   information

Return Registers: AL   1Bh if buffer content valid

Comments: This function works only on the PS/2 series of computers. Even though only 51 bytes of defined data are returned, you need a 64-byte buffer because there are 13 bytes of reserved space in the buffer. Perhaps this is for future system expansion use.

   A detailed explanation of this function is beyond the scope of this book. If you are interested in programming display systems directly, refer to the bibliography for further guidance.

Int 10h   Function 1Ch
Save/Restore Display State

Saves or restores the status of the VGA display system

Calling Registers: AH   1Ch
                         AL   00h, return buffer size needed
                                   01h, save video state
                                   02h, restore video state
                         CX   Bit map of requested states:

```
FEDCBA98 76543210
........ .......1    Video hardware
........ ......1.    Video BIOS
........ .....1..    Video DAC and color
                     registers
00000000 00000...    Not used
```

                         ES:BX   If AL=01 or 02, point to buffer for
                                   video state information

Return Registers: AL   1Ch (if results are valid)
                            BL   Number of 64-byte blocks required for save
                                      buffer

Comments: This function works only on the PS/2 series, models 50, 60, and 80. It is used to save or restore VGA-specific status information such as the state of the video digital-to-analog converters, the color registers, and the driver data area. The state of the VGA is altered while saving; you should follow saves by a restore operation.

   This function returns 1Ch in AL if the results are valid; any other value indicates that the function is not supported (i.e., a VGA is not installed, or a nonstandard VGA is installed).

   A more detailed explanation of this function is beyond the scope of this book. If you are interested in programming display systems directly, refer to the bibliography for further guidance.

Int 11h
Get Equipment Status

Returns a rudimentary list of equipment attached to the computer

Calling Registers: None

Return Registers: AX   Equipment status word (see table BIOS.9)

Comments: During the booting process, the hardware status byte is set to indicate what equipment is attached to the computer. For example, bits 6 and 7 represent the number of floppy disk drives attached to the system. This status byte does not change after you boot the system.

   This function is particularly useful to programmers who must adapt their programs to existing equipment. By checking for serial ports, disk drives, printers, and other equipment, your program can simplify the user's interaction with the program. Programs that have to ask for the characteristics of the system rely on the user to understand the PC well enough to answer the questions. The fewer questions your program has to ask, the easier it is to use.

   As you can see from table BIOS.9, the meaning of the different bits varies according to computer type. To determine which type of machine you are using, check the computer's signature byte at address FFFF:FFFE.

Table BIOS.9. *Equipment Status Word*

Bits	Meaning
0	Disk drive installed = 1
1	Math coprocessor installed = 1
2–3	System board RAM
	00 = 16K
	01 = 32K
	10 = 48K
	11 = 64K
2	Pointing device installed = 1 (PS/2 line only)
3	Not used (PS/2 line only)
4–5	Initial video mode
	01 = 40×25 color
	10 = 80×25 color
	11 = 80×25 mono
6–7	Number of disk drives (if bit 0 = 1)
	00 = 1 drive attached
	01 = 2 drives attached
	10 = 3 drives attached
	11 = 4 drives attached
8	Not used
9–11	Number of serial cards attached
12	Game adapter installed = 1
12	Not used (PS/2 line only)
13	Not used
13	Internal modem installed = 1 (PS/2 line only)
14–15	Number of printers attached

Int 12h

Get Memory Size

Returns the number of contiguous 1K memory blocks available

Calling Registers: None

Return Registers: AX   Number of 1K memory blocks

Comments: This interrupt returns the number of *contiguous* 1K memory blocks found during start-up memory checks of the system. Contrary to what has been written about this interrupt, it has nothing to do with the switches on the mother-board of a standard PC or compatible.

Because the memory is determined from the power-on self test (POST), an incorrect number may be returned if defective memory causes the memory test to fail. (Should this happen, the interrupt will return the number of blocks found before the error.) The POST assumes that all installed memory is functional and that memory in the range of 0 to 640K is contiguous.

The method used to determine available memory depends on the system, but generally consists of an attempt to write to and then read from a memory block. As soon as the write-then-read cycle fails, the end of memory is assumed to have been reached.

When there is more than 640K of memory, Int 15h, Function 88h must be called to determine extended memory size.

On PS/2 systems, this interrupt returns a maximum amount of memory of up to 640K, minus the amount of memory set aside for the extended BIOS data area (EBDA). The EBDA may be as little as 1K. (See Int 15h, Function C1h for more information.)

Int 13h   Function 00h
Reset Disk System

Resets the controller for the disk drive

Calling Registers: AH   00h
                      DL   Drive number (zero based)
                                    Bit 7 = 0 for a diskette, 1 for a fixed disk

Return Registers: Carry flag clear if successful

                      Carry flag set if error
                      AH   Return code (see table BIOS.10)

Comments: This function resets the disk controller in preparation for disk I/O. (A reset of the disk system is essential for handling critical disk-access errors.) This function recalibrates the disk by forcing the drive to pull the heads to track 0 and to start the next I/O operation from track 0.

Invoking this operation does not cause the disk system to react immediately. Rather, a reset flag is set in the disk controller to recalibrate the drives the next time they are used. The recalibration causes the grinding sound one sometimes hears after a disk error.

When the drive number in DL has the high bit set, the diskette system will be reset, after which the hard disk (fixed disk) will be reset. The error return will refer to the hard disk reset. The diskette status can be found in the BIOS data area, at 0040:0041h.

This function is best used when an error has been returned in an attempt to use the diskette system. When a problem occurs, the reset function should be called and the function tried again. Depending on the program, you may want to do several retries. If you get consistent failure, you should notify the user and end the retry cycle.

Int 13h

Function 01h
Get Disk System Status

Returns the disk status byte

Calling Registers: AH   01h
                       DL   Drive code (PS/2 and extended BIOS only)

Return Registers: AH   Status byte (see table BIOS.10)

Table BIOS.10. Disk Controller Status Bits

Bit 76543210	Meaning
.......1	Illegal command to driver
......1.	Address mark not located (bad sector)
......11	Write-protected disk
.....1..	Requested sector not found
.....11.	Diskette change line active
....1...	DMA overrun
....1..1	DMA attempt across 64K boundary
....11..	Invalid media
...1....	CRC error on disk read
..1.....	Controller error
.1......	Seek failure
1.......	Disk time out (failure to respond, drive not ready)

Comments: The status of the controller is set after each disk operation. With this function, your program can get the status of the disk as of the most recent disk operation. For example, you can use this function to detect a write-protected disk in the drive by examining bit 1.

Int 13h   Function 02h
Read Disk Sectors

Retrieves a specific number of disk sectors

Calling Registers:

	AH	02h
	AL	Number of sectors to transfer
	ES:BX	Pointer to user's disk buffer
	CH	Track number (see comments)
	CL	Sector number
	DH	Head number
	DL	Drive number (bit 7 set if hard disk)

Return Registers: Carry flag clear if successful

	AH	0
	AL	Number of sectors transferred

Carry flag set if error

	AH	Status byte (refer to table BIOS.10)

Comments: This function transfers one or more sectors from the disk into memory. Reading the disk is such a standard operation that the lack of any error checking beyond the disk drive number is surprising. All input parameters should be checked carefully before you issue a call for service because passing an invalid value can lead to unpredictable results.

When this function is used with a hard disk, the track number is ten bits rather than eight. The upper two bits are passed to the function in the high two bits of the CL register.

Note: When you use this function, a peculiarity of the system is that the error code AH=9 (DMA Boundary Error) can occur when the DMA operation crosses a memory offset address that ends in three zeros. This type of memory boundary must correspond to a sector boundary in the disk read.

This DMA boundary problem is especially troublesome with the FORMAT.COM program supplied with some versions of DOS; it generates an error message that track 0 is bad and the disk is unusable. If it appears, it can be corrected by adding or removing FILES= or BUFFERS= values from the CONFIG.SYS file and rebooting to change the position in memory of the disk buffer used by FORMAT.COM.

Int 13h   Function 03h
Write Disk Sectors

Writes a specified area of memory to a designated number of disk sectors

Calling Registers:	AH	03h
	AL	Number of sectors to transfer
	ES:BX	Pointer to user's disk buffer
	CH	Track number (see comments)
	CL	Sector number
	DH	Head number
	DL	Drive number (bit 7 set if hard disk)

Return Registers:	Carry flag clear if successful	
	AH	0
	AL	Number of sectors transferred

	Carry flag set if error	
	AH	Status byte (refer to table BIOS.10)

Comments: This function writes one or more sectors from memory to the disk. Except for the disk drive number, none of the values passed to this function are checked for validity. Checking for validity is the programmer's responsibility. Writing to the disk is such a standard operation that this lack of error checking is surprising. You should check all input parameters carefully before you issue a call for service because passing an invalid value may lead to unpredictable results.

When this function is used with a hard disk, the track number is ten bits rather than eight. The upper two bits are passed to the function in the high two bits of the CL register.

IBM documentation indicates that the number of sectors stored in AL is not required when you use this function on the PC XT 286. Leaving AL set will not matter in this case because the passed values are not checked for validity.

Note: When you use this function, a peculiarity of the system is that the error code AH=9 (DMA Boundary Error) can occur when the DMA operation crosses a memory offset address that ends in three zeros. This type of memory boundary must correspond to a sector boundary in the disk write.

Int 13h
Function 04h
Verify Disk Sectors

Checks accuracy of the CRC values of a specified number of disk sectors

Calling Registers:	AH	04h
	AL	Number of sectors to verify
	CH	Track number (see comments)
	CL	Sector number
	DH	Head number
	DL	Drive number (bit 7 set if hard disk)

Return Registers: Carry flag clear if successful
                        AH   0

                        Carry flag set if error
                        AH   Status byte (refer to table BIOS.10)

Comments: Use this function to verify the address fields of the specified disk sectors. No data is transferred to or from the disk during this operation. When this function is used with a hard disk, the track number is ten bits rather than eight. The upper two bits are passed to the function in the high two bits of the CL register.

Disk verification, which takes place on the disk, does not (as some people believe) involve verification of the data on the disk against the data in memory. This function does not read or write a disk; rather, it causes the system to read the data in the designated sector or sectors and to check its computed CRC (cyclic redundancy check) against data stored on the disk.

When a sector is written to disk, the CRC is computed and stored on the disk as part of the sector header information. Because the verify operation checks this value, it is highly probable, but never *certain*, that the data in the disk sector is good.

As with most of the other disk functions, the disk drive number is the only input data that is checked for errors. Errors in input will cause unpredictable results.

This function can be used to check the disk drive for the presence of a readable disk. If the drive does not contain a properly formatted disk, the function will return an error.

Int 13h   Function 05h
                  Format Disk Track

Formats a single disk track

Calling Registers: AH   05h
                         ES:BX   Pointer to track address field list
                         CH   Track number
                         DH   Head number
                         DL   Drive number

Return Registers: AH   Return code (refer to table BIOS.10)

Comments: This function formats a disk track by initializing the disk address fields and data sectors. (See Chapter 8, "Disks," for more information.) Be sure to use this function with great care; it can cause the loss of some or all disk storage on your machine. Test it on a stripped-down system (floppy disk only) until you are absolutely certain of its correctness.

Formatting a disk track is only one part of formatting a disk. To format a disk, you must format each track correctly but, if the disk is to be used with DOS, you must also write the basic DOS disk structure to the disk (including the boot sector, initial FAT tables, and the disk's root directory).

The disk formatting operation is controlled by the track address field list (pointed to by ES:BX). The table is laid out as a series of 4-byte entries, one for each sector on the track. Each 4-byte entry is laid out like this:

Byte Offset	Meaning
00h	Track number
01h	Head number
02h	Sector number
03h	Size code

If this function is used with a hard disk, the track number is ten bits rather than eight. The upper two bits are passed to the function in the high two bits of the sector number.

Table BIOS.11 shows allowable size codes; the entries are laid out in the order in which the sectors will appear on disk. This order need not be sequential; the sectors can be interleaved to improve disk access performance (see Chapter 8, "Disks").

Table BIOS.11. *Track Address Field Size Code*

Size Code	Bytes per Sector
0	128
1	256
2	512
3	1024

Int 13h

Function 06h
Format Cylinder and Set Bad Sector Flags

Formats the specified cylinder only and sets flags for any bad sectors found in the process

Calling Registers:

	AH	08h
	AL	Interleave factor
	CH	Cylinder to format
	CL	Sector number
	DH	Head number
	DL	Drive number (zero based)
		Bit 7 = 0 for a diskette, 1 for a fixed disk

Return Registers: Carry flag clear if successful

Carry flag set if error
AH   Error status (refer to table BIOS.10)

Comments: This function, *which is available only on PC XTs with BIOS dates of 1/10/86 or later, on the Personal Computer AT, and on machines in the PS/2 family,* reformats the specified cylinder, only, of a drive. All data in the reformatted area will be lost. Extreme care should be taken in the use of this function.

Int 13h   Function 07h
Format Drive from Specified Cylinder

Formats the specified cylinder only and sets flags for any bad sectors found in the process

Calling Registers: AH   08h
AL   Interleave factor
CH   Cylinder to format
CL   Sector number
DH   Head number
DL   Drive number (zero based)
Bit 7 = 0 for a diskette, 1 for a fixed disk

Return Registers: Carry flag clear if successful

Carry flag set if error
AH   Error status (refer to table BIOS.10)

Comments: This function, *which is available only on PC XTs with BIOS dates of 1/10/86 or later, on the Personal Computer AT, and on machines in the PS/2 family,* reformats the specified cylinder and all higher-numbered cylinders of a drive. All data in the reformatted area will be lost. Extreme care should be taken in the use of this function.

Int 13h   Function 08h
Return Disk Drive Parameters

Returns information about a specified disk drive

Calling Registers: AH   08h
DL   Drive number (zero based)
Bit 7 = 0 for a diskette, 1 for a fixed disk

Return Registers: Carry flag clear if successful

          CH   Number of tracks per side

          CL   Number of sectors per track

          DH   Number of sides

          DL   Number of consecutive drives attached

          ES:DI Pointer to 11-byte diskette parameter table

          BL   Valid drive-type value from CMOS

               01h $5^{1}/_{4}$ inch, 360K, 40 track

               02h $5^{1}/_{4}$ inch, 1.2M, 80 track

               03h $3^{1}/_{2}$ inch, 720K, 80 track

               04h $3^{1}/_{2}$ inch, 1.44M, 80 track

        Carry flag set if error

          AH   Error status (refer to table BIOS.10)

Comments: This function, *which is available only on the Personal Computer AT and the PS/2,* is used to obtain the physical parameters of the disk.

    Setting bit 7 of the DL register on calling the function refers to hard disks.

    This function allows you to check the characteristics of the disk in the designated drive. On return, the table pointed to by ES:DI has the format shown in table BIOS.12.

Table BIOS.12. Disk Media Characteristic Table

Offset	Meaning
00h	First specify byte
01h	Second specify byte
02h	Number of timer ticks to wait before turning off drive motor
03h	Number of bytes per sector
	00h = 128
	01h = 256
	02h = 512
	03h = 1024
04h	Sectors per track
05h	Gap length
06h	Data length
07h	Gap length for format
08h	Fill byte for format
09h	Head settle time in milliseconds
0Ah	Motor startup time in $^{1}/_{8}$ second

Int 13h

Function 09h
Initialize Fixed Disk Table

Sets the values in the specified fixed disk table to their default values

Calling Registers:	AH	09h
	DL	Fixed disk drive number

Return Registers: Carry flag clear if successful
AH   0

Carry flag set if error
AH   Status byte (refer to table BIOS.10)

Comments: Use this function, *which is available only on the Personal Computer AT and PS/2 line and works only on fixed (hard) disks,* to set the hard disk drive's physical parameters. The drive numbers used are not the standard BIOS drive numbers; rather, they are taken from a special series of numbers for fixed disks only (80h corresponds to the first disk, 81h to the second, and so on). Using an out-of-range disk drive number will lead to unpredictable results.

    Initialization information for the drive is taken from the fixed disk parameter tables. Interrupt vector 41h points to the table for disk 1; vector 46h points to the table for disk 2. If a reference is made for any other disk, the function returns an "invalid command" status byte in AH.

Int 13h

Function 0Ah
Read Long Sector

Reads a specified number of long sectors from a hard disk

Calling Registers:	AH	0Ah
	AL	Number of sectors
	ES:BX	Pointer to data buffer
	CH	Track (see comments)
	CL	Sector
	DH	Head number
	DL	Fixed disk drive number

Return Registers: Carry flag clear if successful
    AH   0

Carry flag set if error
    AH   Status byte (refer to table BIOS.10)

Comments: This function, *which is available only on the Personal Computer AT and works only on fixed (hard) disks,* reads long sectors from the hard disk into memory. Long sectors are standard sectors that contain four bytes of error-correcting code in addition to regular data.

This function, like the other read/write functions, is susceptible to the DMA boundary error (AH=9) that can occur when a DMA crosses a memory offset that ends in three zeros. Because there is no error checking of parameters with this function, errors in parameter values can lead to unexpected results.

The drive numbers used are not the standard BIOS drive numbers; rather, they are taken from a special series of numbers for fixed disks only (80h corresponds to the first disk, 81h to the second, and so on). Using an out-of-range disk drive number will lead to unpredictable results.

Table BIOS.13 gives the valid ranges for all parameters that can be passed to the function. *Note especially that the track number (CH and CL registers) is a 10-bit number stored with the high-order bits in bits 6 and 7 of register CL and the eight low-order bits in register CH.* The sector address (register CL) is a 6-bit number stored in bits 0–5 (the bits not used by the track number).

Table BIOS.13. Valid Parameter Ranges

Register	Parameter	Valid range
AL	# sectors	1–121
CH/CL	Track	0–1023
CL	Sector	1–17
DH	Head	0–15
DL	Drive	80h, 81h, etc.

Figure BIOS.1 shows how the bits in CH and CL are interpreted by this function.

Int 13h   Function 0Bh
Write Long Sector

Writes a specified number of long sectors to the hard disk

Calling Registers:

AH	0Bh
AL	Number of sectors
ES:BX	Pointer to data buffer
CH	Track (see comments)
CL	Sector
DH	Head number
DL	Fixed disk drive number

Return Registers: Carry flag clear if successful
AH   0

Carry flag set if error
AH   Status byte (refer to table BIOS.10)

Comments: *This function is available only on the Personal Computer AT and works only on fixed (hard) disks.* Long sectors are standard sectors that contain four bytes of error-correcting code in addition to regular data. This function, like the other read/write functions, is susceptible to the DMA boundary error (AH=9) which can occur when a DMA crosses a memory offset that ends in three zeros. Because there is no error checking of parameters, errors in parameter values can lead to unexpected results.

The drive numbers used are not the standard BIOS drive numbers; rather, they are taken from a special series of numbers for fixed disks only (80h corresponds to the first disk, 81h to the second, and so on). Using an out-of-range disk drive number will lead to unpredictable results.

The track number is ten bits rather than eight. The upper two bits are passed to the function in the high two bits of the sector number.

Fig. BIOS.1. *Bits in CH and CL, as interpreted by Int 13h, Function 0Ah.*

Int 13h   Function 0Ch
Seek Cylinder

Moves read/write head to a specified cylinder

Calling Registers: AH   0Ch
CH   Low-order track
CL   High-order track
DH   Head number
DL   Fixed disk drive number

Return Registers: Carry flag clear if successful
AH   0

Carry flag set if error
AH   Status byte (refer to table BIOS.10)

Comments: This function, *which is available only on the Personal Computer AT and works only on fixed (hard) disks,* moves the read/write heads to a specified cylinder. The drive numbers used are not the standard BIOS drive numbers; rather, they are taken from a special series of numbers for fixed disks only (80h corresponds to the first disk, 81h to the second, and so on). Using an out-of-range disk drive number will lead to unpredictable results. Unpredictable results can occur also from invalid parameter settings when the function is called.

This function is automatically called when the BIOS performs a read or write function; it does not need to be called separately. Its only use is to preposition the heads when no I/O transfer is expected immediately.

Int 13h   Function 0Dh
Alternate Disk Reset

Resets the hard disk controller

Calling Registers: AH   0Dh
DL   Fixed disk drive number

Return Registers: Carry flag clear if successful
AH   0

Carry flag set if error
AH   Status byte (refer to table BIOS.10)

Comments: *This function is available only on the Personal Computer AT and works only on fixed (hard) disks.* The drive numbers used are not the standard BIOS drive numbers; rather, they are taken from a special series of numbers for fixed disks only (80h corresponds to the first disk, 81h to the second, and so on). Using an out-of-range disk drive number will lead to unpredictable results.

This function is identical to Int 13h, Function 00h, except that in the newer BIOS versions it does not reset the floppy disk controller. Both are used by critical-error handlers to force recalibration (by causing the disk heads to be repositioned to track 0 before the next I/O operation is started). In older BIOS versions, this handler is coded to go to the same routine address as Int 13h, Function 00h.

Int 13h — Function 0Eh
Read Sector Buffer

Reads the sector buffer

Calling Registers: AH   0Eh
                         ES:BX   Point to RAM buffer area

Return Registers: Carry flag clear if successful

                         Carry flag set if error
                         AX   Error code

Comments: *This function is available only on XT models with the original 10M hard disk controller.* It is undefined for all other versions of BIOS, and its use should be avoided.

This function is a carry-over from IBM S/360 usage. The 10M disk controller simply transfers 512 bytes (one sector) of data from an internal sector buffer (on the controller) to RAM, starting at the address contained in ES:BX. This function is obsolete and should not be used by programmers.

Int 13h — Function 0Fh
Write Sector Buffer

Writes the sector buffer

Calling Registers: AH   0Fh
                         ES:BX   Point to RAM buffer area

Return Registers: Carry flag clear if successful

                         Carry flag set if error
                         AX   Error code

Comments: *This function is available only on XT models with the original 10M hard disk controller.* It is undefined for all other versions of BIOS, and its use should be avoided if possible.

This function is a carry-over from IBM S/360 usage. The 10M disk controller simply transfers 512 bytes (one sector) of data from RAM, starting at the address contained in ES:BX, to an internal sector buffer (on the controller). When formatting the 10M XT drive, this function should be used to initialize the controller's buffer before using Function 05h. This function is obsolete and should not be used by programmers.

Int 13h

Function 10h
Test Fixed Disk System Status

Returns the disk status byte (fixed disks only)

Calling Registers: AH   10h
DL   Fixed disk drive number

Return Registers: Carry flag clear if successful
AH   Status byte (see table BIOS.10)

Carry flag set if error
AX   Error code

Comments: *This function is the same as Function 01, but works only on fixed (hard) disks.* It returns the disk status as 00h if no error is present.

    The drive numbers used are not the standard BIOS drive numbers; rather, they are taken from a special series of numbers for fixed disks only (80h corresponds to the first disk, 81h to the second, and so on). Using an out-of-range disk drive number will lead to unpredictable results.

Int 13h

Function 11h
Recalibrate Fixed Disk Drive

Returns the hard disk's heads to cylinder 00 and reports the drive status

Calling Registers: AH   11h
DL   Fixed disk drive number

Return Registers: Carry flag clear if successful
AH   Status byte (see table BIOS.10)

Carry flag set if error
AX   Error code

Comments: *This function works only on fixed (hard) disks.* It returns the disk status as 00h if no error is present.

    The drive numbers used are not the standard BIOS drive numbers; rather, they are taken from a special series of numbers for fixed disks only (80h corresponds to the first disk, 81h to the second, and so on). Using an out-of-range disk drive number will lead to unpredictable results.

Int 13h

Function 12h
Diagnose Controller RAM

Performs built-in diagnostic tests on the internal sector buffer RAM of the fixed disk controller in XT models only

Calling Registers: AH   12h

Return Registers: Carry flag clear if successful

Carry flag set if error
   AX   Error code

Comments: *This function is available only on XT models with the original 10M hard disk controller.* It is undefined for all other versions of BIOS, and its use should be avoided if possible.

Int 13h

Function 13h
Diagnose Drive

Performs built-in diagnostic tests on the fixed disk in XT models only

Calling Registers: AH   13h

Return Registers: Carry flag clear if successful

Carry flag set if error
   AX   Error code

Comments: *This function is available only on XT models with the original 10M hard disk controller.* It is undefined for all other versions of BIOS, and its use should be avoided if possible.

Int 13h

Function 14h
Diagnose Controller

Performs built-in diagnostic tests on the fixed disk controller in XT models only

Calling Registers: AH   14h

Return Registers: Carry flag clear if successful

Carry flag set if error
   AX   Error code

Comments: *This function is available only on XT models with the original 10M hard disk controller.* It is undefined for all other versions of BIOS, and its use should be avoided if possible.

Int 13h

Function 15h
Return DASD Type

Gets the driver's DASD (direct access storage device) type and number of sectors

Calling Registers:
AH	15h
DL	Drive number

Return Registers: Carry flag clear if successful
AH	DASD type of drive
CX	Number of fixed disk sectors (high word)
DX	Number of fixed disk sectors (low word)

Carry flag set if error
AH	Status byte (refer to table BIOS.10)

Comments: This function, *which is available only on the PC XT (BIOS dated 1/10/86 or later), PC XT 286, Personal Computer AT, or PS/2 line*, can use either the standard series of BIOS drive numbers (0 = drive A, 1 = drive B, and so on) or the fixed disk numbers (80h = first drive, 81h = second drive, and so on).

This function is used to determine whether Function 16h can be used to test the drive to see if the floppy disk in the drive has been changed since the last access. Table BIOS.14 lists the function's valid return codes, which indicate whether you can tell anything about the status of the disk in the drive.

Table BIOS.14. *DASD Types*

Code	DASD Type
0	Drive requested is not available
1	Drive present, cannot detect disk change
2	Drive present, can detect disk change
3	Fixed disk

The value returned in CX:DX will be valid only if the DASD type returned in AH is 3.

Int 13h

Function 16h
Read Disk Change Line Status

Determines whether the disk in a specific drive has been changed

Calling Registers: AH   16h

DL   Drive number

Return Registers: Carry flag clear

AH   00h, disk not changed

Carry flag set

AH   06h, disk changed

AH   00h, error

Comments: Use this function, *which is available only on the PC XT (BIOS dated 1/10/86 or later), PC XT 286, Personal Computer AT, or PS/2 line*, to determine whether the disk in a drive has been changed or removed. This function can use either the standard series of BIOS drive numbers (0 = drive A, 1 = drive B, and so on) or the fixed-disk-only numbers (80h = first drive, 81h = second drive, and so on).

    Note, in this function, the unfortunate use of the carry flag, which is confusing and inconsistent with its use in the interrupt's other functions. In this one instance, the presence of the carry flag does *not* indicate that an error has occurred. Rather, it indicates one of two possible conditions: that an error has occurred or that the disk has been removed. All other disk-access functions use the carry flag to indicate that an error has occurred.

Int 13h

Function 17h
Set DASD Type for Disk Format

Specifies the DASD (direct access storage device) type for use by BIOS disk-formatting functions

Calling Registers: AH   17h

AL   DASD format type (see table BIOS.15)

DL   Drive number (zero based)

Return Registers: Nothing

Comments: This function, *which is available only on the PC XT (BIOS dated 1/10/86 or later), PC XT 286, Personal Computer AT, or PS/2 line*, must be called before you format a disk. Its purpose is to tell the format function the DASD format type for formatting operations.

Table BIOS.15 lists the valid disk types that can be formatted on the Personal Computer AT system.

Table BIOS.15. DASD Format Types	
Type	Meaning
1	Formatting 320/360K disk in 320/360K drive
2	Formatting 320/360K disk in 1.2M drive
3	Formatting 1.2M disk in 1.2M drive
4	Formatting 720K floppy disk in 720K drive

The diskette status is kept in the BIOS data area at 0004:0041.

Int 13h   Function 18h
Set Media Type for Format

Specifies the type of media for the BIOS to use in disk-formatting functions

Calling Registers: AH   18h
 CH   Number of tracks (zero based)
 CL   Sectors per track
 DL   Drive number (zero based)
 Bit 7 = 0 for a diskette, 1 for a fixed disk

Return Registers: Carry flag clear if successful
 ES:DI   Pointer to 11-byte parameter table
 (refer to table BIOS.12)

 Carry flag set if error
 AH   Return code

Comments: This function, *which is available only on the Personal Computer AT (BIOS dated after 11/15/86), PC XT (BIOS dated after 1/10/86), PC XT Model 286, and the PS/2 line,* is intended to be used before Int 13h, Function 05h is used to format a disk track. This function specifies to the BIOS the type of media it can expect to find in the disk drive.

Before using this function, you should note the use of the CH and CL registers to specify the track and sector information. The track can be a 10-bit value; as such, it requires the two high-order bits of CL. (Refer to fig. BIOS.1, which shows how this information is stored in the two registers.)

Int 13h — Function 19h
Park Heads

Moves the fixed disk drive's read/write heads to a "safe" position on the disk drive

Calling Registers: AH   18h

                           DL   Drive number (zero based, PS/2 series only)

                                       Bit 7 = 0 for a diskette, 1 for a fixed disk

Return Registers: Carry flag clear if successful

                           AH   Status byte (see table BIOS.10)

                        Carry flag set if error

                           AX   Error code

Comments: This function, *which is available only on the Personal Computer AT (BIOS dated after 11/15/86), PC XT (BIOS dated after 1/10/86), PC XT Model 286, and the PS/2 line,* moves the disk heads to the manufacturer-specified landing zone. It is intended for use before powering down or moving the system, to prevent damage to data.

Int 13h — Function 1Ah
Format ESDI Unit

Formats an ESDI-compatible disk drive connected to a PS/2 system

Calling Registers: AH   18h

                           AL   0, no defect table used

                                       < > 0, use defect table

                           ES:BX   Point to defect table

                           CL   Modifier bits (see comments)

                           DL   Drive number (zero based)

                                       Bit 7 = 1 for a fixed disk

Return Registers: Nothing

Comments: This function, *which is available only on the PS/2 line, models 50, 60, and 80,* formats an ESDI disk. All data on the disk is lost when this function is used. Be extremely careful when you use it. If this is used to format a floppy drive, the results are unknown.

     The CL register contains modifier bits with the following significance when this function is called:

Bits

76543210	*Meaning*
. . . . 1	Ignore primary defect map
. . . . . . 1 .	Ignore secondary defect map
. . . . . 1 . .	Update secondary defect map
. . . . 1 . . .	Perform extended surface analysis
. . . 1	Periodic interrupts ON
xxx	Reserved

Int 14h

Function 00h
Initialize Communications Port

Sets serial port parameters

Calling Registers: AH 00h
                                   AL Initialization parameter
                                   DX Port number (0=COM1, 1=COM2) (2=COM3,
                                                         3=COM4 on Personal Computer AT)

Return Registers: AH Port status
                                  AL Modem status

Comments: Use this function to initialize the communications port specified in DX. You can use the function to initialize COM ports 1 and 2 (DX = 0–1); on Personal Computer AT systems, COM ports 1–4 are allowed.

In AL, you specify how the communications port should be initialized. Use the parameters shown in table BIOS.16 to specify the baud rate, parity, word length, and stop bits.

Table BIOS.16. *Serial Port Initialization Parameters*

7,6,5 Baud Rate	4,3 Parity	2 Stop Bits	1,0 Word Length
000= 110 baud	00=none	0=1 bit	10=7 bits
001= 150 baud	01=odd	1=2 bits	11=8 bits
010= 300 baud	10=none		
011= 600 baud	11=even		
100=1200 baud			
101=2400 baud			
110=4800 baud			
111=9600 baud			

The interrupt returns the status of the port (see table BIOS.17) and the modem (see table BIOS.18). The BIOS adds bit 7 of the port status bits (timeout) to indicate excessive time spent waiting for a response. Otherwise, the status is what you would get directly from the hardware.

Table BIOS.17. *Port Status Bits*

Bit 76543210	Meaning
.......1	Data ready
......1.	Overrun error
.....1..	Parity error
....1...	Framing error
...1....	Break detected
..1.....	Transmit holding register (THR) empty
.1......	Transmit shift register (TSR) empty
1.......	Timeout

Table BIOS.18. *Modem Status Bits*

Bit 76543210	Meaning
.......1	Change in Clear to Send (CTS) status
......1.	Change in Data Set Ready (DSR) status
.....1..	Trailing edge ring indicator
....1...	Change in receive line signal
...1....	Clear to Send (CTS)
..1.....	Data Set Ready (DSR)
.1......	Ring Indicator (RI)
1.......	Receive line signal detected

No matter how you want to use a communications port, initializing the port with this function gives you direct control over important parameters without involving many chip-dependent details. Even programmers who access the serial chips directly through their I/O port addresses will find this function a convenient way to control parameters with minimum complexity.

Int 14h

Function 01h
Write Character to Communications Port

Outputs a character to a serial port

Calling Registers: AH 01h
AL Character to write
DX Communications port (0=COM1, 1=COM2)
(2=COM3, 3=COM4 on Personal Computer AT)

Return Registers: AH bit 7 0 (function successful)
AH bit 7 1 (function failed)
Bits 0–6 show cause of failure (refer to table
BIOS.17)

Comments: This function writes a character to and returns the status of the specified communications port. Ordinarily, writing a character to a serial port is not a time-critical task. It can be done whenever the character is ready. This function can write to serial ports 1 and 2 (COM1 and COM2). Before you call this function, be sure to use Int 14h, Function 00h to initialize the port. (On the Personal Computer AT, you can access ports COM1 to COM4.)

Although communications programs that depend on BIOS read functions can seldom exceed 1200 baud operation, this is not true for the write function. The only effect of failing to supply a new output character as soon as the previous one is sent is a reduction in the effective throughput of the system. No data is lost.

Table BIOS.17 shows the meaning of bits 06 in the AH register on return from the function (if the function failed).

Int 14h

Function 02h
Read Character from Communications Port

Inputs a character from a serial port

Calling Registers: AH 02h
DX Communications port (0=COM1, 1=COM2)
(2=COM3, 3=COM4 on Personal Computer AT)

Return Registers: AH bit 7 0 (function successful)
AL Character

AH bit 7 1 (function failed)
Bits 0–6 show cause of failure (refer to table
BIOS.17)

Comments: This function reads a character from the specified communications port, returns the port's status, and can read from serial ports 1 and 2 (COM1 and COM2). (On the Personal Computer AT, you can access ports COM1 to COM4.) Before calling this function, be sure to initialize the port.

In any communications application, receiving characters is an extremely time-critical operation. When characters are coming in at uncontrolled intervals from an external device, the computer must be ready to respond to them immediately. Although output is controlled by the computer (but intimately tied to input in a communications program), input must respond to the external system. If the computer is not ready to respond before a new character arrives, that character will be lost.

Communications programs that depend on this function can seldom exceed 300 baud for continuous operation. In most cases, a rate of 1200 baud can transfer only a few characters at a time and will lose several characters each time the display fills and has to scroll up one line.

This function is useless in most commercial applications because direct access to the I/O ports is required to achieve the speed necessary for continued operation. Programs that do not depend on human interaction can work acceptably using this function. Reading a serial device with this function is often practical and useful in control and monitoring applications with relatively slow speeds.

Table BIOS.17 shows the meaning of bits 0–6 in the AH register on return from the function (if the function failed).

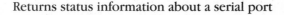

Int 14h

Function 03h
Request Communications Port Status

Returns status information about a serial port

Calling Registers:	AH	03h
	DX	Communications port (0=COM1, 1=COM2)
		(2=COM3, 3=COM4 on Personal Computer AT)

Return Registers:	AH	Port status (refer to table BIOS.17)
	AL	Modem status (refer to table BIOS.18)

Comments: This function, which returns the current status of the specified communications port, requests the status without doing any I/O or affecting the serial port in any other way. The function can access communications ports 1 and 2 (DX = 0–1). (On the Personal Computer AT, this function can access ports COM1–COM4.)

Tables BIOS.17 and BIOS.18 show the meaning of the status bits in the AH and AL registers on return from the call. Table BIOS.17 specifies the bits for the serial port, whereas table BIOS.18 gives the bits for the modem connected to the serial port.

Int 14h

Function 04h
Extended Initialization

Initializes serial port parameters

Calling Registers:	AH	04h
	AL	Break setting
	BH	Parity
	BL	Stop bits
	CH	Data length
	CL	Transmission rate (bps)
	DX	Communications port (0=COM1, 1=COM2, 2=COM3, 3=COM4)

Return Registers:	AH	Port status (refer to table BIOS.17)
	AL	Modem status (refer to table BIOS.18)

Comments: This function, *which is available only on the PS/2 line,* provides (in a simpler fashion than that used by Function 00h) for RS-232 port initialization directly at the BIOS level. Table BIOS.19 shows the possible register settings for this function.

Table BIOS.19. Possible Register Settings

Register	Meaning	Settings	Meaning
AL	Break	00h	No break
		01h	Break
BH	Parity	00h	No parity
		01h	Odd parity
		02h	Even parity
		03h	Stick parity odd
		04h	Stick parity even
BL	Stop Bits	00h	One stop bit
		01h	Two stop bits ($1^1/_2$ if data length setting in CH is 00h)
CH	Data Length	00h	5-bit word length
		01h	6-bit word length
		02h	7-bit word length
		03h	8-bit word length
CL	BPS Rate	00h	110 baud
		01h	150 baud
		02h	300 baud
		03h	600 baud
		04h	1200 baud
		05h	2400 baud
		06h	4800 baud

Register	Meaning	Settings	Meaning
		07h	9600 baud
		08h	19,200 baud

On return from the function, the AH and AL registers reflect the current status of the port. Tables BIOS.17 and BIOS.18 give the meaning of each bit in the registers.

Int 14h

Function 05h
Extended Communications Port Control

Allows extended control of the modem control register

Calling Registers:
AH	05h	
AL	00h, read modem control register	
DX	Communications port (0=COM1, 1=COM2, 2=COM3, 3=COM4)	
AL	01h, write modem control register	
BL	Modem control register (if AL = 01h, see table BIOS.20)	
DX	Communications port (0=COM1, 1=COM2, 2=COM3, 3=COM4)	

Return Registers:
AH	Port status (refer to table BIOS.17)
AL	Modem status (refer to table BIOS.18)
BL	Modem control register (see table BIOS.20)

Comments: This function, *which is available only on the PS/2 line,* allows you to read or write the modem control register associated with the desired RS-232 port. This gives you direct access from the BIOS level to the port's modem-control lines. In a read operation, you get the status of these lines; in a write operation, you set the status. The bits in the BL register are defined in table BIOS.20.

Table BIOS.20. *Modem Control Register Bits*

Bit 76543210	Meaning
. . . . 1	Data Terminal Ready (DTR)
. . . . . . 1 .	Request to Send (RTS)
. . . . . 1 . .	Out1
. . . . 1 . . .	Out2
. . . 1	Loopback test
1 1 1	Reserved

When called, this function also returns the current status of the serial port and modem in registers AH and AL. Tables BIOS.17 and BIOS.18 give the meaning of each bit on return from the call.

Int 15h   Function 00h
Turn On Cassette Motor

Turns on the motor of the cassette tape machine

Calling Registers: AH   00h

Return Registers: Carry flag clear if successful

Carry flag set if error
    AH   Return code (see table BIOS.21)

Comments: Because *this function works only on older PC models,* using it on PC XT, Personal Computer AT, or PS/2 systems will result in the carry flag being set and the return of AH=86h (see table BIOS.21).

Table BIOS.21. Cassette Services Return Codes

Code	Meaning
00h	Invalid command
01h	CRC error
02h	Data transitions lost
03h	No data located on tape
04h	Data not found (PC*jr* only)
86h	No cassette port available

Some owners of older systems with cassette relays have rewired the relays for other control functions. Such a step should be taken carefully, with a full understanding of the equipment's loading and other electrical requirements.

Int 15h   Function 01h
Turn Off Cassette Motor

Turns off the motor of the cassette tape machine

Calling Registers: AH   01h

Return Registers: Carry flag clear if successful

Carry flag set if error
    AH   Return code (refer to table BIOS.21)

Comments: Because *this function works only on older PC models,* using it on a PC XT, Personal Computer AT, or PS/2 system will result in the carry flag being set and the return of AH=86h (refer to table BIOS.21).

Some owners of older systems with cassette relays have rewired the relays for other control functions. Such a step should be taken carefully, with a full understanding of the equipment's loading and other electrical requirements.

Int 15h

Function 02h
Read Data Blocks from Cassette Drive

Reads a specified number of bytes from the cassette

Calling Registers:	AH	02h
	ES:BX	Pointer to data buffer
	CX	Number of bytes to read

Return Registers:	Carry flag clear if successful	
	DX	Number of bytes read
	ES:BX	Pointer to byte following last byte read
	Carry flag set if error	
	AH	Return code (refer to table BIOS.21)

Comments: Because *this function works only on older PC models,* using it on a PC XT, Personal Computer AT, or PS/2 system will result in the carry flag being set and the return of AH=86h (refer to table BIOS.21).

If you are using a cassette on a system with a cassette port, this function will transfer data from the cassette in 256-byte blocks but will deliver to the buffer only the number of bytes called for.

Some owners of older systems with cassette relays have rewired the relays for other control functions. Such a step should be taken carefully, with a full understanding of the equipment's loading and other electrical requirements.

Int 15h

Function 03h
Write Data Blocks to Cassette Drive

Writes a specified number of bytes to the cassette

Calling Registers:	AH	03h
	ES:BX	Pointer to data buffer
	CX	Number of bytes to write

Return Registers: Carry flag clear if successful
> ES:BX   Pointer to byte following last byte written

Carry flag set if error
> AH   Return code (refer to table BIOS.21)

Comments: Because *this function works only on older PC models,* using it on a PC XT, Personal Computer AT, or PS/2 system will result in the carry flag being set and the return of AH=86h (refer to table BIOS.21).

All transfers to the tape occur in 256-byte blocks, but only the number of bytes specified in the CX register will be transferred from the data buffer. Errors during the transfer indicate command, not transfer, errors. If you are writing an application that will use a cassette, the program should provide a way to verify the tape write before destroying the data in memory.

Some owners of older systems with cassette relays have rewired the relays for other control functions. Such a step should be taken carefully, with a full understanding of the equipment's loading and other electrical requirements.

Int 15h   Function 0Fh
ESDI Unit Format Periodic Interrupt

Called by formatting routines at the end of formatting each cylinder

Calling Registers: AH   0Fh
	AL	Phase code
		00h Reserved
		01h Surface analysis
		02h Formatting

Return Registers: Carry flag set, end of formatting or scanning

Carry flag clear, continue formatting or
> scanning

Comments: This function, *which is available only on PS/2 machines,* is used by programmers who want to gain control after formatting or scanning each disk cylinder. At that time, the format routine will call this interrupt.

If this function is invoked from any machine other than a PS/2, the carry flag will be set and AH will contain 80h (PC and PC*jr*) or 86h (all others) on return.

Int 15h   Function 21h
Power-On Self-Test Error Log

Updates or reads the POST error log

Calling Registers:	AH	21h
	AL	00h, read POST error log
		01h, write error code to POST error log
	BX	POST error code if AL=01h
	BH	Device code
	BL	Device error

Return Registers: If *reading* POST error log (AL = 0)

Carry flag clear if successful

	AH	00h
	BX	Number of POST error codes stored
	ES:DI	Pointer to POST error log

Carry flag set if error

| | AH | 80h (PC*jr* and PC) |
| | AH | 86h (all others) |

If *writing* to POST error log (AL = 1)

Carry flag clear if successful

| | AH | 00h |

Carry flag set if error

	AH	01h, POST error log full
	AH	80h (PC*jr* and PC)
	AH	86h (all others)

Comments: This function is used by the POST primarily to write information to the internal error log or by diagnostic routines to gain information about the error codes detected during the POST. The values returned depend on whether you are posting or reading. The use of the POST error log is beyond the scope of this book.

This function works only on PS/2 machines (except the Model 30). If this function is invoked from any machine other than a PS/2, the carry flag will be set and AH will contain 80h (PC and PC*jr*) or 86h (all others, including PS/2 Model 30) on return.

Int 15h

Function 4Fh
Keyboard Intercept

Called by keyboard routines during I/O processing

Calling Registers:	AH	4Fh
	AL	Keyboard scan code
	Carry flag set	

| **Return Registers:** | PC, PC*jr*: | |
| | Carry flag set, AH=80h | |

PC XT BIOS 11/08/82, Personal Computer AT BIOS 1/10/84:
Carry flag set, AH=86h

All Others:
Carry flag set
AL   New keyboard scan code

Carry flag clear
AL   Original keyboard scan code

Comments: *This function is available only on the Personal Computer AT (BIOS dated after 1/10/84), PC XT (BIOS dated after 11/8/82), PC XT Model 286, and PS/2 series computers.* It is called by Int 09h and normally returns the scan code in the AL register with the carry flag set. The purpose of the routine is to translate scan codes for the keyboard interrupt. By providing a function to replace this one, a programmer can change scan codes to do character translations (such as one might do with an alternate keyboard layout).

If the function returns with the carry flag clear, Int 09h ignores the character. In addition to doing character translations, a replacement function can use this to cause the system to ignore certain keystrokes.

Int 15h   Function 80h
Device Open

Opens a device for a specific process

Calling Registers: AH   80h
                          BX   Device ID
                          CX   Process ID

Return Registers: Carry flag clear if successful

                         Carry flag set if error
                          AH   80h (PC, PC*jr*)
                          AH   86h (PC XT with BIOS 11/8/82)

Comments: *This function is available only on the Personal Computer AT, PC XT (BIOS dated after 11/8/82), PC XT Model 286, and PS/2 series computers.* It is intended for use in rudimentary multitasking operations and is beyond the scope of this book.

Int 15h   Function 81h
Device Close

Closes a device associated with a specific process

Calling Registers:	AH	81h
	BX	Device ID
	CX	Process ID
Return Registers:	Carry flag clear if successful	
	Carry flag set if error	
	AH	80h (PC, PC*jr*)
	AH	86h (PC XT with BIOS 11/8/82)

Comments: *This function is available only on the Personal Computer AT, PC XT (BIOS dated after 11/8/82), PC XT Model 286, and PS/2 series computers.* It is intended for use in rudimentary multitasking operations and is beyond the scope of this book.

Int 15h

Function 82h
Program Termination

Used to terminate a process

Calling Registers:	AH	82h
	BX	Process ID
Return Registers:	Carry flag clear if successful	
	Carry flag set if error	
	AH	80h (PC, PC*jr*)
	AH	86h (PC XT with BIOS 11/8/82)

Comments: *This function is available only on the Personal Computer AT, PC XT (BIOS dated after 11/8/82), PC XT Model 286, and PS/2 series computers.* It is intended for use in rudimentary multitasking operations and is beyond the scope of this book.

Int 15h

Function 83h
Event Wait

Waits for a process event to occur

Calling Registers:	AH	83h
	AL	00h, set interval
	CX:DX	Microseconds until posting
	ES:BX	Pointer to byte with high-order bit set as soon as possible after end of interval
	AL	01h, cancel set interval (PS/2 only)

Return Registers: Carry flag clear if successful

Carry flag set if error

AH	80h (PC)
AH	86h (PC XT, Personal Computer AT—BIOS dated after 1/10/84)

Comments: *This function is available only on the Personal Computer AT (BIOS dated after 1/10/84) and PS/2 series computers, except the Model 30.* The function is intended for use in rudimentary multitasking operations and is beyond the scope of this book.

Int 15h   Function 84h
Joystick Support

Returns the status and coordinates of the joystick

Calling Registers:	AH	84h
	DX	00h, read switch settings
		01h, read joystick position

Return Registers: PC, PC*jr:*
        Carry flag set
          AH   80h

        PC XT BIOS 11/08/82:
        Carry flag set
          AH   86h

        All Others:
        If reading switch settings (DX = 0)
          AL Switch settings (bits 4–7)
          Carry flag set if error

        If reading joystick position (DX = 1)
          AX   A(X) value
          BX   A(Y) value
          CX   B(X) value
          DX   B(Y) value

Comments: This function is used to control the operations of the joystick on all IBM computers (including the PS/2 line) *except* the PC, PC*jr*, and early PC XT (BIOS dated 11/08/82). On these computers, the function will return with the carry flag set, which indicates an error. AH will contain the error code: either 80h or 86h (for the PC XT).

    The value in DX is used to indicate the type of information you want from the joystick. If DX is 0, this function will return the switch settings in the four most-significant bits of AL. If DX is 1, the position of the joystick is returned in the four general-purpose registers: AX, BX, CX, and DX. If no joystick is attached to the computer, the carry flag will be set on return.

Int 15h — Function 85h
System Request Key Pressed

Called whenever the SysRq (System Request) key is pressed

Calling Registers: AH   85h

Return Registers: PC, PC*jr*:
          Carry flag set
            AH   80h

          PX XT BIOS 11/08/82:
            Carry flag set
            AH   86h

          All Others:
            AL   00h, key pressed
                  01h, key released

Comments: BIOS calls this function whenever the System Request key (Alt-Print Screen) is pressed or released. *Only the more recent versions of the BIOS support this function, which is accessible only from keyboards with a System Request key.*

     If a computer's BIOS does not support this function, the carry flag will be set and AH will contain either 80h or 86h (early PC XT) on return.

     Ordinarily, the System Request key returns with the flags and registers set. This is of no value, but your program can intercept this function to make effective use of the key. To program the System Request key, you simply revector Int 15h and save the old address. Then your routine should check the contents of AH. If AH does not contain 85h, you should pass control to the original Int 15h handler. If AH does contain 85h, the System Request key was either pressed or released. AL reflects the key's state: if it is 00h, the key was just pressed; if it is 01h, the key was just released.

Int 15h — Function 86h
Delay

Pauses a certain amount of time before returning

Calling Registers: AH   86h
                     CX,DX   Time before return in microseconds (accurate to within 976 microseconds)

Return Registers: PC, PC*jr:*
    Carry flag set
     AH 80h

    PC XT:
    Carry flag set
     AH 86h

    All Others:
    Carry flag set (wait in progress)

    Carry flag clear (successful wait)

Comments: This function, *which works only on the Personal Computer AT and PS/2 line,* is designed to be used (within operating system software) for setting system waits. It is not intended for use by applications programs.

Int 15h

Function 87h
Move Block

Transfers a specified block of memory on 80286 and 80386 machines

Calling Registers: AH   87h
       CX   Word count of storage to be moved
       ES:SI Pointer to global descriptor table

Return Registers: PC, PC*jr:*
    Carry flag set
     AH 80h

    PC XT, PS/2 Model 30:
    Carry flag set
     AH 86h

    All Others:
    Carry flag clear, zero flag set
     Operation successful
     AH 00h

    Carry flag set, zero flag clear
     Operation failed
      AH 01h RAM parity error
         02h Other exception occurred
         03h Gate address line 20h failed

Comments: With this function, IBM computers based on 80286 or 80386 microprocessors can transfer blocks of data to and from memory. (There must be more than 1M of memory.) The computer switches from the processor's real mode to protected mode. No interrupts are allowed during this type of transfer (interrupts may be missed if the move is a large one).

The global descriptor table pointed to by ES:SI is laid out as shown in table BIOS.22.

Table BIOS.22. *Global Descriptor Table*

Offset	Description
00h	Dummy; set to zero.
08h	GDT data segment location; set to zero.
10h	Source GDT. Points to a GDT for the source memory block.
18h	Target GDT. Points to a GDT for the target memory block.
20h	Pointer to BIOS code segment; initialized to zero. BIOS will use this area to create the protected mode code segment.
28h	Pointer to BIOS stack segment; initialized to zero. BIOS will use this area to create the protected mode stack segment.
	—Source/Target GDT Layout—
00h	Segment limit
02h	24-bit segment physical address
05h	Data access rights (set to 93h)
06h	Reserved word (must be zero)

Because the word count loaded into CX has a limit of 8000h, this routine cannot transfer more than 64K bytes of data.

Int 15h — Function 88h
Extended Memory Size Determination

Returns the number of contiguous 1K memory blocks available in extended memory

Calling Registers: AH   88h

Return Registers: PC, PC*jr*:
         Carry flag set
           AH   80h

         PC XT, PS/2 Model 30:
         Carry flag set
           AH   86h

All Others:

    AX   Contiguous 1K blocks of memory
                        beginning at 100000h

Comments: Returns the amount of memory determined available by POST checks above address 100000h. This function is available only for machines using either the 80286 or 80386 microprocessor.

Int 15h — Function 89h
Switch Processor to Protected Mode

Switches the processor to protected mode so that it can access extended memory and take advantage of protected mode instructions

Calling Registers:
AH	89h
BL	IRQ0 interrupt vector offset
BH	IRQ8 interrupt vector offset
ES:SI	Pointer to Global Descriptor Table (GDT)
CX	Offset into protected mode CS to jump to

Return Registers: Carry flag clear if successful

                          Carry flag set if error

Comments: For a programmer with access to a system with extended memory, the capability of switching the processor to protected mode is potentially very interesting. Although protected mode gives you access to additional memory and instructions, the price you pay is incompatibility with many existing systems. Only machines with a 286 or 386 processor have this capability (and they do not necessarily have the extra memory). Furthermore, DOS itself does not use protected mode. Subtle bugs may crop up unless you write all of your own handling for this situation.

    To use this function, you must first set up the global descriptor table (GDT) for the call. (Refer to table BIOS.22 for the GDT layout.)

    While Function 89h is in use, the normal BIOS functions are not available to the user. Programs running in protected mode must create their own I/O commands. Furthermore, the standard interrupt vectors must be moved to accommodate the 80286 interrupt definitions that overlay some of the interrupt vectors assigned for real-mode use of the system. Interrupt handlers for the hardware interrupts must also be defined.

    Interrupt handling is a major part of any shift to protected mode using this function. A more detailed discussion of 80286/80386 interrupts is beyond the scope of this book. For details about the operation of protected mode interrupts and the design of handlers for them, you should consult a reference on the 80286 and 80386 processors.

Int 15h

Function 90h
Device Wait

Used by the BIOS to indicate a waiting state

Calling Registers: AH   90h
                        AL   Device type code
                        ES:BX   Pointer to network control block if waiting for a
                                            network

Return Registers: PC, PC*jr:*
                        Carry flag set
                              AH   80h

                      PC XT BIOS 11/08/82:
                        Carry flag set
                              AH   86h

                      All Others:
                        Carry flag set (minimum wait satisfied)

                        Carry flag clear (wait not satisfied)

Comments: Use this function to tell the operating system that a program is about to wait for a device. This function is designed for developing multitasking software; it is not meant for use by applications programmers. Whenever the BIOS is about to enter a busy loop (when it must wait for a device), it calls this function. Table BIOS.23 lists the type codes passed to the routine in AL.

AL	Type Code
Table BIOS.23. Type Codes Passed in AL	
00h	Disk timeout
01h	Diskette timeout
02h	Keyboard (no timeout)
03h	Pointing device (timeout)
80h	Network (no timeout)
FCh	Fixed disk reset (PS/2 only)
FDh	Diskette drive motor start (timeout)
FEh	Printer (timeout) *576*

This function (called at the beginning of an interrupt) is the opposite of Int 15h, Function 91h (called when the interrupt is complete). If you want to do other things while the computer is busy, you can hook into the Int 15h vector, which passes all functions (except 90h and 91h) to the original handler. After you save the machine's status, you are free to do another task.

Int 15h   Function 91h
Interrupt Complete

Used by the BIOS to indicate the end of a waiting state

Calling Registers: AH   91h

Return Registers: PC, PC*jr:*
　　　　　　　　　Carry flag set
　　　　　　　　　　AH   80h

　　　　　　　　PC XT BIOS 11/08/82:
　　　　　　　　　Carry flag set
　　　　　　　　　　AH   86h

　　　　　　　All Others:
　　　　　　　　AL Type code

Comments: The BIOS uses this function to report that the device interrupt is complete, according to the type code given in table BIOS.24. This function is not meant to be called by applications programmers; it is intended to be used internally by the operating system or to develop multitasking systems. Device interrupts use Int 91h to indicate to the operating system that they are complete (see the comments for Int 09h).

AL	Type Code
Table BIOS.24. Type Codes on Return from Function 91b	
00h	Disk timeout
01h	Diskette timeout
02h	Keyboard (no timeout)
03h	Pointing device (timeout)
80h	Network (no timeout)
FCh	Fixed disk reset (PS/2 only)
FDh	Diskette drive motor start (timeout)
FEh	Printer (timeout)

This function, which is called when an interrupt is complete, is the opposite of Int 15h, Function 90h (called when the interrupt begins).

Int 15h   Function C0h
Return System Configuration Parameters

Returns a pointer to system descriptor information

Calling Registers: AH   C0h

Return Registers: PC, PC*jr:*
              Carry flag set
                 AH   80h

              PC XT BIOS 11/08/82, Personal Computer AT BIOS 1/10/84:
              Carry flag set
                 AH   86h

              All Others:
                 ES:BX   Pointer to system descriptor table in ROM

Comments: The ROM system descriptor table contains useful information about the system. Table BIOS.25 shows the meanings of the entries.

Table BIOS.25. *System Descriptor Table*

Offset	Meaning
00h	Byte count of data that follows (minimum 8)
02h	Model byte
03h	Submodel byte
04h	BIOS revision level (00 = 1st release)
05h	Feature information (see table BIOS.26 for meaning)
06–09h	Reserved

The feature information byte is interpreted as shown in table BIOS.26.

The model byte contained at offset 02h of the system descriptor table should be the same as the system ID byte (stored at F000:FFFE). The submodel byte (offset 03h) can be used for additional system identification. From the information shown in table BIOS.27, you can determine what type of IBM computer is being used. (The BIOS date is provided to indicate differences between table entries for the same type of computer.)

Table BIOS.26. *Feature Information Byte*

Bit 76543210	Meaning
.......x	Reserved
......0.	PC bus I/O channel
......1.	Micro Channel Architecture
.....1..	Extended BIOS data area (EBDA) allocated
....1...	Wait for external event is supported
...1....	Keyboard intercept called by Int 09h
..1.....	Real-time clock present
.1......	Second interrupt chip present
1.......	DMA channel 3 used by hard disk BIOS

Table BIOS.27. *System Model Identifications*

Computer Type	Model Byte (offset 02h)	Submodel (offset 03h)	BIOS Revision (offset 04h)	BIOS Date
PC	FFh			
PC XT	FEh			
PC XT	FBh	00h	01h	1/10/86
PC XT	FBh	00h	02h	5/09/86
PC*jr*	FDh			
AT	FCh			
AT	FCh	00h	01h	6/10/85
AT, COMPAQ 286	FCh	01h	00h	11/15/85
PC XT 286	FCh	02h	00h	
PC Convertible	F9h	00h	00h	
PS/2 Model 30	FAh	00h	00h	
PS/2 Model 50	FCh	04h	00h	
PS/2 Model 60	FCh	05h	00h	
PS/2 Model 80	F8h	00h	00h	

Int 15h

Function C1h
Return Extended BIOS Data Area Segment Address

Returns the segment address of the EBDA

Calling Registers: AH   C1h

Return Registers: PC, PC*jr:*
  Carry flag set
    AH 80h

  PC XT, Personal Computer AT:
  Carry flag set
    AH 86h

  PS/2:
  Carry flag clear if successful
    ES Extended BIOS data area segment address

  Carry flag set if error

Comments: This function is used to determine the segment address of the extended BIOS data area (EBDA). Notice that (so far) this area is used only by the PS/2 line. You can determine whether it is supported on your system through Int 15h, Function C0h (refer to bit 2 of the feature information byte).

  The EBDA is used internally by the BIOS on the Personal System/2 line. It is allocated by the POST routines and resides at the top of the user memory area (usually as the last 1K of the 640K main memory area). POST adjusts the amount of free memory to allow for the EBDA. To determine the amount of free memory available, refer to Int 12h.

Int 15h

Function C2h
Pointing Device BIOS Interface

Interface function for auxiliary pointing devices

Calling Registers: AH   C2h
  AL   00h, Enable/Disable pointing device
    BH   00h, enable
        01h, disable

  AL   01h, reset pointing device

  AL   02h, set sample rate

  AL   03h, set resolution

  AL   04h, read device type

  AL   05h, pointing device interface initialization

  AL   06h, extended commands

  AL   07h, pointing device far call initialization

Return Registers: PC, PC*jr:*
> Carry flag set
>> AH 80h

> PC XT, Personal Computer AT:
> Carry flag set
>> AH 86h

> PS/2:
>> Carry flag clear if successful
>>> Other registers vary by subfunction (see comments)

>> Carry flag set if error
>>> AH 01h, invalid function call
>>> 02h, invalid input
>>> 03h, interface error
>>> 04h, resend
>>> 05h, no far call installed

Comments: This function, *which works only on the PS/2 line,* is designed to interface pointing devices (such as a mouse, digitizer, or puck) to DOS. Because most mouse software currently is interfaced through an Int 33h device driver, information about the mouse is covered under that interrupt. (Later versions of the Int 33h device driver furnished by Microsoft use this BIOS interrupt, if it is available, to accomplish their functions, but programs universally use the Int 33h interface because it has become a standard.)

Although detailed use of this function is beyond the scope of this book, we will touch quickly upon the parameters for each subfunction. Before you issue a subfunction, you should tell BIOS about the interrupt handler for the pointing device (set AL to 7 and ES:BX to the interrupt handler's far address). Next, enable the pointing device by setting AL and BH to 0 and calling this function.

After you have enabled the pointing device, you can reset it by setting AL to 1 and calling the function. On successful completion, BH will be set to the device ID of the pointing device and the device's parameters will be reset.

Note that a similar subfunction (AL=5) is used to initialize the pointer device's interface. This subfunction is invoked with BH set to a number in the range of 1–8, which represents the number of bytes to be used for the data package size.

To allow for setting the pointing device's sampling rate, set AL to 2. A code that indicates the desired sampling rate is loaded into BH as follows:

Code	Sample Rate
00h	10 reports/second
01h	20 reports/second
02h	40 reports/second
03h	60 reports/second
04h	80 reports/second
05h	100 reports/second
06h	200 reports/second

To set the resolution of the pointing device, set AL to 3 and BH to the desired resolution (0 = 1 count per millimeter (cpm), 1 = 2 cpm, 2 = 4 cpm, and 3 = 8 cpm).

By setting AL to 4, you cause the device ID (returned in BH) to be read. This return value is the same as that returned when you reset the device (see AL = 5).

Int 15h

Function C3h
Enable/Disable Watchdog Timeout

Provides control for the PS/2 watchdog timer

Calling Registers: AH C3h
AL 00h, disable watchdog timeout
01h, enable watchdog timeout
BX Watchdog timer count (1–255)

Return Registers: PC, PC*jr*:
Carry flag set
AH 80h

PC XT, Personal Computer AT, PS/2 Model 30:
Carry flag set
AH 86h

PS/2:
Carry flag clear if successful

Carry flag set if error

Comments: This function is used to enable or disable the watchdog timer available with the PS/2 line of computers that use 80286 or 80386 microprocessors. On non-PS/2 computers, this function returns with the carry flag set and an error code in AH.

The watchdog timer uses timer channel 3 and is tied to the IRQ 0 line. When IRQ 0 is active for more than one cycle of the channel 0 timer (main system timer), the watchdog timer count is decremented. When the watchdog timer count reaches 0, a nonmaskable interrupt (NMI) is generated. The main purpose of this function (and the watchdog timer) is to help in the detection of and recovery from errors.

Int 15hz

Function C4h
Programmable Option Select

Provides access to PS/2 system programmable registers on option boards

Calling Registers: AH   C4h

                        AL   00h, return base POS adapter register address
                                        01h, enable slot for setup
                                        02h, adapter enable

Return Registers: PC, PC*jr:*

                          Carry flag set
                              AH   80h

                          PC XT, Personal Computer AT, PS/2 Model 30:
                          Carry flag set
                              AH   86h

                          PS/2:
                          Carry flag clear if successful
                              DL   Base POS adapter register address (function 0)
                              BL   Slot number (function 1)

                          Carry flag set if error

Comments: Programmable Option Select (POS), which is available on PS/2 models that use the 80286 and 80386 microprocessors, eliminates the need for system-board and adapter switches. The function of the switches is replaced by programmable registers accessible through this function.

    On non-PS/2 systems, this function returns an error. The carry flag is set and AH contains an error code.

    This function is intended primarily for use by system configuration software, not by applications programs. Should you decide to use it, be aware that *improper use of the POS can cause loss of system integrity and may damage some adapter boards.* The process for Personal System/2 system configuration and setup is beyond the scope of this book.

Int 16h

Function 00h
Read Keyboard Character

Returns an ASCII value and a scan code from the keyboard buffer

Calling Registers: AH   00h

Return Registers: AH   Keyboard scan code
                                AL   ASCII character code

Comments: This function, which reads a single character from the keyboard buffer and returns the character and its scan code, is the one you most likely will use when you write a TSR that needs a hot key to trigger its operation. By watching requests to this interrupt, you can trap and respond directly to occurrences of the hot key. The keyboard buffer is usually located at 0040:001Ah.

This function waits until a key is pressed and then returns the keyboard scan code and the ASCII code of the keystroke. If a key has no defined ASCII code, a value of 0 is returned for the ASCII code. (The arrow keys and function keys are examples of keys with no defined ASCII code.)

Although the Ctrl, Alt, and Shift keys return no code for themselves, they modify other keystrokes to produce unique codes. (See Int 16h, Function 02h for a way to tell the status of these keys.)

The special keystrokes Ctrl-Alt-Del (press and hold the Ctrl, Alt, and Del keys simultaneously) and PrtSc (press and hold the Shift key and the PrtSc key simultaneously) are not returned. BIOS recognizes these special keystrokes and immediately passes control to other interrupt-servicing routines.

This function allows you to enter any character by holding down the Alt key while you type its corresponding ASCII code on the keypad. For example, if you hold down the Alt key while you type 156, the scan code 156 will be returned. If you type a number greater than 256, the returned code will be the number modulo 256 (the number entered is divided by 256; the code will be the remainder).

Int 16h	**Function 01h**
	Read Keyboard Status

Checks for availability of a keystroke, returning the ASCII code and scan code if available

Calling Registers: AH   01h

Return Registers: Zero flag clear (Key waiting)
                  AH   Scan code
                  AL   ASCII character

               Zero flag set (No key waiting)

Comments: Unlike Function 00h of Int 16h, this function does a quick check of the keyboard and then returns immediately. If a keystroke is ready, the function clears the zero flag and returns the keystroke's ASCII code and the keyboard scan code. If there is no keystroke to be processed, the function sets the zero flag. If the key has no defined ASCII code, a value of 0 is returned for the ASCII code. (The arrow keys and function keys are examples of keys with no defined ASCII code.)

Although the Ctrl, Alt, and Shift keys return no code for themselves, they modify other keystrokes to produce unique codes. (See Function 02h for a way to tell the status of these keys.) The special Ctrl-Alt-Del and PrtSc keystrokes are not returned, but cause other interrupts to occur immediately.

You can enter any ASCII code by holding down the Alt key while typing its corresponding three-digit code number. For example, holding down the Alt key while typing 156 will return the scan code 156. If you type a number greater than 256, the returned code will be the number modulo 256 (the number entered is divided by 256; the code will be the remainder).

Int 16, Function 01h does not end with an IRET instruction, as other interrupt handlers do; rather, it uses a RET instruction with an option that allows the function to flush bytes from the stack. By returning in this way, the function can use the zero flag for a return flag. We do not know why the programmer chose to do this, but it works. Perhaps the intent was to mimic the old CP/M keyboard-status function, which operated in approximately the same way.

Int 16h   Function 02h
Return Keyboard Flags

Returns a status byte indicating the condition of the Shift keys

Calling Registers: AH   02h

Return Registers: AL ROM BIOS keyboard flags byte

Comments: This function returns the status of keyboard toggles and Shift keys from the BIOS status register kept in memory location 0000:0417h.

Unusual key combinations make good triggers for special actions. In older programs, the Escape key (Esc) was often used for getting out of an application. But Esc is not a safe choice for irrevocable actions. The key is too easily pressed. To prevent accidental triggering, you would have to add an Are you sure? question if your program found the Esc key. You can provide a more positive initiator by triggering on a key sequence that is unlikely to occur accidentally (Ctrl-Left Shift-Right Shift, for example). Just be careful not to use key sequences that require double-jointed fingers or other unusual characteristics!

Table BIOS.28 shows the meaning of the bits in the AL register on return from the function.

Table BIOS.28. *BIOS Keyboard Status Flags*

Bit 76543210	*Meaning*
. 1	Right Shift key is depressed
. . . . . .1.	Left Shift key is depressed
. . . . .1. .	Ctrl key is depressed
. . . .1. . .	Alt key is depressed
. . .1. . . .	Scroll Lock is enabled
. .1.	Num Lock is enabled
.1.	Caps Lock is enabled
1.	Insert key has been toggled

Int 16h   Function 03h
Adjust Keyboard Repeat Rate

Sets the keyboard repeat delay time and repeat rate

Calling Registers: AH   03h

AL   Subfunction:
  00h, Restore default rate and delay
    (PC*jr* only)
  01h, Increase initial delay (PC*jr* only)
  02h, Cut repeat rate in half (PC*jr* only)
  03h, Increase initial delay and cut repeat rate
    in half (PC*jr* only)
  04h, Turn off keyboard repeat (PC*jr* only)
  05h, Set repeat rate and delay (Personal
    Computer AT only)

BH   Repeat delay (AT and PS/2 only)
  $(0–3 \times 250 \text{ ms})$

BL   Repeat rate (AT and PS/2 only) (00h-1Fh, lower
  values give higher rates)

Return Registers: Nothing

Comments: This function is not available on the PC or the PC/XT. For details of its use, either experiment or refer to the bibliography.

Int 16h   Function 04h
                    Key-Click On/Off

Turns the key-click sound (issued when a key is struck) on or off

Calling Registers: AH   04h
                         AL   00h, key-click off
                                     01h, key-click on

Return Registers: Nothing

Comments: *This function is available only on the PCjr;* it is not available on the PC, the PC/XT, the Personal Computer AT, or the PS/2.

Int 16h   Function 05h
                    Write to Keyboard Buffer

Writes to an enhanced keyboard's buffer

Calling Registers: AH   05h
                         CH   Scan code
                         CL   Character

Return Registers: AL   1 if buffer is full

Comments: *This function works only on Personal Computer ATs and PS/2s with enhanced keyboards.* To determine whether a system has an enhanced keyboard, follow these steps:

1. Use Function 05h to write FFFFh to the keyboard's buffer.

2. Use Function 10h to read from the keyboard.

   If you do not get FFFFh back within 16 tries (the size of the keyboard buffer), you do not have an enhanced keyboard.

Int 16h   Function 10h
                    Get Keystroke

Gets a keystroke from an enhanced keyboard

Calling Registers: AH   10h

Return Registers: AH   Scan code
                         AL   Character

Comments: This function, *which works only on Personal Computer ATs and PS/2s with enhanced keyboards,* adds to keyboard processing a recognition of similarly named keys. For example, the keyboard has two Alt keys (Left and Right); this function adds recognition of the Left versus the Right Alt key. (For a table of additional available key identifications, see Int 16h, Function 12h.) The discussion of Int 16h, Function 05h tells you how to determine whether an enhanced keyboard is present.

Int 16h Function 11h
Check Keyboard

Checks an enhanced keyboard for a keystroke

Calling Registers: AH 11h

Return Registers: Zero flag clear if keystroke is available
AH Scan code
AL Character

Zero flag set if no keystroke is available

Comments: *This function works only on Personal Computer ATs and PS/2s with enhanced keyboards.* Like other keyboard input routines, this function returns the character and scan code if a character is available and returns the zero flag set if no character is available. This function can be used to implement input routines that poll the keyboard regularly but do other work while waiting for input.

Int 16h Function 12h
Get Keyboard Status Flags

Returns the status of enhanced keyboard Shift keys

Calling Registers: AH 12h

Return Registers: AL Status flag 1
AH Status flag 2

Comments: This function, *which works only on Personal Computer ATs and PS/2s with enhanced keyboards,* is similar in purpose and operation to Int 16h, Function 02h, except extended information is returned. The meaning of the status flags returned by this function is shown in tables BIOS.29 and BIOS.30. Notice that the information provided in table BIOS.29 (returned in AL) is the same as that returned in AL by Int 16h, Function 02h (refer to table BIOS.28).

Table BIOS.29. *BIOS Keyboard Status Flag 1*

Bit 76543210	Meaning
. 1	Right Shift key is depressed
. . . . . .1.	Left Shift key is depressed
. . . . .1..	Either Ctrl key is depressed
. . . .1...	Either Alt key is depressed
. . .1....	Scroll Lock is enabled
. .1.....	Num Lock is enabled
.1......	Caps Lock is enabled
1.......	Insert key has been toggled

Table BIOS.30. *BIOS Keyboard Status Flag 2*

Bit 76543210	Meaning
. 1	Left Ctrl key is depressed
. . . . . .1.	Left Alt key is depressed
. . . . .1..	Right Ctrl key is depressed
. . . .1...	Right Alt key is depressed
. . .1....	Scroll Lock is depressed
. .1.....	Num Lock key is depressed
.1......	Caps Lock key is depressed
1.......	SysReq Key is depressed

Int 17h

Function 00h
Write Character to Printer

Outputs a character to a parallel printer port

Calling Registers:	AH	00h
	AL	Character
	DX	Printer number (0–2)

Return Registers:	AH	Printer status (see table BIOS.31)

Comments: This function writes the specified character to the printer port and returns the printer's current status, as shown in table BIOS.31.

Table BIOS.31. *Print Status Bits*

Bit 76543210	*Meaning*
. 1	Timeout
. . . . .xx.	Unused
. . . .1. . .	I/O error
. . .1. . . .	Printer selected
. .1.	Out of paper
.1.	Acknowledged
1.	Printer *not* busy

Not all printers return the specified items of status information. Because of this lack of standardization among printer manufacturers, it is not advisable to depend on status information unless genuine IBM printers are involved. In particular, if no printer is connected, the BIOS functions will often (but not always) report status indicating that the printer is ready and data is being successfully transferred; if the printer is connected but either powered down or off-line, the "ready" indication is normally *not* given.

Int 17h

Function 01h
Initialize Printer Port

Sends a reset sequence to a parallel printer port

Calling Registers: AH   01h
                               DX   Printer number (0–2)

Return Registers: AH   Printer status (refer to table BIOS.31)

Comments: This function initializes the parallel printer port and returns the port's status (refer to table BIOS.31). The function outputs the byte sequence 08h 0Ch to the printer port (note that these are control signals, not data characters). EPSON and IBM printers respond to this sequence by performing a reset. Other printers, however, may not respond correctly and, if they are not EPSON- or IBM-compatible, may even exhibit undesirable effects from the code sequence.

DOS
PROGRAMMING

Int 17h   Function 02h
Request Printer Port Status

Returns the status of a parallel printer port

Calling Registers: AH   02h
                        DX   Printer number (0–2)

Return Registers: AH   Printer status (refer to table BIOS.31)

Comments: This function returns the current status of the specified parallel printer port (refer to table BIOS.31).

   Note that if you are using a Personal Computer AT, a PC XT 286, or a Personal System/2 machine, and the BIOS determines that the printer is busy (see bit 7 of table BIOS.31), the BIOS will execute an Int 15h, Function 90h. (See the description of that function for additional information.)

Int 18h
Execute ROM BASIC

Starts up BASIC from ROM

Calling Registers: None

Return Registers: Nothing

Comments: On IBM systems, the ROM BASIC interpreter is still included in all BIOS ROM sets. During the boot process, if a floppy disk is not found and no hard disk is present, this interrupt is triggered to execute ROM BASIC (a cassette BASIC interpreter). This interrupt is rarely used directly. User-written software should not trigger this interrupt.

   But ROM BASIC is still necessary because the BASICA interpreter on IBM distribution disks uses ROM BASIC for many of its routines. Because ROM BASIC is not present on compatibles, you cannot start IBM BASIC on a compatible.

   On PS/2 systems, ROM BASIC is still included in the BIOS.

Int 19h
System Warm Boot

Initiates a boot sequence

Calling Registers: None

Return Registers: Nothing

Comments: This function, which is similar to Ctrl-Alt-Del, performs a warm boot of the computer without losing the present status of memory. (Ctrl-Alt-Del performs a warm boot and also resets the machine state and the memory allocations.)

Contrary to some references, neither of these methods is the same as a power-off restart, which causes the entire system to be reset and power-on checks (including memory checks) to be performed.

When this interrupt is executed, it reads track 0, sector 1 (the boot code) from the disk to memory, starting at address 0000:7C00. The DL register is set to the drive number from which the boot is taking place, and then the boot code at that address (0000:7C00h) is executed. If there is a hardware error (the BIOS cannot locate a boot sector that can be loaded), an Int 18h is executed.

Int 1Ah   Function 00h
Get Clock Counter

Returns the value of the system clock counter

Calling Registers:	AH	00h

Return Registers:	AL	Midnight flag
	CX	High-order word clock count
	DX	Low-order word clock count

Comments: This interrupt retrieves the system clock counter, which ticks 18.2065 times per second, starting with zero (at midnight).

Midnight is determined as the number of ticks in a complete day of 86,400 seconds (1,573,040 ticks of the clock, for a total elapsed time of 86,399.9121 seconds). A flag byte in RAM is set to 1 when midnight passes, and calling this function returns the content of that flag byte in the AL register. Note that if midnight passes *twice* before this function is called, the second event is ignored.

You reset AL to zero by executing this function. But be careful—other date routines may need the midnight-passage information.

Int 1Ah   Function 01h
Set Clock Counter

Sets the value of the system clock counter

Calling Registers:	AH	01h
	CX	High-order word clock count
	DX	Low-order word clock count

Return Registers:	Nothing

Comments: This interrupt sets the system clock counter. To set the clock to a particular time, you compute the number of ticks (since midnight) that you want to represent. This number becomes the new setting for the clock.

To determine the number of ticks, you compute the number of seconds since midnight for the desired time setting and multiply that number by 18.2065 (the number of ticks per second). But be careful—the BIOS does not protect you from illegal values. If you specify a value outside a normal day's range (24 hours, or 1800Bh ticks), the BIOS will accept it.

Int 1Ah

Function 02h
Read Real-Time Clock

Returns the time maintained by the real-time clock

Calling Registers: AH   02h

Return Registers: Carry flag clear if successful
           CH   Hours (BCD)
           CL   Minutes (BCD)
           DH   Seconds (BCD)
           DL   Daylight saving time flag (not supported in all
                      BIOS versions)

           Carry flag set if error

Comments: This function, *which is available only on the PC XT 286, Personal Computer AT, or PS/2 line,* returns the clock values in BCD (binary coded decimal). If the Personal Computer AT BIOS is dated before 6/10/85, the value in DL, which indicates the presence of the daylight saving time option, is not returned.

BCD means that each 4-bit nibble is interpreted as a single decimal digit and that hexadecimal digits A through F are ignored. Table BIOS.32 shows the decimal values that correspond to the range of hexadecimal values in a 4-bit nibble representing BCD digits.

To use table BIOS.32, determine which digits correspond to a byte that has been coded BCD, then look at each nibble of the byte. For example, a byte value of 34h represents a decimal value of 34 in BCD. The byte A3h is undefined in BCD coding because the first nibble (A) is outside the range of allowed BCD representations.

If the carry flag is set, the clock is not functioning and the return values should be ignored.

Table BIOS.32. *BCD Correspondence Table*

Hex Value	Decimal Value
0	0
1	1
2	2
3	3
4	4
5	5
6	6
7	7
8	8
9	9
A	Undefined
B	Undefined
C	Undefined
D	Undefined
E	Undefined
F	Undefined

Int 1Ah   Function 03h
Set Real-Time Clock

Sets the time maintained by the real-time clock

Calling Registers:

AH	03h
CH	Hours (BCD)
CL	Minutes (BCD)
DH	Seconds (BCD)
DL	Daylight saving time (not supported in all BIOS versions)

Return Registers: Nothing

Comments: *This function is available only on the PC XT 286, Personal Computer AT, or PS/2 line.* Clock values should be set in BCD (binary coded decimal). Each 4-bit nibble is interpreted as a single decimal digit; hexadecimal digits A through F are ignored. Table BIOS.32 shows the decimal values that correspond to the full range of hexadecimal values in a 4-bit nibble representing a BCD digit.

Register DL is coded to indicate whether the clock is keeping standard time (DL=0) or daylight saving time (DL=1). If the Personal Computer AT BIOS is dated before 6/10/85, the value in DL, which indicates the presence of the daylight saving time option, is not acted upon and does not need to be set.

Int 1Ah

Function 04h
Read Date from Real-Time Clock

Returns the date maintained by the real-time clock

Calling Registers: AH   04h

Return Registers: Carry flag clear if successful
                    CH   Century (BCD)
                    CL   Year (BCD)
                    DH   Month (BCD)
                    DL   Day (BCD)

                  Carry flag set if error

Comments: This function, *which is available only on the PC XT 286, Personal Computer AT, and PS/2 line,* returns the clock values in BCD (binary coded decimal). Each 4-bit nibble is interpreted as a single decimal digit; hexadecimal digits A through F are ignored. Table BIOS.32 shows the decimal values that correspond to the full range of hexadecimal values in a 4-bit nibble representing a BCD digit.

     If the carry flag is set, the clock is not functioning. Return values should be ignored.

Int 1Ah

Function 05h
Set Date of Real-Time Clock

Sets the date maintained by the real-time clock

Calling Registers: AH   05h
                    CH   Century (BCD) (19 or 20)
                    CL   Year (BCD)
                    DH   Month (BCD)
                    DL   Day (BCD)

Return Registers: Nothing

Comments: *This function is available only on the PC XT 286, Personal Computer AT, or PS/2 line.* Clock values should be set in BCD (binary coded decimal). Each 4-bit nibble is interpreted as a single decimal digit; hexadecimal digits A through F are ignored. Table BIOS.32 shows the decimal values that correspond to the full range of hexadecimal values in a 4-bit nibble representing a BCD digit.

     The values provided to the BIOS must be correct because no range checking is done on them. Incorrect values will cause unpredictable settings of the clock.

Int 1Ah

Function 06h
`Set System Alarm`

Sets the system alarm timer to generate an interrupt at a future time

Calling Registers:

AH	06h
CH	Hours (BCD)
CL	Minutes (BCD)
DH	Seconds (BCD)

Return Registers: Carry flag clear if successful

Carry flag set if error

Comments: *This function is available only on the PC XT 286, Personal Computer AT, or PS/2 line.* The alarm settings must be in BCD (binary coded decimal). Each 4-bit nibble is interpreted as a single decimal digit; hexadecimal digits A through F are ignored. Table BIOS.32 shows the decimal values that correspond to the full range of hexadecimal values in a 4-bit nibble representing a BCD digit.

The alarm setting is an offset time from the present time. When the time runs out, the system will trigger Int 04h (arithmetic overflow). The program that sets the alarm must check the validity of the values provided because BIOS does no checking. Before you reset an alarm, you must disable it with function 07h and set up an interrupt handler to deal with the alarm.

On return, a set carry flag indicates that an error has occurred. Either the alarm has been set previously without being disabled, or the clock is not functioning.

Int 1Ah

Function 07h
`Disable Real-Time Clock Alarm`

Turns off the system alarm timer

Calling Registers: AH   07h

Return Registers: Nothing

Comments: This function, *which is available only on the PC XT, Personal Computer AT, and PS/2 lines,* disables the real-time alarm clock. If you have already set the alarm, this function must be called before you can reset it.

Int 1Ah

Function 09h
Read Real-Time Clock Alarm

Returns the status of the system alarm timer

Calling Registers: AH   09h

Return Registers: CH   BCD hours
                         CL   BCD minutes
                         DH   BCD seconds
                         DL   Alarm Status:
                                   0, not enabled
                                   1, enabled, no power on
                                   2, enabled, will power on system
                                      (Convertible only)

Comments: This function, *which is available only on the PC Convertible and the PS/2 Model 30,* reports the setting and status of the real-time alarm clock.

Int 1Ah

Function 0Ah
Get Day Count

Returns a count of the days since 01/01/1980

Calling Registers: AH   0Ah

Return Registers: CX   Total count of days since 01/01/1980

Comments: This function, *which is available only on the PC XT with BIOS dated 01/10/86 or later and on the PS/2 line,* returns in the CX register the total count of days since January 1, 1980.

Int 1Ah

Function 0Bh
Set Day Count

Sets the number of days since 01/01/1980

Calling Registers: AH   0Ah
                         CX   Total count of days since 01/01/1980

Return Registers: Nothing

Comments: This function, *which is available only on the PC XT with BIOS dated 01/10/86 or later and on the PS/2 line,* passes to the BIOS in the CX register the total count of days since January 1, 1980. This value is stored internally to maintain the system calendar; the effect is to change the calendar setting.

Int 1Ah
Function 80h
Set Sound Source

Selects a sound source to be used by the system

Calling Registers: AH   80h
                               AL   Sound source:
                                                   00h, 8253 chip, channel 2
                                                   01h, cassette input
                                                   02h, audio in line of I/O channel
                                                   03h, sound generator chip

Return Registers: Nothing

Comments: This function, *which is available only on the PCjr,* selects one of four sources for the internal sound system. No other computer in the PC line has such sound capabilities.

Int 1Bh
Ctrl-Break Address

Address of the Ctrl-Break interrupt handler

Calling Registers: None

Return Registers: Nothing

Comments: Interrupt vector 1Bh contains the address of the Ctrl-Break interrupt handler. Control is transferred to this address when a program is terminated by a Ctrl-Break key sequence. When the ROM BIOS finds the Ctrl-Break character during keyboard input, the BIOS calls the handler immediately. Because this takes place during the character scan of the keyboard at the BIOS level, it is not guaranteed to be safe with respect to DOS. (See Chapter 11, "Interrupt Handlers," for a discussion of safe interrupt handling.)

During initialization, the ROM BIOS sets this vector to point to an IRET instruction. DOS resets the vector to point to a handler in DOS, which forces a Ctrl-C character into the keyboard buffer that DOS maintains (separate from the one maintained by the BIOS). DOS will then discover that Ctrl-C the next time it checks for one.

This makes the effects of both handlers identical, but delays action on the Ctrl-Break keystroke until it is safe to do something. The Ctrl-C interrupt (Int 23h) is a DOS-level action and is not executed until DOS is in a "safe" position. Ctrl-Break, being handled at ROM BIOS level, cannot tell whether DOS conditions are safe.

The simplest Ctrl-Break (or Ctrl-C) handler for a program points the interrupt to another IRET instruction so that the Ctrl-Break (or Ctrl-C) character is ignored. Then the program can process these characters as they arrive in the input stream.

Int 1Ch
Timer Tick Interrupt

Interrupt called by the system timer interrupts on each clock tick

Calling Registers: None

Return Registers: Nothing

Comments: Vector 1Ch, the timer tick interrupt called by Int 08h (System Metronome), is initialized to point to an IRET instruction. A TSR that needs to be triggered at each clock tick can reset the vector for this interrupt to point to a custom interrupt handler.

Because this function is called from inside the Int 08h code, before the handling of that top-priority action is completed, it shares the top priority and will prevent the system from responding to any other hardware interrupt requests, including those from serial devices or disk units, while it executes. Therefore, it is necessary to keep to an absolute minimum the time spent in any handler for this function, or you will risk the loss of data when time-sensitive applications are running.

The best practice for a TSR is merely to set a flag from this function, then inspect the flag from another handler hooked into the Int 28h (DosOK) chain, which has ample time to take care of any needed processing without blocking hardware interrupts.

Int 1Dh
Video-Initialization Parameter Table

Pointer to a parameter table used for video controller initialization

Calling Registers: None

Return Registers: Nothing

Comments: Int 1Dh (which is not a true interrupt) points to a table of initialization parameters for the video controller. Because Int 1Dh is *not* executable code, this interrupt should not be called by a program. The results of an attempt to execute code at this interrupt will be unpredictable—most likely a system lockup.

Int 1Eh
Disk-Initialization Parameter Table

Pointer to a diskette base table used for disk controller initialization

Calling Registers: None

Return Registers: Nothing

Comments: Int 1Eh (which is not a true interrupt) points to the diskette base table, a table of initialization parameters for the disk controller. Because Int 1Eh is *not* executable code, this interrupt should not be called by a program. The results of an attempt to execute code at this interrupt will be unpredictable—most likely a system lockup.

Although this table can be modified to optimize disk accesses and tune a system, *any modification should be done with extreme care because the procedure can destroy anything and everything you have stored on disk.*

Int 1Fh
Graphics Display Character Bit-Map Table

Pointer to a bit-map table used for video character generation

Calling Registers: None

Return Registers: Nothing

Comments: Int 1Fh (which is not a true interrupt) points to a table of character bit maps for the graphics mode representations of ASCII characters 128 to 255. Because Int 1Fh is *not* executable code, this interrupt should not be called by a program. The results of an attempt to execute code at this interrupt will be unpredictable—most likely a system lockup.

The bit-map table contains 128 characters (a total area of 1K) and is simply constructed. Each entry is eight bytes long and represents one 8-by-8 character. Each byte corresponds to one scan line in the character.

The following sample character represents an uppercase *I*—the coding includes a blank scan line at the top and bottom, one scan line each for the top and bottom bars, and four scan lines for the central vertical bar:

```
  1 2 3 4 5 6 7 8
1 0 0 0 0 0 0 0 0
2 0 1 1 1 1 1 1 0
3 0 0 0 1 1 0 0 0
4 0 0 0 1 1 0 0 0
5 0 0 0 1 1 0 0 0
6 0 0 0 1 1 0 0 0
7 0 1 1 1 1 1 1 0
8 0 0 0 0 0 0 0 0
```

Byte String: 00h, 7Eh, 14h, 14h, 14h, 14h, 7Eh, 00h

By resetting the pointer, you can create your own characters for use in CGA graphics modes.

Int 70h

Real-Time Clock Interrupt

Called 1024 times per second to control periodic and alarm functions

Calling Registers: None

Return Registers: Nothing

Comments: *This function applies only to Personal Computer AT, PC XT 286, and PS/2 product lines.* (The periodic function is not included on the PS/2 Model 30.)

The real-time clock interrupt is called nearly 1024 times per second. Whenever the interrupt is called, a double-word counter is decremented by 976 microseconds (1/1024 of a second). The initial value of this counter is set by calls to Int 15h, Function 83h (Event Wait) or Function 86h (Delay) as part of the call. When the counter reaches a value less than or equal to zero, bit 7 of the designated wait flag is set. For Function 83h, the wait flag is specified by the ES:BX register pointer. For Function 86h, the flag is at BIOS data area location 0040:00A0h (Delay Active Flag).

If the real-time clock is activated as an alarm function by a call to Int 1Ah, Function 06h, when the time runs out, Int 4Ah is called by Int 70h to activate the alarm handler. (The alarm handler must be set up prior to issuing the call to Int 1Ah.)

The VESA BIOS

A new industry standards organization, the Video Electronics Standards Association, has proposed a new set of video BIOS functions that will allow applications to access SuperVGA in a standard fashion. The new functions use interrupt 4Fh.

Int 4Fh

Function 00h
Return SuperVGA Information

Returns data about supported SuperVGA capabilities

Calling Registers: AX   4F00h
ES:DI   Address of a 256-byte buffer

Return Registers: AX   Status (see table BIOS.33)
ES:DI   Address of a 256-byte buffer, structured as follows:

     Bytes 0–3, signature ('VESA')
     Byte 4, minor version number
     Byte 5, major version number
     Bytes 6–9, pointer to ASCIIZ OEM string
     Bytes 10–13, capabilities bitmap currently undefined and unused—should be zero
     Bytes 14–17, pointer to list of supported modes, represented by a list of words terminated by FFFFh. (See table BIOS.34 for standard VESA display modes.)

Comments: Before calling the other VESA functions, this function should be called to find out whether VESA is supported.

Table BIOS.33. *VESA Status Return Values*

Status:	If the function is supported, AL = 4Fh	
	AH = 0	Function returned successfully
	AH = 1	Function failed
	AH = 2–FF	Reserved (should be treated as a failure)

Table BIOS.34. *Standard VESA Display Modes*

Mode	Resolution	Colors
100h	640×400	256
101h	640×480	256
102h	800×600	16
103h	800×600	256
104h	1024×768	16
105h	1024×768	256
106h	1280×1024	16
107h	1280×1024	256
6Ah	800×600	16

Note: 6Ah, if supported, can be set using the standard VGA BIOS Mode Select call (Function 00).

Int 4Fh

Function 01h
Return SuperVGA Mode Information

Returns information about the specified mode

Calling Registers: AX   4F01h
                        CX   Desired mode
                        ES:DI   Address of a 256-byte buffer

Return Registers: AX   Status (see table BIOS.33)
                        ES:DI   Address of a 256-byte buffer, structured as follows:

        Bytes 0–1, mode attributes that are bitmapped as follows:

            Bit 0   Mode is supported by current display
            Bit 1   Optional info block is valid
            Bit 2   BIOS text functions are supported
            Bit 3   Color mode
            Bit 4   Graphics mode

        Byte 2, window A attributes that are bitmapped as follows:

            Bit 0   Window is supported
            Bit 1   Window is readable
            Bit 2   Window is writable

        Byte 3, window B attributes that are bitmapped as above

        Bytes 4–5, window granularity (the smallest increment that can be used in selecting the start address of a display window page)

        Bytes 6–7, window size (the size of a page of display memory in kilobytes)

        Bytes 8–9, window A segment

        Bytes 10–11, window B segment

        Bytes 12–15, pointer to display memory windowing function

        Bytes 16–17, bytes per scan line

    The following are optional fields:

        Bytes 18–19, horizontal resolution in pixels (graphics) or characters (text)

Bytes 20–21, vertical resolution in pixels
(graphics) or characters (text)
Byte 22, character cell width in pixels
Byte 23, character cell height in pixels
Byte 24, number of memory planes
Byte 25, bits per pixel
Byte 26, number of banks
Byte 27, memory model
    0 = text mode
    1 = CGA graphics
    2 = Hercules graphics
    3 = 4-plane graphics
    4 = packed pixel graphics
    5 = nonchain 4, 256-color graphics
    6–0F, reserved by VESA
    10–FF, manufacturer defined
Byte 28, bank size

Comments: Because the options fields are predefined, they are not required for standard VESA video modes.

Int 4Fh   Function 02h
Set Super VGA Display Mode

Sets the display mode

Calling Registers: AX   4F02h
                        BX   Display mode number

Return Registers: AX   Status (see table BIOS.33)

Comments: The mode value should follow VESA numbering conventions:

Bits 0–8   Mode number
Bits 9–14   Reserved for future expansion (should be 0)
Bit 15   0, clear memory
              1, preserve memory

PROGRAMMING

Int 4Fh

Function 03h
Return SuperVGA Display Mode

Gets the current display mode

Calling Registers: AX   4F03h

Return Registers: AX   Status (see table BIOS.33)
                         BX   Current display mode

Comments: The mode value should follow VESA numbering conventions:

Bits 0–8   Mode number
Bits 9–14   Reserved for future expansion (should be 0)
Bit 15   0, clear memory
            1, preserve memory

Int 4Fh

Function 04h
Save/Restore SuperVGA Video State

Saves and restores the video state information

Calling Registers: AX   4F04h
                         DL   Subfunction
                                     0, return state buffer size
                                     1, save state
                                     2, restore state
                         CX   States to be saved or restored
                                     Bit 0, video hardware
                                     Bit 1, video BIOS data
                                     Bit 2, video DAC state
                                     Bit 3, SuperVGA state
                         ES:BX   Pointer to save buffer (Subfunctions 1 and 2)

Return Registers: AX   Status (see table BIOS.33)
                         BX   Number of 64-byte blocks needed to save
                                     specified state(s) (Subfunction 0 only)

Comments: Subfunction 0 should be called by the program to find out the size of
the buffer required, then Subfunctions 1 and 2 can be called safely.

Int 4Fh

Function 05h
Display Memory Window Control

Selects a page of display memory or finds out which page is currently displayed

Calling Registers: AX   4F05h

BH   Subfunction
  0, select display memory page
  1, return current display memory page

BL   Window number
  0, A
  1, B

DX   Page starting address in granularity units
  (Subfunction 0 only)

Return Registers: AX   Status (see table BIOS.33)

DX   Current page starting address in granularity
  units (Subfunction 1 only)

Comments: This function can be called directly by a far call. The address is obtained by executing Function 1, and is a double-word pointer at offset 12 (0Ch) in the buffer. If called directly, AX does not need to be set; no status is returned, and AX and DX are destroyed.

PROGRAMMING

DOS Reference

This section covers services offered by DOS. These services are interrupts in the range of 20–2Fh and include many functions that are important for proper program execution. Separate reference sections cover the use of Int 33h for mouse functions and Int 67h for expanded memory management, as well as DOS extenders, extended memory management, and DOS task-switching.

Before getting into the specifics of the DOS services, a few items must be covered so that you can have a solid understanding of how the services are used.

How DOS Services Are Invoked

DOS services are invoked in much the same fashion as the BIOS services—through the use of software interrupts. How interrupts are directly executed depends on the programming language you are using and, in many cases, on the dialect or implementation of that language. Examples throughout this book are in different languages, such as assembler, BASIC, C, and Pascal.

If the DOS interrupt is used for many different functions, the desired function number is loaded in the

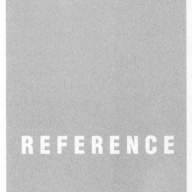

REFERENCE

AH register before the interrupt is called. This may be further modified if the same function number is used for several different subfunctions. In this case, the subfunction number is loaded into the AL register before the interrupt is called.

In addition to the interrupt, function, and subfunction numbers, each DOS service generally requires specific parameters. These parameters usually are provided through the use of CPU registers. Their use varies depending upon the needs of the DOS service and even upon the version of DOS in use.

To recap—in order to use DOS services successfully, you must follow these general steps:

1. Load the necessary registers with the proper parameters for the DOS service.

2. If the DOS interrupt is used for multiple functions, load AH with the proper function number.

3. If the DOS function is used for multiple subfunctions, load AL with the proper subfunction number.

4. Invoke the DOS interrupt.

5. Examine any returned values for validity and use.

Reentrancy

Because DOS was designed as a single-user, single-task system, DOS services are not reentrant. This means that DOS services cannot be called from within other DOS services without running the risk of really mucking things up. For example, if you have developed an interrupt-driven, whiz-bang system and have installed it as a terminate-and-stay-resident (TSR) utility, it is possible that while one interrupt is being handled by your software, another interrupt of the same nature could occur. What do you do? Well, if DOS were reentrant, you could merrily process away, handling each interrupt as it occurred. But this is not possible because DOS is not reentrant. Figure DOS.1 illustrates the possible consequences of such an action.

Notice that at step D, while a DOS command was already in progress, a new interrupt was sensed that started the handler process all over again. The handling of that interrupt was completed with the execution of step I, and control was returned to the original point in the first iteration of the DOS command (step J). At this point, however, all the DOS variables and stack positions previously in use during step C have been changed by steps F and G. The result is predictable: your program loses control of the system, which has locked up in trying to return to the point from which DOS was originally called (at step B) but actually going back to the second call point (at step E).

Fig. DOS.1. *The effects of nonreentrancy in DOS.*

```
A.  Interrupt occurs
          ↓
B.  Interrupt handler
          ↓
C.  DOS command begins
          ↓
D.  New interrupt occurs
          ↓
E.  Interrupt handler
          ↓
F.  DOS command begins
          ↓
G.  DOS command complete
          ↓
H.  Interrupt handler complete
          ↓
I.  Return to original interrupt handler
          ↓
J.  Original DOS command rejoined
```

DOS Function Chart

Table DOS.1 is a quick reference to the DOS functions. In this table, all numbers are in hexadecimal notation. In the register-usage columns, *C* stands for *calling* (meaning that the register is used in calling the function), and *R* stands for *return* (meaning that the register is used to return information). Those interrupts or functions followed by an asterisk are considered undocumented functions (see the section on undocumented functions later in this reference section).

Table DOS.1. DOS Function Chart

Int	Func (AH)	Subfunc (AL)	Purpose	AX	BX	CX	DX	SI	DI	DS	ES	BP
20			Terminate program									
21	00		Terminate program	C								
	01		Keyboard input with Echo	CR								
	02		Display output	C			C					
	03		Auxiliary input	CR								
	04		Auxiliary output	C			C					
	05		Printer output	C			C					
	06		Direct console I/O	CR			C					
	07		Direct STDIN input	CR								
	08		STDIN input	CR								
	09		Display string	C			C			C		
	0A		Buffered STDIN input	C			C			C		
	0B		Check STDIN status	CR								
	0C		Clear buffer and input	CR			C			C		
	0D		Reset disk	C								
	0E		Select disk	CR			C					
	0F		Open file (FCB)	CR			C			C		
	10		Close file (FCB)	CR			C			C		
	11		Search for first entry (FCB)	CR			C			C		
	12		Search for next entry (FCB)	CR			C			C		
	13		Delete file (FCB)	CR			C			C		
	14		Read sequential file (FCB)	CR			C			C		
	15		Write sequential file (FCB)	CR			C			C		
	16		Create file (FCB)	CR			C			C		
	17		Rename file (FCB)	CR			C			C		
	18		Reserved									
	19		Get default drive	CR								
	1A		Set DTA address	C			C			C		
	1B		Get allocation table information	CR	R	R	R			R		

Int	Func (AH)	Subfunc (AL)	Purpose	AX	BX	CX	DX	SI	DI	DS	ES	BP
	1C		Get allocation table information for specific drive	CR	R	R	CR			R		
	1D		Reserved									
	1E		Reserved									
	1F		Get default disk parameter block	CR	R					R		
	20		Reserved									
	21		Random file read (FCB)	CR			C			C		
	22		Random file write (FCB)	CR			C			C		
	23		Get file size (FCB)	CR			C			C		
	24		Set random record field (FCB)	C			C			C		
	25		Set interrupt vector	C			C			C		
	26		Create PSP	C			C					
	27		Random block read (FCB)	CR		CR	C			C		
	28		Random block write (FCB)	CR		CR	C			C		
	29		Parse file name	CR				CR	CR	CR	CR	
	2A		Get system date	CR		R	R					
	2B		Set system date	CR		C	C					
	2C		Get system time	C		R	R					
	2D		Set system time	CR		C	C					
	2E		Set verify flag	C			C					
	2F		Get DTA address	C	R						R	
	30		Get DOS version number	CR	R	R						
	31		Terminate and stay resident	C			C					
	32		Get drive parameter block	CR	R		C			R		
	33	00	Get Ctrl-Break flag	C			R					
	33	01	Set Ctrl-Break flag	C			C					
	33	05	Get boot drive code	C			R					
	33	06	Get MS-DOS version	C	R		R					
	34		Return address of InDOS flag	C	R						R	

continues

Table DOS.1. *continued*

Int	Func (AH)	Subfunc (AL)	Purpose	AX	BX	CX	DX	SI	DI	DS	ES	BP
	35		Get interrupt vector	C	R						R	
	36		Get free disk space	CR	R	R	CR					
	37	00*	Get switchchar	CR			R					
		01*	Set switchchar	CR			C					
		02*	Read device availability	CR			R					
		03*	Sets device availability	CR			CR					
	38		Get/set country information	CR	CR		CR			CR		
	39		Create subdirectory	CR			C			C		
	3A		Remove subdirectory	CR			C			C		
	3B		Set directory	CR			C			C		
	3C		Create/truncate file (handle)	CR		C	C			C		
	3D		Open file (handle)	CR			C			C		
	3E		Close file (handle)	CR	C							
	3F		Read file or device (handle)	CR	C	C	C			C		
	40		Write to a file or device (handle)	CR	C	C	C			C		
	41		Delete file	CR			C			C		
	42		Move file pointer	CR	C	C	CR					
	43	00	Get file attributes	CR		R	C			C		
	43	01	Set file attributes	CR		C	C			C		
	44		Device driver control (IOCTL)									
	44	00	Get device information	CR	C		R					
		01	Set device information	CR	C		C					
		02	Device IOCTL read	CR	C	C	C			C		
		03	Device IOCTL write	CR	C	C	C			C		
		04	Block driver IOCTL read	CR	C	C	C			C		
		05	Block driver IOCTL write	CR	C	C	C			C		
		06	Get input status	CR	C							
		07	Get output status	CR	C							
		08	Block device removable?	CR	C							

Int	Func (AH)	Subfunc (AL)	Purpose	AX	BX	CX	DX	SI	DI	DS	ES	BP
		09	Block device local or remote?	CR	C		R					
		0A	Handle local or remote?	CR	C		R					
		0B	Set sharing retry count	CR		C	C					
		0C	Generic I/O control for handles	CR	C	C	C			C		
		0D	Generic I/O control for block devices	CR	C	C	C			C		
		0E	Get logical drive map	CR	C							
		0F	Set logical drive map	CR	C							
		10	Query IOCTL handle	CR	C	C						
		11	Query IOCTL device	CR	C	C						
	45		Duplicate handle	CR	C							
	46		Force duplicate handle	CR	C	C						
	47		Get current directory	CR			C	CR		CR		
	48		Allocate memory	CR	CR							
	49		Release memory	CR							C	
	4A		Modify memory allocation	CR	CR						C	
	4B	00	Execute program (EXEC)	CR	C		C			C	C	
		01	Load program but do not execute	CR	C		C			C	C	
		03	Load overlay	CR	C		C			C	C	
		05	Enter exec state	CR			C			C		
	4C		Terminate with return code	C								
	4D		Get return code	CR								
	4E		Search for first match	CR		C	C			C		
	4F		Search for next match	CR								
	50		Set PSP segment	C	C							
	51		Get PSP segment	C	R							
	52*		Get disk list	C	R						R	
	53*		Translate BPB to DPB	C				C		C	C	C
	54		Get verify flag	CR								
	55*		Create PSP	C			C					
	56		Rename file	CR			C		C	C	C	

continues

Table DOS.1. *continued*

Int	Func (AH)	Subfunc (AL)	Purpose	AX	BX	CX	DX	SI	DI	DS	ES	BP
	57	00	Get file date and time	CR	C	R	R					
		01	Set file date and time	CR	C	C	C					
	58	00	Get allocation strategy	CR								
		01	Set allocation strategy	CR	C							
		02	Get UMB link status	CR								
		03	Set UMB link	CR	C							
	59		Get extended error information	CR	CR	R						
	5A		Create uniquely named file	CR		C	CR			CR		
	5B		Create new file	CR		C	C			C		
	5C	00	Set file access locks	CR	C	C	C	C	C			
	5C	01	Clear file access locks	CR	C	C	C	C	C			
	5D	00*	Copy data to DOS save area	C			R			R		
		06*	Get critical-error flag address	C			R			R		
		0A	Set error data values	C			C			C		
	5E	00	Get machine name	CR		R	CR	C		CR		
		01*	Set machine name	CR			C			C		
		02	Set network printer setup	CR	C	C		C		C		
		03	Get network printer setup	CR	C	R			CR		CR	
	5F	02	Get redirection list entry	CR	CR	R	R	CR	CR	CR	CR	R
		03	Set redirection list entry	CR	C	C		C	C	C	C	
		04	Cancel redirection list entry	CR			C			C		
	60*		Expand path name string	CR			C	CR	C	CR		
	61		Reserved									
	62		Get PSP address	C	R							
	63	00	Get system lead byte table	C			R			R		

Int	Func (AH)	Subfunc (AL)	Purpose	AX	BX	CX	DX	SI	DI	DS	ES	BP
		01	Set/clear interim console flag	C			C					
		02	Get value of interim console flag	C			R					
	64*		Set current country byte	C								
	65		Get extended country information	CR	C	C	C		CR		CR	
	65	20	Convert character	C			CR					
	65	21	Convert string	C		C	C				C	
	65	22	Convert ASCIIZ string	C			C				C	
	66	01	Get global code page	CR	R		R					
		02	Set global code page	CR	C		C					
	67		Set handle count	CR	C							
	68		Flush buffer	CR	C							
	69		Reserved									
	6A*		Allocate memory	CR	C							
	6B		Reserved									
	6C		Extended open/create	CR	C	CR	C	C		C		
22			Terminate address									
23			Ctrl-C interrupt handler									
24			Critical-error handler	CR				C	C			C
25			Absolute disk read	CR	C	C	C			C		
26			Absolute disk write	CR	C	C	C			C		
27			Terminate and stay resident			C						
28*			DOS safe to use									
29*			Fast putchar	C								
2A*			Microsoft Networks interface									
2B			Reserved									
2C			Reserved									
2D			Reserved									
2E*			Primary shell program loader				C		C			

continues

DOS
PROGRAMMING

Table DOS.1. *continued*

Int	Func (AH)	Subfunc (AL)	Purpose	AX	BX	CX	DX	SI	DI	DS	ES	BP
2F			Multiplex service interrupt									
2F	01	00	Print installation check	CR								
		01	Submit file to print spooler	CR			C			C		
		02	Print file from print queue	CR			C			C		
		03	Cancel all files in print queue	CR								
		04	Hold print jobs	CR			R	R		R		
		05	End print hold	CR								
		06	Get printer device	CR					R		R	
2F	05*		Get outboard critical-error handler installation status	CR								
	06	00	Get ASSIGN.COM/ ASSIGN.EXE installation status	CR								
	08*	00	Get DRIVER.SYS installation status	CR								
	10	00	Get SHARE.EXE installation status	CR								
	11	00	Get network redirector installation status	CR								
	12	00*	Get DOS installation status	CR								
		01*	Flush file	CR	C							
		02*	Get interrupt vector address	C	R						R	
		03*	Get DOS data segment	C					R			
		04*	Normalize path separator	CR								
		05*	Output a character	C								
		06*	Invoke critical error	CR								
		07*	Move disk buffer	C				R	R			
		08*	Decrement user count	CR				C		C		
		0C*	IOCTL open used by DOS	C								
		0D*	Get date and time for file closing	CR		R						

Int	Func (AH)	Subfunc (AL)	Purpose	AX	BX	CX	DX	SI	DI	DS	ES	BP
		0E*	Search buffer chain	C								
		10*	Find modified buffer, Time delay	C								
		11*	Normalize ASCIIZ file name	C				C	CR	C	CR	
		12*	Find ASCIIZ string length	C		R			C		C	
		13*	Case and country conversion	CR								
		14*	Compare 32-bit numbers	C				C	C	C	C	
		16*	Get DCB address	CR	C				R		R	
		17*	Get LDT address	CR				R		R		
		18*	Get user stack address	C				R		R		
		19*	Set LDT pointers	C								
		1A*	Get drive code from path name	CR				CR		CR		
		1B*	Adjust for leap year	CR		C						
		1C*	Calculate days since start-of-month	C		C	CR	C		C		
		1D*	Calculate date	C		CR	CR	C		C		
		1E*	Compare strings	C				C	C	C	C	
		1F*	Initialize LDT	CR								
		20*	Get DCB number	CR	C				R		R	
		21*	Expand ASCIIZ path name	CR				R	CR	R	CR	
		22*	Translate extended error codes	C								
		24*	Execute delay	C								
		25*	Get ASCIIZ string length	C		R		R		R		
		26*	Open file	CR		C	C					
		27*	Close file	CR	C							
		28*	Position file pointer	CR	C	C	CR					C
		29*	Read file	CR	C	C	C			C		
		2B*	IOCTL interface	CR	C	C	CR			C		C
		2D*	Get extended error code	CR								
		2F*	Store DX	C			C					

continues

DOS
PROGRAMMING

Table DOS.1. *continued*

Int	Func (AH)	Subfunc (AL)	Purpose	AX	BX	CX	DX	SI	DI	DS	ES	BP
	14	00	Get NLSFUNC installation status	CR								
	15*		CDROM interface	CR								
	16	80	MS-DOS idle call	C								
	1A	00	Get ANSI.SYS installed state	CR								
	43	00	Get XMS driver installed state	CR								
		10	Get XMS driver entry point address	C	R					R		
	48	00	Get DOSKEY.COM installed state	CR								
		10	Read command line	CR			C		C			
	4B	01	Build notification chain	C	CR	C	C			CR		
		02	Detect switcher	CR	C				CR	CR		
		03	Allocate switcher ID	CR	CR			C		C		
		04	Free switcher ID	CR	CR			C		C		
		05	Identify instance data	C	CR	C	C			CR		
	AD	80	Get KEYB.COM version number	C	R							
		81	Get KEYB.COM active code page	CR	C							
		82	Set KEYB.COM country flag	C	C							
		83	Get KEYB.COM country flag	C	R							
	B0	00	Get GRAFTABL.COM installed state	CR								
	B7	00	Check for APPEND installation	CR								
		02	Get APPEND version	CR								
		04	Get APPEND path pointer	CR					R		R	
		06	Get APPEND function state	CR	R							
		07	Set APPEND function state	CR	C							

Int	Func (AH)	Subfunc (AL)	Purpose	AX	BX	CX	DX	SI	DI	DS	ES	BP
		11	Set return found name state	CR								
33			Mouse interrupt									
	00		Initialize the mouse	CR	R							
	01		Show mouse cursor	CR								
	02		Hide mouse cursor	C								
	03		Get mouse position	C	R	R	R					
	04		Set mouse position	C		C	C					
	05		Get button-press information	CR	CR	R	R					
	06		Get button-release information	CR	CR	R	R					
	07		Set mouse X limits	C		C	C					
	08		Set mouse Y limits	C		C	C					
	09		Set graphics cursor shape	C	C	C	C				C	
	0A		Set text cursor type	C	C	C	C					
	0B		Read motion counters	C		R	R					
	0C		Set user-defined event handler	C		C	C				C	
	0D		Start light pen emulation	C								
	0E		Stop light pen emulation	C								
	0F		Set mickey-to-pixel ratio	C		C	C					
	10		Conditional cursor off	C		C	C	C	C			
	13		Set double speed threshold	C			C					
	14		Swap user event handlers	C		C	C				C	
	15		Get save-state storage size	C	R							
	16		Save mouse driver state	C			C				C	
	17		Restore mouse driver state	C			C				C	
	18		Set alternate mouse user handler	CR		C	C				C	

continues

Table DOS.1. *continued*

Int	Func (AH)	Subfunc (AL)	Purpose	AX	BX	CX	DX	SI	DI	DS	ES	BP
	19		Get user alternate interrupt vector	C	R	CR	R					
	1A		Set mouse sensitivity	C	C	C	C					
	1B		Get mouse sensitivity	C	R	R	R					
	1C		Set interrupt rate	C	C							
	1D		Set CRT page number	C	C							
	1E		Get CRT page number	C	R							
	1F		Disable mouse driver	CR	R						C	
	20		Enable mouse driver	C								
	21		Software reset	CR	R							
	22		Set message language	C	C							
	23		Get message language	C	R							
	24		Get mouse information	C	R	R						
5C			NETBIOS interface									
67	40		Get Manager status	CR								
	41		Get page frame segment	CR	R							
	42		Get page counts	CR	R		R					
	43		Get handle and allocate memory	CR	C		R					
	44		Map/unmap memory	CR	C		C					
	45		Deallocate handle and memory	CR			C					
	46		Get EMM version	CR								
	47		Save page map	CR			C					
	48		Restore page map	CR			C					
	49		Reserved									
	4A		Reserved									
	4B		Get handle count	CR	R							
	4C		Get pages owned by handle	CR	R		C					
	4D		Get pages for all handles	CR	R				C		C	
	4E	00	Get page map registers	CR					C		C	
		01	Set page map registers	CR				C		C		

Int	Func (AH)	Subfunc (AL)	Purpose	AX	BX	CX	DX	SI	DI	DS	ES	BP
							Register Usage					
		02	Get and set page map registers	CR				C	C	C	C	
		03	Get size for page map array	CR								
	4F	00	Get partial page map	CR				C	C	C	C	
		01	Set partial page map	CR				C		C		
		02	Get partial page map size	CR	C							
	50	00	Map/unmap multiple handle pages (physical page number mode)	CR		C	C	C		C		
		01	Map/unmap multiple handle pages (segment address mode)	CR		C	C	C		C		
	51		Reallocate pages	CR	CR		C					
	52	00	Get handle attribute	CR			C					
		01	Set handle attribute	CR	C		C					
		02	Get attribute capability	CR								
	53	00	Get handle name	CR			C		C		C	
		01	Set handle name	CR			C		C		C	
	54	00	Get handle directory	CR					C		C	
		01	Find named handle	CR			R	C		C		
		02	Get handle count	CR	R							
	55		Alter page map and jump	CR			C	C		C		
	56	00	Alter page map and call (physical page number mode)	CR			C	C		C		
		01	Alter page map and call (segment address mode)	CR			C	C		C		
		02	Get stack space size	CR	R							
	57	00	Move memory region	CR				C		C		
		01	Exchange memory regions	CR				C		C		
	58	00	Get mappable physical address array	CR		R			C		C	
		01	Get mappable physical address array size	CR		R						

continues

Table DOS.1. *continued*

Int	Func (AH)	Subfunc (AL)	Purpose	AX	BX	CX	DX	SI	DI	DS	ES	BP
	59	00	Get expanded memory hardware information	CR					C		C	
		01	Get unallocated raw page count	CR	R		R					
	5A	00	Allocate standard pages	CR	C		R					
		01	Allocate raw pages	CR	C		R					
	5B	00	Get alternate map registers	CR	R				R		R	
		01	Set alternate map registers	CR	C				C		C	
		02	Get alternate map register set size	CR			R					
		03	Allocate alternate map register set	CR	R							
		04	Deallocate alternate map register set	CR	C							
		05	Allocate DMA register set	CR	R							
		06	Enable DMA register set	CR	C		C					
		07	Disable DMA register set	CR	C							
		08	Deallocate DMA register set	CR	C							
	5C		Prepare hardware for warm boot	CR								
	5D	00	Enable OS/E functions	CR	R	R						
		01	Disable OS/E functions	CR	CR	CR						
		02	OS/E access key code to EMS	CR	C	C						

Note: Undocumented (reserved) functions are marked with an asterisk (*).

Int 33h for mouse functions is covered in the mouse reference section, and Int 67h for expanded memory management is covered in the EMS reference section of this book.

Int 5Ch, NETBIOS interface, is listed in the chart for your information. Because extensive coverage of local area networks is beyond the scope of this book, Int 5Ch is not covered in the "DOS Reference" section.

Reserved Functions

The functions listed in table DOS.2 are considered reserved by IBM and Microsoft. According to Tim Paterson (the author of MS-DOS's immediate ancestor, 86-DOS), the first four were included in 86-DOS specifically for compatibility with the older CP/M operating system, but IBM chose not to document them in its original DOS version. They have survived to provide backward compatibility to V1. These functions, which are invoked through Int 21h, are not included in the DOS service reference listings later in this section. The reason for the existence of Function 61h is not known, but it uses the same two-instruction code sequence as the older four.

Table DOS.2. Reserved Functions

Int	Function
21h	18h
	1Dh
	1Eh
	20h
	61h
2Bh	
2Ch	
2Dh	

Undocumented Functions

Other functions undocumented by IBM or Microsoft, but whose meaning and use have been documented by programmers over time, are listed in table DOS.3. Many times the function's meaning and use has been accrued by tedious trial-and-error and poring over code listings. The functions are presented here and later in the DOS service reference listings for your information. Keep in mind, however, that because they are officially undocumented, IBM, Microsoft, or other DOS vendors may change them at any time without notice. You should test their operation on your system and verify that the same results are returned for your particular applications. See also Appendix E, "The Reserved DOS Functions," which presents added information concerning the undocumented and reserved functions.

Table DOS.3. *Undocumented Interrupts and Functions*

Int	Function	Purpose
21h	37h	Get/set switchchar
	52h	Get disk list
	53h	Translate BPB
	55h	Create PSP
	5Dh	Get critical-error flag address
	60h	Expand to full path name
29h		Fast putchar
2Eh		Execute command

Later in this section, as each reserved function is presented, you will notice the "stop sign" icon beside the function. This indicates that extreme caution should be used with the function presented. No other warning will be given about the function.

How DOS Services Are Presented

In this section, a standard format is used to present each DOS service. All services are organized in ascending numeric order by interrupt and function number. A sample of this presentation format follows:

Int 21h   **Function 66h   Subfunction 01h**   **V3.3**
                     Get global code page

The first line for each function lists the interrupt number, the function number (if any), the subfunction number (if any), and the DOS version availability. The second line lists the purpose of the function. Additional information includes a quick description, calling registers, return registers, and comments. Let's examine each element of this format.

Interrupt Number

The interrupt number is the one used to invoke the service. DOS interrupts covered in this section include those shown in table DOS.4.

Table DOS.4. *DOS Interrupts*

Interrupt	Purpose
20h	Program termination
21h	Multipurpose DOS interrupt
22h	Terminate address
23h	Ctrl-C interrupt vector
24h	Critical-error vector
25h	Absolute disk read
26h	Absolute disk write
27h	Terminate and stay resident
28h	Keyboard busy loop
29h	Fast putchar
2Ah	Network interface
2Eh	Execute command
2Fh	Multiplex interface
33h	Mouse interface
5Ch	NETBIOS interface
67h	LIM-EMS interface

Function Number

The function number, a designator loaded into the AH register, is used by the DOS interrupt to determine which service is desired. Although it is true that the function number is optional depending upon the interrupt being invoked, in reality it is almost a necessity. For instance, Int 21h has more than 150 functions available as of this writing, all of which are covered in this section except for the five "reserved functions" described earlier.

Subfunction Number

Like the function number, the subfunction is an optional designator that further defines the desired DOS service. Only a few DOS functions are divided into subfunctions, and these subfunctions are covered in this reference section as well. If the DOS function being selected requires the specification of a subfunction, the subfunction number is loaded into the AL register before the DOS interrupt is invoked. If no subfunctions are supported by the function, the use of AL may not be defined, or it may be used to pass other parameters to the DOS service.

DOS Version Availability

"DOS Version Availability" is a designation of the DOS version number in which the service became available. This is of vital importance because you do not want to try to invoke DOS services that are not supported by the operating system in use.

Purpose

The next portion is simply a statement of the meaning of the DOS service. It is designed to give a quick overview of what the service is designed to accomplish. In most instances, the purpose is garnered from technical publications of IBM and Microsoft, the creators of DOS. In a few instances, however, their listed purposes are unclear, ambiguous, or imprecise. In these cases, the stated purposes have been semantically modified for greater clarity.

Description

The description is a quick, one- or two-sentence indication of what the DOS service can do. It is similar to the "Purpose" section but is expanded to provide a brief explanation of the scope of the service.

Calling Registers

A list of the CPU register settings needed by the DOS service to function properly is next. Usually, these are referred to as parameters although they may include pointers to required parameter tables. This portion of the function listing is a quick checklist of register settings required for the service.

Return Registers

Like the "Calling Registers" portion of the DOS function listing, "Return Registers" is a quick checklist of the values returned in registers by the DOS service. It gives a good listing of what is provided by the particular DOS service.

Comments

The "Comments" section is the body of each DOS service listing. It provides a narrative explanation of what the function does, how it is used, possible uses, and any quirks that should be noted. If the DOS function requires the use of parameter tables, they are either described in this section or information that helps you determine the table content is provided.

DOS Services

Int 20h

V1

Terminate Program

Terminates a program's operation and returns control to the process that spawned the program, normally COMMAND.COM

Calling Registers: None

Return Registers: None

Comments: Old DOS hands will recognize this function because it was the standard way to terminate programs on DOS V1. It performs the same basic operations as those provided by Function 00h. With the introduction of DOS Functions 4Ch and 31h, this is no longer the recommended way to terminate a program unless it must maintain compatibility with DOS V1 systems. The newer functions allow exit codes to be returned from higher-level programs or batch files. In fact, the newer versions of DOS handle the Int 20h action by converting it to a call to Int 21h with AX set to 4C00h. Thus, on those systems, this interrupt actually results in an exit code of 00h.

Microsoft recommends that this function no longer be used, unless it is needed to maintain older software. Support for this function may end at any time. Function 4Ch should be used instead.

In addition to terminating the program and freeing the memory space occupied by the program, this interrupt does the following:

1. Restores the termination-handler vector from the program segment prefix (offset 0Ah)

2. Restores the Ctrl-C vector from the program segment prefix (offset 0Eh)

3. In V2 and above, restores the critical-error handler vector from the program segment prefix (offset 12h)

PROGRAMMING

4. Flushes to disk the file buffers used by DOS itself (*not* those within any programs)

5. Frees any memory owned by the terminating program

Item 3 is not done by versions of DOS prior to V2. After these items are completed, system control is transferred to the termination-handler address as restored in item 1.

Although this process sounds complete, it is not complete enough if you are using file control block (FCB) file-handling functions. With FCB functions, the files are not closed by use of this command. Even though the information in the buffers that DOS keeps for itself is written to the disk (they have been flushed), the directory information is *not* updated to reflect changes to the file, nor is there any guarantee that file buffers inside an application have been flushed. Only the close file function for FCBs (Function 10h) will properly close the file, update the directory, and free the buffer space for use by other programs. As a result, and as a practice of good programming style, it is a good idea to explicitly close any open files before using this program-termination function.

EXE programs calling this function must take extra care because the CS register must point to the segment the program segment prefix (PSP) is in. With COM programs, this is usually the case, but there is no such assurance with EXE programs. In most cases, this is not a problem, and a call without explicitly setting the CS register will work.

Upon completion of the program-termination function, system control is returned to the parent program that invoked the recently terminated child with the EXEC function (DOS Function 4Bh). Normally, this parent is COMMAND.COM, but it could be any other program. If returning to DOS, control is passed to the resident portion of COMMAND.COM, where a memory test is done to determine if the transient section needs to be reloaded. If this checksum test fails, the transient portion is reloaded. Finally, if a batch file is in progress, the next line of the batch file is retrieved and executed.

| **Int 21h** | **Function 00h** | **V1** |
| | *Terminate Program* | |

Terminates a program and returns control to the process that spawned the program

Calling Registers: AH   00h
                          CS   PSP segment address

Return Registers: None

Comments: This function is operationally identical to Int 20h. Refer to the "Comments" section of the Int 20h description for more information.

Int 21h	**Function 01h**	**V1**
	Keyboard Input with Echo	

Reads a character from the keyboard (STDIN beginning with DOS V2) and echoes the character to the video display (STDOUT beginning with DOS V2)

Calling Registers: AH   01h

Return Registers: AL   8-bit data

Comments: This is the simplest method of keyboard input that programmers are likely to use. The function simply waits for a character to be entered from the keyboard, echoes the character to the video display, and returns it to the program.

With DOS V1, it was this simple: The function retrieved characters only from the keyboard and displayed them only on the video display. Starting with DOS V2, however, the process was complicated with the introduction of redirection. Now a character is retrieved from the standard input device (STDIN) and displayed on the standard output device (STDOUT). Normally, STDIN is the keyboard and STDOUT is the video display, but these may be redirected by the user.

If no character is available at STDIN, this function will wait until one is available. If STDIN has been redirected to a device other than the keyboard, this can cause problems if the input is variable or sporadic. If working with the keyboard, however, this method of operation is reasonable and usually desirable.

When a character is available and has been displayed, its ASCII value is returned. If the character is an extended ASCII character, a zero will be returned, and another call to this function will be required to return the scan code of the key pressed. The extended ASCII codes are detailed in Appendix A, "The ASCII Character Set."

When STDIN and STDOUT are redirected, problems can occur when using this function:

- If input is coming from a file, a zero byte that does not correspond to an extended keyboard code may be returned.

- The function cannot detect the end of a file in DOS versions before V4. With V4, a fatal error (Out of Data) is reported at the end of file when input is redirected.

These considerations may cause significant problems when STDIN has been redirected so that input is retrieved from a file. Because of this, you may want to use a different DOS input function: 06h, 07h, 08h, or 3Fh (when using handle 0, STDIN).

When you use this function, pressing Ctrl-C or Ctrl-Break causes Int 23h to be invoked before returning from the function.

Like all DOS keyboard input functions that perform Ctrl-C checks, this function can be misled by certain Alt-key input combinations (those which return a scan code with a bit pattern that DOS misinterprets, and responds to, as being Ctrl-Q, Ctrl-S, or Ctrl-P; these keys are, respectively, Alt-W, Alt-R, and Alt-Q).

Microsoft recommends that this function no longer be used, unless it is needed to maintain older software. Support for this function may end at any time. Function 3Fh should be used instead.

Int 21h   Function 02h   V1
Display Output

Outputs a character to the video display (STDOUT beginning with DOS V2.0)

Calling Registers: AH   02h
DL   8-bit character data

Return Registers: None

Comments: Like most of the other low-numbered I/O functions accessed through Int 21h, this function's use depends on the version of DOS being used. If operating under DOS V1, this function directs output to the video display only. Beginning with DOS V2, output is directed to the standard output device (STDOUT), which defaults to the video display.

The system will properly handle a backspace character as a nondestructive backspace on the screen. Ctrl-C and Ctrl-Break are also handled (through Int 23h) if either is detected during the operation.

If output is redirected by the user, this function can cause problems. If output is sent to a file, a disk error can "hang" your system because there is no intrinsic method (before V4) for this function to sense or handle disk errors. (V4 introduced improved error handling that can force a fatal error termination of your program.) Notice that there are no return values for this function, and thus no way to indicate an error while attempting to output a character. Because of this consideration, you may want to use a different DOS output function, such as Function 40h, using the predefined handle 1 (STDOUT).

Microsoft recommends that you no longer use this function, unless it is needed to maintain older software. Support for this function may end at any time. Function 40h should be used instead.

Int 21h   Function 03h   V1
Auxiliary Input

Reads a character from the first serial port (STDAUX beginning with DOS V2)

Calling Registers: AH   03h

Return Registers: AL   8-bit input data from STDAUX

Comments: Unlike the keyboard, a serial device is unbuffered, which means that it handles characters one at a time as they are available. If characters become available faster than they can be handled by your software, they are lost. This function retrieves a character from the serial port. If no character is available, the function will wait until one is available before returning.

Beginning with DOS V2, this function retrieves characters from the standard auxiliary device (STDAUX), which defaults to COM1. Under IBM's version of DOS, COM1 has a default initialization of 2400 bps, 8 data bits, no parity, and 1 stop bit. The DOS MODE command can be used to redirect STDAUX, and the data format settings can be changed either with BIOS functions (see Chapter 7, "Serial Devices," and the BIOS reference) or directly at a hardware level. This latter method is beyond the scope of this book.

Unfortunately, there is no access to information about the status of the serial port through this DOS function. You cannot tell whether a character is waiting or has been lost, nor can you set the parameters for the port. This is a major flaw in a system with serial devices. To do anything serious with serial ports, you must go at least to the BIOS level and generally to the hardware level with custom interrupt-handling software to run the port.

Ctrl-C and Ctrl-Break processing is enabled during this function. If either Ctrl-C or Ctrl-Break is detected, Int 23h is executed immediately.

In addition to this function, you can also use Function 3Fh with the predefined handle 3 (STDAUX) to read information from the serial port.

Microsoft recommends that you no longer use this function, unless it is needed to maintain older software. Support for this function may end at any time. Function 3Fh should be used instead.

Int 21h	**Function 04h**	**V1**
	Auxiliary Output	

Outputs a character to the first serial port (STDAUX beginning with DOS V2)

Calling Registers: AH   04h
                          DL   8-bit data to output to STDAUX

Return Registers: None

Comments: This function is used to send a character out the serial port. Beginning with DOS V2, output is directed to the standard auxiliary device (STDAUX), which defaults to the first serial port. IBM's version of DOS initializes COM1 as the default STDAUX at 2400 bps, 8 data bits, no parity, and 1 stop bit. Although other versions of DOS can differ in the default data format, all should default to COM1 as the standard auxiliary device.

DOS
PROGRAMMING

If the STDAUX device is not free when output is attempted, this function waits until it is. Thus, "hanging" the computer is relatively easy if this function is invoked while STDAUX is not available. A more useful function would return information about the status of the serial port. At present, this function is of limited value to the serious programmer. To do anything serious with serial ports, you must go at least to the BIOS level and generally to the hardware level with custom interrupt handling software to run the port.

Fortunately, Ctrl-C and Ctrl-Break processing is enabled during this call. Upon detection of either a Ctrl-C or Ctrl-Break, Int 23h is invoked. By intercepting the Ctrl-Break handler, it may be possible to recover from a "hung" computer that is waiting for a serial port which will never be available. This, however, is unwieldy and cumbersome. It is better (and more user friendly) to program other methods of controlling the serial port.

As with other DOS device control functions, you can send a character out STDAUX by using DOS Function 40h with the predefined handle 3 (STDAUX).

Microsoft recommends that you no longer use this function, unless it is needed to maintain older software. Support for this function may end at any time. Function 40h should be used instead.

Int 21h   Function 05h   V1
Printer Output

Outputs a character to the printer (STDPRN beginning with DOS V2)

Calling Registers: AH   05h
                      DL   8-bit data to print to STDPRN

Return Registers: None

Comments: This function waits until the printer is ready and then sends a byte. Because no printer-status information is returned, the computer could "hang" while waiting for a printer that is not attached to the system or not ready. You can achieve more satisfactory results with the BIOS printer functions (Int 17h) or through DOS Function 40h using the predefined handle 04.   *574*

Ctrl-C and Ctrl-Break are detected during this function and will cause the execution of Int 23h.

Microsoft recommends that you no longer use this function, unless it is needed to maintain older software. Support for this function may end at any time. Function 40h should be used instead.   *670*

Int 21h   Function 06h   V1
Direct Console I/O

Reads and writes the console without processing by DOS

Calling Registers: AH   06h

DL   Function requested

00h through 0FEh, character to output

0FFh, input character request

Return Registers: If outputting a character, nothing is returned

If inputting a character:

Zero flag set (ZF = 1) if no character is available

Zero flag cleared (ZF = 0) if character is available

AL   8-bit data

Comments: This function is unique in that it inputs or outputs characters depending on the setting of the DL register. Because FFh in the DL register says "input," this function clearly cannot be used to output an FFh character—not a major limitation but, in some cases, significant.

If not being able to output all possible ASCII codes is a drawback for your application, you can accomplish the same type of input and output by using DOS Functions 3Fh and 40h with predefined handles 1 (STDIN) and 2 (STDOUT).

This function is sometimes referred to as the *raw* I/O function: it reads characters without echo and ignores Ctrl-C and Ctrl-Break characters, passing them to the program instead of branching to an interrupt handler. Editing, word processing, and other programs that need complete keyboard control because they have to interpret all keystrokes generally use this function. (The opposite of raw I/O is *cooked* I/O; these terms come from the UNIX terminal-handler world where they have specific meanings. See Chapter 12, "Device Drivers," for a discussion of raw and cooked I/O as it relates to character-oriented device drivers.)

As with Function 01h, the codes returned from the keyboard are ASCII codes, except when there is no corresponding ASCII code for the key pressed. If this function returns a zero in AL, calling the function again will return the scan code corresponding to the key pressed. See Appendix A, "The ASCII Character Set," for extended ASCII code information. This is the only DOS function that will properly read certain Alt-key input combinations (those that return as the scan code a bit pattern that DOS misinterprets, and responds to, as being Ctrl-Q, Ctrl-S, or Ctrl-P; these keys are, respectively, Alt-W, Alt-R, and Alt-Q).

Int 21h   **Function 07h**   **V1**

                    Direct STDIN Input

Reads a character from the standard input device (STDIN) without Ctrl-C intercepting

Calling Registers: AH   07h

Return Registers: AL   8-bit input data

Comments: This function handles input similarly to Function 01h, except that the character is not echoed to the video display, and no Ctrl-C or Ctrl-Break handling is supported. On DOS V1 systems, a character is read only from the keyboard. If no character is ready, it waits for one to become available. On DOS V2 and higher, the function reads from the standard input device (STDIN) and thus supports redirection.

When a character is available, its ASCII value is returned. If the character is an extended ASCII character, a zero is returned and another call to this function is required to return the scan code of the key pressed. The extended ASCII codes are detailed in Appendix A, "The ASCII Character Set."

This function does not echo characters to the display screen, allowing the program to control this function as desired. As with direct I/O (Function 06h), this function ignores Ctrl-C and Ctrl-Break characters. If Ctrl-C or Ctrl-Break intervention is required, use Function 08h.

Int 21h	**Function 08h**	**V1**
	STDIN Input	

Reads a character from the standard input device (STDIN)

Calling Registers: AH   08h

Return Registers: AL   8-bit input data

Comments: This function handles input like other DOS input functions. It is most similar to Function 07h, except that Ctrl-C and Ctrl-Break interception is supported.

On DOS V1 systems, a character is read only from the keyboard. If no character is ready, the function waits for one. On DOS V2 and higher, the function reads from the standard input device (STDIN) and thus supports redirection.

When a character is available, its ASCII value is returned. If the character is an extended ASCII character, a zero is returned and another call to this function is required to return the scan code of the key pressed. The extended ASCII codes are detailed in Appendix A, "The ASCII Character Set."

This function does not echo characters to the display screen, allowing the program to control this function as desired. If either Ctrl-C or Ctrl-Break is detected, an Int 23h is executed.

Like all DOS keyboard input functions that perform Ctrl-C checks, this function can be misled by certain Alt-key input combinations (those that return as the scan code a bit pattern that DOS misinterprets, and responds to, as being Ctrl-Q, Ctrl-S, or Ctrl-P; these keys are, respectively, Alt-W, Alt-R, and Alt-Q).

Int 21h   Function 09h   V1
Display String

Outputs a string of characters to the standard output device (STDOUT)

Calling Registers: AH   09h
                        DS:DX Pointer to string terminated by a dollar sign
                               ($, ASCII code 24h)

Return Registers: None

Comments: Displaying strings of characters on the screen is such a normal operation that it would seem strange if a function were not provided for this purpose. Function 09h allows string output operations by outputting a contiguous series of characters in the same way that Function 02h displays single characters. All characters beginning at the specified address are output until a dollar sign ($, ASCII code 24h) is encountered.

The strings handled by this function are unlike strings handled by any high-level language; they must be terminated by a dollar sign. C functions terminate strings with a NUL character, and Pascal and BASIC strings have a length byte (or word). Because of the choice of string terminator, which is a carryover from CP/M days, you cannot output a dollar sign with this function. This severely limits the usefulness of this function in applications programs. Better results generally are achieved by using one of the other DOS output functions to write an efficient string-output routine matched to your high-level language requirements.

Microsoft recommends that you no longer use this function, unless it is needed to maintain older software. Support for this function may end at any time. Function 40h should be used instead.

Int 21h   Function 0Ah   V1
Buffered STDIN Input

Reads characters from the standard input device (STDIN) and places them in a user-specified buffer

Calling Registers: AH   0Ah
                        DS:DX   Pointer to input buffer
                        Byte 0 Number of bytes the buffer can hold
                        Byte 1 Number of bytes read
                        Byte 2–? Returned characters

Return Registers: None

Comments: Buffered STDIN input is a useful, commonly used function that gives you the full power of the normal input functions for keyboard handling. Input is taken from STDIN, which defaults to the keyboard, and is placed in a user-defined buffer area. The keyboard input buffer, which must be specified from the calling program, is set up as follows:

Byte Offset	Contents
0	Maximum number of bytes to read
1	Number of bytes read
2–?	Actual bytes from the keyboard

To use this function, simply store the number of bytes allowed for input in the first byte of the buffer pointed to by DS:DX. Because the buffer size must allow space for a terminating carriage return (ASCII 0Dh), the minimum buffer size is necessarily 1. In use, this would not allow for any actual keyboard input, because the 1 byte set aside for the buffer would be used by the terminating carriage return—not very useful. The realistic minimum buffer size is 2 bytes (1 byte of input plus the carriage return). The maximum buffer size is 255, which is logical because the buffer length specifier is only a single byte.

The function reads in characters from the keyboard and places them in the buffer, beginning with the third byte of the buffer. Each ASCII character requires one byte of buffer space. When the actual number of characters read reaches one less than the size of the buffer, new characters are ignored and the bell rings with each keystroke. When the Enter key is finally pressed, the number of bytes retrieved and stored is placed in the second byte of the buffer, and control is returned to the calling program.

The input itself allows type-ahead, and all keyboard editing commands are active. Ctrl-C and Ctrl-Break functions are active as well, resulting in the execution of Int 23h.

Notice that the size of the string is determined by the value returned in the length byte. This length does not include the terminating carriage return.

Like all DOS keyboard input functions that perform Ctrl-C checks, this function can be misled by certain Alt-key input combinations (those that return as the scan code a bit pattern that DOS misinterprets, and responds to, as being Ctrl-Q, Ctrl-S, or Ctrl-P; these keys are, respectively, Alt-W, Alt-R, and Alt-Q).

Microsoft recommends that you no longer use this function, unless it is needed to maintain older software. Support for this function may end at any time. Function 3Fh should be used instead.

Int 21h

Function 0Bh   **V1**
Check STDIN Status

Checks whether a character is available from the standard input device (STDIN)

Calling Registers:	AH	0Bh

Return Registers:	AL	FFh, character available from STDIN
		00h, character not available from STDIN (prior to V4)
		< > FFh, character not available from STDIN (V4)

Comments: This function checks whether a character is available from STDIN. Because STDIN normally is set to the keyboard, this function ordinarily is used to determine whether a keystroke is waiting in the keyboard buffer.

When called, this function returns immediately with a status in register AL indicating whether a character is waiting to be read. If a character is available, AL will contain FFh. Notice that the actual character is not returned by this function, which merely provides an indication of availability. This function continues to return the same status on successive calls until one of the DOS input functions (01h, 06h, 07h, 08h, or 0Ah) is used to read the character.

If a Ctrl-C or Ctrl-Break is detected during the execution of this function, an Int 23 is invoked.

Int 21h

Function 0Ch   **V1**
Clear Buffer and Input

Clears the standard input device (STDIN) buffer and then executes the designated input function call

Calling Registers: AH   0Ch

                     AL   Function number to perform after clearing the buffer
                            01h, wait for keyboard input

                            06h, direct console I/O
                                DL = FFh, direct console input
                                DL <> FFh, char to write to STDOUT

                            07h, direct console input without echo

                            08h, console input without echo

Return Registers: Return defined by function:
                            01h, wait for keyboard input
                                AL Character from STDIN

06h, direct console I/O
ZF   1, no character available from STDIN
ZF   0, AL = character from STDIN

07h, direct console input without echo
AL   Character from STDIN

08h, console input without echo
AL   Character from STDIN

Comments: This function is provided to allow the programmer to prevent type-ahead mistakes, which often arise during program operation. It prevents a user from accidentally typing past critical program input points. A good example might be a program that will format a disk. You want to ask the user whether he or she really wants to format the disk, because starting the operation destroys the disk. Using this function, you can prevent problems caused by accidental type-ahead.

This is an alternative entry point for earlier DOS input functions: 01h, 06h, 07h, and 08h. The function's only operation is to clear the input buffer; then control is passed to the DOS input function requested in AL. Return values and programming considerations of each of the available DOS input functions apply when using this function.

Microsoft now states that Subfunction 0AH is reserved and should not be used.

Int 21h   Function 0Dh   V1
Reset Disk

Flushes all disk-buffer contents (if modified) to the appropriate disk files

Calling Registers: AH   0Dh

Return Registers: None

Comments: This function writes the contents of the disk buffers to their corresponding disk files (flushes the disk buffers). It does not update the disk directory and should not be used in place of a file-close operation. No other disk operations are affected, nor are any other disk parameters reset.

On a 3Com network, this function forces a new copy of the network volume file allocation table (FAT) to be loaded into memory when all files are closed.

Int 21h   Function 0Eh   V1
Select Disk

Changes the default disk drive

Calling Registers: AH   0Eh

                          DL   Drive number (A = 0 through Z = 25)

Return Registers: AL   Number of logical drives

Comments: In addition to selecting the default drive, this function can be used to determine the number of logical drives associated with the system. Logical drives are the number of block-oriented devices installed on the system—RAM disks, hard disks, disk emulators, and so forth.

This function always returns a minimum value of 2, indicating the presence of two logical drives (DOS always views a single, physical, floppy disk drive as two logical drives, A and B). If you need to determine the number of physical floppy disk drives attached to the system, use BIOS Function 11h.

Beginning with DOS V3, this function returns a minimum last drive value equal to the number of logical drives or the LASTDRIVE value from the CONFIG.SYS file, whichever is greater. If there are only three logical drives and CONFIG.SYS does not specify a LASTDRIVE value, the default LASTDRIVE value of 5 is returned.

The value returned does not necessarily map to a drive letter; a return value of 5, for example, does not mean that there are A, B, C, D and E drives.

The maximum number of drive designators has varied from one DOS version to another as shown in the following table:

DOS Version	Available Designators
1	16 (00–0Fh)
2	63 (00–3Fh)
3	26 (00–19h)

When compatibility with all versions of DOS is required, applications should be limited to a maximum of 16 drives (the maximum number allowed for DOS V1). Those needing compatibility with only V2 and above should be limited to 26. In most cases, the number actually used will be much smaller.

Notice a peculiarity of this function: the value returned in AL is one-based and represents the number of disk drives attached to the system, but the value used to call the function is zero-based and represents the desired default disk drive. Thus, if you want to set the default drive to the last logical drive, you must complete the following steps:

1. Determine the current default drive (use Function 19h).

2. Call this function with DL set to the current default drive retrieved from step 1.

3. Decrement the value returned from step 2 (make it zero-based).

4. Call this function with the derived value from step 3.

Int 21h

Function 0Fh   **V1**
Open File (FCB)

Searches the current directory for the named file; if the named file is found, it is opened and the file control block (FCB) is filled in

Calling Registers: AH   0Fh
                  DS:DX   Pointer to unopened FCB

Return Registers: AL   00h, file opened successfully
                                FFh, file not opened

Comments: This function is used to open an existing disk file that uses an FCB. This function will not create a file; that operation is left to Function 16h. Chapter 9, "Directories and Files," deals with files and explains FCBs in more detail. The open function is called after filling in the drive, file name, and extension fields of the FCB.

You should note that the proper drive designations are 0 for the default drive, 1 for A, 2 for B, and so on. If the function is called with the drive field set for the default drive (0), the field value is automatically changed to the correct drive number so that subsequent calls to the file will remain correct even if the default drive is changed. In addition, the function sets the FCB block field to zero; the record size to 80h (128-character record length); and the file size, date, and time from the requested file's directory entry. If your file operations require the use of a different block number or record size, these values should be changed after this function is completed but before any other FCB file operations.

For applications operating in a network environment, it is important to note that this function automatically opens a file in compatibility mode. If a different mode is required, the handle operations should be used. If a file was created in a different mode and is subsequently opened in compatibility mode (as with this function), a DOS critical error is generated and Int 24h is executed.

As with other FCB file operations, an error is indicated by the status code returned in the AL register. If AL is 0, no error was detected; if AL is FFh, there was an error during the operation.

Microsoft recommends that you no longer use this function, unless it is needed to maintain older software. Support for this function may end at any time. Function 3Dh should be used instead.

Int 21h

Function 10h   **V1**
Close File (FCB)

Closes a previously opened file that uses a file control block (FCB)

Calling Registers: AH   10h
                  DS:DX   Pointer to opened FCB

Return Registers: AL   00h, file closed successfully
                                      FFh, file not closed

Comments: This function is used to close a previously opened disk file that uses an FCB. The close function is essential to proper operation in FCB files because there is no other way to force DOS to update the file's directory entry. Without properly closing a file, data may be lost. Chapter 9, "Directories and Files," deals with files and explains FCBs in more detail.

To use the function, you must provide information in the FCB's file-name, extension, and drive-designator fields. If you are working with a previously opened file, all this information should already be in place.

A feature of the close command is that the system checks for the position of the file within the directory. If it is not the same, the system is supposed to assume that the disk has changed, and AL will have an FFh character on return. It has been documented that this function does not work as advertised on DOS V2. It will, in fact, overwrite the file allocation table (FAT) and directory, thereby damaging the new disk.

As with other FCB file operations, an error is indicated by the status code returned in the AL register. If AL is 0, no error was detected; if it is FFh, there was an error during the operation. For V3 and above, Get Extended Error (Function 59h) may be used to determine the exact error if one is reported.

Microsoft recommends that you no longer use this function, unless it is needed to maintain older software. Support for this function may end at any time. Function 3Eh should be used instead.

Int 21h   Function 11h   V1
                       Search for First Entry (FCB)

Searches for the first matching entry in the current directory

Calling Registers: AH   11h
                          DS:DX   Pointer to unopened FCB

Return Registers: AL   00h, match was found
                                      FFh, no match was found

Comments: This function is used to search for the first occurrence of a specified directory entry that uses a file control block (FCB). Chapter 9, "Directories and Files," explains FCBs in detail. This function is powerful and makes it easy to look for files in a consistent way without damaging the directory structure.

To use this function, you must provide the file name, extension, and drive designators in the appropriate FCB fields. Beginning with DOS V2.1, the question mark (?) is supported as a wild-card character in file-name specifications. Asterisks (*) are allowed as wild cards only under DOS V3 and above.

To search for a file with a specific attribute, you must use an extended FCB (see Chapter 9). Valid attributes are derived from the various attribute bit settings and include the following:

Value	File Types Matched
00h	Normal
02h	Normal and hidden
04h	Normal and system
06h	Normal, hidden, and system
08h	Volume labels
10h	Directories

When the function completes successfully, the disk transfer area (DTA) holds an unopened FCB for the file that was found. If the search is called with an extended FCB, the DTA has an extended FCB; otherwise it has a normal FCB. For more information on the DTA, refer to Chapter 9 and Function 1Ah.

As with other FCB file operations, an error is indicated by the status code returned in the AL register. If AL is 0, no error was detected; if AL is FFh, there was an error during the operation. For V3 and above, Get Extended Error (Function 59h) can be used to determine the exact error if one is reported.

If you are using wild-card characters to search for files, and no error was returned from this function, you can continue the search for the next matching file by using Function 12h.

Microsoft recommends that you no longer use this function, unless it is needed to maintain older software. Support for this function may end at any time. Function 4Eh should be used instead.

Int 21h   **Function 12h**   **V1**
                     Search for Next Entry (FCB)

Searches for the next matching entry in the current directory

Calling Registers: AH   12h
                         DS:DX   Pointer to FCB returned by either
                                  Function 11h or 12h

Return Registers: AL   00h, match was found
                                  FFh, no match was found

Comments: This function, which continues a search begun with Function 11h, can be called as many times as necessary to locate a given file specification in a directory but will search only for the next matching entry, not the first entry. See Function 11h for further information.

Clearly, this function is of value only if the directory entry being searched uses wild-card characters. The file control block (FCB) pointed to by DS:DX should be the same FCB pointed to when Function 11h was called. Again, see the Function 11h comments for more information.

When this function completes successfully, the disk transfer area (DTA) holds an unopened FCB for the file that was found. If the search was originally initiated with an extended FCB, the DTA will have an extended FCB; otherwise, it will have a normal FCB. For more information on the DTA, refer to Chapter 9, "Directories and Files," and Function 1Ah.

As with other FCB file operations, an error is indicated by the status code returned in the AL register. If AL is 0, no error was detected; if AL is FFh, there was an error during the operation. For V3 and above, Get Extended Error (Function 59h) can be used to determine the exact error if one is reported.

If you are using wild-card characters to search for files, and no error was returned from this function, you can continue the search for the next matching file by using this function again.

Microsoft recommends that you no longer use this function, unless it is needed to maintain older software. Support for this function may end at any time. Function 4Fh should be used instead.

Int 21h   **Function 13h**   **V1**
                     Delete File (FCB)

Deletes all allowable directory entries that match the file specifications provided

Calling Registers: AH   13h
                        DS:DX   Pointer to an unopened FCB

Return Registers: AL   00h, file was deleted
                                 FFh, file was not deleted

Comments: This function is used to delete files through a file control block (FCB). Chapter 9, "Directories and Files," deals with files and explains FCBs in more detail. Only normal files can be deleted. Read-only files, system files, hidden files, volume labels, or directories cannot be deleted with this function.

To use this function, you must provide the file name, extension, and drive designators in the appropriate FCB fields. Beginning with DOS V2.1, the question mark (?) is supported as a wild-card character in file-name specifications. Asterisks (*) are allowed as wild cards only if you are running under DOS V3 or above.

Files deleted with this function are not cleared from the disk. The directory entry is modified to indicate that the file has been deleted and that the directory entry is available for use; the data clusters previously used by the file are made available to other files. The data that was contained in the file is left untouched and may be recovered with special file-recovery programs, such as the Norton Utilities, the Mace utilities, or PC Tools.

As with other FCB file operations, an error is indicated by the status code returned in the AL register. If AL is 0, no error was detected; if AL is FFh, there was an error during the operation. Possible causes for error include trying to delete an illegal file or not finding the specified file name. For V3 and above, Get Extended Error (Function 59h) can be used to determine the exact error if one is reported.

Do not try to delete an open file. This can cause problems later when you try to close the file or during program termination when DOS attempts to flush the disk buffer to the deleted file. Files must be closed before you delete them.

In a network environment, you must have create-access rights in order to delete files.

Microsoft recommends that you no longer use this function, unless it is needed to maintain older software. Support for this function may end at any time. Function 41h should be used instead.

Int 21h   Function 14h   V1
Read Sequential File (FCB)

Beginning at the file pointer's current location, reads the next block of data and updates the file pointer

Calling Registers: AH   14h
                          DS:DX   Pointer to an opened FCB

Return Registers: AL   00h, read was successful
                                    01h, no read, already at EOF
                                    02h, read canceled, DTA boundary error
                                    03h, partial read, now at EOF

Comments: This function facilitates the sequential reading of information from a disk file using a file control block (FCB). You can read information only from a file that has been previously opened (Function 0Fh). Chapter 9, "Directories and Files," deals with files and explains FCBs in more detail.

To use this function, you should ensure that DS:DX points to an FCB created after a file was opened successfully. Sequential reads are controlled by the parameters set in the FCB. The length of the read is given in the record-size field. The location is given by the current block number and the current record number. Before issuing this function, you can change the values of these FCB fields to values appropriate for your application.

When the read is completed, the information read from the disk is placed in the disk transfer area (DTA) and the record address in the FCB is automatically incremented. For more information on the DTA, refer to Chapter 9 and Function 1Ah.

Because the information read from the disk is placed in the DTA, be sure that the DTA is large enough to receive the information. Otherwise, information from the disk could overwrite other data.

As with other FCB file operations, an error is indicated by the status code returned in the AL register. If AL is 0, no error was detected; any other value denotes an error during the operation. If the amount of data read by this function results in crossing a memory segment boundary in the DTA (a memory address ending in 000), a failure is indicated with AL = 2. Partial records (AL = 3) are read and padded with zero characters to the end. For V3 and above, Get Extended Error (Function 59h) can be used to determine the exact error if one is reported.

In a network environment, you must have read-access rights in order to use this function.

Microsoft recommends that you no longer use this function, unless it is needed to maintain older software. Support for this function may end at any time. Function 3Fh should be used instead.

Int 21h	Function 15h	V1
	Write Sequential File (FCB)	

Writes the record to the current block and record locations from the file control block (FCB)

Calling Registers:	AH	15h
	DS:DX	Pointer to an opened FCB

Return Registers:	AL	00h, write was successful
		01h, no write attempted, disk full or read-only file
		02h, write canceled, DTA boundary error

Comments: This function facilitates the sequential writing of data to a disk file using an FCB. You can write data only to a previously opened (Function 0Fh) or created (Function 16h) file. Chapter 9, "Directories and Files," deals with files and explains FCBs in more detail.

To use this function, you should ensure that DS:DX points to an FCB created after a file was opened or created successfully. The parameters set in the FCB control sequential writes. The length of the write is given in the record-size field. The location is given by the current block number and the current record number. Before issuing this function, you can change the values of these FCB fields to values appropriate for your application.

Because information written to disk comes from the disk transfer area (DTA), take care that the record size being written is the amount of data you want. Otherwise, other data (garbage) could be written inadvertently to the disk file. For more information on the DTA, refer to Chapter 9 and Function 1Ah.

If the amount of data being written does not fill the entire DOS disk buffer (internal to DOS), the data simply is added to that already in the disk buffer pending a need to write it to the disk. When this function is completed successfully, the record address in the FCB is updated automatically.

As with other FCB file operations, an error is indicated by the status code returned in the AL register. If AL is 0, no error was detected; any other value denotes an error during the operation. If the disk is full or you try to write to a read-only file, AL is equal to 1. If a memory-segment boundary in the DTA (a memory address ending in 000) is crossed during a write operation, the function will fail and return AL = 2.

In a network environment, you must have write-access rights in order to use this function.

Microsoft recommends that you no longer use this function, unless it is needed to maintain older software. Support for this function may end at any time. Function 40h should be used instead.

Int 21h	**Function 16h**	**V1**
	Create File (FCB)	

Creates a disk file based on the information provided in the file control block (FCB)

Calling Registers: AH   16h
                          DS:DX   Pointer to an unopened FCB

Return Registers: AL   00h, file was created
                                    FFh, file was not created

Comments: This function serves as a complement to opening a file (Function 0Fh). It creates the specified file and leaves it open for subsequent use with an FCB. Chapter 9, "Directories and Files," deals with files and explains FCBs in more detail.

Why not use this function all the time? Because file creation also truncates files that already exist—without warning! First, the function searches the current directory for the specified file. If the file is found, it is truncated and the FCB is updated; the file is open as if it were newly created. If the file doesn't exist, it is created and the FCB is set for access to the new file.

To use this function, the FCB's drive, file-name, and extension fields must be provided. When you use an extended FCB, you also can assign an attribute to create a hidden file or a volume label. For information on file attributes, refer to Chapter 9.

As with other FCB file operations, an error is indicated by the status code returned in the AL register. If AL is 0, no error was detected; if AL is FFh, there was an error during the operation. For V3 and above, Get Extended Error (Function 59h) can be used to determine the exact error if one is reported.

In a network environment, you must have create-access rights in order to use this function.

Microsoft recommends that you no longer use this function, unless it is needed to maintain older software. Support for this function may end at any time. Function 3Ch should be used instead.

Int 21h   Function 17h   V1
Rename File (FCB)

Renames an existing file

Calling Registers: AH   17h
                         DS:DX   Pointer to a modified FCB

Return Registers: AL   00h, file was renamed
                                 FFh, file was not renamed

Comments: This function allows you to change the name of existing disk files using a modified file control block (FCB). Only normal files can be renamed; thus read-only files, system files, hidden files, volume labels, or directories cannot be renamed with this function.

This function uses a modified FCB with the following format:

Offset	Meaning
00h	Drive designation
01h	Original file name
09h	Original file extension
11h	New file name
19h	New file extension

Notice that basically only three pieces of information are required: a drive designator (all renaming must occur on the same drive) and the old and new file names. Beginning with DOS V2.1, the question mark (?) is supported as a wild-card character in file-name specifications. Only under DOS V3 and above are asterisks (*) allowed as wild cards. Putting wild cards in the original file name causes the function to try to rename each file that matches the pattern. Putting wild cards in the new file name causes those character positions to remain unchanged in the new file.

Because file names in any given directory must be unique, this function will stop and return an error if it is asked to rename a file to a name that already exists. Through effective use of wild-card matching, you can build a sophisticated, multifile renamer. For example, suppose that you have a series of files named ABC01.DAT, ABC02.DAT, ABC03.DAT, and so on, and that you want to rename them with the extension .OLD. If you choose the original file name ABC??.DAT and the new file name *.OLD, the rename process will proceed smoothly.

As with other FCB file operations, an error is indicated by the status code returned in the AL register. If AL is 0, no error was detected; if AL is FFh, there was an error during the operation. For V3 and above, Get Extended Error (Function 59h) can be used to determine the exact error if one is reported.

In a network environment, you must have create-access rights in order to use this function.

Microsoft recommends that you no longer use this function, unless it is needed to maintain older software. Support for this function may end at any time. Function 56h should be used instead.

Int 21h   Function 19h   V1
Get Default Drive

Returns the number of the current default drive

Calling Registers: AH   19h

Return Registers: AL   Current drive number (A = 0 through Z = 25)

Comments: This function is used to determine which disk drive DOS is using as the default drive. A number, representing the default drive, is returned in the AL register. The number is zero-based, with 0 for drive A, 1 for drive B, and so on. This is a little different from other functions where a 0 may be used to specify the default drive. This function is related to Function 0Eh, which is used to set the default drive.

Int 21h   Function 1Ah   V1
Set DTA Address

Establishes an address that DOS will use as the beginning of the disk transfer area (DTA)

Calling Registers: AH   1Ah
                          DS:DX   Pointer to a new DTA

Return Registers: None

Comments: This function is used to specify a DTA to be used by DOS for disk operations. The DTA is used by many of the DOS functions, most notably the file control block (FCB) file functions. The handle functions used for file searching (Functions 4Eh and 4Fh) and Int 25h and Int 26h also use the DTA. When a program is started, a default DTA of 128 bytes is set aside at offset 80h in the program segment prefix (PSP). The converse of this function is Function 2Fh, which is used to get the current DTA address.

The programmer is responsible for seeing that the DTA used for disk operations is adequate for the tasks undertaken. Because DOS keeps track only of the DTA's beginning address, the system has no way of knowing whether it has reached the end of the DTA during disk operations. The upshot is that program data or code can easily be overwritten by information transferred from the disk if the amount of data being transferred is more than the DTA can hold.

Int 21h   Function 1Bh   V1
                    Get Allocation Table Information

Gets basic information about disk allocation for the disk in the default drive

Calling Registers: AH   1Bh

Return Registers: AL   Sectors per cluster
                         CX   Bytes per physical sector
                         DX   Clusters per disk
                         DS:BX   Pointer to media descriptor byte

Comments: This function returns the information basic to a knowledge of the capacity of the disk in the default drive. The information itself is seldom used as much as the combination of $CX \times AL \times DX$, which gives the disk's total capacity (in bytes). Function 1Ch returns identical information for a disk in a specific drive, and Function 36h is used to determine the amount of free space on a disk.

Beginning with DOS V2, DS:BX points to the media descriptor byte, contained in the file allocation table (FAT), but on DOS V1 it actually points to the FAT in memory. The media descriptor (or FAT ID) byte can be used to identify the media's formatting from the following table:

Value	Meaning
F0h	Not identifiable
F8h	Fixed disk
F9h	Double sided, 15 sectors per track (1.2M)
F9h	Double sided, 9 sectors per track (720K)
FCh	Single sided, 9 sectors per track
FDh	Double sided, 9 sectors per track (360K)
FEh	Single sided, 8 sectors per track
FFh	Double sided, 8 sectors per track

Notice that the F9h FAT ID byte lets you know only that the disk was formatted in a high-capacity disk drive. You must examine the other information returned by this function to determine the disk's actual capacity. Furthermore, FAT IDs are not supported uniformly by all versions of DOS. The standard as given is from the technical manual for the IBM version of DOS and may not apply to a particular manufacturer's version of DOS.

Microsoft recommends that you no longer use this function, unless it is needed to maintain older software. Support for this function may end at any time. Function 36h should be used instead.

Int 21h

Function 1Ch   V2
Get Allocation Table Information for Specific Drive

Gets the basic information about disk allocation for the disk in a specified drive

Calling Registers: AH   1Ch

                            DL   Drive number (current drive = 0,
                                            A = 1 through Z = 26)

Return Registers: AL   Sectors per cluster

                            CX   Bytes per physical sector

                            DX   Clusters per disk

                            DS:BX   Pointer to media descriptor byte

Comments: This function returns the information basic to a knowledge of the capacity of the disk in a specific drive. The information is exactly the same as that returned by Function 1Bh for the default drive. See the comments on Function 1Bh for details.

       Microsoft recommends that you no longer use this function, unless it is needed to maintain older software. Support for this function may end at any time. Function 36h should be used instead.

Int 21h

Function 1Fh   V2
Get Default Disk Parameter Block

Returns the address of the disk parameter block for the default drive

Calling Registers: AH   1Fh

Return Registers: AL   00h, no error
                                              FFh, error

                            DS:BX   Address of drive parameter block

Comments: Use this function to return, in DS:BX, the address of the disk parameter block (DPB) used by DOS to determine specific structural information about the disk in the default drive. The structure of the DPB is shown in table DOS.5.

Table DOS.5. Drive Parameter Block (DPB)		
Offset Byte	*Field Length*	*Meaning*
All Versions		
00h	Byte	Drive number (0 = A, 1 = B, etc.)
01h	Byte	Device driver unit number
02h	Word	Bytes per sector

Offset Byte	Field Length	Meaning
04h	Byte	Sectors per cluster (zero based)
05h	Byte	Shift factor
06h	Word	First sector containing FAT
08h	Byte	Number of FAT copies
09h	Word	Number of root directory entries
0Bh	Word	First data sector number
0Dh	Word	Highest cluster number plus 1

Version 2 or 3 Only

Offset Byte	Field Length	Meaning
0Fh	Byte	Sectors per FAT (0–255)
10h	Word	Root directory starting sector number
12h	Double word	Drive's device driver address
16h	Byte	Media descriptor byte
17h	Byte	Disk parameter block access flag (0FFh indicates need to rebuild)
18h	Double word	Address of next device parameter block

Version 2 Only

Offset Byte	Field Length	Meaning
1Ch	Word	Starting cluster number for current directory
1Eh	64 bytes	ASCIIZ of current directory path

Version 3 Only

Offset Byte	Field Length	Meaning
1Ch	Word	Last cluster number allocated from this drive
1Eh	Word	Purpose unknown; normally FFFFh

Version 4

Offset Byte	Field Length	Meaning
0Fh	Word	Sectors per FAT (0–65,535)
11h	Word	Root directory starting sector number
13h	Double word	Drive's device driver address
17h	Byte	Media descriptor byte
18h	Byte	Disk parameter block access flag (0FFh indicates need to rebuild)
19h	Double word	Address of next device parameter block
1Dh	Word	Last cluster number allocated from this drive
1Fh	Word	Purpose unknown; normally FFFFh

Version 5

Offset Byte	Field Length	Meaning
0Fh	Word	Sectors per FAT (0–65,535)
11h	Word	Root directory's starting sector number
13h	Double word	Drive's device driver address
17h	Byte	Media descriptor byte
18h	Byte	Disk parameter block access flag (0FFh indicates need to rebuild)
19h	Double word	Address of next device parameter block
1Dh	Word	Last cluster number allocated from this drive
1Fh	Word	Number of free clusters

Note that the DPB structure is different for each DOS version. The purpose of each item in the table should be self-explanatory.

Because this function returns a value in the DS register, you should save the value of DS before you call the function.

Int 21h	**Function 21h**	**V1**
	Random File Read (FCB)	

Reads the record specified by the current-block and current-record fields of an FCB from a disk file, placing the information in the disk transfer area (DTA)

Calling Registers: AH   21h
                         DS:DX   Pointer to open FCB

Return Registers: AL   00h, read was successful
                                01h, no read, EOF encountered
                                02h, read canceled, DTA boundary error
                                03h, partial record read, EOF encountered

Comments: This function facilitates the reading of random (nonsequential) information from a disk file with a file control block (FCB). Chapter 9, "Directories and Files," deals with files and explains FCBs in more detail. You can read information only from a file that has been previously opened (Function 0Fh).

To use this function, be sure that DS:DX points to an FCB created after a file was opened successfully. Random reads are controlled by parameters set in the FCB. The record to read is specified in the FCB by setting the random-record field, and the amount of data is controlled by the record-size field. Before issuing this function, you can change the values of these FCB fields to values appropriate for your application. DOS uses these two values to calculate the actual file position at which reading is begun.

When this function is completed, the information read from the disk is in the DTA. For more information on the DTA, refer to Chapter 9, "Directories and Files," and Function 1Ah. The FCB current-position field is not updated by this function as it is with sequential functions. Unless the random-record field is changed, subsequent accesses of the file return the same data.

Because information read from the disk is placed in the DTA, take care that the DTA is large enough to receive the data. Otherwise, information from the disk may overwrite other data.

As with other FCB file operations, an error is indicated by the status code returned in the AL register. If AL is 0, no error was detected; any other value denotes an error during the operation. If the amount of data read by this function results in crossing a memory segment boundary in the DTA (a memory address ending in 000), the function fails and returns AL = 2. Partial records (AL = 3) are read and padded with zero characters to the end.

In a network environment, you must have read-access rights in order to use this function.

Microsoft recommends that you no longer use this function, unless it is needed to maintain older software. Support for this function may end at any time. Function 3Fh should be used instead.

Int 21h Function 22h V1
Random File Write (FCB)

Writes the record specified by the current-block and current-record fields of an FCB to a disk file, transferring the information from the disk transfer area (DTA)

Calling Registers: AH 22h
 DS:DX Pointer to open FCB

Return Registers: AL 00h, write was successful
 01h, no write attempted, disk full or read-only file
 02h, write canceled, DTA boundary error

Comments: This function facilitates the writing of random (nonsequential) information to a disk file that uses a file control block (FCB). You can write information only to a previously opened (Function 0Fh) or created (Function 16h) file. Chapter 9, "Directories and Files," deals with files and explains FCBs in more detail.

To use this function, make sure that DS:DX points to an FCB created after a file is opened or created successfully. Parameters set in the FCB control random writes. The record to write is specified in the FCB by setting the random-record field; the amount of data is controlled by the record-size field. Before issuing this function, you can change the values of these FCB fields to values appropriate for your application. DOS uses these values to calculate the file position at which writing begins.

Because the information written to disk comes from the DTA, you must be careful that the record size being written is the amount of data you want. Otherwise, other data (garbage) could inadvertently be written to the disk file. For more information on the DTA, refer to Chapter 9 and Function 1Ah.

If the data being written does not fill the entire DOS disk buffer (internal to DOS), it is added to the data already in the disk buffer, pending a need to write it to the disk.

Unlike sequential functions, this function does not update the FCB current-position field. Subsequent random writing to the file will transfer information to the same file record unless the random-record field is changed.

As with other FCB file operations, an error is indicated by the status code returned in the AL register. If AL is 0, no error was detected; any other value denotes an error during the operation. If the disk was full or if you attempted to write to a read-only file, AL is equal to 1. If, during a write operation, a memory segment boundary in the DTA (a memory address ending in 000) is crossed, the function fails and returns AL = 2.

In a network environment, you must have write-access rights in order to use this function.

Microsoft recommends that you no longer use this function, unless it is needed to maintain older software. Support for this function may end at any time. Function 40h should be used instead.

Int 21h   Function 23h   V1
Get File Size (FCB)

Searches a directory for a matching file name; if the file is found, fills in the size information in the designated file control block (FCB)

| **Calling Registers:** | AH | 23h |
| | DS:DX | Pointer to unopened FCB |

| **Return Registers:** | AL | 00h, matching file found |
| | | FFh, no matching file found |

Comments: This function is used to determine the number of records in a specified file through the use of an FCB. Chapter 9, "Directories and Files," deals with files and explains FCBs in more detail. The file should be unopened when using this function.

This function can be used after filling in the drive, file-name, extension, and record-size fields of the FCB. The supplied file name must be complete and unique; wild-card characters are not allowed. To find the size of the file in bytes, simply set the record-size field to 1.

If a file is located that matches the specified file name, the random-record field of the FCB pointed to by DS:DX is updated to indicate the number of records in the file. This number is determined by dividing the file size (in bytes) by the record size, resulting in the number of records. If there is any remainder from the division, the number of records is rounded up. If you forget to set the record-size field before calling this function, or for files in which the file-size portion of the directory entry may be incorrect or rounded to reflect a full sector, the information returned by this function may be of questionable value.

As with other FCB file operations, an error is indicated by the status code returned in the AL register. If AL is 0, no error was detected; if AL is FFh, an error occurred during the operation (generally, this means that the specified file was not found).

Microsoft recommends that you no longer use this function, unless it is needed to maintain older software. Support for this function may end at any time. Function 42h should be used instead.

Int 21h   Function 24h   V1
Set Random Record Field (FCB)

When switching from sequential to random file I/O, used to set the file control block (FCB) random-record field based upon the current file position

Calling Registers: AH   24h
                        DS:DX   Pointer to open FCB

Return Registers: None

Comments: This function modifies an open FCB to prepare it for random access functions. This function can be used after filling in the record-size, record-number, and block-number fields of the FCB. The function modifies the random-record field based on these field values. Chapter 9, "Directories and Files," deals with files and explains FCBs in more detail.

Microsoft recommends that you no longer use this function, unless it is needed to maintain older software. Support for this function may end at any time. Function 42h should be used instead.

Int 21h   Function 25h   V1
Set Interrupt Vector

Safely modifies an interrupt vector to point to a specified interrupt handler

Calling Registers: AH   25h
                        AL   Interrupt number
                        DS:DX   Pointer to interrupt handler

Return Registers: None

Comments: This function makes quick work of what can otherwise be a delicate operation—changing interrupt vectors. Because interrupt vectors are maintained in a table in low memory (see Chapter 11, "Interrupt Handlers"), they could easily be changed directly. This can be dangerous, however, if an interrupt occurs during the process—particularly while only a portion of the address has been transferred to the table.

Rather than write your own code to safely manage setting interrupts, you can use this function, which guarantees to safely update the interrupt vector table to an address you supply. This is the only approved method of altering interrupt vectors.

Changing interrupt vectors can lead to some special problems. Interrupts 22h, 23h, and 24h are reset automatically to their original values when a program terminates in a normal manner (see Int 20h, Int 27h, and Functions 00h, 31h, and 4Ch). If the program modifies any other interrupt vectors, these will remain at their changed values, even after the program terminates. This can cause problems; an interrupt condition that occurs after the program has terminated could cause a jump to a nonexistent interrupt handler.

To prevent such a situation, programs that change the interrupt vectors should first use Function 35h to get the original vector value and store it. The original vector value can be restored when the program ends. This has even greater implications for programs that change interrupt vectors. A program that changes vectors to interrupts other than 22h, 23h, or 24h must be able also to trap all the ways in which the program could be terminated abnormally. This means Ctrl-C and Ctrl-Break interrupt servicing, DOS critical-error servicing, and servicing for any other potential interrupt that might cause the program to terminate, such as dividing by zero.

If the program does not intercept any and all methods that might terminate it, hanging interrupt vectors could remain. If a program crashes without being able to reset the interrupt vectors, the only safe course is to reset the system before you do anything else.

Int 21h   Function 26h   V1
Create PSP

Copies the program segment prefix (PSP) from the currently executing program to the specified segment address and then updates it for use by a new program

Calling Registers: AH   26h
                         DX   Segment address for new PSP

Return Registers: None

Comments: This function creates a PSP preparatory to running another program. A copy is made of the current program's PSP at the specified memory segment address. The PSP is covered in detail in Chapter 3, "The Dynamics of DOS."

In theory, you could copy a COM file directly into the memory space after the new PSP and execute the program, but in actuality it would not be a good practice for the simple reason that this function is out of date. It has been superseded, in V2 and later versions, by the more sophisticated and much easier to use EXEC function (Function 4Bh). All Microsoft and IBM documentation recommends using the EXEC function in preference to Function 26h when spawning programs. EXEC better handles the details of program loading and execution and insulates the program from potential errors in operation. This function does not load or execute another program; it simply prepares a PSP for one. The function invoking the program still must load and execute the program.

If your program has changed the interrupt vectors for Int 22h, 23h, and 24h, the new vectors are copied into the newly created PSP. In addition, the memory allocation information is updated appropriately.

Microsoft recommends that you no longer use this function, unless it is needed to maintain older software. Support for this function may end at any time. Function 4Bh, Subfunction 00h, should be used instead.

Int 21h	**Function 27h**	**V1**
	Random Block Read (FCB)	

Reads one or more consecutive random records from a disk file to the disk transfer area (DTA)

Calling Registers:	AH	27h
	CX	Number of records to read
	DS:DX	Pointer to opened FCB
Return Registers:	AL	00h, all records read successfully
		01h, no read, EOF encountered
		02h, read canceled, DTA boundary error
		03h, partial record read, EOF encountered
	CX	Number of records read

Comments: This function facilitates the reading of a group of consecutive random records from a disk file using a file control block (FCB). You can read information only from a file that has been previously opened (Function 0Fh). Chapter 9, "Directories and Files," deals with files and explains FCBs in more detail.

To use this function, make sure that CX contains the number of records you want and that DS:DX points to an FCB created after a file was opened successfully. Parameters set in the FCB control random reads. The beginning record to read is specified in the FCB by setting the random-record field, and the size of each record is controlled by the record-size field. Before issuing this function, you can change the values of these FCB fields to values appropriate for your application. DOS uses these values to calculate the file position at which reading begins.

When this function is completed, the information read from the disk is in the DTA. (For more information on the DTA, refer to Chapter 9 and Function 1Ah.) When the function is successfully completed, the random-record, current-block, and current-record fields of the FCB are updated.

Because the information read from the disk is placed in the DTA, you must be careful that the DTA is large enough to receive the total block of information. Otherwise, other data or program code could be overwritten with information from the disk.

As with other FCB file operations, an error is indicated by the status code returned in the AL register. If AL is 0, no error was detected; any other value denotes an error during the operation. If the amount of data being read by this function results in crossing a memory segment boundary in the DTA (a memory address ending in 000), the function will fail and return AL = 2. Partial records (AL = 3) are read and padded to the end with zero characters.

In a network environment, you must have read-access rights in order to use this function.

Microsoft recommends that you no longer use this function, unless it is needed to maintain older software. Support for this function may end at any time. Functions 3Fh and 42h should be used instead.

Int 21h   Function 28h   V1
Random Block Write (FCB)

Writes one or more consecutive random records to a disk file from the disk transfer area (DTA)

Calling Registers:	AH	28h
	CX	Number of records to write
	DS:DX	Pointer to opened FCB

Return Registers:	AL	00h, all records successfully written
		01h, no write attempted, disk full or read-only file
		02h, write canceled, DTA boundary error
	CX	Number of records written

Comments: This function facilitates the writing of a group of consecutive random records to a disk file using a file control block (FCB). You can write information only to a previously opened (Function 0Fh) or created (Function 16h) file. Chapter 9, "Directories and Files," deals with files and explains FCBs in more detail.

To use this function, make sure that CX contains the number of records to write and that DS:DX points to an FCB created after a file was successfully opened or created. Parameters set in the FCB control random writes. The beginning record to write is specified in the FCB by setting the random-record field, and the size of each record is controlled by the record-size field. Before issuing this function, you can change the values of these FCB fields to values appropriate for your application. DOS uses these values to calculate the file position at which reading begins.

Because the information written to disk comes from the DTA, you must be careful that the record size and number of records being written correspond to the amount of data you want. Otherwise, other data (garbage) could inadvertently be written to the disk file. For more information on the DTA, refer to Chapter 9, "Directories and Files," and Function 1Ah.

If the amount of data being written does not fill the entire DOS disk buffer (internal to DOS), the data is simply added to that already in the disk buffer pending a need to write it to the disk.

When the function has been completed successfully, the FCB's random-record, current-block, and current-record fields are updated.

As with other FCB file operations, an error is indicated by the status code returned in the AL register. If AL is 0, no error was detected; any other value denotes an error during the operation. If the disk was full or if you attempted to write to a read-only file, AL is equal to 1. During a write operation, if a memory segment boundary in the DTA (a memory address ending in 000) is crossed, the function fails and returns AL = 2.

In a network environment, you must have write-access rights in order to use this function.

Microsoft recommends that you no longer use this function, unless it is needed to maintain older software. Support for this function may end at any time. Functions 40h and 42h should be used instead.

Int 21h
Function 29h
Parse File Name
V1

Parses a file-name string into a file control block (FCB) for use

Calling Registers:	AH	29h
	AL	Parse control flag (see table DOS.6)
	DS:SI	Pointer to text string
	ES:DI	Pointer to FCB
Return Registers:	AL	00h, no wild cards encountered
		01h, wild cards found
		FFh, drive specifier invalid
	DS:SI	Pointer to the first character after the parsed file name
	ES:DI	Pointer to the updated, unopened FCB

Comments: Originally, the purpose of this function was to extract file names from command lines and place them in proper format for opening an FCB. To do so, you start with the pointer to the file-name string and a pointer to the FCB you plan to use. This FCB does not have to be in any sort of format—it can be a block of memory sufficient to hold an FCB.

Separator characters in all versions are the period (.), comma (,), colon (:), semicolon (;), equal sign (=), plus sign (+), tab, and space. In DOS V1, the following additional characters serve as separators: the double quotation mark ("), slash (/), left bracket ([), and right bracket (]).

The function returns a proper, unopened FCB for the desired file and a pointer to the first characters after the file name (clearly useful if you are parsing a command line within which the file name is one of several). Asterisk characters are converted automatically into one or more question-mark characters to the end of the file name or extension in this function.

Because this is an FCB function, it is not compatible with path names; therefore you cannot include directories in file names. This function can refer only to files in the current directory. The interpretation of the file name is controlled by a parse flag shown in table DOS.6.

Table DOS.6. *Parse Control Flag*

Bit 76543210	*Meaning*
.......0	Stop parsing if a file separator is encountered
.......1	Ignore leading separators
......0.	Sets the drive ID in the FCB to 0 (default drive) if the string does not contain a drive letter
......1.	The drive ID in the FCB is left alone if the string does not contain a drive letter
.....0..	The file name in the FCB is set to eight spaces (20H) if the string contains no file name
.....1..	The file name in the FCB is left alone if the string contains no file name
....0...	The extension field in the FCB is set to three spaces if the string contains no extension
....1...	The extension field in the FCB is left alone if the strin contains no extension

When you work with FCB functions, this function is useful for setting up the FCB properly. This function results in a properly formatted FCB, ready to be opened. To use the FCB open or create functions, the pointer in ES must be moved to DS:DX.

If there is no valid file name to parse, the function returns the pointer ES:DI so that ES:DI+1 points to a blank character.

Int 21h   **Function 2Ah**   **V1**
                     Get System Date

Gets the year, month, day, and day of the week from the system

Calling Registers: AH   2Ah

Return Registers: CX   Year (1980–2099)
                         DH   Month (1–12)
                         DL   Day (1–31)
                         AL   Day of week (0 = Sunday, 1 = Monday, and so on), DOS V1.1 or later

Comments: This function returns information about DOS's understanding of the current system date. This is simply a check of the DOS internal clock, not an access to a real-time clock/calendar if one is installed. As a general rule, if the system has an installed clock/calendar, it is checked from the AUTOEXEC.BAT file when the system is started or it is set manually by an operator.

Systems that run for days at a time can drift from accurate time in unexpected ways. The system date or time may not be properly updated, or processes may interfere with or change the internal system time. This function might therefore return an incorrect date (but without access to a clock/calendar chip, you cannot check it).

A common error that affects the accuracy of this function afflicts systems that are left running and unused for more than 24 consecutive hours (for instance, over a weekend). Because the date is advanced only when DOS detects that the midnight flag has been set, and this can happen only when one of a limited number of functions is called, the date does not advance while the system is unused. On the next use, the midnight flag is detected but it has no record of how many midnights have gone by; thus, only one day is added to the date. Note that BIOS function 1Ah (Get Clock Count) resets the midnight flag as part of its activity. It is a simple matter to check and change the date the first time the system is used after an extended period without use.

The function uses the same register format as Function 2Bh (Set System Date) for ease of use.

Int 21h — Function 2Bh — V1
Set System Date

Sets the system date to the specified value without affecting the system time

Calling Registers: AH   2Bh
CX   Year (1980–2099)
DH   Month (1–12)
DL   Day (1–31)

Return Registers: AL   00h, date set successfully
FFh, date invalid, not set

Comments: This function uses the same register format as the Get System Date function. If you have a clock/calendar, you can access it to get the current date and update the system date using this function. Without a clock/calendar, you could prompt the user for input and then correct it in the operating system so that calls to the Get System Date function return the correct date.

The date set with this function is used to mark files during file operations.

If your computer system has a CMOS clock, this function causes its date to be set.

Int 21h

Function 2Ch
Get System Time

V1

Gets the system time in hours, minutes, seconds, and hundredths of seconds

Calling Registers:	AH	2Ch

Return Registers:	CH	Hour (0–23)
	CL	Minutes (0–59)
	DH	Seconds (0–59)
	DL	Hundredths of seconds (0–99)

Comments: Like getting the system date, getting the system time is a clearly useful function that we do not pay much attention to. You frequently need this information for reports or screen displays. However, you need to be aware of the following points:

- This function does not retrieve time from a clock/calendar chip. It gets the DOS internal time, which is only as accurate as its setting.

- On many systems, the system's real-time clock is not accurate enough to provide hundredths-of-a-second resolution. In such a situation, the function could return a discontinuous time value for the hundredths-of-a-second value.

  Applications that use the time function for other than actual system time do not need to worry about the time setting. An application such as a timer that is started by setting the DOS time to zero and then checking elapsed time could be useful in some programs. If you write such a program, however, be aware that other programs expect to get the time of day from this clock. If you use it for elapsed time by setting it to zero and then leave it, the person using your program will be upset when other programs return the wrong system time.

  The register format is the same as that used for Function 2Dh (Set System Time).

Int 21h

Function 2Dh
Set System Time

V1

Sets the system time to the specified hour, minute, second, and hundredth of a second without affecting the system date

Calling Registers:	AH	2Dh
	CH	Hour (0–23)
	CL	Minutes (0–59)

	DH	Seconds (0–59)
	DL	Hundredths of seconds (0–99)
Return Registers:	AL	00h, time set successfully
		FFh, time invalid, not set

Comments: Setting the system time can be useful in a number of cases:

- Your program works with a clock/calendar and can set the date and time exactly from the chip

- Your program queries the user for a time to set

- You are using the clock as an elapsed time clock; you can reset it to zero and display or monitor it in terms of elapsed time rather than system time

The register format, which is the same as that used for Function 2Ch (Get System Time), allows you to get the time, ask about it, and then update only what has changed. It is often best to set to an accuracy of no greater than plus or minus one second when working with a person. Trying to set hundredths of a second goes beyond what the typical user wants. Time setting to greater accuracy (for applications in astronomy, for example) requires special synchronizing techniques.

Programs working from a clock/calendar chip or from a time service, such as a WWV radio link, can set the time to hundredths-of-a-second accuracy. Some computers are unable to return this accuracy on a consistent basis because the real-time clock is not accurate enough.

If your computer system has a CMOS clock, this function will cause its time to be set.

Int 21h

Function 2Eh
Set Verify Flag

V1

Toggles the DOS verify flag; turning it on results in an additional CRC (cyclic redundancy check) when writing to disk and increases disk transfer time

Calling Registers:	AH	2Eh
	AL	00h, turn off verify
		01h, turn on verify
	DH	00h (DOS version earlier than 3.0)
Return Registers:	None	

Comments: How could you *not* want to verify your disk writes to make sure that they are correct? But forcing a disk verify of all data written to a disk increases by a factor of 2 the time needed to do the operation. On some non-IBM BIOS variants, the operation is not supported at all.

So why not do it? Time, obviously. When you do not need absolute assurance that every disk write is correct, leaving the verify flag off makes sense. Only for truly critical functions should you bother to set the flag, and then it should be turned off afterward.

Even when the verify flag is turned on, you do not have absolute assurance that data was properly written because the verification process does not perform a byte-by-byte comparison of the data that was written with the data that was supposed to be written. It waits one revolution, reads the data that was written and has the disk controller calculate its CRC value again, then compares the calculated CRC while reading the value that was calculated and written to the disk the first time.

This process offers no protection against any data error that might occur between memory and the disk controller; it verifies only that the controller wrote to disk the same value it used to calculate the first CRC and that it then performed the same calculation two times running. However, because most disk errors involve failure of the media, which would prevent the read-back CRC from matching that which was written, the test does offer some benefit. For critical work, though, such as archival transfer of data that will then be erased from the hard disk, a byte-by-byte comparison of the copy with the original is the only absolute assurance that the copy was done successfully.

Function 54h can be used to determine the current setting of the verify flag.

Int 21h   **Function 2Fh**   **V2**
                               Get DTA Address

Gets the current value of the disk transfer area (DTA) pointer for file control block (FCB) file operations

Calling Registers: AH   2Fh

Return Registers: ES:BX   Pointer to DTA

Comments: The default DTA is a 128-byte buffer at offset 80h in the program segment prefix (PSP). Most programs do not need more than this for their operations. If you are working with larger record sizes or have special disk transfer requirements, however, setting up another DTA is useful.

Function 1Ah sets the DTA; this function (2Fh) tells you where it is. This function does *not* tell you, however, how large the DTA is (and that information is essential). If you are not sure whether the DTA is big enough for what you are doing, you have no choice but to set it yourself to a block of memory big enough to handle the expected operations.

Int 21h Function 30h V2
Get DOS Version Number

Returns the DOS version number for reference so that an application can determine the capabilities of the software system; DOS versions earlier than 2.0 should return a version number of 0

Calling Registers:	AH	30h
	AL	Version flag
	00h	OEM number
	01h	DOS version flag
Return Registers:	AL	Major version number (2, 3)
	AH	Minor version number (2.1 = 10)
	BH	OEM number or DOS version flag
	BL:CX	24-bit serial number

Comments: The DOS version number is important to programmers who deal directly with DOS; it allows them to customize a program to the system version installed. This function, which was added with DOS V2.0, gives you the major and minor version numbers for the DOS under which your program is expected to run. This is a good way to verify at the beginning of a program that the system can support the DOS calls you need. (Note: With Microsoft C and Borland C++, these values are available as global variables.)

If your program works under a DOS earlier than V2.0, the function returns 0 for both major and minor version numbers. This immediately gives you such important information as no path names, no directories, and no hard disk support. If you are writing programs for DOS V2.0 and then later find yourself on DOS 1.x versions, you should do the following:

1. Display an error message with Int 21h, Function 09h.

2. Exit the program with Int 21h, Function 00h.

If you intend to support DOS versions earlier than 2.0, use this information to restrict your use of DOS functions.

DOS V1.x restrictions are not the only ones of concern when you program. Programmers customarily use functions that extend their abilities, as those functions become available. DOS V3.3 added functions that allow you to increase the number of open files and to flush file buffers to disk. By using these functions in a database program, you can make that database easier to write. But a user without DOS V3.3 would be left out (and would not be a prospective buyer) if you did not provide alternative ways of dealing with the problems for earlier versions of DOS.

If the DOS version flag is returned, bit 3 set means that MS-DOS runs in ROM; otherwise, it runs in RAM. The other bits are undefined. If the OEM number is returned, the OEM-dependent serial number in BL:CX, if unused, will be set to zero.

The DOS version number is the value set by the MS-DOS SETVER command, and may be different from the version number returned by Function 3306h.

Int 21h	**Function 31h**	**V2**
	Terminate and Stay Resident	

Terminates a process and returns control to the parent process

Calling Registers: AH   31h
                          AL   Return code
                          DX   Memory size to reserve (in paragraphs)

Return Registers: None

Comments: Terminate and stay resident (TSR) utilities are so common that you would be hard-pressed to find a system that does not use one or more of them. In addition to utilities like pop-up calculators, calendars, and notepads, TSRs can be used to provide common subroutine services for a series of programs. By building a library of functions activated by calls to a specific interrupt, you can provide standard utility routines for several programs without having to link the routines directly to the program. This reduces the size of such modules and speeds up loading them.

The purpose of the TSR function is to terminate (like Function 4Ch) the operation of a program but *not* to return the program's assigned memory to the pool of memory managed by DOS. This allows the program to remain active and to activate if it ties itself to an interrupt of some kind. For example, you could have a program activate and display a clock on the screen if it tied itself to the clock interrupt. Also, the program could be activated if a key is pressed or if a program calls the interrupt function.

This function replaces the Int 27h TSR function originally provided with DOS V1. The original TSR function allowed only 64K of memory for the function and could not provide a return code. This function allows more than 64K of memory and allows control of the return code, which is available to the parent program through Function 4Dh. This allows batch files to control execution with the ERRORLEVEL parameter available inside the batch file.

The TSR function attempts to allocate the memory requested in the DX register out of the memory allocated when the program was started. It does not deal with memory that was assigned to the process by a call to Function 48h.

This function does not close any files that the program opened; files opened by the program remain open. Handle functions are associated with the currently active process through an undocumented area of the program segment prefix (PSP).

When the TSR function is not the currently active process, the files it might refer to using handles are those opened by the real currently active process. This does not apply to file control block (FCB) functions, which are buffered through the process's own memory area. (See Chapter 9, "Directories and Files," for a discussion of FCB functions.)

Thus, any TSR that uses handle functions to deal with files or devices—and needs to use those functions when popped up or otherwise active—must switch DOS's definition of the currently active process using undocumented Functions 50h and 51h, before using the handles. Otherwise, results will not be what you expect and could do severe damage to other programs or data.

Int 21h   Function 32h   V2
Get Drive Parameter Block

Retrieves the drive parameter block that defines the characteristics of the designated disk drive; if called with DL = 0, this function is identical to Function 1Fh

Calling Registers:	AH	32h
	DL	Drive number (0 = default, 1 = A, and so on)
Return Registers:	AL	FFh if drive number invalid
	DS:BX	Address of drive parameter block

Comments: Use this function to return, in DS:BX, the address of the disk parameter block (DPB) used by DOS to determine specific structural information about the disk in the drive specified by DL at entry.

The structure of the DPB is shown in table DOS.5 (see Function 1Fh). Note that the DPB structure is different for each DOS version. The purpose of each item in the table should be self-explanatory.

Because this function returns a value in the DS register, you should save the value of DS before you call the function.

Int 21h   Function 33h Subfunction:00h   V2
Get Ctrl-Break Flag

Gets the status of the Ctrl-Break/Ctrl-C check flag

Calling Registers:	AH	33h
	AL	00h, getting flag status
Return Registers:	DL	00h, Ctrl-Break checking off
		01h, Ctrl-Break checking on

Comments: Except for a few I/O functions (see character I/O Functions 01h–0Ch for the exceptions), checking for Ctrl-Break or Ctrl-C characters is normally not done during much of the Int 21h function handling. When this checking is turned on, the check is performed for *all* Int 21h functions except the few that merely set or get flag data. This subfunction returns in DL the current state of the Ctrl-Break check flag; see Subfunction 01h to change its state.

When checking is enabled, if a Ctrl-Break or Ctrl-C is found, control is turned over to the handler for Int 23h. You can replace the Int 23h handler and deal with the Ctrl-Break or Ctrl-C in a function of your own rather than disable it.

Be aware that the Ctrl-Break/Ctrl-C flag is a system global that affects all processes running on a DOS system. As a system global, some care must be taken with its handling because it is possible to affect processes other than the one activating or deactivating the function.

Int 21h	Function 33h Subfunction 01h	V2
	Set Ctrl-Break Flag	

Sets the status of the Ctrl-Break/Ctrl-C check flag

Calling Registers:
AH   33h
AL   01h, setting flag status
DL   00h, Ctrl-Break checking off
         01h, Ctrl-Break checking on

Return Registers: None

Comments: Except for a few I/O functions (see character I/O Functions 01h–0Ch for the exceptions), checking for Ctrl-Break or Ctrl-C characters is normally not done during much of the Int 21h function handling. When this checking is turned on, the check is performed for *all* Int 21h functions except the few that merely set or get flag data. This subfunction establishes the current state of the Ctrl-Break check flag; see Subfunction 00h to test its state.

When checking is enabled, if a Ctrl-Break or Ctrl-C is found, control is turned over to the handler for Int 23h. You can replace the Int 23h handler and deal with the Ctrl-Break or Ctrl-C in a function of your own rather than disable it.

Be aware that the Ctrl-Break/Ctrl-C flag is a system global that affects all processes running on a DOS system. As a system global, some care must be taken with its handling because it is possible to affect processes other than the one activating or deactivating the function.

Int 21h   Function 33h Subfunction 05h   V4
Get Boot Drive Code

Returns a code telling which drive the system was most recently booted from

Calling Registers: AH   33h
                         AL   05h, get boot drive code

Return Registers: DL   Boot drive code (1 = A, 2 = B, 3 = C, and
                                   so on)

Comments: With this function, added in V4, the program can determine which drive the system was booted from. This information is stored in the DOS kernel area each time the system initializes itself.

Int 21h   Function 33h Subfunction 06h   V5
Get MS-DOS Version

Returns the MS-DOS version number, revision number, and version flags

Calling Registers: AH   33h
                         AL   06h, get MS-DOS version number

Return Registers: BL   Major version number
                         BH   Minor version number
                         DL   Revision number in bits 0–2; the other bits are
                                   reserved and set to zero
                         DH   Version flag. Bit 3, if set, indicates that MS-DOS
                                   is running from ROM; otherwise, MS-DOS is
                                   running from RAM. Bit 4, if set, indicates that
                                   MS-DOS is running from the high memory
                                   area (HMA); otherwise, MS-DOS is running
                                   from conventional memory. All other bits are
                                   reserved and set to zero.

Comments: This version number is not changed by SETVER.

Int 21h   Function 34h   V2
Return Address of InDOS Flag

This is an internal DOS flag used to tell when DOS is processing an Int 21h function

Calling Registers: AH   34h

Return Registers: ES:BX   Pointer to InDOS flag

Comments: When DOS enters an Int 21h function, DOS increments the InDOS flag; when DOS leaves, it decrements the flag. This flag is used by DOS itself and by terminate and stay resident (TSR) utilities to determine whether DOS is inside the kernel processing an Int 21h function. When a TSR utility determines that DOS is currently in a function, it can do one of two things:

- Go ahead with processing because no Int 21h function will be needed.

- Refuse to process because Int 21h functions will be needed.

This need arises because the operating system kernel is not fully reentrant. This means that if an interrupt occurs while the operating system is already inside the kernel, the servicing routine cannot use Int 21h functions for processing because a call to a function might conflict with the previous call. In this case, you could easily crash the system, but not necessarily in any way that could be traced directly to the interrupt handler.

For operational necessity, a few portions of the DOS kernel code *do* make use of other parts through the Int 21h interface, and the InDOS flag serves as a signal to prevent that code from causing problems. It also permits official TSR programs such as PRINT.COM and its kin to operate properly. At times, however, this flag is misleading.

When DOS waits for keyboard input, it idles in a loop, reading characters as they come in. As long as DOS is waiting at this point, it is safe to use the file-handling and other functions, even though the InDOS flag indicates otherwise. To let you know that you can safely use these functions, DOS continually invokes Int 28h (Keyboard Busy Loop) during its input loop. A TSR can intercept Int 28h, which defaults to a pointer to an IRET, and check for things to do when it comes alive.

For example, if your TSR is started by pressing a hot key but finds that DOS is presently executing an Int 21h function because the InDOS flag is set, the TSR can set an internal flag that means, "I've been invoked, but I can't do anything." Whenever Int 28h is called, this flag could be checked. If the flag is set, the handler can branch immediately to the TSR part that performs the requested function.

A TSR may also intercept the clock interrupt and check the InDOS and TSR invocation flags during clock ticks. The purpose of this is to take care of the situation in which an Int 21h function (other than a character I/O function) was active when the TSR was first called. In this case, the clock interrupt sees the InDOS flag clear and the TSR invocation flag set so that the requested function can be performed.

With DOS V2, however, using Int 28h still can cause the system to crash mysteriously. The reason is that V2 switches to its own internal stack before dispatching control to any requested function; if any function is called while DOS is already processing another function in the range 00 through 0Ch (which it nearly always *is*, when Int 28h is invoked), the second stack switch that results can destroy information needed by the original function call.

The cure is equally simple but extremely subtle: you can trick DOS into believing that it is processing a critical error by manipulating its critical error (CritErr) flag. Setting the CritErr flag before calling a function forces DOS to use its alternate internal stack. You must restore the flag to its original value after return from the function.

In V3, the DOS dispatch code was modified to test for the affected functions before doing any stack switching; if one of them is requested, DOS simply uses the caller's own stack, avoiding the problem. This code remains unchanged in V4.

The CritErr flag is a byte that indicates that DOS has encountered some serious error condition and is processing an Int 24h (Critical Error) handler routine. To let such handlers use as many DOS functions as possible, the flag is set and causes the DOS dispatching code to use an alternate internal stack rather than the normal stack space. Although this is not full reentrant coding, it permits a limited capability to reuse the code.

In all versions of DOS from V2 through V4, the CritErr flag is adjacent to the InDOS flag. Unfortunately, its location flipped between V2 and V3. In V2, it is the byte at the next higher address; in V3 and V4, it is the next lower byte.

Note that this function can cause problems when called from an Int 28h handler. The proper use of this is when you install a TSR, before it is resident. At this point, you can make use of all DOS facilities to determine which correction should be applied for the CritErr address. Use this function to get and save the InDOS flag address, determine the DOS version, apply the increment or decrement as required, and save the CritErr flag address in a separate pointer.

Then, when the TSR pops up, it can use its own InDOS pointer to determine whether DOS is active and, if need be, it can use its own CritErr pointer to get the current value of that flag, save the value, set the flag to force use of the alternate stack, do any processing needed, and restore the original flag value before exiting.

Int 21h   Function 35h   V2
Get Interrupt Vector

Gets the interrupt handler address for the specified interrupt

Calling Registers:	AH	35h
	AL	Interrupt number
Return Registers:	ES:BX	Pointer to interrupt handler

Comments: Although the interrupt handler address is readily available for a given interrupt, this is the only *approved* way to get the current setting of an interrupt vector. This function is guaranteed to work cleanly and return a reliable value for the vector. It is possible that another program, for example a terminate and stay resident (TSR) utility, could change the interrupt vector after this function has returned the value. This is what happens when a single-user, single-tasking operating system is pushed beyond its limits.

When you set up a program that will work from an interrupt, you should use this function to determine the original setting of the interrupt so that you can restore it when you finish. You must be careful in doing this because you could come into conflict with TSRs or other interrupt handlers. If you remember an interrupt value, and a TSR starts and changes it, you might replace the interrupt vector in a way that would disable the TSR.

To guard against such an event, it is best to always compare the current contents of any interrupt vector you are about to restore to the value that your program originally set into it. If these values are not the same, some other program has modified the interrupt vector since you saved it and it is not safe to do the restore or to remove your program from memory. If they do match, you can restore the original value with no danger.

Int 21h	Function 36h	V2
	Get Free Disk Space	

Gets the amount of space available on a designated disk drive along with other selected information about the drive

Calling Registers: AH 36h
DL Disk drive (0 = default, 1 = A, and so on)

Return Registers: AX Sectors per cluster (FFFFh if the drive was invalid)
BX Number of available clusters
CX Bytes per sector
DX Clusters on the drive

Comments: This function, which is similar to Functions 1Bh and 1Ch, returns basic information that can be used to determine the available space on a disk.

You start by specifying the disk drive you want to check. You get back the following raw information:

- Number of sectors per cluster

- Number of available clusters

- Number of bytes per sector

- Number of clusters on the drive

Using this information, the amount of space available is

(available clusters) × (sectors per cluster) × (bytes per sector)

This returns the number of bytes available on the drive. Divide by 1024 to get the number of kilobytes, or divide by a record length to get the available space in numbers of records for a database, and so on.

To get the total usable space on a disk, use

(clusters on the drive) × (sectors per cluster) × (bytes per sector)

With this, you can write a function that prints something like this:

```
XXX bytes free out of YYY
```

Functions 1Bh and 1Ch return similar information.

Int 21h Function 37h Subfunction 00h V2
Get Switchchar

Gets the current switchchar

Calling Registers:	AH	37h
	AL	00h

Return Registers:	AL	FFh, AL subfunction was not in the range 0–3
	DL	Switch character

Comments: The switchchar is the character used by DOS during parsing of strings to designated command switches. Normally, the switchchar is set to be the slash (/), but you can set it to some other character if your application requires it.

Int 21h Function 37h Subfunction 01h V2
Set Switchchar

Allows you to reset the current switchchar

Calling Registers:	AH	37h
	AL	01h
	DL	Switch character

Return Registers:	AL	FFh, AL subfunction was not in the range 0–3

Comments: The switchchar is the character used by DOS during parsing of strings to designated command switches. Normally, the switchchar is set to be the slash (/), but you can set it to some other character if your application requires it.

If you use this function, it is a good idea to determine the current switchchar (Subfunction 0) and store it so that you can restore the original switchchar when your program is completed.

Int 21h   Function 37h Subfunction 02h   V2 only
Read Device Availability

Indicates whether device names must be preceded by the pseudopath name /DEV/

Calling Registers: AH   37h
                            AL   02h

Return Registers: AL   FFh, AL subfunction was not in the range 0–3
                            DL   0, /DEV/ must precede device names
                                      < > 0, /DEV/ does not need to precede device
                                      names

Comments: The device availability flag, present in V2 only, controlled a UNIX-like feature that permitted files and devices to have identical names by forcing all devices to be in the pseudodirectory DEV. When the flag is 00, devices can be opened or closed only in the DEV directory; any nonzero flag permits devices to take precedence over file names, which means that no file anywhere in the system can have a name identical to any device. In V3, the flag was set permanently nonzero, and Subfunction 3 was disabled.

Int 21h   Function 37h Subfunction 03h   V2 only
Set Device Availability

Determines whether device names must be preceded by the pseudopathname /DEV/

Calling Registers: AH   37h
                            AL   03h
                            DL   0, /DEV/ must precede device names
                                      < > 0, /DEV/ need not precede device names

Return Registers: AL   FFh, AL subfunction was not in the range 0–3
                            DL   Device availability flag (same as input)

Comments: The device availability flag, present in V2 only, controlled a UNIX-like feature that permitted files and devices to have identical names, by forcing all devices to be in the pseudodirectory DEV. When the flag is 00, devices can be opened or closed only in the DEV directory; any nonzero flag permits devices to take precedence over file names, which means that no file anywhere in the system can have a name identical to any device. In V3, the flag was set permanently nonzero, and Subfunction 3 was disabled.

Int 21h   Function 38h   V2
Get/Set Current Country Information

Gets the current country information; with DOS V3.0 and later, allows the country information to be set as well

Calling Registers: AH   38h

AL   00, get current country information

With DOS V3.0 and later:
01 to FEh, specified country code less than 255
FFh, country code is in BX register

BX   Country code if AL=FFh

DS:DX   Pointer to buffer for information

DX   FFFFh to set country code (DOS V3.0 and later)

Return Registers: Carry flag clear if successful

BX   Country code (DOS V3 only)

DS:DX   Pointer to returned country information

Carry flag set if error

AX   Error code
02h, invalid country (file not found)

Comments: Because DOS is an international disk operating system, programs sold for DOS may be expected to work in an international setting. This function tells your program what to use for many of the country-dependent parameters used for display of information. For example, date format typical of a certain country is encoded in bytes 0 and 1.

When the function gets the country-dependent information, it returns a pointer to a 32-byte buffer with the information. On DOS V3 and later, the function can be used also to set the country information for use by other programs.

The country code itself is usually the international telephone prefix code (DOS V3 and later). Some typical codes (for example, American Samoa is 684 and Portugal is 351) can be found at the front of almost any telephone book. The important point to notice here is that the numbers can be above 255. To accommodate this, the function provides for using the BX register to hold the country code when the AL register is set to FFh.

Table DOS.7 gives the format of the country information table, which is pointed to by DS:DX.

Table DOS.7. *Country Information Buffer*

Bit Offset	Length	Meaning
		—DOS V2—
00h	Word	Date and time format
		0 = USA m d y, hh:mm:ss
		1 = Europe d m y, hh:mm:ss
		2 = Japan y m d, hh:mm:ss
02h	Byte	Currency symbol
03h	Byte	Zero
04h	Byte	Thousands separator
05h	Byte	Zero
06h	Byte	Decimal separator
07h	Byte	Zero
08h	18 bytes	Reserved
		—DOS V3 or V4—
00h	Word	Date format
		0 = USA m d y
		1 = Europe d m y
		2 = Japan y m d
02h	5 bytes	Currency symbol string (ASCIIZ)
07h	Byte	Thousands separator
08h	Byte	Zero
09h	Byte	Decimal separator
0Ah	Byte	Zero
0Bh	Byte	Date separator
0Ch	Byte	Zero
0Dh	Byte	Time separator
0Eh	Byte	Zero
0Fh	Byte	Currency format
		00h = symbol leads currency, no space
		01h = symbol follows currency, no space
		02h = symbol leads currency, one space
		03h = symbol follows currency, one space
		04h = symbol replaces decimal separator
10h	Byte	Number of digits after decimal
11h	Byte	Time format
		Bit 0 = 0, 12-hour clock
		Bit 0 = 1, 24-hour clock
12h	Double word	Case map call address
16h	Byte	Data list separator
17h	Byte	Zero
18h	8 bytes	Reserved

Bit Offset	Length	Meaning
		—DOS V5—
00h	Word	Date format
		0 = USA m d y
		1 = Europe d m y
		2 = Japan y m d
02h	5 bytes	Currency symbol string (ASCIIZ)
07h	2 bytes	Thousands separator (ASCIIZ)
09h	2 bytes	Decimal separator (ASCIIZ)
0Bh	2 bytes	Date separator (ASCIIZ)
0Dh	2 bytes	Time separator (ASCIIZ)
0Fh	Byte	Currency format
		00h = symbol leads currency, no space
		01h = symbol follows currency, no space
		02h = symbol leads currency, one space
		03h = symbol follows currency, one space
		04h = symbol replaces decimal separator
10h	Byte	Number of digits after decimal
11h	Byte	Time format
		Bit 0 = 0, 12-hour clock
		Bit 0 = 1, 24-hour clock
12h	Double word	Case map call address
16h	2 bytes	Data list separator (ASCIIZ)
18h	10 bytes	Reserved

The case map call address listed at offset 12h in the table is the far address (segment:offset) of a format procedure that performs country-specific, lower- to uppercase mapping for character values above 7Fh. The mapping procedure should be called with the characters to be mapped in the AL register. The adjusted values are returned in the AL register.

Int 21h   Function 39h   V2
Create Subdirectory

Creates a subdirectory at the specified drive and path location

Calling Registers: AH   39h
                              DS:DX   Pointer to ASCIIZ path specification

Return Registers: Carry flag clear if successful

                           Carry flag set if error
                                  AX   Error code
                                               03h, path not found
                                               05h, access denied

Comments: DOS does not provide a way to manipulate directory entries other than through this function and the other directory functions (Functions 3Ah and 3Bh). This particular function allows you to create a new directory, which takes the path name of the directory and the drive designation if necessary.

This function will return an error and not create the requested directory if the directory already exists, if any element of the path name does not exist, or if the directory is from the root and the root is full.

In a network environment, you must have create-access rights in order to be allowed to create a subdirectory.

Int 21h   Function 3Ah   V2
Remove Subdirectory

Removes a subdirectory if it is empty

Calling Registers: AH   3Ah
                         DS:DX   Pointer to ASCIIZ path specification

Return Registers: Carry flag clear if successful

                         Carry flag set if error
                             AX   Error code
                                    03h, path not found
                                    05h, access denied
                                    10h, current directory

Comments: This is one of only three functions provided to manipulate directory entries in other directories. It allows you to delete the specified directory but only if the directory exists and is empty and if the directory to be deleted is not the default directory.

In a network environment, you must have create-access rights in order to be allowed to delete a subdirectory.

Int 21h   Function 3Bh   V2
Set Directory

Sets the current or default directory to match the designated string

Calling Registers: AH   3Bh
                         DS:DX   Pointer to ASCIIZ path string

Return Registers: Carry flag clear if successful

                         Carry flag set if error
                             AX   Error code
                                    03h, path not found

Comments: This function allows you to place your program in a designated location in the directory system.

A useful technique for a program that works in a special directory is to use Function 47h to determine the current directory and save that information before using this function to set a new directory area. Then, when the program is finished, it can return to the original directory. Too few programs perform this simple step.

Int 21h	Function 3Ch	V2
	Create/Truncate File (handle)	

Creates the designated file if it does not exist or truncates it to zero length if it does exist

Calling Registers:

AH	3Ch
CX	File attribute
DS:DX	Pointer to ASCIIZ file specification

Return Registers:

Carry flag clear if successfu
    AX   File handle

Carry flag set if error
    AX   Error code
        03h, path not found
        04h, no handles available
        05h, access denied

Comments: This function is basic to file operations. It does for handle-oriented functions what Function 16h does for file control block (FCB) functions. It creates the named file if it does not exist or truncates it to zero length if it does exist. The desired file is named by an ASCIIZ string, which may contain drive and path specifiers. A 16-bit file handle is returned. The file handle is used for further access to the file. The new file will have the file attributes set in the CX register. The following table describes the file types that are matched according to the different values:

Value	File Types Matched
00h	Normal
02h	Hidden
04h	System
06h	Hidden and system

When the truncate function is not wanted, you have three options, depending on which DOS version is running:

- With DOS V2, try to open the file with Function 3Dh. If the function fails, call this function to create the file.

- With DOS V3, try to create the file with Function 5Bh. If the function fails, call Function 3Dh to open the file.

- With DOS V4, you also can use Function 6Ch, which provides all file-open options in a single function.

Either way, you need to think carefully about the use of this function. More than one programmer has called this function at the wrong time and destroyed important data.

This function will fail if any element of the path name does not exist, if the file is being created in the root directory and the root is full, or if a read-only file exists with the same name.

The file is created as a normal file with read/write permission returned. Function 43h can be used to change the file's attributes if desired. You cannot use this function to create either subdirectories or volume labels.

In a network environment, you must have create-access rights to be allowed to create or truncate a file.

Int 21h	Function 3Dh	V2
	Open File (handle)	

Opens the designated file and returns a file handle (16-bit number) used to reference the opened file

Calling Registers:	AH	3Dh
	AL	Access mode (DOS V2)
		Access and file-sharing mode (DOS V3 and above)
	DS:DX	Pointer to ASCIIZ file specification

Return Registers:	Carry flag clear if successful	
	AX	File handle
	Carry flag set if error	
	AX	Error code
		01h, invalid function
		02h, file not found
		03h, path not found
		04h, no handles available
		05h, access denied
		0Ch, invalid access code

Comments: To open a file, specify the file name as an ASCIIZ string. Normal, hidden, or system files are accessible to the function. Register AL tells the function what access you want to the file. Table DOS.8 shows how to set the AL register for DOS V2 and V3.

Table DOS.8. Access and File-Sharing Modes	
Bits	*Meaning*
—DOS V2—	
76543210	
.....000	Read access
.....001	Write access
.....010	Read/write access
—DOS V3 or V4—	
76543210	
.....000	Read access
.....001	Write access
.....010	Read/write access
....x...	Reserved
.000....	Sharing mode—compatibility mode
.001....	Sharing mode—read/write access denied
.010....	Sharing mode—write access denied
.011....	Sharing mode—read access denied
.100....	Sharing mode—full access permitted
0.......	Inherited by child processes
1.......	Private to current process

In DOS V3 and above, in addition to requesting read/write access, you can request network access (file-sharing modes) and indicate whether the file is to be inherited by any children that this process may execute.

On return, the file is opened for access in the desired mode unless the file cannot be found or the desired access mode is not allowed (for example, accessing a read-only file with the access mode set to read/write). If the file-open function is successful, the read/write pointer will be at the beginning of the file.

In DOS V2, only bits 0–2 of the AL register are significant in this function. The remaining bits should be set to zero. In DOS V3 and above with the file-sharing software loaded, four bits of the AL register are devoted to permissions for other processes (bits 4–6, the sharing mode, and bit 7, the inherit bit). On the dark side, a file-sharing error results in an Int 24h (Critical Error) with error code 02h (Drive Not Ready).

The inherit bit, if set to 1, makes the file private to the process that opened it; it will not pass to any child processes. If this bit is 0, the file passes on to any process spawned after the file is opened. If a file handle is inherited by a child or duplicated by a process, all of its file-sharing modes also are inherited.

Compatibility mode (bits 3–7 set to zero) is the normal mode for most DOS software written before DOS V3, as well as for much of the software written afterward. As long as the software is running on a single workstation, there is no conflict in file access. When networking software is introduced and file sharing becomes a reality, compatibility mode no longer will be suitable for file control.

To work with other programs in a network environment, programs will have to use sharing modes in the open call to provide for access within the limits of the programming task involved. Files opened using FCB functions are assumed to be in compatibility mode unless opened for read-only access, in which case they are assigned deny-write sharing mode. Files opened by handle functions with read-only access also are considered to be in deny-write sharing mode. All other compatibility access modes will deny all outside file access.

To use this function properly, the programmer must carefully think through the required access to the file and the implications of unrestricted write access to the file. The possible modes then are

- *Deny read/write:* Files opened in this mode cannot be opened again by another program (or the current program) either on the current machine or on another machine on the network. This type of access is necessary for control of database operations for critical updating.

- *Deny write:* Files opened in this mode can be opened only for reading by other programs.

- *Deny read:* Files opened in this mode cannot be opened for reading by other programs.

- *Deny none:* No access (read or write) is denied to other programs.

Multiple-program access to data files is a serious concern in a network environment. Databases can be corrupted by programs trying to update the same file record simultaneously. Methods of coordinating file access among different programs are beyond the scope of this book. You should consult books on networked databases or operating systems to learn about such coordination mechanisms.

Int 21h   **Function 3Eh**   **V2**
                  Close File (handle)

Closes a file previously opened with file handles

Calling Registers: AH   3Eh
BX   File handle

Return Registers: Carry flag clear if successful

Carry flag set if error
AX   Error code 06h, invalid handle

Comments: This function is used to close a previously opened or created file using the DOS file-handling functions. The handle is returned to the system for use, and any updates to the file are performed. The file's date, as recorded in its directory entry, is updated if changes are made.

Good programming practice dictates that a program should always close any files it opens to force the operating system to update the file system properly. DOS automatically closes active file handles when a program terminates, but you should not rely on it, particularly if you want your programs to be portable.

Note: Be especially careful about closing file handle zero, which is the standard input device (normally, the keyboard). If you accidentally close file handle zero, you will lose communication through the keyboard unless you immediately reopen the CON device.

Int 21h   Function 3Fh   V2
Read File or Device (handle)

Reads data from the file or device specified by the file-handle argument; this data is written to a designated memory location

Calling Registers: AH   3Fh
BX   File handle
CX   Number of bytes
DS:DX   Pointer to buffer area

Return Registers: Carry flag clear if successful
AX   Number of bytes read

Carry flag set if error
AX   Error code
05h, access denied
06h, invalid handle

Comments: A basic file read gets a designated number of bytes from the file to the buffer as specified. If a read completes successfully, but AX is less than CX, a partial read occurred before the end of file (EOF) was detected. If the EOF already has been reached when this function is called, the carry flag will be set but the AX register will be zero.

As with all file-handle calls, devices can be treated exactly the same as files. We can use this function to read from character devices such as the keyboard. Some special restrictions apply, however, when dealing with a character device. If a character device is in cooked mode (see Function 44h), the read is terminated by a carriage return (it reads a single line only).

In a network environment, you must have read-access rights in order to read a file or device.

Int 21h	**Function 40h**	**V2**
	Write to a File or Device (handle)	

Writes data to a file specified in the handle   ↑ PRINTER 618

Calling Registers: AH   40h
                        BX   File handle
                        CX   Number of bytes to write
                        DS:DX   Pointer to buffer of data to write

Return Registers: Carry flag clear if successful
                        AX   Number of bytes written

                        Carry flag set if error
                        AX   Error code
                                05h, access denied
                                06h, invalid handle

Comments: Writing to a file using the file-handle function is as simple as specifying the file handle and the number of bytes and pointing to the data buffer. The function then writes that number of bytes to the current position in the file.

Register AX returns the number of bytes written or, if the function failed, an error code. Normally, the number of bytes returned in AX is the same as the number of bytes to write (CX register). If the write was successful and if AX is less than CX, a partial record was written. Partial-record writes could result if the disk is out of space; in this case, a check of available space with Function 36h, 1Bh, or 1Ch is a good test. An error code is returned if the file is marked as read-only.

In a network environment, you must have write-access rights in order to write to a file or device.

Int 21h	**Function 41h**	**V2**
	Delete File	

Deletes the specified file from the system

Calling Registers: AH   41h

DS:DX   Pointer to ASCIIZ file specification

Return Registers: Carry flag clear if successful

Carry flag set if error
     AX   Error code
           02h, file not found
           05h, access denied

Comments: This function deletes the file by marking the directory entry with an E5h in the first byte of the file name. This makes it possible to recover the "deleted" file if no other files are created or changed after the deletion. Nothing else is changed in the directory entry. The clusters allocated to the file are returned to the system for reuse. The actual file is not overwritten.

Unlike the file control block (FCB) delete function (13h), wild cards are not allowed here. If you want to delete a group of files by matching a file name that uses wild cards, you must use the search functions (4Eh and 4Fh) to locate the files one by one. Because this function allows access to files in subdirectories, this restriction is easy to live with.

If the file exists but has the read-only attribute, or if the file cannot be found, this function will fail.

To delete a file in a network environment, you must have create-access rights.

Int 21h   Function 42h   V2
Move File Pointer

Changes the current location in the file, the file pointer, to a position relative to the start of file, end of file, or current position

Calling Registers: AH   42h

AL   Method code
           00h, offset from beginning of file
           01h, offset from current position
           02h, offset from end of file

BX   File handle
CX   Most significant part of offset
DX   Least significant part of offset

Return Registers: Carry flag clear if successful
DX:AX   New file-pointer location

Carry flag set if error
     AX   Error code
           01h, invalid function (file sharing)
           06h, invalid handle

Comments: The file read/write pointer is adjusted by this function to a new position set from the beginning, end, or current position in the file. The offset can be specified as a 32-bit number (ranges up to 4096M). Before V4, you could not practically use files of this size because the operating system restricted you to a maximum 32M disk capacity for a single disk volume. In V4, this limit was removed. When the file pointer is moved, this becomes the next point at which data will be written into or read from the file.

A practical use of this function, other than setting the file position, is to determine the file size. You can get this by setting register AL to 2 (relative to end of file) and the CX and DX registers to 0 (offset from end of file). The location returned in the AX and DX registers represents the actual size of the file in bytes. Of course, this leaves the pointer at the end of the file. If this is not satisfactory, you must reset the position to the desired location before a read or write.

Another important use of the function is to implement an open-at-end-of-file or append function. You can use Function 3Dh to open the file and then use this function to reset immediately the read/write pointer to the end of file by the same method used to determine the file size (AL = 2, CX and DX = 0).

With this function, you can set the file pointer to a position before the beginning of the file or after the end of it. Setting the file pointer after the end of the file does not result in an error except when a read is attempted from this nonexistent location. A write to a location past the end of the file causes space to be allocated to the file and makes the file large enough to accommodate the write. Setting the file pointer before the beginning of the file results in an error when a read or write is attempted.

If this function is used on a network system with a file in deny-read or deny-none sharing mode, the file-pointer information is adjusted on the computer that has the file. If the file is in any other sharing mode, the file-pointer information is kept on the remote computer.

Int 21h   Function 43h Subfunction 00h   V2
Get File Attributes

Gets the attributes of a file

Calling Registers: AH   43h
                          AL   00, get file attributes
                          DS:DX   Pointer to ASCIIZ file specification

Return Registers: Carry flag clear if successful
                          CX   Attribute byte (see table)

Carry flag set if error
AX Error code
01h, invalid function (file sharing)
02h, file not found
03h, path not found
05h, access denied

Comments: The file attributes for a directory entry are bit-mapped as shown in the following table:

Bit 76543210	*Meaning*
. 1	Read only
. . . . . .1.	Hidden
. . . . .1..	System
. . . .1...	Volume Label
. . .1....	Directory
. .1.....	Archive
xx......	Unused

Attributes of directory entries for the volume label or for subdirectories are not accessible with this function.

Int 21h Function 43h Subfunction 01h V2
Set File Attributes

Sets the attributes of a file

Calling Registers:
AH	43h
AL	01, set file attributes
CX	New attribute (see table)
DS:DX	Pointer to ASCIIZ file specification

Return Registers: Carry flag clear if successful

Carry flag set if error
AX Error code
01h, invalid function (file sharing)
02h, file not found
03h, path not found
05h, access denied

Comments: The attributes for a file can be set to the values shown in the following table:

Bit

654 3210	*Meaning*
... ...1	Read only
... ..1.	Hidden
... .1..	System
.1.	Archive

You cannot set the subdirectory or volume label attributes with this function. To create a volume label, you must use the file control block (FCB) file-creation function and an extended FCB. Function 39h is the only function that allows you to create a directory.

In a network environment, you must have create-access rights to change any file-attribute bit except the archive bit. Changing the archive bit does not require any restrictive rights.

Int 21h Function 44h V2
Device Driver Control (IOCTL)

Passes or retrieves control information to and from a device driver

Calling Registers:

	AH	44h
	AL	Device subfunction code (see table DOS.9)
	BX	Handle (Subfunction codes 00h, 01h, 02h, 03h, 06h, 07h, 0Ah, 0Ch, and 10h)
	BL	Drive code, 0 = default, 1 = A, and so on (Subfunction codes 04h, 05h, 08h, 09h, 0Dh, and 11h)
	CX	Number of bytes to read or write
	CH	Category code (Subfunction codes 0Ch, 0Dh, 10h, and 11h)
	CL	Function code (Subfunction codes 0Ch, 0Dh, 10h, and 11h)
	DS:DX	Pointer to buffer area (Subfunction codes 02h–05h)
	DS:DX	Pointer to parameter block (Subfunction codes 0Ch, 0Dh, 10h, and 11h)
	DX	Device information (Subfunction code 01h) (see table DOS.9)

Return Registers: Carry flag clear if successful

	AX	Number of bytes transferred (Subfunction codes 02h–05h)

AL	Status (Subfunction codes 06h–07h)
	00h not ready
	FFh ready
AX	Value (Subfunction code 08h)
	00h removable
	01h fixed
DX	Device information (Subfunction code 00)

Carry flag set if error

AX	Error code
	01h, invalid function (file sharing)
	04h, no handles available
	05h, access denied
	06h, invalid handle
	0Dh, invalid data
	0Fh, invalid drive

Comments: The IOCTL function is one of the most comprehensive functions available under DOS. There are 18 separate subfunctions to this function. Table DOS.9 gives an overview of the subfunctions and the DOS version in which the subfunction was officially activated. The meaning of the information passed depends on which specific device driver is addressed.

Table DOS.9. *Device Function Codes*

AL	Meaning	DOS Version
00h	Get device information	2.0
01h	Set device information	2.0
02h	Character device read	2.0
03h	Character device write	2.0
04h	Block device read	2.0
05h	Block device write	2.0
06h	Get input status	2.0
07h	Get output status	2.0
08h	Block device changeable?	3.0
09h	Block device local or remote?	3.1
0Ah	Handle local or remote?	3.1
0Bh	Set sharing retry count	3.0
0Ch	Generic I/O control for handles	3.2
0Dh	Generic I/O control for block devices	3.2
0Eh	Get logical drive map	3.2
0Fh	Set logical drive map	3.2
10h	Query IOCTL handle	5.0
11h	Query IOCTL device	5.0

DOS
PROGRAMMING

The IOCTL function is a generalized device-driver interface program. Its purpose is not to transfer data but to communicate with a driver and tell it how to work.

Int 21h   Function 44h Subfunction 00h   V2
Get Device Information

Gets information about the device or file referred to by the handle

Calling Registers: AH   44h
                           AL   00h
                           BX   Handle

Return Registers: Carry flag clear if successful
                           DX   Device information (see table DOS.10)

                          Carry flag set if error
                           AX   Error code
                                   01h, invalid function
                                   05h, access denied
                                   06h, invalid handle

Comments: The DX register returns coded information from the system about the character device or file referenced by the file handle in the BX register. Table DOS.10 shows the codes and their meaning. The handle must refer to an open file or character device.

Table DOS.10. Device Information Codes

Bit FEDCBA98 76543210	Meaning
—Character Device—	
....1	Standard input device
....1.	Standard output device
....1..	NUL device
....1...	Clock device
....0....	Device does not support Int 28h
....1....	Device supports Int 28h
....0.....	Cooked mode
....1.....	Raw (binary) mode
.... .0......	End of file for input
.... .1......	Not end of file for input
.... 1.......	Character device
..XXXXXX	Reserved

Bit FEDCBA98 76543210	Meaning
.1......	Device can process control strings sent with Subfunctions 02h and 03h. This bit can be read only, not set.
x.......	Reserved
	—*Block Device (Disk File)*—
....xxxxxx	Block device number (0 = A, 1 = B, and so on for first block driver; sequence proceeds for subsequent drivers)
.... .0......	File has been written to
.... .1......	File has not been written to
.... 0.......	Block device (disk file)
..xxxxxx	Reserved; must be set to zero when function is called
.1......	Device can process control strings sent withSubfunctions 02h and 03h. This bit can be read only, not set.
x.......	Reserved

Bit 5 for character devices is a particularly useful information bit. UNIX programmers are familiar with the terms *cooked mode* and *raw mode* when dealing with terminal devices. In DOS, cooked mode means that Ctrl-C, Ctrl-P, Ctrl-Q, Ctrl-S, and Ctrl-Z are processed and also that input is terminated upon detection of a carriage return rather than of the specified number of characters. Cooked mode is the full editing entry mode that many reference manuals describe as the only console input mode.

In raw mode, the supplied I/O system drivers ignore the special meanings of these characters and wait until the full specified number of bytes has been received before returning from a read operation. All bytes received are passed directly to the applications program with no interpretation by either the I/O system or by DOS. Similar differences exist in output processing (expansion of tab characters, automatic addition of carriage return before line feed, and so forth).

The handle in the BX register must refer to an open file or device. If not, the function returns error code 06h (invalid handle).

Bits 8–15 of the DX register on return correspond to the same bits in the device driver's attribute word (see Chapter 12, "Device Drivers," for a more complete discussion of the attribute word and the driver header).

Int 21h   Function 44h Subfunction 01h   V2
Set Device Information

The complement of Subfunction 00h for character devices only, this subfunction allows setting device information codes

Calling Registers: AH   44h
                                         AL   01h
                                         BX   Handle
                                         DX   Device data word

Return Registers: Carry flag clear if successful

                                    Carry flag set if error
                                        AX   Error code
                                                  01h, invalid function
                                                  05h, access denied
                                                  06h, invalid handle
                                                  0Dh, invalid data

Comments: Subfunction 01h allows you to set a limited portion of the device data word for character devices only. The only bit normally modified in this call is bit 5. (For an explanation of raw mode and cooked mode, see the discussion for Subfunction 00h.)

If the DH register is not zero, the subfunction returns error code 01h (invalid function). This subfunction also requires that the handle refer to an open device. If the handle is a file, no information is updated. Table DOS.11 gives the interpretation of the Device Data Word (DX register).

Table DOS.11. Device Data Word

Bit FEDCBA98 76543210	Meaning
....1	Standard input device
....1.	Standard output device
....1..	NUL device
....1...	Clock device
....1....	Device supports Int 28h
....0.....	Cooked mode
....1.....	Raw (binary) mode
.... .0......	End of file for input
.... 1.......	Character device
xxxxxxxx	Reserved

Int 21h   Function 44h Subfunction 02h   V2
Device IOCTL Read

Gets control string information from the driver for use by the calling program

Calling Registers:	AH	44h
	AL	02h
	BX	Handle
	CX	Number of bytes to get
	DS:DX	Pointer to data buffer
Return Registers:	Carry flag clear if successful	
	AX	Number of bytes transferred
	Carry flag set if error	
	AX	Error code
		01h, invalid function
		05h, access denied
		06h, invalid handle
		0Dh, invalid data

Comments: Arbitrary information about a driver can be passed to the calling program in a control string. This can be any kind of information the driver is written to support; there are no standards for format or content of these messages. How the driver responds to the request is up to the driver. Chapter 12, "Device Drivers," goes into more detail about control strings.

Bit 0Eh of Subfunction 00h indicates whether the driver can provide or respond to control strings.

Int 21h   **Function 44h Subfunction 03h**   **V2**
Device IOCTL Write

Sends control-string information to the driver

Calling Registers:	AH	44h
	AL	03h
	BX	Handle
	CX	Number of bytes to send
	DS:DX	Pointer to data buffer
Return Registers:	Carry flag clear if successful	
	AX	Number of bytes transferred
	Carry flag set if error	
	AX	Error code
		01h, invalid function
		05h, access denied
		06h, invalid handle
		0Dh, invalid data

Comments: Arbitrary information about a driver can be passed to the driver in a control string. This can be whatever kind of information the driver is written to support; there are no standards for format or content of these messages. How the driver responds to the request is up to the driver. Chapter 12, "Device Drivers," goes into more detail about control strings. This subfunction is often used to pass configuration information, such as baud rate or word length, to a driver.

Bit 0Eh of Subfunction 00h indicates whether the driver can provide or respond to control strings.

Int 21h	Function 44h Subfunction 04h	V2
	Block Driver IOCTL Read	

Gets control information from a block driver (disk type)

Calling Registers: AH   44h
AL   04h
BL   Drive number
CX   Number of bytes to get
DS:DX   Pointer to data buffer

Return Registers: Carry flag clear if successful
AX   Number of bytes transferred

Carry flag set if error
AX   Error code
01h, invalid function
05h, access denied
06h, invalid handle
0Dh, invalid data

Comments: Arbitrary information about a block driver can be passed from it in a control string. This can be status information or whatever kind of information the driver is written to support. There are no standards for format or content of these messages.

How the driver responds to the request is up to the driver. Chapter 12, "Device Drivers," goes into more detail about control strings. A frequent use of this subfunction involves readiness for the operation of block devices. Devices such as CDROM drives, tape drives, or other devices can be queried if the driver is written for that device.

Bit 0Eh of Subfunction 00h indicates whether the driver can provide or respond to control strings. Block device drivers are not required to support this subfunction. If the driver called does not support it, error code 01h (Invalid Function) is returned.

Int 21h   Function 44h Subfunction 05h   V2
Block Driver IOCTL Write

Sends controlling information to a block device (disk type)

Calling Registers: AH   44h
AL   05h
BL   Drive number
CX   Number of bytes to send
DS:DX Pointer to data buffer

Return Registers: Carry flag clear if successful
AX   Number of bytes transferred

Carry flag set if error
AX   Error code
01h, invalid function
05h, access denied
06h, invalid handle
0Dh, invalid data

Comments: Arbitrary information about a block driver can be passed to it in a control string. This can include commands or whatever kind of information the driver is written to support. There are no standards for format or content of these messages.

How the driver responds to the request is up to the driver. Chapter 12, "Device Drivers," goes into more detail about control strings. Frequent uses of this subfunction include non-I/O device functions, such as tape rewind and disk eject.

Bit 0Eh of Subfunction 00h indicates whether the driver can provide or respond to control strings. Block device drivers are not required to support this subfunction. If the driver called does not support it, error code 01h (Invalid Function) is returned.

Int 21h   Function 44h Subfunction 06h   V2
Get Input Status

Returns status of the device or file for input operations

Calling Registers: AH   44h
AL   06h
BX   Handle

Return Registers: Carry flag clear if successful
AL   Input status code (see table)

Carry flag set if error
    AX   Error code
                   01h, invalid function
                   05h, access denied
                   06h, invalid handle

Comments: With this subfunction, you can tell whether a particular device or file is ready for an input operation. You can test files for position at EOF except when positioned by Function 42h, or you can test whether character devices are ready to operate. The following table gives the input status code (register AH) interpretation:

Code	File	Device
00h	at EOF	Not ready
FFh	not at EOF	Ready

(*Special case:* A file will not return EOF if positioned at EOF using Int 21h, Function 42h.)

Int 21h   Function 44h Subfunction 07h   V2
Get Output Status

Returns status of the device or file for output operations

Calling Registers: AH   44h
                       AL   07h
                       BX   Handle

Return Registers: Carry flag clear if successful
                       AL   Output status code (see table)

                     Carry flag set if error
                     AX   Error code
                              01h, invalid function
                              05h, access denied
                              06h, invalid handle

Comments: With this subfunction, you can tell whether a particular device or file is ready for an output operation. As shown in the following table, files always return *ready* for output; character devices do not.

Code	File	Device
00h	At EOF	Not ready
FFh	Not at EOF	Ready

Int 21h   Function 44h Subfunction 08h   V3
Block Device Removable?

Used to determine whether a block device is removable

Calling Registers: AH   44h
                          AL   08h
                          BL   Drive number

Return Registers: Carry flag clear if successful
                          AX   00h, removable media
                                    01h, nonremovable media

                          Carry flag set if error
                          AX   Error code
                                    01h, invalid function
                                    0Fh, invalid drive

Comments: Applications that need to locate data files or overlays on a particular device can determine with this subfunction whether the device is removable. If the desired file is not located on the device and the device is removable, the program should prompt the user to put in the correct disk to continue.

    Bit 0Bh of the device driver's attribute word indicates whether the driver can support this function. Some drivers do not. In this case, the subfunction returns error code 01h.

Int 21h   Function 44h Subfunction 09h   V3.1
Block Device Local or Remote?

Determines whether the block device is local or remote

Calling Registers: AH   44h
                          AL   09h
                          BL   Drive number

Return Registers: Carry flag clear if successful
                          DX   Device attribute word
                                    Bit 12 = 1, drive is remote
                                    Bit 12 = 0, drive is local

                          Carry flag set if error
                          AX   Error code
                                    01h, invalid function
                                    0Fh, invalid drive

Comments: If the network has not been started, this subfunction returns error code 01h, invalid function.

It is good programming practice to avoid this function. Programs should be written in such a way that they are not dependent on a particular device's location on a network. However, certain undocumented functions operate properly only with respect to local files and cannot be used with remote files; if such a function must be used in a program, this subfunction permits you to avoid some error conditions.

If bit 12 of DX is 0, indicating that the drive is local, other bits in DX have the following meaning:

Bit 1	1 = Drive uses 32-bit sector addressing
Bit 6	1 = Drive supports Function 44h, Subfunctions 0Dh, 0Eh, and 0Fh
Bit 7	1 = Drive supports Function 44h, Subfunction 11h
Bit 9	1 = Drive is local, but is shared by other computers in the network
Bit 11	1 = Drive supports Function 44h, Subfunction 08h
Bit 13	1 = Drive requires media descriptor in FAT
Bit 14	1 = Drive supports Function 44h, Subfunctions 04h and 05h
Bit 15	1 = Substitution drive (e.g., set by the SUBST command)

All other bits are zero.

Int 21h Function 44h Subfunction 0Ah V3.1
Handle Local or Remote?

Determines whether the handle is local or remote

Calling Registers:	AH	44h
	AL	0Ah
	BX	Handle

Return Registers:	Carry flag clear if successful	
	DX	Device attribute word
		Bit 15 = 1, handle is remote
		Bit 15 = 0, handle is local
	Carry flag set if error	
	AX	Error code
		01h, invalid function
		06h, invalid handle

Comments: If the network has not been started, this subfunction returns error code 01h, invalid function.

It is good programming practice to avoid this function. Programs should be written in such a way that they are not dependent on a particular device's location on a network. However, certain undocumented functions operate properly only with respect to local handles and cannot be used with remote handles; if such a function must be used in a program, this subfunction permits you to avoid some error conditions.

If bit 7 of DX is clear, the handle identifies a file, and other bits in DX have the following meaning:

Bits 0–5   Drive number (0 = A, 1 = B, and so on)

Bit 6   1 = File has not been written to

Bit 12   1 = No inherit

Bit 14   1 = Date/time not set at close

All other bits are zero.

If bit 7 of DX is set, the handle is a device handle, and other bits in DX have the following meaning:

Bit 0   1 = Console input device

Bit 1   1 = Console output device

Bit 2   1 = Null device

Bit 3   1 = Clock device

Bit 4   1 = Special device

Bit 5   1 = Binary mode
            0 = ASCII mode

Bit 6   0 = EOF returned if device is read

Bit 11   1 = Network spooler

Bit 12   1 = No inherit

Bit 13   1 = Named pipe

All other bits are zero.

Int 21h	Function 44h Subfunction 0Bh	V3.0
	Set Sharing Retry Count	

Changes the retry parameters for file sharing across a network

Calling Registers:	AH	44h
	AL	0Bh
	CX	Pause between retries
	DX	Number of retries

Return Registers:	Carry flag clear if successful
	Carry flag set if error
	AX Error code
	01h, invalid function

Comments: When working with multiple PCs over a network, the retry parameters are associated with file-locking mechanisms. It is assumed that file locks are temporary and will be cleared after a short update. Such built-in mechanisms will retry automatically to establish access to a file if the file is locked when the first attempt is made.

The two parameters (retry count and pause between retries) are dependent on the system. Differences in CPU and clock speed have a significant effect on the actual length of the pause. The CX register controls the pause by giving the number of times a tight timing loop is executed. The timing loop repeats 65,536 times whenever it is called. Clearly, the retry count is the number of times the access will be attempted before failure is reported. Defaults are PAUSE = 1 and RETRY = 3.

These parameters can be used to tune the system to minimize file-sharing problems. If you expect long periods during which a desired file will be locked, you can extend the pause period when you make another attempt to access the file. If you change any of the defaults, however, restoring the defaults to prevent side effects on other programs is prudent.

Int 21h   Function 44h Subfunction 0Ch   V3.2
Generic I/O Control for Handles

In DOS V3.2, sets or gets the iteration count for a character-oriented device. In DOS V3.3 and above, the function also performs code-page switching. In DOS V5.0, the function also gets and sets the display mode

Calling Registers:	AH	44h
	AL	0Ch
	BX	Handle
	CH	Category code (device type)

     DOS V3.2
         05h, printer

     DOS V3.3 and above
         00h, unknown
         01h, COMx

03h, CON
05h, LPTx

CL   Minor function code

DOS V3.2 and above

    45h, set iteration count
    65h, get iteration count

DOS V3.3 and above

    4Ah, select
    4Ch, prepare start
    4Dh, prepare end
    6Ah, query select
    6Bh, query prepare list

DOS V5.0

    5Fh, set display mode
    7Fh, get display mode

DS:DX   Pointer to iteration count word
                 (minor codes 45h and 65h)
                 Pointer to parameter block (minor
                 codes 4Ah, 4Ch, 4Dh, 5Fh, 6Ah, 6Bh and 7Fh)

Return Registers: Carry flag clear if successful

                      Carry flag set if error
                      AX   Error code
                             01h, invalid function

Comments: The iteration count word specifies the number of times an operation will be attempted before giving up. With DOS V3.2, only category code 05h (printer) was allowed.

    With DOS V3.3 and above, this subfunction changed to handle code-page switching for devices. The minor functions include the following:

- Prepare Start (4Ch) tells the driver to be ready for code-page font loading through Subfunction 03h. A special start operation is a "refresh," which is generated by setting all code-page IDs to FFFFh.

- Prepare End (4Dh) tells the driver that the code-page font loading is complete.

- Select Code Page (4Ah) selects the code page to use.

- Set Display Mode (5Fh) sets the display mode for the device.

- Query Selected Code Page (6Ah) determines the status of the code page from the device.

- Query Prepare List (6Bh) determines the list of code pages on the device.
- Get Display Mode (7Fh) gets the display mode for the device.

Table DOS.12 defines the parameter block, pointed to by DS:DX.

Table DOS.12. *Parameter Block*

Bytes	Meaning
	—Minor Functions 4Ah, 4Dh, 6Ah—
0–1	Length of following data
2–3	Code-page ID
	—Minor Function 4Ch—
0–1	Flags
2–3	Length of parameter block (after this point)
4–5	Number of code pages
.	
.	Code-page designations
.	
	—Minor Function 6Ah—
0–1	Length of parameter block (after this point)
2–3	Number of hardware code pages
.	
.	Hardware code-page designations
.	
n–n+1	Number of prepared code pages
.	
.	Prepared code-page designations
.	
	—Minor Functions 5Fh, 7Fh—
0	Information level (must be zero)
1	Reserved
2–3	Length of parameter block (after this point)
4–5	Control flags
	0 = Intensity off
	1 = Intensity on
6	Display mode
	1 = Text mode
	2 = Graphics mode
7	Reserved
8–9	Number of colors
0A–0B	Screen width, in pixels (graphics mode only)
0C–0D	Screen length, in pixels (graphics mode only)
0E–0F	Columns
10–11	Rows

Device Attribute Codes

Bit 76543210	Meaning
.......0	Removable storage
.......1	Nonremovable storage
......0.	Device does not indicate change line status
......1.	Device does indicate change line status
XXXXXX..	Reserved

Media Type Code

Code	Meaning
00h	1.2M, 5 1/4-inch disk
01h	320/360K, 5 1/4-inch disk

BIOS Parameter Block (BPB) Layout

Offset Byte	Field Length	Meaning
00h	Word	Number of bytes per sector
02h	Byte	Number of sectors per cluster
03h	Word	Number of reserved sectors starting at sector 0
05h	Byte	Number of FATs
06h	Word	Maximum number of root directory entries
08h	Word	Total number of sectors
0Ah	Byte	Media descriptor
0Bh	Word	Number of sectors per FAT
0Dh	Word	Number of sectors per track
0Fh	Word	Number of heads
11h	Double word	Number of hidden sectors
15h	11 bytes	Reserved

Track Layout Table

Length	Meaning
Word	Number of sectors in track
Word	Number of first sector in track
Word	Size of first sector in track
.	
.	
.	
Word	Number of last sector in track
Word	Size of last sector in track

Minor Function 41h: Write Track

The write-track function allows specification of all important parameters for a track (head, cylinder, sector, number of sectors, and location of data). For counting, the sector numbers and cylinder numbers start at zero.

Parameter Block

Offset	Meaning
00h	Special function = 0
01–02h	Number of disk head to use
03–04h	Number of disk cylinder to use
05–06h	First sector to use
07–08h	Number of sectors to transfer
09–0Ch	Pointer to data transfer buffer

Minor Function 42h: Format and Verify Track

This function formats and verifies a track on the disk. You need only to specify the disk head and cylinder to use; all the rest is handled by the driver.

Parameter Block—Format Track

Offset	Meaning
00h	Special function = 0
01–02h	Number of disk head to use
03–04h	Number of disk cylinder to use

Parameter Block—Verify Format Status

Offset	Meaning
00h	Special function = 1
01–02h	Number of disk head to use
03–04h	Number of disk cylinder to use

Upon completion, if the special function field is checked for status, the following return values are possible:

0 = Supported by ROM BIOS, heads/cylinders allowed
1 = Not supported by ROM BIOS
2 = Specified number of heads/cylinders not allowed
3 = Drive is empty

Minor Function 46h: Set Media ID

This function sets the serial number, volume label, and file system type for the specified drive.

Parameter Block

Offset	Meaning
00–01h	Information level
02–05h	Serial number
06–10h	ASCII volume label
11–18h	File system type
"FAT12 "	12-bit FAT
"FAT16 "	16-bit FAT

Minor Function 60h: Get Parameters

This function is the complement to minor Function 40h. This minor function uses the same parameter-block format as minor Function 40h to retrieve information about the device from the driver.

Minor Function 61h: Read Track

This function reads the track into the memory buffer provided in the parameter block. As with the write-track minor function, the location information is provided to the driver.

Parameter Block

Offset	Meaning
00h	Special function = 0
01–02h	Number of disk head to use
03–04h	Number of disk cylinder to use
05–06h	First sector to use
07–08h	Number of sectors to transfer
09–0Ch	Pointer to data transfer buffer

Minor Function 62h: Verify Track

This function performs the track-verify operation part of format/verify in minor Function 42h.

Parameter Block

Offset	Meaning
00h	Special function = 0
01–02h	Number of disk head to use
03–04h	Number of disk cylinder to use

Minor Function 66h: Get Media ID

This function gets the serial number, volume label, and file system type for the specified drive.

Parameter Block

Offset	Meaning
00–01h	Information level
02–05h	Serial number
06–10h	ASCII volume label
11–18h	File system type
"FAT12 "	12-bit FAT
"FAT16 "	16-bit FAT

Minor Function 68h: Sense Media Type

This function returns the media type for the specified drive.

Parameter Block

Offset	Meaning
00h	Default flag
	0 = Media is not default type
	1 = Media is default type
01h	Media type
	2 = 720K disk
	7 = 1.44M disk
	9 = 2.88M disk

Int 21h — Function 44h Subfunction 0Eh — V3.2
Get Logical Drive Map

Determines whether more than one logical drive name is assigned to a device

Calling Registers:

AH	44h
AL	0Eh
BL	Drive number

Return Registers:

Carry flag clear if successful
AL	Drive number
	0 = Only one logical drive assigned
	1 = A, 2 = B, and so on

Carry flag set if error
AX	Error code
	01h, invalid function
	05h, access denied
	0Fh, invalid drive

Comments: The drive number returned by this call tells you the last drive designation used to access the drive if more than one logical drive designation applies to the device.

Int 21h — Function 44h Subfunction 0Fh — V3.2
Set Logical Drive Map

Sets the logical drive name that will be used to access this device next

Calling Registers:

AH	44h
AL	0Fh
BL	Drive number

Return Registers: Carry flag clear if successful
AL   Drive number
0 = Only one logical drive assigned
1 = A, 2 = B, and so on

Carry flag set if error
AX   Error code
01h, invalid function
05h, access denied
0Fh, invalid drive

Comments: When you copy files between two disks, each of which corresponds to a different logical device but both of which must use the same physical device, you normally are prompted to change the disks when you do I/O to the device that is not presently in the drive. This function allows you to force the switch without getting the operating system prompt.

The function works by setting the next drive letter that would be issued to refer to this device. DOS then will not issue the Insert Disk prompt to the user. Subfunction 0Eh determines the name of the last logical drive used to access the device.

Int 21h   Function 44h Subfunction 10h   V5
Query IOCTL handle

Determines whether a specific IOCTL capability is supported by the device specified by the handle

Calling Registers: AH   44h
AL   10h
BX   Device handle
CH   Category code
CL   Function code
DS:DX   Pointer to parameter block

Return Registers: Carry flag clear if successful
AX   0

Carry flag set if error
AL   01h, function not supported
05h, access denied

Comments: The parameter block is set up as it would be for the generic IOCTL call. If the device in question supports Query IOCTL, this can be used to determine whether the specified generic IOCTL call is supported by the driver. Typically, an application will interrogate the driver before making a generic IOCTL call.

Int 21h — Function 44h Subfunction 11h — V5
Query IOCTL device

Determines whether a specific IOCTL capability is supported by the device specified by the handle

Calling Registers:

	AH	44h
	AL	11h
	BL	Drive number
	CH	Category code
	CL	Function code
	DS:DX	Pointer to parameter block

Return Registers: Carry flag clear if successful

    AX   0

Carry flag set if error

    AL   01h, function not supported
             05h, access denied
             0Fh, invalid drive

Comments: The parameter block is set up as it would be for the generic IOCTL call. If the device in question supports Query IOCTL, this can be used to determine whether the specified generic IOCTL call is supported by the driver. Typically, an application will interrogate the driver before making a generic IOCTL call.

The functions supported in DOS 5.0 are

40h	Set device parameters
41h	Write track on logical drive
42h	Format track on logical drive
46h	Set media ID
60h	Get device parameters
61h	Read track on logical drive
62h	Verify track on logical drive
66h	Get media ID
68h	Sense media type

Int 21h — Function 45h — V2
Duplicate Handle

Provides a new handle for an already opened device or file

Calling Registers:

	AH	45h
	BX	File handle

Return Registers: Carry flag clear if successful
AX   New handle

Carry flag set if error
AX   Error code
04h, no handles available
06h, invalid handle

Comments: Duplicating a file handle provides another handle for the same file. The file pointers move together. If you move the file pointer of one file, the file pointer for the other moves as well.

The most common use for this function is to force an update to a file's directory entry without having to incur the overhead of a file open and close. In DOS versions earlier than 3.3, this was the only way to force the update. DOS V3.3 introduced the new Function 68h to do the same thing more easily.

Int 21h   Function 46h   V2
Force Duplicate Handle

Makes two file handles refer to the same opened file at the same location

Calling Registers: AH   46h
BX   First file handle
CX   Second file handle

Return Registers: Carry flag clear if successful

Carry flag set if error
AX   Error code
04h, no handles available
06h, invalid handle

Comments: The result of this function is similar to that of Function 45h; it causes two file handles to refer to the same file and move together. The most significant use of this function is to provide for device redirection. You can control the redirection process from inside another program and then return the device to normal with the following steps:

1. Use Function 45h to duplicate the handle to be redirected. Save the new handle for later restoration.

2. Use Function 46h for redirection by putting the "handle to be redirected" into CX and the "handle to be redirected to" in BX.

When you want to return conditions to normal, call Function 46h again with the redirected handle in CX and the duplicated handle returned by Function 45h in the BX register.

In the calling registers, if the handle in CX refers to an open file, the file will be closed first before the function starts.

Int 21h   **Function 47h**   **V2**
        Get Current Directory

Returns an ASCIIZ string with the full path of the current directory, not including the drive and the leading backslash character (\)

Calling Registers: AH   47h
                          DL   Drive code (0 = default, 1 = A, and so on)
                          DS:SI   Pointer to 65-byte scratch buffer

Return Registers: Carry flag clear if successful
                          DS:SI   Unchanged, buffer contains current
                                        directory path as ASCIIZ string

                          Carry flag set if error
                          AX   Error code
                                    0Fh, invalid drive

Comments: This function returns the path name of the current directory without the drive designator or the leading backslash (\). Because you set the drive code when you call the function, the absence of the drive designator and backslash is okay. (If you want to use the return from this function to build a file name, you will have to supply the drive and initial backslash for the file name.) If the directory is the root directory, the string returned is NUL (first byte 0).

Many programs could benefit from using this function before changing the directory so that the user could be returned to the original directory when the program is complete. Programmers must be careful because an invalid drive code will cause the function to fail. To set the current directory, refer to Function 3Bh.

Int 21h   **Function 48h**   **V2**
        Allocate Memory

Allocates a block of memory for use and returns a pointer to the beginning of the block

Calling Registers: AH   48h
                          BX   Number of paragraphs needed

Return Registers: Carry flag clear if successful
                          AX   Initial segment of allocated block

> Carry flag set if error
>> AX   Error code
>>> 07h, memory control blocks destroyed
>>> 08h, insufficient memory
>> BX   Size of largest available block if function failed

Comments: The pointer is the segment address of the base of the block (the base address is AX:0000h). Because COM programs are always allocated all of memory, this function always fails when called from a COM program unless memory has first been released after entering the program. (For more information, see Chapter 3, "The Dynamics of DOS," and Chapter 10, "Program and Memory Management.")

In multitasking environments, the top of memory seen by the process may not be the actual top of memory. Programs such as DESQview and Windows give each program only as much space as the program is allowed in the program information files.

If the attempt to get space fails, the function returns the size of the largest available memory block. Another call requesting no more than this amount of space will be successful. The EXEC loader function uses this technique to assign all available RAM to a COM program. First, it loads BX with FFFFh, which asks for 1,048,560 bytes of RAM (more than can ever be available). Because error code 8 is certain to result, no check is performed. The Function 48h call is simply repeated; the first call returned in BX is the amount actually available, which the second call allocates.

This same technique can be used in your own programs if you need to know the amount of RAM available (not reserved by any program). If you use Function 48h with BX = FFFFh, the value returned in BX is the number of blocks available.

Int 21h	Function 49h	V2
	Release Memory	

Releases a block of memory to the pool managed by DOS (makes the memory available for other programs)

Calling Registers: AH   49h
                              ES   Segment of block to be released

Return Registers: Carry flag clear if successful

                             Carry flag set if error
                                 AX   Error code
                                           07h, memory control blocks destroyed
                                           09h, invalid memory block address

Comments: This function assumes that the block of memory being freed was acquired from Function 48h. If the block was not acquired from Function 48h, the function may simply fail (if you are lucky), or it may cause unpredictable errors in the program freeing the memory or in other programs residing in memory. The problem arises because the system, in being told to free memory, is expecting the address given to refer to a defined memory block as part of the overall memory allocation scheme. Chapter 10, "Program and Memory Management," goes into memory management in more detail.

Int 21h — Function 4Ah — V2
Modify Memory Allocation

Expands or shrinks a memory block previously allocated by Function 48h

Calling Registers:	AH	4Ah
	BX	New requested block size in paragraphs
	ES	Segment of block to be modified

| **Return Registers:** | Carry flag clear if successful |

Carry flag set if error
AX   Error code
07h, memory control blocks destroyed
08h, insufficient memory
09h, invalid memory block address
BX   Maximum block size available (if AX = 08h)

Comments: Programs can use this function call to modify a memory block they received from a call to Function 48h or to modify their own memory allocation. Because COM programs are allocated all memory when they run, they must call this function if they expect to be able to EXEC other programs. EXE programs also need to call this function to free memory unless their MAXALLOC parameter in the EXE header has been modified to request less than all memory. Chapter 10, "Program and Memory Management," covers in more detail the subject of memory management for program execution.

This function is frequently referred to as SETBLOCK.

Int 21h — Function 4Bh — V2
Execute Program (EXEC)

Executes a program under control of another program

Calling Registers:	AH	4Bh
	AL	00, loading and executing a program
		01, loading but not executing a program
		03, loading an overlay
		05, enter Exec state

ES:BX Pointer to parameter block

DS:DX Pointer to program specification

DS:DX Pointer to ExecState structure, defined as
follows (Subfunction code 05h only):
00h (word), reserved; should be zero
02h (word) type flags; bit 0 = program is an
EXE, bit 1 = program is an overlay
04h (dword), pointer to ASCIIZ program
name (can include path specification)
08h (word), PSP segment for new program
0Ah (dword), CS:IP of new program
0Eh (dword), program size (including PSP)

Return Registers: Carry flag clear if successful. All registers except CS and IP
are destroyed, including the stack pointers. SS and SP must
be stored locally, in a CS-addressable location, before
calling this function and restored after it returns.

Carry flag set if error
 AX Error code
  01h, invalid function
  02h, file not found
  05h, access denied
  08h, insufficient memory
  0Ah, invalid environment
  0Bh, invalid format

Comments: The EXEC function provides for executing programs and managing overlays in the system. The originating program (the parent process) regains control when the new program (the child process) has been completed. The parent may receive an exit code from the child if the child uses a DOS termination function that transfers return codes.

This function can also load overlays. Overlays could consist of program segments or data. A major difference between program execution and overlay operation is that programs are allocated memory from whatever is free in the system, and overlays are loaded to memory already owned by the program invoking the overlay function. If needed, a program should release memory (a necessity for COM programs) before executing another program.

The primary control for the operation is the parameter block pointed to by the ES:BX registers. The format of the parameter block is given in table DOS.13.

Table DOS.13. *Parameter Block Layout*

Offset Byte	Field Length	Contents
		—EXEC Function (AL = 00h)—
00h	Word	Segment pointer to environment block
02h	Word	Offset of command tail
04h	Word	Segment of command tail
06h	Word	Offset of first FCB (offset 5Ch)
08h	Word	Segment of first FCB
0Ah	Word	Offset of second FCB (offset 6Ch)
0Ch	Word	Segment of second FCB
		—Debug Function (AL = 01h)—
00h	Word	Segment pointer to environment block
02h	Word	Offset of command tail
04h	Word	Segment of command tail
06h	Word	Offset of first FCB (offset 5Ch)
08h	Word	Segment of first FCB
0Ah	Word	Offset of second FCB (offset 6Ch)
0Ch	Word	Segment of second FCB
0Eh	Word	SP of loaded program
10h	Word	SS of loaded program
12h	Word	IP of loaded program
14h	Word	CS of loaded program
		—Overlay Function (AL = 03h)—
00h	Word	Segment pointer to load point for the overlay
02h	Word	Relocation factor to be applied to the code image (EXE files only)

The environment block is a series of ASCIIZ strings used to pass environment information to the program being executed. These strings are set at the command level by the SET function, or they can be created internally in the program. Usually, these strings include the COMSPEC variable (where to find the system command processor, COMMAND.COM), the PATH variable (where to look for executables), as well as other variables as specified on the system.

A typical environment block might look like this:

```
          1         2         3         4
12345678901234567890123456789012345678901234567890
COMSPEC=C:\COMMAND.COM*PATH=C:\DOS**
```

The asterisks represent NUL or zero bytes. If the environment block pointer is zero, the child will inherit the same environment that the parent has. In DOS V3 and later, the final zero in the environment block is followed by a two-byte word with a character count followed by an ASCIIZ string with the drive and path name of the program file being executed.

The command tail is a single string that consists of whatever is typed on the command line after the command to be executed. The format is a single-byte length count, followed by the string of characters and terminated with a carriage return. The total length cannot exceed 128 bytes; it will be copied into the program segment prefix (PSP) at offset 80h, giving the command tail only 128 bytes before it runs into the program.

A typical command tail looks like this:

```
         1         2         3         4
1234567890123456789012345678901234567890
#/c CHAPT01.DOC@
```

The # is a single numeric byte with the value 14, and @ represents the single-byte carriage return.

A child process spawned in this way will inherit the parent process I/O files unless the parent explicitly specifies otherwise in the file-open call (Function 3Dh). Standard files remain open. If standard files were redirected for the parent, they will remain redirected for the child. The parent can redirect the files (see Function 46h).

When you call this function, precautions are in order. During any EXEC function, it must be assumed that all registers will be modified in the course of the function call because the purpose of the function is to run another program. When the EXEC function returns, only CS and IP can be assumed to be correct. Before the call, the parent program must store at least SS and SP (plus any other registers you want to retain) in locations that can be addressed by the CS segment register. On return, SS and SP can be restored to their original values, but the restoration must take place with interrupts disabled so that the restoration cannot be stopped in the middle, a condition that would put the system in an unstable state.

The EXEC function cannot complete successfully unless there is sufficient memory to load the desired program. Assembly language programs should release needed memory with Function 4Ah before calling EXEC. When a C program starts, unneeded memory has already been released. For a more detailed discussion of memory allocation, see Chapter 10, "Program and Memory Management."

In DOS V2, this function gained a reputation for problems. Many of them were due to programmers attempting to save registers by pushing them onto the stack, but some versions failed to assure that the CPU direction flag was properly set up and, as a result, the system would hang intermittently. To prevent this problem, simply issue a CLD instruction as part of the setup before calling EXEC. If your programs will be used only with V3 and above, this is not necessary; the check was added to the DOS code.

An interesting sidelight is that this function in IBM's version of DOS 2.x is not physically located in the IBMDOS.COM file but rather forms part of COMMAND.COM. This was done by IBM to save space; other V2.x systems included it as part of MSDOS.SYS, as did IBM beginning with 3.0 (when the requirement that both DOS files be unfragmented was finally relaxed).

Subfunction 01h is used by debuggers to load a program into memory, leaving it ready for execution. This function is used by Microsoft's DEBUG, SYMDEB and CODEVIEW debuggers, as well as by Borland's Turbo Debugger. Of particular use to the debugger is the fact that the loaded program's SS, SP, CS and IP register values are stored at ES:[BX+0Eh] on return. Like the documented Subfunctions 00h and 03h, Subfunction 01h destroys all register contents on return; the programmer must save the ES and BX register values where they can be retrieved relative to CS before the programmer can use the SS:SP and CS:IP values.

Subfunction 05h, which is new to V5, supports programs that intercept the MS-DOS EXEC call and perform the loading themselves. It performs internal fixups such as setting the version number the loaded program will see (the one set by SETVER) and performing load-time patches to the loaded program.

Subfunction 05h should be the last call made before transferring control to the loaded program. In particular, the application should make no MS-DOS or BIOS calls or otherwise issue any software interrupts between the successful return of this function and transferring control to the loaded program.

If DOS is running in the HMA, A20 is turned off on return from the call to Subfunction 05h.

Int 21h   Function 4Ch   V2
Terminate with Return Code

Exits a program to its parent task

Calling Registers: AH   4Ch
                      AL   Return code

Return Registers: None

Comments: On exit, DOS does the following:

- Restores the termination handler vector from PSP:000Ah

- Restores the Ctrl-Break handler vector from PSP:000Eh

- Restores the critical-error handler vector from PSP:0012h (DOS V3 and above)

- Flushes the file buffers (handle files)

- Transfers to the termination-handler address

This is now the approved way to terminate a program. Programs that exist in DOS V2 and later should always use this function in preference to Int 20h or Int 21h, Function 00h. This function has two advantages over the earlier termination functions:

- It allows returning an exit code, which can be used as the ERRORLEVEL parameter in batch files or by the parent process through Function 4Dh to determine return information.

- It does not rely on any register settings for proper operation, such as the CS register pointing to the segment the PSP is in.

Because it automatically closes out file handles and updates the disk directory, this function protects against inadvertent errors in file handling. It will not, however, do anything for file control block (FCB) files.

Int 21h Function 4Dh V2
Get Return Code

Gets the return code from a successful EXEC function call

Calling Registers: AH 4Dh

Return Registers: AH System exit code
00, normal termination
01, termination by Ctrl-C
02, termination by critical device error
03, termination by call to Function 31h

AL Child exit code

Comments: When called, this function returns (once and only once) the exit code returned by a child process through the system. Using this function resets the returned exit code to zero; if you need to pass it on to a parent process, it must be saved and returned as your own process's exit code. The system exit code tells you whether the program terminated normally. The child exit code tells you anything that the program wants to tell you; its interpretation depends on the program you have run.

Int 21h Function 4Eh V2
Search for First Match

Locates the first occurrence of a matching file name, given an ASCII string, which can include wild cards

Calling Registers: AH 4Eh
CX Attribute to use in search
DS:DX Pointer to ASCIIZ file specification

Return Registers: Carry flag clear if successful

Carry flag set if error
AX   Error code
02h, file not found
03h, invalid path
12h, no more files

Comments: This function, when given an ASCIIZ string that contains the full file name of a desired file (possibly including wild cards * and ?), fills information about the returned file into the disk transfer area (DTA). The search is limited by the attribute provided to the function. Only those files that match the attributes specified will be found. The file attributes for the file can include the following values:

Value	File Types Matched
00h	Normal
02h	Normal and hidden
04h	Normal and system
06h	Normal, hidden, and system
08h	Volume labels
10h	Directories

Because the attribute is a byte, you can set CX by setting CL to the desired attribute and CH to zero. When the function returns, the DTA is set as shown here:

Offset Byte	Field Length	Contents
00h	21 bytes	Reserved for DOS use on subsequent searches
15h	Byte	Attribute of matched file
16h	Word	File time
18h	Word	File date
1Ah	Double word	File size
1Eh	13 bytes	File name and extension as ASCIIZ string. Blanks are stripped, and a period is placed in front of the extension

Time and date entries are interpreted as follows:

Bits	
FEDCBA98 76543210	Meaning

—Time Field Encoding—	
xxxxx...	Hours (0–23)
.....xxx xxx.....	Minutes (0–59)
....xxxxx	Two-second increments (0–29)

Bits

FEDCBA98 76543210   *Meaning*

—Date Field Encoding—

xxxxxxx.	Year—1980
.......x xxx.....	Month (1–12)
....xxxxx	Day (1–31)

The DTA may be read to retrieve the information about the located file, which after all will have a different file name than the search string if it includes wild cards. However, the DTA should remain inviolate for use in further searches.

Int 21h   Function 4Fh   V2
Search for Next Match

After a successful call to Function 4Eh, this call continues to find files that match the specified criteria. The DTA must retain the information originally placed there by the call to Function 4Eh.

Calling Registers: AH   4Fh

Return Registers: Carry flag clear if successful

Carry flag set if error
   AX   Error code
         12h, no more files

Comments: If wild cards are used in a first search (Function 4Eh), additional files that match the wild-card specification can be found by repeatedly calling this function. A failed search (carry flag set on return from the function) indicates that no additional file names match the pattern.

Searches with the "next match" function continue to use the same procedures used for the first match. The function updates the DTA to indicate the name of the file and other data regarding the file located by the search. The DTA must not be modified between calls to allow successive searches. The following table shows the layout of the data in the DTA on return from the function:

Offest Byte	Field Length	Contents
00h	21 bytes	Reserved for DOS use on subsequent searches
15h	Byte	Attribute of matched file
16h	Word	File time
18h	Word	File date
1Ah	Double word	File size
1Eh	13 bytes	File name and extension as ASCIIZ string. Blanks are stripped, and a period is placed in front of the extension

Time and date entries are interpreted as follows:

Bits		
FEDCBA98 76543210		*Meaning*

		—Time Field Encoding—
xxxxx...		Hours (0–23)
.....xxx xxx.....		Minutes (0–59)
....xxxxx		Two-second increments (0–29)
		—Date Field Encoding—
xxxxxxx.		Year—1980
.......x xxx.....		Month (1–12)
....xxxxx		Day (1–31)

The DTA may be read to retrieve the information about the located file, which after all will have a different file name than the search string if it includes wild cards. However, the DTA should remain inviolate for use in further searches.

Int 21h	**Function 50h** *Set PSP Segment*	**V2**

Sets the address of the currently executing process's program segment prefix (PSP)

Calling Registers: AH   50h
BX   Segment address of the new PSP

Return Registers: None

Comments: Function 50h allows a terminate and stay resident (TSR) program to implement *context switching* between the TSR process and the interrupted process on a DOS system. Context switching involves making the DOS system think that the TSR is the primary process rather than the interrupted process. To do this, you have to record the original PSP's address (Function 51h) and tell DOS that the TSR's PSP is the current one (Function 50h). When you are ready to return to the interrupted program, you return the PSPs to normal.

It has often been reported that this function is unreliable prior to DOS V3 and that, in particular, it does not work in an Int 28h handler (Keyboard Busy Loop).

The reason for these reports is simple: DOS V2 switches to its own internal stack before dispatching control to any requested function; if this function is called while DOS is already processing another normal input function, the second stack switch that results will destroy information needed by that input function.

The cure is equally simple but extremely subtle: you can trick DOS into believing that it is processing a critical error by manipulating its critical error flag. Setting the critical error flag before calling this function forces DOS to use its alternate internal stack. You must restore the flag to its original value after return from this function. See the comments for Int 21h, Function 34h for details of the critical error flag.

In V3, the DOS dispatch code was modified to test for this function before doing any stack switching; if this function was requested, DOS simply uses the caller's own stack, avoiding the problem entirely.

The PSP segment address has come to be called the process ID (PID) for the running process. This function is often known as SetPID.

Int 21h   **Function 51h**   **V2**
                        Get PSP Segment

Gets the address of the currently executing process's program segment prefix (PSP)

Calling Registers: AH   51h

Return Registers: BX   PSP of currently executing process

Comments: This function is used to determine the PSP of the process interrupted by a terminate and stay resident (TSR) program. The TSR can save this address and then tell DOS that its own PSP is the executing one for the course of its processing. See Function 50h and Chapter 11, "Interrupt Handlers," for a more detailed discussion.

It has often been reported that this function is unreliable prior to DOS V3 and that, in particular, it does not work in an Int 28h handler (Keyboard Busy Loop).

The reason for these reports is simple: DOS V2 switches to its own internal stack before dispatching control to any requested function; if this function is called while DOS is already processing another normal input function, the second stack switch that results will destroy information needed by that input function.

The cure is equally simple but extremely subtle: you can trick DOS into believing that it is processing a critical error by manipulating its critical error flag. Setting the critical error flag before calling this function forces DOS to use its alternate internal stack. You must restore the flag to its original value after return from this function. See the comments for Int 21h, Function 34h for details of the critical error flag.

In V3, the DOS dispatch code was modified to test for this function before doing any stack switching; if this function was requested, DOS simply uses the caller's own stack, avoiding the problem entirely.

The PSP segment address has come to be called the process ID (PID) for the running process. This function is often known as GetPID. In Version 3, Function 62h was added as a documented function to perform this same task; in all versions examined, both functions execute the self-same code.

Int 21h   **Function 52h**   **V2**
                       Get Disk List

This function provides access to the list of drive parameter blocks, where DOS maintains its data about disk configuration, and to many more internal DOS tables

Calling Registers: AH   52h

Return Registers: ES:BX   Pointer to DOS table as described below

Comments: For internal purposes, DOS keeps track of key parameters for disk drive operations as a linked list of drive parameter blocks. This function returns a pointer to the head of that linked list. However, the list of DPBs is only one of a number of items about which DOS maintains data internally, and the pointer returned by this function can be used to locate the other items also, as shown in table DOS.14. Appendix E, "The Reserved DOS Functions," discusses this function more fully.

Notice that the construction of table DOS.14 varies with the DOS version. Only the data from the DPB pointer –02h up through +0Fh remains constant over all three versions. In V2, the number of logical drives is given by a byte at 10h, which is followed by a word giving the maximum block size in bytes and a double word pointing to the first buffer control block.

In V3, six more bytes were added at the front of the table: a double-word pointer to the current buffer control block at –08h, and a word giving the offset into the current buffer (usually 0000) is at –04h. The byte at 10h in V2 was moved to 21h in V3, and the six following bytes were moved up to fill the gap. Then at 16h, a double-word pointer to the logical drive table was added, followed at 1Ah by a double-word pointer to the system FCB chain and at 1Eh by a word telling how many of the FCBs to keep when swapping out during network operations. The byte at 20h gives the number of block devices present, and the byte at 21h (mentioned earlier) tells how many logical drives are present.

As noted in table DOS.14, the only change from V3 to V4 is that the BCB pointer at 12h becomes a pointer to a new EMS linkage block for the file buffers, and the current-BCB pointer at –06h gives direct access to the buffer chain.

There are "holes" in many of the data areas reached by table DOS.14—not because the unknown bytes have no purpose, but because their purpose is not known. What *is* known comes from dedicated DOS hackers who have been digging out the information one piece at a time; Appendix E, "The Reserved DOS Functions," goes into much more detail in this respect. (The format of each DPB is shown in table DOS.15, which appears with the discussion of Function 53h.)

Table DOS.14. *Configuration Variable Table (CVT)*

Offset Byte	Field Length	Meaning
		—DOS V3.x and Above—
-08h	Double word	Current buffer in BUFFERS= chain
-04h	Word	Offset within current buffer
		—DOS V2.x and Above—
-02h	Word	Segment of first memory control block
00h	Double word	Pointer to first drive parameter block
04h	Double word	Pointer to first DCB (system file table device control block)
08h	Double word	Pointer to CLOCK$ device driver
0Ch	Double word	Pointer to CON device driver
		—DOS V2.x Only—
10h	Byte	Number of logical drives
11h	Word	Maximum bytes per sector on any block device
13h	Double word	Pointer to start of disk buffer chain
17h		Beginning of NUL device driver; first device in the device driver chain
		—DOS V3.x and Above—
10h	Word	Maximum bytes per sector on any block device
12h	Double word	Pointer to start of disk buffer chain (in V4, points to EMS link record which in turn points to buffer chain)
16h	Double word	Pointer to logical drive table (see discussion below for layout)
1Ah	Double word	Pointer to start of DOS's FCB chain
1Eh	Word	Number of FCB's to keep when swapping
20h	Byte	Number of block devices
21h	Byte	Number of logical drives, set by value of LASTDRIVE in CONFIG.SYS (defaults to 5 if not specified)
22h		Beginning of NUL device driver; first device in the device driver chain

The following is what is known about the Logical Drive Table pointed to at offset 16h in table DOS.14 (DOS V3 and above). The pointer is to the beginning of this table. There is one table for each logical drive on the system, beginning with drive A:. The minimum is a default of five (A through E) or the value set in LASTDRIVE of the CONFIG.SYS file. The tables, each of which is 81 bytes long in V3 (and 88 bytes in V4), follow one another in memory.

Offset Byte	Field Length	Meaning
00h	2 bytes	Actual drive designator and :
02h	65 bytes	Current path for this drive as an ASCIIZ string (includes root directory slash and room for terminating 00h byte)

43h	Word	Current status of drive (bit map):
		    8000h = unknown
		    4000h = ready for use
		    2000h = unknown
		    1000h = SUBSTed unit
		    0000h = logical drive not mapped to a
		             physical drive

45h	Double word	Pointer to DOS DPB for drive
49h	Word	First cluster of current directory (FFFFh if drive was never accessed, 0 if at the root directory)
4Bh	Word	Unknown
4Dh	Word	Unknown
4Fh	Word	Number of bytes to skip over when reporting directory: 0002 for normal drive, more if SUBSTed unit
		—DOS V4—
51h	7 bytes	Unknown, default values of 0

Int 21h   Function 53h   V2
Translate BPB to DPB

Translates a BIOS parameter block (BPB) into a DOS drive parameter block (DPB)

Calling Registers: AH   53h
                         DS:SI   Pointer to BPB
                         ES:BP   Pointer to area for DPB

Return Registers: None

Comments: The BIOS and DOS both keep their own information about the disks and drives attached to the system. This function allows you to change the BIOS parameter block (BPB) to a DOS drive parameter block (DPB). See also Int 21h, Functions 1Fh and 32h as well as Int 21h, Function 44h, Subfunction 0Dh, minor Function 40h. Table DOS.15 gives the layout of a BPB and a DPB. As you will notice, the information is primarily disk oriented, particularly in the BPB.

Table DOS.15. *BIOS and DOS Parameter Block Layout*

Offset Byte	Field Length	Meaning
		—BIOS Parameter Block Information—
00h	Word	Number of bytes per sector
02h	Byte	Number of sectors per cluster
03h	Word	Number of reserved sectors starting at sector 0
05h	Byte	Number of FATs
06h	Word	Maximum number of root directory entries
08h	Word	Total number of sectors (or 0, in V4 to indicate use of extended BPB format)
0Ah	Byte	Media descriptor
0Bh	Word	Number of sectors per FAT
0Dh	Word	Number of sectors per track
0Fh	Word	Number of heads
11h	Double word	Number of hidden sectors
15h	Double word	In extended BPB format, total number of sectors; used only if word at offset 08h above is zero. Applies to V4 only
19h	7 bytes	Reserved
		—DOS Parameter Block Information—
		—All Versions—
00h	Byte	Drive number (0 = A, 1 = B, etc.)
01h	Byte	Device driver unit number
02h	Word	Bytes per sector
04h	Byte	Sectors per cluster (zero-based)
05h	Byte	Shift factor
06h	Word	Number of reserved boot sectors
08h	Byte	Number of FAT copies
09h	Word	Number of root directory entries
0Bh	Word	First data sector number
0Dh	Word	Highest cluster number plus 1
		—Version 2 or 3 Only—
0Fh	Byte	Sectors per FAT (0–255)
10h	Word	Root directory starting sector number
12h	Double word	Drive's device driver address
16h	Byte	Media descriptor byte
17h	Byte	Disk parameter block access flag (0FFh indicates need to rebuild)
18h	Double word	Address of next device parameter block
		—Version 2 Only—
1Ch	Word	Starting cluster number for current directory
1Eh	64 bytes	ASCIIZ of current directory path

Offset Byte	Field Length	Meaning
		—Version 3 Only—
1Ch	Word	Last cluster number allocated from this drive
1Eh	Word	Purpose unknown; normally FFFFh
		—Version 4 Only—
0Fh	Word	Sectors per FAT (0–65,535)
11h	Word	Root directory starting sector number
13h	Double word	Drive's device driver address
17h	Byte	Media descriptor byte
18h	Byte	Disk parameter block access flag (0FFh indicates need to rebuild)
19h	Double word	Address of next device parameter block
1Dh	Word	Last cluster number allocated from this drive
1Fh	Word	Purpose unknown; normally FFFFh

Int 21h   Function 54h   V2
Get Verify Flag

Gets the current value of the read-after-write (verify) flag

Calling Registers: AH   54h

Return Registers: AL   00h, verify off 01h, verify on

Comments: The verify flag controls whether the system will do a read-after-write verify of disk operations. The default for this flag is OFF (value 00).

Function 2Eh sets the verify flag. The effect of the setting is to slow down disk operations somewhat to allow the verify but increase the assurance that disk operations are successful.

Because network systems do not support the verify function, the return code is meaningless in these cases.

Int 21h   Function 55h   V2
Create PSP

Creates a program segment prefix (PSP) at the designated segment-address location

Calling Registers: AH   55h
                          DX   Segment at which to set up PSP

Return Registers: None

Comments: This function is similar to Int 21h, Function 26h. The difference is that this function does not simply copy the PSP; it creates a separate and distinct "child" PSP in preparation for running another program. Like Int 21h, Function 26h, the usefulness of this function has been superseded by the EXEC function (Int 21h, Function 4Bh).

Int 21h   Function 56h   V2
Rename File

Renames a file or moves it to another directory on the same disk drive

Calling Registers:	AH	56h
	DS:DX	Pointer to ASCIIZ current file name
	ES:DI	Pointer to ASCIIZ new file name

Return Registers: Carry flag clear if successful

Carry flag set if error
      AX   Error code
              02h, file not found
              03h, path not found
              05h, access denied
              11h, not the same device

Comments: The present rename function is both more powerful and less powerful than the one provided for use with file control block (FCB) functions. This rename function allows you to use directory path names to locate files and can even move a file between directories. But because it does not allow wild cards, renaming groups of files is no longer a possibility.

For most normal work, the limitations are not significant. Renaming files in directories and moving them between directories is much more advantageous for general use. Multiple files can be handled by the calling program.

The function will not work if the path name does not exist or if a file of the desired name is already in the target directory. Nor will the function work across disk drives. If files being renamed are open, they should be closed first. Leaving a file open when renaming it can lead to unpredictable results.

In a network environment, you must have create-access rights in order to rename a file.

Int 21h   Function 57h Subfunction 00h   V2
Get File Date and Time

Gets the file's last modified date and time in the directory entry

Calling Registers: AH   57h
AL   00h, get the date and time
BX   File handle

Return Registers: Carry flag clear if successful
    CX   Time if getting date and time
    DX   Date if getting date and time

    Carry flag set if error
    AX   Error code
             01h, invalid function (file sharing)
             06h, invalid handle

Comments: The date and time functions work on files opened with Functions 3Ch, 3Dh, 5Ah, or 5Bh (the handle open or create functions). The following table shows the layout of the bits and how they are interpreted for the date and time:

Bits	
FEDCBA98 76543210	*Meaning*
	—Time Field Encoding—
xxxxx...	Hours (0–23)
.....xxx xxx.....	Minutes (0–59)
....xxxxx	Two-second increments (0–29)
	—Date Field Encoding—
xxxxxxx.	Year—1980
.......x xxx.....	Month (1–12)

Int 21h   **Function 57h Subfunction 01h**   **V2**
                      Set File Date and Time

Sets the file's last modified date and time in the directory entry

Calling Registers: AH   57h
AL   01h, set the date and time
BX   File handle
CX   Time if setting the date and time
DX   Date if setting the date and time

Return Registers: Carry flag clear if successful

Carry flag set if error
AX   Error code
      01h, invalid function (file sharing)
      06h, invalid handle

Comments: The date and time functions work on files opened with Functions 3Ch, 3Dh, 5Ah, or 5Bh (the handle open or create functions). The following table shows the layout of the bits and how they are interpreted for the date and time:

Bits

FEDCBA98 76543210	*Meaning*
	—Time Field Encoding—
XXXXX...	Hours (0–23)
.....XXX XXX.....	Minutes (0–59)
....XXXXX	Two-second increments (0–29)
	—Date Field Encoding—
XXXXXXX.	Year—1980
.......X XXX.....	Month (1–12)
....XXXXX	Day (1–31)

Int 21h   Function 58h Subfunction 00h   V2
Get Allocation Strategy

Gets the code that tells which strategy to use for memory allocation

Calling registers: AH   58h
                     AL   00h, get strategy code

Return registers: Carry flag clear if successful
                   AX   Strategy code
                        00h, first fit, low 640K first (default)
                        01h, best fit, low 640K first
                        02h, last fit, low 640K first
                        40h, first fit, UMBs only
                        41h, best fit, UMBs only
                        42h, last fit, UMBs only
                        80h, first fit, UMBs first
                        81h, best fit, UMBs first
                        82h, last fit, UMBs first

Carry flag set if error
> AX   Error code
> 01h, invalid function (file sharing)

Comments: In V2, Microsoft and IBM officially specified this function as "used internally by DOS." If your copy of DOS V2 is from a third-party vendor, this function may be used for a different purpose. In V3, this function became an official and documented function in Microsoft documentation, but it remains undocumented in IBM versions.

This subfunction permits a program to learn the strategy that DOS is using to allocate memory to processes. In general, this type of parameter is meaningless unless you have reason to believe that one strategy will work better than another.

Possible strategies known to DOS include first fit, best fit, and last fit. These strategies can be modified under V5 to include specifying whether to try the UMBs or the low 640K first. The first-fit strategy searches from low memory to high for the first of memory that is as large as, or larger than, the requested memory size, and returns the first one it finds.

The best-fit strategy checks all available memory blocks to find the smallest block that will meet the allocation requested. Although this strategy results in the most efficient utilization of memory for the available processes, it takes more processor time.

The last-fit strategy is the same as the first-fit strategy except that the search proceeds from high memory to low memroy rather than from low to high, and returns the last block that will meet the requirement.

Under V5, if the first memory arena checked yields a successful result (regardless of whether the arena is the low 640K or the UMBs), the second arena is not checked. Thus, the best-fit strategy will not necessarily give the application the best fit. As long as there is at least one block that can be allocated in the first arena, the second arena, which might yield a better fit, is not checked.

Prior to V5, the last-fit strategy (code 02) could be any value greater than or equal to 02, so a number other than 02 may have been stored. A test for strategy should account for the possibility that the number could be greater than 02.

Int 21h	**Function 58h Subfunction 01h**	**V2**
	Set Allocation Strategy	

Sets the code that tells which strategy to use for memory allocation

Calling registers: AH   58h
                            AL   01h, set strategy code
                            BX   Strategy code
                                          00h, first fit, low 640K first (default)
                                        01h, best fit, low 640K first
                                        02h, last fit, low 640K first

PROGRAMMING

> 40h, first fit, UMBs only
> 41h, best fit, UMBs only
> 42h, last fit, UMbs only
> 80h, first fit, UMBs first
> 81h, best fit, UMBs first
> 82h, last fit, UMBs first

Return registers: Carry flag clear if successful

Carry flag set if error
  AX   Error code
          01h, invalid function (file sharing)

Comments: In V2, Microsoft and IBM officially specified this function as "used internally by DOS." If your copy of DOS V2 is from a third-party vendor, this function may be used for an entirely different purpose. In V3, this function became an official and documented function in Microsoft documentation, but it remains undocumented in IBM versions.

This subfunction selects the strategy that DOS uses to allocate memory to processes when DOS is asked for memory. In general, this type of tuning parameter is meaningless for most programmers, unless they have some reason to think that one strategy will work better than another.

Possible strategies known to DOS include first fit, best fit, and last fit. These strategies can be modified under V5 to include specifying whether to try the UMBs first or the low 640K first. The first-fit strategy searches from low memory to high efor a memory block and returns the first one that is as large as or larger than the requested memory.

The best-fit strategy checks all available memory blocks to find the smallest block that will meet the allocation requested.

The last-fit strategy is the same as the first-fit strategy except the search proceeds from high memory to low memory rather than from low to high.

Under V5, if the first memory arena checked yields a successful result (regardless of whether the arena is the low 640K or the UMBs), the second arena is not checked. Thus, the best-fit strategy will not necessarily give the application the best fit. As long as there is at least one block that can be allocated in the first arena, the second arena, which might yield a better fit, is not checked.

Prior to V5, the last-fit strategy (code 02) could be any value greater than or equal to 02. When setting the strategy, a number other than 02 may be stored.

Int 21h Function 58h Subfunction 02h V5
Get UMB link status

Gets the status of the UMB arena link

Calling registers:	AH	58h
	AL	02h

Return registers: Carry flag clear if successful
AL   Result
     00h, not linked
     01h, linked

     Carry flag set if error
       AX   Error code
          07h, arena trashed

Comments: This subfunction permits a program to learn whether DOS is using UMBs in its memory allocation scheme.

Int 21h Function 58h Subfunction 03h V5
Set UMB link status

Sets the status of the UMB arena link

Calling registers:	AH	58h
	AL	03h
	BX	Link status
		00h, unlink
		01h, link

Return registers: Carry flag clear if successful

     Carry flag set if error
       AX   Error code
          01h, invalid function when MS-DOS
             loaded without DOS=UMB
          07h, arena trashed

Comments: This subfunction permits a program to select whether DOS will use UMBs in its memory allocation scheme.

Int 21h

Function 59h
Get Extended Error Information

V3

Gets extended error return information about a failed call to an Int 21h function, including recommended remedial action. This call destroys registers AX, BX, CX, DX, SI, DI, BP, DS, and ES.

Calling Registers: AH   59h

                      BX   00

Return Registers: AX   Extended error code

                      BH   Error class

                      BL   Recommended action

                      CH   Error locus

Comments: Extended error processing provides a significant extension to DOS error handling by making the DOS system a partner in diagnosing and solving run-time problems. This function adds a significant capability for analyzing and isolating an error that arises from a DOS call. It can be called after an error from any call to Int 21h or from Int 24h when an error status is returned. If there was no error, this function will return AX = 0000h. File control block (FCB) calls that return FFh can also be resolved with this function.

The information returned is classified in the accompanying tables. Register AX returns the extended error code (see table DOS.16). These are general system errors already familiar as the error returned from many Int 21h functions. Register BH contains the error class, which provides further information about the error (see table DOS.17).

The BL register returns the most interesting value, the recommended action to resolve the error (see table DOS.18). Finally, register CH returns the error locus, which helps identify the error's physical location (see table DOS.19). The only problem with all this information is that the wealth of it can be staggering. A generalized error handler would be out of the question. Some general steps, however, can be taken depending on what type of error has occurred.

If a function indicates an error by setting the carry bit on return, its error handling should be written like this:

1. Load the registers for the function.

2. Issue the Int 21h function call.

3. If the carry flag is clear, continue with normal operations.

4. If the carry flag is set, disregard the error code returned from the function and issue a call to Function 59h.

5. Use the suggested action in the BL register to determine the proper course of action.

Some functions indicate an error by returning a code in the AL register (AL = FFh). For these cases, the call should be written like this:

1. Load the registers for the function.

2. Issue the Int 21h function call.

3. If no error is reported in AL, continue with normal operations.

4. If an error is reported in AL, disregard the error code reported and issue a call to Function 59h.

5. Use the suggested action in the BL register to determine the proper course of action.

You must be careful using this function. On return, registers AX, BX, CX, DX, SI, DI, BP, DS, and ES are destroyed. You also must call the function *immediately* after an error has occurred. If another DOS function is executed before the call, the return will not correspond to the desired error.

Table DOS.16. *Extended Error Codes Returned in AX*

Codes		
Decimal	Hex	Meaning
1	01	Invalid function number
2	02	File not found
3	03	Path not found
4	04	No handles available
5	05	Access denied
6	06	Invalid handle
7	07	Memory control blocks destroyed
8	08	Insufficient memory
9	09	Invalid memory block address
10	0A	Invalid environment
11	0B	Invalid format
12	0C	Invalid access code
13	0D	Invalid data
14	0E	Reserved
15	0F	Invalid drive
16	10	Attempt to remove current directory
17	11	Not the same device
18	12	No more files

continues

Table DOS.16. *continued*

Codes		
Decimal	*Hex*	*Meaning*
19	13	Disk write-protected
20	14	Unknown unit
21	15	Drive not ready
22	16	Unknown command
23	17	CRC error
24	18	Bad request structure length
25	19	Seek error
26	1A	Unknown media type
27	1B	Sector not found
28	1C	Out of paper
29	1D	Write fault
30	1E	Read fault
31	1F	General failure
32	20	Sharing violation
33	21	Lock violation
34	22	Invalid disk change
35	23	FCB unavailable
36	24	Sharing buffer overflow
37	25	Code page mismatched
38	26	Unable to complete file operation (V4 only)
39	27	Handle disk full
40–49	28–31	Reserved
50	32	Network request not supported
51	33	Remote computer not listening
52	34	Duplicate name on network
53	35	Network name not found
54	36	Network busy
55	37	Network device no longer exists
56	38	NetBIOS command limit exceeded
57	39	Network adapter error
58	3A	Incorrect network response
59	3B	Unexpected network error
60	3C	Incompatible remote adapter
61	3D	Print queue full
62	3E	Not enough space for print file
63	3F	Print file deleted
64	40	Network name deleted
65	41	Access denied
66	42	Network device type incorrect
67	43	Network name not found
68	44	Network name limit exceeded

Codes		
Decimal	Hex	Meaning
69	45	NetBIOS session limit exceeded
70	46	Sharing temporarily paused
71	47	Network request not accepted
72	48	Print or disk redirection is paused
73–79	49–4F	Reserved
80	50	File already exists
81	51	Dup FCB
82	52	Cannot make directory entry
83	53	Fail on Int 24
84	54	Too many redirections
85	55	Duplicate redirection
86	56	Invalid password
87	57	Invalid parameter
88	58	Network data fault
89	59	Function not supported by network (V4 only)
90	5A	Required system component not installed (V4 only)

Table DOS.17. *Error Class Codes Returned in BH*

Class Codes		
Decimal	Hex	Meaning
1	01	Out of resource
2	02	Temporary situation
3	03	Authorization
4	04	Internal
5	05	Hardware failure
6	06	System failure
7	07	Application program error
8	08	Not found
9	09	Bad format
10	0A	Locked
11	0B	Media
12	0C	Already exists
13	0D	Unknown

DOS
PROGRAMMING

Table DOS.18. *Recommended Action Codes Returned in BL*

Action Code	Meaning
1	Retry. If not cleared, prompt user to Abort or Ignore.
2	Delay, then retry. If not cleared, prompt user to Abort or Ignore.
3	Get correct data from user (bad file name or disk drive).
4	Abort application with cleanup.
5	Abort without cleanup (cleanup may increase problems).
6	Ignore error.
7	Prompt user to correct error, then retry.

Table DOS.19. *Error Locus Codes Returned in CH*

Locus Code	Meaning
1	Unknown
2	Block device (disk or disk emulator)
3	Network
4	Serial device
5	Memory related

Int 21h

Function 5Ah
Create Uniquely Named File

V3

Creates a file with a guaranteed unique name in the specified directory

Calling Registers:

AH	5Ah
CX	Attribute
DS:DX	Pointer to ASCIIZ path specification ending in a backslash (\)

Return Registers:

Carry flag clear if successful

AX	Handle
DS:DX	Pointer to ASCIIZ file specification with file name appended

Carry flag set if error
   AX   Error code
           03h, path not found
           04h, no handles available
           05h, access denied

Comments: Unique files always have uses as temporary files. By using the unique file creation call, you do not have to worry about the exact name created; you can leave that to the operating system.

   To use the function, provide a path name to the directory where you want the temporary file created. Use a full path name ending in a backslash character (for example, \TMP\ to put the file in the \TMP directory). You also can specify the attribute of the file you want created. The following table gives the valid attributes that can be set by this function. The function returns a unique file name according to its own internal rules.

Value	File Types Matched
00h	Normal
02h	Hidden
04h	System
06h	Hidden and system

   The only ways to fail are if the path to the desired directory does not exist, if you have already used all the available handles for the current process, or if you are creating the file in the root directory and it is already full. You have to take some care though. Files created as temporary files have as much existence as files created to have continuing existence. Because such files are not automatically deleted when the program ends, your program should clean up after itself by deleting all such files that it creates.

   In a network environment, you must have create-access rights in order to use this function.

Int 21h	**Function 5Bh**	**V3**
	Create New File	

Creates a new file in the specified directory

Calling Registers: AH   5Bh
                          CX   Attribute
                          DS:DX   Pointer to ASCIIZ file specification

Return Registers: Carry flag clear if successful
                          AX   Handle

Carry flag set if error
AX   Error code
        03h, path not found
        04h, no handles available
        05h, access denied
        50h, file already exists

Comments: This is the normal method of creating a new file that you intend to use as more than just a temporary file. The function returns a file handle for access to the file. If the file cannot be created because the path does not exist, because no handles are available, or because you try to create it in the root directory and the root is full, the function will fail.

Unlike Function 3Ch, this function will fail if the file already exists. You can use this function to test for the existence of a designated file. If creation succeeds, the file did not exist.

The file is created as a normal file with read/write access. You can change the attributes with Function 43h. You cannot, however, create volume labels or subdirectories. The valid attributes are listed in the following table:

Value	File Types Matched
00h	Normal
02h	Hidden
04h	System
06h	Hidden and system

An interesting use for this file-creation function is to implement a semaphore mechanism across a PC network. If this function successfully creates a file, the program has the semaphore and can proceed into its critical code section. If it cannot create the file, you can retest the operation periodically.

When the program that created the file is finished with its critical section, it deletes the file and thereby releases the semaphore.

In a network environment, you must have create-access rights in order to use this function.

Int 21h   Function 5Ch Subfunction 00h   V3
Set File Access Locks

Locks a specified area of a file

Calling Registers: AH   5Ch
                          AL   00h
                           BX   File handle
                           CX   Most significant part of region offset
                           DX   Least significant part of region offset

| SI | Most significant part of region length |
| DI | Least significant part of region length |

Return Registers: Carry flag clear if successful

Carry flag set if error
AX	Error code
	01h, invalid function
	06h, invalid handle
	21h, lock violation
	24h, sharing buffer exceeded

Comments: File locking is an essential operation in network environments for database- and other transaction-oriented functions. If more than one process is allowed to write to the same section of a file, the results of two such writes will be indeterminate. Record locking enforces an ordering on the operations so that one process must complete its write before another starts. It does not guarantee that the order of writes is sensible—it just makes sure that they do not interfere with each other.

Locks and unlocks are like Begin-End pairs in Pascal or braces ({}) in C; they must always be matched. For each file lock, there must be an exact duplicate file unlock in the same program. Failing to unlock a file results in a file whose state is indeterminate.

Programs that use file locking must take pains to trap all possible error exits from the program so that unlocks can be handled even in abnormal conditions. Programs that access files that are or can be locked should not attempt direct access to the file. The proper procedure for using the locking mechanism is not to rely on it to prevent collisions directly. Rather, an attempt should be made to lock the desired portion of the file and check the resulting error code for successful completion. If the lock can be created, file manipulation can proceed. If the lock cannot be created, the program should delay and try again.

The locking mechanism includes an automatic retry function. Using the IOCTL Function (44h), Subfunction 0Bh, you can change the number of retries and the retry interval.

File handles duplicated with Function 45h will inherit access to the locked regions. Programs spawned with the program EXEC Function (4Bh) do not inherit the file locks along with the files.

Int 21h   **Function 5Ch Subfunction 01h**   V3
Clear File Access Locks

Unlocks a specified area of a file that was locked with Subfunction 00h

Calling Registers:
| AH | 5Ch |
| AL | 01h |

BX	File handle
CX	Most significant part of region offset
DX	Least significant part of region offset
SI	Most significant part of region length
DI	Least significant part of region length

Return Registers: Carry flag clear if successful

Carry flag set if error
AX	Error code
	01h, invalid function
	06h, invalid handle
	21h, lock violation
	24h, sharing buffer exceeded

Comments: File locking is an essential operation in network environments for database- and other transaction-oriented functions. If more than one process is allowed to write to the same section of a file, the results of two such writes will be indeterminate. Record locking enforces an ordering on the operations so that one process must complete its write before another starts. It does not guarantee that the order of writes is sensible—it just makes sure that they do not interfere with each other.

Locks and unlocks are like Begin-End pairs in Pascal or braces ({}) in C; they must always be matched. For each file lock, there must be an exact duplicate file unlock in the same program. Failing to unlock a file results in a file whose state is indeterminate.

Refer to the discussion for Subfunction 00h for additional details of this function.

Int 21h   Function 5Dh Subfunction 00h   V3
Copy Data to DOS Save Area

Copies 18 bytes of data from the location pointed to by DS:SI to the DOS internal register-save area so that it will be returned as the register content when DOS returns to the caller

Calling Registers:
AH	5Dh
AL	00h

Return Registers: DS:SI   Pointer to data to be copied

Comments: This function replaces all the saved register values kept by DOS and can transfer control to another part of the system. Its intended purpose is not known.

Int 21h   Function 5Dh Subfunction 06h   V3
Get Critical-Error Flag Address

Returns a pointer to the location at which the system critical-error flag is stored

Calling Registers: AH   5Dh
                         AL   06h

Return Registers: DS:SI   Pointer to critical-error flag

Comments: This function returns a pointer to the error flag used by DOS to determine whether a critical error has occurred.

Int 21h   Function 5Dh Subfunction 0Ah   V3
Set Error Data Values

Changes the system-error data codes stored internally by each DOS operation

Calling Registers: AH   5Dh
                         AL   0Ah
                         DS:SI   Pointer to ERROR structure:
                                   Word, extended error code
                                   Byte, action code to set
                                   Byte, class code to set
                                   Word, locus code to set
                                   Word, DX at time error occurred
                                   Word, SI at time error occurred
                                   Word, DI at time error occurred
                                   Word, DS at time error occurred
                                   Word, ES at time error occurred
                                   Word, reserved
                                   Word, computer ID (0 if local)
                                   Word, program ID (0 if local)

Return Registers: None

Comments: This subfunction changes the internal storage locations used by DOS for returning information through Interrupt 21h, Function 59h (Get Extended Error Information). It can be used with Subfunction 06h (Get Critical-Error Flag Address) to save these codes when an error is detected and then restore them after preliminary processing (which might modify the stored codes) is finished.

These functions can also be used in TSR coding to prevent a pop-up action from accidentally changing an error code and giving rise to inaccurate results. To do so, you first would use Subfunction 06 to get the address, and then save the data to your own storage area. When you do the save, note that the internal DOS structure differs from the one used by Subfunction 0Ah:

Byte, locus code
Word, extended error code
Byte, action code
Byte, class code
Double word, far pointer to driver address

Int 21h   **Function 5Eh Subfunction 00h**   **V3.1**
                     Get Machine Name

Gets the network machine name

Calling Registers: AH   5Eh
                          AL   00h, get machine name
                          DS:DX   Pointer to buffer to receive machine name
                          DS:SI   Pointer to setup string

Return Registers: Carry flag clear if successful
                          CH =   00h, name not defined
                          CH >   00h, name defined
                          CL   NETBIOS name number (CH > 00h)
                          DS:DX   Pointer to identifier (CH > 00h)

                          Carry flag set if error
                          AX   Error code
                                   01h, invalid function

Comments: The *machine name* is a 15-byte, ASCIIZ string used to identify the machine to a network. This function requires that the network be running. If the network is not running, the results of the function will be unpredictable.

Int 21h   **Function 5Eh Subfunction 01h**   **V3.1**
                     Set Machine Name

Sets the network machine name

Calling Registers: AH   5Eh
                          AL   01h, set machine name
                          DS:DX   Pointer to buffer containing machine
                                        name as ASCIIZ string

Return Registers: Carry flag clear if successful

                          Carry flag set if error
                          AX   Error code
                                   01h, invalid function

Comments: The *machine name* is a 15-byte, ASCIIZ string used to identify the machine to a network. This function requires that the network be running. If the network is not running, the results of the function will be unpredictable. This function should be used only by network software because it modifies information essential to the network's operation.

Int 21h   **Function 5Eh Subfunction 02h**   **V3.1**
Set Network Printer Setup

Sets the printer setup

Calling Registers: AH   5Eh
                       AL   02h, set printer setup
                       BX   Redirection list index
                       CX   Length of setup string (maximum of 64 bytes)
                       DS:SI   Pointer to setup string

Return Registers: Carry flag clear if successful

                     Carry flag set if error
                       AX   Error code
                                 01h, invalid function

Comments: The printer setup is a string sent before any print job when accessing the network printer. This function allows setting the string.

Int 21h   **Function 5Eh Subfunction 03h**   **V3.1**
Get Network Printer Setup

Gets the printer setup string

Calling Registers: AH   5Eh
                       AL   03h, get printer setup
                       BX   Redirection list index
                       ES:DI   Pointer to buffer to receive setup string

Return Registers: Carry flag clear if successful
                     CX   Length of printer setup string
                     ES:DI   Pointer to printer setup string

                     Carry flag set if error
                     AX   Error code
                                 01h, invalid function

Comments: The printer setup is a string to be sent before any print job when accessing the network printer. This function allows retrieving the string.

Int 21h — Function 5Fh Subfunction 02h — V3.1
Get Redirection List Entry

Gets the network redirection list entries

Calling Registers:

AH	5Fh	
AL	02h	
BX	Redirection list index	
DS:SI	Pointer to 128-byte buffer for device name	
ES:DI	Pointer to 128-byte buffer for network name	

Return Registers: Carry flag clear if successful

BH	Device status flag	
	Bit 0 = 0, device valid	
	Bit 0 = 1, device invalid	
BL	Device type	
	03h, printer	
	04h, disk drive	
CX	Stored parameter value	
DX	Destroyed	
BP	Destroyed	
DS:SI	Pointer to ASCIIZ local device name	
ES:DI	Pointer to ASCIIZ network name	

Carry flag set if error

AX	Error code	
	01h, invalid function	
	12h, no more files	

Comments: This function is used to get network redirection for devices (printers or disk directories) on the network. The network must be running to support this function. Using this function (together with related Subfunction 03h), you can associate a disk-drive identifier with a network directory, for example. You also can assign a remote printer device to be accessed with a local printer device name. The function supports remote passwords for remote disk access.

The file-sharing module must be loaded to use this function. All identifiers are passed as ASCIIZ strings and are thereby compatible with programming in C but not directly compatible with Pascal or BASIC. When you are getting a redirection entry, each call to Subfunction 02h returns a single entry in the redirection table. The entries are ASCIIZ strings representing the local device name, to which DS:SI points, and the network name, to which ES:DI points.

As you make subsequent calls to Subfunction 02h, you can tell that you have reached the end of the list when error code 12h (no more files) is returned. Calling this function destroys the contents of registers DX and BP, even though they are not used to return values.

Despite the sophisticated redirection available, COM devices, STDOUT, and STDERR cannot be redirected.

Int 21h Function 5Fh Subfunction 03h V3.1
Set Redirection List Entry

Gets or modifies the network redirection list entries

Calling Registers:	AH	5Fh
	AL	03h
	BL	Device type
		03h, printer
		04h, disk drive
	CX	Parameter to save for caller
	DS:SI	Pointer to ASCIIZ local device name
	ES:DI	Pointer to ASCIIZ network name
		followed by ASCIIZ password

Return Registers:	Carry flag clear if successful
	Carry flag set if error
	AX Error code
	01h, invalid function
	03h, path not found
	05h, access denied
	08h, insufficient memory
	0Fh, invalid drive
	12h, no more files
	57h, invalid parameter

Comments: This function is used to set network redirection for devices (printers or disk directories) on the network. It does this by modifying a list of local device names associated with network devices, files, or directories. The network must be running to support this function. Using this function, you can associate a disk-drive identifier with a network directory, for example. You can also assign a remote printer device to be accessed with a local printer device name. The function supports remote passwords for remote disk access.

The file-sharing module must be loaded to use this function. All identifiers are passed as ASCIIZ strings and are thereby compatible with programming in C but not directly compatible with Pascal or BASIC. The entries are ASCIIZ strings representing the local device name, to which DS:SI points, and the network name, to which ES:DI points.

Subfunction 03h allows you to specify a redirection to use. You can specify a printer or disk redirection (BL = device type) and indicate its local name (A, B, and so on for disk redirections; PRN:, LPT1:, and so on for printer redirection). When you redirect a printer, the output for the printer is buffered and sent to the network printer spooler for the desired device. Because this redirection occurs at the Int 17h level, you will trap all but hardware access to the printer itself.

Despite the sophisticated redirection available, COM devices, STDOUT, and STDERR cannot be redirected.

Int 21h	**Function 5Fh Subfunction 04h**	**V3.1**
	Cancel Redirection List Entry	

Cancels network redirection list entries

Calling Registers: AH 5Fh
AL 04h
DS:SI Pointer to ASCIIZ device name

Return Registers: Carry flag clear if successful

Carry flag set if error
AX Error code
01h, invalid function
0Fh, invalid drive

Comments: This function is used to cancel network redirection for devices (printers or disk directories) on the network. It does this by modifying a list of local device names associated with network devices, files, or directories. The network must be running to support this function. Using this function, you can associate a disk-drive identifier with a network directory, for example. You can also assign a remote printer device to be accessed with a local printer device name. The function supports remote passwords for remote disk access.

The file-sharing module must be loaded to use this function. All identifiers are passed as ASCIIZ strings and are thereby compatible with programming in C but not directly compatible with Pascal or BASIC.

Subfunction 04h uses only the local device name. The redirection is broken if that device has been reassigned. When the device name is a string starting with two backslashes, the connection between the local machine and the network directory is broken.

Despite the sophisticated redirection available, COM devices, STDOUT, and STDERR cannot be redirected.

Int 21h	**Function 60h**	**V3**
	Expand Path Name String	

Expands a relative path name, which may include reference to a SUBSTed or ASSIGNed drive, into a fully qualified path name that refers to the physical drive involved

Calling Registers: AH   60h

                      DS:SI   Points to ASCIIZ relative path name

                      ES:DI   Address of 67-byte work buffer

Return Registers: Carry flag clear if successful

                      ES:DI   Unchanged; work buffer contains

                                    fully qualified path name

                      Carry flag set if error

                      AX   Error code

                                02h, illegal character in input string

Comments: This appears to be the function introduced with V3 to permit the EXEC function to add the full path name of a program file to the end of the Environment area. Some reports have indicated that additional token parsing is performed, but our tests indicated that any string that could be a legal path name (including the use of the wild-card characters ? and *) was interpreted to be one. No checks were made by the function to determine whether the named file actually existed. The only error reported was due to illegal characters included in the input string.

Int 21h   Function 62h   V3
Get PSP Address

Gets the segment address of the program segment prefix (PSP) for the current program

Calling Registers: AH   62h

Return Registers: BX   Segment address of PSP

Comments: The purpose of this function is to allow the program to retrieve the address of its PSP at any time without having to explicitly save it in an accessible area during program startup. Because most access to functions should avoid direct access to the PSP, this function has only marginal utility.

    In all DOS versions tested, this function is a duplicate of reserved Function 51h, using the self-same code.

Int 21h   Function 63h Subfunction 00h   V2.25
Get System Lead Byte Table

Gets the address of the system lead byte table

Calling Registers: AH   63h

                         AL   00h

Return Registers: DS:SI   Pointer to lead byte table

Comments: This function retrieves the address of the system lead byte table. These data structures are associated with handling 2-byte-per-character display systems such as Kanji and Hangeul. This function first applied to DOS V2.25 only, was not available on DOS V3, and then reappeared in V4, but without documentation.

In V4, the other subfunctions for Function 63h are not implemented and do not return any error indication if called.

Int 21h   Function 63h Subfunction 01h   V2.25 Only
Set/Clear Interim Console Flag

Controls the interim console flag

Calling Registers: AH   63h
                         AL   01h
                         DL   00h, setting interim console flag
                                 01h, clearing interim console flag

Return Registers: None

Comments: This function allows control of the interim console flag. These data structures are associated with handling 2-byte-per-character display systems such as Kanji and Hangeul. This function applies to DOS V2.25 only; it is not available on DOS V3 or above.

Int 21h   Function 63h Subfunction 02h   V2.25 Only
Get Value of Interim Console Flag

Gets the value of the interim console flag

Calling Registers: AH   63h
                         AL   02h

Return Registers: DL   Value of interim console flag

Comments: This function retrieves the value of the interim console flag. These data structures are associated with handling 2-byte-per-character display systems such as Kanji and Hangeul. This function applies to DOS V2.25 only; it is not available on DOS V3 or above.

Int 21h — Function 64h — V3
Set Current Country Byte

Sets DOS's internal current country byte

Calling Registers: AH   64h
                        AL   Current country byte value

Return Registers: None

Comments: The content of the AL register is stored in the internal current country code location. No tests for validity are made nor is any error condition returned. All flags remain unchanged by this function.

Int 21h — Function 65h — V3.3
Get Extended Country Information

Returns extended information for the specified country

Calling Registers: AH   65h
                        AL   ID of information of interest (1, 2, 4, 5, 6, or 7)
                                or Subfunction (20h, 21h, or 22h)
                        BX   Code page of interest (–1 = active
                                CON device)
                        CX   Amount of data to return
                        DX   Country ID (default –1)
                        ES:DI   Pointer to buffer to return
                                information to

Return Registers: Carry flag clear if successful
                        ES:DI   Pointer to returned information buffer

                        Carry flag set if error
                        AX   Error code
                                01h, invalid function
                                02h, file not found

Comments: Programmers working on international systems must have access to a wide range of country-specific information such as the currency symbol and date format. Function 65h retrieves this information for your program, depending on the country you specify.

   Table DOS.20 can be retrieved by country ID. The default (–1) represents the United States. The call retrieves only as much data as specified in CX. If the table contains additional data, that data will be truncated and no error will be returned.

Table DOS.20. *Extended Country Information*

Offset Byte	Field Length	Meaning
		—Extended Country Information Buffer—
		Info ID: 01
00h	Byte	Info ID = 01
01h	Word	Size (38 or less)
03h	Word	Country ID
05h	Word	Code page
07h	Word	Date and time format code
		0 = USA m d y, hh:mm:ss
		1 = Europe d m y, hh:mm:ss
		2 = Japan y m d, hh:mm:ss
09h	5 bytes	Currency symbol string (ASCIIZ)
0Eh	Byte	Thousands separator
0Fh	Byte	Zero
10h	Byte	Decimal separator
11h	Byte	Zero
12h	Byte	Date separator
13h	Byte	Zero
14h	Byte	Time separator
15h	Byte	Zero
16h	Byte	Currency format
		00h = Symbol leads currency, no space
		01h = Symbol follows currency, no space
		02h = Symbol leads currency, 1 space
		03h = Symbol follows currency, 1 space
		04h = Symbol replaces decimal separator
17h	Byte	Number of digits after decimal
18h	Byte	Time format
		Bit 0 = 0–12 hour clock
		Bit 0 = 1–24 hour clock
19h	Double word	Case map call address
1Dh	Word	Data list separator
1Eh	Byte	Zero
1Fh	10 bytes	Reserved
		—Extended Country Uppercase Table—
		Info ID: 02
00h	Byte	Info ID = 02
01h	Double word	Pointer to uppercase table. Uppercase table is 130 bytes: 2-byte length plus 128 uppercase values.

Offset Byte	Field Length	Meaning
	—Extended Country File Name Uppercase Table—	
	Info ID: 04	
00h	Byte	Info ID = 04
01h	Double word	Pointer to file name uppercase table. File name uppercase table is 130 bytes: 2-byte length plus 128 uppercase values.
	—Extended File Name Character Table—	
	Info ID: 05	
00h	Byte	Info ID = 05
01h	Double word	Pointer to file name character table. Table starts with a 16-bit length, followed by characters that must not be used in file names for the specified country.
	—Extended Country Collating Table—	
	Info ID: 06	
00h	Byte	Info ID = 06
01h	Double word	Pointer to collating table. Collating table is 250 bytes: 2-byte length plus 256 values in collating order.
	—DBCS Lead Byte Table (V4 only)—	
	Info ID: 07	
00h	Word	Number of bytes that follow
02h	2 bytes	Start, end of first lead-byte range
04h	2 bytes	Start, end of next lead-byte range
.	2 bytes	(repeat as necessary)
.	2 bytes	0,0 marks end of table; not included in count

Int 21h Function 65h Subfunction 20h V4
Convert Character

Converts the specified character to uppercase using the current uppercase table

Calling Registers: AH   65h
AL   20h
DL   Character

Return Registers: Carry flag clear if successful
DL   Uppercase character

Carry flag set if error

Comments: This function provides a reliable way to convert a character to uppercase for the current country.

Int 21h   Function 65h Subfunction 21h   V4
Convert String

Converts the specified string to uppercase using the current uppercase table

Calling Registers: AH   65h
                        AL   21h
                        CX   String length
                        DS:DX   Pointer to string

Return Registers: Carry flag clear if successful

Comments: This function provides a reliable way to convert a string to uppercase for the current country.

Int 21h   Function 65h Subfunction 22h   V4
Convert ASCIIZ String

Converts the specified string to uppercase using the current uppercase table

Calling Registers: AH   65h
                        AL   22h
                        DS:DX   Pointer to ASCIIZ string

Return Registers: Carry flag clear if successful

Comments: This function provides a reliable way to convert a string to uppercase for the current country.

Int 21h   Function 66h Subfunction 01h   V3.3
Get Global Code Page

Gets the code page for the current country

Calling Registers: AH   66h
                        AL   01h

Return Registers: Carry flag clear if successful
                        BX   Active code page
                        DX   System code page

Carry flag set if error
AX   Error code
02h, file not found

Comments: This function tells which country data stored in COUNTRY.SYS is in the resident country buffer area, the code page. Devices can be selected automatically for code page switching in the CONFIG.SYS file if the devices support it.

Int 21h   **Function 66h Subfunction 02h**   **V3.3**
Set Global Code Page

Sets the code page for the current country

Calling Registers: AH   66h
AL   02h
BX   Active code page
DX   System code page

Return Registers: Carry flag clear if successful

Carry flag set if error
AX   Error code
02h, file not found

Comments: This function moves the country data stored in COUNTRY.SYS into the resident country buffer area, the code page. Devices can be selected automatically for code page switching in the CONFIG.SYS file if the devices support it.

Int 21h   **Function 67h**   **V3.3**
Set Handle Count

Allows a process to modify dynamically the number of file handles (normally 20) allowed for a process

Calling Registers: AH   67h
BX   Number of open handles to allow

Return Registers: Carry flag clear if successful

Carry flag set if error
AX   Error code

Comments: This function allows a program to control the number of file handles available for use while the program is running. This can be particularly important for complicated database programs, which often require a considerable amount of manipulation to handle the large number of files they need to keep open. Memory is allocated from memory freed by Function 4Ah. If the amount of memory is less than the current number of files open, the memory will become effective when the current number of files drops below the limit.

The CONFIG.SYS entry FILES= can set as many as 255 file handles in DOS V3.3. This function allows the number of file handles to rise to 64K entries. If the number specified is less than 20, the number defaults to 20.

Int 21h   Function 68h   V3
Flush Buffer

Flushes all buffered data for a file to the device

Calling Registers: AH   68h
                          BX   File handle

Return Registers: Carry flag clear if successful

                         Carry flag set if error
                             AX   Error code

Comments: The standard way to flush buffers to disk has always been to close a file and then reopen it. A classic improvement on this was first to duplicate the file handle with Function 45h and then close the duplicate. This got the close without incurring the overhead of another open.

Function 68h eliminates the need to be tricky. If you want to flush the buffers, this function will do it faster and in a more secure fashion.

This function can be used rather than handle duplication or a close/open sequence to flush data buffers.

Int 21h   Function 6Ah   V4
Allocate Memory

Allocates a block of memory for use and returns a pointer to the beginning of the block. This is a duplicate of function 48h.

Calling Registers: AH   6Ah
                          BX   File handle

Return Registers: Carry flag clear if successful

                         Carry flag set if error
                             AX   Error code

Comments: In IBM V4.01, this function uses the same code as documented Function 48h.

Int 21h

Function 6Ch
Extended Open/Create

V4

Combines functions presently provided by Functions 3Ch, 3Dh, and 5Bh into a single multipurpose file-open facility

Calling Registers:

AH	6Ch	
AL	00h (required)	
BX	Open mode (bit map):	

Bits

FEDCBA98 76543210	*Meaning*
....000	Read-only access
....001	Write-only access
....010	Read/write access
....011	Not used, zero
....1xx	Not used, zero
....x...	Not used, zero
.... .000....	Compatibility mode
.... .001....	Deny all sharing
.... .010....	Deny write sharing
.... .011....	Deny read sharing
.... .100....	Deny none
.... .101....	Not used, zero
.... .110....	Not used, zero
.... .111....	Not used, zero
.... 0.......	Child inherits handle
.... 1.......	Handle not passed to child
...xxxxx	Not used, zero
..0.....	Use Int 24h handler
..1.....	Return error only
.0......	Writes may be buffered
.1......	All writes execute immediately
x.......	Not used, zero

CX	File attributes (bit map):	

Bits

FEDCBA98 76543210	*Meaning*
....0	Read/write
....1	Read only
....0.	Visible
....1.	Hidden

DOS
PROGRAMMING

```
........ .....0..  Normal user file
........ .....1..  System file
........ ....0...  Not volume label
........ ....1...  Volume label
........ ...x....  Not used, zero
........ ..0.....  Not modified
........ ..1.....  Modified (archive)
xxxxxxxx xx......  Not used, zero
```

DX   Action flag (bit map):

    Bits

```
FEDCBA98 76543210  Meaning
........ ....0000  Fail if file exists
........ ....0001   Open if file exists
........ ....0010  Replace if file exists
........ ....0011  Not used, zero
........ ....01xx  Not used, zero
........ ....1xxx  Not used, zero
........ 0000....  Fail if file does not exist
........ 0001....  Create file if it does not exist
........ 001x....  Not used, zero
........ 01xx....  Not used, zero
........ 1xxx....  Not used, zero
xxxxxxxx ........  Not used, zero
```

DS:SI Pointer to ASCIIZ path name for file

Return Registers: Carry flag clear if successful
    AX File handle
    CX Action taken
        01, file existed and was opened
        02, file did not exist, created
        03, file existed, was replaced

    Carry flag set if error
    AX Error code

Comments: Like the three older handle-based file open/create functions that it combines, this function is called with DS:SI pointing to an ASCIIZ path name for the file to be opened or created, AL containing a bit map of the access privileges desired, and CX containing a bit map of the permanent attributes to be assigned to the file if it is created by the call. But unlike the older functions, this one carries added information in DX telling the system what to do if the file exists and what to do if it does not exist. It also permits the program to specify that the Int 24h Critical Error handler not be used in case of problems with this file, permitting the program to handle all errors without having to modify DOS actions for other programs that might be running at the same time.

The function was added to DOS for compatibility with OS/2, but fills a long-felt need and should be used on any program that can ignore pre-V4 versions of DOS.

The function fails if any part of the specified path cannot be found (except for the file-name portion, which is controlled by the setting of DX at entry). When running on a network, the user must have access rights at least equal to those specified in the call to the function.

Int 22h   V1
Terminate Address

This is not an interrupt but simply the address of the routine that control is transferred to when the currently executing program ends

Calling Registers: Not applicable

Return Registers: Not applicable

Comments: When a program is loaded, the contents of this memory location are copied into the program segment prefix (PSP) at offset byte 0Ah. When the program terminates, this value is normally restored from the same location. Because it is purely a storage area, it should never be executed directly.

Int 23h   V1
Ctrl-C Interrupt Handler

This interrupt is the routine that receives control when a Ctrl-C (or, indirectly, a Ctrl-Break) detection occurs

Calling Registers: Not applicable

Return Registers: Not applicable

Comments: Whenever detection of a Ctrl-C occurs during I/O operations or at other times when BREAK is on, the system branches to the address given in this vector. (The Ctrl-Break service normally forces a Ctrl-C into the DOS input buffer and thus reaches this routine also, but indirectly.) When a program is loaded, this vector is copied into its program segment prefix (PSP) at byte 0Eh; the vector is restored by program termination.

Ctrl-C and Ctrl-Break handlers are two of the most commonly needed special routines programmers must write. Sophisticated programs cannot afford to relinquish control to a default handler. They must control any break operations to allow proper cleanup in the event of a problem. (Telecommunications programs written by inexperienced programmers are particularly subject to this type of error.)

Because of these control problems, you should never issue an Int 23h to activate the handler. The function will come into play soon enough as the system processes Ctrl-C and Ctrl-Break characters.

Ctrl-C and Ctrl-Break handlers have a number of options they can use to process a break condition:

- The handler can set a local flag, which can be polled by the main program for extensive action. Some limited action can be taken directly and then a *return from interrupt* (IRET) can be executed to return control to DOS. DOS restarts the interrupted function from the beginning and completes the call normally. This is useful for applications where every millisecond spent servicing the interrupt is important. High-speed communications programs can be written this way.

- The handler can take action on the condition that caused the interrupt and then do a *far return* (ret far) to return control to DOS. The carry flag should be set to indicate that the application must be aborted or cleared if the application is to be allowed to continue.

- The handler can take whatever action it needs and then resume operation of the program directly without ever returning to DOS.

All the options are valid; the one you choose depends on what else you are doing. Option 1 should be chosen when it is necessary to minimize the time spent in a handler outside of normal processing. Option 2 is more generally useful as a processing procedure when an abort of the process is a possible option. Option 3 can be used to redirect operation and continue directly when it is not a good idea to return to the original operation in progress. It does no harm, but is not generally a wise idea except in special circumstances for which no other solution exists than a radical break from processing.

While in a Ctrl-C/Ctrl-Break handler, you can use any DOS function needed to process the condition.

Int 24h   V1
Critical-Error Handler

This interrupt is the routine that receives control when a critical error is detected. A critical error generally represents a hardware failure of some sort and is usually the aftermath of a failed device driver call within DOS.

Calling Registers:	AH	Error information
	AL	Drive number
	DI	Error code
	BP:SI	Pointer to device driver header
	STACK	Set up as follows:
High Addr	Flags	Original caller's flags register
	CS	Original caller's CS register
	IP	Original caller's IP register
	ES	Original caller's ES register
	DS	Original caller's DS register
	BP	Original caller's BP register
	DI	Original caller's DI register
	SI	Original caller's SI register
	DX	Original caller's DX register
	CX	Original caller's CX register
	BX	Original caller's BX register
	AX	Original caller's AX register
	Flags	DOS's flags register
	CS	DOS's CS register
Low Addr	IP	DOS's IP register

Return Registers:	AL	Action Code

Comments: When a program is loaded, the contents of this vector are read into the program segment prefix (PSP) starting at offset 12h. When the program terminates, this vector is restored by the system termination handler. This interrupt should never be called directly.

When the critical-error handler is invoked by DOS, the AH, AL, and DI registers contain information about the nature of the error. BP:SI points to a device driver header. The SS, SP, DS, ES, BX, CX and DX registers must be preserved by the critical-error handler.

DOS typically retries the device driver call (normally three times, but this may change in later versions) before invoking the critical-error handler. When invoked, the critical-error handler should preserve the necessary registers and then attempt to deal with the error. Only DOS Functions 00h–0Ch (Traditional Character I/O), 30h (Get DOS Version), and 59h (Get Extended Error Information) can be called in the critical-error handler. Other function calls can destroy DOS's internal stack and should be avoided.

The AH register has bit 7 clear if the error was a disk error; otherwise, bit 7 is set. If the error was a disk error, the rest of the AH register will be as shown in table DOS.21. AL will contain the drive number (0 = A, 1 = B, and so on).

Table DOS.21. *AH Register Usage on Disk Errors*

Bit(s)	Meaning
7	0, to signify a disk error
6	Reserved
5	0 = ignore response not permitted 1 = ignore response permitted
4	0 = retry response not permitted 1 = retry response permitted
3	0 = function call fail response not permitted 1 = function call fail response permitted
1–2	Disk area where error occurred 00 = MS-DOS area 01 = file allocation table 10 = root directory 11 = files area
0	0 = read 1 = write

If the error was a non-disk error, the word at [BP:SI+4] can be examined; if bit 15 is set, the error was due to a character device call. The 8-character name of the device begins at [BP:SI+10].

The error codes returned in the lower byte of DI are the same as the error codes returned in a device driver's request header (see table DOS.22).

Table DOS.22. *Error Code (Lower Byte of DI)*

Code	Meaning
00h	Write-protect error
01h	Unknown unit
02h	Drive not ready
03h	Unknown command
04h	Data error (bad CRC)
05h	Bad request structure length
06h	Seek error
07h	Unknown media type
08h	Sector not found
09h	Printer out of paper
0Ah	Write fault
0Bh	Read fault
0Ch	General failure
0Fh	Invalid disk change

When the critical-error handler is ready to return, it should set an action code in the AL register according to table DOS.23.

Table DOS.23. *Action Codes*

Code	Meaning
00h	Ignore error
01h	Retry operation
02h	Terminate program
03h	Fail system call in progress (V3 and above)

When the action code is set, the saved registers are restored and a return from interrupt (IRET) is performed.

The handler can return directly to the user program, but if it does, it will be responsible for cleaning up the stack and removing all but the last three words from the stack before issuing an IRET. Control then returns to the statement directly after the I/O function that caused the error. This leaves DOS in an "unstable" condition until a call to an Int 21h function above 0Ch is performed. Specifically, the DOS CritErr flag will remain set, causing potential problems with the DOS internal stacks. It is possible for your handler to overcome this by getting the flag's address and clearing it explicitly; refer to Int 21h, Function 34h for details. Such modification of normal DOS actions is recommended only if absolutely necessary; in most cases the best action for an Int 24h handler is to return by DOS rather than directly.

A sidelight concerning the handler's action codes: some programmers have reported that action code 2 does not seem to work in some versions of DOS; however, efforts to identify precisely which versions are involved have not been successful. All documentation for action code 2 in versions before V4 (including the first edition of this book) said that termination occurred through Interrupt 23h; in the *IBM Technical Reference Manual* for V4, this was changed to 22h, which is the normal termination procedure. Apparently the earlier versions were the victims of a longstanding typographical error, because none actually did invoke Interrupt 23h.

The extended file open function added to DOS in V4 provides the capability of specifying that the critical-error handler not be used for a file. That is, if you set the appropriate bit in a register when the file is opened, any critical error will result in an automatic exit code 3 return, with no screen dialog.

Int 25h V1
Absolute Disk Read

Reads data from a specified disk sector to the designated memory area

Calling Registers: AL   Drive number (0 = A, 1 = B, and so on)
                        CX   > 0, number of sectors to read
                                     -1, use extended format (V4)
                        DX   Starting relative (logical) sector number
                        DS:BX   Pointer to DTA if CX > 0
                                      Pointer to parameters if CX = -1

Return Registers: Carry flag clear if successful

                        Carry flag set if error
                        AX   Error code
                                    0207h, wrong format used (V4 only)

Comments: This function reads a disk sector from the disk into memory by accessing the desired logical sector directly. This type of access must be handled with care because it bypasses the DOS directory structure.

Logical sectors are located starting with track 0, head 0. The first sector on this track is disk sector 0. Sectors then go to the next head, then the next track, and so on. Logical sectors correspond to the sequence of sector numbers stored magnetically on the disk itself and may not correspond to the physical sectors. By specifying interleaving factors, logical disk sectors can be physically separated on the disk. This is often done to improve the efficiency of the disk.

If the carry flag is set when the function returns, the AX register is interpreted as shown in the accompanying tables. AH and AL are interpreted as separate error codes (see table DOS.24).

Because the absolute disk read can destroy any registers except the segment registers, care should be taken to preserve needed values before the call.

A special problem with this function makes it difficult to use directly from high-level languages. When the function returns, the word containing the CPU flags, originally pushed on the stack by Int 25h, is still there. To get rid of it and restore the stack to its expected condition, you can do a POPF to take the number off the stack, or you can do an ADD SP,2 to increment the stack pointer past the number. Because high-level languages do not provide direct facilities for this kind of operation, this function has to be called from assembly language to prevent failure of the system. (It could be embedded assembly code, as in Turbo Pascal.)

In DOS V4, the possible size of a logical sector number was extended to 32 bits. To accommodate this larger value, an extended format for Interrupt 25h was created; the extended format must be used when reading from a volume greater than 32M, even if the sector number could be expressed in only 16 bits.

Table DOS.24. *Interpretation of Error Codes Returned by Int 25h*

Code	Meaning
	—AH Register Error Codes—
80h	Attachment failed to respond
40h	Seek operation failed
20h	Controller failed
10h	Data error (bad CRC)
08h	DMA failure
04h	Requested sector not found
03h	Write-protect fault
02h	Bad address mark
01h	Bad command
	—AL Register Error Codes—
00h	Write-protect error
01h	Unknown unit
02h	Drive not ready
03h	Unknown command
04h	Data error (bad CRC)
05h	Bad request structure length
06h	Seek error
07h	Unknown media type
08h	Sector not found
09h	Printer out of paper
0Ah	Write fault
0Bh	Read fault
0Ch	General failure

Use of the extended format is indicated by setting CX to FFFFh (−1). DS:BX is interpreted as the address of a parameter block, rather than as the address of the buffer to read into. This parameter block is arranged as follows:

Offset	Length	Comments
00h	Double word	Logical sector number, zero-based
04h	Word	Number of sectors to transfer
06h	Double word	Pointer to data buffer

Int 26h

V1

Absolute Disk Write

Writes data from the designated transfer area (DTA) to the disk sectors specified

Calling Registers: AL   Drive number (0 = A, 1 = B, and so on)

                         CX   > 0, number of sectors to write

                                     −1, use extended format (V4)

                         DX   Starting relative (logical) sector number

                         DS:BX   Pointer to DTA if CX > 0

                                       Pointer to parameters if CX = −1

Return Registers: Carry flag clear if successful

                       Carry flag set if error

                         AX   Error code

                                     0207h, wrong format used (V4 only)

Comments: This function writes a disk sector from memory by accessing the desired logical sector directly. This type of access must be handled with care because it bypasses the DOS directory structure.

Logical sectors are located starting with track 0, head 0. The first sector on this track is disk sector 0. Sectors then go to the next head, then the next track, and so on. Logical sectors correspond to the sequence of sector numbers stored magnetically on the disk itself and may not correspond to the physical sectors. By specifying interleaving factors, logical disk sectors can be physically separated on the disk. This is sometimes done to improve the disk's efficiency.

If the carry flag is set when the function returns, the AX register is interpreted as shown in the accompanying tables. AH and AL are interpreted as separate error codes (see table DOS.25.)

A special problem with this function makes it difficult to use directly from high-level languages. When the function returns, the word containing the CPU flags, originally pushed onto the stack by Int 26h, is still there. To get rid of it and restore the stack to its expected condition, you can do a POPF to take the number off the stack, or you can do an ADD SP,2 to increment the stack pointer past the number. Because high-level languages do not provide direct facilities for this kind of operation, this function has to be called from assembly language to prevent failure of the system. (It could be embedded assembly code, as in Turbo Pascal.)

In DOS V4, the possible size of a logical sector number was extended to 32 bits. To accommodate this larger value, an extended format for Interrupt 26h was created; the extended format must be used when reading from a volume greater than 32M, even if the sector number could be expressed in only 16 bits.

Table DOS.25. *Interpretation of Error Codes Returned by Int 26h*

Code	Meaning
	—AH Register Error Codes—
80h	Attachment failed to respond
40h	Seek operation failed
20h	Controller failed
10h	Data error (bad CRC)
08h	DMA failure
04h	Requested sector not found
03h	Write-protect fault
02h	Bad address mark
01h	Bad command
	—AL Register Error Codes—
00h	Write-protect error
01h	Unknown unit
02h	Drive not ready
03h	Unknown command
04h	Data error (bad CRC)
05h	Bad request structure length
06h	Seek error
07h	Unknown media type
08h	Sector not found
09h	Printer out of paper
0Ah	Write fault
0Bh	Read fault
0Ch	General failure

Use of the extended format is indicated by setting CX to FFFFh (-1). DS:BX is interpreted as the address of a parameter block, rather than as the address of the buffer to write from. This parameter block is arranged as follows:

Offset	Length	Comments
00h	Double word	Logical sector number, zero-based
04h	Word	Number of sectors to transfer
06h	Double word	Pointer to data buffer

Int 27h V1
Terminate and Stay Resident

Terminates the presently running program but preserves its memory area

| **Calling Registers:** | DX | Offset of last byte plus 1 (relative to PSP) of the program to remain resident |
| | CS | Segment of the PSP |

Return Registers: None (does not return)

Comments: Terminate and stay resident (TSR) utilities are familiar to almost all of us working with PCs. Who doesn't have SideKick or some other utility that gives the feeling of multitasking operations without true multitasking? This interrupt was the original (DOS V1) TSR termination procedure, which allowed a program to set aside its memory after connecting itself to whatever interrupt it needed for processing.

On termination, the procedure restores Int 22h (Terminate Address), Int 23h (Ctrl-C Interrupt Vector), and Int 24h (Critical-Error Vector), then transfers control to the termination address. It allows the program to retain its memory area (DX register sizes the protected area) so that the TSR can remain active.

This termination is subject to some significant limitations. First, you must have the CS register set to the segment of the program segment prefix (PSP) for the program. Generally, this is no problem, but you should make sure. Most significantly, only 64K bytes can be set aside for the TSR program. Under DOS V2 and V3, the preferred TSR termination is Int 21h, Function 31h, which allows any amount of memory and does not require that the CS register be set. Given the improvement in TSR termination handlers, Int 27h should be called only on DOS V1.x systems.

Unlike the normal terminate action, this interrupt does not close any files that may be open. If you want them closed, you must explicitly close them before using this interrupt.

Int 28h   V1
DOS Safe To Use

Called regularly during the DOS console I/O polling loops to let terminate and stay resident (TSR) programs (such as the DOS-supplied utility PRINT.COM) know that it is safe to use file operations and other Int 21h functions above 0Ch

Calling Registers: Not applicable

Return Registers: Not applicable

Comments: This interrupt is called by DOS at several points in its console input-polling loop where it is safe to do file system operations or most other DOS functions above 0Ch.

Normally, the vector for Interrupt 28h points to a single IRET instruction, making it a dummy handler stub. Any handler you write should chain to the next handler in line, letting the original default IRET take care of returning to DOS. This will assure that all processes which are depending on it will get an opportunity to run while COMMAND.COM is waiting for input at a command-line prompt.

Note that in DOS V2, not *all* DOS functions above 0Ch are safe to use from this interrupt because of internal stack-usage conflicts. Refer to the comments on Int 21h, Function 34h for a discussion of this problem and a method for overcoming it.

Int 29h
V2

Fast Putchar

DOS output routine interrupt

Calling Registers: AL   Character to display

Return Registers: Not applicable

Comments: This interrupt is called by DOS output routines if the output is going to a device and the device driver's attribute word has bit 3 set to 1.

All ASCII characters are output as if going to a display, with no processing, except the carriage return, line feed, and bell characters. These are processed as control characters.

This interrupt is intended for use with DOS device drivers and is not documented as being supported beyond DOS V2.0. Nevertheless, it is the output method used by ANSI.SYS in later versions and thus can be expected to be supported without change. Any use in applications programs, however, is at your own risk.

Int 2Ah
V3

Microsoft Networks Interface

This interrupt, which has many functions, provides protection against interference between multiple users on a networked system

Calling Registers: Not applicable

Return Registers: Not applicable

Comments: Calls to this interrupt appear frequently in the code of DOS itself to provide protection against interference between multiple processes when operating in a network. When no network is present, the routines that call it are disabled; when the network is installed, the disabling code is automatically patched out and the interrupt is called to control access to critical regions of code. It is *not* to be used in applications programs. Because it is not a part of DOS unless network software has been installed, its actions are beyond the scope of this book.

Int 2Eh   V3 (?)
Primary Shell Program Loader

Loads program under primary command interpreter shell for execution

Calling Registers: DS:SI   Pointer to counted, CR-terminated
                                      command string identical to that
                                      supplied to DOS by Interrupt 21h,
                                      Function 0Ah

Return Registers: Returns to address pointed to by Int 22h vector

Comments: This function permits access to the main environment area. It has been essentially superceded by EXEC function (Int 21h, Function 4Bh, Subfunction 00h).

The only known reason for using this function rather than EXEC would be to gain access to the master environment area of the system to make changes to it. Programs that make use of this function may not operate in a network or multiuser situation.

Int 2Fh   V3
Multiplex Service Interrupt

Multiplex service, only partially documented; controlled by content of AH register at entry, which may range from 01h through FFh

Comments: Only Function 12h, DOS internal services, is present in "vanilla" DOS operation; additional functions graft themselves into this service when the corresponding program is installed. For example, Function 01h has no meaning unless the resident portion of the DOS print spooler (PRINT.COM) has been installed.

Functions 00h through BFh for this interrupt have been reserved for use by DOS; Functions C0h through FFh are documented as being available for users. The dividing line originally was set at 80h rather than C0h, until Function B7h was taken for use (at V3.3) by the DOS function APPEND. A number of user programs take over functions below C0h. At least one third-party utility searches the Int 2Fh chain looking for any available code and uses the first it can find.

To preserve some semblance of order, Subfunction 00h (the content of AL) of *all* functions has been officially reserved for use as the "get installed status" operation and returns that status as documented for Function 01h: 00h in AL upon return indicates that the function is not yet installed, but may be installed; 01h indicates that the function is not installed and may not be; and FFh indicates that the function is already in place. Adherence to this standard makes it possible to avoid multiple installation of the same resident utility. Unfortunately, not all functions that employ Int 2Fh follow this standard, but the majority seem to do so. One notable exception is described in appendix D, "A Standard TSR-Identification Technique."

Int 2Fh Function 01h Subfunction 00h V3
Print Installation Check

Interface to resident portion of DOS print spooler (PRINT.COM)

Calling Registers: AH   01h
                           AL   00h

Return Registers: Carry flag clear if successful
                           AL   Status
                                   00h, okay to install if not installed
                                 01h, not okay to install if not installed
                                 FFh, installed

Comments: Print spooling has become a normal method of operation for many people who are too busy to stop what they are doing to wait for a printout. This function gives a program access to the printer spooler. Subfunction 00h lets a program determine whether the spooler is installed.

Int 2Fh Function 01h Subfunction 01h V3
Submit File to Print Spooler

Interface to resident portion of DOS print spooler (PRINT.COM)

Calling Registers: AH   01h
                           AL   01h
                           DS:DX   Pointer to packet address

Return Registers: Carry flag clear if successful

                          Carry flag set if error
                           AX   Error code
                                 01h, function invalid
                                 02h, file not found
                                 03h, path not found
                                 04h, too many open files
                                 05h, access denied
                                 08h, queue full
                                 09h, spooler busy
                                 0Ch, name too long
                                 0Fh, drive invalid

Comments: Print spooling has become a normal method of operation for many people who are too busy to stop what they are doing to wait for a printout. This function gives a program access to the printer spooler.

For Subfunction 01h, you provide a 5-byte packet with a priority level in the first byte and a pointer to an ASCIIZ file specification to be printed. The spooler takes over and automatically prints the file unless you intervene.

Int 2Fh   Function 01h Subfunction 02h   V3
Remove File from Print Queue

Interface to resident portion of DOS print spooler (PRINT.COM)

Calling Registers: AH   01h
                   AL   02h
                   DS:DX   Pointer to ASCIIZ file specification

Return Registers: Carry flag clear if successful

                      Carry flag set if error
                   AX   Error code
                             01h, function invalid
                             02h, file not found
                             03h, path not found
                             04h, too many open files
                             05h, access denied
                             08h, queue full
                             09h, spooler busy
                             0Ch, name too long
                             0Fh, drive invalid

Comments: Print spooling has become a normal method of operation for many people who are too busy to stop what they are doing to wait for a printout. This function gives a program access to the printer spooler.

Subfunction 02 accepts wild cards (* and ?) in the file specification, allowing multiple print file terminations from a single call to the function.

Int 2Fh   Function 01h Subfunction 03h   V3
Cancel All Files in Print Queue

Stops the current print job and removes all files from the print queue

Calling Registers: AH   01h
                   AL   03h

Return Registers: None

Comments: This function makes no attempt to clean up the last page of the file that was being printed, so you may want the calling program to send a form feed.

Int 2Fh Function 01h Subfunction 04h V3
Hold Print Jobs

Interface to resident portion of DOS print spooler (PRINT.COM)

Calling Registers: AH 01h
AL 04h

Return Registers: Carry flag clear if successful
DX Error count
DS:SI Pointer to print queue

Carry flag set if error
AX Error code
01h, function invalid
09h, spooler busy

Comments: Print spooling has become a normal method of operation for many people who are too busy to stop what they are doing to wait for a printout. This function gives a program access to the printer spooler.

    Subfunction 04 returns a pointer to a series of file-name entries, each 64 bytes long and containing an ASCIIZ string that is the file specification for one of the print files. The first in the list is the file presently being printed. The last entry has a NUL character in the first byte (zero length file-name string). This function also puts the spooler's action into a HOLD status so that none of the information can become obsolete before the caller can act on it. Subfunction 05 releases the HOLD status.

Int 2Fh Function 01h Subfunction 05h V3
End Print Hold

Interface to resident portion of DOS print spooler (PRINT.COM)

Calling Registers: AH 01h
AL 05h

Return Registers: Carry flag clear if successful

Carry flag set if error
AX Error code
01h, function invalid
09h, spooler busy

Comments: Print spooling has become a normal method of operation for many people who are too busy to stop what they are doing to wait for a printout. This function gives a program access to the printer spooler.

Subfunction 05 cancels the HOLD status established by use of Subfunction 04; all print-spooling action stops between these two calls.

Int 2Fh   Function 01h Subfunction 06h   V3
Get Printer Device

Returns the address of the device header for the current printer

Calling Registers: AH   01h
                        AL   06h

Return Registers: Carry flag clear if queue empty
                        AX   0

                        Carry flag set if queue not empty
                        DS:SI Pointer to device header
                        AX   0008

Comments: This function can be used to determine whether the printer queue is empty.

Int 2Fh   Function 05h   V3
Get Outboard Critical-Error Handler Installation Status

Interface to the outboard critical-error handler

Calling Registers: AH   05h
                        AL   00h

Return Registers: Carry flag clear if successful
                        AL   Status
                              00h, okay to install if not installed
                              01h, not okay to install if not installed
                              FFh, installed

Comments: Action of this undocumented function is not fully understood. It appears to permit direct communication with the DOS critical-error handler routines.

Int 2Fh   Function 06h   V3
Get ASSIGN.COM/ASSIGN.EXE Installation Status

Checks to determine if ASSIGN.COM or ASSIGN.EXE is loaded

Calling Registers: AH   06h
                               AL   00h

Return Registers: Carry flag clear if successful
                               AL   Status
                                         00h, okay to install if not installed
                                       01h, not okay to install if not installed
                                     FFh, installed

Comments: This function interfaces to ASSIGN.EXE and does nothing if ASSIGN is not loaded.

Int 2Fh   Function 08h   V3
Get DRIVER.SYS Installation Status

Checks to see if DRIVER.SYS is installed

Calling Registers: AH   08h
                               AL   00h

Return Registers: Carry flag clear if successful
                               AL   Status
                                       00h, okay to install if not installed
                                     01h, not okay to install if not installed
                                     FFh, installed

Comments: This function interfaces to DRIVER.SYS and does nothing if that file is not loaded.

Int 2Fh   Function 10h   V3
Get SHARE.EXE Installation Status

Checks to determine if SHARE.EXE is loaded

Calling Registers: AH   10h
                               AL   00h

Return Registers: Carry flag clear if successful
                               AL   Status
                                       00h, okay to install if not installed
                                     01h, not okay to install if not installed
                                     FFh, installed

Comments: This function interfaces to SHARE.EXE and does nothing if SHARE is not loaded.

Int 2Fh   **Function 11h**   **V3**
Get Network Redirector
Installation Status

Checks to see if the network redirector interface has been installed

Calling Registers: AH   11h
                         AL   00h

Return Registers: Carry flag clear if successful
                         AL   Status
                                 00h, okay to install if not installed
                                 01h, not okay to install if not installed
                                 FFh, installed

Comments: This function interfaces with the standard network redirector routines and does nothing unless Microsoft Networks or a fully compatible similar program is loaded.

Int 2Fh   **Function 12h Subfunction 00h**   **V3**
Get DOS Installation Status

Checks to see if DOS is installed; mainly for conformity with other DOS functions

Calling Registers: AH   12h
                         AL   00h

Return Registers: AL   FFh (function always installed)

Comments: Function 12h provides access to certain DOS internal services (00h–25h in Version 3, 00h–2Fh in Version 4). Note that many of these can be called only when all segment registers are set to the DOS kernel's segment; *if this restriction is not met, damage to data is extremely likely.* Nevertheless, they do provide information that is difficult to obtain by any other means and can be useful to developers who take proper precautions.

Subfunction 00h always returns the *installed* condition because this function is hard-coded into the DOS kernel. It is the standard "Is the function available?" test and appears to have been included for consistency with other DOS functions that do installation checks.

Int 2Fh   **Function 12h Subfunction 01h**   **V3**
Flush File

Accesses internal services of DOS to flush a file

Calling Registers:	AH	12h
	AL	01h
	BX	File handle

Return Registers:	Carry flag clear if successful
	Carry flag set if error
	AX	Error code

Comments: Function 12h provides access to certain DOS internal services (00h–25h in Version 3, 00h–2Fh in Version 4). Note that many of these can be called only when all segment registers are set to the DOS kernel's segment; *if this restriction is not met, damage to data is extremely likely.* Nevertheless, they do provide information that is difficult to obtain by any other means and can be useful to developers who take proper precautions.

Subfunction 01h appears to flush the file whose handle is passed to it. That is, it writes to disk all accumulated buffers for the file. It assumes that all segment registers point to the DOS kernel area. It is uncertain whether the file is closed by this action.

Int 2Fh   **Function 12h Subfunction 02h**   **V3**
Get Interrupt Vector Address

Accesses internal services of DOS to retrieve an interrupt vector

Calling Registers:	AH	12h
	AL	02h
	STACK	Number of interrupt to get

Return Registers:	ES:BX	Far pointer to interrupt vector

Comments: Function 12h provides access to certain DOS internal services (00h–25h in Version 3, 00h–2Fh in Version 4). Note that many of these can be called only when all segment registers are set to the DOS kernel's segment; *if this restriction is not met, damage to data is extremely likely.* Nevertheless, they do provide information that is difficult to obtain by any other means and can be useful to developers who take proper precautions.

Subfunction 02h provides direct access to the internal routine used by Interrupt 21h, Functions 25h and 35h to address the interrupt vector table. Subfunction 02h must be passed the number of the interrupt vector desired, in the low byte of the word on top of the stack. It returns a far pointer to the interrupt vector itself (not the interrupt service routine) in ES and BX.

PROGRAMMING

Int 2Fh   Function 12h Subfunction 03h   V3
Get DOS Data Segment

Accesses internal services of DOS to return the DOS-kernel data segment value

Calling Registers: AH   12h
                                 AL   03h

Return Registers: DS   DOS kernel segment address

Comments: Function 12h provides access to certain DOS internal services (00h–25h in Version 3, 00h–2Fh in Version 4). Note that many of these can be called only when all segment registers are set to the DOS kernel's segment; *if this restriction is not met, damage to data is extremely likely.* Nevertheless, they do provide information that is difficult to obtain by any other means and can be useful to developers who take proper precautions.

    Subfunction 03h obtains the segment address of the DOS kernel, which then can be used to make other segment registers point to the DOS kernel area. Because DS is destroyed by this call, the caller's DS value should be saved first so that it can be restored.

Int 2Fh   Function 12h Subfunction 04h   V3
Normalize Path Separator

Accesses internal services of DOS to normalize a path delimiter

Calling Registers: AH   12h
                                   AL   04h
                                   STACK   Separator to process (in low byte)

Return Registers: AL   5Ch (ASCII "\")

Comments: Function 12h provides access to certain DOS internal services (00h–25h in Version 3, 00h–2Fh in Version 4). Note that many of these can be called only when all segment registers are set to the DOS kernel's segment; *if this restriction is not met, damage to data is extremely likely.* Nevertheless, they do provide information that is difficult to obtain by any other means and can be useful to developers who take proper precautions.

    Subfunction 04h translates the alternate path delimiter (/) into the DOS standard delimiter (\).

Int 2Fh Function 12h Subfunction 05h V3
Output a Character

Accesses internal services of DOS to output a character with Int 29h

Calling Registers: AH   12h
AL   05h
STACK Character to output (in low byte)

Return Registers: None

Comments: Function 12h provides access to certain DOS internal services (00h–25h in Version 3, 00h–2Fh in Version 4). Note that many of these can be called only when all segment registers are set to the DOS kernel's segment; *if this restriction is not met, damage to data is extremely likely.* Nevertheless, they do provide information that is difficult to obtain by any other means and can be useful to developers who take proper precautions.

Subfunction 05h sends the character found on top of the stack to the CRT using interrupt 29h. This function is redundant and adds to overhead for programmers who already use Int 29h.

Int 2Fh Function 12h Subfunction 06h V3
Invoke Critical Error

Accesses internal services of DOS to invoke the critical-error handler as though an error had been encountered

Calling Registers: AH   12h
AL   06h

Return Registers: AL   Action code (see interrupt 24h)

Comments: Function 12h provides access to certain DOS internal services (00h–25h in Version 3, 00h–2Fh in Version 4). Note that many of these can be called only when all segment registers are set to the DOS kernel's segment; *if this restriction is not met, damage to data is extremely likely.* Nevertheless, they do provide information that is difficult to obtain by any other means and can be useful to developers who take proper precautions.

Subfunction 06h invokes the critical-error handler as if an error had been detected and then returns its action code.

Int 2Fh — Function 12h Subfunction 07h — V3 only
Move Disk Buffer

Accesses internal services of DOS to move a disk buffer under DOS V3 (only)

Calling Registers: AH   12h
                                   AL   07h

Return Registers: DS:DI   Pointer to disk buffer

Comments: Function 12h provides access to certain DOS internal services (00h–25h in Version 3, 00h–2Fh in Version 4). Note that many of these can be called only when all segment registers are set to the DOS kernel's segment; *if this restriction is not met, damage to data is extremely likely*. Nevertheless, they do provide information that is difficult to obtain by any other means and can be useful to developers who take proper precautions.

    Subfunction 07h manipulates the internal DOS disk buffers set up by BUFFERS= in CONFIG.SYS. This function should *not* be used unless you are more confident of your knowledge of the buffering algorithms than are the authors of this book; any *mistakes in its use could destroy all data on your hard disk* because the file allocation tables usually reside in these buffers.

Int 2Fh — Function 12h Subfunction 08h — V3
Decrement User Count

Accesses internal services of DOS to decrement the user count word in a device control block

Calling Registers: AH   12h
                                   AL   08h
                                   ES:DI   Pointer to DCB for file or device

Return Registers: AX   New user count

Comments: Subfunction 08h decrements the user count word in a DOS internal device control block. It is called with ES:DI pointing to the appropriate DCB (because the user count is the first word in the DCB, DI automatically points to the count word itself), and it returns with the DCB user count decremented and the new user count in AX. This routine usually is called as part of processing the Close Handle function but, by pointing ES:DI to some other word in RAM, it could be used to decrement that word instead. It makes no assumptions about the segment registers.

Int 2Fh Function 12h Subfunction 0Ch V3
IOCTL Open Used by DOS

Accesses internal services of DOS to open a file or device using IOCTL routines

Calling Registers: AH 12h
AL 0Ch

Return Registers: Carry flag clear if successful

Comments: Function 12h provides access to certain DOS internal services (00h–25h in Version 3, 00h–2Fh in Version 4). Note that many of these can be called only when all segment registers are set to the DOS kernel's segment; *if this restriction is not met, damage to data is extremely likely*. Nevertheless, they do provide information that is difficult to obtain by any other means and can be useful to developers who take proper precautions.

Subfunction 0Ch uses the Open subfunction of the IOCTL call to open the device or file previously tagged by DOS internal pointers as being current. It can be used only by DOS itself or by programs that control all the DOS internal tables and flags.

Int 2Fh Function 12h Subfunction 0Dh V3
Get Date and Time for File Closing

Accesses internal services of DOS to retrieve the system date and time for file date and time stamping

Calling Registers: AH 12h
AL 0Dh

Return Registers: AX System date in packed (file) format
DX System time in packed (file) format

Comments: Function 12h provides access to certain DOS internal services (00h–25h in Version 3, 00h–2Fh in Version 4). Note that many of these can be called only when all segment registers are set to the DOS kernel's segment; *if this restriction is not met, damage to data is extremely likely*. Nevertheless, they do provide information that is difficult to obtain by any other means and can be useful to developers who take proper precautions.

Subfunction 0Dh is used by DOS to obtain the system date and time, in the file-directory format, when closing a modified file. This function assumes that all segment registers point into the DOS kernel.

Int 2Fh   Function 12h Subfunction 0Eh   V3 (only)
Search Buffer Chain

Accesses internal services of DOS, apparently to search a buffer chain under DOS V3

Calling Registers: AH   12h
AL   0Eh

Return Registers: Unknown

Comments: Function 12h provides access to certain DOS internal services (00h–25h in Version 3, 00h–2Fh in Version 4). Note that many of these can be called only when all segment registers are set to the DOS kernel's segment; *if this restriction is not met, damage to data is extremely likely*. Nevertheless, they do provide information that is difficult to obtain by any other means and can be useful to developers who take proper precautions.

   The purpose of Subfunction 0Eh is not fully known. It *appears* to search the disk buffering used in DOS and should be approached with care. See the comments concerning Subfunction 07h.

Int 2Fh   Function 12h Subfunction 10h   V3
Find Modified Buffer (V3 only),
Time Delay (V4)

Accesses internal services of DOS to either find a disk buffer that had been modified (under DOS V3) or execute a time delay (under DOS V4)

Calling Registers: AH   12h
AL   10h

Return Registers: Carry flag clear if successful

Comments: Function 12h provides access to certain DOS internal services (00h–25h in Version 3, 00h–2Fh in Version 4). Note that many of these can be called only when all segment registers are set to the DOS kernel's segment; *if this restriction is not met, damage to data is extremely likely*. Nevertheless, they do provide information that is difficult to obtain by any other means and can be useful to developers who take proper precautions.

   Subfunction 10h was used in V3 to locate a "dirty" buffer (that is, one that had been modified and needed to be written out to disk). With the total rewrite of the buffering scheme introduced in V4, this subfunction became obsolete and was pointed to the time-delay routine to provide a harmless no-op action. It should never be used outside of DOS itself.

Int 2Fh   Function 12h Subfunction 11h   V3
Normalize ASCIIZ File Name

Accesses internal services of DOS to perform normalization conversion on a path name

Calling Registers:

AH	12h	
AL	11h	
DS:SI	Pointer to file name to normalize	
ES:DI	Pointer to buffer to receive output	

Return Registers:

ES:DI	Unchanged, point to normalized file name with all alpha characters in uppercase and all / characters changed to \ characters

Comments: Subfunction 11h converts a file or path name into standard format for use by the other DOS functions. All lowercase characters are converted to uppercase and all forward-slash characters are changed to backslashes. Both the input and output are ASCIIZ strings. This function makes no assumptions about the segment registers.

Int 2Fh   Function 12h Subfunction 12h   V3
Find ASCIIZ String Length

Accesses internal services of DOS to determine the length of the ASCIIZ string pointed to by ES:DI

Calling Registers:

AH	12h	
AL	12h	
ES:DI	Pointer to ASCIIZ string	

Return Registers: CX   Length of string in bytes

Comments: Function 12h provides access to certain DOS internal services (00h–25h in Version 3, 00h–2Fh in Version 4). Note that many of these can be called only when all segment registers are set to the DOS kernel's segment; *if this restriction is not met, damage to data is extremely likely*. Nevertheless, they do provide information that is difficult to obtain by any other means and can be useful to developers who take proper precautions.

    Subfunction 12h counts the number of bytes in the ASCIIZ string pointed to by ES:DI at entry and then returns the count (not including the NUL that terminates the ASCIIZ string) in the CX register. The SS register is assumed to point into the DOS kernel area.

DOS
PROGRAMMING

Int 2Fh   Function 12h Subfunction 13h   V3
Case and Country Conversion

Accesses internal services of DOS to convert the case (and country information, if necessary) of an ASCII character

Calling Registers: AH   12h
                         AL   13h
                         STACK   Character to be converted

Return Registers: AL   Uppercase (and translated) version
                                        of character

Comments: Function 12h provides access to certain DOS internal services (00h–25h in Version 3, 00h–2Fh in Version 4). Note that many of these can be called only when all segment registers are set to the DOS kernel's segment; *if this restriction is not met, damage to data is extremely likely*. Nevertheless, they do provide information that is difficult to obtain by any other means and can be useful to developers who take proper precautions.

   Subfunction 13h takes the word from the top of the stack, converts its low byte to uppercase, and if country translation is in effect, translates it from the extended ASCII character set to normal ASCII. The result is returned in AX. This function assumes that the SS register points into the DOS kernel code in order to locate the country conversion tables and the translation flag; for this reason, it will not be useful in most cases.

Int 2Fh   Function 12h Subfunction 14h   V3
Compare 32-bit Numbers

Accesses internal services of DOS to compare two 32-bit values (typically pointers)

Calling Registers: AH   12h
                         AL   14h
                         DS:SI   First pointer
                         ES:DI   Second pointer

Return Registers: Zero flag set if pointers equal, clear if not equal

Comments: Subfunction 14h can be used to compare any two 32-bit numbers by loading them into the appropriate registers. It is used by DOS as a general pointer-compare function. No assumptions about segment registers are made.

Int 2Fh

Function 12h Subfunction 16h   V3
Get DCB Address

Accesses internal services of DOS to retrieve the device control block address for a specified handle

Calling Registers:	AH	12h
	AL	16h
	BX	File handle

Return Registers: Carry flag clear if successful
          ES:DI   Pointer to DCB that corresponds to the handle

          Carry flag set if error
          AX   Error code

Comments: Function 12h provides access to certain DOS internal services (00h–25h in Version 3, 00h–2Fh in Version 4). Note that many of these can be called only when all segment registers are set to the DOS kernel's segment; *if this restriction is not met, damage to data is extremely likely*. Nevertheless, they do provide information that is difficult to obtain by any other means and can be useful to developers who take proper precautions.

Subfunction 16h provides direct access to the device control block being used by any file or device handle. However, this function assumes that all segment registers point into the DOS kernel and so is useful primarily to DOS itself.

Int 2Fh

Function 12h Subfunction 17h   V3
Get LDT Address

Accesses internal services of DOS to return an address for the logical drive table

Calling Registers:	AH	12h
	AL	17h
	Stack	Word, drive code (0 = A, 1 = B, and so on)

Return Registers: Carry flag clear if successful
          DS:SI   Pointer to logical drive table for that drive
                  (DOS internal pointers also set)

          Carry flag set if error
          AX   Error code

Comments: Function 12h provides access to certain DOS internal services (00h–25h in Version 3, 00h–2Fh in Version 4). Note that many of these can be called only when all segment registers are set to the DOS kernel's segment; *if this restriction*

is not met, damage to data is extremely likely. Nevertheless, they do provide information that is difficult to obtain by any other means and can be useful to developers who take proper precautions.

Subfunction 17h assumes that all segment registers point into the DOS kernel code and so is useful mainly to DOS itself. This function sets the current drive pointers and returns the address of the logical drive table for the specified drive.

Int 2Fh   Function 12h Subfunction 18h   V3
Get User Stack Address

Accesses internal services of DOS to retrieve the user's stack address

Calling Registers: AH   12h
                          AL   18h

Return Registers: DS:SI   Pointer to area of DOS stack where registers
                                    were saved at entry to Interrupt 21h

Comments: Subfunction 18h loads DS and SI from the locations at which DOS saved SS and SP after pushing all registers at entry to Interrupt 21h. This permits direct control of the values that will be returned by Interrupt 21h (unless subsequent code changes the values again). This function is of limited value and makes no assumptions about segment registers.

Int 2Fh   Function 12h Subfunction 19h   V3
Set LDT Pointers

Accesses internal services of DOS to set the logical drive table pointers

Calling Registers: AH   12h
                          AL   19h

Return Registers: None

Comments: Function 12h provides access to certain DOS internal services (00h–25h in Version 3, 00h–2Fh in Version 4). Note that many of these can be called only when all segment registers are set to the DOS kernel's segment; *if this restriction is not met, damage to data is extremely likely*. Nevertheless, they do provide information that is difficult to obtain by any other means and can be useful to developers who take proper precautions.

Subfunction 19h uses the DOS internal data to set up the LDT pointer to correspond to the currently selected drive. It assumes that all segment registers point into the DOS kernel and is of limited value outside of DOS itself.

Int 2Fh   Function 12h Subfunction 1Ah   V3
Get Drive Code from Path Name

Accesses internal services of DOS to parse, from a supplied ASCIIZ path name, the drive code

Calling Registers: AH   12h
                          AL   1Ah
                          DS:SI   Pointer to ASCIIZ path name

Return Registers: AL   Drive code (0 = default, 1 = A, and so on)
                         DS:SI   Advanced past drive specification if one was
                                  present, otherwise unchanged

Comments: Subfunction 1Ah determines whether a drive has been specified as part of the path name passed to it, and if so, translates the drive letter into a numeric value and advances SI to point past the drive specification. This function makes no assumptions about segment registers.

Int 2Fh   Function 12h Subfunction 1Bh   V3
Adjust for Leap Year

Accesses internal services of DOS to set the number of days in February based on whether the supplied year is a leap year

Calling Registers: AH   12h
                          AL   1Bh
                          CX   Year (full value, such as 1989)

Return Registers: AL   29 if leap year, else 28

Comments: Function 12h provides access to certain DOS internal services (00h–25h in Version 3, 00h–2Fh in Version 4). Note that many of these can be called only when all segment registers are set to the DOS kernel's segment; *if this restriction is not met, damage to data is extremely likely*. Nevertheless, they do provide information that is difficult to obtain by any other means and can be useful to developers who take proper precautions.

Subfunction 1Bh assumes that all segment registers point into the DOS kernel and is of limited usefulness outside of DOS. It tests the value in CL to determine whether the year is a leap year and, if it is, modifies the DOS days-per-month table accordingly. In any event, the number of days in February for the specified year is returned in AL. This function is part of DOS time/date processing.

Int 2Fh   Function 12h Subfunction 1Ch   V3
Calculate Days Since Start-of-Month

Accesses internal services of DOS to return the number of elapsed days since the beginning of the month

Calling Registers: AH   12h
                          AL   1Ch
                          CX   Number code of current month
                          DX   Total days in prior years (0, if day
                                      in this year desired)
                          DS:SI   Pointer to days-per-month table

Return Registers: DX   Total days to start of current month

Comments: Function 12h provides access to certain DOS internal services (00h–25h in Version 3, 00h–2Fh in Version 4). Note that many of these can be called only when all segment registers are set to the DOS kernel's segment; *if this restriction is not met, damage to data is extremely likely.* Nevertheless, they do provide information that is difficult to obtain by any other means and can be useful to developers who take proper precautions.

Subfunction 1Ch assumes that all segment registers point into the DOS kernel and is of limited usefulness outside of DOS. It calculates a tally of the total number of days elapsed from the DOS "zero day" (January 1, 1980) or from the start of the current year (if DX = 0) to the start of the current month. This function is part of DOS time/date processing.

Int 2Fh   Function 12h Subfunction 1Dh   V3
Calculate Date

Accesses internal services of DOS to calculate the month and day of the year when supplied with a count of the number of elapsed days

Calling Registers: AH   12h
                          AL   1Dh
                          CX   00h
                          DX   Total day count *this year*
                          DS:SI   Pointer to days-per-month table

Return Registers: CX   Month
                          DX   Day

Comments: Function 12h provides access to certain DOS internal services (00h–25h in Version 3, 00h–2Fh in Version 4). Note that many of these can be called only when all segment registers are set to the DOS kernel's segment; *if this restriction*

is not met, damage to data is extremely likely. Nevertheless, they do provide information that is difficult to obtain by any other means and can be useful to developers who take proper precautions.

Subfunction 1Dh assumes that all segment registers point into the DOS kernel and is of limited usefulness outside of DOS. It accepts a count of total days *in the year* and calculates the current month and day values. This function is part of DOS time/date processing.

This function is the inverse of Function 12h, Subfunction 1Ch. It assumes that DX is less than 367 at entry, but no error is reported if this condition is not true. If DX is outside this range, the results are unpredictable. Because this function was never intended for general public use, no error detection was included.

Int 2Fh **Function 12h Subfunction 1Eh** **V3**
    Compare Strings

Accesses internal services of DOS to provide a comparison test of two ASCIIZ strings

Calling Registers:	AH	12h
	AL	1Eh
	DS:SI	Pointer to one string
	ES:DI	Pointer to other string

Return Registers: Zero flag set if strings match identically, clear otherwise

Comments: Subfunction 1Eh provides a generic test for equality of two ASCIIZ strings. It makes no assumptions about segment registers, but if the two strings differ, it returns no information beyond the fact that they *do* differ. In particular, it will not tell you the location at which they differ or the nature of the difference.

Int 2Fh **Function 12h Subfunction 1Fh** **V3**
    Initialize LDT

Accesses internal services of DOS to set up the logical drive table for a specified drive

Calling Registers:	AH	12h
	AL	1Fh
	STACK	Drive letter in ASCII

Return Registers: Carry flag clear if successful

Carry flag set if error
    AX   Error code

Comments: Function 12h provides access to certain DOS internal services (00h–25h in Version 3, 00h–2Fh in Version 4). Note that many of these can be called only when all segment registers are set to the DOS kernel's segment; *if this restriction*

is not met, damage to data is extremely likely. Nevertheless, they do provide information that is difficult to obtain by any other means and can be useful to developers who take proper precautions.

Subfunction 1Fh assumes that all segment registers point into the DOS kernel and is of limited usefulness outside of DOS. It is used as a part of the SUBST function, which permits a subdirectory to be identified as a separate logical drive. Because it modifies internal DOS pointers, it should be explored with the utmost caution.

 ## Int 2Fh Function 12h Subfunction 20h V3
Get DCB Number

Accesses internal services of DOS to return a drive control block number (not address) for a specifed file handle

Calling Registers: AH   12h
 AL   20h
 BX   File handle

Return Registers: Carry flag clear if successful
 ES:DI Pointer to appropriate byte in the handle table
 for the current process (address of DCB
 number for that handle)

 Carry flag set if error
 AX   Error code

Comments: Subfunction 20h assumes that the SS register points into the DOS kernel, in order to locate the handle table for the current process. No other segment register assumptions are made. Upon successful return, ES:DI points to the byte in the handle table that contains the DCB number for the specified handle. This DCB number, in turn, may be used to locate the DCB itself by means of Subfunction 16h.

The SS register may be forced into the DOS area by setting SS:SP to offset 40h of the logical drive table for an unused drive; the LDT is always in the DOS kernel. To locate the LDT, refer to the information in Appendix E, "Reserved DOS Functions."

 ## Int 2Fh Function 12h Subfunction 21h V3
Expand ASCIIZ Path Name

Accesses internal services of DOS to expand a partial path name to a full path name

Calling Registers: AH   12h
 AL   21h
 DS:SI Pointer to path name for expansion

	ES:DI	Pointer to 65-byte buffer to receive expanded string
Return Registers:	Carry flag clear if successful	
	ES:DI	Unchanged, pointer to expanded string
	Carry flag set if error	
	AX	Error code
		02, illegal character in input string

Comments: Function 12h provides access to certain DOS internal services (00h–25h in Version 3, 00h–2Fh in Version 4). Note that many of these can be called only when all segment registers are set to the DOS kernel's segment; *if this restriction is not met, damage to data is extremely likely.* Nevertheless, they do provide information that is difficult to obtain by any other means and can be useful to developers who take proper precautions.

Subfunction 21h accesses the same routine used by undocumented Function 60h of Interrupt 21h. This function assumes that the SS register points into the DOS kernel, in order to access a number of internal tables that are used during the expansion. The expanded string will include the drive letter and full path name (if the input string referred to a SUBSTed drive, the actual physical drive letter will replace it in the output expansion).

Int 2Fh Function 12h Subfunction 22h V3
Translate Extended Error Codes

Accesses internal services of DOS to determine the extended error codes of an error

Calling Registers:	AH	12h
	AL	22h

Return Registers:	None

Comments: Function 12h provides access to certain DOS internal services (00h–25h in Version 3, 00h–2Fh in Version 4). Note that many of these can be called only when all segment registers are set to the DOS kernel's segment; *if this restriction is not met, damage to data is extremely likely.* Nevertheless, they do provide information that is difficult to obtain by any other means and can be useful to developers who take proper precautions.

Subfunction 22h is useful only to DOS itself. This function uses internal DOS tables to translate an error condition into the appropriate extended error code, class code, action code, and locus; it then places those values in the DOS internal storage locations from which Int 21h, Function 59h will retrieve them. It should not be used by other programs.

Int 2Fh

Function 12h Subfunction 24h   V3
Execute Delay

Accesses internal services of DOS to execute a variable-length delay based on internal DOS values

Calling Registers: AH   12h
                          AL   24h

Return Registers: None

Comments: Function 12h provides access to certain DOS internal services (00h–25h in Version 3, 00h–2Fh in Version 4). Note that many of these can be called only when all segment registers are set to the DOS kernel's segment; *if this restriction is not met, damage to data is extremely likely*. Nevertheless, they do provide information that is difficult to obtain by any other means and can be useful to developers who take proper precautions.

Subfunction 24h executes a delay loop, using delay values stored in the DOS kernel. It assumes that all segment registers point into the DOS kernel and should not be used outside of DOS.

Int 2Fh

Function 12h Subfunction 25h   V3
Get ASCIIZ String Length

Accesses internal services of DOS to determine the length of an ASCIIZ string pointed to by DS:SI

Calling Registers: AH   12h
                          AL   25h
                          DS:SI   Pointer to ASCIIZ string

Return Registers: CX   Length of string in bytes

Comments: Function 12h provides access to certain DOS internal services (00h–25h in Version 3, 00h–2Fh in Version 4). Note that many of these can be called only when all segment registers are set to the DOS kernel's segment; *if this restriction is not met, damage to data is extremely likely*. Nevertheless, they do provide information that is difficult to obtain by any other means and can be useful to developers who take proper precautions.

Subfunction 25h counts the number of bytes in the ASCIIZ string pointed to by DS:SI at entry and then returns the count in the CX register. The SS register is assumed to point into the DOS kernel area.

Int 2Fh   Function 12h Subfunction 26h   V4
Open File

Accesses internal services of DOS to open a file through Int 21h, Function 3Dh

Calling Registers: AH   12h
                          AL   26h
                          CL   Access mode (same as AL for Int 21h,
                                        Function 3Dh)
                          DS:DX   Pointer to ASCIIZ file specification

Return Registers: Carry flag clear if successful
                          AX   Handle

                          Carry flag set if error
                          AX   Error code
                                    01h, invalid function
                                    02h, file not found
                                    03h, path not found
                                    04h, no handles available
                                    05h, access denied
                                    0Ch, invalid access code

Comments: Function 12h provides access to certain DOS internal services (00h–25h in Version 3, 00h–2Fh in Version 4). Note that many of these can be called only when all segment registers are set to the DOS kernel's segment; *if this restriction is not met, damage to data is extremely likely*. Nevertheless, they do provide information that is difficult to obtain by any other means and can be useful to developers who take proper precautions.

Subfunction 26h transfers CL into AL and then executes the same routine reached by Interrupt 21h, Function 3Dh (Open File). It assumes that all segment registers point into the DOS kernel. Thus, in most cases, this function is useful only to DOS itself.

Int 2Fh   Function 12h Subfunction 27h   V4
Close File

Accesses internal services of DOS to close a file through Int 21h, Function 3E

Calling Registers: AH   12h
                          AL   27h
                          BX   File handle

Return Registers: Carry flag clear if successful

Carry flag set if error
AX   Error code

Comments: Function 12h provides access to certain DOS internal services (00h–25h in Version 3, 00h–2Fh in Version 4). Note that many of these can be called only when all segment registers are set to the DOS kernel's segment; *if this restriction is not met, damage to data is extremely likely.* Nevertheless, they do provide information that is difficult to obtain by any other means and can be useful to developers who take proper precautions.

    Subfunction 27h executes the same routine reached by Int 21h, Function 3Eh (Close File). It assumes that all segment registers point into the DOS kernel. Thus, in most cases, this function is useful only to DOS itself.

Int 2Fh   Function 12h Subfunction 28h   V4
Position File Pointer

Accesses internal services of DOS to position a file pointer through Int 21h, Function 42h

Calling Registers:
AH	12h
AL	28h
BX	File handle
CX	Most significant part of offset
DX	Least significant part of offset
BP	Normal values of AX for Int 21h, Function 42h

Return Registers: Carry flag clear if successful
    DX:AX   New file-pointer location

Carry flag set if error
    AX   Error code
          01h, invalid function (file sharing)
          06h, invalid handle

Comments: Function 12h provides access to certain DOS internal services (00h–25h in Version 3, 00h–2Fh in Version 4). Note that many of these can be called only when all segment registers are set to the DOS kernel's segment; *if this restriction is not met, damage to data is extremely likely.* Nevertheless, they do provide information that is difficult to obtain by any other means and can be useful to developers who take proper precautions.

    Subfunction 28h transfers BP into AX and then executes the same routine reached by Int 21h, Function 42h (Move File handle). It assumes that all segment registers point into the DOS kernel. Thus, in most cases, this function is useful only to DOS itself.

Int 2Fh   Function 12h   Subfunction 29h   V4
Read File

Accesses internal services of DOS to read a file through Int 21h, Function 3Fh

Calling Registers: AH   12h
                         AL   29h
                         BX   File handle
                         CX   Number of bytes
                         DS:DX   Pointer to buffer area

Return Registers: Carry flag clear if successful
                         AX   Number of bytes read

                      Carry flag set if error
                         AX   Error code
                                       05h, access denied
                                       06h, invalid handle

Comments: Function 12h provides access to certain DOS internal services (00h–25h in Version 3, 00h–2Fh in Version 4). Note that many of these can be called only when all segment registers are set to the DOS kernel's segment; *if this restriction is not met, damage to data is extremely likely.* Nevertheless, they do provide information that is difficult to obtain by any other means and can be useful to developers who take proper precautions.

    Subfunction 29h executes the same routine reached by Int 21h, Function 3Fh (Read File or Device). It assumes that all segment registers point into the DOS kernel. Thus, in most cases, this function is useful only to DOS itself.

Int 2Fh   Function 12h   Subfunction 2Bh   V4
IOCTL Interface

Accesses internal services of DOS to interface with IOCTL services of Int 21h, Function 44h

Calling Registers: AH   12h
                         AL   2Bh
                         BX   Handle (Subfunction codes 00h, 01h, 02h, 03h, 06h, 07h, and 0Ah)
                         BL   Drive code: 0 = default, 1 = A, and so on Subfunction codes 04h, 05h, 08h, and 09h)
                         CX   Number of bytes to read or write
                         BP   Normal values of AX for IOCTL function

	DS:DX	Pointer to buffer area (Subfunction codes 02h–05h)
	DX	Device information (Subfunction code 01h); see table DOS.9

Return Registers: Carry flag clear if successful

	AX	Number of bytes transferred (Subfunction codes 02h–05h)
	AL	Status (Subfunction codes 06h–07h)
		00h, not ready
		FFh, ready
	AX	Value (Subfunction code 08h)
		00h, removable
		01h, fixed
	DX	Device information (Subfunction code 00h)

Carry flag set if error

	AX	Error code
		01h, invalid function (file sharing)
		04h, no handles available
		05h, access denied
		06h, invalid handle
		0Dh, invalid data
		0Fh, invalid drive

Comments: Function 12h provides access to certain DOS internal services (00h–25h in Version 3, 00h–2Fh in Version 4). Note that many of these can be called only when all segment registers are set to the DOS kernel's segment; *if this restriction is not met, damage to data is extremely likely.* Nevertheless, they do provide information that is difficult to obtain by any other means and can be useful to developers who take proper precautions.

Subfunction 2Bh transfers BP into AX and then executes the same routine reached by Int 21h, Function 44h (IOCTL). It assumes that all segment registers point into the DOS kernel. Thus, in most cases, this function is useful only to DOS.

Int 2Fh Function 12h Subfunction 2Dh V4
Get Extended Error Code

Accesses internal services of DOS to retrieve extended error code information

Calling Registers:	AH	12h
	AL	2Dh

Return Registers:	AX	Error code

Comments: Function 12h provides access to certain DOS internal services (00h–25h in Version 3, 00h–2Fh in Version 4). Note that many of these can be called only when all segment registers are set to the DOS kernel's segment; *if this restriction is not met, damage to data is extremely likely*. Nevertheless, they do provide information that is difficult to obtain by any other means and can be useful to developers who take proper precautions.

    Subfunction 2Dh returns in AX the current value of the extended error code that would be returned by Int 21h, Function 59h. It assumes that the SS and DS registers point into the DOS kernel.

Int 2Fh   Function 12h Subfunction 2Fh   V4
`Store DX`

Accesses internal services of DOS to store the value of DX in the DOS kernel

Calling Registers: AH   12h
                           AL   2Fh
                           DX   New value to set

Return Registers: None

Comments: Function 12h provides access to certain DOS internal services (00h–25h in Version 3, 00h–2Fh in Version 4). Note that many of these can be called only when all segment registers are set to the DOS kernel's segment; *if this restriction is not met, damage to data is extremely likely*. Nevertheless, they do provide information that is difficult to obtain by any other means and can be useful to developers who take proper precautions.

    Subfunction 2Fh stores the value in the DX register into an internal DOS word, the purpose of which is not known. Extreme caution should be used when you experiment with this function. It assumes that all segment registers point into the DOS kernel.

Int 2Fh   Function 14h Subfunction 00h   V3
`Get NLSFUNC Installation Status`

Interfaces with NLSFUNC.COM and does nothing unless that program is loaded

Calling Registers: AH   14h
                           AL   00h

Return Registers: Carry flag clear if successful
                           AL   Status
                                      00h, okay to install if not installed
                                      01h, not okay to install if not installed
                                      FFh, installed

Comments: Function 14h, Subfunction 00h is used for interfacing with NLSFUNC.COM. The uses of other subfunctions are not known at this time.

Int 2Fh

Function 15h   **V3**
CDROM Interface

Interfaces with the CDROM routines and does nothing unless that program is loaded

Calling Registers: AX   1500h, get installed status

Return Registers: Carry flag clear if successful
AL   Status
00h, not installed, okay to install
01h, not okay to install
FFh, installed

Comments: Used for CDROM interface routines, most notably those provided by Microsoft in the CDROM extensions. A discussion of these services is beyond the scope of this book.

Int 2Fh

Function 16h Subfunction 80h   **V5**
MS-DOS Idle Call

Informs the system that the calling program is idle

Calling Registers: AH   16h
AL   80h

Return Registers: None

Comments: Programs should use this interrupt when idle, such as when waiting for user input. Before doing so, the calling program should make sure that the Int 2Fh vector is not zero.

   The interrupt is non-blocking; if the system does not have another program to run, it will return immediately and the calling program will continue to run.

Int 2Fh

Function 1Ah Subfunction 00h   **V4**
Get ANSI.SYS Installed State

Returns the installation state of ANSI.SYS

Calling Registers: AH   1Ah
AL   00h

Return Registers: AL   FFh, ANSI.SYS loaded
00h, ANSI.SYS not loaded

Comments: This function is used to determine whether ANSI.SYS is loaded. The ANSI.SYS driver provides a subset of the ANSI screen-handling codes. Before a program uses such codes, it should call this function to find out whether the codes will be supported.

Int 2Fh ·   Function 43h Subfunction 00h   V5
Get XMS Driver Installed State

Returns the installation state of an XMS driver

Calling Registers:	AH	43h
	AL	00h

Return Registers:	AL	80h, XMS driver loaded
		00h, XMS driver not loaded

Comments: This function must be called before calling Function 4310 to verify the presence of the XMS driver.

Int 2Fh   Function 43h Subfunction 10h   V5
Get XMS Driver Entry-Point Address

Returns the address of the XMS driver function call

Calling Registers:	AH	43h
	AL	10h

Return Registers:	ES:BX	Pointer to function

Comments: This function should be called only after calling Function 43h, Subfunction 00h to verify the installation of an XMS driver.

    Programs should not take advantage of the XMS driver's HMA and UMB management if MS-DOS is already managing those areas.

Int 2Fh   Function 48h Subfunction 00h   V5
Get DOSKEY.COM Installed State

Returns the installation state of DOSKEY.COM

Calling Registers:	AH	48h
	AL	00h

Return Registers:	AL	Nonzero, DOSKEY.COM loaded
		00h, DOSKEY.COM not loaded

Comments: This function is used to determine whether DOSKEY.COM, an enhanced command-line interpreter, is installed.

Int 2Fh Function 48h Subfunction 10h V5
Read Command Line

Reads a line of up to 126 characters and copies it the specified buffer

Calling Registers:

	AH	48h
	AL	10h
	DS:DX	Pointer to buffer
		Byte 0, maximum buffer size
		Byte 1, returned line length
		Byte 2, first byte of input line

Return Registers: AX 0 if successful

Comments: During the call, DOSKEY macros and function keys are enabled. If a macro name is entered, AX will be zero, but a second call must be made to expand the macro.

The returned line has a carriage return (0Dh) added to the end. The returned line length does not include the carriage return.

The line entered is added to the DOSKEY history.

Int 2Fh Function 4Bh Subfunction 01h V5
Build Notification Chain

Creates a linked list of notification function handlers

Calling Registers:

	AH	4Bh
	AL	01h
	ES:BX	0
	CX:DX	Service function handler address

Return Registers:

	ES:BX	0, no notification chain
		Nonzero, address of SWCALLBACKINFO
		structure, formatted as follows:

Dword	Address of next SWCALLBACKINFO structure in chain
Dword	Address of notification function handler
Dword	Reserved
Dword	Address of SWAPIINFO structure

Comments: The client program must handle this call as part of its Int 2Fh handling to support the task switching API. If this call is not handled, the client must jump to the previously installed Int 2Fh handler.

If the client program chooses to handle this call, it must first call the previously loaded Int 2F handler. On return, it should fill its own SWCALLBACKINFO structure, set the address of the next SWCALLBACKINFO structure to the ES:BX value returned by the previous Int 2Fh handler, and set ES:BX to the address of its own SWCALLBACKINFO structure. Thus, the most recently loaded client is the first in the chain.

Int 2Fh — Function 4Bh Subfunction 02h — V5
Detect Switcher

Detects the presence a task switcher

Calling Registers:

AH	4Bh	
AL	02h	
BX	0	
DI	0	
ES:BX	0	

Return Registers:

ES:BX	0 if no task switcher installed	
	Address of service-function handler if task switcher installed	

Comments: Programs that need to prevent or control the interruptions caused by task switching should call this function during initialization.

Int 2Fh — Function 4Bh Subfunction 03h — V5
Allocate Switcher ID

Returns a unique switcher identifier

Calling Registers:

AH	4Bh	
AL	03h	
BX	0	
ES:DI	Service function handler	

Return Registers:

BX	00, could not allocate an identifier	
	01h–0Fh, identifier	

Comments: This function must be called only by a task switcher, not by a client program.

A task switcher must first find out whether it is the first task switcher installed by calling Function 4B, Subfunction 02h. If it is, it must handle the processing of this call by other task switchers. Otherwise, it must call this function and get a switcher ID. If it fails to do so, it must exit or disable itself.

A task switcher uses its switch ID as the high 4 bits of any session identifiers it creates, thus assuring that no two session identifiers are the same.

The task switcher must disable interrupts while examining and changing its record of allocated switch identifiers. At any other time, the task switcher may enable interrupts and call any MS-DOS function. It may modify the AX and BX registers, but it must preserve the other registers.

Int 2Fh   Function 4Bh Subfunction 04h   V5
Free Switcher ID

Frees a switch identifier allocated by Function 4B, Subfunction 03h

Calling Registers: AH   4Bh
                          AL   04h
                          BX   Identifier
                          ES:DI   Service handler address

Return Registers: BX   0, valid identifier freed
                                    Nonzero, invalid identifier

Comments: When a task switcher exits, it should call this function to free its identifier.

Int 2Fh   Function 4Bh Subfunction 05h   V5
Identify Instance Data

Identifies instance data maintained by a client program

Calling Registers: AH   4Bh
                          AL   05h
                          ES:BX   0
                          CX:DX   Service function handler

Return Registers: ES:BX   0, no instance data chain
                                    Nonzero, address of SWSTARTUPINFO
                                    structure:

Word	Version
Dword	Previous handler's SWSTARTUPINFO structure address
Dword	Ignored
Dword	Ignored
Dword	SWINSTANCEITEM structure address

Comments: The client program must handle this call as part of its Int 2Fh handling to support the task switching API. If this call is not handled, the client must jump to the previously installed Int 2Fh handler.

If the client program chooses to handle this call, it must first call the previously loaded Int 2F handler. On return, it should fill its own SWSTARTUPINFO structure, set the address of the previous handler's SWSTARTUPINFO structure to the ES:BX value returned by the previous Int 2Fh handler, and set ES:BX to the address of its own SWSTARTUPINFO structure. Thus, the most recently loaded client is the first in the chain.

Int 2Fh   Function ADh   Subfunction 80h   V3.3
Get KEYB.COM Version Number

Returns KEYB.COM's version number

Calling Registers: AH   ADh
                       AL   80h

Return Registers: BH   Major version number
                      BL   Minor version number

Comments: The version number will be zero if KEYB.COM is not installed.

Int 2Fh   Function ADh   Subfunction 81h   V3.3
Set KEYB.COM Active Code Page

Sets the active code page for KEYB.COM

Calling Registers: AH   ADh
                       AL   81h
                       BX   Code page id

Return Registers: Carry flag clear, if successful

                      Carry flag set, if error
                       AX   0001

Comments: This function is used to select the code page for the keyboard driver.

Int 2Fh   Function ADh   Subfunction 82h   V3.3
Set KEYB.COM Country Flag

Sets the KEYB.COM country flag

Calling Registers: AH   ADh
                       AL   82h
                       BL   Country flag
                                     00h, domestic
                                     FFh, foreign

Return Registers: Carry flag clear, if successful

Carry flag set, if error

Comments: This function is used to select between USA and non-USA for the country flag.

Int 2Fh   Function ADh Subfunction 83h   V3.3
Get KEYB.COM Country Flag

Gets the KEYB.COM country flag

Calling Registers: AH   ADh
                          AL   83h

Return Registers: BL   Country flag

Comments: This function is used to get the country flag. Values are 00h (domestic) and FFh (foreign).

Int 2Fh   Function B0h Subfunction 00h   V3.3
Get GRAFTABL.COM Installed State

Returns the installation state of GRAFTABL.COM

Calling Registers: AH   B0h
                          AL   00h

Return Registers: AL   FFh, GRAFTABL.COM loaded
                                      00h, GRAFTABL.COM not loaded

Comments: This function determines whether GRAFTABL is installed. GRAFTABL enables MS-DOS to display characters in the range 80h to FFh in graphics mode.

Int 2Fh   Function B7h Subfunction 00h   V3.3
Check for APPEND Installation

Returns a value indicating whether APPEND has been installed at the DOS level

Calling Registers: AH   B7h
                          AL   00h

Return Registers: AH   < > 0 if APPEND installed

Comments: This function is used to determine whether APPEND has been installed by checking the value returned in AH. APPEND is installed at the DOS level through the APPEND command. Because there has been little standardization in networking over the past several years, not all networks will respond correctly to this interrupt.

Int 2Fh Function B7h Subfunction 02h V4
Get APPEND Version

Determines which version of APPEND is installed

Calling Registers: AH   B7h
              AL   02h

Return Registers: Carry flag clear if successful
                AX   FFFFh if V4 APPEND installed; otherwise,
                      APPEND is not MS-DOS V4 version

              Carry flag set if error
                AX   Error code

Comments: This function is used to determine whether all the features added to APPEND at V4 are available. Subfunction 00h will return `installed` if any version is present; this function establishes that the version present is V4.

Int 2Fh Function B7h Subfunction 04h V4
Get APPEND Path Pointer

If APPEND is installed, returns a pointer to the currently active APPEND path

Calling Registers: AH   B7h
              AL   04h

Return Registers: Carry flag clear if successful
                ES:DI Pointer to active APPEND path

              Carry flag set if error
                AX   Error code

Comments: This function is used to determine the address of the currently active APPEND path.

Int 2Fh Function B7h Subfunction 06h V4
Get APPEND Function State

Returns a bit map of the APPEND fuctions currently in use (if APPEND is installed)

Calling Registers: AH   B7h
                            AL   06h

Return Registers: Carry flag clear if successful
                            BX   APPEND state (bit map):

                                  Bits

FEDCBA98 76543210	*Meaning*
....0	APPEND disabled
....1	APPEND enabled
...xxxxx xxxxxxx.	Not used (zero)
..0.....	/PATH inactive
..1.....	/PATH active
.0......	/E switch inactive
.1......	/E switch active
0.......	/X switch inactive
1.......	/X switch active

                     Carry flag set if error
                         AX   Error code

Comments: This function is used to read the current state of the APPEND function. For details of the various switches, see the DOS V4 documentation for APPEND.

Int 2Fh   Function B7h Subfunction 07h   V4
Set APPEND Function State

Changes the state of the APPEND functions using bit-mapped codes

Calling Registers: AH   B7h
                            AL   07h
                            BX   APPEND state (bit map):

                                    Bits

FEDCBA98 76543210	*Meaning*
....0	APPEND disabled
....1	APPEND enabled
...xxxxx xxxxxxx.	Not used (zero)
..0.....	/PATH inactive
..1.....	/PATH active
.0......	/E switch inactive
.1......	/E switch active
0.......	/X switch inactive
1.......	/X switch active

Return Registers: Carry flag clear if successful

Carry flag set if error
     AX   Error code

Comments: This function is used to set the state of the APPEND function by passing it a bit map describing the desired state. For details of the various switches, see the DOS V4 documentation for APPEND.

Int 2Fh   **Function B7h Subfunction 11h**   **V4**
Set Return Found Name State

Modifies action of APPEND for the next DOS access only

Calling Registers: AH   B7h
                     AL   11h

Return Registers: Carry flag clear if successful

Carry flag set if error
     AX   Error code

Comments: This function is used to cause APPEND to modify the action of Functions 3Dh, 43h, and 6Ch of Interrupt 21h. When this function is executed, the next call to any of those functions will return the fully qualified file name, in the same location at which the file name was passed to the function. You must be sure that the buffer is large enough (67 bytes) to accept any possible return value.

After a fully expanded file name has been returned, the flag set by this function is cleared, and operation of the Interrupt 21h functions returns to normal. Thus, each use of this APPEND subfunction affects only a single use of the Interrupt 21h functions.

PROGRAMMING

Mouse Functions: Int 33h

The DOS mouse functions operate through an installed driver (MOUSE.SYS or MOUSE.COM) that ties itself to Int 33h for access to the functions. The driver constantly updates the mouse cursor's position on the screen relative to the movement of the mouse itself. No action by the program is needed to maintain the driver's action.

At any time, a program can query the driver to find the current status of the mouse.

Several versions of mouse-driver software exist. This section describes the functions provided by Microsoft's Version 6 drivers. These are generally accepted as an industry standard. Some older drivers and some drivers from other mouse makers omit functions (especially those numbered above 18h). For use with DOS V1, which did not permit installable device drivers, most are supplied also as TSRs; whether installed as a driver or as a TSR, the functions are identical. Many mouse users use the TSR version with all DOS versions.

Int 33h	**Function 00h**	**V2**
	Initialize the Mouse	

Determines whether a mouse is installed, resets the driver, and returns the number of buttons on the mouse

Calling Registers: AX   0000h

Return Registers: AX   0, mouse not installed
                                    –1, mouse installed
                         BX   Number of buttons (2 for Microsoft, 3 for some
                                       other brands)

Comments: When a program in which you want to use the mouse starts, that program must verify the mouse's presence. The usual way to do this is to call Function 00h. This function resets the mouse to the center of the screen, makes sure that the mouse is off, and sets the default mouse cursor and default movement ratios.

In DOS V2.x, it is best to verify that the vector for Interrupt 33h points to code before using this function. If the four bytes of the vector are not all 00, it should be safe to use Function 00h to determine whether the driver is present.

The initial conditions established for the mouse driver by this function are

Display page:	Page 0
Cursor range:	Entire screen (x=0 to 639, y=0 to 199)
Exclusion area:	None
Cursor position:	At screen center (x=320, y=100)
Cursor state:	Hidden
Cursor shape:	Arrow for graphics modes
	Reverse block for text modes
User Interrupts:	Disabled
Light pen emulator:	Enabled
Mickey/Pixel ratio:	Horizontal = 8 to 8
	Vertical = 16 to 8
Speed threshold:	64 mickeys per second. (Mickey is the unit of mouse motion. One mickey is approximately 1/200 inch.)

Int 33h   Function 01h   V2
Show Mouse Cursor

Causes the mouse cursor to appear on the display

Calling Registers: AX   0001h

Return Registers: None

Comments: Turns on the mouse cursor, allowing display on the screen. This is not an absolute function; rather, it increments an internal mouse-cursor flag. Initially, this flag is set to a – 1. Whenever the flag is zero, the mouse cursor will be displayed. Function 02h decrements the cursor flag, causing the cursor to disappear if the original value was zero. Thus, multiple calls to Function 02h require multiple calls to this function. The software prevents the flag's value from becoming greater than zero, however.

Int 33h   Function 02h   V2
Hide Mouse Cursor

Turns off display of the mouse cursor

Calling Registers: AX   0002h

Return Registers: None

Comments: This function turns off the display function but does not disable the driver. As noted in the comment for Function 01h, Function 02h decrements a cursor flag. If the value is not zero, the cursor is turned off. Because the flag can never be greater than zero, a single call to this function is guaranteed to hide the cursor.

Int 33h   **Function 03h**   **V2**
                         Get Mouse Position

Returns current mouse position and button status

Calling Registers: AX   0003h

Return Registers: BX   Button status
                      CX   X-coordinate (horizontal)
                      DX   Y-coordinate (vertical)

Comments: This function tells you where the mouse is located. No matter what mode the screen is in, Function 03h always returns an x-coordinate (column) between 0 and 639 and a y-coordinate (row) between 0 and 199. Table M.1 shows the mouse cursor's allowable positions for each display mode, in terms of screen (pixel) coordinates.

Table M.1. *Mouse Cursor's Position*

Screen Mode	Mouse Coordinates
00h, 01h	$x = 16 \times$ column
	$y = 8 \times$ row
02h, 03h	$x = 8 \times$ column
	$y = 8 \times$ row
04h, 05h	$x = 2 \times$ screen X
	$y =$ screen Y
06h	$x =$ screen X
	$y =$ screen Y
07h	$x = 8 \times$ screen column
	$y = 8 \times$ screen row
0Eh–10h	$x =$ screen X
	$y =$ screen Y

     The status of the mouse buttons is returned in BX; only the low-order bits are significant. Table M.2 illustrates the meaning of the bits. Because each button acts independently, the value can be anything from 0 to 3 for a two-button mouse or 0 to 7 for the three-button version.

Table M.2. *Mouse Button Status Bits*

Bit 76543210	*Meaning*
. . . . 0	Left button up
. . . . 1	Left button down
. . . . . . 0 .	Right button up
. . . . . . 1 .	Right button down
. . . . . 0 . .	Center button (if present) up
. . . . . 1 . .	Center button (if present) down
XXXXX . . .	Undefined

Int 33h   **Function 04h**   V2
              Set Mouse Position

Sets the mouse's position on the screen

Calling Registers: AX   0004h
                          CX   New x-coordinate (horizontal)
                          DX   New y-coordinate (vertical)

Return Registers: None

Comments: You can use this function to place the mouse cursor anywhere on the screen. (The mouse driver will resume operating from that location.) This function is useful, for example, when you want to start the mouse at the first item on a menu that is brought up on the screen.

    If either coordinate has a value inappropriate for the current screen mode as defined for Function 03h, it will be adjusted to the nearest appropriate value. If the specified position lies outside the display range established by calls to Functions 07h and 08h, the cursor will be placed as close to the specified position as possible while remaining within the range limits. If the position lies within an exclusion area defined by Function 10h, it will be hidden.

Int 33h   **Function 05h**   V2
              Get Button-Press Information

Returns information about button presses

Calling Registers: AX   0005h
                          BX   Button
                                        0, left

                                        1, right
                                        2, center (if present)

Return Registers: AX   Button status (see table M.2)
                        BX   Count of button presses (reset to zero at
                                    each call)
                        CX   Cursor's horizontal position at last button press
                        DX   Cursor's vertical position at last button press

Comments: Function 05h provides information about what has happened to the specified cursor button since your last call to this function. You can tell whether the button has been pressed, the number of times it was pressed since this function was called, and the location of the mouse when the button was last pressed.

The button status is returned in register AX. This status is the same as that returned in BX for Function 03h (see table M.2).

Int 33h   Function 06h   V2
                    Get Button-Release Information

Returns information about button releases

Calling Registers: AX   0006h
                        BX   Button
                                    0, left
                                    1, right
                                    2, center (if present)

Return Registers: AX   Button status (see table M.2)
                        BX   Count of button releases since last call
                        CX   Cursor's horizontal position when button was
                                    last released
                        DX   Cursor's vertical position when button was
                                    last released

Comments: Function 06h returns information about the release of a mouse button. (Function 05h returns information about presses.) A button release (you let go of the button) is distinct from a press (you press down on the button) and can be identified if you use these two functions. Registers for this function contain information corresponding to the release operation.

Int 33h   Function 07h   V2
                    Set Mouse X Limits

Sets the X limits of the mouse's travel on the screen

Calling Registers: AX   0007h
                           CX   Minimum X bound
                           DX   Maximum X bound

Return Registers: None

Comments: When you want to limit the movement of the mouse cursor in the X (horizontal) direction, call Function 07h. This function is useful when you want to keep the mouse cursor within a defined area on-screen, as you might, for example, with a menu. Function 08h (Y Limits) is also useful for restricting the mouse cursor's movement.

The mouse driver is initialized to have its X limits set at 0 for minimum and 639 for maximum. The values passed to this function should be between those limits. If the value in CX is greater than that in DX, the two values are swapped. If the mouse cursor position is outside the limit after this function is executed, it automatically moves to the limit position.

Int 33h   Function 08h   V2
Set Mouse Y Limits

Sets the Y limits of the mouse's travel on the screen

Calling Registers: AX   0008h
                           CX   Minimum Y bound
                           DX   Maximum Y bound

Return Registers: None

Comments: When you want to limit the movement of the mouse cursor in the Y (vertical) direction, call Function 08h. This function is useful when you want to keep the mouse cursor within a defined area on the screen, as you might, for example, with a menu. Function 07h (X Limits) is also useful for restricting the mouse cursor's movement.

The mouse driver is initialized to have its Y limits set at 0 for minimum and 199 for maximum. The values passed to this function should be between those limits. If the value in CX is greater than that in DX, the two values are swapped. If the mouse cursor position is outside the limit after this function is executed, it automatically moves to the limit position.

Int 33h   Function 09h   V2
Set Graphics Cursor Shape

Sets shape of cursor for use in graphics mode

Calling Registers: AX   0009h
                           BX   Hot spot x position (−16 to 16)

      CX   Hot spot y position (–16 to 16)

      ES:DX   Pointer to screen and cursor masks

Return Registers: None

Comments: In graphics mode, the cursor is defined by a *screen mask*, a *cursor mask*, and the *hot spot*. Function 09h specifies them all.

    This concept is one of the most confusing items in the mouse driver and requires detailed examination. To provide a framework for the examination, keep in mind that the visible mouse cursor is always defined to the software as a 16-pixel-by-16-pixel area, and the hot spot is a single pixel addressed relative to the upper left corner of this 16 × 16 square, which is the official cursor location. Within the square, the visible pointer shape is established by the screen and cursor masks.

    When the mouse cursor is generated in graphics mode, the screen mask is ANDed to the screen, and then the cursor mask is XORed with the result. When two bytes are ANDed together, the resulting byte has a 1 bit wherever *both* of the two original bytes have a 1; all the other bits are set to 0. An XOR on two bytes results in a byte with a 1 bit wherever *only one* of the original bytes has a 1; all the other bits are set to 0.

    As an example, if the screen mask is 9Ch and the byte is 3Bh, the result of ANDing them together is the following:

```
        9Ch    10011100
AND     3Bh    00111011
               --------
               00011000
```

    If the cursor mask is 9Ch and the byte is 3Bh, the result of XORing them together is as follows:

```
        9Ch    10011100
XOR     3Bh    00111011
               --------
               10100111
```

    The practical effect of these operations for graphics modes 1 through 6 is as follows for each bit:

			Screen Mask	
C			0	1
u M				
r a		0	0	1
s s				
o k		1	No change	Inverted
r				

For screen modes 7 and over, the effect is

Screen Mask

			0	1
C				
u	M			
r	a	0	Black	White
s	s			
o	k	1	No change	No change
r				

The masks stored at the location pointed to by ES:DX are bit-mapped blocks of 16-bit words. Each word of the bit map corresponds to one of the 16 rows of the cursor (starting at the top row, screen mask first). Words 0 through 15 are the screen mask; words 16 through 31 are the cursor mask. Figure M.1 shows how the bytes correspond to cursor locations.

Fig. M.1. *Bytes corresponding to cursor locations.*

There are two bits per cursor pixel in graphics modes 4–6 and 14–16, even though the cursor size may differ.

The screen mask temporarily erases anything behind the cursor area; the cursor mask then draws the pointer shape within the space that is left. This makes the mouse pointer appear to overlay on-screen data. By providing several sets of masks and switching between them using this function, you can use different pointer shapes in different parts of your programs.

The hot-spot coordinates are always relative to the upper left corner of the 16 × 16 pixel area covered by the two masks and define the specific coordinates that will be returned as the mouse position whenever any function requests that information.

Setting the hot spot to 0,0 would cause the upper left corner of the image to be the official mouse position (the tip of the default arrow image), a setting of 8,8 would make the center of the area the official position, and 16,16 would move it to the lower right corner. Because –16,–16 is a valid hot-spot setting, it can even be moved outside the actual image—though it is difficult to envision any good reason for doing so.

Int 33h

Function 0Ah   **V2**
Set Text Cursor Type

Sets up the text mode cursor

Calling Registers:	AX	000Ah
	BX	0, select attribute cursor
		1, select hardware cursor
	CX	Screen mask (AND value) if BX = 0
		Starting scan line if BX = 1
	DX	Cursor mask (XOR value) if BX = 0
		Ending scan line if BX = 1

Return Registers: None

Comments: In text mode, the cursor is an attribute cursor or a hardware cursor, depending on how BX is set. With the attribute cursor, the CX and DX registers are screen and cursor masks, respectively, which operate on the CRT attribute-character byte pairs in the same way that the graphics-mode masks operate on pixels. The screen mask preserves most of the original character's attributes. The cursor mask determines which attributes will be changed. To preserve the character unchanged, the low byte of the screen mask should be FFh and the low byte of the cursor mask should be 00h.

The attribute and character bytes at the mouse cursor's location are ANDed with the screen mask and XORed with the cursor mask.

If the hardware mode of operation is selected, the CX and DX registers select the start and stop scan lines for the mouse cursor in the same way that CH and CL do for Int 10h, Function 01h. With this option, set the mouse cursor to a different shape than the normal text cursor so that they are easy to distinguish on the screen. Because the number of usable shapes is limited, the attribute mode usually is used instead.

Int 33h   Function 0Bh   V2
Read Motion Counters

Determines the amount of actual mouse motion, if any, since the last call to this function

Calling Registers: AX   000Bh

Return Registers: CX   Number of mickeys moved horizontally
                                 (−32768 to 32768, negative means to left)
                      DX   Number of mickeys moved vertically
                                   (−32768 to 32768, negative means up)

Comments: Function 0Bh will tell you the *relative* movement of the mouse cursor between calls. The internal software keeps track of the mouse cursor's location at all times and records its location at each call to this function.

    The CX and DX registers return the relative movement (positive values correspond to right and down the screen). The numbers returned are in mickeys, the unit of mouse motion. Each mickey is equal to approximately 0.5 millimeters (0.02 inches).

Int 33h   Function 0Ch   V2
Set User-Defined Event Handler

Establishes a vector to a function that will be called by the device driver whenever a condition defined by the supplied call mask occurs

Calling Registers: AX   000Ch
                        CX   Call mask (see "Comments")
                        ES:DX   Pointer to user-interrupt routine

Return Registers: None

Comments: This function sets up a special handler for conditions recognized by the mouse device driver. A function can be written to respond to button presses, button releases, changes in the cursor's position, or any combination of these events. Operation is essentially identical to that of an interrupt handler, particularly in that the routine can be invoked during the execution of any program as long as it is active, but all details are in the mouse driver and the handler need not be concerned with them.

    Operation of the handler is controlled by a *call mask* in CX that identifies which conditions will trigger the handler's invocation. Wherever the call mask has a 1 bit, the function pointed to by ES:DX will be executed when the condition occurs.

A 0 bit in the same position cancels the function. Table M.3 shows the assignment of bits in the call mask, and table M.4 shows the state of the CPU registers upon entry to the user's event-handler routine.

Table M.3. *Call Mask Bits*

Bit 76543210	*Meaning*
. 1	Mouse moved
. . . . . .1.	Left button pressed
. . . . .1. .	Left button released
. . . .1. . .	Right button pressed
. . .1. . . .	Right button released
. .1.	Center button (if present) pressed
.1.	Center button (if present) released

Table M.4. *Register Setup When User Function Is Called*

Register	Contents
AX	Event trigger bit (same as condition mask presented in table M.3, but only the bit that triggered this call is present)
BX	Button state (same as Functions 05h and 06h)
CX	Cursor's horizontal coordinate (same as Function 03h)
DX	Cursor's vertical coordinate (same as Function 03h)
DI	Horizontal counts (same as CX for Function 0Bh)
SI	Vertical counts (same as DX for Function 0Bh)

When Function 00h is called, the entire call mask is reset to zero. Before a program that sets up a special handler for these conditions ends, the call mask should be reset by a call to Function 00h, 0Ch, or 14h. Remember to restore the initial value of the call mask and subroutine addresses before you end your program.

Int 33h

Function 0Dh
Start Light Pen Emulation

V2

Turns on light pen emulation mode

Calling Registers: AX   000Dh

Return Registers: None

Comments: In light pen emulation mode, the mouse position is the light pen position. Pressing both mouse buttons corresponds to pressing the light pen to the screen. Not all mouse-driver programs provide this interface.

Int 33h   **Function 0Eh**   **V2**
                 Stop Light Pen Emulation

Turns off light pen emulation mode

Calling Registers: AX   000Eh

Return Registers: None

Comments: This function is used to instruct the device driver to stop handling the mouse inputs as though they originated from a light pen. Function 0Eh causes the mouse to work in its normal manner, without driver translation. Not all mouse-driver programs provide this interface.

Int 33h   **Function 0Fh**   **V2**
                 Set Mickey-to-Pixel Ratio

Sets the ratio between physical movement of the cursor (in mickeys, 1/200th of an inch) and coordinate changes (in pixels)

Calling Registers: AX   000Fh
                            CX   Number of mickeys required to cause
                                            an 8-pixel change in horizontal position
                                            (default 8)
                            DX   Number of mickeys required to cause
                                            an 8-pixel change in vertical position
                                            (default 16)

Return Registers: None

Comments: In both the CX and DX registers, the high bit must be zero. The minimum value for each ratio is 1. The higher the ratio, the slower the mouse cursor will move on the screen.

Int 33h Function 10h V2
Conditional Cursor Off

Defines a screen area (exclusion area) in which the cursor is hidden

Calling Registers: AX — 0010h
CX — Upper x screen coordinate
DX — Upper y screen coordinate
SI — Lower x screen coordinate
DI — Lower y screen coordinate

Return Registers: None

Comments: Function 10h specifies an area on the screen in which the cursor disappears. After using this function, be sure to call Function 01h again when the cursor has moved out of the hidden region to restore the cursor's visibility.

Int 33h Function 13h V2
Set Double Speed Threshold

Sets the threshold speed above which the cursor will move at twice the normal rate

Calling Registers: AX — 0013h
DX — Threshold speed in mickeys per second

Return Registers: None

Comments: When the mouse moves at or above the threshold value (of mickeys per second), the cursor-movement factor across the screen is increased by a factor of 2.

Int 33h Function 14h V2
Swap User Event Handlers

Sets the user-interrupt function and call mask while returning their previous values

Calling Registers: AX — 0014h
CX — User-interrupt call mask
ES:DX — Point to user-interrupt routine

Return Registers: CX — Old user-interrupt mask
ES:DX — Old user-interrupt vector

Comments: Like Function 0Ch, this function sets a user-defined handling function to respond to special events recognized by the mouse device driver. The call mask is the same one used in Function 0Ch (see table M.5). Function 14h is enabled when the call-mask bit is set to 1; when it is set to 0, the function is disabled.

Table M.5. *Call Mask Bits*

Bit 76543210	Meaning
. . . . 1	Mouse moved
. . . . . . 1 .	Left button pressed
. . . . . 1 . .	Left button released
. . . . 1 . . .	Right button pressed
. . . 1	Right button released
. . 1	Center button (if present) pressed
. 1	Center button (if present) released

Unlike Function 0Ch, with this function you get the old values in return, permitting you to save them and restore them later. Except for this, the two functions are identical.

When the handler is called, the CPU registers are set up with the information shown in table M.4. The DS register points to the mouse-driver data segment. If the user function needs to get its own data, the function will have to set DS to its own data segment.

The major difference between this function and Function 0Ch is that you can save the original values of the call mask and user-interrupt vector. Remember to restore them before you end your program.

Int 33h **Function 15h** V2
Get Save-State Storage Size

Returns the size of the buffer for the current state of the mouse device driver

Calling Registers: AX   0015h

Return Registers: BX   Buffer size (bytes) needed to hold current mouse state

Comments: This function, which is used in preparation for Function 16h or 17h, determines the amount of memory needed to save the mouse's current state before you use another program that also needs the mouse. The value returned is the exact number of bytes necessary to save the driver state.

DOS PROGRAMMING

Int 33h   Function 16h   V2
Save Mouse Driver State

Copies the state of the mouse driver to the buffer pointed to by ES:DX

Calling Registers: AX   0016h
                           ES:DX   Pointer to buffer to hold mouse state

Return Registers: None

Comments: This function copies the mouse's current state into the buffer pointed to by ES:DX. The buffer size needed is determined by a call to Function 15h.

Use this function whenever you suspend one program that is using the mouse and execute another such program. When the second program ends, you can restore the mouse's state to what it was before the second program started.

Int 33h   Function 17h   V2
Restore Mouse Driver State

Restores the mouse driver to the state saved by Function 16h

Calling Registers: AX   0017h
                           ES:DX   Pointer to buffer in which mouse state is saved

Return Registers: None

Comments: When one program resumes after having executed another program that used the mouse, this function allows you to restore the mouse's state as it was immediately before the second program was executed (provided that you saved the state using Function 16h).

Int 33h   Function 18h   V2
Set Alternate Mouse User Handler

Allows setup of as many as three special-event handlers (similar to those defined in Function 0Ch or 14h)

Calling Registers: AX   0018h
                           CX   Call mask (see "Comments")
                           ES:DX   Address offset to function

Return Registers: AX   0018h if function successful
                                   FFFFh if function failed

Comments: This function creates a special handler for conditions recognized by the mouse device driver. A function can be written to respond to button presses or releases or to changes in cursor position. As many as three such handlers can be defined by separate calls to Function 18h. The difference between the handler established by this function and one established by Function 0Ch or 14h is that this handler responds when the Shift, Alt, or Ctrl key is pressed. The driver will permit a total of four handlers simultaneously: the three permitted by this function and the one set by Function 0Ch. Combinations such as Shift-Alt and Ctrl-Alt are *not* supported, contrary to descriptions published elsewhere.

The operation of the interrupt is controlled by a *call mask* that identifies which conditions will trigger the special handler. Wherever the call mask has a 1 bit, the function pointed to by the DX register will be executed when the condition occurs. A zero bit in the same position cancels the function. Table M.6 shows the assignment of bits in the call mask. Note that because the bits to specify the center button on a 3-button mouse in the call mask are used for the Shift and Ctrl key indicators, this function cannot respond to the center button on a 3-button mouse.

Table M.6. *Call Mask Bits*

Bit 76543210	*Meaning*
. . . . 1	Mouse moved
. . . . . . 1 .	Left-button down event
. . . . . 1 . .	Left-button up event
. . . . 1 . . .	Right-button down event
. . . 1	Right-button up event
. . 1	Shift button pressed during event
. 1	Ctrl key pressed during event
1	Alt key pressed during event

The entire call mask is reset to zero when Function 00h is called. Before it ends, a program that sets up a special handler for these conditions should reset the call mask by calling Function 18h or Function 00h.

When the handler is called, the CPU registers are set up with the information shown in table M.4.

Int 33h **Function 19h** **V2**
Get User Alternate Interrupt Vector

Returns a pointer to a function defined by a call to Function 18h

Calling Registers: AX   0019h

CX   Call mask

Return Registers: BX:DX   User interrupt vector

CX   Call mask (0 if no match was found)

Comments: This function searches the event handlers defined by Function 18h for one whose call mask matches the CX register. When one is found, it returns its segment in BX and its offset in DX.

Int 33h   Function 1Ah   V2
Set Mouse Sensitivity

Sets the mouse speed *and* double speed threshold values

Calling Registers: AX   001Ah

BX   Horizontal mickeys (1–100, default is 8)

CX   Vertical mickeys (1–100, default is 16)

DX   Double speed threshold (default is 64)

Return Registers: None

Comments: This function combines Functions 0F and 13h into a single call. The values are not reset by a call to Function 00h. The maximum value for BX and CX is 100.

Int 33h   Function 1Bh   V2
Get Mouse Sensitivity

Returns the sensitivity values set by Function 1Ah

Calling Registers: AX   001Bh

Return Registers: BX   Horizontal mickeys per pixel

CX   Vertical mickeys per pixel

DX   Double speed threshold

Comments: This function returns the sensitivity of the mouse, represented as the number of mickeys (horizontal and vertical) the mouse must move to move the cursor each pixel on the screen.

Int 33h

Function 1Ch
Set interrupt rate

V2

Sets the rate at which the mouse driver polls the mouse status

Calling Registers: AX   001Ch
                          BX   Interrupt rate code:
                                1, no polling
                                2, poll 30 times per second
                                4, poll 50 times per second
                                8, poll 100 times per second
                                16, poll 200 times per second

Return Registers: None

Comments: *This function applies only to the Microsoft InPort mouse.* If any value other than those listed is put into BX, the lowest bit will apply (for example, 3 = no polling, because it contains the bit for 1).

Int 33h

Function 1Dh
Set CRT Page Number

V2

Sets the page on which the mouse cursor will be displayed

Calling Registers: AX   001Dh
                          BX   CRT page number

Return Registers: None

Comments: This function is used to set the screen page on which the mouse cursor will be displayed. Valid page numbers depend on both the video hardware in place and the display mode; refer to the discussion of Interrupt 10h, Function 05h for valid combinations.

Int 33h

Function 1Eh
Get CRT Page Number

V2

Gets the CRT page number on which the mouse cursor is displayed

Calling Registers: AX   001Eh

Return Registers: BX   CRT page number

Comments: This function is used to determine the screen page on which the mouse cursor will be displayed. Valid page numbers depend on both the video hardware in place and the display mode; refer to the discussion of Interrupt 10h, Function 05h for valid combinations.

Int 33h

Function 1Fh   V2
Disable Mouse Driver

Disables the mouse driver by restoring interrupt vectors used by the mouse driver

Calling Registers: AX   001Fh

Return Registers: AX   001Fh, successful

                               FFFFh, unsuccessful

                ES:BX   Previous vector for Int 33h (only if successful)

Comments: This function disables mouse operation by restoring the interrupt vectors for Int 10h and either Int 71h (8086 processor based systems) or Int 74h (80286- or 80386-based systems). Int 33h (the mouse function interrupt itself) is not affected directly by this call. But the original value of the Int 33h vector is returned in the ES:BX register pair. This value can be used to restore Int 33h to its original value, which will disable the handler completely.

      Disabling any interrupt handler can be tricky. There is no way of knowing whether another handler has also attached itself to these interrupts after the mouse handler installed itself. The restored interrupt vectors will be the values from when the mouse driver was first installed. If another handler attached itself after that, calling this function will disable the other handler also. This could lead to a system crash or worse.

Int 33h

Function 20h   V2
Enable Mouse Driver

Reinstalls the mouse driver for use

Calling Registers: AX   0020h

Return Registers: None

Comments: If the Interrupt 33h vector was left alone, this function restores the interrupt vectors for Int 10h and 71h or 74h, which were removed by the call to Function 1Fh.

Int 33h

Function 21h
Software Reset

V2

Resets the mouse software (but not the mouse)

Calling Registers: AX   0021h

Return Registers: AX   FFFFh, mouse driver installed
                                    0021h, mouse driver not installed
                BX   Number of buttons mouse has (2 for
                                      Microsoft mice, could be 3 for other makes)

Comments: This function is identical to Function 00h except that it does not reset the mouse hardware.

Int 33h

Function 22h
Set Message Language

V2

Selects language used by the mouse driver for prompts and error messages (not in all versions)

Calling Registers: AX   0022h
                               BX   Language number
                                        0, English
                                        1, French
                                        2, Dutch
                                          3, German
                                          4, Swedish
                                          5, Finnish
                                          6, Spanish
                                          7, Portuguese
                                          8, Italian

Return Registers: None

Comments: This function is available only in international versions of the mouse drivers.

Int 33h

Function 23h
Get Message Language

V2

Returns language used by the mouse driver for prompts and error messages (not in all versions)

Calling Registers: AX   0023h

Return Registers: BX   Language number
0, English
1, French
2, Dutch
3, German
4, Swedish
5, Finnish
6, Spanish
7, Portuguese
8, Italian

Comments: This function is available only in international versions of the mouse drivers.

Int 33h   Function 24h   V2
Get Mouse Information

Returns driver version number, mouse type, and IRQ number being used

Calling Registers: AX   0024h

Return Registers: BH   Major version (for example, 6 for 6.11)
BL   Minor version (for example, 11 for 6.11)
CH   Mouse type
1, bus mouse
2, serial mouse
3, InPort mouse
4, PS/2 mouse
5, HP mouse
CL   IRQ being used
0, PS/2 system
2–7, IRQ number

Comments: This function returns the version number of the driver, the mouse type, and the interrupt request line in use for the standard Microsoft drivers. Drivers from other firms might not support this function or might return different results.

The EGA Register Interface

Unlike its predecessors and successors, much of the EGA hardware is controlled through write-only registers, making control of the video unusually difficult. To simplify the task of keeping track of the EGA controller's registers, the driver creates a virtual EGA controller through which it controls the physical EGA hardware. An interface to the mouse driver's virtual EGA controller, the EGA Register Interface, is provided to the programmer through new Video BIOS functions (Interrupt 10h). If an application uses the mouse and intends to manipulate either the EGA or VGA registers, it should manipulate the registers through this interface.

Int 10h   **Function F0h**
Read One Register

Returns data from a specified EGA register

Calling Registers: AH   F0h
BX   Index for pointer/data chips
BH   0
BL   Index (this register is ignored for single registers)
DX   Port number (refer to table EGA.1)

Return Registers: BL   Data

Comments: Drivers from firms other than Microsoft may not support this function.

Table EGA.1. *EGA Register Values*

Port Number	EGA Register
00h	CRT Controller
08h	Sequencer
10h	Graphics Controller
18h	Attribute Controller
20h	Miscellaneous Output Register
28h	Feature Control Register
30h	Graphics 1 Control Register
38h	Graphics 2 Control Register

Int 10h

Function F1h
Write One Register

Writes data to a specified EGA register

Calling Registers:	AH	F1h
	BL	Index for pointer/data chips or data for single registers
	BH	Data for pointer/data chips (ignored for single registers)
	DX	Port number (refer to table EGA.1)
Return Registers:	BH	Contents modified
	DX	Contents modified

Comments: Drivers from firms other than Microsoft may not support this function. *The function does not check the values used; be sure of your input values before making this function call. Some combinations of register values can cause physical damage to the EGA adapter or monitor.* The contents of the BH and DX registers are not preserved by this function call.

Int 10h

Function F2h
Read Register Range

Returns data from a specified range of EGA registers (several registers on a single chip with consecutive indexes)

Calling Registers:	AH	F2h
	CH	Starting index
	CL	Number of registers (must be greater than 1)
	DX	Port number
		00h, CRT controller
		08h, sequencer
		10h, graphics controller
		18h, attribute controller
	ES:BX	Pointer to a table of one-byte entries whose length is the value in CL
Return Registers:	CX	Contents modified

Comments: Drivers from firms other than Microsoft may not support this function. The contents of the CX register are not preserved by this function call.

Int 10h

Function F3h
Write Register Range

Writes data to a specified range of EGA registers (several registers on a single chip with consecutive indexes)

Calling Registers:

AH	F3h	
CH	Starting index	
CL	Number of registers (must be greater than 1)	
DX	Port number	
	00h, CRT controller	
	08h, sequencer	
	10h, graphics controller	
	18h, attribute controller	
ES:BX	Pointer to a table of one-byte entries whose length is the value in CL	

Return Registers:

BX	Contents modified
CX	Contents modified
DX	Contents modified

Comments: Drivers from firms other than Microsoft may not support this function. *The function does not check the values used; be sure of your input values before making this function call. Some combinations of register values can cause physical damage to the EGA adapter or monitor.* The contents of the BX, CX and DX registers are not preserved by this function call.

Int 10h

Function F4h
Read Register Set

Returns data from a specified set of EGA registers (several registers which may not be on the same chip and, if on the same chip, may not have consecutive indexes)

Calling Registers:

AH	F4h	
CX	Number of registers (must be greated than 1)	
ES:BX	Pointer to a table of records whose format is as follows:	
	Byte 0	Port number (refer to table EGA.1)
	Byte 1	Must be zero
	Byte 2	Index value for pointer registers, 0 for single registers
	Byte 3	Data is written here

Return Registers: CX   Contents modified

Comments: Drivers from firms other than Microsoft may not support this function. The contents of the CX register are not preserved by this function call.

Int 10h

Function F5h
Write Register Set

Writes data to a specified set of EGA registers (several registers which may not be on the same chip and, if on the same chip, may not have consecutive indexes)

Calling Registers: AH   F5h
                        CX   Number of registers (must be greater than 1)
                        ES:BX   Pointer to a table of records whose format is as follows:

Byte 0	Port number (refer to table EGA.1)
Byte 1	Must be zero
Byte 2	Index value for pointer registers, 0 for single registers
Byte 3	Data to be written

Return Registers: CX   Contents modified

Comments: Drivers from firms other than Microsoft may not support this function. *The function does not check the values used; be sure of your input values before making this function call. Some combinations of register values can cause physical damage to the EGA adapter or monitor.* The contents of the CX register are not preserved by this function call.

Int 10h

Function F6h
Revert to Default Registers

Restores the default settings of any registers that were changed through the EGA Register Interface. The default values are those set up by calls to Function F7h.

Calling Registers: AH   F6h

Return Registers: Nothing

Comments: Drivers from firms other than Microsoft may not support this function. If Int 10h, Function 00h is used to set the display mode, the default register values will be the BIOS values for the selected mode.

Int 10h

Function F7h
Define Default Register Table

Defines the default settings of a single register or for all the registers in a pointer/data chip

Calling Registers:	AH	F7h
	CX	VGA color select flag 5448h: Byte offset 14h of the table pointed to by ES:BX is the value for the VGA color select register
	DX	Port number (refer to table EGA.1)
	ES:BX	Pointer to a table of one-byte entries; the table must contain values for all registers in a pointer/data chip
Return Registers:	BX	Contents modified
	DX	Contents modified

Comments: Drivers from firms other than Microsoft may not support this function. *The function does not check the values used; be sure of your input values before making this function call. Some combinations of register values can cause physical damage to the EGA adapter or monitor.* The contents of the BH and DX registers are not preserved by this function call.

Int 10h

Function FAh
Interrogate Driver

Interrogates the mouse driver to determine whether the EGA Register Interface is present

Calling Registers:	AH	FAh
	BX	0
Return Registers:	BX	0 if the EGA Register Interface is not present
	ES:BX	Points to the EGA Register Interface version number. The format is
		Byte 0 Major release number
		Byte 1 Minor release number (in 100ths)

Comments: Drivers from firms other than Microsoft may not support this function.

EMS Functions: Int 67h

PROGRAMMING

Expanded memory (EMS memory, as explained in Chapter 2, "The Structure of a DOS System") allows as much as eight megabytes of RAM to be accessed through a technique called *bank switching*.

In this technique, we define small sections of an extra memory area (the EMS memory) that can be switched into a processor's physical address area. Each section is called a *bank*. Bank switching has been used on computers for years as a way to extend access to high-speed temporary storage. With EMS memory, the 16K banks (referred to as *pages* in the EMS documentation) are switched to appear as normal memory in a defined *page frame*. (See Chapter 2, "The Structure of a DOS System," and Chapter 10, "Program and Memory Management," for more detailed descriptions of the operation of EMS memory.)

A special driver is loaded to allow programs to access EMS memory. You access EMS memory as you would a file. After opening access to EMS memory with Int 67h, Function 43h, you tell the board (with Int 67h, Function 44h) which memory pages to make accessible. While a memory page is accessible, you can read from and write to the page. When you are finished, you use Int 67h, Function 45h to close the handle.

Version 3.0 of the EMS standard (the earlier versions never saw public use) was developed jointly by Lotus, Intel, and Microsoft Corporations (hence LIM memory). Version 3.2 added support for such multitasking operating systems as Windows and DESQview. Later, a new version (4.0) was defined. Under the new version, you can run programs from and store information in expanded memory. This reference section was developed using information applicable to LIM Version 4.0; those functions present in earlier versions are indicated by the "LIM Specification Version" line at the top of each description.

The only drawback to expanded memory is that programmers must keep track of where things are located in expanded memory. A great deal of effort has gone into creating programming languages that hide the way memory works. You do not have to remember, for example, which memory block your variables are stored in. Even in assembly language, if you use labels to refer to the variables, an assembler keeps track of which one you are dealing with.

But with expanded memory, you, the programmer, must remember which expanded memory blocks are currently in the page frame and which blocks contain data. You have to ask to have the correct block moved into the page frame when you want something that is not there. In other words, you are responsible for whether the right piece of memory is in use. Assembly language programmers who use multiple data segments have the same sorts of problems, but high-level language programmers do not.

Int 67h   Function 40h   LIM Spec V3.0
Get Manager Status

Tests whether expanded memory hardware (if installed) is functional

Calling Registers: AH   40h

Return Registers: AH   00h, no error
                                       80h, internal error in EMS software
                                       81h, malfunction in EMS hardware
                                       84h, undefined function

Comments: When you are sure that an expanded memory board is installed, this function will test to see whether it is functional. (Chapter 10 contains some techniques for determining whether a board is installed.)

Int 67h   Function 41h   LIM Spec V3.0
Get Page Frame Segment

Gets the segment address of the page frame used by the EMS

Calling Registers: AH   41h

Return Registers: If successful
                AH   00h
                BX   Segment of page frame

              If unsuccessful
                AH   80h, internal error in EMS software
                         81h, malfunction in EMS hardware
                         84h, undefined function

Comments: After you have determined that a board is installed and functional, you need to determine its location in memory. The board maps four 16K pages (a total of 64K) into an area of memory between 640K (segment A000h) and 1M (segment 10000h). From the memory maps of up to 1M on the PC shown in Chapter 2, you can see that most of this space is taken up by video displays and ROMs, but that substantial amounts of free space are unused in any single system. When the board is installed, you usually select the address of the EMS window with switches on the board. You must be careful to select memory not being used for any other purposes.

    The segment address returned is the base of the first 16K page. All other pages are offset from this location.

Int 67h

Function 42h
Get Page Counts

LIM Spec V3.0

Gets the total number of pages of EMS memory in the system and the number of pages available

Calling Registers: AH   42h

Return Registers: If successful
          AH   00h
          BX   Number of unallocated pages
          DX   Total number of pages in system

    If unsuccessful
          AH   80h, internal error in EMS software
                    81h, malfunction in EMS hardware
                    84h, undefined function

Comments: Use this function to determine whether there is enough memory for your application (or to scale the application to the memory). With a single call, you can tell how much memory there is and how much of it is available. For instance, regardless of the number of pages returned in DX, if BX is equal to 0, all expanded memory has been allocated and none is available for other uses.

Note that this function might return inaccurate results when running under DOS V4.0x because the operating system might take pages from EMS without marking them as allocated to protect them from normal programs, if the /X (EMS) switches are used in any of the CONFIG.SYS commands. If the pages taken happen to be used for disk buffers and contain part of the FAT for your hard disk when some other program uses them, your data will be lost. For this reason, the /X switch of DOS V4 should be avoided.

Int 67h

Function 43h
Get Handle and Allocate Memory

LIM Spec V3.0

Opens an EMS handle for use and allocates a specified number of pages for the process

Calling Registers: AH   43h
          BX   Number of logical pages to allocate

Return Registers: If successful
          AH   00h
          DX   Handle (0001h to 00FEh)

If unsuccessful
>
> | AH | 80h, internal error in EMS software |
> |----|----|
> | | 81h, malfunction in EMS hardware |
> | | 84h, undefined function |
> | | 85h, no more handles available |
> | | 87h, allocation requested more pages than are physically available; no pages allocated |
> | | 88h, specified more logical pages than are currently available; no pages allocated |
> | | 89h, zero pages requested |

Comments: Use this function as a file open for EMS memory. Although it does not perform the same functions as a regular file open call, this function does provide a file-like interface to memory.

The handle returned in this call is used for all accesses to the board. This call associates the handle with a specified number of EMS memory pages that you can control with Function 44h.

More than one EMS handle can be assigned to a single process during operation, but the process must close each handle properly by calling Function 45h. Otherwise, the memory assigned to the handle will simply disappear and be unavailable for reuse until you restart the system.

One handle, 0000h, is reserved for use by the operating system and will never be returned by this function.

Int 67h   Function 44h   LIM Spec V3.0
Map/Unmap Memory

Maps one of the EMS pages assigned to the handle into one of the four physical pages in the calling process's page frame; also can unmap a page, making it inaccessible, by setting its logical page to FFFFh

Calling Registers:

AH	44h
AL	Physical page number (0–3)
BX	Logical page number (zero-based, FFFFh to unmap physical page)
DX	Handle

Return Registers: If successful

AH	00h

If unsuccessful

AH	80h, internal error in EMS software
	81h, malfunction in EMS hardware
	83h, invalid handle

84h, undefined function
8Ah, logical page not assigned to this handle
8Bh, physical page number invalid

Comments: The logical pages are the EMS memory pages assigned to the handle by function call 43h. Logical pages are numbered from 0 to n–1, with *n* being the number of pages requested. The special logical page number FFFFh is used to specify unmapping.

On the EMS board, the pages are not accessible to the program because they are outside the computer's physical address space. This function maps one logical page into the computer's physical address space so that memory instructions can be used to manipulate information in the page area. As many as four physical pages can be mapped from a single board (number 0–3).

Int 67h	**Function 45h**	**LIM Spec V3.0**
	Deallocate Handle and Memory	

Closes the specified handle and returns the memory for use by other processes

Calling Registers: AH 45h
DX EMS handle

Return Registers: If successful
AH 00h

If unsuccessful
AH 80h, internal error in EMS software
81h, malfunction in EMS hardware
83h, invalid handle
84h, undefined function
86h, error in save or restore of mapping context

Comments: The EMS memory equivalent of a file close operation, this simple function is particularly important. Because the EMS memory manager functions as an add-on driver to the operating system, the operating system will not close an open EMS handle for you when your program ends. Before a program terminates, it *must* close all EMS handles allocated to it. If it does not, the memory it has allocated *remains allocated* and cannot be used by any other program. The only way to free up the memory is to reboot the computer.

When the close function is executed, the memory that was assigned to the handle is returned to the pool of available EMS memory. If the function does not complete successfully, the memory has not been returned to the pool—you must keep trying.

Most programs simply close files without checking whether the function was successful. Generally, this does not pose a problem for files (handle files, anyway) because DOS closes the file when the program terminates. But with EMS memory, you must verify the proper exit code and respond with a retry if the function was not successful.

Int 67h   **Function 46h**   **LIM Spec V3.0**
Get EMM Version

Returns the software version number

Calling Registers: AH   46h

Return Registers: If successful
           AH   00h
           AL   EMM version number

              If unsuccessful
           AH   80h, internal error in EMS software
                   81h, malfunction in EMS hardware
                   84h, undefined function

Comments: This function returns (in BCD) the version number of the EMM (expanded memory management) software. The upper four bits of the AL register represent the major version number (the part to the left of the decimal point); the lower four bits represent the minor version number (the part to the right of the decimal). For example, Version 3.2 returns 32h in AL, and 4.0 returns 40h. A program should always be prepared to accept a version number *greater* than that for which it was designed; the EMS specification requires drivers to be upwardly compatible.

Int 67h   **Function 47h**   **LIM Spec V3.0**
Save Page Map

Saves the current state of the EMS hardware map

Calling Registers: AH   47h
                    DX   Handle

Return Registers: If successful
           AH   00h

              If unsuccessful
           AH   80h, internal error in EMS software
                   81h, malfunction in EMS hardware
                   83h, invalid handle

84h, undefined function

8Ch, page-mapping hardware state save area full

8Dh, save of mapping context failed because one is already associated with the specified handle

Comments: If you are writing a resident program (TSR), an interrupt service routine, or a device driver that uses EMS memory, you must save the state of the mapping hardware before doing any EMS operations so that other programs do not interfere with your use of the memory. This function saves the state of the mapping hardware. Int 67h, Function 48h is used to restore the hardware map.

This function saves the map register states for only the 64K page frame defined by Version 3.x of the LIM specification. Applications that use a mappable memory region outside of the LIM-3.x page frame should use Functions 4Eh and 4Fh to save and restore the state of the map registers.

Int 67h **Function 48h** **LIM Spec V3.0**
Restore Page Map

Restores the EMS hardware map associated with the designated file handle

Calling Registers: AH 48h

  DX Handle

Return Registers: If successful

  AH 00h

  If unsuccessful

  AH 80h, internal error in EMS software

  81h, malfunction in EMS hardware

  83h, invalid handle

  84h, undefined function

  8Eh, restore failed, save area has no context for the handle

Comments: If you are writing a resident program (TSR), an interrupt service routine, or a device driver that uses EMS memory, you must restore the state of the mapping hardware upon completion of your program. Failure to do so may cause unpredictable results. While your software executes, for example, an applications program that uses EMS memory may be running and expecting the EMS mapping registers to be unchanged. This function restores the state of the mapping hardware. Int 67h, Function 47h is used to save the state of the hardware map.

This function restores the map register states for only the 64K page frame defined by Version 3.x of the LIM specification. Applications that use a mappable memory region outside of the LIM-3.x page frame should use Functions 4Eh and 4Fh to save and restore the state of the map registers.

Int 67h   Function 49h   LIM Spec V3.0
Reserved

This function is undefined in Version 3.2 and above of the EMS standard

Comments: In previous versions of LIM/EMS, this function was used to retrieve the page-mapping register I/O array from the EMS hardware. This function is now reserved. New software should not use it.

Functions 49h and 4Ah were removed from the specification because they were specific to the hardware on certain Intel EMS boards and could not be guaranteed to work with boards from other firms. Programs that use the new functions added in Version 4 of the LIM specification must not use either of these two functions. Programs that do use these functions will not be compatible with the IBM Micro Channel Architecture, but may work with other hardware.

Int 67h   Function 4Ah   LIM Spec V3.0
Reserved

This function is undefined in Version 3.2 and above of the EMS standard

Comments: In previous versions of LIM/EMS, this function was used to retrieve the logical-to-physical page translation array from the EMS hardware. This function is now reserved. New software should not use it.

Functions 49h and 4Ah were removed from the specification because they were specific to the hardware on certain Intel EMS boards and could not be guaranteed to work with boards from other firms. Programs that use the new functions added in Version 4 of the LIM specification must not use either of these two functions. Programs that do use these functions will not be compatible with the IBM Micro Channel Architecture, but may work with other hardware.

Int 67h   Function 4Bh   LIM Spec V3.0
Get Handle Count

Returns the number of active EMS handles

Calling Registers: AH   4Bh

Return Registers: If successful
          AH   00h
          BX   Number of active EMS handles (0–255)

            If unsuccessful
          AH   80h, internal error in EMS software
                   81h, malfunction in EMS hardware
                   84h, undefined function

DOS
PROGRAMMING

Comments: This function tells you how many handles are in active use at any given time. If BX=0, expanded memory is not being used. BX can range from 0 to 255 (the maximum number of EMS handles).

Your program's interpretation of this number is less clear than it may seem. The number of active handles is not necessarily the same as the number of programs presently using expanded memory. Nothing restricts a program from using more than one EMS handle to access expanded memory. In fact, some programs use more than one handle to simplify bookkeeping for the data they are managing. Perhaps a more reasonable use of this function is to determine the number of handles still available, which is derived by subtracting the value in BX from 255. A program that knows how many EMS handles it needs to function properly can quickly determine whether it will be able to function with the number of handles remaining in EMS.

Int 67h   **Function 4Ch**   **LIM Spec V3.0**
                 Get Pages Owned by Handle

Determines the number of pages associated with a specific handle

| **Calling Registers:** | AH | 4Ch |
| | DX | Handle |

Return Registers:	If successful	
	AH	00h
	BX	Number of logical pages (1–2048)
	If unsuccessful	
	AH	80h, internal error in EMS software
		81h, malfunction in EMS hardware
		83h, invalid handle
		84h, undefined function

Comments: Any single handle can refer to from 1 to 2048 (512 before LIM 4) pages of expanded memory. Because each page represents 16K of memory, a single handle can access from 16K to 32M (8M before LIM 4). This function never returns 0 pages because at least 1 page must be assigned to a handle by the Expanded Memory Manager.

Int 67h   **Function 4Dh**   **LIM Spec V3.0**
                 Get Pages for All Handles

Returns the handles and the number of logical pages for all handles

Calling Registers:	AH	4Dh
	ES:DI	Pointer to array to hold information
		(may need to be 1020 bytes in size)

Return Registers: If successful

AH	00h
BX	Number of active EMS handles (1–255)

If unsuccessful

AH	80h, internal error in EMS software
	81h, malfunction in EMS hardware
	84h, undefined function

Comments: This function returns an array of values that indicate the current handles and the number of pages assigned to each of the handles. The EMS handle table is composed of a variable number of two-word entries, each arranged as follows:

Word	Meaning
0	EMS handle
1	Number of pages

The formula for determining the amount of memory required for the table can be expressed as $4 \times BX$. Because there can be a maximum of 255 handles, 4×255 (or 1020 bytes) is the maximum reasonable allocation for the table. BX will tell you the number of valid table entries. In LIM 4 systems, BX cannot be less than 1 because of the special OS handle always reserved; in earlier versions, if BX is 0, the EMS manager is idle.

Be careful not to place the table (as specified by ES:DI) so that it will cause a segment wrap when the table is transferred to memory. This would result in an error.

Int 67h   Function 4Eh   Subfunction 00h   LIM Spec V3.2
Get Page Map Registers

Gets the EMS page-mapping registers into a local array without using a handle

Calling Registers:

AH	4Eh
AL	00h
ES:DI	Pointer to array to receive information

Return Registers: If successful

AH	00h

If unsuccessful

AH	80h, internal error in EMS software
	81h, malfunction in EMS hardware
	84h, undefined function
	8Fh, subfunction parameter invalid

Comments: This function was added in Version 3.2 of the EMM software to support multitasking systems such as Windows or DESQview. Function 4Eh gives the program direct access to the page-mapping information used internally by the EMS board, information that is extremely hardware-dependent. The array will hold information about the page-mapping registers and additional control information.

   Multitasking systems are the only programs that should use this type of information—they cannot work effectively without it. Single programs cannot use this type of information.

   Be careful not to place the table (as specified by ES:DI) so that it will cause a segment wrap when the table is transferred to memory. This would result in an error.

Int 67h   Function 4Eh   Subfunction 01h   LIM Spec V3.2
Set Page Map Registers

Sets the EMS page-mapping registers from a local array without using a handle

Calling Registers: AH   4Eh
                          AL   01h
                          DS:SI   Pointer to array from which to set information

Return Registers: If successful
                             AH   00h

                         If unsuccessful
                             AH   80h, internal error in EMS software
                                      81h, malfunction in EMS hardware
                                      84h, undefined function
                                      8Fh, subfunction parameter invalid

Comments: This function was added in Version 3.2 of the EMM software to support multitasking systems such as Windows or DESQview. Function 4Eh gives the program direct access to the page-mapping information used internally by the EMS board, information that is extremely hardware-dependent. The array will hold information about the page-mapping registers and additional control information.

Int 67h   Function 4Eh   Subfunction 02h   LIM Spec V3.2
Get and Set Page Map Registers

Simultaneously gets the EMS page-mapping registers from a local array and sets them from another, without using handles

Calling Registers: AH   4Eh
                          AL   02h
                          DS:SI   Pointer to array from which to set information
                          ES:DI   Pointer to array to receive information

Return Registers: If successful
         AH   00h

         If unsuccessful
         AH   80h, internal error in EMS software
                  81h, malfunction in EMS hardware
                  84h, undefined function
                  8Fh, subfunction parameter invalid

Comments: This function was added in Version 3.2 of the EMM software to support multitasking systems such as Windows or DESQview. Function 4Eh gives the program direct access to the page-mapping information used internally by the EMS board, information that is extremely hardware-dependent. The array will hold information about the page-mapping registers and additional control information.

Int 67h   Function 4Eh   Subfunction 03h   LIM Spec V3.2
Get Size for Page Map Array

Gets the size needed for a local array to hold the EMS page-mapping registers

Calling Registers: AH   4Eh
                     AL   03h

Return Registers: If successful
         AH   00h
         AL   Bytes in page-mapping array

         If unsuccessful
         AH   80h, internal error in EMS software
                  81h, malfunction in EMS hardware
                  84h, undefined function
                  8Fh, subfunction parameter invalid

Comments: This function was added in Version 3.2 of the EMM software to support multitasking systems such as Windows or DESQview. Function 4Eh gives the program direct access to the page-mapping information used internally by the EMS board, information that is extremely hardware-dependent. The array will hold information about the page-mapping registers and additional control information.

    Subfunction 03h can be used to get the array size needed, before using either Subfunctions 00h and 01h separately or 02h to swap the registers in one operation.

Int 67h   Function 4Fh   Subfunction 00h   LIM Spec V4.0
Get Partial Page Map

Saves partial mapping context for only specified mappable memory regions; may be much faster than Function 4Eh, which deals with all mappable memory

Calling Registers:

AH	4Fh	
AL	00h	
DS:SI	Point to page list	
ES:DI	Point to destination array	

Return Registers:

If successful

AH	00h

If unsuccessful

AH	80h, internal error in EMS software
	81h, malfunction in EMS hardware
	84h, undefined function
	8Bh, one of the specified segments is not mappable
	8Fh, subfunction parameter invalid
	A3h, partial page-map structure corrupt

Comments: This function is passed two pointers, one to a list of segments to be mapped and the other to an array in which the maps are to be saved. The page list consists of one word that holds the count of the number of pages in the list, followed by that many additional words, each of which contains the number of a page to be mapped.

The destination array must contain at least the number of bytes returned by Subfunction 03h (Get Partial Page Map Size). Its format is not specified by LIM 4 because the only use of this array is to provide input to Subfunction 01h (Set Partial Page Map).

Int 67h   Function 4Fh   Subfunction 01h   LIM Spec V4.0
Set Partial Page Map

Restores partial mapping context saved by Subfunction 00h; may be much faster than Function 4Eh, which deals with all mappable memory

Calling Registers:

AH	4Fh
AL	01h
DS:SI	Point to source array

Return Registers:

If successful

AH	00h

If unsuccessful

AH	80h, internal error in EMS software
	81h, malfunction in EMS hardware
	84h, undefined function
	8Fh, subfunction parameter invalid

Comments: This function is passed from a pointer to an array in which the maps were saved by Subfunction 00h. Its format is not specified by LIM 4 because the only use of this array is to provide input to this subfunction. The subfunction then restores the mapping for each page that was saved in the array.

Int 67h   Function 4Fh   Subfunction 02h   LIM Spec V4.0
Get Partial Page Map Size

Returns the byte count telling how large an array is required to save page maps using Subfunction 00h

Calling Registers:

	AH	4Fh
	AL	02h
	BX	Number of pages in page list

Return Registers: If successful

	AH	00h
	AL	Number of bytes required for array used by Subfunctions 00h and 01h

If unsuccessful

	AH	80h, internal error in EMS software
		81h, malfunction in EMS hardware
		84h, undefined function
		8Bh, specified number of pages is outside the range of physical pages in the system
		8Fh, subfunction parameter invalid

Comments: This function tells the array size required to perform partial page mapping. It should be called before a partial page-mapping function to verify that the array passed to that function is of adequate size.

Int 67h   Function 50h   Subfunction 00h   LIM Spec V4.0
Map/Unmap Multiple Handle Pages
(Physical Page Number Mode)

Maps or unmaps logical pages into physical pages using the physical page number method

Calling Registers:

	AH	50h
	AL	00h
	CX	Number of pages to process
	DX	EMM handle
	DS:SI	Point to logical/physical page correspondence list

Return Registers: If successful
          AH   00h

            If unsuccessful
          AH   80h, internal error in EMS software
                     81h, malfunction in EMS hardware
                     83h, could not find specified EMM handle
                     84h, undefined function
                     8Ah, logical page out of range
                     8Bh, one of the segments is not mappable
                     8Fh, subfunction parameter invalid

Comments: This function, an extension of the LIM 3.2 function that mapped a single page for a handle, can deal with multiple pages at one call. The correspondence list pointed to by DS:SI consists of one word pair for each page to be mapped or unmapped; the first word of each pair is the logical page number to be assigned or FFFFh if the page is to be unmapped, and the second word is the corresponding physical page number. Both values are zero-based.

Int 67h   Function 50h   Subfunction 01h   LIM Spec V4.0
Map/Unmap Multiple Handle Pages
(Segment Address Mode)

Maps or unmaps logical pages into physical pages using the segment address method

Calling Registers: AH   50h
                     AL   01h
                     CX   Number of pages to process
                     DX   EMM handle
                     DS:SI   Point to logical page/segment
                                     address correspondence list

Return Registers: If successful
          AH   00h

            If unsuccessful
          AH   80h, internal error in EMS software
                     81h, malfunction in EMS hardware
                     83h, could not find specified EMM handle
                     84h, undefined function
                     8Ah, logical page out of range
                     8Bh, one of the segments is not mappable
                     8Fh, subfunction parameter invalid

Comments: This function is an alternate for Subfunction 00h, which produces identical results but is sometimes easier to work with. The correspondence list pointed to by DS:SI consists of one word pair for each page to be mapped or unmapped; the first word of each pair is the logical page number to be assigned or FFFFh if the page is to be unmapped, and the second word is the segment address at which that page is to be mapped or unmapped. The logical page values are zero-based, but the segment addresses are those obtained with Function 58h (Get Mappable Physical Address Array Size) and must correspond exactly.

Int 67h   **Function 51h**   **LIM Spec V4.0**
                            Reallocate Pages

Allows an application to increase or decrease the number of logical pages allocated to an EMM handle

Calling Registers: AH   51h
                        BX   Number of logical pages desired
                        DX   EMM handle

Return Registers: If successful
                        AH   00h
                        BX   Number of logical pages allocated

                  If unsuccessful
                        AH   80h, internal error in EMS software
                                 81h, malfunction in EMS hardware
                                 83h, could not find specified EMM handle
                                 84h, undefined function
                                 87h, not enough pages in system
                                 88h, not enough pages available

Comments: This function permits any of four cases: the new page count can be zero, smaller than the original page count, equal to the original count, or greater than the original count. If zero, the handle remains open but all its pages are returned to the available pool. In the other three cases, all allocated pages after the function is completed from a continuous sequence of page numbers based at zero.

    The handle determines what type of logical pages are allocated; if its pages were originally allocated using Function 43h or Function 5Ah, Subfunction 00h, they will be 16K standard pages. If they were originally allocated with Function 5Ah, Subfunction 01h, they will be raw pages and their size will be defined by the EMS software.

Int 67h   **Function 52h**   **Subfunction 00h**   **LIM Spec V4.0**
   Get Handle Attribute

Returns attribute associated with a handle

Calling Registers: AH   52h
                          AL   00h
                          DX   EMM handle

Return Registers: If successful
                             AH   00h
                             AL   Attribute associated with specified EMM handle
                                       0, volatile
                                       1, nonvolatile

                         If unsuccessful
                             AH   80h, internal error in EMS software
                                       81h, malfunction in EMS hardware
                                       83h, could not find specified EMM handle
                                       84h, undefined function
                                       8Fh, subfunction parameter invalid
                                       91h, feature not supported

Comments: This function is an option that probably will not be available in most systems because the hardware prevents memory content from surviving a warm boot operation. If it is not available, the function will return AH=91h.

    If the function is available, Subfunction 00h returns in AL the current attribute associated with the specified handle. Volatile (AL=0) indicates that the handle's content will not survive a warm boot operation, and nonvolatile (AL=1) indicates that it will.

Int 67h   **Function 52h**   **Subfunction 01h**   **LIM Spec V4.0**
   Set Handle Attribute

Sets attribute associated with a handle

Calling Registers: AH   52h
                          AL   01h
                          BL   New attribute for specified EMM handle
                                    0, volatile
                                    1, nonvolatile
                          DX   EMM handle

Return Registers: If successful
                             AH   00h

If unsuccessful
AH   80h, internal error in EMS software
           81h, malfunction in EMS hardware
           83h, could not find specified EMM handle
           84h, undefined function
           8Fh, subfunction parameter invalid
           90h, attribute not 0 or 1
           91h, feature not supported

Comments: This function is an option that probably will not be available in most systems because the hardware prevents memory content from surviving a warm boot operation. If it is not available, the function will return AH=91h.

    If the function is available, Subfunction 01h sets the current attribute associated with the specified handle to the value specified by BL. Volatile (BL=0) indicates that the handle's content will not survive a warm boot operation, and nonvolatile (BL=1) indicates that it will.

Int 67h   Function 52h   Subfunction 02h   LIM Spec V4.0
Get Attribute Capability

Returns system's attribute capability

Calling Registers: AH   52h
                      AL   02h

Return Registers: If successful
                      AH   00h
                      AL   Attribute capability of EMS software
                              and hardware
                            0, only volatile handles supported
                            1, nonvolatile and volatile both supported

If unsuccessful
           AH   80h, internal error in EMS software
                      81h, malfunction in EMS hardware
                      84h, undefined function
                      8Fh, subfunction parameter invalid

Comments: Subfunction 02h returns in AL the attribute capability of the EMS software and hardware. A value of zero indicates that only volatile handles are supported, and a value of one indicates that both volatile and nonvolatile support is provided.

Int 67h   Function 53h   Subfunction 00h   LIM Spec V4.0
Get Handle Name

Gets the 8-character name associated with the specified EMM handle

Calling Registers: AH   53h
                           AL   00h
                           DX   EMM handle
                           ES:DI   Point to 8-byte buffer to accept handle name

Return Registers: If successful
                           AH   00h

                          If unsuccessful
                           AH   80h, internal error in EMS software
                                       81h, malfunction in EMS hardware
                                       83h, could not find specified EMM handle
                                       84h, undefined function
                                       8Fh, subfunction parameter invalid

Comments: This function gets the name associated with the specified handle. The name's length is always eight characters, and each character may be any 8-bit value; it is not restricted to the ASCII character set. The system initializes the name to eight NUL (00h) characters when a handle is allocated or deallocated; by definition, a handle which has that character string associated with it has no name. When a handle is assigned a name, at least one of the eight bytes must be nonzero to distinguish it from the "no name" case.

Int 67h   Function 53h   Subfunction 01h   LIM Spec V4.0
Set Handle Name

Sets 8-character name associated with specified EMM handle

Calling Registers: AH   53h
                           AL   01h
                           DX   EMM handle
                           ES:DI   Point to 8-byte handle name

Return Registers: If successful
                           AH   00h

                          If unsuccessful
                           AH   80h, internal error in EMS software
                                       81h, malfunction in EMS hardware
                                       83h, could not find specified EMM handle

84h, undefined function
8Fh, subfunction parameter invalid
A1h, duplicates existing name

Comments: This function sets the name associated with the specified handle. The name's length is always eight characters, and each character may be any 8-bit value; it is not restricted to the ASCII character set. The system initializes the name to eight NUL (00h) characters when a handle is allocated or deallocated; by definition, a handle which has that character string associated with it has no name. When a handle is assigned a name, at least one of the eight bytes must be nonzero to distinguish it from the "no name" case.

Int 67h   Function 54h   Subfunction 00h   LIM Spec V4.0
Get Handle Directory

Makes local copy of handle directory for all open EMM handles

Calling Registers: AH   54h
                          AL   00h
                          ES:DI   Point to destination array

Return Registers: If successful
                          AH   00h
                          AL   Number of entries in the array (same as
                                  number of open handles)

                          If unsuccessful
                          AH   80h, internal error in EMS software
                                  81h, malfunction in EMS hardware
                                  84h, undefined function
                                  8Fh, subfunction parameter invalid

Comments: Subfunction 00h copies into an array all active handles and the name associated with each (a copy of the EMM handle-to-name directory). Format of each entry in the array is a word containing the EMM handle, followed by eight bytes that contain the name. The array size in bytes is ten times the number of open handles at the time this function is called.

Int 67h   Function 54h   Subfunction 01h   LIM Spec V4.0
Find Named Handle

Given handle name, returns handle value

Calling Registers: AH   54h
                          AL   01h
                          DS:SI   Point to handle name

Return Registers: If successful

AH	00h
DX	EMM handle associated with name

If unsuccessful

AH	80h, internal error in EMS software
	81h, malfunction in EMS hardware
	84h, undefined function
	8Fh, subfunction parameter invalid
	A0h, no handle could be found
	A1h, handle had no name

Comments: Subfunction 01h searches the handle-name directory for the specified name, and if found, returns the associated handle value. At entry to this function, DS:SI points to an 8-byte string that is the name to be searched for.

Int 67h   Function 54h   Subfunction 02h   LIM Spec V4.0
Get Handle Count

Return total number of handles supported by the memory manager system

Calling Registers:

AH	54h
AL	02h

Return Registers: If successful

AH	00h
BX	Number of handles supported

If unsuccessful

AH	80h, internal error in EMS software
	81h, malfunction in EMS hardware
	84h, undefined function
	8Fh, subfunction parameter invalid

Comments: Subfunction 02h returns the maximum number of handles that the system is capable of allocating, including the reserved OS handle 0. This function can be used to determine the maximum array size that may be necessary to support Subfunction 00h (Get Handle Directory).

Int 67h   Function 55h   LIM Spec V4.0
Alter Page Map and Jump

Alters page mapping permanently and transfers control

Calling Registers:	AH	55h
	AL	Physical page/segment selector
		0, physical page numbers used
		1, segment addresses used
	DX	EMM handle
	DS:SI	Point to map/jump structure

Return Registers: If successful

    AH   00h

If unsuccessful

AH	80h, internal error in EMS software
	81h, malfunction in EMS hardware
	83h, could not find specified EMM handle
	84h, undefined function
	8Ah, logical page out of range
	8Bh, physical page out of range
	8Fh, subfunction parameter invalid

Comments: This function permits applications programs to run from EMS memory by altering a page map and then transferring control into the mapped area. It is the equivalent of the assembly language FAR JUMP operation. The memory-mapping context that existed before use of this function is lost.

    At entry to function 55h, DX contains the EMM handle, and DS:SI points to a structure that has the following layout:

Byte Offset	Field Length	Meaning
00h	Double word	Far pointer to address to which control is to transfer
04h	Byte	Number of word pairs in map array
05h	Double word	Far pointer to map array

    The map array is a variable-sized set of word pairs that map logical pages into either physical page numbers or segment addresses, depending on the value passed in AL. Its arrangement is as follows:

Byte Offset	Field Length	Meaning
00h	Word	Number of the logical page to be mapped
04h	Word	Physical page number or segment address, depending on value in AL

    Values in all registers not containing required parameters maintain their values across the jump, as do the flag conditions.

Int 67h   Function 56h   LIM Spec V4.0
Alter Page Map and Call

Alters page mapping temporarily and transfers control; mapping is restored upon return

Calling Registers: AH   56h
                        AL   Physical page/segment selector
                                  0, physical page numbers used
                                  1, segment addresses used
                        DX   EMM handle
                        DS:SI   Point to map/jump structure

Return Registers: If successful
                        AH   00h

                        If unsuccessful
                            AH   80h, internal error in EMS software
                                      81h, malfunction in EMS hardware
                                      83h, could not find specified EMM handle
                                      84h, undefined function
                                      8Ah, logical page out of range
                                      8Bh, physical page out of range
                                      8Fh, subfunction parameter invalid

Comments: This function permits applications programs to run from EMS memory by altering a page map and then transferring control into the mapped area. It is the equivalent of the assembly language FAR CALL operation. The memory mapping context that existed before use of this function is saved; it is restored upon return from the called procedure by means of a normal RETF (RET FAR) operation.

At entry to this function, DX contains the EMM handle, and DS:SI points to a structure that has the following layout:

Byte Offset	Field Length	Meaning
00h	Double word	Far pointer to address to which control is to transfer
04h	Byte	Number of word pairs in new map array
05h	Double word	Far pointer to new map array
09h	Byte	Number of word pairs in old map array
0Ah	Double word	Far pointer to old map array
0Eh	4 words	Reserved; used by EMS software

Each map array is a variable-sized set of word pairs that map logical pages into either physical page numbers or segment addresses, depending on the value passed in AL. The new map array specifies the context to be used during the CALL, and the old map array preserves the original context so that it can be restored. Their arrangement is as follows:

Byte Offset	Field Length	Meaning
00h	Word	Number of the logical page to be mapped
04h	Word	Physical page number or segment address, depending on value in AL

Values in all registers not containing required parameters maintain their values across the jump, as do the flag conditions.

Int 67h   **Function 56h**   **Subfunction 02h**   **LIM Spec V4.0**
Get Stack Space Size

Returns number of bytes of additional stack space required for use of Function 56h

Calling Registers: AH   56h
                           AL   02h

Return Registers: If successful
                           AH   00h
                           BX   Number of bytes of stack space required by Alter Page Map and Call subfunctions

                          If unsuccessful
                           AH   80h, internal error in EMS software
                                  81h, malfunction in EMS hardware
                                  84h, undefined function
                                  8Fh, subfunction parameter invalid

Comments: This function returns in BX the number that must be added to the stack pointer to remove all saved elements from the stack. It should be called before using the Alter Page Map and Call function in order to correct the value of SP upon returning from that function.

Int 67h   **Function 57h**   **Subfunction 00h**   **LIM Spec V4.0**
Move Memory Region

Moves memory region

Calling Registers: AH   57h
                           AL   00h
                           DS:SI Point to parameter block for move

Return Registers: If successful

AH   00h, no problem encountered

92h, overlap, source destroyed

If unsuccessful

AH   80h, internal error in EMS software

81h, malfunction in EMS hardware

83h, could not find specified EMM handle

84h, undefined function

8Ah, logical page out of range

8Fh, subfunction parameter invalid

93h, region too big for handle

94h, conventional and expanded regions
overlap

95h, offset in logical page is outside logical page

96h, length exceeds 1M bytes

98h, source and destination types not defined

A2h, 1M wraparound occurred; no data was
moved

Comments: This function moves the content of one region of memory to another region, overwriting what was originally located at the destination. The move can be any combination of conventional and expanded areas: conventional to conventional, conventional to expanded, expanded to conventional, or expanded to expanded.

It is not necessary to modify page mapping to perform this function; the current context is maintained throughout the operation. Length of the region moved can be from 0 to 1M bytes, but in general it will be some multiple of 16K bytes.

If source and destination handles are identical, the source and destination regions are tested for overlap before the move. If overlap exists, the move is made in such a way that the destination receives an intact copy of the source although the source may be destroyed in the process. A status code indicating that overlap has occurred is returned in such a case.

Operation of this function is controlled by a parameter block pointed to by DS:SI. Layout of this block is as follows:

Byte Offset	Field Length	Meaning
00h	Double word	Number of bytes to be moved
04h	Byte	Source memory type (0=conventional, 1=expanded, others undefined)
05h	Word	Source handle
07h	Word	Source initial offset
09h	Word	Source segment or page; if type is conventional, this is a segment address; if type is expanded, this is a logical page number

Byte Offset	Field Length	Meaning
0Bh	Byte	Destination memory type (0=conventional, 1=expanded, others undefined)
0Ch	Word	Destination handle
0Eh	Word	Destination initial offset
10h	Word	Destination segment or page; if type is conventional, this is a segment address; if type is expanded, this a logical page number

Int 67h   Function 57h   Subfunction 01h   LIM Spec V4.0
Exchange Memory Regions

Exchanges two memory regions

Calling Registers: AH   57h

AL   01h

DS:SI   Point to parameter block for move

Return Registers: If successful

AH   00h No problem encountered

If unsuccessful

AH   80h, internal error in EMS software

81h, malfunction in EMS hardware

83h, could not find specified EMM handle

84h, undefined function

8Ah, logical page out of range

8Fh, subfunction parameter invalid

93h, region too big for handle

94h, conventional and expanded regions overlap

95h, offset in logical page is outside logical page

96h, length exceeds 1M bytes

97h, source and destination overlap

98h, source and destination types not defined

A2h, 1M wraparound occurred; no data was moved

Comments: This function exchanges the content of one region of memory with that of another. They may be any combination of conventional and expanded areas: conventional and conventional, conventional and expanded, expanded and conventional, or expanded and expanded.

It is not necessary to modify page mapping to perform this function; the current context is maintained throughout the operation. Length of the region moved can be from 0 to 1M bytes, but in general it will be some multiple of 16K bytes.

If source and destination handles are identical, the source and destination regions are tested for overlap before the move. If overlap exists, no exchange takes place and an error status is returned.

Operation of this function is controlled by a parameter block pointed to by DS:SI. Layout of this block is as follows:

Byte Offset	Field Length	Meaning
00h	Double word	Number of bytes to be moved
04h	Byte	Source memory type (0=conventional, 1=expanded, others undefined)
05h	Word	Source handle
07h	Word	Source initial offset
09h	Word	Source segment or page; if type is conventional, this is a segment address; if type is expanded, this is a logical page number
0Bh	Byte	Destination memory type (0=conventional, 1=expanded, others undefined)
0Ch	Word	Destination handle
0Eh	Word	Destination initial offset
10h	Word	Destination segment or page; if type is conventional, this is a segment address; if type is expanded, this is a logical page number

Int 67h   Function 58h   Subfunction 00h   LIM Spec V4.0
Get Mappable Physical Address Array

Returns an array containing the segment address and physical page number for each mappable physical page in a system

Calling Registers:	AH	58h
	AL	00h
	ES:DI	Point to destination array
Return Registers:	If successful	
	AH	00h
	CX	Number of entries in array
	If unsuccessful	
	AH	80h, internal error in EMS software
		81h, malfunction in EMS hardware
		84h, undefined function
		8Fh, subfunction parameter invalid

Comments: This function fills a user-supplied array with word pairs that correlate actual segment addresses to physical page numbers. The array is sorted into segment sequence, which does not imply any sequence at all in the physical page numbers. Each word pair in the array has the following structure:

Byte Offset	Field Length	Meaning
00h	Word	Segment address of mappable physical page
02h	Word	Logical page number associated with page

Int 67h   Function 58h   Subfunction 01h   LIM Spec V4.0
Get Mappable Physical Address Array Size

Returns the number of entries that a call to Subfunction 00h will return

Calling Registers: AH   58h
                         AL   01h

Return Registers: If successful
                          AH   00h
                          CX   Number of entries in array

                        If unsuccessful
                          AH   80h, internal error in EMS software
                               81h, malfunction in EMS hardware
                               84h, undefined function
                               8Fh, subfunction parameter invalid

Comments: This function returns in CX the number of entries that a call to Subfunction 00h will return. Multiplying the returned value by 4 will yield the size in bytes required for the array to be supplied to Subfunction 00h.

Int 67h   Function 59h   Subfunction 00h   LIM Spec V4.0
Get Expanded Memory Hardware Information

Returns hardware configuration array

Calling Registers: AH   59h
                         AL   00h
                         ES:DI Point to destination array

Return Registers: If successful
                           AH   00h

                          If unsuccessful
                           AH   80h, internal error in EMS software
                                   81h, malfunction in EMS hardware
                                   84h, undefined function
                                   8Fh, subfunction parameter invalid
                                   A4h, access to function denied by operating
                                        system

Comments: This function fills in a 5-word array with details of the system's hardware configuration. Layout of the destination array, pointed to by ES:DI at entry to the function, is

Byte Offset	Field Length	Meaning
00h	Word	Size of a raw mappable physical page in paragraphs (16 bytes)
02h	Word	Number of alternate mapping register sets available
04h	Word	Number of bytes required to save a mapping context
06h	Word	Number of register sets that can be assigned to DMA channels
08h	Word	0 if DMA register sets behave as described for Function 5Bh; 1 if hardware has only one DMA register set. LIM standard boards have 0 value here.

Int 67h   Function 59h   Subfunction 01h   LIM Spec V4.0
Get Unallocated Raw Page Count

Returns the number of unallocated raw mappable pages and the total number of raw pages

Calling Registers: AH   59h
                          AL   01h

Return Registers: If successful
                           AH   00h
                           BX   Number of raw pages currently available for use
                           DX   Total number of raw pages in EMS

                          If unsuccessful
                           AH   80h, internal error in EMS software
                                   81h, malfunction in EMS hardware

84h, undefined function
8Fh, subfunction parameter invalid

Comments: Some EMS hardware has a page size that is a submultiple of the standard 16K bytes. Such a nonstandard page size is termed a *raw page*. This function returns the counts of raw pages available. For hardware using the standard page size, this function is identical to Function 42h, Get Page Counts.

Int 67h   Function 5Ah   Subfunction 00h   LIM Spec V4.0
Allocate Standard Pages

Returns handle after allocating the requested number of standard pages to process

Calling Registers:

	AH	5Ah
	AL	00h
	BX	Number of pages desired

Return Registers: If successful

	AH	00h
	DX	EMM handle

If unsuccessful

	AH	80h, internal error in EMS software
		81h, malfunction in EMS hardware
		84h, undefined function
		85h, all EMM handles in use
		87h, not enough pages in system
		88h, not enough pages available
		8Fh, subfunction parameter invalid

Comments: This function allocates the requested number of standard (16K) pages for use by the calling process and returns a unique handle that the process uses to refer to the assigned memory. This is analogous to the file open process.

Int 67h   Function 5Ah   Subfunction 01h   LIM Spec V4.0
Allocate Raw Pages

Returns handle after allocating the requested number of raw pages to process

Calling Registers:

	AH	5Ah
	AL	01h
	BX	Number of pages desired

Return Registers: If successful

	AH	00h
	DX	EMM raw handle

If unsuccessful

AH	80h, internal error in EMS software
	81h, malfunction in EMS hardware
	84h, undefined function
	85h, all EMM handles in use
	87h, not enough pages in system
	88h, not enough pages available
	8Fh, subfunction parameter invalid

Comments: This function allocates the requested number of raw (nonstandard) pages for use by the calling process and returns a unique handle that the process uses to refer to the assigned memory. This is analogous to the file open process. Applications should not use this subfunction because the size of a raw page may vary from one make of EMS board to another; by using only standard pages, portability is retained.

Int 67h   Function 5Bh   Subfunction 00h   LIM Spec V4.0
Get Alternate Map Registers

Operating-system-only function to control usage of EMS hardware; gets alternate map register set

Calling Registers: AH 5Bh
              AL 00h

Return Registers: If successful

AH	00h
BL	If nonzero, this is the current alternate map register set number and ES:DI is not affected by this function. If zero, ES:DI is set as described here ES:DI Point to operating-system-supplied context save area that has the state of all map registers for all boards in the system plus any additional data necessary to restore the boards' original state
ES:DI	Point to operating-system-supplied context save area that has the state of all map registers for all boards in the system plus any additional data necessary to restore the boards' original state

If unsuccessful

AH	80h, internal error in EMS software
	81h, malfunction in EMS hardware
	84h, undefined function

8Fh, subfunction parameter invalid
A4h, operating system denied access to this
function

Comments: This function is for use only by the operating system and can be disabled by the operating system at any time by means of Function 5Dh, OS/E Functions. Details of its operation are extremely complex, and implementors should refer to the official LIM 4 specification.

Int 67h   Function 5Bh   Subfunction 01h   LIM Spec V4.0
Set Alternate Map Registers

Operating-system-only function to control usage of EMS hardware; sets alternate map

Calling Registers:	AH	5Bh
	AL	01h
	BL	New alternate map register set number
		0, ES:DI contains pointer to save area that has all required information
		<>0, specifies alternate map register set to activate; function responds by activating it if possible. Content of ES:DI is unaffected and ignored.
	ES:DI	Point to map-register-context restore area originally supplied by Subfunction 00h of this function

Return Registers:	If successful	
	AH	00h
	If unsuccessful	
	AH	80h, internal error in EMS software
		81h, malfunction in EMS hardware
		84h, undefined function
		8Fh, subfunction parameter invalid
		9Ah, requested register set not supported
		9Ch, no alternate register sets are supported and BL was nonzero
		9Dh, requested register set either undefined or unallocated
		A3h, restore array, or pointer to it, is corrupted
		A4h, operating system denied access to this function

DOS
PROGRAMMING

Comments: This function is for use only by the operating system and can be disabled by the operating system at any time by means of Function 5Dh, OS/E Functions. Details of its operation are extremely complex, and implementors should refer to the official LIM 4 specification.

Int 67h   **Function 5Bh**   **Subfunction 02h**   **LIM Spec V4.0**
Get Alternate Map Register Set Size

Operating-system-only function to control usage of EMS hardware; gets alternate map save array size

Calling Registers: AH   5Bh
                          AL   02h

Return Registers: If successful
                         AH   00h
                         DX   Number of bytes that will be transferred to the
                               memory area supplied by the operating
                               system whenever a get, set, or get and set
                               subfunction is requested

                         If unsuccessful
                         AH   80h, internal error in EMS software
                               81h, malfunction in EMS hardware
                               84h, undefined function
                               8Fh, subfunction parameter invalid
                               A4h, operating system denied access to this
                               function

Comments: This function is for use only by the operating system and can be disabled by the operating system at any time by means of Function 5Dh, OS/E Functions. Details of its operation are extremely complex, and implementors should refer to the official LIM 4 specification.

Int 67h   **Function 5Bh**   **Subfunction 03h**   **LIM Spec V4.0**
Allocate Alternate Map Register Set

Operating-system-only function to control usage of EMS hardware; allocates alternate map register set

Calling Registers: AH   5Bh
                          AL   03h

Return Registers: If successful

        AH   00h

        BL   Alternate map register set number; if no set available, will be 0

        If unsuccessful

        AH   80h, internal error in EMS software

                     81h, malfunction in EMS hardware

                     84h, undefined function

                     8Fh, subfunction parameter invalid

                     9Bh, all alternate map register sets already allocated

                     A4h, operating system denied access to this function

Comments: This function is for use only by the operating system and can be disabled by the operating system at any time by means of Function 5Dh, OS/E Functions. Details of its operation are extremely complex, and implementors should refer to the official LIM 4 specification.

Int 67h   Function 5Bh   Subfunction 04h   LIM Spec V4.0
Deallocate Alternate Map Register Set

Operating-system-only function to control usage of EMS hardware; deallocates alternate map register set

Calling Registers: AH   5Bh

        AL   04h

        BL   Number of alternate map registers set to deallocate; cannot be zero

Return Registers: If successful

        AH   00h

        If unsuccessful

        AH   80h, internal error in EMS software

                     81h, malfunction in EMS hardware

                     84h, undefined function

                     8Fh, subfunction parameter invalid

                     9Ch, no alternate register sets are supported

                     9Dh, requested register set either undefined or unallocated

                     A4h, operating system denied access to this function

Comments: This function is for use only by the operating system and can be disabled by the operating system at any time by means of Function 5Dh, OS/E Functions. Details of its operation are extremely complex, and implementors should refer to the official LIM 4 specification.

Int 67h Function 5Bh Subfunction 05h LIM Spec V4.0
Allocate DMA Register Set

Operating-system-only function to control usage of EMS hardware; allocates DMA register set

Calling Registers: AH 5Bh
AL 05h

Return Registers: If successful
AH 00h
BL Number of DMA register set that was allocated. Zero if no set available

If unsuccessful
AH 80h, internal error in EMS software
81h, malfunction in EMS hardware
84h, undefined function
8Fh, subfunction parameter invalid
9Bh, all DMA register sets already allocated
A4h, operating system denied access to this function

Comments: This function is for use only by the operating system and can be disabled by the operating system at any time by means of Function 5Dh, OS/E Functions. Details of its operation are extremely complex, and implementors should refer to the official LIM 4 specification.

Int 67h Function 5Bh Subfunction 06h LIM Spec V4.0
Enable DMA Register Set

Operating-system-only function to control usage of EMS hardware; enables DMA on alternate set

Calling Registers: AH 5Bh
AL 06h
BL DMA register set number to be enabled; if zero, no special action will be taken for DMA on specified channel

DL   DMA channel number to associate with
             specified set

Return Registers: If successful
                AH   00h

                If unsuccessful
                AH   80h, internal error in EMS software
                          81h, malfunction in EMS hardware
                          84h, undefined function
                          8Fh, subfunction parameter invalid
                          9Ah, specified alternate DMA register set is not
                             supported
                          9Ch, no alternate DMA register sets
                             are supported and BL was nonzero
                          9Dh, requested DMA register set either
                             undefined or unallocated
                          9Eh, dedicated DMA channels not supported
                          9Fh, specified DMA channel not supported
                          A4h, operating system denied access to this
                             function

Comments: This function is for use only by the operating system and can be disabled by the operating system at any time by means of Function 5Dh, OS/E Functions. Details of its operation are extremely complex, and implementors should refer to the official LIM 4 specification.

Int 67h   Function 5Bh   Subfunction 07h   LIM Spec V4.0
Disable DMA Register Set

Operating-system-only function to control usage of EMS hardware; disables DMA on alternate set

Calling Registers: AH   5Bh
                AL   07h
                BL   DMA register set number to disable;
                          if zero, no action will be taken

Return Registers: If successful
                AH   00h

                If unsuccessful
                AH   80h, internal error in EMS software
                          81h, malfunction in EMS hardware
                          84h, undefined function

8Fh, subfunction parameter invalid

9Ah, specified alternate DMA register set is
not supported

9Ch, no alternate DMA register sets are
supported and BL was nonzero

9Dh, requested DMA register set either
undefined or unallocated

9Eh, dedicated DMA channels not supported

9Fh, specified DMA channel not supported

A4h, operating system denied access to this
function

Comments: This function is for use only by the operating system and can be disabled by the operating system at any time by means of Function 5Dh, OS/E Functions. Details of its operation are extremely complex, and implementors should refer to the official LIM 4 specification.

Int 67h   **Function 5Bh**   **Subfunction 08h**   **LIM Spec V4.0**
Deallocate DMA Register Set

Operating-system-only function to control usage of EMS hardware; deallocates DMA register set

Calling Registers: AH   5Bh

AL   08h

BL   Number of DMA register set that is to be
deallocated; if zero, no action will be taken

Return Registers: If successful

AH   00h

If unsuccessful

AH   80h, internal error in EMS software

81h, malfunction in EMS hardware

84h, undefined function

8Fh, subfunction parameter invalid

9Ch, no DMA register sets are supported and
BL was nonzero

9Dh, requested DMA register set either
undefined or unallocated

A4h, operating system denied access
to this function

Comments: This function is for use only by the operating system and can be disabled by the operating system at any time by means of Function 5Dh, OS/E Functions. Details of its operation are extremely complex, and implementors should refer to the official LIM 4 specification.

Int 67h	Function 5Ch	LIM Spec V4.0

Prepare Hardware For Warm Boot

Prepares EMS system for warm boot operation

Calling Registers: AH   5Ch

Return Registers: If successful
                        AH   00h

   If unsuccessful
   AH   80h, internal error in EMS software
        81h, malfunction in EMS hardware
        84h, undefined function

Comments: This function prepares the EMS hardware for an impending warm boot operation. In general, the current mapping context, the alternate register set in use, and any other EMS information requiring initialization will be affected. Any application that maps memory below 640K must trap all possible conditions that would result in a warm boot and call this function before performing the boot.

Int 67h	Function 5Dh	Subfunction 00h	LIM Spec V4.0

Enable OS/E Functions

Operating-system-only function that enables access to operating system functions

Calling Registers: AH   5Dh
                        AL   00h
                        BX/CX   32-bit access key (except on first
                                   use of function)

Return Registers: If successful
                        AH   00h
                        BX/CX   32-bit access key (first use of function, only)

If unsuccessful

AH	80h, internal error in EMS software
	81h, malfunction in EMS hardware
	84h, undefined function
	8Fh, subfunction parameter invalid
	A4h, operating system denied access to this function

Comments: This function is for use only by the operating system and can be disabled at any time. Subfunction 00h enables the use of Functions 59h, 5Bh, and 5Dh.

Int 67h   **Function 5Dh**   **Subfunction 01h**   **LIM Spec V4.0**
Disable OS/E Functions

Operating-system-only function that disables access to operating-system functions

Calling Registers:
AH	5Dh
AL	01h
BX/CX	32-bit access key (except on first use of function)

Return Registers: If successful
AH	00h
BX/CX	32-bit access key (first use of function, only)

If unsuccessful
AH	80h, internal error in EMS software
	81h, malfunction in EMS hardware
	84h, undefined function
	8Fh, subfunction parameter invalid
	A4h, operating system denied access to this function

Comments: This function is for use only by the operating system and can be disabled at any time. Subfunction 01h disables the use of Functions 59h, 5Bh, and 5Dh. Access to them may be regained by use of Subfunction 02h.

Int 67h   Function 5Dh   Subfunction 02h   LIM Spec V4.0
OS/E Access Key Code to EMS

Operating-system-only function that controls access to other operating-system functions

Calling Registers: AH   5Dh
                           AL   02h
                           BX/CX   32-bit access key

Return Registers: If successful
                           AH   00h

                         If unsuccessful
                           AH   80h, internal in EMS software
                                          81h, malfunction in EMS hardware
                                          84h, undefined function
                                          8Fh, subfunction parameter invalid
                                          A4h, operating system denied access
                                          to this function

Comments: This function is for use only by the operating system and can be disabled at any time. Subfunction 02h returns the access key code to the EMS and places the system back in its initial state; the OS/E functions then will be enabled (if they had been disabled), and the next call to any of the subfunctions of this function will return a new access key code.

XMS Functions

PROGRAMMING

The XMS functions operate through an installed drive. They provide access to the upper memory blocks (UMBs), which consist of the memory between the standard 640K and 1M, the high memory area (HMA), and extended memory.

Function 000h   XMS Spec   V2.0
Get XMS Version Number

Determines what version of XMS is used and returns information as to whether the HMA exists

Calling Registers: AH   000h

Return Registers: AX   XMS version number
                         BX   XMS driver revision number
                         DX   HMA existence flag
                                     00000h, HMA does not exist
                                     00001h, HMA exists

Comments: The version number returned is a 16-bit BCD value. Thus, a value in AX of 01234h would mean that the driver implements XMS version 12.34. The driver revision number is of value mainly for debugging. The existence of the HMA does not imply its availability.

Function 001h   XMS Spec   V2.0
Request High Memory Area

Assigns the 65520-byte HMA to the caller

Calling Registers: AH   001h
                         DX   Space requested in bytes

Return Registers: AX   Status
                                     00000h, failure
                         BL   Error code
                                     080h, function not implemented
                                     081h, VDISK device detected
                                     090h, HMA does not exist
                                     091h, HMA already in use

092h, number of bytes requested is
less than the /HMAMIN= parameter

Comments: The value placed in DX should be 0FFFFh if the caller is an applications program; otherwise, as in the cases of device drivers or TSRs, the value should reflect the number of bytes needed. Assignment of the HMA is an all-or-nothing proposition, and the XMS driver can be told, through the /HMAMIN= parameter, how large a request must be before the driver can hand over the HMA to the caller.

Function 002h   XMS Spec   V2.0
Release High Memory Area

Releases the HMA

Calling Registers: AH   002h

Return Registers: AX   Status
                                   00000h, failure
                                   00001h, success
          BL   Error code
                                   080h, function not implemented
                                   081h, VDISK device detected
                                   090h, HMA does not exist
                                   093h, HMA was not allocated

Comments: Programs that allocate the HMA must release it before exiting. Code or data stored in it becomes invalid and should not be accessed.

Function 003h   XMS Spec   V2.0
Global Enable A20

Enables the A20 line

Calling Registers: AH   003h

Return Registers: AX   Status
                                   00000h, failure
                                   00001h, success
          BL   Error code
                                   080h, function not implemented
                                   081h, VDISK device detected
                                   082h, A20 error occurred

Comments: This call should be made only by programs with control of the HMA. Before exiting, Function 004h should be called. On many machines, toggling the A20 line is a relatively slow operation.

DOS
PROGRAMMING

Function 004h XMS Spec   V2.0
Global Disable A20

Disables the A20 line

Calling Registers: AH   004h

Return Registers: AX   Status
                                   00000h, failure
                                   00001h, success
                    BL   Error code
                                   080h, function not implemented
                                   081h, VDISK device detected
                                   082h, A20 error occurred
                                   094h, A20 line still enabled

Comments: This call should be made only by programs with control of the HMA. On many machines, toggling the A20 line is a relatively slow operation.

Function 005h XMS Spec   V2.0
Local Enable A20

Enables the A20 line

Calling Registers: AH   005h

Return Registers: AX   Status
                                   00000h, failure
                                   00001h, success
                    BL   Error code
                                   080h, function not implemented
                                   081h, VDISK device detected
                                   082h, A20 error occurred

Comments: This call should be made only by programs that need direct access to extended memory. Before exiting, Function 006h should be called. On many machines, toggling the A20 line is a relatively slow operation.

Function 006h XMS Spec   V2.0
Local Disable A20

Disables the A20 line

Calling Registers: AH   006h

Return Registers: AX Status
         00000h, failure
         00001h, success
      BL Error code
         080h, function not implemented
         081h, VDISK device detected
         082h, A20 error occurred
         094h, A20 line still enabled

Comments: This call should be made only by programs that need direct access to extended memory. On many machines, toggling the A20 line is a relatively slow operation.

Function 007h XMS Spec   V2.0
Query A20

Checks the status of the A20 line

Calling Register: AH 007h

Return Registers: AX Status
         00000h, failure
         00001h, success
      BL Error code
         000h, no error
         080h, function not implemented
         081h, VDISK device detected

Comments: As implemented by the Microsoft HIMEM.SYS driver, this function is performed in a hardware-independent fashion by checking for memory wrap.

Function 008h XMS Spec   V2.0
Query Free Extended Memory

Checks the availability of extended memory

Calling Registers: AH 008h

Return Registers: AX Size of the largest free extended memory block
         in K-bytes
      DX Total amount of free extended memory in
         K-bytes

DOS PROGRAMMING

	BL	Error code
		080h, function not implemented
		081h, VDISK device detected
		0A0h, all extended memory is allocated

Comments: The HMA is not included in the returned values even if it is unassigned.

Function 009h   XMS Spec   V2.0
Allocate Extended Memory Block

Allocates a block of the given size from the pool of free extended memory

Calling Registers:	AH	009h
	DX	Size of memory block in K-bytes
Return Registers:	AX	Status
		00000h, failure
		00001h, success
	DX	Handle of allocated block
	BL	Error code
		080h, function not implemented
		081h, VDISK device detected
		0A0h, all extended memory is allocated
		0A1h, all extended memory handles are
		in use

Comments: The handle returned in DX should be used in all subsequent extended memory calls. If no memory is allocated, the handle returned is null. The memory allocated should be freed with a call to Function 00Ah before exiting.

Function 00Ah   XMS Spec   V2.0
Free Extended Memory Block

Deallocates a block of extended memory

Calling Registers:	AH	00Ah
	DX	Handle of block to be freed
Return Registers:	AX	Status
		00000h, failure
		00001h, success
	BL	Error code
		080h, function not implemented
		081h, VDISK device detected

0A2h, handle is invalid

0ABh, handle is locked

Comments: When a block is freed, its handle and all data stored in it become invalid and should not be accessed.

Function 00Bh XMS Spec   V2.0
Move Extended Memory Block

Transfers a block of data from one memory location to another

Calling Registers:	AH	00Bh
	DS:SI	Pointer to extended memory move structure (see table XMS.1)
Return Registers:	AX	Status
		00000h, failure
		00001h, success
	BL	Error code
		080h, function not implemented
		081h, VDISK device detected
		082h, A20 error occurred
		0A3h, invalid source handle
		0A4h, invalid source offset
		0A5h, invalid destination handle
		0A6h, invalid destination offset
		0A7h, length is invalid
		0A8h, move has invalid overlap
		0A9h, parity error occurred

Comments: Although this function is intended to move blocks of data between conventional DOS memory and extended memory, it also can move blocks of data within conventional DOS memory and within extended memory.

Neither source nor destination handles have to be locked.

The length must be even. Performance is improved if the blocks are word-aligned, or double word-aligned on 80386 and 80486 machines. If the blocks overlap, only a forward move (the source base is less than the destination base) is guaranteed to work correctly.

The caller should not attempt to manipulate the A20 line before calling this function. The state of the A20 line is preserved by this function.

A reasonable number of interrupt windows are guaranteed during long transfers.

Table XMS.1. *Structure of Extended Memory Block Structure*

Offset	Meaning
000h – 003h	32-bit number of bytes to be transferred
004h – 005h	Source block handle
006h – 009h	32-bit source offset
00Ah – 00Bh	Destination block handle
00Ch – 00Fh	32-bit destination offset

Function 00Ch XMS Spec   V2.0
Lock Extended Memory Block

Prevents a memory block from being moved and returns its physical address

Calling Registers: AH   00Ch
                        DX   Handle of block to be locked

Return Registers: AX   Status
                                      00000h, failure
                                      00001h, success
                        DX:BX   32-bit linear address of block
                        BL   Error code
                                      080h, function not implemented
                                      081h, VDISK device detected
                                      0A2h, handle is invalid
                                      0ACh, block's lock count overflowed
                                      0ADh, lock failed

Comments: The pointer returned is valid only while the block is locked. A locked block should be unlocked as soon as possible. A lock count is maintained for extended memory blocks.

Function 00Dh XMS Spec   V2.0
Unlock Extended Memory Block

Unlocks a memory block

Calling Registers: AH   00Dh
                        DX   Handle of block to be unlocked

Return Registers: AX   Status
00000h, failure
00001h, success

BL   Error code
080h, function not implemented
081h, VDISK device detected
0A2h, handle is invalid
0AAh, block is not locked

Comments: Any 32-bit pointers used to access the block are no longer valid after unlocking the memory block.

This function decrements the block's lock count. To unlock a block, you must make the same number of unlock calls as lock calls.

Function 00Eh   XMS Spec   V2.0
Get EMB Handle Information

Gets additional information about an extended memory block

Calling Registers: AH   00Eh
DX   Handle of block

Return Registers: AX   Status
00000h, failure
00001h, success

BH   Block's lock count
BL   Number of free EMB handles in the system if
successful
Error code if unsuccessful
080h, function not implemented
081h, VDISK device detected
0A2h, handle is invalid

Comments: To get the block's base address, use Function 00Ch.

Function 00Fh   XMS Spec   V2.0
Reallocate Extended Memory Block

Changes the size of an extended memory block

Calling Registers: AH   00Fh
BX   New size in K-bytes
DX   Handle of block to be resized

Return Registers:	AX	Status
		00000h, failure
		00001h, success
	BL	Error code
		080h, function not implemented
		081h, VDISK device detected
		0A0h, all extended memory is allocated
		0A1h, all available extended memory handles in use
		0A2h, handle is invalid
		0ABh, block is locked

Comments: If the new size is smaller than the old block's size, all data at the upper end of the old block is lost.

Function 010h XMS Spec   V2.0
Request Upper Memory Block

Allocates an upper memory block

Calling Registers:	AH	010h
	DX	Size of block in paragraphs
Return Registers:	AX	Status
		00000h, failure
		00001h, success
	BX	Segment number of UMB if successful
	BL	Error code
		080h, function not implemented
		0B0h, a smaller UMB is available
		0B1h, no UMBs are available
	DX	Actual size of allocated block in paragraphs if successful; size of largest available UMB in paragraphs if not successful

Comments: Upper memory blocks (UMBs) are below the 1M address boundary, making manipulation of the A20 line unnecessary. UMBs are always paragraph-aligned. To find out the largest available UMB, attempt to allocate one with a size of 0FFFFh.

Function 011h XMS Spec   V2.0
Release Upper Memory Block

Releases an upper memory block

Calling Registers: AH   011h
DX   Segment number of the UMB

Return Registers: AX   Status
00000h, failure
00001h, success
BL   Error code
080h, function not implemented
0B2h, UMB segment number is invalid

Comments: When an upper memory block (UMB) is released, the code or data stored in it becomes invalid and should not be accessed.

If a block is in extended memory, the block handle is a valid handle obtained from a call to Function 009h. If the block is in conventional memory, the block handle is set to zero and the offset is a standard segment:offset pair.

DPMI Functions

PROGRAMMING

As Intel created more and more powerful microprocessors and these microprocessors found their way into DOS systems, the constraints of running with only 1M of memory and 16-bit code became more and more chafing. The marketplace has spawned a number of systems designed to get around these constraints. These systems take advantage of the 80286, 80386, and 80486 architectures to provide access to memory above 1M (EMS and XMS memory managers), multitasking environments (Windows, OS/2, DESQView), and environments called DOS extenders to run protected mode programs.

DOS extenders provide a protected mode with the capability to access 16-bit DOS functions and BIOS functions. They also typically allow access to more than 1M of memory. One popular DOS extender is the DOS protected mode interface (DPMI).

DPMI is a DOS extended specification developed by Borland International, Ergo Computer Inc., Intelligent Graphics Corporation, IBM Corporation, Intel Corporation, Locus, Lotus Development Corporation, Microsoft Corporation, Phar Lap Software, Inc., Phoenix Technologies Ltd., Quarterdeck Office Systems and Rational Systems, Inc. DPMI can be implemented on any CPU supporting 80286 protected mode execution. Full utilization of DPMI, however, requires an 80386 or 80486.

DPMI Version 0.9 is part of the support structure of Windows 3.0. Version 1.0 adds enhancements to better support multitasking.

Under DPMI, a *DPMI client* is created when a real mode program calls the DPMI interface to request the initial switch into protected mode. A DOS environment and the one or more protected mode DPMI clients launched from it are collectively referred to as a *DPMI virtual machine*. A multitasking host can run several DPMI virtual machines concurrently. It is therefore crucial that a DPMI client not assume it owns the resources of the entire machine. DPMI implementations on an 80386 or 80486 may choose to use hardware protection to virtualize I/O and interrupts and to enforce the supervisor/user privilege model; therefore, the DPMI client cannot make any assumptions about its privilege level.

Int 2Fh   **DPMI Version 1.0**
Release Current Virtual Machine's
Time Slice

Allows the operating system to switch control to another client or to take power-conserving measures on laptop and notebook computers

Calling Registers:	AX	1680h

Return Registers:	AL	00h if supported by host
		80h if not supported by host

Comments: This call should be made whenever the program is idle, such as when waiting for keyboard input. As it regains control at intervals, it should continue to make this call as long as it is idle.

Int 2Fh
Get CPU Mode
DPMI Version 0.9

Returns information about the current CPU mode

Calling Registers:	AX	1686h

Return Registers:	AX	00h if in protected mode
		Nonzero if in real mode or virtual 86 mode

Comments: Some environments support programs or libraries that can execute in either real or protected mode (*bimodal code*). This call allows such programs to determine at run time which CPU mode they are running under and to make use of system facilities accordingly. Programs and libraries that execute only in protected mode do not need to call this function.

This call should only be made after determining that a DPMI host is present; otherwise, the results may not be valid.

Int 2Fh
Obtain Real-to-Protected Mode Switch
Entry Point
DPMI Version 0.9

Tests for the presence of a DPMI host and obtains the address of a mode switch routine that can be called to begin execution in protected mode; call can be made only in real mode

Calling Registers:	AX	1687h

Return Registers:	AX	Status
		00, success
		Nonzero, failure

If successful:
	BX	Flags	
		Bit 0	If set, 32-bit programs are supported; otherwise, 32-bit programs are not supported
		Bits 1–15	Unused

CL	Processor type
	02h, 80286
	03h, 80386
	04h, 80486
	05h–FFh, reserved for future Intel processors
DH	DPMI major version as a decimal number (in binary)
DL	DPMI minor version as a decimal number (in binary)
SI	Number of paragraphs required for DPMI host private data (may be 0)
ES:DI	Segment:offset of procedure to call to enter protected mode

Comments: This call is made before entering protected mode for the first time. To enter protected mode, the caller must allocate the private memory required (the size in paragraphs is returned in SI), and a far call must be made to ES:DI with AX containing a flag indicating whether the application is 16 bits (bit 0 is 0) or 32 bits (bit 0 is 1) and with ES containing the real mode segment containing the DPMI private data (if SI was zero, ES is ignored).

If the carry flag is set on return, the mode switch failed, the client is still in real mode, and AX contains either 8011h (descriptor unavailable; could not allocate descriptors for CS, DS, ES, SS, the PSP, and the environment pointer) or 8021h (a 32-bit program was specified, but is not supported).

If the carry flag is clear on return, the switch was successful. CS, DS and SS will be 16-bit selectors with bases of the real mode CS, DS and SS, and 64K limits. ES will be a selector with a base of the program's PSP and a limit of 100h. FS and GS will be null selectors if they exist. The environment pointer in the program's PSP will also be converted into a selector; if the client wants to free the environment space, it must do so before entering protected mode and must clear the word at PSP:2Ch (the environment segment address). The program may free or modify the CS, DS or SS descriptors; the program may change the environment pointer in the PSP after entering protected mode, but should restore it before exiting. The program should not modify or free the PSP or environment descriptors at any time.

Int 2Fh   **DPMI Version 1.0**
                      Get Vendor-Specific API Entry Point

Returns an address that can be called to access host-specific extensions to DPMI

Calling Registers: AX   168Ah

DS:(E)SI Selector:offset of ASCIIZ string
identifying the DPMI host vendor

Return Registers: AL 00h if successful
8Ah if unsuccessful
ES:(E)DI Extended API entry point

Comments: This call can be made only in protected mode. This call supersedes the equivalent function of calling Int 31h, Function 0A00h. DPMI 1.0 clients should use this function. It will work also under Version 0.9, although not documented as such.

Clients must use a far call to the entry point. The string passed is case-sensitive.

Int 31h **Function 0000h** **DPMI Version 0.9**
Allocate LDT Descriptors

Allocates one or more descriptors in the task's local descriptor table (LDT)

Calling Registers: AX 0000h
CX Number of descriptors to allocate

Return Registers: If successful
Carry flag clear
AX Base selector

If unsuccessful
Carry flag set
AX 8011h, descriptor unavailable

Comments: The descriptors allocated are initialized to "data" with the present bit set and a base and limit of zero. The privilege level matches the caller's code segment privilege level.

If multiple selectors were allocated, AX references the first of a contiguous array of descriptors. The selector values for subsequent descriptors in the array can be calculated by adding the value returned by Int 31h Function 0003h.

Int 31h **Function 0001h** **DPMI Version 0.9**
Free LDT Descriptor

Frees an LDT descriptor

Calling Registers: AX 0001h
BX Selector for the descriptor to be freed

Return Registers: If successful
Carry flag clear

If unsuccessful
　　Carry flag set
　　AX　　8022h, invalid selector

Comments: Each descriptor allocated by Int 31h, Function 0000h must be freed individually even if it was allocated as part of a contiguous array of descriptors.

　　Under Version 1.0, any segment registers containing the selector being freed will be zeroed by this function.

Int 31h　　　　　　**Function 0002h**　　　　　　**DPMI Version 0.9**
　　　　　　　　　　　　Segment to Descriptor

Converts a real mode segment address into an LDT descriptor that can be used by a protected mode program to access the same memory

Calling Registers:　　AX　　　　0002h
　　　　　　　　　　　　　BX　　　　Real mode segment address

Return Registers:　　If successful
　　　　　　　　　　　　Carry flag clear
　　　　　　　　　　　　AX　　Selector for real mode segment

　　　　　　　　　　　　If unsuccessful
　　　　　　　　　　　　Carry flag set
　　　　　　　　　　　　AX　　8011h, descriptor unavailable

Comments: This function provides easy access to commonly used real mode segments such as the BIOS data area at segment 0040h and the video memory at segments A000h, B000h, or B800h. The descriptors created by calls to this function cannot be modified or freed. If a client needs to access various real mode addresses using the same selector, a descriptor should be allocated by a call to Int 31h, Function 0000h, and the base address changed by calls to Int 31h, Function 0007h.

　　The descriptor limit is set to 64K. Multiple calls to this function with the same segment address will return the same selector.

Int 31h　　　　　　**Function 0003h**　　　　　　**DPMI Version 0.9**
　　　　　　　　　　　　Get Selector Increment Value

Returns the selector increment value used for accessing successive elements of a contiguous array of descriptors, such as that allocated by a call to Int 31h, Function 0000h or Int 31h, Function 0100h

Calling Registers:　　AX　　　　0003h

Return Registers:　　Carry flag clear
　　　　　　　　　　　　AX　　Selector for increment value

Comments: The value returned is always a power of two.

Int 31h   **Function 0006h**   **DPMI Version 0.9**
                            Get Segment Base Address

Returns the 32-bit linear base address from the LDT descriptor for the specified segment

Calling Registers: AX   0006h
                          BX   Selector

Return Registers: If successful
                          Carry flag clear
                          CX:DX   32-bit linear base address of segment

                          If unsuccessful
                          Carry flag set
                          AX   8022h, invalid selector

Comments: Client programs must use the LSL instruction to query the limit of the descriptor. On 80386 or 80486 machines, this must be the 32-bit form if the segment size is greater than 64K.

Int 31h   **Function 0007h**   **DPMI Version 0.9**
                            Set Segment Base Address

Sets the 32-bit linear base address field in the LDT descriptor for the specified segment

Calling Registers: AX   0007h
                          BX   Selector
                          CS:DX   32-bit linear base address of segment

Return Registers: If successful
                          Carry flag clear

                          If unsuccessful
                          Carry flag set
                          AX   Error code
                                          8022h, invalid selector
                                          8025h, invalid linear address

Comments: DPMI 1.0 automatically reloads any segment register that contains the selector specified in the BX register. DPMI 0.9 hosts may or may not do this.

Int 31h   **Function 0008h**   **DPMI Version 0.9**
                     Set Segment Limit

Sets the limit field in the LDT descriptor for the specified segment

Calling Registers: AX   0008h
                          BX   Selector
                          CX:DX   32-bit segment limit

Return Registers: If successful
                             Carry flag clear

                          If unsuccessful
                             Carry flag set
                             AX   Error code
                                    8021h, invalid value
                                    8022h, invalid selector
                                    8025h, invalid linear address

Comments: The value in CX:DX must be the byte length of the segment minus 1. If the limit is greater than or equal to 1M, it must be page-aligned (that is, the least significant 12 bits must be set).

The DPMI host sets or clears the descriptor's granularity bit as required.

DPMI 1.0 reloads any segment registers loaded with the selector in the BX register.

Int 31h   **Function 0009h**   **DPMI Version 0.9**
                     Set Descriptor Access Rights

Modifies the access rights and type fields in the LDT descriptor for the specified segment

Calling Registers: AX   0009h
                          BX   Selector
                          CL   Access rights type byte
                          CH   80386 extended access rights type byte

Return Registers: If successful
                             Carry flag clear

                          If unsuccessful
                             Carry flag set
                             AX   Error code
                                    8021h, invalid value
                                    8022h, invalid selector
                                    8025h, invalid linear address

Comments: The access rights type byte in the CL register has the following format:

Bit	Meaning
0	0 = not accessed, 1 = accessed
1	Data: 0 = read, 1 = read/write
	Code: must be 1 (readable)
2	Data: 0 = expand-up, 1 = expand-down
	Code: must be 0 (nonconforming)
3	0 = data, 1 = code
4	Must be 1
5–6	Must equal caller's CPL
7	0 = absent, 1 = present

The extended access rights type byte in the CH register has the following format:

Bit	Meaning
0–3	Ignored
4	Can be 0 or 1
5	Must be 0
6	0 = 16-bit, 1 = 32 bit
7	0 = byte granular, 1 = page granular

Client programs should use the LAR instruction to examine the descriptor's access rights.

DPMI 1.0 reloads any segment registers referencing the affected descriptor.

Int 31h   Function 000Ah   DPMI Version 0.9
Create Alias Descriptor

Creates a new LDT descriptor with the same base and limit as the specified descriptor

Calling Registers: AX   000Ah
                        BX   Selector

Return Registers: If successful
                        Carry flag clear
                        AX   Data selector (alias)

                        If unsuccessful
                        Carry flag set
                        AX   Error code
                                      8011h, descriptor unavailable
                                      8022h, invalid selector

PROGRAMMING

Comments: The selector can be a data or code selector. The published DPMI 0.9 specification states that an error is generated if the selector is a data selector; this is untrue.

The descriptor alias returned does not track changes made to the original descriptor. Thus, if the base or limit of the original segment is modified after creating an alias, the segment and its alias no longer map the same memory.

Int 31h	**Function 000Bh**	**DPMI Version 0.9**
	Get Descriptor	

Copies the LDT entry for the specified selector into an 8-byte buffer

Calling Registers:
AX	000Bh	
BX	Selector	
ES:(E)DI	Selector:offset of 8-byte buffer	

Return Registers: If successful
  Carry flag clear
  Buffer pointed to by ES:(E)DI contains descriptor

If unsuccessful
  Carry flag set
  AX   8022h, invalid selector

Comments: 16-bit code should use ES:DI; 32-bit programs should use ES:EDI.

Int 31h	**Function 000Ch**	**DPMI Version 0.9**
	Set Descriptor	

Copies the contents of an 8-byte buffer into the LDT descriptor for the specified selector

Calling Registers:
AX	000Ch	
BX	Selector	
ES:(E)DI	Selector:offset of 8-byte buffer containing descriptor	

Return Registers: If successful
  Carry flag clear

If unsuccessful
  Carry flag set
  AX   Error code
            8021h, invalid value
            8022h, invalid selector
            8025h, invalid linear address

Comments: 32-bit programs must use ES:EDI; 16-bit programs should use ES:DI. DPMI 1.0 reloads segments that contain the specified selector.

Int 31h | **Function 000Dh** | **DPMI Version 0.9**
Allocate Specific LDT Descriptor

Allocates a specific LDT descriptor

Calling Registers: AX   000Dh

                       BX   Selector

Return Registers: If successful
                        Carry flag clear

                  If unsuccessful
                        Carry flag set
                        AX   Error code
                                    8011h, descriptor unavailable
                                    8022h, invalid selector

Comments: The first 16 descriptors (values 04h–7Ch) are reserved for this function. Under DPMI 0.9, another application may have already been loaded and allocated some of these descriptors, making them unavailable. Under DPMI 1.0, every client has its own LDT and has access to all 16 descriptors.

     Resident service providers (protected mode TSRs) should not use this function.

Int 31h | **Function 000Eh** | **DPMI Version 1.0**
Get Multiple Descriptors

Copies one or more LDT entries into a client buffer

Calling Registers: AX   000Eh

                       CX   Number of descriptors to copy

                       ES:(E)DI   Selector:offset of a buffer in the following format:

Offset	Length	Contents
0000h	2	Selector #1 (set by client)
0002h	8	Descriptor #1 (returned by host)
000Ah	2	Selector #2 (set by client)
000Ch	8	Descriptor #2 (returned by host)

.
.
.

Return Registers: If successful
Carry flag clear
Buffer contains copies of the descriptors for the
specified selectors

If unsuccessful
Carry flag set
AX   8022h, invalid selector
CX   Number of descriptors successfully copied

Comments: If an invalid selector or descriptor is detected, all descriptor copies prior to the one that failed are valid.

32-bit programs must use ES:EDI; 16-bit programs should use ES:DI.

Int 31h   Function 000Fh   DPMI Version 1.0
Set Multiple Descriptors

Copies one or more descriptors from a client buffer into the LDT

Calling Registers: AX   000Fh
CX   Number of descriptors to copy
ES:(E)DI Selector:offset of a buffer in the following
format:

Offset	Length	Contents
0000h	2	Selector #1
0002h	8	Descriptor #1
000Ah	2	Selector #2
000Ch	8	Descriptor #2

.
.
.

Return Registers: If successful
Carry flag clear

If unsuccessful
Carry flag set
AX   Error code
8021h, invalid value
8022h, invalid selector
8025h, invalid linear address
CX   Number of descriptors successfully copied

Comments: If an error occurs because of an invalid selector or descriptor, the number of successfully copied descriptors is returned in CX. All descriptors copied up to the one that failed are valid. The remaining descriptors are not updated.

32-bit programs must use ES:EDI; 16-bit programs should use ES:DI.

Any segment register containing a selector specified in the data structure is reloaded.

Int 31h	**Function 0100h**	**DPMI Version 0.9**
	Allocate DOS Memory Block	

Allocates a block of memory from the memory below the 1M boundary

Calling Registers:	AX	0100h
	BX	Number of paragraphs desired

Return Registers: If successful
     Carry flag clear

	AX	Real mode segment base address of allocated block
	DX	Selector for allocated block

     If unsuccessful
     Carry flag set

	AX	Error code
		0007h, memory control blocks damaged
		0008h, insufficient memory
		8011h, descriptor unavailable
	BX	Size of largest block in paragraphs

Comments: If the size of the block is greater than 64K and the client is a 16-bit program, contiguous descriptors are allocated and the base selector is returned. Consecutive selectors can be calculated using the value returned from Int 31h, Function 0003h. The descriptors have limits of 64K, except the last one, which has a limit of block size MOD 64K. The first descriptor has a limit on the size of the entire block if the host is 32 bits; the limit of the first descriptor is 64K if the host is 16 bits, even if it is running on an 80386.

If the client is 32 bits, only one descriptor is allocated.

Client programs must never modify or free any descriptors allocated by this function. The descriptors are deallocated by a call to Int 31h, Function 0101h.

The DOS allocation function (Int 21h, Function 48h) is used to allocate the DOS memory.

Int 31h | **Function 0101h** | **DPMI Version 0.9**
Free DOS Memory Block

Frees a memory block previously allocated by Int 31h, Function 0100h

Calling Registers: AX 0101h
DX Selector of block to be freed

Return Registers: If successful
Carry flag clear

If unsuccessful
Carry flag set
AX Error code
0007h, memory control blocks damaged
0009h, incorrect memory segment specified
8022h, invalid selector

Comments: All descriptors allocated for the memory block are automatically freed and are no longer valid.

Under DPMI 1.0, any segment registers containing a selector being freed are zeroed.

Int 31h | **Function 0102h** | **DPMI Version 0.9**
Resize DOS Memory Block

Changes the size of a memory block previously allocated by Int 31h, Function 0100

Calling Registers: AX 0102h
BX New block size in paragraphs
DX Selector of block to modify

Return Registers: If successful
Carry flag clear

If unsuccessful
Carry flag set
AX Error code
0007h, memory control blocks damaged
0008h, insufficient memory specified
8011h, descriptor unavailable
8022h, invalid selector
BX Maximum possible block size

Comments: A request to increase size may fail if DOS memory is fragmented, if there is insufficient DOS memory, or if the block grows past a 64K boundary and the next descriptor in the LDT is unavailable.

A request to decrease size may free some descriptors and decrease the limit of the new last descriptor.

Under DPMI 1.0, any segment registers containing a selector being modified are reloaded, and any segment register containing a selector being freed will be zeroed.

Client programs should never modify or free any descriptors allocated by this function. Int 31h, Function 0101h deallocates them automatically.

Int 31h   **Function 0200h**   **DPMI Version 0.9**
Get Real Mode Interrupt Vector

Returns the contents of the current virtual machine's real mode interrupt vector

Calling Registers: AX   0200h
                         BL   Interrupt number

Return Registers: Carry flag clear
                        CX:DX   Segment:offset of real mode interrupt handler

Comments: The value returned in CX is a real mode segment address, not a selector. Attempts to place this value into a segment register may cause a general protection fault.

Int 31h   **Function 0201h**   **DPMI Version 0.9**
Set Real Mode Interrupt Vector

Sets the current virtual machine's real mode interrupt vector for the specified interrupt

Calling Registers: AX   0201h
                         BL   Interrupt Number
                         CX:DX   Segment:offset of real mode interrupt handler

Return Registers: Carry flag clear

Comments: The address passed in CX must be a real mode segment address, not a selector. The handler must reside in DOS memory or the client must allocate a real mode callback address.

If the interrupt being hooked is a hardware interrupt, the memory used by the handler must be locked.

Int 31h   Function 0202h   DPMI Version 0.9
Get Processor Exception Handler Vector

Returns the address of the current client's protected mode exception handler for the specified exception number

Calling Registers: AX   0202h

                          BL   Exception number (00h–1Fh)

Return Registers: If successful

                           Carry flag clear

                           CX:(E)DX Selector:offset of exception handler

                      If unsuccessful

                           Carry flag set

                           AX   8021h, invalid value

Comments: This function is supported under DPMI 1.0 for backward compatibility; DPMI 1.0 clients should use Int 31h, Functions 0210h and 0211h. The value in CX is a selector, not a segment address. A 32-bit offset in EDX is returned for 32-bit clients.

Int 31h   Function 0203h   DPMI Version 0.9
Set Processor Exception Handler Vector

Sets the address of a handler for a CPU exception or fault

Calling Registers: AX   0203h

                          BL   Exception number (00h–1Fh)

                          CX:(E)DX   Selector:offset of exception handler

Return Registers: If successful

                           Carry flag clear

                      If unsuccessful

                           Carry flag set

                           AX   Error code

                                        8021h, invalid value

                                        8022h, invalid selector

Comments: The value in CX should be a valid protected mode code selector, not a segment address. 32-bit clients must supply a 32-bit offset in EDX.

     DPMI 1.0 clients should avoid this function, which is provided for backward compatibility, and use Int 31h, Functions 0212h and 0213h instead.

Int 31h　　　Function 0204h　　　DPMI Version 0.9
Get Protected Mode Interrupt Vector

Returns the address of the current protected mode interrupt handler for the specified interrupt

Calling Registers:　AX　　　　02024h
　　　　　　　　　　　BL　　　　Interrupt number

Return Registers:　Carry flag clear
　　　　　　　　　　　CX:(E)DX Selector:offset of interrupt handler

Comments: The value in CX is a valid protected mode selector, not a real mode segment. A 32-bit offset in EDX is returned for 32-bit clients.

Int 31h　　　Function 0205h　　　DPMI Version 0.9
Set Protected Mode Interrupt Vector

Sets the address of a protected mode interrupt handler for the specified interrupt to the specified address

Calling Registers:　AX　　　　0205h
　　　　　　　　　　　BL　　　　Interrupt number
　　　　　　　　　　　CX:(E)DX Selector:offset of interrupt handler

Return Registers:　If successful
　　　　　　　　　　　　Carry flag clear

　　　　　　　　　　　If unsuccessful
　　　　　　　　　　　　Carry flag set
　　　　　　　　　　　　AX　　　8022h, invalid selector

Comments: The value passed in CX must be a valid protected mode selector, not a real mode segment address. 32-bit clients must pass a valid 32-bit offset in EDX.

Int 31h　　　Function 0210h　　　DPMI Version 1.0
Get Extended Processor Exception Handler Vector (Protected Mode)

Returns the address of the client's protected mode handler for the specified protected mode exception

| Calling Registers: | AX | 0210h |
| | BL | Exception number (00h–1Fh) |

Return Registers:	If successful	
	Carry flag clear	
	CX:(E)DX	Selector:offset of exception handler
	If unsuccessful	
	Carry flag set	
	AX	8021h, invalid value

Comments: DPMI 1.0 clients should use this function instead of Int 31h, Function 0202h.

Int 31h   Function 0211h   DPMI Version 1.0
Get Extended Processor Exception Handler Vector (Real Mode)

Returns the address of the client's protected mode handler for the specified real mode exception

| Calling Registers: | AX | 0211h |
| | BL | Exception number (00h–1Fh) |

Return Registers:	If successful	
	Carry flag clear	
	CX:(E)DX	Selector:offset of exception handler
	If unsuccessful	
	Carry flag set	
	AX	8021h, invalid value

Comments: CX:(E)DX is a selector:offset pair, not a segment:offset pair. The address returned is the address of the function that will receive control in protected mode after the real mode handler performs the mode switch into protected mode.

Int 31h   Function 0212h   DPMI Version 1.0
Set Extended Processor Exception Handler Vector (Protected Mode)

Sets the address of the client's protected mode handler for the specified protected mode exception

Calling Registers:	AX	0212h
	BL	Exception number (00h–1Fh)
	CS:(E)DX	Selector:offset of exception handler

Return Registers: If successful
   Carry flag clear

   If unsuccessful
   Carry flag set
   AX   Error code
   8021h, invalid value
   8022h, invalid selector

Comments: DPMI 1.0 clients should use this function instead of Int 31h, Function 0203h.

Int 31h   **Function 0213h**   **DPMI Version 1.0**
Set Extended Processor Exception Handler Vector (Real Mode)

Sets the address of the client's protected mode handler for the specified real mode exception

Calling Registers: AX   0213h
   BL   Exception number (00h–1Fh)
   CS:(E)DX   Selector:offset of exception handler

Return Registers: If successful
   Carry flag clear

   If unsuccessful
   Carry flag set
   AX   Error code
   8021h, invalid value
   8022h, invalid selector

Comments: The address specified is the address of the protected mode handler to which control is passed by the real mode exception handler after performing a mode switch.

Int 31h   **Function 0300h**   **DPMI Version 0.9**
Simulate Real Mode Interrupt

Simulates an interrupt in real mode

Calling Registers: AX   0300h
   BL   Interrupt number
   BH   Flags (all zero)
   CX   Number of words to copy from the protected
      mode stack to the real mode stack

ES:(E)DI   Selector:offset of real mode register
data structure

Return Registers: If successful
Carry flag clear
ES:(E)DI   Selector:offset of modified real mode
register data structure

If unsuccessful
Carry flag set
AX   Error code
8012h, linear memory unavailable
8013h, physical memory unavailable
8014h, backing store unavailable
8021h, invalid value

Comments: This function transfers control to the real mode interrupt handler specified by the real mode interrupt vector. The CS:IP values are ignored. The SS:SP values are used by the real mode handler unless set to zero; in that case, the DPMI host supplies a real mode stack. The flags specified are pushed onto the real mode interrupt handler's IRET frame; the interrupt and trace flags are cleared. The segment register values must be real mode segment addresses, not selectors. 16-bit hosts are not required to pass the high word of 32-bit registers or the FS and GS registers, even if running on an 80386 machine. On return from the interrupt handler, the data structure contains the values returned by the real mode interrupt handler.

The real mode register structure is set up as follows:

Offset	Contents
0000h	(E)DI
0004h	(E)SI
0008h	(E)BP
000Ch	Reserved; should be zero
0010h	(E)BX
0014h	(E)DX
0018h	(E)CX
001Ch	(E)AX
0020h	CPU flags
0022h	ES
0024h	DS
0026h	FS
0028h	GS
002Ah	IP (ignored)
002Ch	CS (ignored)
002Eh	SP
0030h	SS

Int 31h   Function 0301h   DPMI Version 0.9
Call Real Mode Procedure with
Far Return Frame

Simulates a far call to a real mode procedure

Calling Registers:	AX	0301h
	BH	Flags (should be zero)
	CX	Number of words to copy from the protected mode stack to the real mode stack
	ES:(E)DI	Selector:offset of the real mode register data structure

Return Registers: If successful
       Carry flag clear
       ES:(E)DI   Selector:offset of modified real
                        mode register data structure

     If unsuccessful
       Carry flag set
       AX   Error code
                8012h, linear memory unavailable
                8013h, physical memory unavailable
                8014h, backing store unavailable
                8021h, invalid value

Comments: This function transfers control to the real mode procedure specified by the CS:IP values. The SS:SP values are used by the real mode handler unless set to zero; in that case, the DPMI host supplies a real mode stack. The segment register values must be real mode segment addresses, not selectors. 16-bit hosts are not required to pass the high word of 32-bit registers or the FS and GS registers, even if running on an 80386 machine. On return from the procedure, the data structure contains the values returned by the real mode procedure.

     The real mode register structure is set up as follows:

Offset	Contents
0000h	(E)DI
0004h	(E)SI
0008h	(E)BP
000Ch	Reserved; should be zero
0010h	(E)BX
0014h	(E)DX
0018h	(E)CX
001Ch	(E)AX
0020h	CPU flags

Offset	Contents
0022h	ES
0024h	DS
0026h	FS
0028h	GS
002Ah	IP
002Ch	CS
002Eh	SP
0030h	SS

The procedure must return by executing the RETF (far return) instruction.

Int 31h   **Function 0302h**   **DPMI Version 0.9**
Call Real Mode Procedure with
IRET Frame

Simulates a far call with flags pushed on the stack to a real mode procedure

Calling Registers: AX   0302h

BH   Flags (should be zero)

CX   Number of words to copy from the protected mode stack to the real mode stack

ES:(E)DI   Selector:offset of the real mode register data structure

Return Registers: If successful

Carry flag clear

ES:(E)DI   Selector:offset of modified real mode register data structure

If unsuccessful

Carry flag set

AX   Error code

8012h, linear memory unavailable

8013h, physical memory unavailable

8014h, backing store unavailable

8021h, invalid value

Comments: This function transfers control to the real mode procedure specified by the CS:IP values. The SS:SP values are used by the real mode handler unless set to zero; in that case, the DPMI host supplies a real mode stack. The flags value is pushed onto the real mode stack's IRET frame with interrupt and trace flags clear. The segment register values must be real mode segment addresses, not selectors. 16-bit hosts are not required to pass the high word of 32-bit registers or the FS and GS registers, even if running on an 80386 machine. On return from the procedure, the data structure contains the values returned by the real mode procedure.

The real mode register structure is set up as follows:

Offset	Contents
0000h	(E)DI
0004h	(E)SI
0008h	(E)BP
000Ch	Reserved; should be zero
0010h	(E)BX
0014h	(E)DX
0018h	(E)CX
001Ch	(E)AX
0020h	CPU flags
0022h	ES
0024h	DS
0026h	FS
0028h	GS
002Ah	IP
002Ch	CS
002Eh	SP
0030h	SS

The procedure must return by executing the IRET or RETF(2) instruction.

Int 31h   Function 0303h   DPMI Version 0.9
Allocate Real Mode Callback
Address

Returns a unique real mode segment:offset known as a *real mode callback* that will transfer control from real mode to a protected mode procedure

Calling Registers: AX   0303h

DS:(E)SI   Selector:offset of protected mode procedure to call

ES:(E)DI   Selector:offset of 32h-byte buffer for real mode register data structure used when calling callback routine

If successful
  Carry flag clear
  CX:DX Segment:offset of real mode callback

If unsuccessful
  Carry flag set
  AX   8015h, callback unavailable

Comments: DPMI hosts are required to provide a minimum of 16 callback addresses per client. Callback addresses are limited resources, however, and should be freed when no longer necessary.

The data structure contains no valid data until the time of the actual callback.

Int 31h   **Function 0304h**   **DPMI Version 0.9**
Free Real Mode Callback Address

Releases a callback address previously allocated by Int 31h, Function 0303h

Calling Registers: AX   0304h
                         CX:DX   Real mode callback address to be freed

Return Registers: If successful
                         Carry flag clear

                         If unsuccessful
                         Carry flag set
                         AX   8024h, invalid callback address

Comments: Real mode callbacks are a limited system resource. Clients should release callbacks when no longer necessary.

Int 31h   **Function 0305h**   **DPMI Version 0.9**
Get State Save/Restore Addresses

Returns the addresses of two routines used to save the current task's registers

Calling Registers: AX   0305h

Return Registers: Carry flag clear
                         AX   Size of buffer in bytes
                         BX:CX   Real mode address of save/restore function
                         SI:(E)DI   Protected mode address of save/restore function

Comments: The real mode address is the address of a routine, called *from real mode only,* that will save or restore the state of the protected mode registers. The protected mode address is the address of a routine, called *from protected mode only,* that will save or restore the state of the real mode registers.

These routines do not need to be called unless the client is using the raw switch services. Functions 0300h, 0301h, and 0302h do not require these routines.

The routines are called by setting AL to 0 to save the state or to 1 to restore the state, by setting ES:(E)DI to the address of a state save buffer, and by making a FAR CALL to the appropriate routine. The buffer must be at least as large as the value returned in AX. A DPMI host may not require that registers be saved; in that case, this function may return a size of zero. A call to the save/restore routine will still be safe, but will do nothing.

Int 31h Function 0306h DPMI Version 0.9
Get Raw Mode Switch Addresses

Returns the address of routines that can be called to perform low-level mode switching

Calling Registers: 0306h

Return Registers: Carry flag clear
BX:CX   Address of real-to-protected mode switch
          routine
SI:(E)DI Address of protected-to-real mode switch
          routine

Comments: The real-to-protected mode switch routine must be called only from real mode, and the protected-to-real mode switch routine must be called only from protected mode. The mode switch routines are entered by a FAR JUMP with the following parameters:

AX	new DS value
CX	new ES value
DX	new SS value
(E)BX	new (E)SP value
SI	new CS value
(E)DI	new (E)IP value

The values of (E)AX, (E)BX, (E)CX, (E)DX, (E)DI and (E)SI are undefined after the mode switch. (E)BP is preserved across the mode switch. In 80386 and 80486 CPUs, FS and GS are set to zero. If interrupts are disabled when the mode switch is invoked, they are not reenabled by the DPMI host; the client must do this after the mode switch.

If the specified selector values are invalid when switching to protected mode, an exception will occur.

If the register state must be preserved, the functions accessible through Function 0305h must be used.

Int 31h   **Function 0400h**   **DPMI Version 0.9**
                             Get Version

Returns the version number of the DPMI specification supported by the host and additional information about the host's capabilities

Calling Registers: AX   0400h

Return Registers: Carry flag clear
                         AH   DPMI major version (binary)
                         AL   DPMI minor version (binary)
                         BX   Flags
                         Bit 0   0 = 16-bit implementation
                                   1 = 32-bit implementation
                         Bit 1   0 = CPU returned to virtual 86 mode
                                       for reflected interrupts
                                   1 = CPU returned to real mode for
                                       reflected interrupts
                         Bit 2   0 = Virtual memory not supported
                                   1 = Virtual memory supported
                         Bits 3–15 Reserved
                         CL   Processor type
                                   02h, 80286
                                   03h, 80386
                                   04h, 80486
                         DH   Current value of virtual master PIC base
                                       interrupt
                         DL   Current value of virtual slave PIC base interrupt

Comments: Version 0.9 shows AH = 0, AL = 5A (90 decimal); Version 1.0 shows AH = 1, AL = 0.

Int 31h   **Function 0401h**   **DPMI Version 1.0**
                             Get DPMI Capabilities

Returns information about the DPMI host

Calling Registers: AX   0401h

Return Registers: If successful
                         Carry flag clear
                         AX   Capabilities flag
                         Bit 0   0 = Page accessed/dirty not supported
                                   1 = Page accessed/dirty supported

Bit 1	0 = Exception restartability not supported
	1 = Exception restartability supported
Bit 2	0 = Device mapping not supported
	1 = Device mapping supported
Bit 3	0 = Conventional memory mapping not supported
	1 = Conventional memory mapping supported
Bit 4	0 = Demand zero-fill not supported
	1 = Demand zero-fill supported
Bit 5	0 = Write-protect client not supported
	1 = Write-protect client supported
Bit 6	0 = Write-protect host not supported
	1 = Write-protect host supported
CX	0
DX	0
ES:(E)DI	Selector:offset of 128-byte host information buffer

If unsuccessful
Carry flag set

Comments: This function always fails under Version 0.9.

Page accessed/dirty is the capability of the host to maintain page accessed and page dirty bits that can be read with Function 0506h and written with Function 0507h. If the DPMI host does not provide demand-paged virtual memory, this functionality must be supported. Otherwise, it is optional and, if present, gives the client the capability to read from and write to the virtual-page-accessed and page-dirty bits maintained by the host.

Exception restartability is the capability of restarting a faulting instruction inside the host kernel if the client's exception handler corrects the reason for the exception and returns.

Device mapping indicates whether or not Function 0508h is supported.

Conventional memory mapping indicates whether Function 0509h is supported.

Demand zero-fill, if supported, means that all committed pages are initialized to zero when created. If unsupported, the page contents are undefined.

Write-protect client is the capability to protect pages from the client's writes and to generate a page fault.

Write-protect host is the capability to protect pages from the host's writes and to generate page faults.

The host information buffer is defined as follows:

Offset	Length	Contents
0	Byte	Host major version number
1	Byte	Host minor version number
2	126 byte	Null-terminated string identifying the host

The host major and minor version numbers are OEM-specific and are not the DPMI version.

Int 31h   Function 0500h   DPMI Version 0.9
Get Free Memory Information

Returns information about the amount of memory available

Calling Registers: AX   0500h
                                ES:(E)DI   Selector:offset of 48-byte buffer

Return Registers: Carry flag clear

Comments: This function is superseded by Function 050Bh for Version 1.0.
The buffer is defined as follows:

Offset	Length	Contents
00h	Dword	Largest available free block in bytes (largest block of contiguous linear memory that could be allocated if the memory were to be allocated and left unlocked)
04h	Dword	Maximum unlocked page allocation in bytes. This is the value of offset 0 divided by the page size. If unsupported, this is FFFFFFFFh.
08h	Dword	Maximum locked page allocation in pages (the largest block that could be allocated and locked). If unsupported, this is FFFFFFFFh.
0Ch	Dword	Linear address space size in bytes, including linear space already allocated. If unsupported, this is FFFFFFFFh.
10h	Dword	Total number of unlocked pages. These pages can be paged out and can include any free pages. If unsupported, this is FFFFFFFFh.
14h	Dword	Total number of free pages (number of physical pages not currently in use). If unsupported, this is FFFFFFFFh.
18h	Dword	Total number of physical pages. This includes free, locked, and unlocked pages. If unsupported, this is FFFFFFFFh.
1Ch	Dword	Free linear address space in pages. If unsupported, this is FFFFFFFFh.
20h	Dword	Size of paging/file partition in pages. If unsupported, this is FFFFFFFFh.
24h	12 bytes	Reserved; all bytes set to FFh.

The page size can be obtained from Function 0604h.

Int 31h   **Function 0501h**   **DPMI Version 0.9**
Allocate Memory Block

Allocates a block of linear memory

Calling Registers: AX   0501h

                     BX:CX   Size of block in bytes; must be nonzero

Return Registers: If successful

           Carry flag clear

           BX:CX   Linear address of allocated memory block

           SI:DI   Memory block handle

         If unsuccessful

           Carry flag set

           AX   Error code

                     8012h, linear memory unavailable

                     8013h, physical memory unavailable

                     8014h, backing store unavailable

                     8016h, handle unavailable

                     8021h, invalid value

Comments: The block is guaranteed to be at least paragraph-aligned. Pages created are committed; if virtual memory is supported, the pages are unlocked. Unlocked pages can be locked with Function 0600h. No descriptors are allocated; it is the client's responsibility to allocate and initialize descriptors needed to access the block.

Under many DPMI hosts, allocations are page granular; if the request is for n pages plus 1 byte, $n+1$ pages are allocated. Therefore, it is often best to allocate memory in units of granularity. Function 0604h can be called to get the unit of granularity; if it fails, a value of 4K is recommended.

Int 31h   **Function 0502h**   **DPMI Version 0.9**
Free Memory Block

Frees a memory block allocated by a call to Function 0501h or 0504h

Calling Registers: AX   0502h

                     SI:DI   Memory block handle

Return Registers: If successful

           Carry flag clear

> If unsuccessful
>> Carry flag set
>> AX   8023h, invalid handle

Comments: This function correctly frees committed pages, uncommitted pages, and mapped pages. It does not free descriptors mapped to the block. Descriptors should be free before linear memory blocks.

Int 31h   **Function 0503h**   **DPMI Version 0.9**
Resize Memory Block

Changes the size of a block allocated by Function 0501h or 0504h

Calling Registers: AX   0503h
                          BX:CX New size of block, in bytes (must be nonzero)
                          SI:DI   Memory block handle

Return Registers: If successful
                          Carry flag clear
                          BX:CX New linear address of block
                          SI:DI   New memory block handle

                    If unsuccessful
                          Carry flag set
                          AX   Error code
                                    8012h, linear memory unavailable
                                    8013h, physical memory unavailable
                                    8014h, backing store unavailable
                                    8016h, handle unavailable
                                    8021h, invalid value
                                    8023h, invalid handle

Comments: This function invalidates the old handle; the old handle should not be used. When increasing a block size, the pages created are committed. When decreasing the size, unused pages are correctly freed. It is the client's responsibility to update descriptors that map the memory block.

Int 31h   **Function 0504h**   **DPMI Version 1.0**
Allocate Linear Memory Block

Allocates a block of page-aligned linear address space

Calling Registers: AX   0504h
                          EBX   Desired page-aligned linear address or zero if
                                      calling program does not care

ECX	Size of block, in bytes (must be nonzero)
EDX	Flags
Bit 0	0, create uncommitted pages
	1, create committed pages
Bits 1–31	Reserved

Return Registers: If successful

           Carry flag clear

EBX	Linear address of memory block
ESI	Handle of memory block

    If unsuccessful

           Carry flag set

AX	Error code
	8011h, unsupported function
	8012h, linear memory unavailable
	8013h, physical memory unavailable
	8014h, backing store unavailable
	8016h, handle unavailable
	8021h, invalid size
	8025h, linear address not page-aligned

Comments: A 16-bit host will not support this function. A 16-bit client of a 32-bit host, however, can use this function.

    Function 0501h, which also can allocate linear memory, does not guarantee page-alignment, create uncommitted pages, or allocate a block at a specific linear address.

Int 31h   Function 0505h   DPMI Version 1.0
Resize Linear Memory Block

Changes the size of a block of memory previously allocated with Function 0504h

Calling Registers:

AX	0505h
ESI	Memory block handle
ECX	New block size, in bytes (must be nonzero)
EDX	Flags
Bit 0	0, create uncommitted pages
	1, create committed pages
Bit 1	0, do not update segment descriptors
	1, update segment descriptors
Bits 2–31	Reserved

DOS
PROGRAMMING

If bit 1 of EDX is set

ES:EBX Selector:offset of buffer containing an array of selectors, 1 word (16 bits) per selector

EDI   Count of selectors in the array

Return Registers: If successful

Carry flag clear

EBX   New linear address of memory block

ESI   New handle for memory block

If unsuccessful

Carry flag set

AX   Error code

8001h, unsupported function

8012h, linear memory unavailable

8013h, physical memory unavailable

8014h, backing store unavailable

8016h, handle unavailable

8021h, invalid size

8023h, invalid handle

Comments: A 16-bit implementation will not support this function. A 16-bit client of a 32-bit host, however, can use it. On return, the old handle is no longer valid and should not be used.

On failure, the block's size and base address are unchanged.

If the block increases in size, the base address may change. If the size of the block decreases, pages at the end of the block are freed; the base address does not change.

If the block's base address is changed, and if bit 1 of EDX was set, the descriptors of selectors in the update list are modified when the segments fall within the memory block. Expand-up segments fall within the block if the base address is within the block; expand-down segments fall within the block if (base address + limit −1) is within the block. If the block must be moved, no hardware interrupts will be delivered to the client during the move.

Function 0503h, which can be used also to resize linear memory blocks, does not necessarily page-align blocks, create uncommitted pages, or update descriptors.

Int 31h   **Function 0506h**   **DPMI Version 1.0**
                            Get Page Attributes

Returns the attributes of one or more pages of linear memory allocated by Function 0504h

Calling Registers:	AX	0506h
	ESI	Memory block handle
	EBX	Base offset in the page's memory block or in the first page of multiple pages
	ECX	Number of pages
	ES:EDX	Selector:offset of a buffer in which to receive page attributes

Return Registers:	If successful
	Carry flag clear
	Buffer updated
	If unsuccessful
	Carry flag set
	AX Error code
	8001h, unsupported function
	8023h, invalid handle
	8025h, offset is not within specified block

Comments: A 16-bit host will not support this function. A 16-bit client of a 32-bit host, however, can use it.

If EBX is not page-aligned, it will be rounded down to the next lower page boundary.

The page attribute buffer is an array of words, 1 per page, formatted as follows:

Bits 0–2 Page type
> 0 = Uncommitted page
> 1 = Committed page
> 2 = Mapped page

Bit 3
> 0 = Page is read-only
> 1 = Page is read/write

Bits 4–6
> 0 = Page accessed/page dirty bits not available
> 1 = Page has not been accessed, page is not dirty
> 3 = Page has been accessed, page is not dirty
> 5 = Page has not been accessed, page is dirty
> 7 = Page has been accessed, page is dirty

Bits 7–15 Reserved

Int 31h   Function 0507h   DPMI Version 1.0
Set Page Attributes

Sets the attributes of one or more pages in a linear memory block allocated with Function 0504h

Calling Registers:
AX   0507h
ESI   Memory block handle
EBX   Offset in memory block of page(s) whose attributes are to be changed
ECX   Number of pages
ES:EDX   Selector:offset of a buffer containing page attributes

Return Registers:
If successful
    Carry flag clear

If unsuccessful
    Carry flag set
    AX   Error code
         8001h, unsupported function
         8002h, page is in wrong state
         8013h, physical memory unavailable
         8014h, backing store unavailable
         8021h, illegal value in bits 0–2 of one or more page attribute words
         8023h, invalid handle
         8025h, linear address not in memory block

Comments: A 16-bit host will not support this function. A 16-bit client on a 32-bit host, however, can use this function.

An uncommitted page can be created from a committed page or a mapped page. A committed page can be created from an uncommitted page or a mapped page.

The attribute word has the following format:

Bits 0–2 Page type
         0 = Change page type to uncommitted
         1 = Change page type to committed
         2 = Invalid
         3 = Modify attributes without changing page type
         4–7 Invalid
Bit 3
         0 = Make page read-only
         1 = Make page read/write
Bits 4–6
         0 = Do not modify page accessed/page dirty bits
         1 = Mark page as not accessed, not dirty
         3 = Mark page as accessed, not dirty
         5 = Mark page as not accessed, dirty
         7 = Mark page as accessed, dirty
Bits 7–15   Reserved; should be zero

The page accessed/page dirty bits are modified only if the host supports Page Accessed/Dirty.

Int 31h **Function 0508h** **DPMI Version 1.0**
Map Device in Memory Block

Maps the physical address assigned to a device onto the linear addresses of a memory block allocated by Function 0504h

Calling Registers: AX 0508h
ESI Memory block handle
EBX Offset within memory block of page(s) to be mapped (must be page-aligned)
ECX Number of pages to map
EDX Physical address of device (must be page-aligned)

Return Registers: If successful
Carry flag clear

If unsuccessful
Carry flag set
AX Error code
8001h, unsupported function
8003h, invalid device address
8023h, invalid handle
8025h, linear address not in memory block or not page-aligned

Comments: 16-bit hosts will not support this function 16-bit clients running under 32-bit hosts, however, can use it.

This function is optional; applications programs or DOS extenders that require this function are *not* DPMI compliant.

Committed or mapped pages will be uncommitted or unmapped by the host.

Unlike Function 0800h, this function supports mapping a physical device within an existing memory block (which gives 32-bit programs the capability to access the device with near pointers) and can map addresses below 1M, such as display adapter refresh buffers.

Int 31h   Function 0509h   DPMI Version 1.0
Map Conventional Memory in Memory Block

Maps physical addresses below 1M to the linear addresses of a memory block allocated by Function 0504h

Calling Registers: AX   0509h
  ESI   Memory block handle
  EBX   Offset within memory block of page(s) to be
    mapped (must be page-aligned)
  ECX   Number of pages to map
  EDX   Linear address of conventional memory
    (must be page-aligned)

Return Registers: If successful
  Carry flag clear

  If unsuccessful
  Carry flag set
  AX   Error code
    8001h, unsupported function
    8003h, invalid conventional memory address
    8023h, invalid handle
    8025h, linear address not in memory block or
      not page-aligned

Comments: 16-bit hosts will not support this function. 16-bit clients running under 32-bit hosts, however, can use it.

This function is optional; applications programs or DOS extenders that require this function are *not* DPMI compliant.

Committed or mapped pages will be uncommitted or unmapped by the host.

A client may map only conventional memory it already owns, either with a call to Function 0100h or with a call to DOS's Int 21h, Function 48h through the translation services.

Int 31h   Function 050Ah   DPMI Version 1.0
Get Memory Block Size and Base

Returns the size of a memory block that was allocated by Function 0501h or 0504h

Calling Registers: AX   050Ah
  SI:DI   Memory block handle

Return Registers: If successful
Carry flag clear
SI:DI   Size of memory block in bytes
BX:CX   Base address of memory block

If unsuccessful
Carry flag set
AX   8023h, invalid handle

Comments: This function will fail in DPMI Version 0.9.

Int 31h	**Function 050Bh** *Get Memory Information*	**DPMI Version 1.0**

Returns information about available physical and virtual memory

Calling Registers: AX   050Bh
ES:(E)DI   Selector:offset of 128-byte buffer

Return Registers: If successful
Carry flag clear
Buffer updated

If unsuccessful
Carry flag set

Comments: This function will fail in DPMI 0.9.
The buffer is formatted as follows:

Offset	Length	Contents
00h	Dword	Total allocated bytes of physical memory controlled by the host
04h	Dword	Total allocated bytes of virtual memory controlled by the host
08h	Dword	Total available bytes of virtual memory controlled by the host
0Ch	Dword	Total allocated bytes of virtual memory for this virtual machine
10h	Dword	Total available bytes of virtual memory for this virtual machine
14h	Dword	Total allocated bytes of virtual memory for this client
18h	Dword	Total available bytes of virtual memory for this client
1Ch	Dword	Total locked bytes of memory for this client
20h	Dword	Maximum locked bytes of memory for this client
24h	Dword	Highest linear address available to this client
28h	Dword	Size in bytes of largest available free memory block
2Ch	Dword	Size of minimum allocation unit in bytes
30h	Dword	Size of allocation alignment unit in bytes
34h	76 bytes	Reserved

Int 31h   **Function 0600h**   **DPMI Version 0.9**
Lock Linear Region

Locks the specified linear address range

Calling Registers: AX   0600h
BX:CX   Starting linear address
SI:DI   Size of region in bytes

Return Registers: If successful
Carry flag clear

If unsuccessful
Carry flag set
AX   Error code
8013h, physical memory unavailable
8017h, lock count exceeded
8025h, invalid linear address

Comments: If the function returns unsuccessfully, none of the region is locked. If the region overlaps part of a page at either end, the page(s) will be locked. This function may be called more than once; a lock count is maintained.

Int 31h   **Function 0601h**   **DPMI Version 0.9**
Unlock Linear Region

Unlocks a region that was locked by Function 0600h

Calling Registers: AX   0601h
BX:CX   Starting address of region
SI:DI   Size of region

Return Registers: If successful
Carry flag clear

If unsuccessful
Carry flag set
AX   Error code
8002h, page not locked
8025h, invalid address

Comments: If the function returns an error, none of the memory was unlocked. The region is not unlocked until the lock count is zero; i.e., there must be the same number of calls to this function as to Function 0600h.

Int 31h — Function 0602h — DPMI Version 0.9
Mark Real Mode Region as Pageable

Marks a region of memory below 1M as pageable to disk

Calling Registers: AX   0602h
                           BX:CX   Starting address
                           SI:DI   Size of region in bytes

Return Registers: If successful
                               Carry flag clear

                           If unsuccessful
                               Carry flag set
                               AX   Error code
                                           8002h, region already marked pageable
                                           8025h, address is above 1M boundary

Comments: If an error occurs, none of the memory is marked pageable. Unlike the lock state, if the region overlaps a page at either end, the overlapped pages will not be marked pageable and multiple calls to this function have no effect.

On termination, the client program should relock the memory with a call to Function 0603.h DPMI 1.0 hosts will do so automatically on client termination, but DPMI 0.9 won't. Failure to do so could result in fatal page faults when another program executes in the same space.

The client should mark only the space that it owns, meaning the space acquired through calls to Function 0100h or by a direct call to the DOS memory allocation service. In particular, areas owned by DOS or the DPMI host should not be marked as pageable; to do so could result in a fatal page fault.

Int 31h — Function 0603h — DPMI Version 0.9
Relock Real Mode Region

Relocks a memory region previously marked pageable by Function 0602h

Calling Registers: AX   0603h
                           BX:CX   Starting address of memory to relock
                           SI:DI   Size of region in bytes

Return Registers: If successful
                               Carry flag clear

                           If unsuccessful
                               Carry flag set
                               AX   Error code

8002h, region not marked pageable
8013h, physical memory not available
8025h, region is above 1M boundary

Comments: If an error occurs, none of the region is relocked. Pages that overlap either end of the region are not relocked.

Int 31h	**Function 0604h**	**DPMI Version 0.9**
	Get Page Size	

Returns the size of a single memory page in bytes

Calling Registers: AX   0604h

Return Registers: If successful
Carry flag clear
BX:CX Page size in bytes

If unsuccessful
Carry flag set
AX   8001h, unsupported function

Comments: This function returns the basic memory allocation block size.

Int 31h	**Function 0702h**	**DPMI Version 0.9**
	Mark Page as Demand Paging Candidate	

Marks a page or set of pages to be placed at the head of the pageout candidacy list

Calling Registers: AX   0702h
BX:CX   Starting linear address
SI:DI   Size of region in bytes

Return Registers: If successful
Carry flag clear

If unsuccessful
Carry flag set
AX   8025h, range unallocated

Comments: This function does not force the indicated pages out of memory, and may be treated by the host as advisory. Partial pages will not be marked.

This function is useful if a client knows that the contents of the region will not be accessed for a long period of time and that the memory it occupies could be better utilized.

Int 31h	**Function 0703h**	**DPMI Version 0.9**
	Discard Page Contents	

Discards the contents of a specified linear address range so that it will not be paged to disk unnecessarily

Calling Registers: AX   0703h
BX:CX   Starting linear address
SI:DI   Size of region to discard in bytes

Return Registers: If successful
Carry flag clear

If unsuccessful
Carry flag set
AX   8025h, range unallocated

Comments: Partial pages and locked pages will not be discarded. The contents of the discarded pages are not defined.

Int 31h	**Function 0800h**	**DPMI Version 0.9**
	Physical Address Mapping	

Converts a physical address into a linear address

Calling Registers: AX   0800h
BX:CX   Physical address
SI:DI   Size of region in bytes

Return Registers: If successful
Carry flag clear
BX:CX   Linear address

If unsuccessful
Carry flag set
AX   Error code
8003h, address is in DPMI host memory region
8021h, address is below 1M boundary

Comments: This function should be used only by clients that require direct access to a memory mapped device above the 1M boundary.

The client is responsible for allocating and initializing a descriptor to access the region.

Int 31h   Function 0801h   DPMI Version 0.9
Free Physical Address Mapping

Releases a mapping of physical addresses to linear addresses previously obtained with Function 0800h

Calling Registers: AX   0801h

                          BX:CX   Linear address to be released

Return Registers: If successful

                          Carry flag clear

                          If unsuccessful

                          Carry flag set

                          AX   8025h, invalid address

Comments: The client should use this function when finished using the device mapped with Function 0800h.

Int 31h   Function 0900h   DPMI Version 0.9
Get and Disable Virtual Interrupt State

Disables the virtual interrupt flag and returns the previous state of the flag

Calling Registers: AX   0900h

Return Registers: Carry flag clear

                          AL   Previous status

                                        0, virtual interrupts previously disabled

                                        1, virtual interrupts previously enabled

Comments: AH is not modified by this function call; a client can restore the previous state without knowing what it was by simply calling Int 31h again.

      The user can use CLI also to disable interrupts; the DPMI host will probably trap the instruction, however. The client must assume that CLI will execute very slowly.

Int 31h   Function 0901h   DPMI Version 0.9
Get and Enable Virtual Interrupt State

Enables the virtual interrupt flag and returns the previous state of the flag

Calling Registers: AX   0901h

Return Registers: Carry flag clear
                      AL   Previous status
                                  0, virtual interrupts previously disabled
                                  1, virtual interrupts previously enabled

Comments: AH is not modified by this function call; a client can restore the previous state without knowing what it was by simply calling Int 31h again.

      The user can use STI also to disable interrupts; the DPMI host will probably trap the instruction, however. The client must assume that CLI will execute very slowly.

Int 31h   Function 0902h   DPMI Version 0.9
`Get Virtual Interrupt State`

Returns the current state of the virtual interrupt flag

Calling Registers: AX   0902h

Return Registers: Carry flag clear
                      AL   Virtual interrupt state
                                  0, virtual interrupts are disabled
                                  1, virtual interrupts are enabled

Comments: This function should be used instead of the PUSHF instruction, because PUSHF returns the physical interrupt flag instead of the virtualized, per-client, interrupt flag.

Int 31h   Function 0A00h   DPMI Version 0.9
`Get Vendor-Specific API Entry Point`

Returns the address of a routine that can be called to access host-specific extensions to DPMI

Calling Registers: AX   0A00h
                      DS:(E)SI   Selector:offset of null-terminated
                                     string identifying the DPMI host vendor

Return Registers: If successful
                      Carry flag clear
                      ES:(E)DI   Selector:offset of extended API entry point
                      Other registers may be modified as well

If unsuccessful
Carry flag set
AX   8001h, extension not found

Comments: The address returned should be accessed by a far call. Additional requirements are specified by the vendor. The string comparison is case-sensitive. DPMI 1.0 clients should use Int 2Fh, Function 168Ah instead of this function.

Int 31h   **Function 0B00h**   **DPMI Version 0.9**
Set Debug Watchpoint

Sets a debug watchpoint at the specified address

Calling Registers: AX   0B00h
BX:CX   Linear address
DL   Size of watchpoint (1, 2, or 4 bytes)
DH   Type of watchpoint
0, execute
1, write
2, read/write

Return Registers: If successful
Carry flag clear
BX   Watchpoint handle

If unsuccessful
Carry flag set
AX   Error code
8016h, too many watchpoints
8021h, invalid size or type of watchpoint
8025h, linear address not mapped or
    alignment error

Comments: The handle returned is in the range 0–14 under DPMI 1.0; the range is unrestricted under DPMI 0.9.

Int 31h   **Function 0B01h**   **DPMI Version 0.9**
Clear Debug Watchpoint

Clears a watchpoint previously set with Function 0B00h and releases the handle

Calling Registers: AX   0B01h
BX   Watchpoint handle

Return Registers: If successful
          Carry flag clear

          If unsuccessful
          Carry flag set
          AX   8023h, invalid handle

Comments: This function should be called before terminating.

Int 31h   Function 0B02h   DPMI Version 0.9
Get State of Debug Watchpoint

Returns the state of a watchpoint previously set with Function 0B00h

Calling Registers: AX   0B02h
                     BX   Watchpoint handle

Return Registers: If successful
          Carry flag clear
          AX   Status
          Bit 0   0, watchpoint not encountered
                     1, watchpoint encountered
          Bits 1–15 Reserved

          If unsuccessful
          Carry flag set
          AX   8023h, invalid handle

Comments: Use Function 0B03h to clear the watchpoint's status without releasing the watchpoint.

Int 31h   Function 0B03h   DPMI Version 0.9
Reset Debug Watchpoint

Resets the state of the watchpoint so that a subsequent call to Function 0B02h will show no encounter

Calling Registers: AX   0B03h
                     BX   Watchpoint handle

Return Registers: If successful
          Carry flag clear

          If unsuccessful
          Carry flag set
          AX   8023h, invalid handle

Comments: This function should be called after a watchpoint is encountered.

Int 31h	**Function 0C00h**	**DPMI Version 1.0**
	Install Resident Service	
	Provider Callback	

Used by resident service providers to request notification from the host whenever another DPMI client in the same virtual machine is loaded or terminated

Calling Registers: AX   0C00h

ES:(E)DI   Selector:offset of 40-byte buffer,
structured as follows:

Offset	Length	Contents
00h	8 bytes	Descriptor for a 16-bit data segment
08h	8 bytes	Descriptor for a 16-bit code segment
10h	2 bytes	Offset of a 16-bit callback procedure
12h	2 bytes	Reserved
14h	8 bytes	Descriptor for a 32-bit data segment
1Ch	8 bytes	Descriptor for a 32-bit code segment
24h	4 bytes	Offset of a 32-bit callback procedure

Return Registers: If successful
Carry flag clear

If unsuccessful
Carry flag set
AX   Error code
8015h, callback unavailable
8021h, invalid access rights or type
bytes; offset outside segment limits
8025h, descriptor references an
illegal linear address range

Comments: Only a DPMI client that intends to provide resident protected mode services should call this function; the client must subsequently terminate and stay resident using Function 0C01h. DPMI clients that intend to provide only resident real mode services should not use this function.

The buffer is easily initialized by using Function 000Bh to get copies of its code and data descriptors. If only one mode, 16 or 32 bits, is to be provided, the code descriptor for the unsupported mode should be set to zero.

Int 31h	**Function 0C01h**	**DPMI Version 1.0**

Terminate and Stay Resident

Terminates the DPMI client's execution while leaving its protected mode and memory, and possibly some real mode memory, allocated

Calling Registers: AX   0C01h
BL   Return code
DX   Number of paragraphs of DOS memory to
       reserve

Return Registers: None; does not return

Comments: This function should be used only by DPMI clients providing resident services to other DPMI protected mode clients. A client desiring to provide resident services to only real mode programs should use Function 0300h to invoke DOS's Int 21h, Function 31h directly.

The value in DX is the number of DOS memory paragraphs; the DPMI host automatically leaves allocated all protected mode memory. The value in DX must be either 0 or a minimum of 6. If DX is 0, the DOS Int 21h, Function 4Ch function is called instead of Function 31h.

If the client has not called Function 0C00h beforehand, the client will be simply terminated.

Int 31h	**Function 0D00h**	**DPMI Version 1.0**

Allocate Shared Memory

Allocates a block of memory that may be shared by DPMI clients

Calling Registers: AX   0D00h
ES:(E)DI Selector:offset of shared memory
          allocation request structure,
          formatted as follows:

Offset	Length	Contents
00h	4 bytes	Length of memory block (set by client) may be zero
04h	4 bytes	Length actually allocated (set by host)
08h	4 bytes	Handle (set by host)

Offset	Length	Contents
0Ch	4 bytes	Linear address of block (set by host)
10h	6 bytes	32-bit offset:selector of null-terminated ASCII name of block (set by client)
16h	2 bytes	Reserved
18h	4 bytes	Reserved; must be zero

Return Registers: If successful
  Carry flag clear
  Fields at offsets 04h, 08h, and 0Ch updated

If unsuccessful
  Carry flag set
  AX   Error code
      8012h, linear memory unavailable
      8013h, physical memory unavailable
      8014h, backing store unavailable
      8016h, handle unavailable
      8021h, name too long

Comments: 16-bit clients must set the high word of the 32-bit offset to zero. The maximum name length is 128 bytes, including the terminating null.

The linear address provided is guaranteed to be the same for all clients in the same virtual machine using the shared memory block. The client must establish addressability by allocating and initializing a descriptor itself.

No assumptions should be made about handle values; successive allocations of the same block by the same client may return different values.

The first client to allocate a shared memory block determines its size. Other clients may allocate the same block with a different size, but the size allocated will be the same as that reported to the first client.

A size of 0 is legal; the handle returned can be used with the serialization Functions 0D02h and 0D03h. The linear address is undefined, and referencing it may result in a page fault.

The first 16 bytes of the block will be set to zero on the first allocation. Clients can use this as an "area initialized" indicator.

Int 31h   **Function 0D01h**   **DPMI Version 1.0**
           Free Shared Memory

Frees a block of shared memory allocated by Function 0D00h

Calling Registers: AX   0D01h
                        SI:DI   Handle of block

Return Registers: If successful
                     Carry flag clear

                  If unsuccessful
                     Carry flag set
                     AX   8023h, invalid handle

Comments: The handle is invalidated by a successful call.

It is the client's responsibility to free any descriptors used to map the block.

Two counts are maintained by the host: a virtual machine use count, which is the count of successful allocation calls for the block within the virtual machine, and a global use count, which is a count of virtual machines with access to the block. When the virtual machine count is zero, clients in that virtual machine no longer can address the block. When the global use count is zero, the block is destroyed by the host.

Int 31h   **Function 0D02h**   **DPMI Version 1.0**
                       Serialize on Shared Memory

Requests serialization of a shared memory block

Calling Registers: AX   0D02h
                     SI:DI   Handle of block
                     DX   Flags
                     Bit 0   0, suspend client until
                                     serialization available
                               1, return immediately with error if
                                     serialization unavailable
                     Bit 1   0, exclusive serialization request
                               1, shared serialization request
                     Bits 2–15   Reserved; must be zero

Return Registers: If successful
                     Carry flag clear

                  If unsuccessful
                     Carry flag set
                     AX   Error code
                               8004h, host detected deadlock
                               8005h, request canceled by Function 0D03h
                               8017h, lock count exceeded
                               8018h, exclusive serialization owned
                                     by another client

> 8019h, shared serialization owned by
> another client
> 8023h, invalid handle

Comments: Successful serialization equates to ownership and right of access to the block. This system is used by DPMI clients to synchronize inspection and modification of the block.

Exclusive serialization is equivalent to ownership for writing; shared serialization is equivalent to read-only access. A successful request for exclusive serialization will block other requests, both exclusive and shared. A successful request for shared serialization will block requests for exclusive serialization.

Clients that poll a block by setting bit 0 of DX should yield the CPU with calls to Int 2F, Function 1680h when appropriate.

Clients blocked waiting for the block can still service interrupts. A suspended serialization call may return when a client interrupt service routine calls Function 0D03h, freeing serialization. Error code 8005 is returned in this case.

The host is not required to detect deadlock.

Int 31h	**Function 0D03h**	**DPMI Version 1.0**
	Free Serialization on Shared Memory	

Releases a shared memory serialization previously obtained by a successful call to Function 0D02h

Calling Registers:

	AX	0D03h
	SI:DI	Handle
	DX	Flags
	Bit 0	0, release exclusive serialization
		1, release shared serialization
	Bit 1	0, do not free pending serialization
		1, free pending serialization
	Bits 2–15	Reserved; must be zero

Return Registers: If successful
Carry flag clear

If unsuccessful
Carry flag set
AX   Error code
8002h, client does not own the specified type
of serialization
8023h, invalid handle

Comments: This function should be called when the caller has finished using the shared memory.

Int 31h   **Function 0E00h**   **DPMI Version 1.0**
                      Get Coprocessor   Status

Returns status about the existence of a coprocessor, the type of coprocessor, and whether the host supports coprocessor emulation

Calling Registers: AX   0E00h

Return Registers: If successful
                         Carry flag clear
                         AX   Coprocessor status
                         Bit 0   0, numeric coprocessor disabled for
                                        this client
                                     1, numeric coprocessor enabled for
                                        this client
                         Bit 1   0, client is not emulating
                                        coprocessor instructions
                                     1, client is emulating coprocessor instructions
                         Bit 2   0, numeric coprocessor is not present
                                     1, numeric coprocessor is present
                         Bit 3   0, host is not emulating
                                        coprocessor instructions
                                     1, host is emulating coprocessor
                                        instructions
                         Bits 4–7   Coprocessor type
                                     00h, no coprocessor
                                     02h, 80286
                                     03h, 80386
                                     04h, 80486 with numeric coprocessor
                         Bits 8–15   Reserved

                         If unsuccessful (DPMI version 0.9)
                         Carry flag set

Comments: If bit 2 and bits 4–7 are in conflict, ignore bit 2.

Int 31h   **Function 0E01h**   **DPMI Version 1.0**
                      Set Processor   Emulation

Enables or disables the numeric processor for the virtual machine and the reflection of coprocessor exceptions to the client

Calling Registers:	AX	0E01h
	BX	Flags
	Bit 0	0, disable numeric coprocessor for this client
		1, enable numeric coprocessor for this client
	Bit 1	0, client will not supply coprocessor emulation
		1, client will supply coprocessor emulation
	Bits 2–15	Reserved

Return Registers: If successful
        Carry flag clear

   If unsuccessful
      Carry flag set
      AX   8026h, invalid request

Comments: The client should register an exception handler for coprocessor-not-present faults before setting bit 1.

Task Switching

Task switching is a feature introduced with Version 5.0. Provided by DOS 5.0's shell, it allows the user to suspend one program and start another, then resume the suspended program where it left off. It is not a true multitasking system; the suspended program is removed from memory, its image is saved to disk, and the new program is loaded. Thus, the suspended program does no work, and the newly loaded program works alone.

In the environment of task switching, there are two classes of programs: *task switchers*, which manage the task sessions, and *client programs*, which are the user programs that run under the management of a task switcher. Microsoft has documented three classes of functions required for task switching: notification services, service functions, and task switcher services. *Notification services* are provided by the client programs and used by the task switcher to notify the client programs of task switches and session events. *Service functions* are provided by the task switcher for client programs to control switching, to get information about the task switcher, and to get information about other client programs. *Task switcher services* are functions provided by task switchers for other task switchers.

Data Structures

Several data structures are used in task switching. The functions invariably involve pointers to one or more of these structures. This section describes these structures in both C and assembler format.

SWAPIINFO

The SWAPIINFO structure describes the level of support that a client program provides for a particular type of asynchronous API. This structure is provided for the use of network managers operating under a task switcher.

```
SWAPIINFO struc
    aisLength       dw      10
    aisAPI          dw      ?
    aisMajor        dw      ?
    aisMinor        dw      ?
    aisSupport      dw      ?
SWAPIINFO ends
```

```
struct SWAPIINFO
    {
    unsigned int   aisLength;
    unsigned int   aisAPI;
    unsigned int   aisMajor;
    unsigned int   aisMinor;
    unsigned int   aisSupport;
    };
```

aisLength is the length of the structure, in bytes. It should be 10.

aisAPI identifies the interface supported by the client program. Valid values and their meanings follow:

Value	Meaning
0001h	NETBIOS interface
0002h	802.2 interface
0003h	TCP/IP interface
0004h	LAN Manager named pipes interface
0005h	NetWare IPX interface

All other values are reserved.

aisMajor identifies the highest major version of the application for which the client program provides the support described in the aisSupport field.

aisMinor identifies the highest minor version of the application for which the client program provides the support described in the aisSupport field.

aisSupport identifes the level of support provided by the client program for the interface described by the aisAPI, aisMajor, and aisMinor fields. Valid values and their meanings follow:

Value	Meaning
0001h	Minimal support. The client program prevents a session switch after an application has called a function supported by the API, even after the request has been completed.
0002h	API-level support. The client program tracks asynchronous requests, prevents task switches when requests are outstanding, and allows task switches when all requests have been completed.
0003h	Switcher compatibility. The API provider allows switches to occur even when asynchronous requests are outstanding. This may be limited by resource limitations; some requests may fail.
0004h	Seamless compatibility. The API provider always allows session switches to occur.

SWCALLBACKINFO

The SWCALLBACKINFO structure contains information about the client program:

```
SWCALLBACKINFO struc
    scbiNext        dd   ?
    scbiEntryPoint  dd   ?
    scbiReserved    dd   ?
    scbiAPI         dd   ?
SWCALLBACKINFO ends

struct SWCALLBACKINFO
    {
    struct SWCALLBACKINFO far    *scbiNext;
    void far                     *scbiEntryPoint;
    long                          scbiReserved;
    struct SWAPIINFO far         *scbiAPI;
    };
```

scbiNext is a 32-bit pointer (segment:offset) to the next SWCALLBACKINFO structure in the notification chain.

scbiEntryPoint is a 32-bit pointer (segment:offset) to the client's notification function handler. The task switcher uses this address to call the client program's notification functions.

scbiReserved is a reserved area; do not use it.

scbiAPI is a 32-bit pointer (segment:offset) of a zero-terminated list of SWAPIINFO structures that specify the type of support the client program provides for various asynchronous APIs.

SWINSTANCEITEM

The SWINSTANCEITEM structure contains information about a block of instance data. It is uncertain what such a block is; it is free-form enough to contain just about anything:

```
SWINSTANCEITEM struc
    iisPtr    dd   ?
    iisSize   dw   ?
SWINSTANCEITEM ends

struct SWINSTANCEITEM
    {
    void far      *iisPtr;
    unsigned int   iisSize;
    };
```

iisPtr is a 32-bit pointer (segment:offset) of a block of instance data.
iisSize is the size of the block of instance data in bytes.

SWSTARTUPINFO

The SWSTARTUPINFO structure contains information about a client program's instance data:

```
SWSTARTUPINFO struc
     sisVersion          dw   ?
     sisNextDev          dd   ?
     sisVirtDevFile      dd   0
     sisReferenceData    dd   ?
     sisInstanceData     dd   ?
SWSTARTUPINFO ends

struct SWSTARTUPINFO
     {
     int                       sisVersion;
     struct SWSTARTUPINFO far  *sisNextDev;
     long                      sisVirtDevFile;
     long                      sisReferenceData;
     struct SWINSTANCEITEM far *sisInstanceData;
     };
```

sisVersion is not used.

sisNextDev is a 32-bit pointer (segment:offset) to the next SWSTARTUPINFO structure in the notification chain.

sisVirtDevFile is not used.

sisReferenceData is not used.

sisInstaceData is a 32-bit pointer (segment:offset) to a zero-terminated list of SWINSTANCEITEM structures.

SWVERSION

The SWVERSION structure contains information about the task switcher:

```
SWVERSION struc
     svsAPIMajor         dw   ?
     svsAPIMinor         dw   ?
     svsProductMajor     dw   ?
     svsProductMinor     dw   ?
     svsSwitcherID       dw   ?
     svsFlags            dw   ?
     svsName             dd   ?
     svsPrevSwitcher     dd   ?
SWVERSION ends

struct SWVERSION
     {
     unsigned int   svsAPIMajor;
```

```
unsigned int    svsAPIMinor;
unsigned int    svsProductMajor;
unsigned int    svsProductMinor;
unsigned int    svsSwitcherID;
unsigned int    svsFlags;
char far        *svsName;
void far        *svsPrevSwitcher;
};
```

svsAPIMajor is the highest major version of the task-switching protocol supported by the task switcher.

svsAPIMinor is the highest minor version of the task-switching protocol supported by the task switcher.

svsProductMajor is the major version of the task switcher.

svsProductMinor is the minor version of the task switcher.

svsSwitcherID is the switcher identifier. Each switcher has a unique 4-bit identifier; the identifier is the low-order 4 bits of this field.

svsFlags is the task switcher's operation flags. Currently, only bit 0 is defined; the others are reserved and must be zero. If bit 0 is set, the switcher is currently disabled; if bit 0 is zero, the switcher is enabled.

svsName is the 32-bit pointer (segment:offset) to the zero-terminated ASCII string containing the task switcher's name.

svsPrevSwitcher is the 32-bit pointer (segment:offset) to the previously loaded task switcher. This address can be used to call the previously loaded task switcher's service-function handler.

Notification Functions

This section describes the notification functions in a fashion similar to the way interrupt functions are described elsewhere in this book.

The client program's notification function handler address is provided to the task switcher and the program that invokes and controls the task switcher by Interrupt 2F, Function 4B, Subfunction 01 (Build Notification Chain). The task switcher, or the program that controls and invokes it, calls the notification handlers with AX containing the function number, and with other registers in use as well.

Notification Function 0000h — V5
Init Switcher

Notifies client programs that a new task switcher is being initialized

Calling Registers: AX   0000h
                           ES:DI   Service function handler

Return Registers: AX   Status

> 0000h, task switcher can be loaded safely
> Nonzero, task switcher cannot be loaded safely

Comments: Task switchers or their controlling programs or both must call this function when they are initialized. The task switcher's service function handler, if present, must support Service Function 0000h (Get Version). The service function handler can be a NULL pointer, however, especially if the task switcher's control program is calling the notification function.

If any client program responds negatively (that is, sets AX to nonzero on return), the task switcher should disable itself. The task switcher may make Notification Handler 0007 (Switcher Exit) calls to the other client programs. Client programs should ignore this call if it occurs without a preceding Init Switcher call.

Interrupts are enabled before the notification function is called. The client program may call any MS-DOS system function while servicing the notification call. The client program is allowed to modify the AX register, but must preserve the other registers.

Notification Function 0001h   V5
Query Suspend

Notifies the client programs that the task switcher is preparing to perform a session switch

Calling Registers: AX   0001h
                          BX   Current session identifier
                          ES:DI   Service function handler

Return Registers: AX   Status

> 0000, switch is allowed
> 0001, switch is not allowed
> All other values are reserved

Comments: Client programs in global memory can tell by the session identifier which session is about to be suspended when the switch occurs.

By calling Service Function 0001h (Test Memory Region), client programs can tell whether or not specific code or data in memory will be affected by the switch and whether the switch should be allowed.

Before blocking a session switch because of the state of an asynchronous API, the client should call Service Function 0006 (Query API Support) to make sure another client program is not handling the API.

If any client program sends a nonzero response, the task switcher may make a Notification Handler 0002 (Session Active) call to all client programs. Client programs should ignore the Session Active call without a preceding call to Query Suspend or Suspend Session.

Interrupts are enabled before the notification function is called. The client program may call any MS-DOS system function while servicing the notification call. The client program is allowed to modify the AX register, but must preserve the other registers.

Notification Function 0002h   V5
Suspend Session

Notifies client programs that a session switch is about to take place

Calling Registers: AX   0002h
                           BX   Session ID
                           ES:DI   Service function handler

Return Registers: Status
                              0000h, switch is allowed
                              0001h, switch is not allowed
                              All other values are reserved

Comments: If all client programs return 0000h to Notification Function 0001 (Query Suspend), the task switcher disables interrupts and calls Suspend Session. This is the client programs' last chance to prevent the session switch. Client programs must not issue software interrupts or make any calls that might enable interrupts.

If all client programs return 0000h, the task switcher replaces the current interrupt table with a saved copy before enabling interrupts; this is to assure that no local interrupt handlers are called between the time that Suspend Session is called and Active Session is called.

Client programs in global memory can receive interrupts but must not use non-global memory.

Before blocking a session switch because of the state of an asynchronous API, the client should call Service Function 0006 (Query API Support) to make sure another client program is not handling the API.

If any client program sends a nonzero response, the task switcher may make a Notification Handler 0002 (Session Active) call to all client programs. Client programs should ignore the Session Active call without a preceding call to Query Suspend or Suspend Session.

Interrupts are disabled before the notification function is called. The client program may not call any MS-DOS system functions while servicing the notification call. The client program is allowed to modify the AX register, but must preserve the other registers.

Notification Function 0003h   V5
Activate Session

Notifies client programs that a session is about to become active

Calling Registers: AX   0003h
                        BX   Session ID
                        CX   Session status flags
                                Bit 0
                                        1, session is being activated for the first time
                                        0, session was suspended and is now being
                                           resumed
                                All other bits are reserved and must be zero
                        ES:DI   Service function handler

Return Registers: AX   0000h

Comments: If a suspended session is being resumed, local memory has been
reloaded, including the vector table.

    If the session is being activated for the first time, it will be preceded by a Create
Session call.

    Interrupts are disabled before the notification function is called. The client
program may not call any MS-DOS system functions while servicing the notification
call. The client program must clear the AX register and preserve the other registers.

Notification Function 0004h   V5
Session Active

Notifies client programs that a session has become active

Calling Registers: AX   0004h
                        BX   Session ID
                        CX   Session status flags
                                Bit 0
                                        1, session is active for the first time
                                        0, session was suspended and has now
                                           resumed
                                All other bits are reserved and must be zero
                        ES:DI   Service function handler

Return Registers: AX   0000h

Comments: If any client fails a Query Suspend or Suspend Session call, the task
switcher may call all client programs with a Session Active call, whether or not they
had received a Query Suspend or Suspend Session call. Client programs should
ignore the call.

Interrupts are enabled by the task switcher, and the client program may make any MS-DOS system function calls. The client must clear the AX registers, and must preserve the other registers.

Notification Function 0005h   V5
Create Session

Notifies client programs that the task switcher is about to create a new session

Calling Registers: AX   0005h
BX   Session ID for the new session
ES:DI   Service function handler

Return Registers: AX   Status
0000h, new session can be created safely
0001h, new session cannot be created safely
All other values are reserved

Comments: This call is made to allow client programs to block creation of a new session.

If any client program responds with 0001, the task switcher may make a Destroy Session call to all client programs. Client programs that receive a Destroy Session without a preceding Create Session should ignore that call.

Interrupts are enabled by the task switcher, and the client program may make any MS-DOS system function calls. The client must modify the AX register and must preserve the other registers.

Notification Function 0006h   V5
Destroy Session

Notifies client programs that the task switcher is about to destroy a session

Calling Registers: AX   0006h
BX   Session ID for session to be destroyed
ES:DI   Service function handler

Return Registers: AX   0000h

Comments: The task switcher typically makes this call when the program in the current session terminates. It may be made, however, at the behest of the session manager, and may apply to the current session while the program is running or to a suspended session.

This call may be made without a preceding Create Session for the session if another client program has failed a Create Session call. Client programs should take no action in this case.

Interrupts are enabled by the task switcher, and the client program may make any MS-DOS system function calls. The client program must clear the AX register and preserve all other registers.

Notification Function 0007h   V5
Switcher Exit

Notifies client programs that the task switcher is no longer active

Calling Registers: AX   0007h
                        BX   Flags
                                 Bit 0
                                     1, the task switcher is the only one present
                                     0, at least one other task switcher is active
                                 All other bits are reserved and must be zero
                        ES:DI   Service function handler

Return Registers: AX   0000h

Comments: To coexist with the task switcher, global client programs should stop any additional processing they are running.

   This function may be called by the program controlling the task switcher rather than by the task switcher. Thus, the service function pointer may be different from the pointer passed to other notification handle functions, and it may be a NULL pointer.

   Interrupts are enabled, and the client program may make any MS-DOS system function calls. The client program must clear the AX register and preserve all other registers.

Service Functions

This section describes the service functions in a fashion similar to the way interrupt functions are described elsewhere in this book.

   When the task switcher makes notification calls or task switcher service calls, it provides the client program with access to the service function handler. Because these calls may be made by different task switchers or by programs controlling the task switcher, the client program must not assume that the service function handler pointer is reusable. As far as the client program is concerned, that pointer is valid only while it is processing the call from the switcher. The client program calls the service function handlers with AX containing the function number, and with other registers in use as well.

Service Function 0000h   V5
Get Version

Returns the address of the current task switcher's SWVERSION structure

Calling Registers: AX   0000h

Return Registers: Carry flag clear if successful
                              AX   0000h
                              ES:BX   Pointer to SWVERSION structure

Carry flag set if not supported by task switcher

Comments: The task switcher may enable interrupts and call any MS-DOS system functions. It must preserve all registers except the AX, ES, and BX registers.

Service Function 0001h   V5
Test Memory Region

Determines whether a given block of memory is global or local to the current session; local blocks are swapped out when a session switch occurs

Calling Registers: AX   0001h
                              CX   Size of buffer in bytes
                              ES:DI   Address of buffer

Return Registers: Carry flag clear if successful
                              AX   Memory status
                                            0000h, buffer is in global memory
                                            0001h, buffer is in both global and local memory
                                            0002h, buffer is in local memory
                                            All other values are reserved

Carry flag set if function not supported

Comments: A client program should make this call whenever it receives a Query Suspend or a Session Active call to determine whether its memory is deemed global or local by the task switcher. Client programs such as network managers that provide services to other programs should identify those programs as either global or local.

The task switcher must not enable interrupts or make any MS-DOS system function calls while servicing this call. While the task switcher modifies the AX register, it must preserve all other registers.

Service Function 0002h   V5
Suspend Switcher

Notifies the task switcher that it should suspend operations

Calling Registers: AX   0002h
                          ES:DI   Pointer to new task switcher's service function
                                    handler

Return Registers: Carry flag clear if successful
                          AX   Status
                                    0000h, current task switcher has suspended
                                        operations
                                    0001h, current task switcher has not
                                        suspended operations; the new task switcher
                                        must not start
                                    0002h, current task switcher has not
                                        suspended operations, but the new task
                                        switcher may start anyway
                                    All other values are reserved

                          Carry flag set if not supported

Comments: This function should be called only by another task switcher. Client programs should respond negatively to a Query Suspend call in order to stop a task switcher from switching sessions.

   When a task switcher receives this call, it should continue to service functions, but it should not respond to keyboard interrupts or attempt to switch sessions until it receives a Resume Switcher call.

   Suspend Switcher calls may be nested, and normal operations should stay suspended until an equal number of calls to Resume Switcher have been received. An exception to this is when a child program running another task switcher suspends its session manager's task switcher and fails to resume it before returning control to the session manager. In that case, the session manager may safely reactivate its task switcher.

   Interrupts may be enabled by the task switcher and MS-DOS system function calls may be made while servicing this call.

   The new task switcher acquires the previous task switcher's service function handler pointer by a call to Detect Switcher (Interrupt 2Fh, Function 4B02h).

Service Function 0003h   V5
Resume Switcher

Notifies a suspended task switcher that it can resume operations

Calling Registers: AX   0003h
                         ES:DI   Caller's service function handler

Return Registers: Carry flag clear if successful
                         AX   0000h

                         Carry flag set if not supported

Comments: A task switcher that has suspended another task switcher by a Suspend Switcher call should make this call to reactivate the task switcher. The task switcher should use the same service function handle address it used to make the Suspend Switcher call.

    Interrupts may be enabled by the task switcher and MS-DOS system function calls may be made while servicing this call.

Service Function 0004h   V5
Hook Notification Chain

Directs the task switcher to add a SWCALLBACKINFO structure to its notification chain

Calling Registers: AX   0004h
                         ES:DI   Pointer to SWCALLBACKINFO structure

Return Registers: Carry flag clear if successful
                         AX   0000h

                         Carry flag set if not supported

Comments: Client programs can use the Detect Switcher (Interrupt 2Fh, Function 4B02h) call to detect a task switcher and get its service function handler's address. If a task switcher is present, the client program should then call this function. The client program must fill the SWCALLBACKINFO structure before making the call.

    Some task switchers may choose to call Build Notification Chain (Interrupt 2Fh, Function 4B01h) prior to each session switch. In this case, the task switcher may simply return from this call with no action.

    If the task switcher does not make the Build Notification Chain calls, it must modify its notification chain through client programs making this call.

    Before terminating, a client program must unhook itself from the notification chain by calling Unhook Notification Chain (Service Function 0005h).

    Interrupts may be enabled by the task switcher and MS-DOS system function calls may be made while servicing this call.

Service Function 0005h   V5
Unhook Notification Chain

Directs the task switcher to remove a SWCALLBACKINFO structure from its notification chain

Calling Registers: AX   0005h

ES:DI   Pointer to SWCALLBACKINFO structure

Return Registers: Carry flag clear if successful

AX   0000h

Carry flag set if not supported

Comments: The client program must make this call before terminating, whether its notification handler is added to the list by a Hook Notification Chain or a Build Notification Chain call.

A task switcher that rebuilds its notification chain by calling Build Notification Chain before each session switch may return from this call with no action.

Interrupts may be enabled by the task switcher and MS-DOS system function calls may be made while servicing this call.

Service Function 0006h   V5
Query API Support

Returns the address of the SWAPIINFO structure of the client program that provides the highest level of support for the specified asynchronous API

Calling Registers: AX   0006h

BX   API ID

0001h, NETBIOS interface

0002h, 802.2 interface

0003h, TCP/IP interface

0004h, LAN Manager named pipes interface

0005h, NetWare IPX interface

All other values are reserved

Return Registers: Carry flag clear if successful

AX   0000h

ES:BX   Pointer to SWAPIINFO structure

Carry flag set if unsuccessful

Comments: Before making any decisions regarding session switching, client programs that provide API support should make this call to find out whether another client program is providing a higher level of support for the same API. If a pointer to its own SWAPIINFO structure is returned, it must decide whether to suspend a session switch. If the pointer is to another client program's SWAPIINFO structure, that client program should make the decision.

If interrupts are disabled, the task switcher must not reenable interrupts or make any MS-DOS system function calls.

PROGRAMMING

The ASCII Character Set

Hex	Dec	Screen	Ctrl	Key
00h	0		NUL	^@
01h	1	☺	SOH	^A
02h	2	☻	STX	^B
03h	3	♥	ETX	^C
04h	4	♦	EOT	^D
05h	5	♣	ENQ	^E
06h	6	♠	ACK	^F
07h	7	•	BEL	^G
08h	8	◘	BS	^H
09h	9	○	HT	^I
0Ah	10	◙	LF	^J
0Bh	11	♂	VT	^K
0Ch	12	♀	FF	^L
0Dh	13	♪	CR	^M
0Eh	14	♫	SO	^N
0Fh	15	☼	SI	^O
10h	16	►	DLE	^P
11h	17	◄	DC1	^Q
12h	18	↕	DC2	^R
13h	19	‼	DC3	^S
14h	20	¶	DC4	^T
15h	21	§	NAK	^U
16h	22	▬	SYN	^V
17h	23	↨	ETB	^W
18h	24	↑	CAN	^X
19h	25	↓	EM	^Y

A

APPENDIX

Hex	Dec	Screen	Ctrl	Key	Hex	Dec	Screen
1Ah	26	→	SUB	^Z	48h	72	H
1Bh	27	←	ESC	^[	49h	73	I
1Ch	28	∟	FS	^\	4Ah	74	J
1Dh	29	↔	GS	^]	4Bh	75	K
1Eh	30	▲	RS	^^	4Ch	76	L
1Fh	31	▼	US	^_	4Dh	77	M
20h	32				4Eh	78	N
21h	33	!			4Fh	79	O
22h	34	"			50h	80	P
23h	35	#			51h	81	Q
24h	36	$			52h	82	R
25h	37	%			53h	83	S
26h	38	&			54h	84	T
27h	39	'			55h	85	U
28h	40	(			56h	86	V
29h	41	)			57h	87	W
2Ah	42	*			58h	88	X
2Bh	43	+			59h	89	Y
2Ch	44	,			5Ah	90	Z
2Dh	45	-			5Bh	91	[
2Eh	46	.			5Ch	92	\
2Fh	47	/			5Dh	93	]
30h	48	0			5Eh	94	^
31h	49	1			5Fh	95	_
32h	50	2			60h	96	`
33h	51	3			61h	97	a
34h	52	4			62h	98	b
35h	53	5			63h	99	c
36h	54	6			64h	100	d
37h	55	7			65h	101	e
38h	56	8			66h	102	f
39h	57	9			67h	103	g
3Ah	58	:			68h	104	h
3Bh	59	;			69h	105	i
3Ch	60	<			6Ah	106	j
3Dh	61	=			6Bh	107	k
3Eh	62	>			6Ch	108	l
3Fh	63	?			6Dh	109	m
40h	64	@			6Eh	110	n
41h	65	A			6Fh	111	o
42h	66	B			70h	112	p
43h	67	C			71h	113	q
44h	68	D			72h	114	r
45h	69	E			73h	115	s
46h	70	F			74h	116	t
47h	71	G			75h	117	u

Hex	Dec	Screen	Hex	Dec	Screen	Hex	Dec	Screen
76h	118	v	A5h	165	Ñ	D3h	211	╙
77h	119	w	A6h	166	ª	D4h	212	╘
78h	120	x	A7h	167	º	D5h	213	╒
79h	121	y	A8h	168	¿	D6h	214	╓
7Ah	122	z	A9h	169	⌐	D7h	215	╫
7Bh	123	{	AAh	170	¬	D8h	216	╪
7Ch	124	|	ABh	171	½	D9h	217	┘
7Dh	125	}	ACh	172	¼	DAh	218	┌
7Eh	126	~	ADh	173	¡	DBh	219	█
7Fh	127	Δ	AEh	174	«	DCh	220	▄
80h	128	Ç	AFh	175	»	DDh	221	▌
81h	129	ü	B0h	176	░	DEh	222	▐
82h	130	é	B1h	177	▒	DFh	223	▀
83h	131	â	B2h	178	▓	E0h	224	α
84h	132	ä	B3h	179	│	E1h	225	β
85h	133	à	B4h	180	┤	E2h	226	Γ
86h	134	å	B5h	181	╡	E3h	227	π
87h	135	ç	B6h	182	╢	E4h	228	Σ
88h	136	ê	B7h	183	╖	E5h	229	σ
89h	137	ë	B8h	184	╕	E6h	230	µ
8Ah	138	è	B9h	185	╣	E7h	231	τ
8Bh	139	ï	BAh	186	║	E8h	232	Φ
8Ch	140	î	BBh	187	╗	E9h	233	θ
8Dh	141	ì	BCh	188	╝	EAh	234	Ω
8Eh	142	Ä	BDh	189	╜	EBh	235	δ
8Fh	143	Å	BEh	190	╛	ECh	236	∞
91h	145	æ	BFh	191	┐	EDh	237	φ
92h	146	Æ	C0h	192	└	EEh	238	∈
93h	147	ô	C1h	193	┴	EFh	239	∩
94h	148	ö	C2h	194	┬	F0h	240	≡
95h	149	ò	C3h	195	├	F1h	241	±
96h	150	û	C4h	196	─	F2h	242	≥
97h	151	ù	C5h	197	┼	F3h	243	≤
98h	152	ÿ	C6h	198	╞	F4h	244	⌠
99h	153	Ö	C7h	199	╟	F5h	245	⌡
9Ah	154	Ü	C8h	200	╚	F6h	246	÷
9Bh	155	¢	C9h	201	╔	F7h	247	≈
9Ch	156	£	CAh	202	╩	F8h	248	°
9Dh	157	¥	CBh	203	╦	F9h	249	•
9Eh	158	₧	CCh	204	╠	FAh	250	·
9Fh	159	ƒ	CDh	205	═	FBh	251	√
A0h	160	á	CEh	206	╬	FCh	252	ⁿ
A1h	161	í	CFh	207	╧	FDh	253	²
A2h	162	ó	D0h	208	╨	FEh	254	■
A3h	163	ú	D1h	209	╤	FFh	255	
A4h	164	ñ	D2h	210	╥			

Selected Memory Locations

Note: This table of selected memory locations is provided to help you understand the way the system functions. Direct access to any of these memory locations makes a program extremely nonportable and should be avoided unless there is no other way to provide the features or response you want.

At best, knowing the locations of this information in memory can help you get information. Changing the information in the BIOS and DOS data areas can be extremely damaging, however (and a lot of fun if you don't mind crashing your system).

Address	Description
00000–00400	**Interrupt Vector Tables:**
00000	Int 00, Hardware divide by zero
00004	Int 01, Hardware single step trap
00008	Int 02, Nonmaskable
0000C	Int 03, Debugger breakpoint set
00010	Int 04, Arithmetic overflow
00014	Int 05, BIOS print screen
00020	Int 08, IRQ0—Clock tick

Address	Description
00024	Int 09, IRQ1—Keyboard action
00028	Int 0A, IRQ2
0002C	Int 0B, IRQ3—COM2
00030	Int 0C, IRQ4—COM1
00034	Int 0D, IRQ5—PC/XT Hard Disk Int 0D, IRQ5—PC AT LPT2
00038	Int 0E, IRQ6—Diskette
0003C	Int 0F, IRQ7—LPT1
00040	Int 10, BIOS video services
00044	Int 11, BIOS equipment list services
00048	Int 12, BIOS memory size services
0004C	Int 13, BIOS disk/diskette services
00050	Int 14, BIOS communications services
00054	Int 15, BIOS system services
00058	Int 16, BIOS keyboard services
0005C	Int 17, BIOS printer services
00060	Int 18, Executes ROM BASIC
00064	Int 19, Reboots system
00068	Int 1A, BIOS time-of-day services
0006C	Int 1B, Ctrl-Break handler address
00070	Int 1C, Called by Int 08 handler
00074	Int 1D, Video-initialization parameter table
00078	Int 1E, Disk-initialization parameter table
0007C	Int 1F, Graphics character table
00080	Int 20, DOS program terminate
00084	Int 21, DOS function services
00088	Int 22, Program terminate
0008C	Int 23, DOS Ctrl-Break interrupt
00090	Int 24, Critical-error handler
00094	Int 25, DOS absolute disk read
00098	Int 26, DOS absolute disk write
0009C	Int 27, DOS TSR
000A0	Int 28, DOS Idle interrupt
000A4	Int 29, DOS fast putchar
000A8	Int 2A, MS-Net access
000B8	Int 2E, DOS primary shell program loader
000BC	Int 2F, DOS multiplex interrupt
0009C	Int 33, Mouse interrupt

Address	Description
00100	Int 40, Diskette Int Vector if hard disk is installed
00104	Int 41, Fixed disk parameter table
00108	Int 42, EGA BIOS uses this to redirect the video interrupt
0010C	Int 43, EGA-initialization parameter table
00110	Int 44, EGA character table
00128	Int 4A, PC AT: Int 70 alarm
00168	Int 5A, Cluster
0016C	Int 5B, Used by cluster program
00170	Int 5C, NetBIOS interface
0019C	Int 67, Expanded memory manager services
001C0	Int 70, IRQ8—PC AT Real-time clock
001C4	Int 71, IRQ9—PC AT redirect to Int 0A
001D4	Int 75, IRQ13—PC AT math coprocessor
00400–00500	**ROM BIOS Data Area:**
00400	COM1 address (zero if unused)
00402	COM2 address (zero if unused)
00404	COM3 address (zero if unused)
00406	COM4 address (zero if unused)
00408	LPT1 address (zero if unused)
0040A	LPT2 address (zero if unused)
0040C	LPT3 address (zero if unused)
00410	Equipment flag
00412	Initialization flag
00413	Memory size in K
00415	Amount of memory in I/O channel
00417	Keyboard status flags
00419	Alternate keypad entry storage
0041A	Keyboard type-ahead buffer
0043E	Diskette data
00449	Current display mode
0044A	Number of screen columns
0044C	Size in bytes of display memory page
0044E	Offset to current display page
00450	Cursor position for display page 0
00452	Cursor position for display page 1
00454	Cursor position for display page 2

Address	Description
00456	Cursor position for display page 3
00458	Cursor position for display page 4
0045A	Cursor position for display page 5
0045C	Cursor position for display page 6
0045E	Cursor position for display page 7
00460	Current cursor mode
00462	Number of active video page
00463	Port address of active display card
00465	Hardware mode select register value
00466	Color palette setting
00467	Cassette data
0046C	Low word of time data
0046E	High word of time data
00470	Midnight flag (set if midnight passed since last read)
00471	Break flag
00472	Reset flag
00474	Fixed disk data area
00478	PC*jr* printer and serial time-outs
00480	Start of keyboard data area
00482	End of keyboard data area
00484	EGA additional video parameters
004F0	User communication area
00500–00600	**DOS/BASIC Data Area:**
00500	Print screen status flag

PROGRAMMING

A Resource List

Hardware

Hogan, Thom. *The Programmer's PC Sourcebook*. Microsoft Press, Redmond, Wash., 1988.

Intel Corporation. *iAPX 286 Programmer's Reference Manual*. Intel Corp., Santa Clara, Calif., 1983.

International Business Machines Corporation. *Personal Computer Technical Reference*. IBM, Boca Raton, Fla., 1984.

International Business Machines Corporation. *Mouse Technical Reference*. IBM, Boca Raton, Fla., 1987.

International Business Machines Corporation. *Personal System/2 and Personal Computer BIOS Technical Reference*. IBM, Boca Raton, Fla., 1987.

Morse, Stephen P. *The 8086/8088 Primer*, 2nd Edition. Hayden Book Company, Rochelle Park, N.J., 1982.

Woram, John. *The PC Configuration Handbook*. Bantam Books, New York, N.Y., 1987.

C

APPENDIX

MS-DOS and BIOS Programming

Angermeyer, John and Keven Jaeger. *MS-DOS Developer's Guide*, 2nd Edition. Howard W. Sams and Company, Indianapolis, Ind., 1989.

Campbell, Joe. *C Programmer's Guide to Serial Communications*. Howard W. Sams and Company, Indianapolis, Ind., 1987.

Chesley, Harry R. and Mitchell Waite. *Supercharging C with Assembly Language*. Addision-Wesley, Reading, Mass., 1987.

Duncan, Ray. *Advanced MS-DOS Programming*, Second Edition. Microsoft Press, Redmond, Wash., 1988.

Hyman, Michael. *Memory Resident Utilities, Interrupts, and Disk Management with MS and PC DOS*. MIS Press, Portland, Ore., 1986.

International Business Machines Corporation. *Disk Operating System Technical Reference Version 3.3*. IBM, Boca Raton, Fla., 1987.

International Business Machines Corporation. *Disk Operating System Version 4.00, Technical Reference*. IBM, Boca Raton, Fla., 1988.

Jourdain, Robert. *Programmer's Problem Solver*. Brady Books, New York, N.Y., 1986.

Jump, Dennis N. *Programmer's Guide to MS-DOS*. Brady Books, New York, N.Y., 1987.

Lai, Robert S. *Writing MS-DOS Device Drivers*. Addison-Wesley, Reading, Mass., 1987.

Porter, Kent. *Stretching Turbo Pascal*. Brady Books, New York, N.Y., 1987.

Wadlow, Thomas A. *Memory Resident Programming on the IBM PC*. Addison-Wesley, Reading, Mass., 1987.

Wilton, Richard. *Programmer's Guide to PC and PS/2 Video Systems*. Microsoft Press, Redmond, Wash., 1987.

Young, Michael J. *Performance Programming Under MS-DOS*. Sybex, San Francisco, Calif., 1987.

Programming Languages

Abel, Peter. *Assembler for the IBM PC and PC-XT*. Reston Publishing, Reston, Va., 1984.

Duntemann, Jeff. *Complete Turbo Pascal*. Scott, Foresman and Company, Glenview, Ill., 1986.

Feldman, Phil and Tom Rugg. *Using QuickBASIC 4*. Que Corporation, Carmel, Ind., 1988.

Harbison, Samuel P. and Guy L. Steele, Jr. *C: A Reference Manual*. Prentice Hall, Englewood Cliffs, N.J., 1987.

Holzner, Steve. *Advanced Assembly Language on the IBM PC*. Brady Books, New York, N.Y., 1987.

Lafore, Robert. *Microsoft C Programming for the PC*, 2nd Edition. Howard W. Sams and Company, Indianapolis, Ind., 1990.

Plantz, Alan et al. *Turbo C Programming*. Que Corporation, Carmel, Ind., 1989

Scanlon, Leo. *IBM PC and XT Assembly Language*. Brady Books, Bowie, Md., 1983.

Wyatt, Allen. *Using Assembly Language*, 2nd Edition. Que Corporation, Carmel, Ind., 1990.

Yester, Michael. *Using Turbo Pascal 6*, 2nd Edition. Que Corporation, Carmel, Ind., 1991.

General Programming

Birrell, N.D. and M.A. Ould. *A Practical Handbook for Software Development*. Cambridge University Press, Cambridge, England, 1986.

Ledgard, Henry. *Software Engineering Concepts*. Addison-Wesley, Reading, Mass., 1987.

Liffick, Blaise W. *The Software Developer's Handbook*. Addison-Wesley, Reading, Mass., 1985.

Yourdon, Edward. *Techniques of Program Structure and Design*. Prentice Hall, Englewood Cliffs, N.J., 1975.

General DOS

DeVoney, Chris. *MS-DOS User's Guide,* Special Edition. Que Corporation, Carmel, Ind., 1989.

DeVoney, Chris. *Using PC DOS*, 3rd Edition. Que Corporation, Carmel, Ind., 1989.

International Business Machines Corporation. *Disk Operating System Version 3.3*. IBM, Boca Raton, Fla., 1987.

International Business Machines Corporation. *Disk Operating System Version 4.00*. IBM, Boca Raton, Fla., 1988.

Microsoft Corporation. *MS-DOS Programmer's Reference*. Microsoft Corporation, Redmond, Wa., 1991.

A
Standard TSR-
Identification
Technique

An ongoing problem with using several TSR programs at the same time is the lack of standards for managing conflicts between such programs.

In early 1986, a group of TSR developers organized a team to establish such a standard. A majority of the leading independent TSR developers participated.

After first attempting to produce a full Applications Program Interface (API) for use by both independent and commercial programs (an effort that could not get strong enough support from commercial TSR publishing houses), followed by a period during which many of the original team moved on to other activities, the team developed and published an interface that permits developers to communicate with their own (and other) TSRs. In addition to the interface, a prewritten library of routines for Microsoft and Turbo C, Turbo Pascal versions 4 and 5, and assembler programs, known as TesSeRact, is available as shareware from team headquarters.

The TesSeRact Standard specifies a group of functions that chain into DOS's multiplex interrupt (2Fh). Because DOS uses this interrupt to communicate with its own TSRs (such as ASSIGN, PRINT, and SHARE), the TesSeRact Development Team felt that it was appropriate to use the same interface to service independently developed TSR programs. These functions are accessed by generating an Interrupt 2Fh, with a special code (5453h, or TS in ASCII) in the AX register.

This usage is *not* in accord with the standard documented usage of Int 2Fh: DOS specifies that the identification code should be in the AH register (and in the 80h–FFh range), with AL=0 used for the "Installed?" function.

The team developed its standard before the official usage was documented, and preliminary copies were too widely distributed to permit a change in such a basic aspect. The inconsistency should pose no problems because at present no known function uses the 54h code. (Even if one did, the chances of it also having a 53h function code are vanishingly small.)

It is also worthy of note that DOS did not follow its own rules when APPEND was introduced in V3.3; it uses the B7h code, which is officially reserved for non-DOS applications.

In keeping with the original goal of reducing conflict between TSRs from different sources, the team encourages all developers to support the TesSeRact Standard in their own code. All that is required to do so is a handler for Int 2Fh that can support the User Parameters block and the two functions described in this appendix, through the special TS identification code.

The User Parameters Block

One requirement for TesSeRact compatibility is to support the UserParms data area. The area is described in the following (this must be at the start of the TSR's handler for Int 2Fh):

```
New_2F:    jmp OverParms       ;Int 2F vector points here
UserParms  db  8 dup (' ')     ;8-byte program ID string
IdNum      dw  0               ;TSR identification number
FuncFlag   dd  0ffffffffh      ;supported function bit map
HotKey     db  0               ;scan code of hot key to use
ShiftSt    db  0               ;shift state to use for popup
HotFlag    db  0               ;which hot key is in use
ExtCnt     db  0               ;number of extra hot keys
ExtHot     dd  0               ;pointer to extra hot keys
Status     dw  0               ;TSR status flags
OurPSP     dw  0               ;our PSP segment
OurDTA     dd  0               ;our DTA region
DSeg       dw  0               ;user's default data Segment
```

Note: This is only a partial listing of the structure; the elements not shown here are used and maintained only by the TesSeRact library.

FuncFlag is a bit-mapped, four-byte variable that shows all Multiplex functions that this TSR supports. In every case, the function number must be passed to the handler in BX rather than the standard AL, as already explained. This variable is mapped as follows:

```
Bit 0              Function 00h (check install--required)
Bit 1              Function 01h (return userparms--required)
Bit 2              Function 02h (check hot key)
Bit 3              Function 03h (replace INT 24h)
Bit 4              Function 04h (return data pointer)
Bit 5              Function 05h (set extra hot keys)
Bits 6--7          Undefined--reserved for future use
Bit 8              Function 10h (enable TSR)
Bit 9              Function 11h (disable TSR)
Bit 10             Function 12h (release TSR from RAM)
Bit 11             Function 13h (restart TSR)
Bit 12             Function 14h (get current status)
Bit 13             Function 15h (set TSR status)
Bit 14             Function 16h (get popup type)
Bit 15             Undefined--reserved for future use
Bit 16             Function 20h (call user procedure)
Bit 17             Function 21h (stuff keyboard)
Bits 18--31        Undefined--reserved for future use
```

If the TSR supports the function, the bit should be set (1); otherwise, it should be 0. A program that uses the TesSeRact Library will return with `FuncFlag` set to FFFFFFFFh. Other TSRs should set the undefined variables to 0 to differentiate themselves.

Function 00h (Check Install)

Check Install (Function 00h) determines whether the program has been loaded before. It is called in the following fashion:

```
mov     ax,5453h          ; TS code
mov     si,offset IDStr   ; see below
mov     ds,seg IDStr
xor     cx,cx             ; handle counter
xor     bx,bx             ; function 0000
int     2Fh
```

IDStr is an eight-byte data area that contains a unique TSR identification string. The Int 2Fh routine should compare the string passed (as shown in the next example) with its own eight-byte string. If the two strings match, the TSR should return with the CX register set to its own TSR handle and the AX register set to 0FFFFh.

If the identification strings do not match, restore all the registers, increment the CX register, and pass the interrupt down the chain. If every TesSeRact-compatible TSR in a system increments the CX register before chaining to the next with this function, when the interrupt procedure eventually returns to the caller, the CX register will contain either the handle of the TSR being sought or the next available handle if no match could be found for IDStr.

If no match can be found, AL will *not* be equal to FFh upon return; the TSR installation program can then use the content of CX as the handle by which it identifies itself and store it in the *IdNum* word of the parameter block.

The following code, based on the TesSeRact Library's Int 2Fh handler but edited for clarity, shows what the handler must do to confirm program identity:

```
overparms:
        cmp     ax,5453h                ;ax=5453h for TesSeRact
        jne     not_our_2F              ;some other multiplex function
        push    ds                      ;save for next handler
        push    cs
        pop     ds                      ;set DS while here
        push    ax
        push    bx
        or      bx,bx                   ;do check for install first,
        jnz     test_for_1              ;try other function test
; following is the CHECK INSTALL code
;DS:SI points to ID string
;CX is current number in chain
        push    cx
        push    si                      ;save SI for next one
        lea     di,UserParms            ;the program copy of IDStr
        push    cs
        pop     es
        mov     cx,8                    ;test for match
        rep     cmpsb
        pop     si
        pop     cx
        jnz     next_one                ;no match, not us
        pop     bx                      ;matched, empty stack
        pop     ax
        mov     cx,es:[di]              ;return IdNum in CX
        xor     ax,ax
        dec     ax                      ;AX=-1 means already here
        jmp     short done_2F
```

```
next_one                             ;try next higher ID code:
    inc    cx
    pop    bx                        ;restore for next to use
    pop    ax
    pop    ds
not_our_2F:                          ;chain to next 2F handler
    jmp    dword ptr [oldint2F]      ;via saved pointer to it

done_2F:                             ;return to caller
    pop    ds
    iret
```

Function 01h (Return User Parameter Pointer)

The other function necessary for minimal support of the TesSeRact standard is Function 01h, which must return a far pointer to the User Parameters Block area. This function is called as follows:

```
    mov    ax,5453h
    mov    bx,01h          ;function number
    mov    cx,TsrIdNum      ;identification number
    int    2Fh
```

If the identification number in CX matches the TSR's ID number (which was returned by Function 00h), the function should return with ES:BX pointing to the UserParms area and AX equal to zero. The following code fragment shows one way to do this:

```
test_for_1:               ;if not Function 00h
    cmp    cx,IdNum        ;the program copy
    jne    not_our_2F
    push   cs              ;got it, set up for return
    pop    es
    lea    bx,UserParms
    xor    ax,ax           ;success status code
    pop    ds
    jmp    done_2F
```

Other TesSeRact Functions

The other TesSeRact functions are described in detail in the full TesSeRact documentation, which can be obtained from the development team or by downloading from a BBS or on-line service that distributes the library. If you want a copy of the source code for TesSeRact's Int 2Fh handler, send a self-addressed, stamped envelope to

> TesSeRact Development Team1657
> The Fairways, Suite 101
> Jenkintown, PA 19046

For more information, the TesSeRact Development Team can be contacted at this address, at CompuServe 70731,20, or at MCIMAIL 315-5415 (TESSERACT).

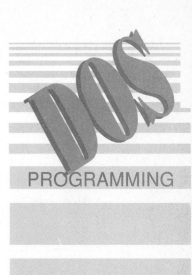

The Reserved DOS Functions

In the reference section, we have attempted to describe *all* the functions to which Int 21h responds; this includes those officially labeled as "reserved" and not documented in most reference manuals.

The descriptions we provide of the reserved functions, derived from wholly unofficial sources (in many cases, as the result of disassembling portions of DOS code and analyzing what it might possibly be accomplishing), may be less than totally accurate, although we have made every attempt to provide the best information available.

These functions fall into four general groups, which we describe in this appendix. After examining all four groups, we present a pair of programs that use one of the "useful" functions to provide otherwise unobtainable information.

One of the primary reasons these functions are "reserved" is to make it possible for designers to change them in any way required, between versions. This happened between V2 and V3, and then again between V3 and V4, with the data areas reached by way of the function we chose as our sample. Such an occurrence is not only possible but also likely when these undocumented functions are used; it is one of the major risks you take when you design a program around them.

APPENDIX

Four Types of Reserved DOS Functions

The four types of reserved DOS functions are

- The useful ones, which include such things as SetPID and GetDPB

- Those not actually used, all of which simply return after doing nothing

- Hooks for "future" features, which may or may not ever be implemented

- Those whose true nature has not yet been determined, mostly new numbers added with the release of DOS V4

Let's see which function is which. Note that functions numbered 59h and above did not appear until V3, and that those numbered 69h and above were not added until V4. Those between 59h and 68h were added piecemeal as V3 evolved into V4.

The Useful Group

In DOS V1, the only undocumented function was 1Fh (Details for Default Drive). It was "undocumented" only in the IBM version; the original Seattle Computer Products 86-DOS left no functions undocumented. This was a functional equivalent of the CP/M 2.2 function with the same number, which Microsoft and IBM chose not to support.

With the advent of V2, seven more such functions made their appearance. They were 32h (Detail for Specified Drive), 34h (Get InDOS Address), 50h (SetPID), 51h (GetPID), 52h (GetCVT), 53h (GetDrive Parameter Block), and 55h (Make PSP). Most of these functions were needed to permit such DOS utility programs as PRINT.COM, FORMAT.COM, and so on to access information they had to have.

These functions were not present before V3: 5Dh (CritErr), 60h (ExpandPath), and 64h (Set Country Code). They seem to fill the needs of networking software that requires private access to DOS internal data.

Finally, one more function appeared at V4: 6Ah (Commit File). The function's reason for existence is unknown; it executes exactly the same code as does documented function 68h.

Numbers Not Really Used

Five of the reserved functions (18h, 1Dh, 1Eh, 20h, and 61h) are do-nothing codes. The first four of these were provided in the original SCP operating system for compatibility with CP/M, according to designer Tim Paterson, and have never had any meaning in MS-DOS; the reason for the fifth function, which did not appear until V3, is unknown. All five functions execute the selfsame routine, which merely zeroes the AL register and then returns to the caller.

Hooks for the Future

Two of the reserved functions (37h and 63h) form the "future hooks" class. The first function was documented in some OEM versions of V2; it provided the capability of making DOS look and act more like UNIX. However, most of its capability was taken away in V3, and what remains is not recognized by all the official DOS utilities. The other function appeared in only one variant of V2 and then was resurrected in somewhat different form in V4.

Neither of these functions is useful for general program development.

Who Knows?

This list leaves the two functions 69h and 6Bh, both added in V4, still not fully understood. Both appear to involve critical areas of DOS, but their intended purpose is still a mystery.

Using Function 52h: The Configuration Variable Table

Starting with V3 and the introduction of network support, DOS found it necessary to standardize system-configuration information so that all the add-in optional programs required for network operation could obtain the information they needed. The result was what Dr. Edwin Floyd (one of the first people outside Microsoft and IBM to discover its existence and purpose) dubbed the configuration variable table (CVT). Actually, much of the table was already there in V2, but it was significantly expanded in V3, and its exact location in RAM was also moved slightly.

The configuration variable table is located near the front of the MSDOS.SYS program. The table contains pointers to the memory control block (MCB) chain and other essential control information, and the number of drives present or permitted.

Content and Layout of the CVT

In DOS V2, the CVT is only 25 bytes long. In both V3 and V4, it occupies 42 bytes. In all three versions, the CVT immediately precedes the NUL device driver, which is always the first driver in the chain. (Installable drivers are fitted between the NUL driver and the remaining drivers, which are part of the IO.SYS file.)

To locate the CVT, undocumented Function 52h of Int 21h is used. When this function is called with no parameters, it returns in ES:BX a pointer to the address of the first drive parameter block maintained by DOS. In V2, this is the second item in the CVT (the segment address of the start of the memory control block chain, a 2-byte value, precedes it). In V3 or V4, this address is the eighth byte of the CVT because the 32-bit far pointer to the current buffer control block and the 16-bit offset value for the current buffer location were added in front of the MCB segment word.

Thus, in V2 you must subtract 2 from BX after returning from the function, and in V3 and V4 you must subtract 8, to be at the front of the CVT.

Now that you have learned how to access the CVT, let's see what it contains.

The Version 2 CVT

The following layout of the configuration variable table shows how it first appeared in DOS V2. The asterisk indicates the address returned by undocumented Function 52h of Interrupt 21h, and all byte offsets listed are relative to that address.

Offset Byte	Field Length	Meaning
−02h	Word	Segment of first memory control block
*00h	Double word	Pointer to first drive parameter block
04h	Double word	Pointer to first DCB (system file table device control block)
08h	Double word	Pointer to CLOCK$ device driver
0Ch	Double word	Pointer to CON device driver
10h	Byte	Number of logical drives
11h	Word	Maximum bytes per sector on any block device
13h	Double word	Pointer to start of disk buffer chain
17h		Beginning of NUL device driver; first device in device-driver chain

The format of the memory control blocks pointed to by the word at offset −02 for both V2 and V3 was simple:

Offset Byte	Field Length	Meaning
00h	Byte	MCB identifier; 'M' for every MCB except last one, and 'Z' for last block. Always at offset 0000h within segment.

Offset Byte	Field Length	Meaning
01h	Word	PSP address of process that owns this MCB, or 0000h to indicate that memory in this block is unassigned
03h	Word	Size of following memory block in paragraphs, not including this 16-byte MCB area
05h	11 bytes	Remainder of paragraph unused

The drive parameter block, pointed to by the double word at offset 00h in the CVT, is the structure described in the reference section of this book in connection with undocumented Function 53h of Interrupt 21h. It remained unchanged between DOS V2 and V3. Because the drive parameter block is fully covered in the reference section, it is not repeated here. Each physical drive in the system (including drive B in a single-floppy system) has its own DPB; the next-block pointer of the last DPB contains FFFF:FFFFh to flag the end of the chain.

The number of DCBs in a system is established by the FILES= line in CONFIG.SYS. The default number is 5, if no FILES= value is specified. The DCBs are grouped in "links," and each link is preceded by a three-word link header:

Offset Byte	Field Length	Meaning
00h	Double word	Far pointer to next link header, or FFFF:FFFFh to indicate that this is final link in chain
04h	Word	Number of blocks in this link

The double word at offset 04h in the CVT points to the header of the link containing the first device control block in the DCB chain. In DOS V2, the 40-byte DCB layout was a slightly modified version of the documented FCB structure:

Offset Byte	Field Length	Meaning
00h	Byte	Number of current users for this DCB
01h	Byte	Access mode in which DCB was opened
02h	Byte	Attribute byte from directory entry, or 00h for device
03h	Byte	Drive code (1 = A, and so on)
04h	8 bytes	File or device name
0Ch	3 bytes	File extension, or blanks
0Fh	13 bytes	Not deciphered; may be same as FCB for a file
1Ch	Double word	Far pointer to device driver for device; not deciphered for file
20h	8 bytes	Not deciphered

The word at offset 11h indicates the maximum sector size on any block device. It is set during power-up initialization as the block device drivers are installed, and it establishes the size of the buffers created during configuration. This assures that each buffer is large enough to hold the largest sector present in the system, but no larger than necessary to do so.

The disk buffer chain pointed to by the double word at offset 13h of the CVT was laid out as follows (very little was deciphered of the buffer organization for version 2):

Offset Byte	Field Length	Meaning
00h	Double word	Far pointer to next buffer, or FFFF:FFFFh to indicate end of chain
04h	4 words	Control information not fully decoded, including flag bytes, logical sector number, and drive code
0Ch	Double word	Far pointer to DPB associated with this buffer
10h	varies	The buffer itself, usually 512 bytes, but the actual size is set by the value stored at offset 11h in CVT

The Version 3 CVT

The configuration variable table in DOS V3 grew at both ends, as listed here. As in the V2 listing, the asterisk indicates the address returned by undocumented Function 52h of Interrupt 21h, and all byte offsets listed are relative to that address.

Offset Byte	Field Length	Meaning
−08h	Double word	Current buffer in BUFFERS= chain
−04h	Word	Offset within current buffer
−02h	Word	Segment of first memory control block
*00h	Double word	Pointer to first drive parameter block
04h	Double word	Pointer to first DCB (system file table device control block)
08h	Double word	Pointer to CLOCK$ device driver
0Ch	Double word	Pointer to CON device driver
10h	Word	Maximum bytes per sector on any block device
12h	Double word	Pointer to start of disk buffer chain
16h	Double word	Pointer to logical drive table
1Ah	Double word	Pointer to start of DOS's FCB chain

Offset Byte	Field Length	Meaning
1Eh	Word	Number of FCBs to keep when swapping
20h	Byte	Number of block devices
21h	Byte	Number of logical drives, set by value of LASTDRIVE in CONFIG.SYS (defaults to 5 if not specified)
22h		Beginning of NUL device driver; first device in the device-driver chain

The double word at offset –08 points to the current buffer in the disk buffer chain; the layout of the buffer control blocks is described later. The word at offset –04 is the byte offset within the current buffer, relative to the buffer's first byte; a value of 0000h indicates that the last byte in the buffer has been used and the next buffer in the chain should be accessed.

As in V2, the word at offset –02 is the segment address of the first memory control block in the MCB chain. The layout is the same as in V2. The DPB chain, the first entry of which is pointed to by the double word at offset 00h, is the same as in V2.

The drive control blocks for V3 underwent extensive changes from V2, to accommodate the addition of networking and multiple processes sharing use of the same files or devices. As in V2, however, the drive control blocks still were collected into links with link headers, and the link header layout was not changed. The new structure layout for each DCB was as follows:

Offset Byte	Field Length	Meaning
00h	Word	Number of users for this DCB
02h	Word	Access mode per open
04h	Word	Disk attribute byte
05h	Byte	Device attributes
06h	Byte	Second device attribute byte
07h	Double word	Far pointer to driver
0Bh	Word	First cluster number
0Dh	Word	File time word
0Fh	Word	File date word
11h	Double word	Total file size
15h	Double word	Current byte position
19h	Word	Total cluster count
1Bh	Word	Current cluster number

Offset Byte	Field Length	Meaning
1Dh	Word	Directory sector
1Fh	Byte	Directory entry index (within sector)
20h	8 bytes	Device or file name
28h	3 bytes	File extension or blanks
2Bh	Word	Unknown
2Dh	Word	Unknown
2Fh	Word	Unknown
31h	Word	PSP segment address of owner
33h	Word	Unknown

The word at offset 10h indicates the maximum sector size on any block device. The size is set during power-up initialization as the block device drivers are installed. It is used to establish the size of the buffers created during configuration, to assure that each buffer is large enough to hold the largest sector present in the system, but no larger than necessary to do this.

The double word at offset 12h points to the start of the disk buffer chain. Each buffer in the chain is as large as specified by the word at 10h (usually 512 bytes), plus a 16-byte header that precedes the data area. The layout follows:

Offset Byte	Field Length	Meaning
00h	Double word	Far pointer to next buffer, or FFFF:FFFFh to indicate end of chain
04h	Byte	Logical drive code
05h	Byte	Action code
06h	Word	Logical sector number
08h	Byte	Number of FATs, or 01
09h	Byte	Sectors per FAT, or 00
0Ah	Double word	Far pointer to DPB associated with this buffer
0Eh	Word	Unknown
10h	varies	The buffer itself, usually 512 bytes, but the actual size set by the value stored at offset 10h in CVT

The "current directory" area that was part of the DPB in V2 became a separate table, the logical drive table, at V3. The double word at offset 16h of the CVT points to the LDT, which contains one entry for each system logical drive, up to the value set in LASTDRIVE of the CONFIG.SYS file. The minimum number of entries defaults to five (A: through E:) beginning with drive A. The tables, each of which is 81 bytes long in V3, follow one another in memory. Each is laid out as follows:

Offset Byte	Field Length	Meaning
00h	2 bytes	Actual drive designator and ' : '
02h	65 bytes	Current path for this drive as an ASCIIZ string (includes root directory slash and room for terminating 00h byte)
43h	Word	Current status of drive (bitmap):
		8000h = unknown, may indicate remote network drive
		4000h = ready for use
		2000h = unknown
		1000h = SUBSTed unit
45h	Double word	Pointer to DPB for drive
49h	Word	Current directory first cluster
4Bh	Word	Unknown
4Dh	Word	Unknown
4Fh	Word	Number of bytes to skip over when reporting directory; 0002 for normal drive, more if SUBSTed unit.

The double word at offset 1Ah and the word that follows it are related to the FCBS= line in CONFIG.SYS. They are, respectively, a far pointer to the chain of system FCBs, and the number of FCBs to protect against swapping should swaps be required. Though FCBs are intended primarily for network usage, they are used at times by programs in a single-user environment also. The system FCBs follow the same layout as the DCBs and, like the DCBs, are organized into links, each of which contains multiple blocks.

The final two items in the V3 CVT, at offsets 20h and 21h, are the number of block devices and the number of logical drives. The first is established by the total number of units encountered while installing block devices, and the other by the *LASTDRIVE=* line in CONFIG.SYS.

The Version 4 CVT

The changes made to the CVT and its tables between DOS V3 and V4 were minor in comparison to what happened between V2 and V3. However, the addition of EMS support did have some effect in the CVT area, as did the change from 16-bit to 32-bit logical sector numbers. And the rewrite of the buffering algorithms had a major impact on the buffer structures. Here's the CVT itself as used in V4; the only significant change is that the old buffer-chain-head pointer at offset 12h became a pointer to a new EMS link record.

Offset Byte	Field Length	Meaning
–08h	Double word	Current buffer in BUFFERS= chain
–04h	Word	Offset within current buffer
–02h	Word	Segment of first memory control block
*00h	Double word	Pointer to first drive parameter block
04h	Double word	Pointer to first DCB (system file table device control block)
08h	Double word	Pointer to CLOCK$ device driver
0Ch	Double word	Pointer to CON device driver
10h	Word	Maximum bytes per sector on any block device
12h	Double word	Pointer to EMS link record that leads to DOS buffer chain (only change between V3 and V4)
16h	Double word	Pointer to logical drive table (see the discussion following this table for layout, which did change slightly)
1Ah	Double word	Pointer to start of DOS's FCB chain
1Eh	Word	Number of FCBs to keep when swapping
20h	Byte	Number of block devices
21h	Byte	Number of logical drives, set by value of LASTDRIVE in CONFIG.SYS (defaults to 5 if not specified)
22h		Beginning of NUL device driver; first device in the device-driver chain

Everything located at addresses below that returned by Function 52h of Interrupt 21h remained unchanged in V4, but the buffer control block pointed to from the double word at offset –08 underwent drastic change. Previously, each buffer had its own unique segment address, and the buffers were linked by a chain of far pointers in the forward direction only. In V4, all buffers reached by way of a single EMS linkage block (described in this section) are in the same segment, and they are doubly linked (both forward and backward) by means of near pointers into an endless chain.

To accommodate the new buffering algorithms, the buffer control block size was extended from 16 to 20 bytes. Its structure in V4 is as follows:

Offset Byte	Field Length	Meaning
00h	Word	Offset of previous buffer in chain, within segment or EMS physical page
02h	Word	Offset of next buffer in chain, within segment or EMS physical page
04h	Byte	Logical drive code (same as V3)
05h	Byte	Action code (same as V3?)
06h	Double word	Logical sector number, expanded from V3
0Ah	Byte	Number of FATs, or 01; full meaning not known
0Bh	Word	Sectors per FAT if FAT in buffer; else meaning not known
0Dh	Double word	Far pointer to DPB for physical drive associated with this buffer
11h	Word	Meaning not known
13h	Word	Meaning not known
14h	512 bytes	The buffer itself; as in V3, size actually is set by word in CVT, but 512 bytes is normal

To speed up the buffer searching, a brand new linkage record was added to the buffering algorithm at V4. This 11-byte record holds a hash value and points to the associated BCB. Not all its details are fully understood, but the structure is as follows:

Offset Byte	Field Length	Meaning
00h	Word	Hash value
02h	Double Word	Far pointer to associated BCB
06h	Byte	Usage counter
07h	Double word	Meaning not known

A second new record was added to accommodate the new capability to store the buffers in EMS rather than in conventional memory. This record associates an EMM handle and physical page with a linkage record. Because of compatibility problems between the system software and non-IBM EMS hardware, we were not able to test in detail exactly how this record is used when EMS is active; the description that follows applies in a non-EMS environment:

Offset Byte	Field Length	Meaning
00h	Double word	Far pointer to linkage record described above
04h	Word	Number of pages controlled by this record
06h	Double word	Meaning not known
0Ah	Word	Meaning not known
0Ch	Byte	Flag; value is FF if EMS not being used
0Dh	Word	EMS handle value
0Eh	Byte	EMS physical page number

The next area to undergo change was the DPB structure, reached from the pointer at offset 00h of the CVT. The only change to the drive parameter blocks themselves was that the "sectors per FAT" value changed from 8 bits to 16, increasing the offset for all subsequent entries by one byte.

Everything above the DPB pointer, up to offset 12h, remained the same. The far pointer at offset 12h, though, became a pointer to the EMS record for the disk buffering, already described in connection with the BCB changes.

The LDT, reached by way of the far pointer at offset 16h in the CVT, was extended by seven bytes whose purpose could not be determined. The new structure is

Offset Byte	Field Length	Meaning
00h	2 bytes	Actual drive designator and :
02h	65 bytes	Current path for this drive as an ASCIIZ string (includes root directory slash and room for terminating 00h byte)
43h	Word	Current status of drive (bit map):
		8000h = unknown
		4000h = ready for use
		2000h = unknown
		1000h = SUBSTed unit
45h	Double word	Pointer to DPB for drive
49h	Word	Current directory first cluster
4Bh	Word	Unknown
4Dh	Word	Unknown
4Fh	Word	Number of bytes to skip over when reporting directory; 0002 for normal drive, more if SUBSTed unit
51h	Byte	Unknown

Offset Byte	Field Length	Meaning
52h	Word	Unknown
54h	Word	Unknown
56h	Word	Unknown

The rest of the CVT escaped change from what it was in V3, so far as could be determined by disassembly and testing.

CVT3: A Program for V3

The accompanying program, CVT3.PAS, provides both an example of a practical use for undocumented Function 52h of Interrupt 21h, and a tool for exploring just how the CVT is laid out in your own system running under DOS V3 (see the next section if you are using V4; unfortunately, no program was developed for V2).

CVT3 is written in Turbo Pascal and should compile properly with either version 4.0 or 5.0, although it was tested only with 5.0 (for 4.0, the compiler directives might require slight change).

While the listing for CVT3.PAS may look formidable at first glance, do not be dismayed. The listing is actually a collection of relatively simple procedures. The first few pages of the listing simply define all the CVT structures so that they can be referenced by the program. Following the declarations, a number of utility functions to assist in displaying output are defined. Then the individual tracing functions for each major structure are built, and finally it is all pulled together into the main program. Let's go through it in detail, a little bit at a time.

The Data Structures

The CVT3 program begins by declaring a number of special data types, one for each CVT structure and another as a pointer to that structure. Thus, bcb defines the format of the buffer control block as a *record* (the Pascal equivalent of the C *struct*), and bcbptr defines a pointer to such a record.

Similarly, mcb and mcbptr define the memory control block format, dpb and dpbptr define the drive parameter block format, chn and chnptr define the link header used in the DCB and FCB chains, dcb and dcbptr define the format of the device control block (also used by system FCBs), ldt and ldtptr define the logical drive table, and cvt defines the CVT itself.

The remaining special types defined are dtstr (the size of string used for date and time reporting), pstrg (the size used when reporting pointer values), and memst (the size used when reporting memory usage). These types are defined because

Turbo Pascal considers two different string[8] definitions as being two unique types; defining special types permits the compiler's type checking to work properly and also documents the usage of the shorter strings.

With all the special types defined, they are in turn used to declare the global working variables that the rest of the program uses: cvtbase is the pointer that will be returned as the base of the CVT; curbuf, curmcb, curdpb, curchn, curdcb, curfcb, and curldt are the current pointers to the various records being traced, and the remaining variables are used by the report-generating process.

Utility Functions

With the types and variables declared, the program next defines a number of utility functions. Hexn is passed a single byte, and converts its low four bits to a hex digit returned as an ASCII character. Hexb, in turn, uses hexn twice (shifting by four bits on the first call) to convert a full byte to a two-character string; hexw uses hexb in the same way to convert a 16-bit word to a string of hex digits, and hexl does it again with hexw to convert 32-bit values. When something is simple and it works, keep using it!

The procedure holdup, which is called after each line of output is generated during the tracing procedures, does nothing if the global PawsFlag is false. This permits continuous output if you are redirecting the report to the printer or to a file. If PawsFlag is true, however, holdup increments the line counter lctr and, if its value is greater than 23 (a full screen for comfortable viewing), resets lctr and waits for you to press Enter before returning.

Function xp is a special function that converts pointer values into the conventional ASCII representation *ssss:oooo*, using hexw to do the binary-to-hex conversion of the pointer.

The final utility procedure, dmp, is a general building block that you can use anywhere to generate a DEBUG-like listing of any 16 consecutive bytes in both hex and ASCII format. It accepts a far pointer as input, then writes to the screen the pointer value, the 16 bytes in hex format, and the same 16 bytes converted to ASCII (with the high bit stripped off and control characters converted to '.' to prevent confusion). Most of the procedures described earlier are used by dmp, either directly or indirectly. The reporting procedures use dmp to display the content of memory areas such as buffers.

Tracing the DPBs

Procedure dpbtrc performs both the tracing and the reporting of drive parameter block content. It defines a local procedure, dpbrpt, which does the actual reporting. This procedure can be called only from within dpbtrc and is not available to other routines; the capability of using such a "local" procedure is one of the most significant differences between Pascal and C.

The `dpbrpt` procedure depends on the pointer `curdpb` being set properly and simply converts data from the DPB, which is pointed to, into a more descriptive format for display by translating drive codes to letters and so forth. Some of its display is presented in hex format, and some values are output in decimal, all to increase the readability of the report. This might be considered a bare-bones "expert system" procedure that translates the knowledge of the DPB format into relatively plain language that is easier to understand.

Following the definition of `dpbrpt`, the actual `dpbtrc` procedure begins by setting global pointer `curdpb` to the value of the pointer passed in (from the CVT). Next, local variable `ofsv` is set to zero; this saves the offset of the next DPB pointer inside each record, and when its value becomes FFFFh the trace loop terminates.

With variables set up, the procedure prints a title line and goes into the tracing loop controlled by `ofsv`. On each pass through the loop, the value of `ofsv` is changed, `dpbrpt` is called to report everything contained in the current DPB, and `curdpb` is set to the value found in the next-DPB pointer. Until `ofsv` becomes FFFFh, the loop continues so that all valid DPBs are reported. Each time the screen fills during this process, `holdup` introduces a wait, which gives you time to read the screen.

After the last DPB report is displayed, `dpbtrc` sends a form-feed character to its output with `"write(#12)"`. This simply displays a graphics character on the CRT, but if output is sent to the printer, it forces the next trace function's output to appear on a fresh page. Most of the tracing procedures do this immediately before returning to the main calling routine.

Tracing the BCBs

Tracing and reporting the buffer control blocks is done by procedure `bcbtrc`. This procedure, like `dpbtrc`, includes a local reporting function appropriately called `bcbrpt`.

Like `dpbrpt`, `bcbrpt` translates the information from the buffer headers into a more comprehensible format and displays the information on the screen. It then uses `dmp` to display the complete contents of the buffer, before returning to `bcbtrc`.

And like `dpbtrc`, the `bcbtrc` routine is essentially a shell that first initializes its associated variables and then loops through calls to `bcbrpt` until it reaches the end of the buffer chain. When the end of the chain is reached, the procedure outputs a form-feed and returns to its caller.

Unlike `dpbtrc`, however, `bcbtrc` cannot use a global variable to hold its pointer for `bcbrpt` because `bcbtrc` is called for two different chains. Instead, the pointer is passed as the sole argument to each of these procedures.

Tracing the DCBs

The procedure that traces and reports both the device control blocks and the system FCBs (which share the same structure) is a bit more complex. In addition to its local reporting routine dcbrpt, it also defines a pair of functions: f_tm, which translates the time value kept in the DCB into conventional display format, and f_dt, which does the same for the date value.

Both f_tm and f_dt are straightforward examples of what is often called *brute force* programming. In f_tm, for example, the input time variable—packed tightly in the DOS-prescribed file-directory format—is shifted and masked as required to extract the hour as a single byte, then this byte is converted to a two-digit decimal by a sequence of DIV and MOD operations (the value 48 added here is the binary value of an ASCII '0' character). The same is done for the minutes and for the seconds.

When the packed value thus has been expanded to a string of type dtstr, that string is returned as the function's value. The f_dt function works in the same way for month, day, and year values.

Because the DCB can hold information about either a file or a device, and the descriptions of that information differ depending on which is present, dcbrpt is a bit more complex too. It includes code to determine whether each DCB refers to a file or to a device, and decision structures to change the report accordingly.

Another complicating factor is the way in which DCBs are grouped sequentially into links, with the links chained by pointers. To track this, dcbrpt receives a count (n) telling it how many DCBs to report on before returning to dcbtrc; the dcbtrc routine takes care of the linkage between chains. Because dcbrpt can refer to either DCBs or FCBs, the appropriate string is passed to it as t, an argument of type dtstr.

When you finally reach the beginning of dcbtrc, where the global and local variables are initialized, it is almost an anticlimax. As in the previous tracing routines, it is just a loop that cycles through the chains until it reaches the end of the chain, indicated by an offset value of FFFFh in the nxtlnk pointer. When the loop is through, a form-feed character is written to the output and dcbtrc returns.

Tracing the MCB Chain

The MCB tracer procedure, memtrc, repeats the now familiar pattern: a local reporting procedure, memrpt, contains a local function, memu. These, however, are significantly shorter than the ones you have seen.

The memu function interprets the first character of the memory block controlled by each MCB, to make an educated guess of the usage of that block. Because all programs begin with a PSP, which in turn begins with the two bytes CDh and 20h (the opcode for Int 20h), if memu finds CDh as the first byte, it assumes that a *program* is there. If not, then if the first byte is an uppercase alphabetic character in ASCII, it is assumed to be an *environment* block; otherwise, it is reported as containing *data*. One of these three description strings is returned by memu as its value.

The memrpt procedure is given three arguments: s, o, and a. They are, respectively, the size, owner process, and address of the first byte. If the owner is 0000, that means the memory block is free; otherwise, it is the process ID of the process for which the block is reserved.

The `memtrc` routine itself initializes the `curmcb` global pointer from the value passed to it by the main program, displays a title banner for the report, then enters a loop. This loop calls `memrpt` for the current MCB, calculates the next MCB segment value from the size of the current one, and sets `curmcb` to that address. The loop continues as long as the MCB identifier byte, `M`, is found in the first byte of each MCB. When the loop fails, a `Z` in the first byte identifies the valid last-MCB block; any other value indicates that the MCB chain has been corrupted. All of this checking is done by `memtrc` in only a few statements.

LDT Tracing

The final tracer routine is `ldttrc`, which displays the area used to keep the current-directory information for each logical drive in the system and used also to record SUBSTed and ASSIGNed drive information.

The local reporting routine, `ldtrpt`, gets a pointer to the first LDT when called and also a drive code numeric value in the range 0 through the number of logical drives (minus one because this drive code is zero-based). It converts the drive code to a letter value for reporting use, then checks the status byte in the LDT to determine whether the drive has in fact been defined.

If the drive has been defined, the physical drive and current directory information stored in the LDT are printed along with the logical drive letter, and the status byte (and other LDT entries whose meanings have been decoded) is translated and displayed.

The `ldttrc` procedure first sets `curldt` and displays a title. Next it decrements the logical drive count that was passed to it in order to adjust for the zero-based drive-code usage. It then loops through the LDT for each possible logical drive, calling `ldtrpt` for each and then setting `curldt` to point to the next, calculating the address from the size of each entry.

The Main Routine

Now that we have examined each of the tracing modules, we can put them together into the main calling sequence. It begins by verifying that the program is running under DOS V3.x, by using Function 30h of Interrupt 21h (invoked through the Turbo Pascal library procedure `MsDos`). If the program is not running under DOS V3.x, the program displays an error message and terminates with an errorlevel code of 255.

If the DOS version is correct, operation continues and the global variable `PawsFlag` is set to true if an argument accompanied the program name on the DOS command line, or to false if only the name was given. This lets you control the full-screen pause feature by furnishing or omitting an argument; no other use is made of any argument that you supply.

The program then initializes the `lctr` global variable that `holdup` uses, in case full-screen pauses are needed, and it displays a banner line. Next, it uses undocumented Function 52h of Interrupt 21h to obtain the address of the CVT from DOS, subtracts 8 from the returned offset, and stores the result in the global pointer cvtbase.

The CVT address is used to obtain a number of system statistics that are then displayed to the screen—not necessarily in the sequence in which the CVT holds them but rather in a sequence that may be more informative.

Following the display of these items, each of the trace/report routines is called. The holdup routine assures that you have ample time to read each screenful of information supplied. This step completes the CVT3 program.

You can easily adapt any part of the program to deal with only one area. For instance, by changing the memtrc routines to search but not display data, you could create a program using only the routines that could access the master DOS environment no matter how deeply its running shell was nested.

CVT4: Updating the Program to V4

The changes made to the undocumented DOS structures at the introduction of V4 rendered CVT3 unusable with the new version. And because of the way in which all the structures were defined, it was not practical to make the program capable of running under either version. Instead, the required changes were put into a new program, CVT4.PAS. In the following discussion, only changes are described; the rest of the program is identical to what we have already examined.

Buffer Control Block and EMS Links

The first major change in CVT4, as compared with CVT3, is in the definition of the bcb record. The old 4-byte far pointer to the next buffer (nxcb) changes to a pair of 2-byte near pointers to the previous buffer (prcb) and the next one (nxcb). The remaining functions in the control block are the same, except the lsect element (logical sector number) changes from a 16-bit value to 32 bits and the secf element (sectors per FAT) expands from a single byte to a 16-bit word. These changes increase the size of the BCB from 16 to 20 bytes.

To accommodate DOS's use of expanded memory, introduced in V4, two new structures were added. They are defined in CVT4 as bcblnk, a link record that contains a hash word (bxval) and points to the corresponding BCB (pagebase), and bufctl, a record that associates the EMM handle with a bcblnk record and also maintains other data used by the EMS software. Not all the fields in either record have been fully decoded as of this writing. The corresponding pointer types defined are bcblkp (to a bcblnk record) and bcptr (to a bufctl record).

Because of the extensive changes in buffer handling, the bcbtrc and bcbrpt procedures were almost completely rewritten, while retaining as much as possible of the original modularity. The changes in bcbrpt reflect the added information in the V4 BCB. The bcbtrc routine was replaced by two new procedures (bcbtrc1 and bcbtrc2) that deal with the changed method of accessing the buffers and accommodate the new EMS link structures. An additional new procedure, bcbtrl, was added in bcbtrc1.

The loop that calls bcbrpt, which was originally in bcbtrc, now is located in bcbtrc2. The bcbtrl procedure reports page base data from the bcblnk record and then calls bcbtrc2; bcbtrc1 passes a bcblnk pointer to bcbtrl after reporting data from the bufctl record. The apparent simplicity of these changes, which are required to handle a major change to the input data, is a strong testimonial to the power of the modular design used for these programs.

The Memory Control Block

One minor change was made to the MCB in V4; an MCB used for program loading now includes the program's name (that is, the name, minus the extension, of the file from which it was loaded). CVT4 handles this change by defining a new type, nam8 (which is an array of char rather than a string because the MCB contains neither a Pascal length byte nor a C end-of-string byte), and extends the definition of the mcb record to include the nam8 field.

The addition of the program name required a modification to the memrpt procedure so that the nam8 field would be reported if a program name is present. No other change was made, however.

The Drive Parameter Block

The only change to the DPB between V3 and V4 was that the sectors-per-FAT field changed in size from a byte to a word. The definition of the dpb record was modified to accommodate the change. This change was conceptually minor, but it was one of the major reasons why CVT3 cannot trace a DOS V4 system; the change in size for the spf element in the dpb record changes the position of the nxt pointer used to trace through the DPB chain, and the program goes wild.

The Device Control Block

In DOS V4, the size of the DCB was extended by six bytes. Three words (of unknown meaning) were added to the definition of the dcb record to account for this change.

The dcbrpt procedure was changed to report the added words, but no other change to the tracing or reporting of DCBs and FCBs was required.

The Logical Drive Table

The LDT size also was extended in DOS V4, by seven bytes. The program adds one byte and three words, all of unknown meaning, to the definition of the ldt record to keep things synchronized.

Because of the added data, the ldtrpt procedure was modified slightly to report the content of the new fields.

The CVT Definition Itself

Only one change was made in the definition of the cvt record and it was so small that it is easy to overlook: the type for the pointer bfrchn changed from bcbptr (in V3) to bcblkp (in V4). The effect of this change, however, is significant.

Utility Routines

One utility routine, outcstr, was added to CVT4 to provide output capability for the new nam8 data type used by the modified MCB. This routine is passed the address of a nam8 variable and outputs its characters until either all eight have been processed or a 00h byte is encountered. It is used only by the memrpt routine.

The Main Routine

The first change in the main calling sequence is that CVT4 tests for operation with DOS V4 rather than V3 and terminates if the version is not 4.

The wording of the summary statistics report changed slightly, reflecting the changed meaning of the curbfr field in the cvt record. Similarly, the heading for the buffer tracing changed somewhat, because the entire EMS link page (or all buffers if no EMS is in use) is reported at the same point that CVT3 reported only the current buffer.

In general, however, the changes between programs are far less complex than were the actual changes between DOS versions.

Summary

In this appendix, you have seen one method for using the undocumented DOS functions to explore the internal working of DOS itself, together with an example that you can modify to make use of the information available to you as DOS runs.

Keep in mind, however, that making use of such features can and will cause you headaches whenever a major version change occurs in DOS. Because of this, use of undocumented features should be held to an absolute minimum in any program that will be distributed widely, either commercially or by way of the public domain.

Listing E.1

```pascal
{ cvt3.pas - Turbo Pascal V5.0 version for DOS 3.x
 *      Copyright 1987, 1988, 1989 Jim Kyle - All Rights Reserved
 *
 *      The program, and the information it contains, may be freely
 *      distributed and used as long as this entire comment section
 *      is not altered.
 }
PROGRAM CVT3;
{$A-,B-,D+,E-,F-,I+,L+,N+,O-,R-,S+,V-}
{$M 8192,0,0 }
USES DOS;

TYPE

    bcb = RECORD                 { Buffer Control Block format     }
            nxcb   : pointer;         { +00 next one in chain  }
            ldrv   : byte;            { +04 logical drive code }
            action : byte;            { +05 action code        }
            lsect  : word;            { +06 logical sector #   }
            nf     : byte;            { +08 nbr FATs or 01     }
            secf   : byte;            { +09 sectors/FAT or 00  }
            pdrv   : pointer;         { +0A phys drv tbl ptr   }
            fill   : integer;         { +0E unknown            }
            buf    : array[0..511] of byte; { +10 the buffer itself  }
          END;
    bcbptr = ^bcb;

    mcb = RECORD                 { Mem Alloc Block header format   }
            flag  : char;             { +00 must be M or Z     }
            owner : word;             { +01 PSP seg or 0000    }
            siz   : word;             { +03 Number paragraphs  }
          END;
    mcbptr = ^mcb;

    dpb = RECORD                 { Drive Parameter Block format    }
            drvc   : byte;            { +00 drive code         }
            dunit  : byte;            { +01 unit number        }
            bps    : integer;         { +02 bytes per sector   }
            spc    : byte;            { +04 sec per cluster -1 }
            pwr2   : byte;            { +05 power of 2         }
            rsrvs  : integer;         { +06 reserved sectors   }
            nfats  : byte;            { +08 number of FATs     }
            dirsiz : word;            { +09 root dir size      }
            fus    : word;            { +0B first usable sectr }
            tcc    : word;            { +0D total clstr ct +1  }
            spf    : byte;            { +0F sec per FAT        }
```

continues

Listing E.1 continued

```
            fds     : word;                  { +10 first dir sector   }
            drvr    : pointer;               { +12 driver pointer     }
            mcode   : byte;                  { +16 media code         }
            accflg  : byte;                  { +17 access flag        }
            nxt     : pointer;               { +18 next table ptr     }
            lastused : word;                 { +1C last used cluster  }
            filler  : word;                  { +1E usually FFFF       }
        END;
    dpbptr = ^dpb;


    chn = RECORD              { Chain links for DCB, FCB chains    }
            nxtlnk : pointer;           { +00 next link or FFFF   }
            nmbr    : integer;          { +04 number blocks here  }
        END;
    chnptr = ^chn;


    dcb = RECORD              { Device Control Block format         }
            nusers : integer;           { +00 users for this DCB }
            mode    : integer;          { +02 0,1,2 per OPEN     }
            datrb  : byte;              { +04 disk attrib byte   }
            dvatr  : byte;              { +05 device attrib (hi) }
            atrb2  : byte;              { +06 2nd device attrib  }
            pdrvr  : pointer;           { +07 points to driver   }
            frstc  : word;              { +0B first cluster nbr  }
            modtm  : word;              { +0D file time word     }
            moddt  : word;              { +0F file date word     }
            totsiz : longint;           { +11 total file size    }
            curpos : longint;           { +15 current byte pos   }
            clsctr : word;              { +19 total cluster ctr  }
            curcls : word;              { +1B current cluster    }
            dirsec : word;              { +1D directory sector   }
            dirndx : byte;              { +1F dir entry index 0..}
            name   : array[0..7] of char; { +20 dev/file name    }
            ext    : array[0..3] of char; { +28 file extension   }
            fill2  : word;              { +2B unknown            }
            fill3  : word;              { +2D unknown            }
            fill4  : word;              { +2F unknown            }
            owner  : word;              { +31 PSP of owner proc  }
            fill5  : word;              { +33 unknown            }
        END;
     dcbptr = ^dcb;


    ldt = RECORD                     { Logical Drive Table format  }
            name   : array[0..67] of char;{ +00 drive and path    }
            code    : byte;             { +44 drive in use code  }
            mydpb  : dpbptr;            { +45 DPB for this drive }
            dirclu : word;              { +49 directory cluster  }
```

```
                filler2: word;           { +4B FFFF                }
                filler3: word;           { +4D FFFF                }
                patlen : word;           { +4F SUBST path length  }
            END;
    ldtptr = ^ldt;

    cvt = RECORD                  { Configuration Variable Table      }
            curbfr : bcbptr;             { current buffer pointer }
            memchn : mcbptr;             { start of MCB chain      }
            pdrvs  : dpbptr;             { Fn $52 points to here  }
            dcbchn : dcbptr;             { set up by FILES=        }
            clkdev : pointer;            { set by DEVICE= (clock$)}
            condev : pointer;            { set by DEVICE= (con)   }
            secsiz : integer;            { maximum block size      }
            bfrchn : bcbptr;             { set up by BUFFERS=      }
            ldrvs  : ldtptr;             { set up by LASTDRIVE=   }
            fcbchn : chnptr;             { set up by FCBS=         }
            filler : integer;            { number of FCBs to keep }
            npdrvs : byte;               { set by driver list      }
            nldrvs : byte;               { set by LASTDRIVE=       }
        END;
    cvtptr = ^cvt;

    dtstr = string[8];                   { date-time strings       }
    pstrg = string[9];                   { pointer-conversion fmt }
    memst = string[12];                  { memory usage string     }

VAR
  cvtbase : cvtptr;
  curbuf  : bcbptr;
  curmcb  : mcbptr;
  curdpb  : dpbptr;
  curchn  : chnptr;
  curdcb,
  curfcb  : dcbptr;
  curldt  : ldtptr;
  bcbctr,
  dcbctr  : integer ;          { counters                        }
  b       : Registers;
  PawsFlag: Boolean;           { controls screen-full pausing }
  lctr    : integer;           { counts lines displayed          }

function hexn(b:byte) : char;  { converts nibble to char         }
  begin
    b := b and 15;            { force to only 4 bits           }
    if b > 9 then inc(b,7);   { adjust for hex digits           }
    hexn := chr(b+48);        { convert to character            }
  end;
```

continues

Listing E.1 continued

```
function hexb(b:byte) : string;
  begin
    hexb := hexn(b shr 4) + hexn(b);      { assemble the nibbles    }
  end;

function hexw(w:word) : string;
  begin
    hexw := hexb(w shr 8) + hexb(w);      { assemble the bytes      }
  end;

function hexl(l:longint) : string;
  begin
    hexl := hexw(l shr 16) + hexw(l);     { assemble the words      }
  end;

PROCEDURE holdup;                         { count lines and wait if full }
  BEGIN
    IF PawsFlag THEN
      BEGIN
        inc(lctr);
        if lctr > 23 then
          BEGIN
            lctr := 0;
            readln;
          END
      END
  END;

FUNCTION xp( p : pointer ) : pstrg;           { displays pointer P }
  BEGIN
    xp := hexw(seg(p^)) + ':' + hexw(ofs(p^));
  END;

PROCEDURE  dmp(f : pointer);        { display hex dump of data to CRT }
  VAR
    x : ^byte;
    i : integer;
    c : char;
  BEGIN
    x := f;
    write( xp(f), '> ');
    FOR i:=0 to 15 DO
      BEGIN
        write( hexb(x^) );
        if i=7 then write('-')
               else write(' ');
        x := pointer(longint(x) + 1);
      END;
```

```
      write(' ');
      x := f;
      FOR i:=0 to 15 DO
        BEGIN
          c := char($7f AND x^);
          if c<' ' then c := '.';
          write( c );
          if i=7 then write(' ');
          x := pointer(longint(x) + 1);
        END;
      writeln;
      holdup;
   END;

PROCEDURE dpbtrc(a: pointer);      { trace and report DPB data  }
   VAR
     ofsv : word;

   PROCEDURE dpbrpt;                     { reports each DPB's content }
     BEGIN
       writeln;
       holdup;
       write('Drive ', char (curdpb^.drvc+ord('A')) );
       write(': (unit ', curdpb^.dunit, ' of driver at ', xp(curdpb^.drvr) );
       writeln(') media code = ', hexb(curdpb^.mcode) );
       holdup;
       write(' ', curdpb^.bps:3, ' bytes per sector,');
       write(' ', curdpb^.spc+1:2, ' sectors per cluster,');
       writeln(' ', curdpb^.tcc-1:4, ' total cluster count');
       holdup;
       write(' Res sectors: ', curdpb^.rsrvs, ' ');
       write(' ', curdpb^.nfats, ' FAT''s, ', curdpb^.spf:2, ' sec ea ');
       write(' FAT entry: ');
       IF (curdpb^.tcc) > $0FFC
          THEN  write( 16 )
          ELSE  write( 12 );
       writeln(' bits  Root: ', curdpb^.dirsiz:3, ' entries');
       holdup;
       write(' First root sector: ', curdpb^.fds:3  );
       write(' First data sector: ', curdpb^.fus:3  );
       writeln(' Last cluster used: ', hexw(curdpb^.lastused));
       holdup;
     END;        { of dpbrpt proc }
```

continues

```
          BEGIN
            curdpb := a;
            ofsv := 0;
            writeln;
            holdup;
            writeln('DRIVE PARAMETER BLOCK (DPB) DATA--');
            holdup;
            WHILE (ofsv <> $FFFF) DO
              BEGIN
                ofsv := word(longint( curdpb^.nxt ));
                dpbrpt ;
                curdpb := dpbptr(curdpb^.nxt);
              END;
            write(#12);
          END;   { of dpbtrc proc }

        PROCEDURE bcbtrc(a : pointer);
          VAR
            ofsv : word;

          PROCEDURE  bcbrpt(a : bcbptr);
            VAR
              i : integer;
              x : pointer;
            BEGIN
              writeln;
              holdup;
              inc(bcbctr);
              writeln('Buffer Control Block ', bcbctr:2, ' at ', xp(a));
              holdup;
              write('     Logical ''', char(ord('A')+a^.ldrv));
              write(':'',     Sector ', hexw(a^.lsect));
              writeln('     Action code: ', hexb(a^.action));
              holdup;
              write('     NFATS: ', hexb( a^.nf));
              write('   SPF: ', hexb(a^.secf));
              write('   DPB: ', xp(a^.pdrv));
              writeln('   FILL: ', hexw(a^.fill));
              holdup;
              x := addr(bcbptr(a)^.buf[0]);
              FOR i:=0 to 31 DO
                dmp(pointer(longint(x)+(i SHL 4)));
            END;        { of bcbrpt proc }

        BEGIN           { bcbtrc routine }
          bcbctr := 0;
          ofsv := 0;
```

```
      WHILE (ofsv <> $FFFF) DO
        BEGIN
          ofsv := word(longint( bcbptr(a)^.nxcb ));
          bcbrpt (a);
          a := bcbptr(a)^.nxcb;
        END;
      write(#12);
  END;              { bcbtrc routine }

PROCEDURE dcbtrc(t : dtstr; a : pointer);
  VAR
    ofsv : word;

  FUNCTION f_tm(n : word) : dtstr;
    VAR
      buf : dtstr;
      b   : byte;
    BEGIN
      b := ((n SHR 11) AND 31);
      buf[1] :=char((b DIV 10) + 48);
      buf[2] :=char((b MOD 10) + 48);
      buf[3] := ':';
      b := ((n SHR  5) AND 63);
      buf[4] :=char((b DIV 10) + 48);
      buf[5] :=char((b MOD 10) + 48);
      buf[6] := ':';
      b := ((n SHL  1) AND 63);
      buf[7] :=char((b DIV 10) + 48);
      buf[8] :=char((b MOD 10) + 48);
      f_tm := buf;
    END;

  FUNCTION f_dt(n : word) : dtstr;
    VAR
      buf : dtstr;
      b   : byte;
    BEGIN
      b :=((n SHR  5) AND 15);
      buf[1] :=char((b DIV 10) + 48);
      buf[2] :=char((b MOD 10) + 48);
      buf[3] := '/';
      b := ( n        AND 31);
      buf[4] :=char((b DIV 10) + 48);
      buf[5] :=char((b MOD 10) + 48);
      buf[6] := '/';
      b := ((n SHR  9) AND 15) + 80;
      buf[7] :=char((b DIV 10) + 48);
      buf[8] :=char((b MOD 10) + 48);
      f_dt := buf;
    END;
```

continues

```
PROCEDURE dcbrpt( var t : dtstr; n : integer );
  type
    acctyp = array[0..3] of string[7];
  const
    actyp : acctyp = ('READ', 'WRITE', 'R/W', 'unknown');
  var
    isdvc : Boolean;
  BEGIN
    WHILE (n > 0) DO
    BEGIN
      INC (dcbctr);
      writeln;
      holdup;
      write (t, ' ', dcbctr:2 );
      IF (curdcb^.name[0] = #0)  THEN
      BEGIN
        writeln(' at ', xp(curdcb), ' not used since bootup');
        holdup;
      END
      else
      BEGIN
        isdvc := (curdcb^.dvatr and 128) <> 0;
        write(' for ');
        IF isdvc
          THEN write( 'device ' )
          ELSE write( 'file ' );
        write(curdcb^.name[0], curdcb^.name[1], curdcb^.name[2]);
        write(curdcb^.name[3], curdcb^.name[4], curdcb^.name[5]);
        write(curdcb^.name[6], curdcb^.name[7]);
        IF (NOT isdvc) THEN   { block driver }
          write('.', curdcb^.ext[0], curdcb^.ext[1], curdcb^.ext[2]);
        write(' at ', xp( curdcb ) );
        write(' shows ', curdcb^.nusers);
        writeln(' OPENs');
        holdup;
        write('  Opened for ', actyp[3 AND (curdcb^.mode)]);
        write(' access' );
        IF ($FFFC AND (curdcb^.mode))<>0 THEN
          write(' (', hexw(curdcb^.mode), ')');
        writeln(' by process ', hexw(curdcb^.owner));
        holdup;
        IF( isdvc ) THEN              { Device       }
          BEGIN
            write('  Device driver at ', xp(curdcb^.pdrvr) );
            write(' is in ');
            if ((curdcb^.dvatr) AND 32)<>0 THEN write('Raw')
                                            ELSE write( 'Cooked' );
```

```
            write(' mode and is ');
            if ((curdcb^.dvatr) AND 64)=0 THEN  write('not ');
            writeln('ready');
            holdup;
          END
        else                           { File        }
          BEGIN
            write('  File is on drive ', char(ord('A')+((curdcb^.dvatr) AND 31)));
            write(': (driver at ', xp(curdcb^.pdrvr));
            write(') and has ');
            if ((curdcb^.dvatr) AND 64)<>0 THEN  write('not ');
            writeln('been written to.');
            holdup;
            writeln('  File''s attribute byte = ', hexb(curdcb^.datrb));
            holdup;
          END;
        write  ('  Mod Time/date: ');
        write  (f_tm(curdcb^.modtm), ', ');
        writeln(f_dt(curdcb^.moddt));
        holdup;
        write  ('       Dir Sector:  ', hexw(curdcb^.dirsec), ' ');
        writeln('         Dir Index:  ', curdcb^.dirndx:4, ' ');
        holdup;
        write  ('    First Cluster:  ', hexw(curdcb^.frstc), ' ');
        write  ('    Prev Clusters:  ', curdcb^.clsctr:4, ' ');
        writeln('  Current Cluster:  ', hexw(curdcb^.curcls), ' ');
        holdup;
        write  ('   Directory size:',   curdcb^.totsiz:6, ' ');
        writeln('  Curr byte count:',   curdcb^.curpos:6      );
        holdup;
        write  (' Fill2=', hexw(curdcb^.fill2), ' ');
        write  (' Fill3=', hexw(curdcb^.fill3), ' ');
        write  (' Fill4=', hexw(curdcb^.fill4), ' ');
        writeln(' Fill5=', hexw(curdcb^.fill5)      );
        holdup;
      END;
      curdcb := pointer(longint(curdcb) + sizeof(dcb) - 1);
      DEC( n );
    END;       { n >= 0 loop   }
  END;          { of dcbrpt     }

BEGIN
  curchn := chnptr(a);
  dcbctr := 0;
  ofsv := 0;
  WHILE (ofsv <> $FFFF) DO
```

continues

Listing E.1 *continued*

```
        BEGIN
          ofsv := word(longint(curchn^.nxtlnk));
          curdcb := dcbptr(longint(curchn)+sizeof(chn));
          writeln;
          holdup;
          write  ( 'Link at ', xp(curchn), ' contains ');
          writeln( curchn^.nmbr, ' ', t, 's--');
          holdup;
          dcbrpt (t, curchn^.nmbr);
          curchn := chnptr(curchn^.nxtlnk);
        END;
      write(#12);
    END;

  PROCEDURE memtrc(a : pointer);
    VAR
      z : longint;

    PROCEDURE memrpt(s,o,a : word);

      FUNCTION memu(a : word) : memst;      { determine memory use }
        var
          x : char;
      BEGIN
        x := char( mem[a:0] );
        CASE x OF
          #$CD:
            memu := 'Program';
          'A'..'Z':
            memu := 'Environment';
          else
            memu := 'Data';
          End;
      END;

    BEGIN
      z := longint(s) SHL 4;
      write( z:6, ' bytes ' );
      IF (o<>0) THEN
        writeln('USED by proc ', hexw(o), ', at ', hexw( a ), ':0000, for ', memu(a))
      else
        writeln('FREE at ', hexw( a ), ':0000' );
      holdup;
    END;  { of memrpt      }
```

```
BEGIN
  curmcb := mcbptr(a);
  writeln;
  holdup;
  writeln('MEMORY ALLOCATION CHAIN');
  holdup;
  WHILE (curmcb^.flag = 'M') DO
    BEGIN
      memrpt( curmcb^.siz, curmcb^.owner, SEG(curmcb^)+1);
      curmcb := ptr( seg(curmcb^) + (curmcb^.siz + 1), 0 );
    END;
  IF (curmcb^.flag <> 'Z') THEN
    BEGIN
      writeln(#13, #10, 'MEMORY ALLOCATION ERROR at ', xp(curmcb) );
      halt(255);
    END;
  memrpt( curmcb^.siz, curmcb^.owner, SEG(curmcb^)+1);
  write(#12);
END;    { of memtrc }

PROCEDURE ldttrc( a: ldtptr; n: byte );

  PROCEDURE ldtrpt( l: ldtptr; d: byte );
    VAR
      ldrive : char;
      i      : integer;
    BEGIN
      ldrive := chr( $41 + d );
      if (l^.code AND byte($40))=0 then
        writeln( 'Logical Drive ', ldrive, ' not yet defined' )
      else
        begin
          write ( 'Logical Drive ', ldrive );
          writeln( ' = Physical drive ', l^.name[0] );
          holdup;
          write ( 'The current (full) pathspec is: ' );
          i := 0;
          repeat
            write ( l^.name[i] );
            inc( i );
          until (l^.name[i] = #0);
          writeln;
        end;
      holdup;
      if(l^.code = $50) then
        writeln( 'Code = 0x50 -- result of SUBST command')
      else if(l^.code = $40) then
        writeln( 'Code = 0x40 -- physical (or aliased) device')
```

continues

```
      else
        writeln( 'Code = 0x', hexb(l^.code), ' -- unknown');
      holdup;
      writeln( 'Directory Cluster = ', hexw( l^.dirclu ));
      holdup;
      writeln( 'Path Length to ignore = ', hexw( l^.patlen ));
      holdup;
      writeln;
      holdup;
    END; { of ldtrpt }

VAR
  o  : byte;

BEGIN
  curldt := a;
  writeln;
  holdup;
  writeln('LOGICAL DRIVE TABLES (set by LASTDRIVE=, SUBST, etc.):');
  holdup;
  dec( n );                        { convert for zero-based reference  }
  for o := 0 to n do               { loop thru contiguous tables       }
    begin
      ldtrpt(curldt, o);
      curldt := ptr(seg(curldt^), ( ofs(curldt^) + sizeof(ldt)));
    end;
  write(#12);
END; { of ldttrc }

{ main  }
BEGIN
  b.ah := $30;                     { Check for correct DOS version     }
  MsDos(b);
  if b.al <> 3 then                { If not version 3.x, get right out }
    begin
      writeln( 'Wrong DOS version: ', b.al, '.', b.ah );
      halt(255);                   { return ErrorLevel=255             }
    end;
  PawsFlag := ParamCount = 0;   { else set up for paging output        }
  lctr := 0;
  writeln( 'Configuration Variables, DOS version ', b.al, '.', b.ah );
  holdup;
  b.ah := $52;                     { Get CVT pointer set up            }
  msdos(b);                        {   (using undocumented function)   }
  cvtbase := ptr(b.es, b.bx-8); { hold pointer to CVT                  }
```

```
writeln;
holdup;
writeln('CVT is located at ', xp(cvtbase));
 holdup;
write  ('No. of Phys Drives (at ', xp(@cvtbase^.npdrvs));
writeln('): ', cvtbase^.npdrvs);
holdup;
write  ('No. of Log. Drives (at ', xp(@cvtbase^.nldrvs));
writeln('): ', cvtbase^.nldrvs);
holdup;
write  ('  Clock Device (ptr at ', xp(@cvtbase^.clkdev));
writeln('): ', xp(cvtbase^.clkdev));
holdup;
write  ('    CON Device (ptr at ', xp(@cvtbase^.condev));
writeln('): ', xp(cvtbase^.condev));
holdup;
write  ('    Sector Size(?) (at ', xp(@cvtbase^.secsiz));
writeln('):      ',hexw(cvtbase^.secsiz));
holdup;
write  ('     FCBs to keep (at ', xp(@cvtbase^.filler));
writeln('):      ',hexw(cvtbase^.filler));
holdup;
write  ('1.    Memory Chain (ptr at ', xp(@cvtbase^.memchn));
writeln('): ', xp(cvtbase^.memchn));
holdup;
write  ('2.       DCB Chain (ptr at ', xp(@cvtbase^.dcbchn));
writeln('): ', xp(cvtbase^.dcbchn));
holdup;
write  ('3.       DPB Chain (ptr at ', xp(@cvtbase^.pdrvs));
writeln('): ', xp(cvtbase^.pdrvs));
holdup;
write  ('4.       FCB Chain (ptr at ', xp(@cvtbase^.fcbchn));
writeln('): ', xp(cvtbase^.fcbchn));
holdup;
write  ('5.       LDT Chain (ptr at ', xp(@cvtbase^.ldrvs));
writeln('): ', xp(cvtbase^.ldrvs));
holdup;
write  ('6. Current Buffer (ptr at ', xp(@cvtbase^.curbfr));
writeln('): ', xp(cvtbase^.curbfr));
holdup;
write  ('7.    Buffer Chain (ptr at ', xp(@cvtbase^.bfrchn));
writeln('): ', xp(cvtbase^.bfrchn));
holdup;

writeln;
holdup;
writeln('TRACING     MCB Chain===');
```

continues

```
      holdup;
      memtrc(cvtbase^.memchn);

      writeln;
      holdup;
      writeln('TRACING      DCB Chain===');
      holdup;
      dcbtrc('DCB', cvtbase^.dcbchn);

      writeln;
      holdup;
      writeln('TRACING      DPB Chain===');
      holdup;
      dpbtrc(cvtbase^.pdrvs);

      writeln;
      holdup;
      writeln('TRACING      FCB Chain===');
      holdup;
      dcbtrc('FCB', cvtbase^.fcbchn);

      writeln;
      holdup;
      writeln('TRACING      LDT Chain===');
      holdup;
      ldttrc(cvtbase^.ldrvs, cvtbase^.nldrvs);

      writeln;
      holdup;
      writeln('TRACING Current Buffer===');
      holdup;
      bcbtrc(cvtbase^.curbfr);

      writeln;
      holdup;
      writeln('TRACING   Buffer Chain===');
      holdup;
      bcbtrc(cvtbase^.bfrchn);
   END.
```

Listing E.2

```
{ cvt4.pas - Turbo Pascal V5.0 version for DOS 4.x, 5.0
 *      Copyright 1987, 1988, 1989 Jim Kyle - All Rights Reserved
 *
 *      The program, and the information it contains, may be freely
 *      distributed and used so long as this entire comment section
 *      is not altered.
 }
PROGRAM CVT4;
{$A-,B-,D+,E-,F-,I+,L+,N+,O-,R-,S+,V-}
{$M 8192,0,0 }
USES DOS;

TYPE

  bcb = RECORD                    { Buffer Control Block format, V4    }
          prcb   : word;              { +00 prev one in chain     }
          nxcb   : word;              { +02 next one in chain     }
          ldrv   : byte;              { +04 logical drive code  }
          action : byte;              { +05 action code           }
          lsect  : longint;           { +06 logical sector #      }
          nf     : byte;              { +0A nbr FATs or 01        }
          secf   : word;              { +0B sectors/FAT or 00     }
          pdrv   : pointer;           { +0D phys drv tbl ptr      }
          fill2  : word;              { +11 unknown               }
          fill3  : byte;              { +13 unknown               }
          buf    : array[0..511] of byte; { +14 the buffer itself  }
        END;
  bcbptr = ^bcb;

  bcblnk = RECORD              { BCB link record, new in V4         }
          bxval : word;            { +00, unknown             }
          pagebase : bcbptr;       { +02, points to a BCB     }
          usrs   : byte;           { +06, count of usage      }
          fill   : longint;        { +07, unknown             }
        END;
  bcblkp = ^bcblnk;

  bufctl = RECORD                  { EMS control for buffers, new in V4 }
          lnkptr   : bcblkp;          { +00, point to pagebase }
          pgs      : word;            { +04, number of pages   }
          fill1    : longint;         { +06, unknown           }
          fill2    : word;            { +0A, unknown           }
          emsflg   : byte;            { +0C, FF if no EMS used }
          emshdl   : word;            { +0D, EMS handle        }
          emsppg   : byte;            { +0F, EMS physical page }
        END;
  bcptr = ^bufctl;
```

continues

Listing E.2 *continued*

```
nam8 = array[1..8] of char;

mcb = RECORD                      { Mem Alloc Block header format    }
        flag  : char;               { +00 must be M or Z             }
        owner : word;               { +01 PSP seg or 0000            }
        siz   : word;               { +03 Number paragraphs          }
        junk  : array[5..7] of byte; { +05-+07 not used              }
        name  : nam8;               { +08 Name of owner              }
      END;
mcbptr = ^mcb;

dpb = RECORD                      { Physical Drive Table format      }
        drvc  : byte;               { +00 drive code                 }
        dunit : byte;               { +01 unit number                }
        bps   : integer;            { +02 bytes per sector           }
        spc   : byte;               { +04 sec per cluster -1         }
        pwr2  : byte;               { +05 power of 2                 }
        rsrvs : integer;            { +06 reserved sectors           }
        nfats : byte;               { +08 number of FATs             }
        dirsiz : word;              { +09 root dir size              }
        fus   : word;               { +0B first usable sectr         }
        tcc   : word;               { +0D total clstr ct +1          }
        spf   : word;               { +0F sec per FAT **CHG**        }
        fds   : word;               { +11 first dir sector           }
        drvr  : pointer;            { +13 driver pointer             }
        mcode : byte;               { +17 media code                 }
        accflg : byte;              { +18 access flag                }
        nxt   : pointer;            { +19 next table ptr             }
        lastused : word;            { +1D last used cluster          }
        filler : word;              { +1F usually FFFF               }
      END;
dpbptr = ^dpb;

chn = RECORD                      { Chain links for DCB, FCB chains  }
        nxtlnk : pointer;           { +00 next link or FFFF          }
        nmbr  : integer;            { +04 number blocks here         }
      END;
chnptr = ^chn;

dcb = RECORD                      { Device Control Block format      }
        nusers : integer;           { +00 users for this DCB         }
        mode  : integer;            { +02 0,1,2 per OPEN             }
        datrb : byte;               { +04 disk attrib byte           }
        dvatr : byte;               { +05 device attrib (hi)         }
        atrb2 : byte;               { +06 2nd device attrib          }
        pdrvr : pointer;            { +07 points to driver           }
        frstc : word;               { +0B first cluster nbr          }
```

```
          modtm  : word;                  { +0D file time word      }
          moddt  : word;                  { +0F file date word      }
          totsiz : longint;               { +11 total file size     }
          curpos : longint;               { +15 current byte pos     }
          clsctr : word;                  { +19 total cluster ctr   }
          curcls : word;                  { +1B current cluster     }
          dirsec : word;                  { +1D directory sector    }
          dirndx : byte;                  { +1F dir entry index 0..}
          name   : array[0..7] of char; { +20 dev/file name       }
          ext    : array[0..3] of char; { +28 file extension      }
          fill2  : word;                  { +2B unknown             }
          fill3  : word;                  { +2D unknown             }
          fill4  : word;                  { +2F unknown             }
          owner  : word;                  { +31 PSP of owner proc   }
          fill5  : word;                  { +33 unknown             }
          fill6  : word;                  { +35 unknown             }
          fill7  : word;                  { +37 unknown             }
          fill8  : word;                  { +39 unknown             }
       END;
  dcbptr = ^dcb;


    ldt = RECORD                   { Logical Drive Table format  }
          name   : array[0..67] of char;{ +00 drive and path      }
          code   : byte;                  { +44 drive in use code   }
          mydpb  : dpbptr;                { +45 DPB for this drive }
          dirclu : word;                  { +49 directory cluster   }
          filler2: word;                  { +4B unknown             }
          filler3: word;                  { +4D unknown             }
          patlen : word;                  { +4F SUBST path length   }
          filler4: byte;                  { +51 unknown             }
          filler5: word;                  { +52 unknown             }
          filler6: word;                  { +54 unknown             }
          filler7: word;                  { +56 unknown             }
       END;
  ldtptr = ^ldt;


    cvt = RECORD              { Configuration Variable Table      }
          curbfr : bcbptr;                { current pos in chain    }
          memchn : mcbptr;                { start of MCB chain      }
          pdrvs  : dpbptr;                { Fn $52 points to here   }
          dcbchn : dcbptr;                { set up by FILES=        }
          clkdev : pointer;               { set by DEVICE= (clock$)}
          condev : pointer;               { set by DEVICE= (con)    }
          secsiz : integer;               { maximum block size      }
          bfrchn : bcblkp;                { set up by BUFFERS=      }
          ldrvs  : ldtptr;                { set up by LASTDRIVE=    }
          fcbchn : chnptr;                { set up by FCBS=         }
```

continues

```pascal
              filler : integer;             { number of FCBs to keep }
              npdrvs : byte;                { set by driver list     }
              nldrvs : byte;                { set by LASTDRIVE=      }
           END;
      cvtptr = ^cvt;

      dtstr = string[8];                     { date-time strings      }
      pstrg = string[9];                     { pointer-conversion fmt }
      memst = string[12];                    { memory usage string    }

   VAR
      cvtbase : cvtptr;
      curbuf  : bcbptr;
      curmcb  : mcbptr;
      curdpb  : dpbptr;
      curchn  : chnptr;
      curdcb,
      curfcb  : dcbptr;
      curldt  : ldtptr;
      bcbctr,
      dcbctr  : integer ;                    { counters               }
      b       : Registers;
      PawsFlag: Boolean;                     { controls screen-full pausing }
      lctr    : integer;                     { counts lines displayed }

   function hexn(b:byte) : char;             { converts nibble to char }
      begin
         b := b and 15;                      { force to only 4 bits   }
         if b > 9 then inc(b,7);             { adjust for hex digits  }
         hexn := chr(b+48);                  { convert to character   }
      end;

   function hexb(b:byte) : string;
      begin
         hexb := hexn(b shr 4) + hexn(b);    { assemble the nibbles   }
      end;

   function hexw(w:word) : string;
      begin
         hexw := hexb(w shr 8) + hexb(w);    { assemble the bytes     }
      end;

   function hexl(l:longint) : string;
      begin
         hexl := hexw(l shr 16) + hexw(l);   { assemble the words     }
      end;
```

```pascal
procedure outcstr( var s : nam8);  { output ASCIIZ string          }
  VAR
    i : integer;
  BEGIN
    i := 1;
    while (s[i] <> #0) and (i < 9) do
      begin
        write(s[i]);
        inc(i);
      end;
  END;

PROCEDURE holdup;                    { count lines and wait if full }
  BEGIN
    IF PawsFlag THEN
      BEGIN
        inc(lctr);
        if lctr > 23 then
          BEGIN
            lctr := 0;
            readln;
          END
      END
  END;

FUNCTION xp( p : pointer ) : pstrg;    { displays pointer P }
  BEGIN
    xp := hexw(seg(p^)) + ':' + hexw(ofs(p^));
  END;

PROCEDURE  dmp(f : pointer);         { display hex dump of data to CRT }
  VAR
    x : ^byte;
    i : integer;
    c : char;
  BEGIN
    x := f;
    write( xp(f), '> ');
    FOR i:=0 to 15 DO
      BEGIN
        write( hexb(x^) );
        if i=7 then write('-')
               else write(' ');
        x := pointer(longint(x) + 1);
      END;
    write('  ');
    x := f;
    FOR i:=0 to 15 DO
```

continues

DOS Programmer's Reference, 3rd Edition

DOS Programmer's Reference, 3rd Edition

Listing E.2 continued

```
      BEGIN
        c := char($7f AND x^);
        if c<' ' then c := '.';
        write( c );
        if i=7 then write(' ');
        x := pointer(longint(x) + 1);
      END;
    writeln;
    holdup;
  END;

  PROCEDURE dpbtrc(a: pointer);      { trace and report DPB data }
    VAR
      ofsv : word;

    PROCEDURE dpbrpt;                { reports each DPB's content }
      BEGIN
        writeln;
        holdup;
        write('Drive ', char (curdpb^.drvc+ord('A')) );
        write(': (unit ', curdpb^.dunit, ' of driver at ', xp(curdpb^.drvr) );
        writeln(') media code = ', hexb(curdpb^.mcode) );
        holdup;
        write(' ', curdpb^.bps:3, ' bytes per sector,');
        write(' ', curdpb^.spc+1:2, ' sectors per cluster,');
        writeln(' ', curdpb^.tcc-1:4, ' total cluster count');
        holdup;
        write(' Res sectors: ', curdpb^.rsrvs, ' ');
        write(' ', curdpb^.nfats, ' FAT''s, ', curdpb^.spf:2, ' sec ea ');
        write(' FAT entry: ');
        IF (curdpb^.tcc) > $0FFC
          THEN  write( 16 )
          ELSE  write( 12 );
        writeln(' bits  Root: ', curdpb^.dirsiz:3, ' entries');
        holdup;
        write(' First root sector: ', hexw(curdpb^.fds)  );
        write(' First data sector: ', hexw(curdpb^.fus)  );
        writeln(' Last cluster used: ', hexw(curdpb^.lastused));
        holdup;
      END;          { of dpbrpt proc }

    BEGIN
      curdpb := a;
      ofsv := 0;
      writeln;
      holdup;
```

```
          writeln('DRIVE PARAMETER BLOCK (DPB) DATA--');
          holdup;
          WHILE (ofsv <> $FFFF) DO
            BEGIN
              ofsv := word(longint( curdpb^.nxt ));
              dpbrpt ;
              curdpb := dpbptr(curdpb^.nxt);
            END;
          write(#12);
      END;  { of dpbtrc proc }

    PROCEDURE bcbtrc2(a : pointer);
      VAR
        ofsv : word;
        ofst : word;

      PROCEDURE  bcbrpt(a : bcbptr);
        VAR
          i : integer;
          x : pointer;
        BEGIN
          writeln;
          holdup;
          inc(bcbctr);
          write('Buffer Control Block ', bcbctr:2, ' at ', xp(a));
          write('      Prev: ', hexw(a^.prcb));
          writeln('      Next: ', hexw(a^.nxcb));
          holdup;
          write('    Logical ''', char(ord('A')+a^.ldrv));
          write(':'',    Sector ', hexl(a^.lsect));
          writeln('    Action code: ', hexb(a^.action));
          holdup;
          write('    NFATS: ', hexb( a^.nf));
          write('        SPF: ', hexw(a^.secf));
          writeln('        DPB address: ', xp(a^.pdrv));
          holdup;
          write('    FILL2: ', hexw(a^.fill2));
          writeln('      FILL3: ', hexb(a^.fill3));
          holdup;
          x := addr(bcbptr(a)^.buf[0]);
          FOR i:=0 to 31 DO
            dmp(pointer(longint(x)+(i SHL 4)));
        END;         { of bcbrpt proc }

    BEGIN           { bcbtrc2 routine }
      bcbctr := 0;
      ofsv := 0;
      ofst := ofs(a^);
      WHILE (ofsv <> ofst) DO
```

continues

Listing E.2 continued

```
        BEGIN
          ofsv := bcbptr(a)^.nxcb;
          bcbrpt (a);
          a := ptr(seg(a^),ofsv);
        END;
      write(#12);
    END;           { bcbtrc2 routine }

  PROCEDURE bcbtrc1(a:pointer);

    PROCEDURE bcbtrl(a:bcblkp);
      BEGIN
        writeln;
        holdup;
        writeln( 'Page base is at ', xp(a^.pagebase));
        holdup;
        write  ( 'BX Val = ', hexw(a^.bxval) );
        write  ( '   Users = ', hexb(a^.usrs) );
        writeln( '    Fill = ', hexl(a^.fill) );
        holdup;
        bcbtrc2(a^.pagebase);
      END;

    BEGIN
      writeln( 'Link table is at ', xp(bcptr(a)^.lnkptr));
      holdup;
      write  ( 'Page count = ', bcptr(a)^.pgs:4 );
      write  ( '    Fill1 = ', hexl(bcptr(a)^.fill1) );
      writeln( '    Fill2 = ', hexw(bcptr(a)^.fill2) );
      holdup;
      write  ( 'EMS Flag = ', hexb(bcptr(a)^.emsflg) );
      write  ( '       Handle = ', hexw(bcptr(a)^.emshdl) );
      writeln( '    PhysPg = ', hexb(bcptr(a)^.emsppg) );
      holdup;
      bcbtrl( bcptr(a)^.lnkptr);
    END;

  PROCEDURE dcbtrc(t : dtstr; a : pointer);
    VAR
      ofsv : word;

    FUNCTION f_tm(n : word) : dtstr;
      VAR
        buf : dtstr;
        b   : byte;
      BEGIN
        b := ((n SHR 11) AND 31);
        buf[1] :=char((b DIV 10) + 48);
        buf[2] :=char((b MOD 10) + 48);
```

```
        buf[3] := ':';
        b := ((n SHR  5) AND 63);
        buf[4] :=char((b DIV 10) + 48);
        buf[5] :=char((b MOD 10) + 48);
        buf[6] := ':';
        b := ((n SHL  1) AND 63);
        buf[7] :=char((b DIV 10) + 48);
        buf[8] :=char((b MOD 10) + 48);
        f_tm := buf;
      END;

FUNCTION f_dt(n : word) : dtstr;
  VAR
    buf : dtstr;
    b   : byte;
  BEGIN
    b :=((n SHR  5) AND 15);
    buf[1] :=char((b DIV 10) + 48);
    buf[2] :=char((b MOD 10) + 48);
    buf[3] := '/';
    b := ( n         AND 31);
    buf[4] :=char((b DIV 10) + 48);
    buf[5] :=char((b MOD 10) + 48);
    buf[6] := '/';
    b := ((n SHR  9) AND 15) + 80;
    buf[7] :=char((b DIV 10) + 48);
    buf[8] :=char((b MOD 10) + 48);
    f_dt := buf;
  END;

PROCEDURE dcbrpt( var t : dtstr; n : integer );
  type
    acctyp = array[0..3] of string[7];
  const
    actyp : acctyp = ('READ', 'WRITE', 'R/W', 'unknown');
  var
    isdvc : Boolean;
  BEGIN
    WHILE (n > 0) DO
    BEGIN
      INC (dcbctr);
      writeln;
      holdup;
      write  (t, ' ', dcbctr:2 );
      IF (curdcb^.name[0] = #0)  THEN
      BEGIN
        writeln(' at ', xp(curdcb), ' not used since bootup');
        holdup;
      END
```

continues

DOS
PROGRAMMING

```
else
BEGIN
  isdvc := (curdcb^.dvatr and 128) <> 0;
  write(' for ');
  IF isdvc
    THEN write( 'device ' )
    ELSE write( 'file ' );
  write(curdcb^.name[0], curdcb^.name[1], curdcb^.name[2]);
  write(curdcb^.name[3], curdcb^.name[4], curdcb^.name[5]);
  write(curdcb^.name[6], curdcb^.name[7]);
  IF (NOT isdvc) THEN  { block driver }
    write('.', curdcb^.ext[0], curdcb^.ext[1], curdcb^.ext[2]);
  write(' at ', xp( curdcb ) );
  write(' shows ', curdcb^.nusers);
  writeln(' OPENs');
  holdup;
  write('  Opened for ', actyp[3 AND (curdcb^.mode)]);
  write(' access' );
  IF ($FFFC AND (curdcb^.mode))<>0 THEN
    write(' (', hexw(curdcb^.mode), ')');
  writeln(' by process ', hexw(curdcb^.owner));
  holdup;
  IF( isdvc ) THEN            { Device         }
    BEGIN
      write('  Device driver at ', xp(curdcb^.pdrvr) );
      write(' is in ');
      if ((curdcb^.dvatr) AND 32)<>0 THEN write('Raw')
                                ELSE write( 'Cooked' );
      write(' mode and is ');
      if ((curdcb^.dvatr) AND 64)=0 THEN  write('not ');
      writeln('ready');
      holdup;
    END
  else                        { File          }
    BEGIN
      write('  File is on drive ', char(ord('A')+((curdcb^.dvatr) AND 31)));
      write(': (driver at ', xp(curdcb^.pdrvr));
      write(') and has ');
      if ((curdcb^.dvatr) AND 64)<>0 THEN  write('not ');
      writeln('been written to.');
      holdup;
      writeln('  File''s attribute byte = ', hexb(curdcb^.datrb));
      holdup;
    END;
```

```
            write  ('  Mod Time/date: ');
            write  (f_tm(curdcb^.modtm), ', ');
            writeln(f_dt(curdcb^.moddt));
            holdup;
            write  ('       Dir Sector:  ', hexw(curdcb^.dirsec), ' ');
            writeln('        Dir Index:  ', curdcb^.dirndx:4, ' ');
            holdup;
            write  ('    First Cluster:  ', hexw(curdcb^.frstc), ' ');
            write  ('    Prev Clusters:  ', curdcb^.clsctr:4, ' ');
            writeln(' Current Cluster:  ', hexw(curdcb^.curcls), ' ');
            holdup;
            write  ('   Directory size:',   curdcb^.totsiz:6, ' ');
            writeln('  Curr byte count:',   curdcb^.curpos:6     );
            holdup;
            write  ('  Fill2=', hexw(curdcb^.fill2), ' ');
            write  ('  Fill3=', hexw(curdcb^.fill3), ' ');
            write  ('  Fill4=', hexw(curdcb^.fill4), ' ');
            writeln('  Fill5=', hexw(curdcb^.fill5)     );
            holdup;
            write  ('  Fill6=', hexw(curdcb^.fill6), ' ');
            write  ('  Fill7=', hexw(curdcb^.fill7), ' ');
            writeln('  Fill8=', hexw(curdcb^.fill8)     );
            holdup;
          END;
          curdcb := pointer(longint(curdcb) + sizeof(dcb) - 1);
          DEC( n );
        END;        { n >= 0 loop   }
      END;          { of dcbrpt     }

BEGIN
  curchn := chnptr(a);
  dcbctr := 0;
  ofsv := 0;
  WHILE (ofsv <> $FFFF) DO
    BEGIN
      ofsv := word(longint(curchn^.nxtlnk));
      curdcb := dcbptr(longint(curchn)+sizeof(chn));
      writeln;
      holdup;
      write ( 'Link at ', xp(curchn), ' contains ');
      writeln( curchn^.nmbr, ' ', t, 's--');
      holdup;
      dcbrpt (t, curchn^.nmbr);
      curchn := chnptr(curchn^.nxtlnk);
    END;
  write(#12);
END;
```

continues

```
PROCEDURE memtrc(a : pointer);
  VAR
    z : longint;

  PROCEDURE memrpt(s,o,a : word; var n : nam8);

    FUNCTION memu(a : word) : memst;      { determine memory use }
      var
        x : char;
    BEGIN
      x := char( mem[a:0] );
      CASE x OF
        #$CD:
          memu := 'Program';
        'A'..'Z':
          memu := 'Environment';
        else
          memu := 'Data';
        End;
    END;

  BEGIN
    z := longint(s) SHL 4;
    write( z:6, ' bytes ' );
    IF (o<>0) THEN
      begin
        write  ('USED by proc ', hexw(o));
        write  (', at ', hexw( a ), ':0000, for ', memu(a));
        if n[1] in ['A'..'Z'] then
          begin
            write('. Pgm name: ' );
            outcstr( n );
            writeln;
          end
        else
          writeln('. No program name');
      end
    else
      writeln('FREE at ', hexw( a ), ':0000' );
    holdup;
  END;  { of memrpt      }

BEGIN
  curmcb := mcbptr(a);
  writeln;
  holdup;
  writeln('MEMORY ALLOCATION CHAIN');
```

```
      holdup;
      WHILE (curmcb^.flag = 'M') DO
        BEGIN
          memrpt( curmcb^.siz, curmcb^.owner, SEG(curmcb^)+1, curmcb^.name);
          curmcb := ptr( seg(curmcb^) + (curmcb^.siz + 1), 0 );
        END;
      IF (curmcb^.flag <> 'Z') THEN
        BEGIN
          writeln(#13, #10, 'MEMORY ALLOCATION ERROR at ', xp(curmcb) );
          halt(255);
        END;
      memrpt( curmcb^.siz, curmcb^.owner, SEG(curmcb^)+1, curmcb^.name);
      write(#12);
    END;    { of memtrc }

    PROCEDURE ldttrc( a: ldtptr; n: byte );

      PROCEDURE ldtrpt( l: ldtptr; d: byte );
        VAR
          ldrive : char;
          i      : integer;
        BEGIN
          ldrive := chr( $41 + d );
          if (l^.code AND byte($40))=0 then
            writeln( 'Logical Drive ', ldrive, ' not yet defined' )
          else
            begin
              write  ( 'Logical Drive ', ldrive );
              writeln( ' = Physical drive ', l^.name[0] );
              holdup;
              write  ( 'The current (full) pathspec is: ' );
              i := 0;
              repeat
                write  ( l^.name[i] );
                inc( i );
              until (l^.name[i] = #0);
              writeln;
            end;
          holdup;
          if(l^.code = $50) then
            writeln( 'Code = 0x50 -- result of SUBST command')
          else if(l^.code = $40) then
            writeln( 'Code = 0x40 -- physical (or aliased) device')
          else
            writeln( 'Code = 0x', hexb(l^.code), ' -- unknown');
          holdup;
          writeln( 'Directory Cluster = ', hexw( l^.dirclu ));
          holdup;
```

continues

```
          writeln( 'Path Length to ignore = ', hexw( l^.patlen ));
          holdup;
          write  ( 'Filler2 = ', hexw(l^.filler2), '  ');
          write  ( 'Filler3 = ', hexw(l^.filler3), '  ');
          writeln( 'Filler4 = ', hexb(l^.filler4)       );
          holdup;
          write  ( 'Filler5 = ', hexw(l^.filler5), '  ');
          write  ( 'Filler6 = ', hexw(l^.filler6), '  ');
          writeln( 'Filler7 = ', hexw(l^.filler7)       );
          holdup;
          writeln;
          holdup;
        END; { of ldtrpt }

    VAR
      o  : byte;

    BEGIN
      curldt := a;
      writeln;
      holdup;
      writeln('LOGICAL DRIVE TABLES (set by LASTDRIVE=, SUBST, etc.):');
      holdup;
      dec( n );                      { convert for zero-based reference   }
      for o := 0 to n do             { loop thru contiguous tables        }
        begin
          ldtrpt(curldt, o);
          curldt := ptr(seg(curldt^), ( ofs(curldt^) + sizeof(ldt)));
        end;
      write(#12);
    END; { of ldttrc }

{ main  }
BEGIN
  b.ah := $30;                   { Check for correct DOS version      }
  MsDos(b);
  if b.al < 4 then               { If not V4.x or higher, get out     }
    begin
      writeln( 'Wrong DOS version: ', b.al, '.', b.ah );
      halt(255);                 { return ErrorLevel=255              }
    end;
  PawsFlag := ParamCount = 0;    { else set up for paging output      }
  lctr := 0;
  writeln( 'Configuration Variables, DOS version ', b.al, '.', b.ah );
  holdup;
  b.ah := $52;                   { Get CVT pointer set up             }
  msdos(b);                      {    (using undocumented function)   }
  cvtbase := ptr(b.es, b.bx-8); { hold pointer to CVT                 }
```

```
writeln;
holdup;
writeln('CVT is located at ', xp(cvtbase));
holdup;
write  ('No. of Phys Drives (at ', xp(@cvtbase^.npdrvs));
writeln('): ', cvtbase^.npdrvs);
holdup;
write  ('No. of Log. Drives (at ', xp(@cvtbase^.nldrvs));
writeln('): ', cvtbase^.nldrvs);
holdup;
write  ('  Clock Device (ptr at ', xp(@cvtbase^.clkdev));
writeln('): ', xp(cvtbase^.clkdev));
holdup;
write  ('    CON Device (ptr at ', xp(@cvtbase^.condev));
writeln('): ', xp(cvtbase^.condev));
holdup;
write  ('    Sector Size(?) (at ', xp(@cvtbase^.secsiz));
writeln('):      ',hexw(cvtbase^.secsiz));
holdup;
write  ('      FCBs to keep (at ', xp(@cvtbase^.filler));
writeln('):      ',hexw(cvtbase^.filler));
holdup;
write  ('1.    Memory Chain (ptr at ', xp(@cvtbase^.memchn));
writeln('): ', xp(cvtbase^.memchn));
holdup;
write  ('2.      DCB Chain (ptr at ', xp(@cvtbase^.dcbchn));
writeln('): ', xp(cvtbase^.dcbchn));
holdup;
write  ('3.      DPB Chain (ptr at ', xp(@cvtbase^.pdrvs));
writeln('): ', xp(cvtbase^.pdrvs));
holdup;
write  ('4.      FCB Chain (ptr at ', xp(@cvtbase^.fcbchn));
writeln('): ', xp(cvtbase^.fcbchn));
holdup;
write  ('5.      LDT Chain (ptr at ', xp(@cvtbase^.ldrvs));
writeln('): ', xp(cvtbase^.ldrvs));
holdup;
write  ('6.  Current Buffer (ptr at ', xp(@cvtbase^.curbfr));
writeln('): ', xp(cvtbase^.curbfr));
holdup;
write  ('7.  Buffer Chain (link at ', xp(@cvtbase^.bfrchn));
writeln('): ', xp(cvtbase^.bfrchn));
holdup;
```

continues

```
      writeln;
      holdup;
      writeln('TRACING      MCB Chain===');
      holdup;
      memtrc(cvtbase^.memchn);

      writeln;
      holdup;
      writeln('TRACING      DCB Chain===');
      holdup;
      dcbtrc('DCB', cvtbase^.dcbchn);

      writeln;
      holdup;
      writeln('TRACING      DPB Chain===');
      holdup;
      dpbtrc(cvtbase^.pdrvs);

      writeln;
      holdup;
      writeln('TRACING      FCB Chain===');
      holdup;
      dcbtrc('FCB', cvtbase^.fcbchn);

      writeln;
      holdup;
      writeln('TRACING      LDT Chain===');
      holdup;
      ldttrc(cvtbase^.ldrvs, cvtbase^.nldrvs);

      writeln;
      holdup;
      writeln('TRACING Buffer Chain from current buffer===');
      holdup;
      bcbtrc2(cvtbase^.curbfr);

      writeln;
      holdup;
      writeln('TRACING   Buffer Chain thru EMS link record===');
      holdup;
      bcbtrc1(cvtbase^.bfrchn);
   END.
```

Index

Symbols

#define directives, 100
#define preprocessor directives, 100
. (dot) current directory entries, 265, 270
.. (dot-dot) parent directory entries, 265, 270
1-2-3, 118
12-bit FAT, 241-243
16-bit FAT, 243-245
32M barrier, 240-241
80186 processor, hardware interrupt conflicts, 364
80286 processor
    hardware interrupts, 363
    memory addressing, 32-33
80386 processor chips, memory addressing, 33
80486 processor chips, memory addressing, 33
8086 processor
    family of, 22-24, 36
        interrupts, 363-365
    hardware interrupts, 363
    register set, 27-28
        flags, 32
        general-purpose, 28-29
        offset, 31-32
        segment, 29-30
    segmented memory addressing, 24-26
8250 serial interface chip (UART), 191, 196-197
    accessing directly, 206-207, 220-221
    baud rate divisor (BRD), 197-199
    interrupt enable register (IER), 197-200
    interrupt identification register (IIR), 197, 200
    line control register (LCR), 197, 200-201
    line status register (LSR), 197, 202
    modem control register (MCR), 197, 200-202

modem status register (MSR), 197, 202-203

receiver data register (RDR), 197-198

transmitter holding register (THR), 197-198

8259 Programmable Interrupt Controller chip, 79

8259A Programmable Interrupt Controller (PIC), 362

86-DOS, 11-12

A

_a20_stat function, 327

Abort, Retry, Ignore? message, 80

absolute addresses, 24

Absolute Disk Read (Int 25h), 751-753

Absolute Disk Write (Int 26h), 753-755

accessing
8250 serial interface chip (UART) directly, 206-207, 220-221

DOS and BIOS from programs, 88-89

files with wild cards, 92

registers
in C language, 93-95
in QuickBASIC, 109-110
in Turbo Pascal, 104-105
segment, 248-250

video displays, 120

Activate Session (0003h, notification function), 930

active TSRs (terminate and stay resident), 356, 406

addresses
absolute, 24
base (segment), 24
offset, 24
string, passing to DOS, 90-91

Adjust for Leap Year (Int 2Fh, Function 12h, Subfunction 1Bh), 775

Adjust Keyboard Repeat Rate (Int 16, Function 03h), 571

all-points addressable (APA) modes, 127-128

Allocate Alternate Map Register Set (Int 67h, Function 5Bh, Subfunction 03h), 854-855

Allocate DMA Register Set (Int 67h, Function 5Bh, Subfunction 05h), 856

Allocate DOS Memory Block (Int 31h, Function 0100h), 883

Allocate Extended Memory Block (XMS Function 009h), 866

Allocate LDT Descriptors (Int 31h, Function 0000h), 875

Allocate Linear Memory Block (Int 31h, Function 0504h), 900-901

Allocate Memory (Int 21h, Function 48h), 699-700

Allocate Memory (Int 21h, Function 6Ah), 744

Allocate Memory Block (Int 31h, Function 0501h), 899

Allocate Raw Pages (Int 67h, Function 5Ah, Subfunction 01h), 851-852

Allocate Real Mode Callback Address (Int 31h, Function 0303h), 893-894

Allocate Shared Memory (Int 31h, Function 0D00h), 917-918
Allocate Specific LDT Descriptor (Int 31h, Function 000Dh), 881
Allocate Standard Pages (Int 67h, Function 5Ah, Subfunction 00h), 851
Allocate Switcher ID (Int 2Fh, Function 4Bh, Subfunction 03h), 789-790
allocating memory, 82-85
alphanumeric mode
    see text mode
Alt key, 171
Alter Page Map and Call (Int 67h, Function 56h), 844-845
Alter Page Map and Jump (Int 67h, Function 55h), 842-843
_alter_a20 function, 327
Alternate Disk Reset (Int 13, Function 0Dh), 536-537
Alternate Select (Int 10, Function 12h), 519-520
ANSI.SYS, 54
    driver, accessing video displays, 120
Applications Program Interface (API), 949
    task switcher, 16
applications programs
    COM, 61-64
    EXE, 64-72
    level within system layering, 18
arena chain, 292-293
arena entries
    see memory blocks
Arithmetic Overflow (Int 04h), 495
ASCII
    character set, 937-939
    keystroke values, 164-167

ASCIIZ (ASCII plus zero)
    strings, 276
    formats, 89
assembly language
    accessing 8250 serial interface chip (UART) directly, 220
    allocating memory, 294
    bright CGA backgrounds, 126
    building routines, 372
    calling DOS, 90
    COM program, 62-64
    comparing to high-level languages, 72-73
    EXE program, 65-66
    interrupt handlers, 370-371
    passing string addresses to DOS, 90-91
    reasons for coding device drivers, 418
    resource list, 946-947
asynchronous communication, 193
attributes, character, 125
AUTOEXEC.BAT file, 59
auxiliary
    carry flag (AF), 32
    device (AUX), 59
Auxiliary Input (Int 21h, Function 03h), 616-617
Auxiliary Output (Int 21h, Function 04h), 617-618
AX (AH and AL) general purpose register, 28-29, 66, 204, 466, 475-477

B

bank switching, 822
base addresses, 24
BASIC language, 18
    accessing 8250 serial interface chip (UART) directly, 221

and DOS data area, 944
ASCIIZ strings, 89
building video displays, 120
memory allocation, 85,
    294-295
reading keyboard from,
    168-169
retrieving DOS version num-
    bers, 463-464
BASICA, 108
BAT file extension, 53
batch files, 52-53
    device driver assembly, 456
    executing with EXEC function,
    345
baud rate, 194
    divisor (BRD), 197-199
Beginning Disk Cluster (Offset
    1Ah) of directory entry struc-
    ture, 268
Best Fit memory allocation, 83,
    292
bimodal code, 873
BIN file extension, 422
BIOS (basic input/output
    system), 10, 50-51
    accessing
        from programs, 88-89
        keyboard, 170-174
        video displays through
            function calls, 120
    calling to, with high-level
        languages, 91-93
    data area, 943-944
    identifying level of keyboard
        support, 181-183
    initializing communications
        port, 203-207
    keyboard interrupt handler,
        164, 168
    level within system layering, 17

programming
    chips, 33
    resource list, 946
video functions, 145-153,
    586-591
BIOS interrupts, 485-492
    00h (Divide-by-Zero), 493
    01h (Single Step), 493-494
    02h (Non-Maskable Interrupt
        [NMI]), 494-495
    03h (Breakpoint), 495
    04h (Arithmetic Overflow),
        495
    05h (Print Screen), 496
    08h (System Timer), 496-497
    09h (Keyboard), 42, 408-409,
        497-498
    0Bh
        COM1 and COM3 Interrupt
            Service (PC, PC XT), 499
        COM2 and COM4 Interrupt
            Service (Personal
            Computer AT), 499
        Reserved (PS/2), 499
    0Ch
        COM1 and COM3 Interrupt
            Service (Personal
            Computer AT), 499-500
        COM2 and COM4 Interrupt
            Service (PC, PC XT),
            499-500
        Reserved (PS/2), 499-500
    0Dh
        Hard Disk Management
            (Disk Controller) (PC XT),
            500
        LPT2 Control (Personal
            Computer AT), 500
        Reserved (PS/2), 500
    0Eh (Floppy Disk Manage-
        ment), 500

0Fh
Printer Management (LPT1),
501
Reserved (PS/2), 501
10h
00h (Set Video Mode),
501-502
01h (Set Cursor Type), 503
02h (Set Cursor Position),
503-504
03h (Read Cursor Position
and Configuration), 505
04h (Read Light Pen Posi-
tion), 505-506
05h (Select Active Display
Page), 506-507
06h (Scroll Window Up),
507-508
07h (Scroll Window Down),
508-509
08h (Read Character and
Attribute), 509
09h (Write Character and
Attribute), 509-510
0Ah (Write Character at
Cursor), 510-511
0Bh (Set Color Palette),
511-512
0Ch (Write Graphics Pixel),
512-513
0Dh (Read Graphics Pixel),
513
0Eh (Write Text in Teletype
Mode), 513-514
0Fh (Get Current Display
Mode), 514-515
10h (Set Palette Registers),
515-517
11h (Character Generator),
517-518

12h (Alternate Select),
519-520
13h (Write String), 520-521
1Ah (Read/Write Display
Codes), 521
1Bh (Get Display State), 522
1Ch (Save/Restore Display
State), 522-523
10h (Video BIOS), 817
F0h (Read One Register),
817
F1h (Write One Register),
818
F2h (Read Register Range),
818
F3h (Write Register Range),
819
F4h (Read Register Set),
819-820
F5h (Write Register Set),
820
F6h (Revert to Default
Registers), 820
F7h (Define Default Register
Table), 821
FAh (Interrogate Driver),
821
11h (Get Equipment Status),
466-469, 523-524
12h (Get Memory Size),
524-525
13h
00h (Reset Disk System),
525-526
01h (Get Disk System
Status), 526
02h (Read Disk Sectors),
527
03h (Write Disk Sectors),
527-528

04h (Verify Disk Sectors),
528-529
05h (Format Disk Track),
254-255, 529-530
06h (Format Cylinder and
Set Bad Sector Flags),
530-531
07h (Format Drive from
Specified Cylinder), 531
08h (Return Disk Drive
Parameters), 531-532
09h (Initialize Fixed Disk
Table), 533
0Ah (Read Long Sector),
533-535
0Bh (Write Long Sector),
534-535
0Ch (Seek Cylinder), 536
0Dh (Alternate Disk Reset),
536-537
0Eh (Read Sector Buffer),
537
0Fh (Write Sector Buffer),
537-538
10h (Test Fixed Disk System
Status), 538
11h (Recalibrate Fixed Disk
Drive), 538
12h (Diagnose Controller
RAM), 539
13h (Diagnose Drive), 539
14h (Diagnose Controller),
539-540
15h (Return DASD Type),
540
16h (Read Disk Change Line
Status), 541
17h (Set DASD Type for
Disk Format), 541-542
18h (Set Media Type for
Disk Format), 542

19h (Park Heads), 543
1Ah (Format ESDI Unit),
543-544
14h
00h (Initialize Commu-
nications Port), 544-545
01h (Write Character to
Communications Port),
546
02h (Read Character from
Communications Port),
546-547
03h (Request Commu-
nications Port Status), 547
04h (Extended Initial-
ization), 548-549
05h (Extended
Communications Port
Control), 549-550
15h
00h (Turn On Cassette
Motor), 550
01h (Turn Off Cassette
Motor), 550-551
02h (Read Data Blocks from
Cassette Drive), 551
03h (Write Data Blocks to
Cassette Drive), 551-552
0Fh (ESDI Unit Format
Periodic Interrupt), 552
21h (Power-On Self-Test
Error Log), 552-553
4Fh (Keyboard Intercept),
553-554
80h (Device Open), 554
81h (Device Close), 554-555
82h (Program Termination),
555
83h (Event Wait), 555-556
84h (Joystick Support),
556-557

85h (System Request Key Pressed), 557

86h (Delay), 557-558

87h (Move Block), 289, 558-559

88h (Extended Memory Size Determination), 289, 559-560

89h (Switch Processor to Protected Mode), 560

90h (Device Wait), 561-562

91h (Interrupt Complete), 562-563

C0h (Return System Configuration Parameters), 563-564

C1h (Return Extended BIOS Data Area Segment Address), 564-565

C2h (Pointing Device BIOS Interface), 565-567

C3h (Enable/Disable Watchdog Timeout), 567

C4h (Programmable Option Select), 568

16h

00h (Read Keyboard Character), 170, 568-569

01h (Read Keyboard Status), 170-171, 569-570

02h (Return Keyboard Flags), 171-174, 570-571

03h (Adjust Keyboard Repeat Rate), 571

04h (Key-Click On/Off), 572

05h (Write to Keyboard Buffer), 181-183, 572

10h (Get Keystroke), 181, 572-573

11h (Check Keyboard), 573

12h (Get Keyboard Status Flags), 573-574

17h (printer functions), 157-158

00h (Write Character to Printer), 574-575

01h (Initialize Printer Port), 575

02h (Request Printer Port Status), 96, 105, 110, 576

18h (Execute ROM BASIC), 576

19h (System Warm Boot), 576-577

1Ah

00h (Get Clock Counter), 577

01h (Set Clock Counter), 577-578

02h (Read Real-Time Clock), 578-579

03h (Set Real-Time Clock), 579

04h (Read Date from Real-Time Clock), 580

05h (Set Date of Real-Time Clock), 580

06h (Set System Alarm), 581

07h (Disable Real-Time Clock Alarm), 581

09h (Read Real-Time Clock Alarm), 582

0Ah (Get Day Count), 582

0Bh (Set Day Count), 582

80h (Set Sound Source), 583

1Bh (Ctrl-Break Address), 583

1Ch (Timer Tick), 409, 584

1Dh (Video-Initialization Parameter Table), 584

1Eh (Disk-Initialization Parameter Table), 585

1Fh (Graphics Display
Character Bit-Map Table),
585-586
4Fh
00h (Return SuperVGA
Information), 587-588
01h (Return SuperVGA
Mode Information),
588-589
02h (Set SuperVGA Display
Mode), 589
03h (Return SuperVGA
Display Mode), 590
04h (Save/Restore
SuperVGA Video State),
590
05h (Display Memory
Window Control), 591
70h (Real-Time Clock
Interrupt), 586
BIOS parameter block (BPB),
57-58
building in device drivers,
441-443
layout of, 237-239
bits
data, 193-194
masks, 100
rate, 194
set archive, 100
settings, color text mode, 127
start, 193
stop, 193-194
swapped, 195
blink feature, disabling, 126
Block Device Local or Remote?
(Int 21h, Function 44h,
Subfunction 09h), 683-684
Block Device Removable? (Int
21h, Function 44h, Subfunction
08h), 683

block devices, 53
drivers, 419
Block Driver IOCTL Read (Int
21h, Function 44h, Subfunction
04h), 680
Block Driver IOCTL Write (Int
21h, Function 44h, Subfunction
05h), 681
blocks
environment, 346
file control (FCBs), 346
memory, 82-83
boot
record, 9, 49, 234, 237-239
sectors, 56-58
sequence, 55-59
bootstrap initialization
procedure, 56
border() function, 148
Borland C++, pseudovariables,
94
BP (base pointer) register, 28, 31
Breakpoint (Int 03h), 495
Btrieve file-management system,
81
buffer control block (BCB),
964-965, 969, 972-973
Buffered STDIN Input (Int 21h,
Function 0Ah), 180-181,
621-622
build BIOS parameter block
(BPB), 441-443
Build Notification Chain (Int 2Fh,
Function 4Bh, Subfunction
01h), 788-789
busy waits, 76
buttons, mouse, 46
BX (BH and BL) general purpose
register, 28-29, 205, 477-478
bytes, keyboard flag, 173

C

C language, 18-19, 93
accessing
  8250 serial interface chip
  (UART) directly, 221
  registers and generating
  interrupts, 93-96
ASCIIZ strings, 89
exec() function, 348
getting and setting file
  attributes, 96-103
memory allocation, 85
  dynamic, 294-296
resource list, 947
retrieving DOS version
  numbers, 462-463
sample program, 73-74
working with video display
  and printer, 118
Calculate Date (Int 2Fh, Function
12h, Subfunction 1Dh),
776-777
Calculate Days Since Start-of-
Month (Int 2Fh, Function 12h,
Subfunction 1Ch), 776
Call Real Mode Procedure with
Far Return Frame (Int 31h,
Function 0301h), 891-892
Call Real Mode Procedure with
IRET Frame (Int 31h, Function
0302h), 892-893
calling registers, 612
Cancel All Files in Print Queue
(Int 2Fh, Function 01h,
Subfunction 03h), 760
Cancel Redirection List Entry (Int
21h, Function 5Fh, Subfunction
04h), 736
Caps Lock key, 171
carry flag (CF), 32, 91

Case and Country Conversion
(Int 2Fh, Function 12h,
Subfunction 13h), 772
Cathode Ray Tube Controller
(CRTC) chips, 122-123
  Motorola 6845, 120
cdate() function, 471-472
CDROM Interface (Int 2Fh,
Function 15h), 786
central processing unit (CPU),
24, 88
  80286+ memory addressing,
  32-33
  8086
    memory addressing, 24-26
    register set, 27-32
  identifying chips, 33-36
  math coprocessors, 36-39
character
  attributes, 125
  device drivers, 419
  devices, 53
    basic, 117-118
Character Generator (Int 10,
Function 11h), 517-518
characters
  ASCII set (3 pages of), 937
  extended sets, 175
  receiving in terminal
    programs, 216-219
charwait() function, 178
Check for APPEND Installation
(Int 2Fh, Function B7h,
Subfunction 00h), 792-793
Check Install (Int 2Fh, Function
00h), 951-953
Check Keyboard (Int 16,
Function 11h), 573
Check STDIN Status (Int 21h,
Function 0Bh), 177-178, 623
child programs, 344-348

chk_mouse() function, 187
chkver() function, 462-464
_chmod function, 103
chrdy() function, 217, 221
chromablizzard, 123
Clear Buffer and Input (Int 21h, Function 0Ch), 623-624
Clear Debug Watchpoint (Int 31h, Function 0B01h), 914-915
Clear File Access Locks (Int 21h, Function 5Ch, Subfunction 01h), 729-730
clear interrupt instruction (CLI), 79
clearwin() function, 148
client programs, 923
clock interrupt handler, 415
CLOCK$ device drivers, 469
clock() function, 414
Close File
    Int 2Fh, Function 12h, Subfunction 27h, 781-782
    FCB (Int 21h, Function 10h), 626-627
    handle (Int 21h, Function 3Eh), 668-669
cls() function, 151
clusters, 230, 239-240
cold boots, 56
Color Graphics Adapter (CGA), 43, 118-119
    bright backgrounds, 126
    displaying test line, 156
    identifying, 128-145
    memory configuration, 122
    monitors driven by, 119
    snow problem, 123
    video display mode, 124
color text mode
    bit meanings, 125
    bit settings, 127

COM file extension, 52
COM programs, 61-64
    dump of, 64-65
    failure to convert EXE programs to, 353
    memory allocation, 84, 293
    versus EXE programs, 75-76
COM1 and COM3 Interrupt Service
    PC, PC XT (Int 0Bh), 499
    Personal Computer AT (Int 0Ch), 499-500
COM2 and COM4 Interrupt Service
    PC, PC XT (Int 0Ch), 499-500
    Personal Computer AT (Int 0Bh), 499
command processor, 10, 52-53, 59-61
    level within system layering, 18
command tail, 346, 355
COMMAND.COM
    command processing, 59-61
    copying trick, 345-348
    loading, 59
    structure of, 52-53
    superseding DOS internal commands, 352
commands
    DATE, 469
    entering to DOS, 350
    external, 52-53
    internal, 52
        superseding, 352
    processing, 59-61
    TIME, 469
Commit File (Int 21h, Function 6Ah), 956
communication
    asynchronous, 193
    synchronous, 192-193

communications port, initializing, 203-207

Compare 32-bit Numbers (Int 2Fh, Function 12h, Subfunction 14h), 772

Compare Strings (Int 2Fh, Function 12h, Subfunction 1Eh), 777

compilers, comparing, 72-74

composite
  color monitors, 119
  monochrome monitors, 119

Conditional Cursor Off (Int 33h, Function 10h), 808

CONFIG.SYS file, adding device drivers, 54

configuration variable table (CVT), 957
  accessing, 957-958
  DOS Version 2.0, 958-960
  DOS Version 3.0, 960-963, 967-972
  DOS Version 4.0, 963-967, 972-974

console device (CON), 59

context switching, 410

control flags, 32

Convert ASCIIZ String (Int 21h, Function 65h, Subfunction 22h), 742

Convert Character (Int 21h, Function 65h, Subfunction 20h), 741-742

Convert String (Int 21h, Function 65h, Subfunction 21h), 742

converting data between parallel and serial format, 192-193

cooked mode, 419

Copy Data to DOS Save Area (Int 21h, Function 5Dh, Subfunction 00h), 730

copying
  COMMAND.COM trick, 345-348
  groups of files to floppy disks, 253

CP/M operating system, 11

Create Alias Descriptor (Int 31h, Function 000Ah), 879-880

Create File (FCB) (Int 21h, Function 16h), 632

Create New File (Int 21h, Function 5Bh), 727-728

Create PSP
  Int 21h, Function 55h, 715-716, 956
  Int 21h, Function 26h, 642-643

Create Session (Notification Function 0005h), 931

Create Subdirectory (Int 21h, Function 39h), 663-664

Create Uniquely Named File (Int 21h, Function 5Ah), 726-727

Create/Truncate File (handle) (Int 21h, Function 3Ch), 665-666

CritErr (Int 21h, Function 5Dh), 956

critical error handlers, writing, 375-405

Critical-Error Handler (Int 24h), 59, 79-81, 748-751

CS (code segment) register, 28-30

ctime() function, 471-472

Ctrl key, 171

Ctrl-Alt-Del key combination, 56

Ctrl-Break Address (Int 1Bh), 583

Ctrl-Break key combination, 168

Ctrl-Break/Ctrl-C handler, 361

Ctrl-C handlers, writing, 369-375

Ctrl-C Interrupt Handler (Int 23h), 59, 747-748

ctrlbrk() function, 368-370

CX (CH and CL) general purpose
register, 28-29, 205-206, 479
cylinders, 230

D

data
  bits, 193-194
  converting between parallel
    and serial format, 192-193
  structures
    SWAPIINFO, 923-924
    SWCALLBACKINFO,
      924-925
    SWINSTANCEITEM, 925
    SWSTARTUPINFO, 926
    SWVERSION, 926-927
  video, storing and displaying,
    120-123
data terminal ready (DTR) line,
  201
date
  functions, 469-474
  stamps, 268
    reading in Turbo Pascal,
      105-108
DATE command, 469
Date of Last Update (Offset 18h)
  of directory entr, 268
Deallocate Alternate Map Register
  Set (Int 67h, Function 5Bh,
  Subfunction 04h), 855-856
Deallocate DMA Register Set (Int
  67h, Function 5Bh,
  Subfunction 08h), 858-859
Deallocate Handle and Memory
  (Int 67h, Function 45h),
  826-827
debugging
  device drivers, 457-458
  system date, 469

Decrement User Count (Int 2Fh,
  Function 12h, Subfunction
  08h), 768
Define Default Register Table (Int
  10h, Function F7h), 821
Delay (Int 15, Function 86h),
  557-558
Delete File
  FCB (Int 21h, Function 13h),
    629-630
  Int 21h, Function 41h, 670-671
depth_search() function, 278-280
descriptor tables, 33
DESQview, 16
Destroy Session (Notification
  Function 0006h), 931
Detect Switcher (Int 2Fh,
  Function 4Bh, Subfunction
  02h), 789
device close, 449
Device Close (Int 15, Function
  81h), 554-555
Device Driver Control (IOCTL)
  (Int 21h, Function 44h),
  674-676
device drivers, 53-54, 417-418
  assembling, 456
  block, 419
  build BIOS parameter block
    (BPB), 441-443
  character, 419
  CLOCK$, 469
  debugging, 457-458
  device close, 449
  device headers, 423-427
  driver initialization, 435-438
  EMM.SYS, 289-290
  Extended Memory
    Specification (XMS), 305
  flush input buffers, 447
  flush output buffers, 448
  generic IOCTL, 450-452

get/set logical device, 450-451
I/O control (IOCTL)
    read, 443-445
    write, 448
input status, 446
installing, 457
interrupt routines, 430-435
media check, 438-441
MOUSE.SYS, 184
nondestructive read, 445-447
open, 449
output
    status, 448
    until busy, 450
read, 445
removable media, 449
strategy routines, 428-430
structure of, 422-423
using, 459-460
workings of, 420-422
write, 447-448
    with verify, 448
device headers, 423-427
Device IOCTL Read (Int 21h,
    Function 44h, Subfunction
    02h), 678-679
Device IOCTL Write (Int 21h,
    Function 44h, Subfunction
    03h), 679-680
Device Open (Int 15, Function
    80h), 554
Device Wait (Int 15, Function
    90h), 561-562
devices
    auxiliary (AUX), 59
    basic character, 117-118
    block, 53
    character, 53
    console (CON), 59
    memory-mapped, 121
    printer (PRN), 59

DI (destination index) register,
    28-32
Diagnose Controller (Int 13,
    Function 14h), 539-540
Diagnose Controller RAM (Int 13,
    Function 12h), 539
Diagnose Drive (Int 13, Function
    13h), 539
Digital Research, CP/M, 11
Direct Console I/O (Int 21h,
    Function 06h), 178-180,
    618-619
direct monochrome monitors,
    119
Direct STDIN Input (Int 21h,
    Function 07h), 619-620
direction flag (DF), 32
directives
    #define, 100
    #define preprocessor, 100
directories
    entry structure, 264
        Beginning Disk Cluster
            (Offset 1Ah), 268
        Date of Last Update (Offset
            18h), 268
        File Attribute (Offset 0Bh),
            266-267
        File Extension (Offset 08h),
            266
        File Name (Offset 00h),
            264-265
        File Size (Offset 1Ch), 269
        Time of Last Update (Offset
            16h), 267
    hierarchical, 262
    root, 49-50, 246-264
    searching, 277-281
    subdirectories, 262-270
    volume labels, 270-271

Disable DMA Register Set (Int
    67h, Function 5Bh,
    Subfunction 07h), 857-858
Disable Mouse Driver (Int 33h,
    Function 1Fh), 814
Disable OS/E Functions (Int 67h,
    Function 5Dh, Subfunction
    01h), 860
Disable Real-Time Clock Alarm
    (Int 1Ah, Function 07h), 581
Discard Page Contents (Int 31h,
    Function 0703h), 911
disk bootstrap code, 56-57
disk drives, calling for
    information of, 247-253
disk transfer area (DTA), 111, 278
Disk-Initialization Parameter
    Table (Int 1Eh), 585
disks
    boot records, 234-239
    file allocation table (FAT),
        239-246
    formatting, 254-260
    functions, 246-253
    internals, 230
    logical structure, 48
        boot record, 49
        file allocation table (FAT),
            49
        root directory, 49-50
    partition tables, 231-234
    physical structure, 47-48
display adapters
    identifying, 128-145
    memory configurations, 122
    memory contained, 121
    memory mapping and, 44-45
    types of, 43-44
Display Memory Window Control
    (Int 4Fh, Function 05h), 591
display monitors
    composite color, 119

composite monochrome, 119
direct monochrome, 119
enhanced RGB, 119
multisync, 119
RGB, 119
standards in use, 118-119
Display Output (Int 21h,
    Function 02h), 90, 616
display pages, 121
    using multiple, 154-156
Display String (Int 21h, Function
    09h), 621
Divide-by-Zero (Int 00h), 493
do-nothing codes
    Int 21h, Function 18h, 956
    Int 21h, Function 1Dh, 956
    Int 21h, Function 1Eh, 956
    Int 21h, Function 20h, 956
    Int 21h, Function 61h, 956
DOS
    32M barrier, 240-241
    accessing
        from programs, 88-89
        keyboard, 174-181
        video displays through
            function calls, 120
    and BASIC data area, 944
    calling to, 90
        with high-level languages,
            91-93
    entering commands to, 350
    extenders, 33, 872
    functions
        chart, 595-608
        format of, 610-613
        reserved, 609
        undocumented, 609-610
    future of, 16
    handling files, 271-272
    hardware for, 23-50
    history of, 10-12
    invoking, 593-594

kernel, 51
modules, 9-10
passing string addresses to, 90-91
programmer's interface to, 18-19
programs, 10
reentrancy, 594-595
resource list, 947
software for, 50-54
structure of, 16-18
Version 1.0, 12-13
  memory requirement, 12
  reserved functions, 956
Version 1.1, 12-13
Version 1.25, 12-13
Version 2.0, 12-14
  accessing video displays, 120
  carry flag (CF) for error, 91
  configuration variable table (CVT), 958-960
  context switching, 410
  device driver structure, 422
  EXEC function problems, 349
  function codes in interrupt routine, 430
  hierarchical directories, 262
  Int 29h, 146
  memory requirement, 12
  reserved functions, 957
  retrieving DOS version numbers, 461
Version 2.1, 12-14
Version 3.0, 12-15
  16-bit FAT, 243-245
  BIOS parameter block (BPB), 57
  BIOS parameter block (BPB) extension, 238

configuration variable table (CVT), 960-972
date bug, 469
device driver structure, 423
extended error information function, 474
function codes in interrupt routine, 430
initialized Int 33h vector, 184
last volume-ID read pointer, 440
memory requirement, 12
MSDOS.SYS file location, 57
reserved functions, 956-957
superseding internal commands, 352
Version 3.1, 12, 15
Version 3.2, 12, 15
  function codes in interrupt routine, 430
  memory-allocation strategy, 84
Version 3.3, 12, 15
  Abort, Retry, Fail? message, 80
  superseding internal commands, 352
Version 4.0, 12, 15-16
  configuration variable table (CVT), 963-974
  memory requirement, 12
  removing 32M limit on hard disks, 234-245
  reserved functions, 956-957
Version 4.01, 16
Version 5.0, 12, 16
  automatic detection of enhanced keyboard, 182
versions, 11
  information, 461-465, 612

video functions, 145-153
virtual machine concept, 21-22
DOS interrupts
  20h (Terminate Program),
    613-614
  21h
    see functions interrupts
  22h (Terminate Address), 59,
    747
  23h (Ctrl-C Interrupt
    Handler), 59, 747-748
  24h (Critical-Error Handler),
    59, 79-81, 748-751
  25h (Absolute Disk Read),
    751-753
  26h (Absolute Disk Write),
    753-755
  27h (Terminate and Stay
    Resident), 356, 755-756
  28h (DOSOK)/(DOS Safe To
    Use), 369, 409, 756-757
  29h (Fast Putchar), 146, 757
  2Ah (Microsoft Networks
    Interface), 757
  2Eh (Primary Shell Program
    Loader), 758
  2Fh (Multiplex Services)
    see Multiplex Services
    interrupts
  33h (Mouse Functions)
    see Mouse Functions
    interrupts
  36h (free drive space), 250-253
  67h (EMS Functions)
    see EMS Functions
    interrupts
  device driver, 436
DOS protected mode interface
  (DPMI), 33, 872
  2Fh
    1680h (Release Current
      Virtual Machine's Time
      Slice), 872-873

1686h (Get CPU Mode), 873
1687h (Obtain Real-to
  Protected Mode Switch
  Entry Point), 873-874
168Ah (Get Vendor-Specific
  API Entry Point), 874-875
31h
  0000h (Allocate LDT
    Descriptors), 875
  0001h (Free LDT
    Descriptor), 875-876
  0002h (Segment to
    Descriptor), 876
  0003h (Get Selector
    Increment Value), 876
  0006h (Get Segment Base
    Address), 877
  0007h (Set Segment Base
    Address), 877
  0008h (Set Segment Limit),
    878
  0009h (Set Descriptor
    Access Rights), 878-879
  000Ah (Create Alias
    Descriptor), 879-880
  000Bh (Get Descriptor),
    880
  000Ch (Set Descriptor),
    880-881
  000Dh (Allocate Specific
    LDT Descriptor), 881
  000Eh (Get Multiple
    Descriptors), 881-882
  000Fh (Set Multiple
    Descriptors), 882-883
  0100h (Allocate DOS
    Memory Block), 883
  0101h (Free DOS Memory
    Block), 884
  0102h (Resize DOS Memory
    Block), 884-885

0200h (Get Real Mode Interrupt Vector), 885

0201h (Set Real Mode Interrupt Vector), 885

0202h (Get Processor Exception Handler Vector), 886

0203h (Set Processor Exception Handler Vector), 886

0204h (Get Protected Mode Interrupt Vector), 887

0205h (Set Protected Mode Interrupt Vector), 887

0210h (Get Extended Processor Exception Handler Vector [Protected Mode]), 887-888

0211h (Get Extended Processor Exception Handler Vector [Real Mode]), 888

0212h (Set Extended Processor Exception Handler Vector [Protected Mode]), 888-889

0213h (Set Extended Processor Exception Handler Vector [Real Mode]), 889

0300h (Simulate Real Mode Interrupt), 889-890

0301h (Call Real Mode Procedure with Far Return Frame), 891-892

0302h (Call Real Mode Procedure with IRET Frame), 892-893

0303h (Allocate Real Mode Callback Address), 893-894

0304h (Free Real Mode Callback Address), 894

0305h (Get State Save/ Restore Addresses), 894-895

0306h (Get Raw Mode Switch Addresses), 895

0400h (Get Version), 896

0401h (Get DPMI Capabilities), 896-898

0500h (Get Free Memory Information), 898

0501h (Allocate Memory Block), 899

0502h (Free Memory Block), 899-900

0503h (Resize Memory Block), 900

0504h (Allocate Linear Memory Block), 900-901

0505h (Resize Linear Memory Block), 901-902

0506h (Get Page Attributes), 902-903

0507h (Set Page Attributes), 903-905

0508h (Map Device in Memory Block), 905

0509h (Map Conventional Memory in Memory Block), 906

050Ah (Get Memory Block Size and Base), 906-907

050Bh (Get Memory Information), 907

0600h (Lock Linear Region), 908

0601h (Unlock Linear Region), 908

0602h (Mark Real Mode Region as Pageable), 909

0603h (Relock Real Mode Region), 909-910

0604h (Get Page Size), 910

0702h (Mark Page as Demand Paging Candidate), 910

0703h (Discard Page Contents), 911

0800h (Physical Address Mapping), 911

0801h (Free Physical Address Mapping), 912

0900h (Get and Disable Virtual Interrupt State), 912

0901h (Get and Enable Virtual Interrupt State), 912-913

0902h (Get Virtual Interrupt State), 913

0A00h (Get Vendor-Specific API Entry Point), 913-914

0B00h (Set Debug Watchpoint), 914

0B01h (Clear Debug Watchpoint), 914-915

0B02h (Get State of Debug Watchpoint), 915

0B03h (Reset Debug Watchpoint), 915-916

0C00h (Install Resident Service Provider Callback), 916-917

0C01h (Terminate and Stay Resident), 917

0D00h (Allocate Shared Memory), 917-918

0D01h (Free Shared Memory), 918-919

0D02h (Serialize on Shared Memory), 919-920

0D03h (Free Serialization on Shared Memory), 920-921

0E00h (Get Coprocessor Status), 921

0E01h (Set Processor Emulation), 921-922

_dos_getvect function, 367

_dos_setvect function, 367

DOSOK/DOS Safe To Use (Int 28h), 369, 409, 756-757

dot (.) current directory entries, 265, 270

dot-dot (..) parent directory entries, 265, 270

DPMI
clients, 872
virtual machines, 872

drive control block (DCB), 959-973

drive parameter block (DPB), 959-962, 966-969, 973

driver initialization, 435-438

drivers
see device drivers

DS (data segment) register, 28-30, 66, 110

DS:DX register pair, 344-345

dual-ported memory, 123

dumps
COM program, 64-65, 72
EXE program, 67, 72
root directory, 263
subdirectory, 269

duplex considerations for writing terminal programs, 208-209

Duplicate Handle (Int 21h, Function 45h), 697-698

DX general purpose register, 28-29

E

EGA Register Interface, 817-821
EMM.SYS driver, 54, 289-290
emmalloc() function, 304
emmclose() function, 304
emmget() function, 304
emmmap() function, 304
emmmove() function, 304
emmok() function, 304
emmtest() function, 304
EMS Functions interrupts (Int 67), 81, 822
  40h (Get Manager Status), 823
  41h (Get Page Frame Segment), 823
  42h (Get Page Counts), 824
  43h (Get Handle and Allocate Memory), 824-825
  44h (Map/Unmap Memory), 825-826
  45h (Deallocate Handle and Memory), 826-827
  46h (Get EMM Version), 827
  46h (Save Page Map), 827
  48h (Restore Page Map), 828
  49h (Reserved), 829
  4Ah (Reserved), 829
  4Bh (Get Handle Count), 829
  4Ch (Get Pages Owned by Handle), 830
  4Dh (Get Pages for All Handles), 830-831
  4Eh
    00h (Get Page Map Registers), 831-832
    01h (Set Page Map Registers), 832
    02h (Get and Set Page Map Registers), 832
    03h (Get Size for Page Map Array), 833
  4Fh
    00h (Get Partial Page Map), 833-834
    01h (Set Partial Page Map), 834
    02h (Get Partial Page Map Size), 835
  50h
    00h (Map/Unmap Multiple Handle Pages), 835-836
    01h (Map/Unmap Multiple Handle Pages), 836-837
  51h (Reallocate Pages), 837
  52h
    00h (Get Handle Attribute), 838
    01h (Set Handle Attribute), 838
    02h (Get Attribute Capability), 839
  53h
    00h (Get Handle Name), 840
    01h (Set Handle Name), 840
  54h
    00h (Get Handle Directory), 841
    01h (Find Named Handle), 841
    02h (Get Handle Count), 842
  55h (Alter Page Map and Jump), 842-843
  56h (Alter Page Map and Call), 844-845
    02h (Get Stack Space Size), 845
  57h
    00h (Move Memory Region), 845-847
    01h (Exchange Memory Regions), 847-848

58h
00h (Get Mappable Physical
Address Array), 848-849
01h (Get Mappable Physical
Address Array Size), 849
59h
00h (Get Expanded Memory
Hardware Information),
849-850
01h (Get Unallocated Raw
Page Count), 850-851
5Ah
00h (Allocate Standard
Pages), 851
01h (Allocate Raw Pages),
851-852
5Bh
00h (Get Alternate Map
Registers), 852-853
01h (Set Alternate Map
Registers), 853-854
02h (Get Alternate Map
Register Set Size), 854
03h (Allocate Alternate Map
Register Set), 854-855
04h (Deallocate Alternate
Map Register Set),
855-856
05h (Allocate DMA Register
Set), 856
06h (Enable DMA Register
Set), 856-857
07h (Disable DMA Register
Set), 857-858
08h (Deallocate DMA
Register Set), 858-859
5Ch (Prepare Hardware For
Warm Boot), 859
5Dh
00h (Enable OS/E
Functions), 859-860

01h (Disable OS/E
Functions), 860
02h (OS/E Access Key Code
to EMS), 861
Enable DMA Register Set (Int
67h, Function 5Bh,
Subfunction 06h), 856-857
Enable Mouse Driver (Int 33h,
Function 20h), 814
Enable OS/E Functions (Int 67h,
Function 5Dh, Subfunction
00h), 859-860
Enable/Disable Watchdog
Timeout (Int 15, Function
C3h), 567
End Print Hold (Int 2Fh,
Function 01h, Subfunction
05h), 761-762
enhanced
keyboard (101-key), 163-167
RGB monitors, 119
Enhanced Expanded Memory
Specification (EEMS), 291
Enhanced Graphics Adapter
(EGA), 43, 118-119
chips, 120-121
color display, 127-128
displaying test line, 156
identifying, 128-145
memory configuration, 122
monitors driven by, 119
toggling blink bit, 126
video display mode, 124
entry points, 78
environment block, 346
environments, level within
system layering, 17
equipment() function, 468
Error in CONFIG.SYS
message, 437
errors, extended information,
474-479

ES (extra segment) register, 28-30, 110

ES:BX register pair, 345-346

ESDI Unit Format Periodic Interrupt (Int 15, Function 0Fh), 552

Event Wait (Int 15, Function 83h), 555-556

Exchange Memory Regions (Int 67h, Function 57h, Subfunction 01h), 847-848

EXE file extension, 53

EXE programs, 64-72
dump of, 67
failure to convert to COM programs, 353
identifying as, 69
memory allocation, 85, 293
versus COM programs, 75-76

EXE2BIN program, 64
failure to convert EXE to COM programs, 353

EXEC function, 60, 344-349

exec() function, 348

EXECOM program, 64

Execute Delay (Int 2Fh, Function 12h, Subfunction 24h), 780

Execute Program (EXEC) (Int 21h, Function 4Bh), 344, 701-705

Execute ROM BASIC (Int 18h), 576

exits, program, 348-349

Expand ASCIIZ Path Name (Int 2Fh, Function 12h, Subfunction 21h), 778-779

Expand Path Name String (Int 21h, Function 60h), 736-737, 956

expanded memory (EMS), 40, 289, 290-291

determining availability, 296-299
link records, 964-966
links, 972-973
using, 299-304

expanded memory manager (EMM), 289

extended
character sets, 175
error information, 474-479
file control blocks (FCB), 272-274
memory, 40, 287, 304-343

Extended Communications Port Control (Int 14, Function 05h), 549-550

Extended Initialization (Int 14, Function 04h), 548-549

Extended Memory Size Determination (Int 15, Function 88h), 289, 559-560

Extended Memory Specification (XMS), 304
driver, 305

Extended Open/Create (Int 21h, Function 6Ch), 745-747

extenders, DOS, 872

external
commands, 52-53
hardware interrupts, 365

F

far pointers, 297

FAR procedure, 66, 427

Fast Putchar (Int 29h), 146, 757

file allocation table (FAT), 49, 239-241
12-bit, 241-243
16-bit, 243-245
allocating file space, 245-246

File Attribute (Offset 0Bh) of
directory entry structure,
266-267
file attributes, getting/setting in C
language, 96-103
file control blocks (FCB), 271,
346, 963
basic file handling, 273-274
extended, 272-274
functions
comparing to handle files,
271-272
standard FCB, 272
when to use, 274-275
standard, 272-273
File Extension (Offset 08h) of
directory entry structure, 266
File Name (Offset 00h) of
directory entry structure,
264-265
File Size (Offset 1Ch) of directory
entry structure, 269
files, 271
AUTOEXEC.BAT, 59
batch, 52-53
CONFIG.SYS, 54
date stamps, 268
extensions
BAT, 53
BIN, 422
COM, 52
EXE, 53
SYS, 422
finding with wild-card file
specifications, 111-113
groups of, copying to floppy
disks, 253
handles, 107, 271
handling through DOS,
271-272

IO.SYS, 56-58
MSDOS.SYS, 56-59
searching for, 277-281
setting size, 276
time stamps, 267
Find ASCIIZ String Length (Int
2Fh, Function 12h, Subfunction
12h), 771
Find First File
see Search for First Match
Find Modified Buffer (V3) (Int
2Fh, Function 12h, Subfunction
10h), 770
Find Named Handle (Int 67h,
Function 54h, Subfunction
01h), 841
Find Next File
see Search for Next Match
first fit memory allocation, 83-84
fixed disk drives
see hard drives
flags register, 32-33
testing, 170-171
flat-file operating systems, 262
Floppy Disk Management (Int
0Eh), 500
floppy disks
capacities, 46
copying groups of files to, 253
Flush Buffer (Int 21h, Function
68h), 744
Flush File (Int 2Fh, Function 12h,
Subfunction 01h), 764-765
flush input buffers, 447
flush output buffers, 448
fmt_trk() function, 258-260
Force Duplicate Handle (Int 21h,
Function 46h), 698-699
Format Cylinder and Set Bad
Sector Flags (Int 13, Function
06h), 530-531

Format Disk Track (Int 13, Function 05h), 254-255, 529-530

Format Drive from Specified Cylinder (Int 13, Function 07h), 531

Format ESDI Unit (Int 13, Function 1Ah), 543-544

FORMAT program, 48

formats
converting data between parallel and serial, 192-193
video displays, 123-124

formatting disks, 254-260

fragmented memory, 84

Free DOS Memory Block (Int 31h, Function 0101h), 884

free drive space (Int 36h), 250-253

Free Extended Memory Block (Function 00Ah), 866-867

Free LDT Descriptor (Int 31h, Function 0001h), 875-876

Free Memory Block (Int 31h, Function 0502h), 899-900

Free Physical Address Mapping (Int 31h, Function 0801h), 912

Free Real Mode Callback Address (Int 31h, Function 0304h), 894

Free Serialization on Shared Memory (Int 31h, Function 0D03h), 920-921

Free Shared Memory (Int 31h, Function 0D01h), 918-919

Free Switcher ID (Int 2Fh, Function 4Bh, Subfunction 04h), 790

full duplex communications, 194, 208-209

function number (DOS functions), 611

functions
_a20_stat, 327
_alter_a20, 327
border(), 148
cdate(), 471, 472
charwait(), 178
chk_mouse(), 187
chkver(), 462-464
_chmod, 103
chrdy(), 217, 221
clearwin(), 148
clock(), 414
cls(), 151
ctime(), 471-472
ctrlbrk(), 368-370
date and time, 469-474
depth_search(), 278-280
DOS version information, 461-465
_dos_getvect, 367
_dos_setvect, 367
emmalloc(), 304
emmclose(), 304
emmget(), 304
emmmap(), 304
emmmove(), 304
emmok(), 304
emmtest(), 304
equipment(), 468
EXEC, 60, 344-349
exec(), 348
FCB, 271-275
fmt_trk(), 258-260
get_ch(), 214-215
get_drive(), 248
get_drvinfo(), 250
get_drvspace(), 250-251
get_free(), 251-253
GetDateAndTime, 105-108
GetFileHandle, 107
GetIntVec, 367

getvect(), 367, 414
getversion(), 464-465
gotoxy(), 151
handle, 271-277
hardware information, 466-469
_hma_alloc, 327
_hma_free, 327
_hma_move, 327
int86(), 95
intdos(), 95
intdosx, 248-250
intr(), 95
IOCTL, 296
keybd(), 213-216
keyin(), 176
loopback(), 223-224
MEMSET, 294
notification, 927-932
pgprint(), 156
PrinterOnline, 105
put_ch(), 219
putch(), 178
putscrn(), 218
putwin(), 148
rch(), 217-222
reserved, 955-957
SADD(TheString$), 111
savewin(), 148
search(), 279-280
serial(), 216-219
service, 932-936
set_dta(), 280
SetIntVec, 367
setpage(), 154-156
setup(), 210-213
setvect, 367
showattr(), 103
signal(), 368
streql(), 280-281
test(), 414
_umb_alloc, 327

_umb_free, 327
undocumented, 480
upwin(), 148
xmit(), 214-216, 222
_xms_alloc, 326
_xms_avail, 326
_xms_bstat, 327
_xms_free, 327
_xms_lock, 327
_xms_move, 327
_xms_realloc, 327
_xms_stat, 326
_xms_test, 326
_xms_unlock, 327
functions interrupts (Int 21h), 81
00h (Terminate Program), 614
01h (Keyboard Input with
Echo), 174-175, 615-616
02h (Display Output), 90, 616
03h (Auxiliary Input), 616-617
04h (Auxiliary Output),
617-618
05h (Printer Output), 157, 618
06h (Direct Console I/O),
178-180, 618-619
07h (Direct STDIN Input),
619-620
08h (STDIN Input), 175-176,
620
09h (Display String), 621
0Ah (Buffered STDIN Input),
180-181, 621-622
0Bh (Check STDIN Status),
177-178, 623
0Ch (Clear Buffer and Input),
623-624
0Dh (Reset Disk), 624
0Eh (Select Disk), 624-625
0Fh (Open File [FCB]), 626
10h (Close File [FCB]),
626-627

11h (Search for First Entry [FCB]), 627-628

12h (Search for Next Entry [FCB]), 628-629

13h (Delete File [FCB]), 629-630

14h (Read Sequential File [FCB]), 630-631

15h (Write Sequential File [FCB]), 631-632

16h (Create File [FCB]), 632

17h (Rename File [FCB]), 633-634

18h (do-nothing code), 956

19h (Get Default Drive), 634

1Ah (Set DTA Address), 634

1Bh (Get Allocation Table Information), 635

1Ch (Get Allocation Table Information for Specific Drive), 636

1Dh (do-nothing code), 956

1Eh (do-nothing code), 956

1Fh (Get Default Disk Parameter Block), 636-638, 956

20h (do-nothing code), 956

21h (Random File Read [FCB]), 638-639

22h (Random File Write [FCB]), 639-640

23h (Get File Size [FCB]), 640

24h (Set Random Record Field [FCB]), 641

25h (Set Interrupt Vector), 366-367, 641-642

26h (Create PSP), 642-643

27h (Random Block Read [FCB]), 643-644

28h (Random Block Write [FCB]), 644-645

29h (Parse File Name), 645-646

2Ah (Get System Date), 470, 646-647

2Bh (Set System Date), 470, 647

2Ch (Get System Time), 470-471, 648

2Dh (Set System Time), 471, 648-649

2Eh (Set Verify Flag), 649-650

2Fh (Get DTA Address), 650

30h (Get DOS Version Number), 462, 651-652

31h (Terminate and Stay Resident), 356, 652-653

32h (Get Drive Parameter Block), 653, 956

33h
00h (Get Ctrl-Break Flag), 653-654

01h (Set Ctrl-Break Flag), 654

05h (Get Boot Drive Code), 655

06h (Get MS-DOS Version), 655

34h (Return Address of InDOS Flag), 368, 409, 655-956

35h (Get Interrupt Vector), 366-367, 657-658

36h (Get Free Disk Space), 658-659

37h (hook for future features), 957
00h (Get Switchchar), 659

01h (Set Switchchar), 659

02h (Read Device Availability), 660

03h (Set Device Availability), 660

38h (Get/Set Current Country Information), 661-663

39h (Create Subdirectory), 663-664

3Ah (Remove Subdirectory), 664

3Bh (Set Directory), 664-665

3Ch (Create/Truncate File [handle]), 665-666

3Dh (Open File [handle]), 91, 107, 666-668

3Eh (Close File [handle]), 668-669

3Fh (Read File or Device [handle]), 669-670

40h (Write to a File or Device [handle]), 670

41h (Delete File), 670-671

42h (Move File Pointer), 671-672

43h (get and set file attribute), 97-99, 103

    00h (Get File Attributes), 672-673

    01h (Set File Attributes), 673-674

44h (Device Driver Control [IOCTL]), 674-676

    00h (Get Device Information), 676-677

    01h (Set Device Information), 677-678

    02h (Device IOCTL Read), 678-679

    03h (Device IOCTL Write), 679-680

    04h (Block Driver IOCTL Read), 680

    05h (Block Driver IOCTL Write), 681

    06h (Get Input Status), 681-682

    07h (Get Output Status), 682

    08h (Block Device Removable?), 683

    09h (Block Device Local or Remote?), 683-684

    0Ah (Handle Local or Remote?), 684-685

    0Bh (Set Sharing Retry Count), 685-686

    0Ch (Generic I/O Control for Handles), 686-688

    0Dh (Generic I/O Control for Block Devices), 689-695

    0Eh (Get Logical Drive Map), 695

    0Fh (Set Logical Drive Map), 695-696

    10h (Query IOCTL handle), 696

    11h (Query IOCTL device), 697

45h (Duplicate Handle), 697-698

46h (Force Duplicate Handle), 698-699

47h (Get Current Directory), 699

48h (Allocate Memory), 699-700

49h (Release Memory), 700-701

4Ah (Modify Memory Allocation), 294, 701

4Bh (Execute Program [EXEC]), 344, 701-705

    000h, 350

4Ch (Terminate with Return
Code), 348, 705-706

4Dh (Get Return Code), 349,
706

4Eh (Search for First Match),
111-113, 279-280, 706-708

4Fh (Search for Next Match),
111-113, 280, 708-709

50h

  Set PSP Segment, 410,
709-710

  SetPID, 956

51h

  Get PSP Segment, 410,
710-711

  GetPID, 956

52h

  Get Disk List, 711-713

  GetCVT, 956-974

53h

  Get Drive Parameter Block,
956

  Translate BPB to DPB,
713-715

54h (Get Verify Flag), 715

55h (Create PSP), 715-716, 956

56h (Rename File), 716

57h (get date and time),
105-108

  00h (Get File Date and
Time), 716-717

  01h (Set File Date and
Time), 717-718

58h

  00h (Get Allocation Strategy), 718-719

  01h (Set Allocation Strategy), 719-720

  02h (Get UMB link status),
721

  03h (Set UMB link status),
721

59h (Get Extended Error
Information), 474-479,
722-726

5Ah (Create Uniquely Named
File), 726-727

5Bh (Create New File),
727-728

5Ch

  00h (Set File Access Locks),
728-729

  01h (Clear File Access
Locks), 729-730

5Dh (CritErr), 956

  00h (Copy Data to DOS
Save Area), 730

  06h (Get Critical-Error Flag
Address), 731

  0Ah (Set Error Data Values),
731-732

5Eh

  00h (Get Machine Name),
732

  01h (Set Machine Name),
732-733

  02h (Set Network Printer
Setup), 733

  03h (Get Network Printer
Setup), 733

5Fh

  02h (Get Redirection List
Entry), 734-735

  03h (Set Redirection List
Entry), 735-736

  04h (Cancel Redirection List
Entry), 736

60h (Expand Path Name
String), 736-737, 956

61h (do-nothing code), 956

62h (Get PSP Address), 737

63h (hook for future features), 957
  00h (Get System Lead Byte Table), 737-738
  01h (Set/Clear Interim Console Flag), 738
  02h (Get Value of Interim Console Flag), 738
64h (Set Current Country Byte), 739, 956
65h (Get Extended Country Information), 739-741
  20h (Convert Character), 741-742
  21h (Convert String), 742
  22h (Convert ASCIIZ String), 742
66h
  01h (Get Global Code Page), 742-743
  02h (Set Global Code Page), 743
67h (Set Handle Count), 743-744
68h (Flush Buffer), 744
69h (unknown purpose), 957
6Ah
  Allocate Memory, 744
  Commit File, 956
6Bh (unknown purpose), 957
6Ch (Extended Open/Create), 745-747

G

garbage collection, 84
general-purpose registers, 28-33
Generic I/O Control for Block Devices (Int 21h, Function 44h, Subfunction 0Dh), 689-695

Generic I/O Control for Handles (Int 21h, Function 44h, Subfunction 0Ch), 686-688
generic IOCTL function, 450-452
Get Allocation Strategy (Int 21h, Function 58h, Subfunction 00h), 718-719
Get Allocation Table Information (Int 21h, Function 1Bh), 635
Get Allocation Table Information for Specific Drive (Int 21h, Function 1Ch), 636
Get Alternate Map Register Set Size (Int 67h, Function 5Bh, Subfunction 02h), 854
Get Alternate Map Registers (Int 67h, Function 5Bh, Subfunction 00h), 852-853
Get and Disable Virtual Interrupt State (Int 31h, Function 0900h), 912
Get and Enable Virtual Interrupt State (Int 31h, Function 0901h), 912-913
get and set file attribute (Int 21h, Function 43h), 97-99, 103
Get and Set Page Map Registers (Int 67h, Function 4Eh, Subfunction 02h), 832
Get ANSI.SYS Installed State (Int 2Fh, Function 1Ah, Subfunction 00h), 786-787
Get APPEND Function State (Int 2Fh, Function B7h, Subfunction 06h), 793-794
Get APPEND Path Pointer (Int 2Fh, Function B7h, Subfunction 04h), 793
Get APPEND Version (Int 2Fh, Function B7h, Subfunction 02h), 793

Get ASCIIZ String Length (Int 2Fh, Function 12h, Subfunction 25h), 780

Get ASSIGN.COM/ASSIGN.EXE Installation Status (Int 2Fh, Function 06h), 762-763

Get Attribute Capability (Int 67h, Function 52h, Subfunction 02h), 839

Get Boot Drive Code (Int 21h, Function 33h, Subfunction 05h), 655

Get Button-Press Information (Int 33h, Function 05h), 799-800

Get Button-Release Information (Int 33h, Function 06h), 800

Get Clock Counter (Int 1Ah, Function 00h), 577

Get Coprocessor Status (Int 31h, Function 0E00h), 921

Get CPU Mode (Int 2Fh, Function 1686h), 873

Get Critical-Error Flag Address (Int 21h, Function 5Dh, Subfunction 06h), 731

Get CRT Page Number (Int 33h, Function 1Eh), 813-814

Get Ctrl-Break Flag (Int 21h, Function 33h, Subfunction 00h), 653-654

Get Current Directory (Int 21h, Function 47h), 699

Get Current Display Mode (Int 10, Function 0Fh), 514-515

get date and time (Int 21h, Function 57h), 105-108

Get Date and Time for File Closing (Int 2Fh, Function 12h, Subfunction 0Dh), 769

Get Day Count (Int 1Ah, Function 0Ah), 582

Get DCB Address (Int 2Fh, Function 12h, Subfunction 16h), 773

Get DCB Number (Int 2Fh, Function 12h, Subfunction 20h), 778

Get Default Disk Parameter Block (Int 21h, Function 1Fh), 636-638, 956

Get Default Drive (Int 21h, Function 19h), 634

Get Descriptor (Int 31h, Function 000Bh), 880

Get Device Information (Int 21h, Function 44h, Subfunction 00h), 676-677

Get Disk List (Int 21h, Function 52h), 711-713

Get Disk System Status (Int 13, Function 01h), 526

Get Display State (Int 10, Function 1Bh), 522

Get DOS Data Segment (Int 2Fh, Function 12h, Subfunction 03h), 766

Get DOS Installation Status (Int 2Fh, Function 12h, Subfunction 00h), 764

Get DOS Version Number (Int 21h, Function 30h), 462, 651-652

Get DOSKEY.COM Installed State (Int 2Fh, Function 48h, Subfunction 00h), 787-788

Get DPMI Capabilities (Int 31h, Function 0401h), 896-898

Get Drive Code from Path Name (Int 2Fh, Function 12h, Subfunction 1Ah), 775

Get Drive Paramter Block (Int 21h, Function 32h), 653-956

Get DRIVER.SYS Installation Status (Int 2Fh, Function 08h), 763

Get DTA Address (Int 21h, Function 2Fh), 650

Get EMB Handle Information (Function 00Eh), 869

Get EMM Version (Int 67h, Function 46h), 827

Get Equipment Status (Int 11h), 466-469, 523-524

Get Expanded Memory Hardware Information (Int 67h, Function 59h, Subfunction 00h), 849-850

Get Extended Country Information (Int 21h, Function 65h), 739-741

Get Extended Error Code (Int 2Fh, Function 12h, Subfunction 2Dh), 784-785

Get Extended Error Information (Int 21h, Function 59h), 474-479, 722-726

Get Extended Processor Exception Handler Vector
Protected Mode (Int 31h, Function 0210h), 887-888
Real Mode (Int 31h, Function 0211h), 888

Get File Attributes (Int 21h, Function 43h, Subfunction 00h), 672-673

Get File Date and Time (Int 21h, Function 57h, Subfunction 00h), 716-717

Get File Size (Int 21h, Function 23h), 640

Get Free Disk Space (Int 21h, Function 36h), 658-659

Get Free Memory Information (Int 31h, Function 0500h), 898

Get Global Code Page (Int 21h, Function 66h, Subfunction 01h), 742-743

Get GRAFTABL.COM Installed State (Int 2Fh, Function B0h, Subfunction 00h), 792

Get Handle and Allocate Memory (Int 67h, Function 43h), 824-825

Get Handle Attribute (Int 67h, Function 52h, Subfunction 00h), 838

Get Handle Count
Int 67h, Function 4Bh, 829
Int 67h, Function 54h, Subfunction 02h, 842

Get Handle Directory (Int 67h, Function 54h, Subfunction 00h), 841

Get Handle Name (Int 67h, Function 53h, Subfunction 00h), 840

Get Input Status (Int 21h, Function 44h, Subfunction 06h), 681-682

Get Interrupt Vector (Int 21h, Function 35h), 366-367, 657-658

Get Interrupt Vector Address (Int 2Fh, Function 12h, Subfunction 02h), 765

Get KEYB.COM Country Flag (Int 2Fh, Function ADh, Subfunction 83h), 792

Get KEYB.COM Version Number (Int 2Fh, Function ADh, Subfunction 80h), 791

Get Keyboard Status Flags (Int 16, Function 12h), 573-574

Get Keystroke (Int 16h, Function 10h), 181, 572-573

Get LDT Address (Int 2Fh, Function 12h, Subfunction 17h), 773-774

Get Logical Drive Map (Int 21h, Function 44h, Subfunction 0Eh), 695

Get Machine Name (Int 21h, Function 5Eh, Subfunction 00h), 732

Get Manager Status (Int 67h, Function 40h), 823

Get Mappable Physical Address Array (Int 67h, Function 58h, Subfunction 00h), 848-849

Get Mappable Physical Address Array Size (Int 67h, Function 58h, Subfunction 01h), 849

Get Memory Block Size and Base (Int 31h, Function 050Ah), 906-907

Get Memory Information (Int 31h, Function 050Bh), 907

Get Memory Size (Int 12h), 524-525

Get Message Language (Int 33h, Function 23h), 815-816

Get Mouse Information (Int 33h, Function 24h), 816

Get Mouse Position (Int 33h, Function 03h), 798-799

Get Mouse Sensitivity (Int 33h, Function 1Bh), 812

Get MS-DOS Version (Int 21h, Function 33h, Subfunction 06h), 655

Get Multiple Descriptors (Int 31h, Function 000Eh), 881-882

Get Network Printer Setup (Int 21h, Function 5Eh, Subfunction 03h), 733

Get Network Redirector Installation Status (Int 2Fh, Function 11h), 764

Get NLSFUNC Installation Status (Int 2Fh, Function 14h, Subfunction 00h), 785-786

Get Outboard Critical-Error Handler Installation Status (Int 2Fh, Function 05h), 762

Get Output Status (Int 21h, Function 44h, Subfunction 07h), 682

Get Page Attributes (Int 31h, Function 0506h), 902-903

Get Page Counts (Int 67h, Function 42h), 824

Get Page Frame Segment (Int 67h, Function 41h), 823

Get Page Map Registers (Int 67h, Function 4Eh, Subfunction 00h), 831-832

Get Page Size (Int 31h, Function 0604h), 910

Get Pages for Handles (Int 67h, Function 4Dh), 830-831

Get Pages Owned by Handle (Int 67h, Function 4Ch), 830

Get Partial Page Map (Int 67h, Function 4Fh, Subfunction 00h), 833-834

Get Partial Page Map Size (Int 67h, Function 4Fh, Subfunction 02h), 835

Get Printer Device (Int 2Fh, Function 01h, Subfunction 06h), 762

Get Processor Exception Handler Vector (Int 31h, Function 0202h), 886

Get Protected Mode Interrupt Vector (Int 31h, Function 0204h), 887

Get PSP Address (Int 21h, Function 62h), 737

Get PSP Segment (Int 21h, Function 51h), 710-711

Get Raw Mode Switch Addresses (Int 31h, Function 0306h), 895

Get Real Mode Interrupt Vector (Int 31h, Function 0200h), 885

Get Redirection List Entry (Int 21h, Function 5Fh, Subfunction 02h), 734-735

Get Return Code (Int 21h, Function 4Dh), 349, 706

Get Save-State Storage Size (Int 33h, Function 15h), 809

Get Segment Base Address (Int 31h, Function 0006h), 877

Get Selector Increment Value (Int 31h, Function 0003h), 876

Get SHARE.EXE Installation Status (Int 2Fh, Function 10h), 763

Get Size for Page Map Array (Int 67h, Function 4Eh, Subfunction 03h), 833

Get Stack Space Size (Int 67h, Function 56h, Subfunction 02h), 845

Get State of Debug Watchpoint (Int 31h, Function 0B02h), 915

Get State Save/Restore Addresses (Int 31h, Function 0305h), 894-895

Get Switchchar (Int 21h, Function 37h, Subfunction 00h), 659

Get System Date (Int 21h, Function 2Ah), 470, 646-647

Get System Lead Byte Table (Int 21h, Function 63h, Subfunction 00h), 737-738

Get System Time (Int 21h, Function 2Ch), 470-471, 648

Get UMB link status (Int 21h, Function 58h, Subfunction 02h), 721

Get Unallocated Raw Page Count (Int 67h, Function 59h, Subfunction 01h), 850-851

Get User Alternate Interrupt Vector (Int 33h, Function 19h), 811-812

Get User Stack Address (Int 2Fh, Function 12h, Subfunction 18h), 774

Get Value of Interim Console Flag (Int 21h, Function 63h, Subfunction 02h), 738

Get Vendor-Specific API Entry Point
Int 2Fh, Function 168Ah, 874-875
Int 31h, Function 0A00h, 913-914

Get Verify Flag (Int 21h, Function 54h), 715

Get Version
Service Function 0000h, 933
Int 31h, Function 0400h, 896

Get Virtual Interrupt State (Int 31h, Function 0902h), 913

Get XMS Driver Entry-Point Address (Int 2Fh, Function 43h, Subfunction 10h), 787

Get XMS Driver Installed State (Int 2Fh, Function 43h, Subfunction 00h), 787

Get XMS Version Number (Function 000h), 862

Get/Set Current Country Information (Int 21h, Function 38h), 661-663 get/set logical device functions, 450-451

get_ch() function, 214-215

get_drive() function, 248

get_drvinfo() function, 250

get_drvspace() function, 250-251

get_free() function, 251-253

GetCVT (Int 21h, Function 52h), 956-974

GetDateAndTime function, 105-108

GetDrive Parameter Block (Int 21h, Function 53h), 956

GetFileHandle function, 107

GetIntVec function, 367

GetPID (Int 21h, Function 51h), 956

getvect() function, 367, 414

getversion() function, 464-465

Global Disable A20 (Function 004h), 864

Global Enable A20 (Function 003h), 863

gotoxy() function, 151

graphics display modes, 127-128

Graphics Display Character Bit-Map Table (Int 1Fh), 585-586

GW-BASIC, 108

H

half duplex communications, 194, 208-209, 214

handle functions, 271-272, 275
   basic handling, 276
   when to use, 276-277

Handle Local or Remote? (Int 21h, Function 44h, Subfunction 0Ah), 684-685

handlers
   see interrupt handlers

handles, file, 107, 271

Hard Disk Management (Disk Controller) (PC XT) (Int 0Dh), 500

hardware
   accessing video displays through, 120
   for DOS, 23
      central processing unit (CPU), 24-39
      I/O devices, 40-46
      memory, 40
      storage devices, 46-50
   information, 466-469
   interrupts, 79, 362
      external, 365
      internal, 363-365
   power-on self test (POST), 56
   resource list, 945

Hayes Smartmodem internal board, 202

headers, EXE program, 64-70

heap, 85

Heath-Zenith, 13

Hercules Graphics Adapter (HGA), 43, 118-119
   identifying, 129-145
   monitors driven by, 119

Hercules Graphics Card, identifying, 128-145

Hercules Graphics Card Plus, identifying, 128-145

Hercules InColor Card, identifying, 128-145

Hide Mouse Cursor (Int 33h, Function 02h), 797

hierarchical directories, 262

high memory area (HMA),
304-305
high-level languages
avoiding unnecessary work, 92
calling DOS and BIOS
routines, 91-93
comparing to assembly
languages, 72-73
_hma_alloc function, 327
_hma_free function, 327
_hma_move function, 327
Hold Print Jobs (Int 2Fh,
Function 01h, Subfunction
04h), 761
Hook Notification Chain (Service
Function 0004h), 935
hooks for future features
Int 21h, Function 37h, 957
Int 21h, Function 63h, 957
horizontal retrace interval (HRI),
122
huge pointers, 297

I

IBM, 11, 15-16
IBMBIO.COM
see IO.SYS
IBMDOS.COM
see MSDOS.SYS
Identify Instance Data (Int 2Fh,
Function 4Bh, Subfunction
05h), 790-791
identifying
CPU chips, 33-36
math coprocessors, 37-39
IF (interrupt flag), 32
inactive TSRs (terminate and stay
resident), 356
index registers, 31-32
InDOS flag, 368-369

infinity values, 37
Init Switcher (Notification
Function 0000h), 927-928
Initialize Communications Port
(Int 14, Function 00h), 544-545
Initialize Fixed Disk Table (Int 13,
Function 09h), 533
Initialize LDT (Int 2Fh, Function
12h, Subfunction 1Fh), 777-778
Initialize Printer Port (Int 17,
Function 01h), 575
Initialize the Mouse (Int 33h,
Function 00h), 796-797
initializing
communications port, 203-207
mouse drivers, 184
terminal programs, 210-213
input status, 446
input/output (I/O)
control (IOCTL)
function, 296
read, 443-445
terminal programs, 214-216
write, 448
devices, 40
display adapters, 43-45
keyboard, 41-42
mouse, 46
printers, 45
serial ports, 45-46
system, 10
level within system layering,
17
Ins key, 171
Install Resident Service Provider
Callback (Int 31h, Function
0C00h), 916-917
installing device drivers, 457
INT instruction, 90
int86() function, 95
intdos() function, 95

intdosx function, 248-250
interleaving, 255-256
internal
   commands, 52
      superseding, 352
   hardware interrupts, 363-365
   interrupts, 78
Interrogate Driver (Int 10h,
   Function FAh), 821
Interrupt Complete (Int 15,
   Function 91h), 562-563
interrupt
   enable register (IER), 197-200
   handlers, 79-81, 362
      BIOS keyboard, 164, 168
      clock, 415
      critical error, 375-405
      Ctrl-Break/Ctrl-C, 361
      Ctrl-C, 369-375
      writing, 367-369
   identification register (IIR),
      197, 200
   request level (IRQ), 362
   routines, 430-435
   service routines (ISRs), 357
   vector tables, 362, 366,
      941-943
   vectors, 360, 366
      getting and setting, 366-367
      IBM assigned, 364-365
interrupts, 76-78, 360-362
   generating
      in C language, 93-95
      in QuickBASIC, 109-110
      in Turbo Pascal, 104-105
   hardware, 362
      external, 365
      internal, 363-365
   Intel 8086 microprocessor
      family, 363-365
      internal, 78
      maskable (INTR), 79, 365
      nonmaskable (NMI), 78, 365
      return from (IRET), 371
      service routines
         see interrupt handlers
      software, 19, 79-82, 365
intr() function, 95
Invoke Critical Error (Int 2Fh,
   Function 12h, Subfunction
   06h), 767
IO.SYS file, 56-58
IOCTL Interface (Int 2Fh,
   Function 12h, Subfunction
   2Bh), 783-784
IOCTL Open Used by DOS (Int
   2Fh, Function 12h, Subfunction
   0Ch), 769
IP (instruction pointer) register,
   28, 31

J-K

Joystick Support (Int 15,
   Function 84h), 556-557

key combinations
   Ctrl-Alt-Del, 56
   Ctrl-Break, 168
   Shift-PrintScreen, 168
Key-Click On/Off (Int 16,
   Function 04h), 572
keybd() function, 213-216
keyboard, 41-42, 162
   accessing with
      Int 16h, 170-174
      Int 21h, 174-181
   controlling in terminal
      programs, 213-216
   flag byte, 173

identifying level of support,
181-183
reading from
BASIC, 168-169
QuickBASIC, 169
scan codes, 162-167
Keyboard Input with Echo (Int
21h, Function 01h), 174-175,
615-616
Keyboard Intercept (Int 15,
Function 4Fh), 553-554
Keyboard Interrupt (Int 09h), 42,
408-409, 497-498
keyin() function, 176
keys
Alt, 171
Caps Lock, 171
Ctrl, 171
Ins, 171
Num Lock, 171
scan codes for, 41-42
Scroll Lock, 171
Shift, 171
Kyle, Jim, 195, 408

L

labels, volume, 267, 270-271
languages, comparing, 74-75
Last Fit memory allocation, 83,
293
last-in first-out (LIFO) structures,
30
line control register (LCR), 197,
200-201
line status register (LSR), 197,
202
link records, EMS, 964
linked lists of memory blocks,
82-83

linking programs, memory
allocation, 85
listings
allocating memory in assembly
language, 294
BASIC version of
chkver(), 463-464
equipment installed,
468-469
getversion(), 465
BIOS printer-status request
in C language, 95
in QuickBASIC, 110
in Turbo Pascal, 105
C sample, 74
C version of
chkver(), 462-463
equipment installed,
466-467
getversion(), 464
calling DOS interrupt with C
library functions, 100-103
chario.c functions, 152-153
checking keyboard status,
171-173
Chrdy.c, 217
Chrdy2.c, 221
clock.c, 410-416
clock.pas, 472-474
COMMAND.COM copying
trick, 347-348
CPU identification, 34-36
critical error handlers, 375-405
Date and time functions,
471-472
declaring interrupt directives
as interrupt handle, 373-374
depth_search(), 278-279
determining free memory, 295
direct call to DOS interrupt,
97-99

dispatch table for sample driver drvr.asm, 431

drvinfo.c, 247-250

emmchk(), 298

emmtest(), 297

extended memory functions, 306-326

FileDateAndTime program, 107-108

Find.c, 277-278

finding files by wild-card file specifications, 111-113

fmt_trk(), 259-260

free.bas, 252

free.c, 251

Get_ch.c, 214-215

get_drvspace(), 250-251

get_free(), 252

GetDateAndTime procedure, 106-107

handler.c, 370

handler2.c, 374-375

identifying
display adapters, 130-145
level of keyboard support, 182-183

indicating keystrokes waiting, 170-171

Int 67 memory functions, 299-304

interrupt routine for sample driver drvr.asm, 431-432

KEYBD.BAS program, 168-169

Keybd.c, 213

KEYBD2.BAS program, 169

keyboard input, 170

keyin.c, 174-175

keyin2.c, 176

keyin3.c, 177-178

keyin4, 178-180

keyin5.c, 180-181

loopback testing, 223-224

MAKEDRVR.BAT file, 456

makefile for clock program, 415

math coprocessor identification, 38-39

Mouse.c, 185-187

NULL program, 371-372

opening sample driver drvr.asm, 460

printer functions (Int 17h), 158

printer output (Int 21h, Function 05h), 157

Put_ch.c, 219

Putscrn.c, 218

Rch.c, 217-218

Rch2.c, 221-222

sample COM program in assembly language, 62-63

sample driver drvr.asm, 433-434, 451-455
with write function, 458-459

sample EXE program in assembly language, 65-66

screen.c functions, 151-152
with setpage() function, 154-156

search(), 279-280

Serial.c, 216-217

setting interrupt vectors in assembly language, 367

Setup.c, 210-211

Setup2.c, 211-213

strategy routine for sample driver drvr.asm, 429-430

Term.c, 209-210

testing for expanded memory, 299

testpage.c sample program, 156

testscn.c program, 147-148
Turbo Pascal sample, 73
window.c, 148-151
Xmit.c, 215-216
Xmit2.c, 222
XMS library functions, 327-343
loading and initializing software
for DOS, 55-59
Local Disable A20 (Function
006h), 864-865
Local Enable A20 (Function
005h), 864
Lock Extended Memory Block
(Function 00Ch), 868
Lock Linear Region (Int 31h,
Function 0600h), 908
logical drive table (LDT),
962-963, 966-967, 971, 974
loopback testing, 223-224
loopback() function, 223-224
Lotus-Intel-Microsoft Expanded
Memory Specification (LIM
EMS), 291
LPT2 Control (Personal
Computer AT) (Int 0Dh), 500

M

machines
physical, 23
virtual, 21-22
macro, streql(), 280
MAKE utility, 415
Map Conventional Memory in
Memory Block (Int 31h,
Function 0509h), 906
Map Device in Memory Block (Int
31h, Function 0508h), 905
Map/Unmap Memory (Int 67h,
Function 44h), 825-826

Map/Unmap Multiple Handle
Pages
Int 67h, Function 50h,
Subfunction 00h, 835-836
Int 67h, Function 50h,
Subfunction 01h, 836-837
Mark Page as Demand Paging
Candidate (Int 31h, Function
0702h), 910
Mark Real Mode Region as
Pageable (Int 31h Function
0602h), 909
mark state, 193
maskable interrupts (INTR), 79,
365
math coprocessors, 36-39
maximum command number
(MAXCMD), 427
media check, 438-441
memory, 287-291
80286+ addressing, 32-33
8086 segmented addressing,
24-26
allocating, 82-85
arena, 82, 291
blocks, 82-83
allocating, 84
freeing, 84
resizing, 84
classes of, 40
configuration of display
adapters, 122
control blocks (MCB), 82-83,
958-959, 970-973
DOS versions requirements, 12
dual-ported, 123
expanded, 289-291, 296-304
extended, 287, 304-343
fragmented, 84
getting more, 294-296

heap, 85
  management, 291-293
  mapping, 44-45
  selected locations, 941--944
  shrinking, 293-294
Memory Allocation Error
  message, 83, 293
memory-allocation strategy,
  determining, 84
memory-mapped devices, 121
MEMSET function, 294
messages
  Abort, Retry, Ignore?, 80
  Error in CONFIG.SYS, 437
  Memory Allocation Error, 83,
    293
  Please check the printer!, 96
  Ready to print, 96
Microsoft, 11, 15-16
  C, 19
    absence of pseudovariables,
      94, 100
    handling signal traps, 368
    memory allocation, 293
    resource list, 947
  C Compiler (Version 5.0),
    setting interrupt vectors, 367
  Macro Assembler (MASM), 90
  Networks Interface (Int 2Ah),
    757
  QuickBASIC (Version 4.0),
    calling DOS and BIOS, 91-92
  Windows, 16
    using mouse, 183-184
  Word, 118
modem control register (MCR),
  197, 200-202
modem status register (MSR),
  197, 202-203
modems, 207-208
  signals, 203

modes
  all-points addressable (APA),
    127-128
  cooked, 419
  protected, 288
  raw, 419
  real, 288
  text (alphanumeric), 125-127
  video display, 123-124
Modify Memory Allocation (Int
  21h, Function 4Ah), 294, 701
Monochrome Display Adapter
  (MDA), 43, 118-119
  memory configuration, 122
  monitors driven by, 119
  identifying, 128-145
  video display modes, 124
monochrome text mode, 125
Motorola 6845 Cathode Ray Tube
  Controller (CRTC) chips, 120
mouse, 46, 183-184
  initializing driver, 184
  on-screen position, 188
  polling, 184-187
Mouse Functions interrupts (Int
  33h), 46, 81, 796
  00h (Initialize the Mouse),
    184, 796-797
  01h (Show Mouse Cursor),
    188, 797
  02h (Hide Mouse Cursor), 797
  03h (Get Mouse Position),
    188, 798-799
  04h (Set Mouse Position), 799
  05h (Get Button-Press
    Information), 799-800
  06h (Get Button-Release
    Information), 800
  07h (Set Mouse X Limits),
    800-801

08h (Set Mouse Y Limits), 801

09h (Set Graphics Cursor
Shape), 801-804

0Ah (Set Text Cursor Type),
804

0Bh (Read Motion Counters),
805

0Ch (Set User-Defined Event
Handler), 805-806

0Dh (Start Light Pen
Emulation), 806-807

0Eh (Stop Light Pen
Emulation), 807

0Fh (Set Mickey-to-Pixel Ratio),
807

10h (Conditional Cursor Off),
808

13h (Set Double Speed
Threshold), 808

14h (Swap User Event
Handlers), 808-809

15h (Get Save-State Storage
Size), 809

16h (Save Mouse Driver State),
810

17h (Restore Mouse Driver
State), 810

18h (Set Alternate Mouse User
Handler), 810-811

19h (Get User Alternate
Interrupt Vector), 811-812

1Ah (Set Mouse Sensitivity),
812

1Bh (Get Mouse Sensitivity),
812

1Ch (Set interrupt rate), 813

1Dh (Set CRT Page Number),
813

1Eh (Get CRT Page Number),
813-814

1Fh (Disable Mouse Driver),
814

20h (Enable Mouse Driver),
814

21h (Software Reset), 815

22h (Set Message Language),
815

23h (Get Message Language),
815-816

24h (Get Mouse Information),
816

MOUSE.SYS driver, 54, 184

Move Block (Int 15, Function
87h), 289, 558-559

Move Disk Buffer (Int 2Fh,
Function 12h, Subfunction
07h), 768

Move Extended Memory Block
(Function 00Bh), 867-868

Move File Pointer (Int 21h,
Function 42h), 671-672

Move Memory Region (Int 67h,
Function 57h Subfunction
00h), 845-847

MS-DOS
resource list, 946
Version 1.0, 11
Version 2.11, 14
Version 3.2 date bug, 469

MS-DOS Idle Call (Int 2Fh,
Function 16h, Subfunction
80h), 786

MSDOS.SYS file, 56-59

MultiColor Graphics Array
(MCGA), 43, 119
identifying, 129-145
memory configuration, 122
video display mode, 124

Multiplex Services interrupts (Int
2Fh), 758, 950
00h (Check Install), 951-953
01h (Return User Parameter
Pointer), 953

00h (Print Installation Check), 759

01h (Submit File to Print Spooler), 759-760

02h (Remove File from Print Queue), 760

03h (Cancel All Files in Print Queue), 760

04h (Hold Print Jobs), 761

05h (End Print Hold), 761-762

06h (Get Printer Device), 762

05h (Get Outboard Critical-Error Handler Installation Status), 762

06h (Get ASSIGN.COM/ ASSIGN/EXE Installation Status), 762-763

08h (Get DRIVER.SYS Installation Status), 763

10h (Get SHARE.EXE Installation Status), 763

11h (Get Network Redirector Installation Status), 764

12h

00h (Get DOS Installation Status), 764

01h (Flush File), 764-765

02h (Get Interrupt Vector Address), 765

03h (Get DOS Data Segment), 766

04h (Normalize Path Separator), 766

05h (Output a Character), 767

06h (Invoke Critical Error), 767

07h (Move Disk Buffer), 768

08h (Decrement User Count), 768

0Ch (IOCTL Open Used by DOS), 769

0Dh (Get Date and Time for File Closing), 769

0Eh (Search Buffer Chain), 770

10h (Find Modified Buffer [V3]), 770

10h (Time Delay [V4]), 770

11h (Normalize ASCIIZ File Name), 771

12h (Find ASCIIZ String Length), 771

13h (Case and Country Conversion), 772

14h (Compare 32-bit Numbers), 772

16h (Get DCB Address), 773

17h (Get LDT Address), 773-774

18h (Get User Stack Address), 774

19h (Set LDT Pointers), 774

1Ah (Get Drive Code from Path Name), 775

1Bh (Adjust for Leap Year), 775

1Ch (Calculate Days Since Start-of-Month), 776

1Dh (Calculate Date), 776-777

1Eh (Compare Strings), 777

1Fh (Initialize LDT), 777-778

20h (Get DCB Number), 778

21h (Expand ASCIIZ Path Name), 778-779

22h (Translate Extended Error Codes), 779

24h (Execute Delay), 780

25h (Get ASCIIZ String
Length), 780
26h (Open File), 781
27h (Close File), 781-782
28h (Position File Pointer),
782
29h (Read File), 783
2Bh (IOCTL Interface),
783-784
2Dh (Get Extended Error
Code), 784-785
2Fh (Store DX), 785
14h, 00h (Get NLSFUNC
Installation Status), 785-786
15h (CDROM Interface), 786
16h, 80h (MS-DOS Idle Call),
786
1Ah, 00h (Get ANSI.SYS
Installed State), 786-787
43h
00h (Get XMS Driver
Installed State), 787
10h (Get XMS Driver Entry-
Point Address), 787
48h
00h (Get DOSKEY.COM
Installed State), 787-788
10h (Read Command Line),
788
4Bh
01h (Build Notification
Chain), 788-789
02h (Detect Switcher), 789
03h (Allocate Switcher ID),
789-790
04h (Free Switcher ID), 790
05h (Identify Instance
Data), 790-791
ADh
80h (Get KEYB.COM
Version Number), 791

81h (Set KEYB.COM Active
Code Page), 791
82h (Set KEYB.COM
Country Flag), 791-792
83h (Get KEYB.COM
Country Flag), 792
B0h, 00h (Get
GRAFTABL.COM Installed
State), 792
B7h
00h (Check for APPEND
Installation), 792-793
02h (Get APPEND Version),
793
04h (Get APPEND Path
Pointer), 793
06h (Get APPEND Function
State), 793-794
07h (Set APPEND Function
State), 794-795
11h (Set Return Found
Name State), 795
multisync monitors, 119

N

near pointers, 297
NEAR procedures, 63
Non-Maskable Interrupt (NMI)
(Int 02h), 494-495
nondestructive read, 445-447
nonmaskable interrupts (NMI),
78, 365
Normalize ASCIIZ File Name (Int
2Fh, Function 12h, Subfunction
11h), 771
Normalize Path Separator (Int
2Fh, Function 12h, Subfunction
04h), 766
Norton Utilities FA (file attribute)
program, 96

Notification Functions
0000h (Init Switcher), 927-928
0001h (Query Suspend), 928-929
0002h (Suspend Session), 929
0003h (Activate Session), 930
0004h (Session Active), 930
0005h (Create Session), 931
0006h (Destroy Session), 931
0007h (Switcher Exit), 932
notification services, 923
Novell Netware, 81
NULL program, 371-372
Num Lock key, 171

O

Obtain Real-to-Protected Mode Switch Entry Point (Int 2Fh, Function 1687h), 873-874
offset addresses, 24
offset registers, 31-33
Open File
Int 2Fh, Function 12h, Subfunction 26h, 781
FCB (Int 21h, Function 0Fh), 626
handle (Int 21h, Function 3Dh), 91, 107, 666-668
open function, 449
operating systems
DOS
see DOS
flat-file, 262
OS/2, 15
optical mouse, 46
order of precedence of program types for execution, 60
original equipment manufacturers (OEMs), 13
OS/2 operating system, 15
BIOS, 486-487

OS/E Access Key Code to EMS (Int 67h, Function 5Dh, Subfunction 02h), 861
Output a Character (Int 2Fh, Function 12h, Subfunction 05h), 767
output status, 448
output until busy function, 450
overflow flag (OF), 32
overlays, 286
Owl International's Hypertext system, 184

P

p-system, 11
pages
display, 121
using multiple, 154-156
expanded memory, 289
frames, 289, 822
printing strings to current, 156
parent programs, 344-348
parity, 193-194
parity flag (PF), 32
Park Heads (Int 13, Function 19h), 543
Parse File Name (Int 21h, Function 29h), 645-646
partition tables, 231-234
Pascal language, 18
accessing 8250 serial interface chip (UART) directly, 221
ASCIIZ strings, 89
memory allocation, 85
passive TSRs (terminate and stay resident), 406
Paterson, Tim, 11-13
path names, 344-345
PC (83-key) keyboard, 163, 166-167

PC XT, 12
PCjr, 12-13
Personal Computer AT (PC AT),
    12-14
    keyboard (84-key), 163-167
Personal System/2 (PS/2), 12, 15
    BIOS, 486-488
    controling communications
        interface, 205
    display monitors used with,
        119
    identifying compatible display
        monitors, 129
    Multi-Color Graphics Array
        (MCGA), 43-44
    Video Graphics Array (VGA),
        43-44
pgprint() function, 156
Physical Address Mapping (Int
    31h, Function 0800h), 911
physical machine, 23
PIC
    see 8259A Programmable
        Interrupt Controller
pixels, 122, 127-128
platters, 230
Please check the printer!
    message, 96
pointers
    far, 297
    huge, 297
    near, 297
    registers, 31
Pointing Device BIOS Interface
    (Int 15, Function C2h), 565-567
polling, 77, 177-181
    mouse, 184-187
POP operations, 30
Portable PC, 12

ports
    communications, 203-207
    serial, 45-46
Position File Pointer (Int 2Fh,
    Function 12h, Subfunction
    28h), 782
power-on self test (POST), 56
Power-On Self-Test Error Log (Int
    15, Function 21h), 552-553
Prepare Hardware For Warm
    Boot (Int 67h, Function 5Ch),
    859
Primary Shell Program Loader
    (Int 2Eh), 758
Print Installation Check (Int 2Fh,
    Function 01h, Subfunction
    00h), 759
Print Screen (Int 05h), 496
printer device (PRN), 59
printer functions (Int 17h),
    157-158
Printer Management (LPT1) (Int
    0Fh), 501
Printer Output (Int 21h, Function
    05h), 157, 618
PrinterOnline function, 105
printers, 45
    functions, 157-159 _574-6, 618, 670_
printing
    DOS version numbers,
        464-465
    strings to current page, 156
procedures
    FAR, 66
    NEAR, 63
program segment prefix (PSP),
    60-61, 346, 353-355
Program Termination (Int 15,
    Function 82h), 555
Programmable Option Select (Int
    15, Function C4h), 568

programmable read-only memory (PROM), 40

programmers' interface to DOS, 18-19

programming resource list, 946-947

programs

COM, 61-64, 293

versus EXE, 75-76

disk operating system (DOS), 10

EXE, 64-72, 293, 353

EXE2BIN, 64

EXECOM, 64

exits, 348-349

FORMAT, 48

I/O system, 10

linking, memory allocation, 85

MAKE, 415

overlays, 286

running child from within parent, 344-348

SideKick, 355

states, 77

SYS.COM, 57

Term.c, 209-210, 219-224

terminal, 208-224

terminate and stay resident (TSRs), 355-357, 406-416

protected mode, 32-33, 288

PUSH operations, 30

put_ch() function, 219

putch() function, 178

putchar(','), 173

putscrn() function, 218

putwin() function, 148

Q

Query A20 (Function 007h), 865

Query API Support (Service Function 0006h), 936

Query Free Extended Memory (XMS Function 008h), 865-866

Query IOCTL device (Int 21h, Function 44h, Subfunction 11h), 697

Query IOCTL handle (Int 21h, Function 44h, Subfunction 10h), 696

Query Suspend (Notification Function 0001h), 928-929

QuickBASIC, 109

accessing registers and generating interrupts, 109-110

finding files by wild-card file specifications, 111-113

handling events, 368

reading keyboard from, 169

resource list, 947

R

Random Block Read (Int 21h, Function 27h), 643-644

Random Block Write (Int 21h, Function 28h), 644-645

Random File Read (Int 21h, Function 21h), 638-639

Random File Write (Int 21h, Function 22h), 639-640

random-access memory (RAM), 40

raw mode, 419

rch() function, 217-222

Read Character and Attribute (Int 10, Function 08h), 509

Read Character from Communications Port (Int 14, Function 02h), 546-547

Read Command Line (Int 2Fh, Function 48h, Subfunction 10h), 788

Read Cursor Position and Configuration (Int 10, Function 03h), 505

Read Data Blocks from Cassette Drive (Int 15, Function 02h), 551

Read Date from Real-Time Clock (Int 1Ah, Function 04h), 580

Read Device Availability (Int 21h, Function 37h, Subfunction 02h), 660

Read Disk Change Line Status (Int 13, Function 16h), 541

Read Disk Sectors (Int 13, Function 02h), 527

Read File (Int 2Fh, Function 12h, Subfunction 29h), 783

Read File or Device (handle) (Int 21h, Function 3Fh), 669-670

read function, 445

Read Graphics Pixel (Int 10, Function 0Dh), 513

Read Keyboard Character (Int 16, Function 00h), 170, 568-569

Read Keyboard Status (Int 16, Function 01h), 170, 171, 569-570

Read Light Pen Position (Int 10, Function 04h), 505-506

Read Long Sector (Int 13, Function 0Ah), 533-535

Read Motion Counters (Int 33h, Function 0Bh), 805

Read One Register (Int 10h, Function F0h), 817

Read Real-Time Clock (Int 1Ah, Function 02h), 578-579

Read Real-Time Clock Alarm (Int 1Ah, Function 09h), 582

Read Register Range (Int 10h, Function F2h), 818

Read Register Set (Int 10h, Function F4h), 819-820

Read Sector Buffer (Int 13, Function 0Eh), 537

Read Sequential File (FCB) (Int 21h, Function 14h), 630-631

read-only memory (ROM), 40
  BIOS data area, 943-944
  bootstrap initialization procedure, 56

Read/Write Display Codes (Int 10, Function 1Ah), 521

Ready to print message, 96

real mode, 32, 288

Real-Time Clock Interrupt (Int 70h), 586

Reallocate Extended Memory Block (XMS Function 00Fh), 869-870

Reallocate Pages (Int 67h, Function 51h), 837

Recalibrate Fixed Disk Drive (Int 13, Function 11h), 538

receiver data register (RDR), 197-198

records, boot, 234-239

registers, 88
  8086
    AF (auxiliary carry flag), 32
    AX (AH and AL) general purpose, 28, 66, 29, 204, 466, 475-477
    BP (base pointer), 31
    BX (BH and BL) general purpose, 28-29, 205, 477-478
    CF (carry flag), 32, 91
    CS (code segment), 29-30
    CX (CH and CL) general purpose, 28-29, 205-206, 479

DF (direction flag), 32
DI (destination index),
    31-32
DS (data segment), 29-30,
    66, 110
DS:DX, 344-345
DX general purpose, 28-29
ES (extra segment), 29-30,
    110
ES:BX, 345-346
IF (interrupt flag), 32
IP (instruction pointer), 31
OF (overflow flag), 32
PF (parity flag), 32
SF (sign flag), 32
SI (source index), 31-32
SP (stack pointer), 30-31
SS (stack segment), 29-30
TF (trap flag), 32
ZF (zero flag), 32
8086 set, 27-28
    flags, 32
    general-purpose, 28-29
    offset, 31-32
    segment, 29-30
8250 UART
    baud rate divisor (BRD),
        197-199
    interrupt enable register
        (IER), 197-200
    interrupt identification
        register (IIR), 197, 200
    line control register (LCR),
        197, 200-201
    line status register (LSR),
        197, 202
    modem control register
        (MCR), 197, 200-202
    modem status register
        (MSR), 197, 202-203

receiver data register (RDR),
    197-198
transmitter holding register
    (THR), 197-198
accessing
    in C language, 93-95
    in QuickBASIC, 109-110
    in Turbo Pascal, 104-105
calling, 612
flags, testing, 170-171
index, 31-32
pointer, 31
return, 612
Release Current Virtual Machine's
    Time Slice (Int 2Fh, Function
    1680h), 872-873
Release High Memory Area
    (Function 002h), 863
Release Memory (Int 21h,
    Function 49h), 700-701
Release Upper Memory Block
    (Function 011h), 871
Relock Real Mode Region (Int
    31h, Function 0603h), 909-910
removable media, 449
Remove File from Print Queue
    (Int 2Fh, Function 01h,
    Subfunction 02h), 760
Remove Subdirectory (Int 21h,
    Function 3Ah), 664
Rename File
    FCB (Int 21h, Function 17h),
        633-634
    Int 21h, Function 56h, 716
Request Communications Port
    Status (Int 14, Function 03h),
    547
request header (RH), 428-429
Request High Memory Area (XMS
    Function 001h), 862-863

Request Printer Port Status (Int 17, Function 02h), 96, 105, 110, 576
request to send (RTS) line, 201
Request Upper Memory Block (XMS Function 010h), 870
Reserved
    Int 67h, Function 49h, 829
    Int 67h, Function 4Ah, 829
    PS/2
        Int 0Bh, 499
        Int 0Ch, 499-500
        Int 0Dh, 500
        Int 0Fh, 501
reserved functions, 955-956
    DOS, 609
    hooks for the future, 957
    numbers not really used, 956-957
    see undocumented functions, 480
    useful group, 956
    who knows?, 957
Reset Debug Watchpoint (Int 31h, Function 0B03h), 915-916
Reset Disk (Int 21h, Function 0Dh), 624
Reset Disk System (Int 13, Function 00h), 525-526
resident drivers, 53
Resize DOS Memory Block (Int 31h, Function 0102h), 884-885
Resize Linear Memory Block (Int 31h, Function 0505h), 901-902
Resize Memory Block (Int 31h, Function 0503h), 900
Restore Mouse Driver State (Int 33h, Function 17h), 810
Restore Page Map (Int 67h, Function 48h), 828
Resume Switcher (Service Function0003h), 934-935

retrace intervals, 122
Return Address of InDOS Flag (Int 21h, Function 34h), 368, 409, 655-657, 956
Return DASD Type (Int 13, Function 15h), 540
Return Disk Drive Parameters (Int 13, Function 08h), 531-532
Return Extended BIOS Data Area Segment Address (Int 15, Function C1h), 564-565
return from interrupt (IRET), 371
Return Keyboard Flags (Int 16, Function 02h), 171-174, 570-571
return registers, 612
Return SuperVGA Display Mode
    Int 4Fh, Function 02h, 589
    Int 4Fh, Function 03h, 590
Return SuperVGA Information (Int 4Fh, Function 00h), 587-588
Return SuperVGA Mode Information (Int 4Fh, Function 01h), 588-589
Return System Configuration Parameters (Int 15, Function C0h), 563-564
Return User Parameter Pointer (Int 2Fh, Function 0), 953
Revert to Default Registers (Int 10h, Function F6h), 820
RGB monitors, 119
root directories, 49-50, 262-264
    location of, 246

S

SADD(TheString$) function, 111
Save Mouse Driver State (Int 33h, Function 16h), 810

Save Page Map (Int 67h, Function 47h), 827

Save/Restore Display State (Int 10, Function 1Ch), 522-523

Save/Restore SuperVGA Video State (Int 4Fh, Function 04h), 590

savewin() function, 148

scan codes, 41-42, 162-167

screens
  clearing window in center of filled, 147-153
  display
    see display pages
  pixels, 122, 127-128

Scroll Lock key, 171

Scroll Window Down (Int 10, Function 07h), 508-509

Scroll Window Up (Int 10, Function 06h), 507-508

Search Buffer Chain (Int 2Fh, Function 12h, Subfunction 0Eh), 770

Search for First Entry (FCB) (Int 21h, Function 11h), 627-628

Search for First Match (Int 21h, Function 4Eh), 111-113, 279-280, 706-708

Search for Next Entry (FCB) (Int 21h, Function 12h), 628_629

Search for Next Match (Int 21h, Function 4Fh), 111-113, 280, 708-709

search() function, 279-280

searching directories, 277-281

Seattle Computer Products, 11-12

sectors, 230
  boot, 56

Seek Cylinder (Int 13, Function 0Ch), 536

segment
  addresses, 24
  registers, 29-30
    accessing, 248-250
  selectors, 33

Segment to Descriptor (Int 31h, Function 0002h), 876

segmented memory addressing, 24-26

Select Active Display Page (Int 10, Function 05h), 506-507

Select Disk (Int 21h, Function 0Eh), 624-625

serial interface chip (8250 UART), 191, 196-197

serial
  interfaces, 192-196
    evaluation of, 224
  links, 192
  ports, 45-46
    checking status in terminal programs, 217

serial() function, 216-219

Serialize on Shared Memory (Int 31h, Function 0D02h), 919-920

Service Functions, 923, 932
  0000h (Get Version), 933
  0001h (Test Memory Region), 933
  0002h (Suspend Switcher), 934
  0003h (Resume Switcher), 934-935
  0004h (Hook Notificaton Chain), 935
  0005h (Unhook Notificaton Chain), 935-936
  0006h (Query API Support), 936

Session Active (Notification Function 0004h), 930

Set Allocation Strategy (Int 21h, Function 58h, Subfunction 01h), 719-720

Set Alternate Map Registers (Int 67h, Function 5Bh, Subfunction 01h), 853-854

Set Alternate Mouse User Handler (Int 33h, Function 18h), 810-811

Set APPEND Function State (Int 2Fh, Function B7h, Subfunction 07h), 794-795

Set Clock Counter (Int 1Ah, Function 01h), 577-578

Set Color Palette (Int 10, Function 0Bh), 511-512

Set CRT Page Number (Int 33h, Function 1Dh), 813

Set Ctrl-Break Flag (Int 21h, Function 33h, Subfunction 01h), 654

Set Current Country Byte (Int 21h, Function 64h), 739, 956

Set Cursor Position (Int 10, Function 02h), 503-504

Set Cursor Type (Int 10, Function 01h), 503

Set DASD Type for Disk Format (Int 13, Function 17h), 541-542

Set Date of Real-Time Clock (Int 1Ah, Function 05h), 580

Set Day Count (Int 1Ah, Function 0Bh), 582

Set Debug Watchpoint (Int 31h, Function 0B00h), 914

Set Descriptor (Int 31h, Function 000Ch), 880-881

Set Descriptor Access Rights (Int 31h, Function 0009h), 878-879

Set Device Availability (Int 21h, Function 37h, Subfunction 03h), 660

Set Device Information (Int 21h, Function 44h, Subfunction 01h), 677-678

Set Directory (Int 21h, Function 3Bh), 664-665

Set Double Speed Threshold (Int 33h, Function 13h), 808

Set DTA Address (Int 21h, Function 1Ah), 634

Set Error Data Values (Int 21h, Function 5Dh, Subfunction 0Ah), 731-732

Set Extended Processor Exception Handler Vector
    Protected Mode (Int 31h, Function 0212h), 888-889
    Real Mode (Int 31h, Function 0213h), 889

Set File Access Locks (Int 21h, Function 5Ch, Subfunction 00h), 728-729

Set File Attributes (Int 21h, Function 43h, Subfunction 01h), 673-674

Set File Date and Time (Int 21h, Function 57h, Subfunction 01h), 717-718

Set Global Code Page (Int 21h, Function 66h, Subfunction 02h), 743

Set Graphics Cursor Shape (Int 33h, Function 09h), 801-804

Set Handle Attribute (Int 67h, Function 52h, Subfunction 01h), 838

Set Handle Count (Int 21h, Function 67h), 743-744

Set Handle Name (Int 67h, Function 53h, Subfunction 01h), 840

Set interrupt rate (Int 33h, Function 1Ch), 813

Set Interrupt Vector (Int 21h, Function 25h), 641-642

Set Interrupt Vector (Int 21h, Function 25h), 366-367

Set KEYB.COM Active Code Page (Int 2Fh, Function ADh, Subfunction 81h), 791

Set KEYB.COM Country Flag (Int 2Fh, Function ADh, Subfunction 82h), 791-792

Set LDT Pointers (Int 2Fh, Function 12h, Subfunction 19h), 774

Set Logical Drive Map (Int 21h, Function 44h, Subfunction 0Fh), 695-696

Set Machine Name (Int 21h, Function 5Eh, Subfunction 01h), 732-733

Set Media Type for Disk Format (Int 13, Function 18h), 542

Set Message Language (Int 33h, Function 22h), 815

Set Mickey-to-Pixel Ratio (Int 33h, Function 0Fh), 807

Set Mouse Position (Int 33h, Function 04h), 799

Set Mouse Sensitivity (Int 33h, Function 1Ah), 812

Set Mouse X Limits (Int 33h, Function 07h), 800-801

Set Mouse Y Limits (Int 33h, Function 08h), 801

Set Multiple Descriptors (Int 31h, Function 000Fh), 882-883

Set Network Printer Setup (Int 21h, Function 5Eh, Subfunction 02h), 733

Set Page Attributes (Int 31h, Function 0507h), 903-905

Set Page Map Registers (Int 67h, Function 4Eh Subfunction 01h), 832

Set Palette Registers (Int 10, Function 10h), 515-517

Set Partial Page Map (Int 67h, Function 4Fh, Subfunction 01h), 834

Set Processor Emulation (Int 31h, Function 0E01h), 921-922

Set Processor Exception Handler Vector (Int 31h, Function 0203h), 886

Set Protected Mode Interrupt Vector (Int 31h, Function 0205h), 887

Set PSP Segment (Int 21h, Function 50h), 709-710

Set Random Record Field (Int 21h, Function 24h), 641

Set Real Mode Interrupt Vector (Int 31h, Function 0201h), 885

Set Real-Time Clock (Int 1Ah, Function 03h), 579

Set Redirection List Entry (Int 21h, Function 5Fh, Subfunction 03h), 735-736

Set Return Found Name State (Int 2Fh, Function B7h, Subfunction 11h), 795

Set Segment Base Address (Int 31h, Function 0007h), 877

Set Segment Limit (Int 31h, Function 0008h), 878

Set Sharing Retry Count (Int 21h, Function 44h, Subfunction 0Bh), 685-686

Set Sound Source (Int 1Ah, Function 80h), 583

Set Switchchar (Int 21h, Function 37h, Subfunction 01h), 659

Set System Alarm (Int 1Ah, Function 06h), 581

Set System Date (Int 21h, Function 2Bh), 470, 647

Set System Time (Int 21h, Function 2Dh), 471, 648-649

Set Text Cursor Type (Int 33h, Function 0Ah), 804

Set UMB link status (Int 21h, Function 58h, Subfunction 03h), 721

Set User Event Handlers (Int 33h, Function 14h), 808-809

Set User-Defined Event Handler (Int 33h, Function 0Ch), 805-806

Set Verify Flag (Int 21h, Function 2Eh), 649-650

Set Video Mode (Int 10, Function 00h), 501-502

Set/Clear Interim Console Flag (Int 21h, Function 63h, Subfunction 01h), 738

set_dta() function, 280

SetIntVec function, 367

setpage() function, 154-156

SetPID (Int 21h, Function 50h), 956

setup() function, 210-213

setvect function, 367

shell
    see command processor

Shift keys, 171

Shift-PrintScreen key combination, 168

Show Mouse Cursor (Int 33h, Function 01h), 797

showattr() function, 103

SI (source index) register, 28, 31-32

SideKick program, 355

sign flag (SF), 32

signal() function, 368

Simulate Real Mode Interrupt (Int 31h, Function 0300h), 889-890

Single Step (Int 01h), 493-494

snow, 123

software
    for DOS
        BIOS (basic input/output system), 50-51
        command processor, 52-53
        device drivers, 53-54
        DOS kernel, 51
        loading and initializing, 55-59
    interrupts, 19, 79-82, 365
        generating in C language, 94-95

Software Reset (Int 33h, Function 21h), 815

SP (stack pointer) register, 28-31

space state, 193

SS (stack segment) register, 28-30

stacks, 30

start bits, 193

Start Light Pen Emulation (Int 33h, Function 0Dh), 806-807

state of programs, 77

status flags, 32

STDIN Input (Int 21h, Function 08h), 175-176, 620

stepper motors, 230

stop bits, 193-194

Stop Light Pen Emulation (Int 33h, Function 0Eh), 807

storage devices, 46-50

Store DX (Int 2Fh, Function 12h, Subfunction 2Fh), 785

strategy routines, 428-430

streql() function, 280-281

string descriptors, 111

strings
  ASCIIZ (ASCII plus zero), 276
    format, 89
  passing addresses to DOS,
    90-91
  printing to current page, 156
subdirectories, 262, 269-270
subfunction number (DOS
  functions), 611
Submit File to Print Spooler (Int
  2Fh, Function 01h, Subfunction
  01h), 759-760
SuperVGA, identifying, 129-145
Suspend Session (Notification
  Function 0002h), 929
Suspend Switcher (Service
  Function 0002h), 934
SWAPIINFO data structure,
  923-924
swapped bits, 195
SWCALLBACKINFO data struc-
  ture, 924-925
SWINSTANCEITEM data structure, 925
Switch Processor to Protected
  Mode (Int 15, Function 89h),
  560
Switcher Exit (Notification
  Function 0007h), 932
SWSTARTUPINFO data structure,
  926
SWVERSION data structure,
  926-927
synchronous communication,
  192-193
SYS file extension, 422
SYS.COM program, 57
SYSINIT module, 58-59
system, 266
  crashes caused by TSRs,
    407-408

layering, 16-17
System Request Key Pressed (Int
  15, Function 85h), 557
System Timer (Int 08h), 496-497
System Warm Boot (Int 19h),
  576-577

T

tables
  configuration variable (CVT),
    957-974
  descriptor, 33
  file allocation (FAT), 239-246
  interrupt vector, 362, 366,
    941-943
  logical drive (LDT), 962-963,
    966-967, 971, 974
  partition, 231-234
  track-address, 258
Tandy, 14
task switcher API (application
  program interface), 16
task switchers, 923
Technical Reference Manual, 406
Term.c program, 209-210,
  219-220
  loopback testing, 223-224
  modifying, 221-223
terminal programs
  accessing 8250 serial interface
    chip (UART) direct, 220-221
  controlling
    keyboard, 213-216
    program, 209-210
  duplex considerations for
    writing, 208-209
  initializing, 210-213
  loopback testing, 223-224
  modifying, 221-223
  receiving characters, 216-219

supporting functions, 210-220
writing, 208
Terminate Address (Int 22h), 59, 747
Terminate and Stay Resident
Int 21h, Function 31h, 356, 652-653
Int 27h, 356, 755-756
Int 31h, Function 0C01h, 917
terminate and stay resident
programs (TSRs), 355-357, 406-408
interrupts essential to, 408-416
managing conflicts between multiple, 949-950
Terminate Program
Int 20h, 613-614
Int 21h, Function 00h, 614
Terminate with Return Code (Int 21h, Function 4Ch), 348, 705-706
TesSeRact shareware, 408, 9 49-954
Test Fixed Disk System Status (Int 13, Function 10h), 538
Test Memory Region (Service Function 0001h), 933
test() function, 414
testing, loopback, 223-224
text mode, 125-127
Time Delay (V4) (Int 2Fh, Function 12h, Subfunction 10h), 770
time
functions, 469-474
stamps, 267
reading in Turbo Pascal, 105-108
TIME command, 469
Time of Last Update (Offset 16h) of directory entry structure, 267

Timer Tick (Int 1Ch), 409, 584
track-address table, 258
tracks, 230
formatting, 255-260
transient program area (TPA), 287
controlling memory in, 291-293
Translate BPB to DPB (Int 21h, Function 53h), 713-715
Translate Extended Error Codes (Int 2Fh, Function 12h, Subfunction 22h), 779
transmitter holding register (THR), 197-198
trap flag (TF), 32
Turbo BASIC
handling events, 368
memory allocation, 295
Version 1.0, calling DOS and BIOS, 91-92
Turbo C, 19
compiling under small memory model, 100
memory allocation, 293
resource list, 947
setting
Ctrl-C interrupt handlers, 368
interrupt vectors, 367
Version 1.5, MAKE utility, 415
Turbo Pascal, 103-104
accessing registers and generating interrupts, 104-105
dynamic memory allocation, 294-296
handling interrupts, 368
memory allocation, 293
reading date/time stamp, 105-108

resource list, 946-947

sample program, 73

Version 3.0, accessing files with wild cards, 92

Version 4.0
  accessing files with wild cards, 92
  declaring interrupt directives as interrupt handle, 372
  exec() function, 348
  memory allocation, 85
  setting interrupt vectors, 367

Version 5.0, accessing files with wild cards, 92

Turn Off Cassette Motor (Int 15, Function 01h), 550-551

Turn On Cassette Motor (Int 15, Function 00h), 550

U

_umb_alloc function, 327

_umb_free function, 327

undocumented functions, 480, 609-610

Unhook Notification Chain (Service Function 0005h), 935-936

UNIX operating system, 52
  compatibility with, 118
  parallel processes, 344
  porting applications in C to DOS, 275

unknown purpose
  Int 21h, Function 69h, 957
  Int 21h, Function 6Bh, 957

Unlock Extended Memory Block (XMS Function 00Dh), 868-869

Unlock Linear Region (Int 31h, Function 0601h), 908

upper memory blocks (UMBs), 304

upwin() function, 148

User Parameters block (TesSeRact), 950-951

V

vectors, interrupt, 360, 364-367

Verify Disk Sectors (Int 13, Function 04h), 528-529

vertical retrace interval (VRI), 123

video adapters
  see display adapters

Video BIOS (Int 10h), 817

video BIOS functions, 586-591

video display mode, 123-124

video displays
  accessing, 120
  formats, 123-124
  storing and displaying data, 120-123

Video Electronics Standards Association, 586

video functions, 145-153

Video Graphics Array (VGA), 44
  identifying, 129-145

Video-Initialization Parameter Table (Int 1Dh), 584

virtual control program interface (VCPI), 33

Virtual Graphics Array (VGA), 119
  chips, 120-121
  memory configuration, 122
  memory contained, 121
  video display mode, 124

virtual machine concept, 21-22

VisiCalc, 120

volume labels, 267, 270-271

volume serial numbers, 270

W

warm boots, 56
Western Digital floppy disk controllers, 195
wild cards
    accessing files with, 92
    file specifications, 111-113
windows, clearing in center of filled screen, 147-153
Write Character and Attribute (Int 10, Function 09h), 509-510
Write Character at Cursor (Int 10, Function 0Ah), 510-511
Write Character to Communications Port (Int 14, Function 01h), 546
Write Character to Printer (Int 17, Function 00h), 574-575
Write Data Blocks to Cassette Drive (Int 15, Function 03h), 551-552
Write Disk Sectors (Int 13, Function 03h), 527-528
write function, 447-448
Write Graphics Pixel (Int 10, Function 0Ch), 512-513
Write Long Sector (Int 13, Function 0Bh), 534-535
Write One Register (Int 10h, Function F1h), 818
Write Register Range (Int 10h, Function F3h), 819
Write Register Set (Int 10h, Function F5h), 820
Write Sector Buffer (Int 13, Function 0Fh), 537-538
Write Sequential File (FCB) (Int 21h, Function 15h), 631-632
Write String (Int 10, Function 13h), 520-521
Write Text in Teletype Mode (Int 10, Function 0Eh), 513-514
Write to a File or Device (handle) (Int 21h, Function 40h), 670
Write to Keyboard Buffer (Int 16h, Function 05h), 181-183, 572
write with verify function, 448

X-Z

XENIX, compatibility with, 118
xmit() function, 214-216, 222
XMS
    see Extended Memory Specification
XMS Functions
    000h (Get XMS Version Number), 862
    001h (Request High Memory Area), 862-863
    002h (Release High Memory Area), 863
    003h (Global Enable A20), 863
    004h (Global Disable A20), 864
    005h (Local Enable A20), 864
    006h (Local Disable A20), 864-865
    007h (Query A20), 865
    008h (Query Free Extended Memory), 865-866
    009h (Allocate Extended Memory Block), 866
    00Ah (Free Extended Memory Block), 866-867
    00Bh (Move Extended Memory Block), 867-868
    00Ch (Lock Extended Memory Block), 868

00Dh (Unlock Extended
  Memory Block), 868-869
00Eh (Get EMB Handle
  Information), 869
00Fh (Reallocate Extended
  Memory Block), 869-870
010h (Request Upper Memory
  Block), 870
011h (Release Upper Memory
  Block), 871
_xms_alloc function, 326
_xms_avail function, 326
_xms_bstat function, 327
_xms_free function, 327
_xms_lock function, 327
_xms_move function, 327
_xms_realloc function, 327
_xms_stat function, 326
_xms_test function, 326
_xms_unlock function, 327
Zbikowski, Mark, 69
ZDOS, 12-13
zero flag (ZF), 32

Computer Books from Que Mean PC Performance!

Que Gives You The Most Comprehensive Programming Information Available!

Count On Que
For The Latest
In DOS Information!

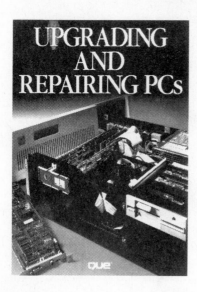

Find It Fast With Que's Quick References!

Que's Quick References are the compact, easy-to-use guides to essential application information. Written for all users, Quick References include vital command information under easy-to-find alphabetical listings. Quick References are a must for anyone who needs command information fast!

To Order, Call:
(800) 428-5331 OR (317) 573-2500

Teach Yourself
With QuickStarts From Que!

The ideal tutorials for beginners, Que's QuickStart books use graphic illustrations and step-by-step instructions to get you up and running fast. Packed with examples, QuickStarts are the perfect beginner's guides to your favorite software applications.

1-2-3 for DOS Release 2.3 QuickStart

Release 2.3

$19.95 USA

0-88022-716-8, 500 pp., 7 3/8 x 9 1/4

1-2-3 for Windows QuickStart

1-2-3 for Windows

$19.95 USA

0-88022-723-0, 500 pp., 7 3/8 x 9 1/4

1-2-3 Release 3.1 + QuickStart, 2nd Edition

Releases 3 & 3.1

$19.95 USA

0-88022-613-7, 569 pp., 7 3/8 x 9 1/4

dBASE IV 1.1 QuickStart,

Through Version 1.1

$19.95 USA

0-88022-614-5, 400 pp., 7 3/8 x 9 1/4

Excel 3 for Windows QuickStart

Version 3 fo rWindows

$19.95 USA

0-88022-762-1, 500 pp., 7 3/8 x 9 1/4

MS-DOS QuickStart, 2nd Edition

Version 3.X & 4.X

$19.95 USA

0-88022-611-0, 420 pp., 7 3/8 x 9 1/4

Q&A 4 QuickStart

Versions 3 & 4

$19.95 USA

0-88022-653-6, 400 pp., 7 3/8 x 9 1/4

Quattro Pro 3 QuickStart

Through Version 3.0

$19.95 USA

0-88022-693-5, 450 pp., 7 3/8 x 9 1/4

WordPerfect 5.1 QuickStart

WordPerfect 5.1

$19.95 USA

0-88022-558-0, 427 pp., 7 3/8 x 9 1/4

Windows 3 QuickStart

Ron Person & Karen Rose

This graphics-based text teaches Windows beginners how to use the feature-packed Windows environment. Emphasizes such software applications as Excel, Word, and PageMaker and shows how to master Windows' mouse, menus, and screen elements.

Version 3

$19.95 USA

0-88022-610-2, 440 pp., 7 3/8 x 9 1/4

MS-DOS 5 QuickStart

Que Development Group

This is the easy-to-use graphic approach to learning MS-DOS 5. The combination of step-by-step instruction, examples, and graphics make this book ideal for all DOS beginners.

DOS 5

$19.95 USA

0-88022-681-1, 420 pp., 7 3/8 x 9 1/4

To Order, Call:
(800) 428-5331 OR (317) 573-2500